MEMORIAL VOLUME

OF THE

POPHAM CELEBRATION,

August 29, 1862:

COMMEMORATIVE OF THE PLANTING OF THE

POPHAM COLONY ON THE PENINSULA OF SABINO,

August 19, O. S., 1607,

ESTABLISHING THE TITLE OF ENGLAND TO THE CONTINENT.

PUBLISHED UNDER THE DIRECTION OF THE

REV. EDWARD BALLARD,

SECRETARY OF THE EXECUTIVE COMMITTEE OF THE CELEBRATION.

PORTLAND:

BAILEY & NOYES.

1863.

PRINTED BY BROWN THURSTON,

COR. OF EXCHANGE AND MIDDLE STS.

MAP OF SABINO.

THE well executed map, which forms the frontispiece to this volume, is taken from the "Coast Survey," made by the General Government. It will be found to be a valuable illustrative aid, enabling the reader of these pages, as well as of the history of the early times to which they relate, to identify the locality of the original FORT ST. GEORGE, within the limits of the ancient "Mawooshen."[1]

In regard to this location, the minds of many persons in years past have been influenced by Sullivan, who in 1806 gave his opinion in a communication to the Massachusetts Historical Society, that the Popham Colony made their settlement "on an island within Georgetown, called Parker's Island." The following extract conveys his statement: "Upon this island the Europeans who first colonized to New England made their landing. Virginia was planted in the year 1606, and has, therefore, assumed the dignified title of 'The Ancient Dominions.' But the Colony of Parker's Island, which has since been called Sagadahoc, was but one year behind her. In the year 1607, George Popham, Rawleigh Gilbert, Edmund Harlow, Edmund Davis, and about one hundred other adventurers, in form of a colony, landed and took possession of Parker's Island. Had the leaders of this little colony survived the severities of the winter next after their landing, Plymouth might have been deprived of the honor of being the mother of New England."[2] In his history at an earlier date (1795), he had taken Stage Island, from tradition, as the place of this settlement.[3] Williamson, adopting this opinion, connects it with another, and

1 This aboriginal name [Purchas, vol. 4, p. 1837] indicated a large portion of the maritime region of Maine ; embracing its two large rivers, the Kennebec and the Penobscot. The Bashaba was chief of its confederated tribes. The word was written "Moasham" by Gorges, [Me. H. C., vol. 2, p. 62,] and "Moassons" by Popham, to denote the Indians therein. [*Post*, 224.] Another form, "Mavooshen," should be "Mauooshen," as the third letter was not used by the natives.

2 Mass. Hist. Col., vol. 1, p. 251.

3 Hist., pp. 53, 169, 170, 174.

states of the colonists, that, "Although according to some accounts, they first went ashore upon *Erascohegan*, [1] or the western *Peninsula*; [2] yet it is believed they finally disembarked upon an Island 200 rods eastward, called Stage Island." He also adds, that after they had "erected on the Island some slight habitations or cottages, and sunk two or three wells," they deemed the Island [3] "too small for the permanent foundation of a colony. * * * Therefore they concluded to change their situation; and passing across the river to the western bank, they selected a convenient site on the southeast side of a creek, near what is now called Atkins' Bay, which stretches west into the land half a league, and forms a peninsula at the southerly corner of the present town of Phipsburg. To this place they themselves removed, and during the autumn located and established a settlement, which was subsequently denominated the SAGADAHOC COLONY." [4]

But the earlier and better testimony to their first and only choice of the place and its occupancy, is solely in favor of the "Peninsula of Sabino." Strachey, the historian of the settlement, says, "they made choise of a place for their plantation at the mouth or entry of the river on the west side, (for the river bendeth yt self towards the nor-east and by east,) being almost an island, of a good bignes, being in a province called by the Indians, Sabino, so called of a sagamo or chief commander under the graund bassaba." [5] Purchas, on the authority of a letter from George Popham to Sir John Gilbert, asserts that "they chose the place of their plantacion at the mouth of the Sagadahoc, *in a westerly peninsula*." [6] Heylin says, "S. Gorges' Fort, the first plantation of the English, was built by them at the mouth of the Sagadahoc, in a Demi-Island, *Anno* 1607." [7] Ogilby says, that "a hundred men were sent to settle a colony at Sagadahoc, under the command of George Popham, who seated themselves in a Peninsula at the mouth of this River." [8] Prince is explicit, saying that these colonists "settle on a westerly peninsula at the mouth of Sagadahoc." [9] Belknap is confirmatory: "They landed at the mouth of Sagadahock or Kennebeck River, on a peninsula." [10] Holmes, to the same purport, has been quoted above by Williamson. In the year 1807, two hundred years after the settlement, the Rev. Dr. Jenks, then a resident of Bath, with a party of friends,

1 Now Parker's Island.

2 "On a peninsula." Holmes' Annals, vol. 1, p. 160.

3 "On Stage Island are the remains of a fort; brick chimneys; and some wells of water; several cellars; — the bricks must have come from England. Sullivan, p. 170."

4 Williamson, vol. 1, pp. 198, 199.

5 Hist. Trav., p. 172.

6 Cited in Me. Hist. Col., vol. 2, p. 28. Folsom's Address.

7 Cosmog. Lib., 4, p. 95.

8 Hist., p. 141.

9 Chron., p. 116.

10 Amer. Biog., vol. 1, p. 350.

visited the mouth of the Kennebec River. He says, "To the spot that bore the best claims to this distinction, and which is on a 'peninsula,' they gave the name of Point Popham."[1] The author of the "Ancient Dominions of Maine" describes the precise position, as remembered in deeply marked traditions related by aged residents in the neighborhood. He also gives "a sketch of the outline remains," as they are now traceable on the shore of Atkins' Bay.[2]

These many concurrent testimonies, running through two centuries and a half, are sufficient to show the *peninsular* location of Fort St. George on the *west* side of the Kennebec.[3]

1 This statement is derived from the Rev. William S. Bartlett, of Chelsea, Mass,, [Me. H. C., vol. 3, p. 285,] to whom our local history is greatly indebted for the prominence given to the Popham Colony in his "Frontier Missionary," and for introducing the work of Strachey to the practical knowledge of the Maine Historical Society. See also *post*, p. 227.

2 Sewall's Ancient Dominions, p. 228.

3 *Post*, p. 251. In later years Hunnewell, whose name has been given to the Point, had his dwelling on or near the same spot, as appears in an old map among the Pejepscot Papers.

THE AUTOGRAPH OF SIR JOHN POPHAM. (1590.)

Samuel G. Drake, Esq., the learned antiquary of Boston, during a residence of a year and a half in Europe, from November, 1858, to May, 1860, devoted much time in examining colonial papers in the British State Paper Office in London. In these researches, he fortunately discovered an original paper in the hand writing of Sir John Popham, and signed by him, bearing date 1590.

Annexed is Mr. Drake's letter, communicating a copy of the autograph to the Hon. William Willis, President of the Maine Historical Society, who has thus made a welcome addition to the present publication.

"Boston, Sept. 27, 1862.

Mr. Willis,

Dear Sir: — I am to thank you for your kindness in sending me a paper containing an account of the Popham Celebration. In my rummaging among the British Archives, I met with an original paper in the autograph of the Lord Chief Justice Popham. Thinking it may interest you, I send you a tracing of his signature. * * *

Very truly yours,

Sam'l G. Drake."

CONTENTS.

THE POPHAM CELEBRATION.

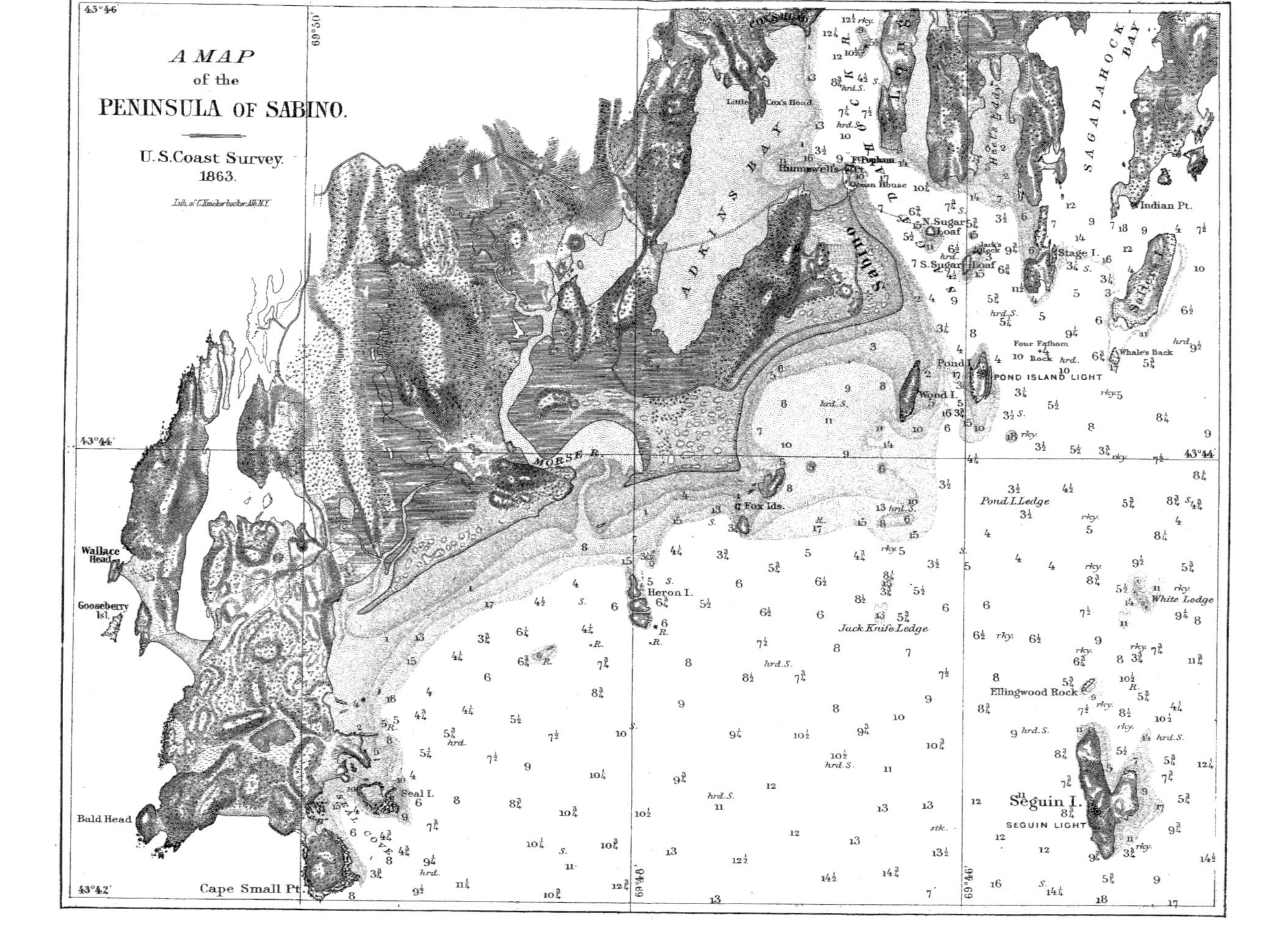
A MAP
of the
PENINSULA OF SABINO.
U.S.Coast Survey.
1863.
43°46'
69°50'
43°44'
43°42'
69°48'
69°46'
SAGADAHOCK BAY
ADKINS BAY
Sabino
Little Cox's Head
Cox's Head
Hunnewell's Pt.
Ft. Popham
Ocean House
N. Sugar Loaf
S. Sugar Loaf
Jack's Rock
Stage I.
Indian Pt.
Salter's I.
Whale's Back
Four Fathom Rock
Pond I.
POND ISLAND LIGHT
Wood I.
Fox Ids.
MORSE R.
Pond I. Ledge
Heron I.
Jack Knife Ledge
White Ledge
Ellingwood Rock
Seguin I.
SEGUIN LIGHT
Seal I.
SEAL COVE
Wallace Head
Gooseberry Isl.
Bald Head
Cape Small Pt.

THE POPHAM CELEBRATION.

PRELIMINARY.

In the arrangements made by the government of the United States for protecting the coast of Maine, the defense of the entrance of the Kennebec River and its valley received mature consideration. For the accomplishment of this purpose, the point of land on its west side and near its mouth was selected, and a fort of the first class was authorized by Congress to be built thereon. The ancient name of this portion of the river was "Sagadahoc,"[1] and the part of the territory where the structure was to be placed, was the Peninsula of Sabino.[2] On this shore and near the spot thus chosen, was the site of

1 *Sagadahoc.* This orthography of the name, out of twenty varieties, is the present generally adopted representative of the Indian "Sank-ta-onk." The first part of this word is abbreviated, as is usual in these formations, from "Sanktaiiwi;" the meaning of which is given in Ràle's Dictionary, "To finish." The last syllable is a common locative termination, as in "Ken-neb-onk," equivalent to "here," or "there." The compound name means, "It ends here," i. e. "the mouth" of this river; and it is so explained in Jeffries' Maps, of 1775.

2 The usage, in the pronunciation of aboriginal names, indicates that in words of this formation, the accent should be on the first syllable, as in "Kineo," "Orono," and others. Its origin is in the Abnaki word "sĕbĕ," meaning "a river." It is also written by Strachey, "Sĕb′-e-nōā," the last three letters forming one syllable, as in "oak."

the ancient Fort St. George, where, in the month of August, 1607, the first English colony, led by the venerable GEORGE POPHAM, planted the emblems of the authority of their sovereign. By acts of formal occupation and possession, attended with the solemn sanctions of religious worship and instruction, in accordance with the usages of their country and time, these early settlers established the title of England to the continent, under the Royal Charter of April 10, 1606.

The location of this fort on the soil, thus made prominent in its historical relations, suggested to several gentlemen, interested in the history of this State, the name of POPHAM, as the appropriate designation for this great work of national defense. The late Hon. Reuel Williams of Augusta, and the Hon. John A. Poor of Portland,—Commissioners at Washington from the State of Maine to the general government on the subject of its coast defenses,—took means to bring this name before the proper authorities. The proposal received the favor and the prompt approval of the government of the United States through the Hon. Simon Cameron, Secretary of War.

The work of construction having been commenced, suggested the plan of reviving the recollection of the important events, which have given to this spot its great historical value and interest, and of connecting them more closely with the name and the destinies of this fortification; thus making it serve the double purpose of national defense and the preservation of these leading occurrences of our early history. Measures were adopted for erecting, in the walls of the Fort, a "Memorial Stone," with inscriptions recording the facts; and for the commemorative services of a public historical celebration.

After much consultation with several members of the Maine Historical Society in Portland and Brunswick, a visit by two gentlemen of the latter place was made to Bath,—the city nearest to the locality,—to confer with its influential citizens on the subject. The idea was met with cordial favor everywhere. On the 10th of July, 1862, the following editorial appeared in the Bath Daily "Sentinel and Times," introducing a communication from a writer, who is understood to be the Hon. B. C. Bailey.

SIR JOHN POPHAM'S COLONY.

We publish below, a communication from one of our old and highly respected citizens, relating to an important fact in the history of our State, and suggesting the propriety of some public observance of the circumstance by our community. We heartily concur in the suggestion, and trust measures will be at once inaugurated to carry the same into effect. Local events, of such a nature as that mentioned, ought not certainly to be overlooked. In fact, it may well he questioned whether our people, to any extent, are familiar with the history of George Popham's settlement on our coast, and its attendant results. We hold it to be wise, therefore, to mark the anniversary of the event in some public manner; if in no other way, by the selection of some person conversant with our local history, to prepare an address relating to the colony and its attendant circumstances, that thus information may be imparted to the people and knowledge be diffused among us. We repeat that we trust some early action will be taken to carry out the suggestion in the communication, which is as follows:

MR. LINCOLN: — Bath being the natural seaport of and for the Kennebec River, as also the Androscoggin, and in fact of all North-western Maine, it would seem proper that she should be a little more before the public.

Two hundred and fifty-five years ago the 19th day of this coming August, George Popham, with his colony, landed at the mouth of the Kennebec and commenced a settlement, near where they are now building a Fort, which is to be called by the name of Popham.

Would it not be well for the citizens of Bath to call a meeting and choose a committee of arrangements, for the purpose of celebrating the day this coming 19th of August (old style), making it the 29th or 30th of August this year (new style), and invite the Historical Society of Maine to be present with their orator and proclaim the past history of that settlement, it being the very first one on this part of the continent.

I would suggest, with humble submission to public opinion, that we have a meeting the first of next week, and make some arrangement for such a commemoration of the day as would seem proper.

A CITIZEN OF BATH.

The Standing Committee of the Maine Historical Society were ready to lend their aid to the enterprise. As the proposed commemoration embraced subjects fitly coming within the range and purposes of this institution, they deemed it a duty to take the initiatory steps; and at their suggestion the President of the Society, the Hon. William Willis of Portland, addressed a letter to the Mayor of Bath, in the following words:

LETTER OF THE HON. WILLIAM WILLIS.

To the Honorable the Mayor of Bath.

SIR: — The government of the United States, having selected the peninsula at the mouth of Kennebec River as the site of a fortress, and made preparations for a large and expensive structure, to bear the name of "Popham," in honor of George Popham, President of the company of adventurers who planted, on the same spot, the first English colony on the shores of New England: — it is thought by the Maine Historical Society, that the occasion ought to be improved to commemorate this most signal event in the history of our State.

By a singular coincidence, the new fort will occupy the same ground on which was erected, two hundred and fifty-five years ago, the first English fort, which was built on the Atlantic coast of America, north of Virginia. This little colony, —"one hundred landmen," — left England, May 31, 1607, in two small vessels, prepared with all things needful to establish a civilized society on this continent. Their historian thus speaks of their early movements: "August 17, Capt. Popham in his pynnace with thirty persons, and Capt. Gilbert in his long boat with eighteen persons more, went early in the morning from their shipps in the river Sachadehoc to view the river, and to search where they might find a fitt place for their plantation. 18th. They all went ashore and there made choice of a place for their plantation at the mouth or entrance of the river, on the west side, being almost an island." The next day, in true Puritan style, although they were not strictly Puritans, they commenced their grand undertaking, the opening a new world to civilization, by *religious services*. The historian says: "19th. They all went ashore, where they had made choice of their plantation, and where they had a sermon delivered unto them by their preacher." They then entered on their work in earnest. "Aug. 20. All went to shore again and there began to entrench and make a fort, and to build a store-house."

The place selected for their settlement was Hunnewell's Point, precisely the spot chosen by the government for the new fortress; it was there this company spent a cold and dreary winter, and there the gallant Popham lies buried.

The work of construction is already begun, and the superintending engineer has given assurance that he will permit a commemorative tablet to be inserted in the wall, which shall perpetuate the first attempt to colonize the State, and mark the wonderful progress of our country.

I am instructed by the Standing Committee of the Historical Society to call the attention of the citizens of Bath to this subject, and to urge that they will not only co-operate in a suitable commemoration of this great event, but that they will take the lead in making arrangements for the occasion.

It is a custom not less honorable than useful, in all nations, to celebrate the leading events of their history; thus reviving and keeping alive in posterity the virtuous deeds, the patient fortitude, and the gallant services of the founders of their States, and of those who have illustrated their annals by their lives. If the Rock of Plymouth is annually remembered, — if the landing at Jamestown finds a perpetual echo in song, — if the 4th of July and the 22d of February, shall never fail to inspire the hearts of loyal Americans, let not the landing of the first English colony in Maine sink into oblivious silence!

Your obedient servant,

WILLIAM WILLIS,

President of the Maine Historical Society.

The request, so suitably presented in this communication, was promptly responded to by the Mayor, who accordingly issued the following call for a preliminary meeting, to be held as therein indicated:

CALL OF THE MEETING BY THE MAYOR OF BATH.

NOTICE. — In compliance with the request of the Maine Historical Society, as expressed in a communication of its President, Hon. William Willis, as to some commemoration in a public manner by our community, of the landing of Popham's Colony on the shores of Maine, I invite the citizens of Bath and vicinity to meet at the City Hall, on Monday evening the 28th inst., at 7 1-2 o'clock, for consultation and cöoperation. I. PUTNAM, *Mayor.*

BATH, July 21, 1862.

The issuing of this call at once led to inquiry and discussion in private circles and in the newspapers, not only of Maine, but of other States.

The "Maine State Press" of Portland, gave the following account of the meeting, held in accordance with the call:

CELEBRATION AT FORT POPHAM.

In accordance with a suggestion of the Maine Historical Society, made through its President to the Mayor of Bath, and a notice by said Mayor published in the papers of that city, a meeting was held in the City Hall at that place, on Monday evening, to take preliminary action relative to the proper observance of the landing and settlement of the first English Colony in New England, at the mouth of the Kennebec River, near the present site of Fort Popham, in the month of August, 1607. The meeting was largely attended, not only by influential citizens of Bath, but by a large delegation from this city, and by gentlemen from Wiscasset, Phipsburg, Bowdoin College, Brunswick, Gorham, Biddeford, Kennebunk, and other places.

The meeting was called to order by Hon. B. C. Bailey of Bath, on whose motion Hon. Israel Putnam, Mayor of that city was invited to preside. Rev. Henry W. Rugg of Bath, was chosen Secretary. Various remarks, explanatory of the objects of the meeting, and of the importance to American colonization and the spread of English civilization, of the event proposed to be celebrated, were made; when, on motion of Rev. John O. Fiske of Bath, a committee of five was selected to propose to the meeting a suitable list of gentlemen to act as an Executive Committee to carry into effect the objects of the meeting. This Committee consisted of Hon. Amos Nourse and John Hayden, Esq., of Bath, John A. Poor, Esq., of this city, R. K. Sewall, Esq., of Wiscasset, and Rev. Edward Ballard of Brunswick.

The committee, after mature deliberation, reported the following gentlemen for the proposed committee, which report was unanimously accepted, to wit:

BATH, — Hon. B. C. Bailey, Rev. John O. Fiske, Oliver Moses, Esq., Col. Frederick D. Sewall, Col. James T. Patten, John B. Swanton, Esq.

BRUNSWICK, — Rev. Edward Ballard, Hon. Charles J. Gilman.

TOPSHAM, — Rev. A. D. Wheeler, D. D.

PHIPSBURG, — Rev. Francis Norwood, Moses Riggs, Esq.

GEORGETOWN, — Thomas M. Reed, Esq.

GARDINER, — Hon. Noah Woods, Rev. Frederick Gardiner.

HALLOWELL, — Charles Dummer, Esq., Ebenezer Rowell, Esq.

AUGUSTA, — Hon. James W. Bradbury, Hon. James G. Blaine.

WISCASSET, — Alexander Johnston, Esq., Rufus K. Sewall, Esq.

GORHAM, — Hon. Josiah Pierce.

PORTLAND, — Rev. Alexander Burgess, Hon. Jedediah Jewett, William P. Preble, Esq.

SACO, — Hon. Philip Eastman.
BIDDEFORD, — Hon. William P. Haines.
KENNEBUNK. — Hon. Edward E. Bourne.
ALFRED, — Hon. John H. Goodenow.
BANGOR, — Hon. Elijah L. Hamlin, Hon. John E. Godfrey.
OLDTOWN, — Hon. George Popham Sewall.
WINSLOW, — Hon. Joseph Eaton.
BELFAST, — Joseph Williamson, Esq.
WATERVILLE, — Rev. J. T. Champlin, D. D.
LEWISTON, — Hon. John M. Frye.
FARMINGTON, — Hon. Robert Goodenow, Hon. Hannibal Belcher.
CALAIS, — Hon. George Downes.
EASTPORT, — Hon. Bion Bradbury.
HOULTON, — Hon. Shepard Cary.
NORRIDGEWOCK, — Hon. John S. Tenney.
MACHIAS, — William B. Smith, Esq.

It was voted that the gentlemen of the foregoing list, selected from Bath, Brunswick, Topsham, Phipsburg, and Georgetown, being in the immediate neighborhood, shall constitute the Executive Committee, with power to increase their numbers, and that the other gentlemen named be an advisory, or assistant committee.

During the evening exceedingly interesting and felicitous remarks were made by Hon. C. J. Gilman, Brunswick; John A. Poor, Esq., Hon. John Neal, Hon. Woodbury Davis, and Rev. Alex. Burgess, of Portland; Rev. J. O. Fiske, Hon. Amos Nourse, Hon. William D. Sewall, Hon. D. C. Magoun, and John Hayden, Esq., of Bath; R. K. Sewall, Esq., of Wiscasset; Hon. William P. Haines, of Biddeford; Prof. Alpheus S. Packard, of Bowdoin College; Hon. Edward E. Bourne, of Kennebunk, and others. The meeting was very enthusiastic, and the speakers were frequently interrupted by applause.

The affair has opened very auspiciously; and a circular, to be issued in a few days, will more definitely set forth the reasons why such an observance as is proposed, should be had; and give some of the proposed details to be observed. The celebration is designed to be *the* event, to Maine, of the year; and to be worthy of our great and glorious commonwealth.

The members of the Executive Committee present organized themselves, after the meeting was adjourned, by choosing the Hon. B. C. Bailey, Chairman, and the Rev. J. O. Fiske, Secretary, both of Bath. At a meeting held at Bath on the next week, Mr. Fiske, in consequence of a pressure of duties, resigned his office, and the Rev. Edward Ballard, of Brunswick, was elected in his place. The Hon. Charles J. Gilman of Brunswick, was appointed Marshal of the day, with power to appoint assistants and secure conveyance by railroad. The Hon. Mr. Bailey and Col. James T. Patten of Bath, were requested to secure means of transportation, by water, from that city to the Fort, and provide platforms and seats for the accommodation of the speakers and the assembly. The members of the committee in Portland were also requested to make arrangements for procuring a tent, and for transportation from that city. On the nomination of the Rev. J. O. Fiske, the Right Rev. George Burgess, Bishop of the Diocese of Maine, was requested to take charge of the religious services of the occasion; and on motion of the Hon. C. J. Gilman, the Hon. John A. Poor was appointed the orator of the day. It was also voted that the Grand Lodge of the Masonic Fraternity of the State be invited to be present on the occasion, and contribute their aid in placing the "Memorial Stone" according to the usages and ceremonies of their ancient Order.

The Executive Committee resolved to fill vacancies and add to the number of members already appointed, as might be desirable; and thereupon, at a subsequent meeting, held on August 1st, they elected Rev. S. F. Dike, of Bath; Hon. John A. Poor, John Neal, Esq., Rev. Wm. Stevens Perry, of Portland; Capt. James Drummond, E. S. J. Neally, Esq., of Bath; Samuel Fairhaven, Esq., of Woolwich; H. S. Hagar, Esq., of Richmond; Edward S. Little, Esq., of Auburn; Hon. George C. Gatchell, of North Anson; Hon. Abner Coburn, of Skowhegan; Capt. Horace A. Gray, of Bowdoinham; and Hon. Franklin Smith, of Waterville.

On the 7th of August, at the Annual Meeting of the Maine Historical Society, held at Brunswick, the following resolution was proposed and unanimously adopted:

On motion,

Resolved, That this Society has heard with great satisfaction, of the proposed celebration to commemorate the founding of the *First English Colony* on the shores of New England, under Captain George Popham, on the 29th day of August current; and approves the action of the Standing Committee in causing public attention to be called thereto; and will prepare a "Memorial Stone," to be placed, with the consent of the General Government, in the walls of the Fort now building, which is to bear his honored name."

On the same day the Executive Committee met again at Brunswick, and adopted the following form of invitation:

PUBLIC HISTORICAL CELEBRATION.

AUGUST 12, 1862.

The undersigned solicit the honor of the company of __________ and ladies at the public celebration, on the two hundred and fifty-fifth anniversary of the founding of the first English Colony on the shores of New England, August 19, 1607 [O. S.]; to take place at the site of Fort Popham, near the place of the original Fort St. George, at the mouth of the Kennebec River, in the ancient Province of Sabino, August 29, 1862 [N. S.].

EXECUTIVE COMMITTEE. — B. C. Bailey, John O. Fiske, Oliver Moses, F. D. Sewall, J. T. Patten, John B. Swanton, James Drummond, E. S. J. Nealley, S. F. Dike, C. J. Gilman, A. D. Wheeler, Francis Norwood, Thomas M. Reed, Moses Riggs.

EDWARD BALLARD, *Secretary.*

The favor of an answer is requested.

The following circular, having been considered and approved, was sent on a printed sheet with the cards of invitation.

ENGLISH COLONIZATION IN AMERICA. — PUBLIC CELEBRATION.

The colonization of the continent of North America by the Anglo-Saxon race, first attempted by Sir Humphrey Gilbert, and followed by Sir Walter Raleigh and Sir Richard Grenville, without success, was finally accomplished by Sir Ferdinando Gorges, who obtained from King James the charter of April 10, 1606, under the broad basis of which the subsequent settlements were made. The voyages of Bartholomew Gosnold, in 1602; of Martin Pring, in 1603, and of George Weymouth, in 1605, — all incipient measures towards a common end, — were under the guidance or patronage of Sir Ferdinando Gorges, the Governor of the Island and Fort of Plymouth, and his friend, the Earl of Southampton, the illustrious friend and patron of Shakespeare. In May, 1606, the Lord Chief Justice of England, Sir John Popham, having become associated in the enterprise, sent out Captain Haines, " in a tall ship belonging to Bristol and the river Severne, to settle a plantation in the river of Sagadahoc," but from the failure of the master to follow the course ordered, the ship fell into the hands of the Spaniards by capture, and the expedition failed of success. In August of the same year, a ship sent out by Sir Ferdinando Gorges, under command of Henry Challong, for the same purpose, — the two designed to form one expedition, — shared a similar fate. So that in consequence of these mishaps, Virginia was occupied prior to Maine. The expedition of Captain Newport, to the Chesapeake, which sailed December 19th, 1606, landed at Jamestown, May 13th, 1607.

On the 31st of May, 1607, the first colony to New England sailed from Plymouth for the Sagadahoc, in two ships, — one, called the "*Gift of God*," whereof George Popham, brother of the chief justice, was commander; the other, the "*Mary and John*," which Raleigh Gilbert commanded, — on board which ships were one hundred and twenty persons, for planters. They came to anchor under an island, supposed to be Monhegan, the 31st of July. After exploring the coast and islands, on Sunday, the 9th of Aug., 1607, they landed on an island they called St. George, where they had a sermon delivered unto them by Mr. Seymour, their preacher, and returned aboard again. On the 15th of Aug., they anchored under Seguin, and on that day the "Gift of God" got into the river of Sagadahoc. On the 16th, both ships got safely in and came to anchor. On the 17th, in two boats, they sailed up the river,— Captain Popham in his pinnace, with thirty persons, and Captain Gilbert in his long boat, with eighteen persons, and " found it a very gallant river; with many good islands therein, and many branches of other small rivers falling into it," and returned. On the the 18th, they all went ashore, and then made choice of a place for their plantation, at the mouth or entry of the river, on the west side, (for the river bendeth towards the nor-east and by east), being almost an island, of good bigness, in a province called by the Indians, "Sabino," — so called of a Sagamore, or chief commander, under the grand bashaba.

On the 19th, they all went ashore, where they had made choice of their plantation, and where they had a sermon delivered unto them by their preacher, and after the sermon the President's commission was read, with the laws to be observed and kept.

George Popham, gent., was nominated President.

Captain Raleigh Gilbert,
James Davies,
Richard Seymour, Preacher,
Captain Richard Davies,
Captain Harlowe,

were all sworn assistants; and so they returned back again.

Thus commenced the first occupation and settlement of New England, and from which date the title of England to the new world remained unquestioned. At this place they opened a friendly trade with the natives, put up houses, and built a small vessel, during the autumn and winter.

On the 5th of February, 1608, George Popham died, and his remains were deposited within the walls of his fort, which was named Fort St. George.

We necessarily pass over the next two hundred and fifty years of history.

Congress having made an appropriation for a fort at the mouth of the Kennebec, — the ancient Sagadahoc, — the following correspondence, copied from the files of the War Office, shows the action of the Secretary of War in the matter, and the fitness of the name selected for the new fort, which is called Fort Popham:

"To the Hon. Simon Cameron, *Secretary of War:*

The undersigned, citizens of Maine, respectfully request that the new fort to be erected at the mouth of the Kennebec River, in Maine, may be named Fort Popham, in honor of Captain George Popham, brother of the learned Chief Justice Popham, of England.

Captain George Popham, as the Governor of the first English Colony in New England, built a fort at or near the site of the proposed fort, in the year 1607, where he died, February 5th, 1608, and was buried, being the first person of his race whose bones were laid beneath the soil of New England, and whose grave will be approriately marked by the fort that rises over his place of burial.

[Signed] John A. Poor,
Reuel Williams.

Washington, Nov. 18, 1861."

This proposal for a name was favorably received at the Engineer Bureau, by General Totten, who laid the matter before the Secretary of War.

On the 23d of November, General Cameron acted on the foregoing petition, and entered thereon :—"Name approved.

Simon Cameron, *Secretary of War.*

War Department, Washington, Nov. 23, 1861."

It has been proposed that a memorial stone, with an appropriate inscription, be inserted in the wall of this new fort, and this event made the occasion of a public celebration, commemorating not only the first settlement of New England, but doing honor to the memory of the man, who led to it, the first British Colony, and who, after honorably discharging the duties of his office, and presenting a report, in the form of a letter, to the King, dated Fort St. George,

December 13th, 1607, here laid down his life, — the first man of the English race whose bones are laid beneath the soil of New England.

The 19th of August, 1607, *Old Style*, corresponds to the 29th of August of the present calendar. The day on which, with religious services, they dedicated the spot and inaugurated their government, is appropriately fixed upon for the proposed celebration. This year the anniversary day falls on Friday, August 29th.

The following programme having been prepared by the part of the Executive Committee, to whom the charge of this portion of the arrangements had been entrusted, was advertised in the newspapers of the State, and distributed in the form of handbills:

HISTORICAL CELEBRATION AT FORT POPHAM, AUGUST 29, 1862.

There will be a public celebration of the founding of the first British Colony on the shores of New England, under the authority of the Royal Charter of April 10th, 1606, at the site of the ancient Fort St. George, on the Peninsula of Sabino, at the mouth of the Kennebec River, which will take place on Friday, August 29th, 1862, the two hundred and fifty-fifth anniversary of the inauguration of the first civil government on these shores.

Special Trains, leaving Portland and Augusta at 7 A. M., will be run over the Kennebec and Portland Railroad, leaving Brunswick at 8 A. M., connecting at Bath with the steamers running to and from the site of Fort Popham, returning to Portland and to Augusta, stopping at the intermediate places on the same evening after the celebration services are completed.

Excursion tickets over the railroad will be sold at half price, or $1.25 down and back. From Brunswick and Topsham, fifty cents for tickets both ways. Trains will also run over the Androscoggin Railroad at half price, connecting at Brunswick with the trains to Bath. Fares from all other intermediate stations at half price; and on the steamers, twenty-five cents.

Tickets admitting parties upon the parade of the fort and to the collation will be thirty-seven cents. Parties arriving on the ground by the other modes of conveyance will also be furnished with tickets to the grounds of the celebration and to the collation at the same price. The collation will be spread in the great tent, and no one admitted to it without a ticket.

The Hon. C. J. Gilman of Brunswick will be chief marshal of the day, with assistant marshals, who will assign places to the various parties admitted to the grounds, and within the tent. At 10½ o'clock A. M., the chief marshal will call to order and announce the objects and purposes of the celebration.

The Hon. William Willis, President of the Maine Historical Society, will then make a brief historical statement, and invite the Rev. George Burgess, D. D., Episcopal Bishop of the Diocese of Maine, to conduct the religious services in those forms of the church made use of at the time of the founding of Popham's Colony. Printed forms will then be distributed.

The service concluded, the President of the Historical Society will invite his Excellency, Israel Washburn, Jr., Governor of Maine, to cause the Memorial Stone to be put in place, by the consent of the United States Government, in accordance with the request of the Maine Historical Society. Accepting this trust with an allusion to the historic importance of the occasion, Gov. Washburn will invite Leonard Woods, D. D., President of Bowdoin College, to take charge of the work.

Addressing Gen. Totten or Capt. T. L. Casey, the officer in charge, and receiving in reply the assent of the government, Dr. Woods will invite the Masonic Fraternity to cause the Memorial Stone to be put into its place, wlth the appropriate forms of their ancient order. Hon. Josiah H. Drummond, Grand Master of the Grand Lodge of Maine, will then proceed with the ceremony, and its conclusion will be followed by appropriate music. This will be followed by an address by John A. Poor, Esq., of Portland, the orator of the day.

From the fort the company will march to the pavilion, where Judge Kent of Bangor will preside, assisted by vice-presidents, one from each county, as follows:

York, ... Hon. Philip Eastman.
Cumberland, ... Hon. John B. Brown.
Lincoln, ... Hon. Isaac Reed.
Hancock, ... Hon. Andrew Peters.
Washington, ... Hon. Aaron Hayden.
Kennebec, ... Hon. Joseph H. Williams.
Oxford, ... Dr. Isaiah B. Bradley.
Penobscot, ... Hon. William C. Hammatt.
Somerset, ... Hon. Abner Coburn.
Waldo, ... Hon. William G. Crosby.
Franklin, ... Hon. Samuel Belcher.
Piscataquis, ... Hon. John H. Rice.
Androscoggin, ... A. D. Lockwood, Esq.
Sagadahoc, ... Hon. B. C. Bailey.
Aroostook, ... Hon. E. Woodbury.
York, ... Hon. N. A. Farwell.

Toastmaster, — Hon. George Popham Sewall.

In response to appropriate sentiments, speeches will be made by eminent men from different parts of the United States and the British Provinces.

Per Order of the Executive Committee,

Edward Ballard, *Secretary.*

By subsequent arrangements the committee agreed on the following Toasts, — the order to be changed as circumstances might require, — to each of which they invited responses from distinguished gentlemen in different parts of the United States and of British North America:

TOASTS FOR THE POPHAM CELEBRATION.

The 19th of August [*O. S.*], 1607, — ever memorable as the day that witnessed the consummation of the title of England to the New World, by the formal occupation and possession of New England, under the Royal Charter of April 10, 1606.

The President of the United States.

The Queen of Great Britain.

The Memory of George Popham, — who led hither the first English Colony; became the head of its government by the election of his companions, and left his bones to mingle with the soil of New England, upon the Peninsula of Sabino.

The Memory of Sir Ferdinando Gorges, — the Father of English Colonization in America.

Henry Wriothesley, Earl of Southampton, — patron of Letters and of American Colonization; the friend and associate of Sir Ferdinando Gorges; whose joint labors procured the Royal Charter of April 10, 1606; the basis on which rests the title of our race to the New World.

Sir John Popham,— the able, learned, and upright Chief Justice of England, by the appointment of Elizabeth; under the shadow of whose great name was laid the foundation of the Colossal Empire of the Western World.

Maritime Adventure and Discovery, — illustrated by the men of Bristol and the Severne; whose Cabots and Gilberts pointed the way to the northern shores of the New World. The name of Raleigh Gilbert shall ever be honored for his fidelity in conducting to these shores the colony of Popham.

The Memory of Sieur de Champlain, — the fearless navigator and accomplished statesman; the first to explore and designate these shores; whose plans of empire, more vast and sagacious than any of his time, failed of success only through the short-sightedness of his sovereign, in allowing the Atlantic shores of New England to fall into the hands of his rivals, thereby changing the history of the New World.

Richard Vines,— the faithful friend of Sir Ferdinando Gorges, whose occupation of the country, to the time of his appointment as Deputy Governor of the

"Province of Mayne," in 1644, upheld the title of his nation against the French, and saved New England to his country.

Pierre du Gas, Seigneur De Monts, — the Patentee of the first charter of Henry of Navarre, who sacrificed empire and fortune rather than his religious faith, and beheld the fairest portion of the continent, which he had apparently secured to his nation, pass into the hands of his rivals.

George Weymouth,— the early explorer of the coast of New England; memorable for his description of our own coast and his exploration of "the most excellent and beneficyall river of Sachadehoc."

The Ancient Dominions of Maine, — Sabino, Sagadahoc, Sheepscot, Pemaquid, and Monhegan; the theater of early maritime discovery and settlement; the designed seat of empire of our colonial ancestors.

The Colonization of Manhattan — by the Hollanders; whose tolerant spirit and commercial enterprise laid the foundation of the great metropolis of the New World.

Captain John Smith, — the daring soldier and navigator; whose efforts in acts of government in Virginia, and of naval skill in exploring and defining the boundaries of New England, which he made known by maps and description, give his name a place among the great men of his time.

The Mountains and the Seas, — Hindrances to the sluggish, — helps to the adventurous.

The Brotherhood of Nations, — the holiest of all brotherhoods; requiring only that mankind should remember their parentage, their relationship, and their inheritance.

The Fall of Quebec,— under the leadership of the heroic Wolfe, in 1759, which gave peace, security, and progress to the frontier settlements of the colonies, and supremacy to English power in North America.

Sir William Phips, — the ship carpenter of Woolwich, — the bold seaman and adventurer, the Baronet, the successful General and Governor. His life and character illustrated the spirit and genius of New England.

The Coast Line of Maine, — the nursery of seamen; affording the highest advantages for maritime and commercial pursuits; more deeply indented than any on the globe. The efforts and skill of modern science have laid open its most secret recesses to the uses of commerce.

The Eastern Coast of New England, — the arena of the conflict of the races, where alternated the fortunes of the French and English.

The Saco, — the home of Vines and companions in 1616, and the first seat of justice, in which the forms of the common law were put into practice.

Pennsylvania, — to whose archives we are indebted for the only exact account of Arnold's expedition to Canada.

The Memory of Ex-Governor King. — the first Governor of Maine after she ceased to be a Province of Massachusetts, and became one of the States of the Union.

Change and Progress, — these make up the history of the world, mental, moral, and physical. Slowly were they written upon its pages, till Fulton, Stephenson, Henry, and Morse, solved the problem of intercommunication by steam and lightning.

The Virginia of Sagadahoc, — the *first* vessel built on the North American continent; the germ of that naval architecture which has made Maine the foremost community of the world in shipbuilding.

Plymouth Plantation, — founded by men of strong faith, of earnest piety; educated under the teachings of Robinson and Brewster at Leyden, they were fitted to become pioneers in the new movement toward civil and religious liberty.

Nova Scotia, — the earliest battle ground of the races upon this continent; the home of the loyalist in Revolutionary times. Distinguished for the fascinations of its scenery and its treasures of mineral wealth, but still more distinguished for the intelligence of its people and the ability of its public men.

New Brunswick, — cotemporaneous with Maine in origin and neighboring in territory; may our bonds of good fellowship never be broken.

The Colony of Massachusetts' Bay, — founded in 1629, by men of the same unconquerable will as those that brought royalty to the block, and discarded prescription as heresy. Their descendants have ever shown a faithful adherence to the doctrine of "*Uniformity.*"

The Heroes of 1776, — may the men of to-day prove themselves worthy to be called their sons.

New Jersey, — where the Northmen of the Scandinavian Peninsula founded their first colony in the New World.

The Valley of the Mississippi, — the garden of the world. Its development in population, wealth, and power, — in all that constitutes progress in the highest civilization, finds no parallel in history.

The Art of War, — the only guarantee of the blessings of peace. For the vast improvements in the means of attack and defense of the present day, our country is mainly indebted to the ability, caution, and consummate skill of the distinguished Chief of the Bureau of Engineers of the Army of the United States.

The West, — The proudest achievement of modern civilization. The march of empire Westward, — unlike the conquering hordes of Atilla, or the advance of the Tartar tribes of Tamerlane, — diffuses peace, plenty, and content among the teeming millions, that throng the vast domain of the Mississippi valley.

Rhode Island, — the early home of toleration, and of civil and religious freedom, — the greatness of whose example is in inverse proportion to the extent of her territory.

The Clergy of New England, — who, by their early and assiduous devotion to popular education, became the architects of our civilization. Their teachings and influence have saved our prosperity from degenerating into luxury, and have helped to preserve in our children the fidelity to principle and the fear of God, which characterized the fathers and founders of the New England colonies.

The Rights of New England Citizenship, — Hard Work with Freedom; Hard Thought with Generosity; Hard Fighting with Patience unto Victory.

Poetry and Art, — twin products of civilization, at once the loftiest expressions of human genius and the most elevating in their influence on mankind, — the works of a Longfellow and an Akers attest that their growth is native to our soil, and that after the lapse of two centuries and a half, the wilderness, in this highest efflorescence of humanity, has indeed been made "to blossom as the rose."

Diplomacy: the Instrument of International Conciliation, — wisely used by the Master's hand; may it guide us as it has guided our periled ship of State past the threatened dangers of foreign intervention, and while restoring our own, preserve the world's peace.

The Memory of Governor Sullivan, — the earliest Historian of his native State, and the honored Chief Magistrate of the Commonwealth of Massachusetts, of which Maine then constituted a part; his residence on the banks of the Kennebec fitted him for the study of the earliest annals of our State, and made him eminent not only in the department of law and of statesmanship, but of history.

THE CELEBRATION.

The day, — Friday, August 29th,[1] — appointed for the fulfilment of the design of the various actions of the committee,

[1] Some inquiries were made for the reasons of the selection of the 29th day, rather than the 30th, for the commemoration; as the opinion had been held that *eleven* days, in that century, instead of *ten*, should be added to the date in the Old Style to bring it to the proper day in the New. The following article, from the "Brunswick Telegraph," furnishes a suitable explanation:

Old Style and New Style.—When the announcement of the day for the celebration at Fort Popham was made, it was thought, spoken, and written, that a mistake had been committed in adding *ten* days to change the date, August 19, 1607, O. S., to August 29, 1862, N. S., instead of *eleven*. But the decision was right for the years in that century. In a late number of the Historical and Genealogical Register, published in Boston, there is an allusion to the real error, made in regard to the day for commemorating the landing of the Pilgrims at Plymouth, in placing it one day too late. The first celebration of that event was held on "Friday, December 22, 1769." The writer proceeds to say: "A mistake was then made in reducing the Old Style date (Dec. 11), to New Style, which caused them to select the wrong day for the celebration. The mistake was not noticed for some time; and when it was discovered, the error was too firmly fixed in the public mind to be easily removed. An effort, however, was made in 1849, to change the celebration to the true day. A committee was appointed by the Pilgrim Society, December 15th, of that year, who reported, May 27th, 1850, that the 21st of December was the true anniversary of the landing, and recommended that this day be celebrated in future, instead of the 22d. The report was accepted by the Society, and a vote passed in accordance with the recommendation of the committee. We believe, however, that the force of habit has proved stronger that the love of truth, and that the Pilgrim Society has rescinded its vote, and again celebrates the 22d of December." Thus it is evident, that the believers in Popham celebrate a true event on the right day and place; but the believers in Plymouth Rock commemorate a true event in the right place, but on the wrong day.

was as clear and beautiful as the season could allow. The response to the notice and invitations was given by thousands of persons of both sexes, from this and other States, and from the British Provinces. The railroad accommodations, though specially provided and judiciously intended to be ample, were insufficient to afford passage to many, who were seeking to participate in the expected enjoyments of the day. Difficulty also was feared in finding means of conveyance by water from Bath to the mouth of the Kennebec, as the government had taken into its employ the principal steamers that had usually plied on the river and on the other steamboat routes in Maine. Two tug boats with two barges each had been secured by Col. J. T. Patten, the committee, for the purpose. But they were filled to the utmost, and had departed before the arrival of the cars from Portland, Augusta, and Lewiston, as had also a stern wheel boat from Augusta, which made a second trip at a later hour. Fortunately for the accommodation of the multitude thus arriving, a steamboat from Bangor, independently of the efforts of the committee, had been placed at the depot wharf, and with its capacious barges, fully met the emergency.

After the necessary delay in receiving on board this large number of persons, the trip commenced favorably, and was enlivened at intervals with patriotic and other music of the Band from Fort Preble, engaged for the occasion, and another provided by the boat from Bangor. The waters of the river had already been made historical by the entrance of Captain George Weymouth [1605], in the ship "Archangel," and his explorations on its western shore;[1] and minds, familiar with the records of those first events of English enterprise, delighted to recall the distant past, to compare it with the changes to the present, and to dwell on other topics suited to the time, the

[1] See the statements of Strachey, Hubbard, and Prince. Purchase added to the narrative of Rosier, and thus led Belknap into an error, as has been truly shown by the late John McKeen, Esq.—Me. Hist. Col. Vol. 5.

excursion, and its object. Large numbers of persons reached the place also from different quarters by steamboats, yachts, and small boats on the water, and by vehicles of various kinds on the land, and were ready to greet the large crowd on the fourth boat from Bath with welcoming cheers. The vessels in the harbor were gaily dressed, and conspicuous among them was the Revenue Cutter, decorated with the flags of Old and New England, and which had been furnished by the Hon. Jedediah Jewett, Collector of the port of Portland, to give aid on the festive occasion, and which had brought the President and members of the Historical Society, and other gentlemen of distinction. When all were assembled on the shore the numbers were variously estimated at from five to seven thousand. So large a multitude had hardly been expected; and, coming from many different places, near and distant, with thoughts converging to one object, it was an unexpected incident, that showed the interest of the public mind in the purpose of the gathering, and will be long remembered as one of the most cheering circumstances of the commemoration, to show that the design had already in good part been accomplished.

AT THE FORT.

The first place of gathering was on the parade of the Fort, now in process of erection, on the eastern point of the peninsula of the ancient province of Sabino, where a platform for the opening services had been judiciously prepared by the Hon. B. C. Bailey, who also provided the platform, seats, and tables in the tent. This position was in full view of the mouth of the river, the high grounds of the peninsula, the opposite shore, the broad ocean, and the neighboring islands. On this platform were assembled the President and members of the Historical Society, the Bishop of the Diocese and the clergy of different denominations, Presidents and Professors of Bowdoin and Waterville Colleges, Representatives of the State and General Governments, the Orator of the day, and gentlemen of distinction from this and neighboring States and from the British Provinces. The large audience was called to order by the Hon. C. J. Gilman, the Marshal of the day, who thereupon made the following remarks:

ADDRESS OF THE HON. C. J. GILMAN.

Two hundred and fifty-five years ago this day, under the auspices of a Royal charter granted by King James, there assembled on the Peninsula of Sabino, and near to this spot, a party of Englishmen, who formed the first civil and Protestant government of the New World, and by formal occupation and possession, established the title of England to the continent. In the year 1607, in the month of August, on the 19th day of the month, the Commission of George Popham for the Presidency of the new Government was read. Captain Raleigh Gilbert, James Davies, Richard Seymour, the preacher, Capt. Richard Davies, and Capt. Harlow, were all sworn assistants.

In commemoration of this event, the Historical Society of this State, in correspondence with citizens in different parts of the State, have concurred in this celebration; and it is proposed from time to time, in the valley of the Sagadahoc, on the Peninsula of Sabino, to recall and to illustrate the events of the past, and by this and future celebrations to assign to Maine her true historic position. On this spot, under the direction of the distinguished Chief of the Bureau of Engineers, and his accomplished assistants, a Fort is in process of construction. In compliance with a petition of John A. Poor and Reuel Williams, dated Washington, November 18th, 1861, Simon Cameron, then Secretary of War, with the approval of Gen. Totten, determined to associate this Fort with the name of "Popham" and the history of his colony.

In order that the record of events, which here transpired, may be made still more vivid and impressive, it has been thought fit and proper to insert in the wall of the Fort a "Memorial Stone." The President of the Historical Society, the President of Bowdoin College, the representative of the government of the State, the representative of the government of the United States, and the Grand Masonic Lodge of Maine, in the disposition and adjustment of this stone, will participate. Before the commencement of these interesting exercises, let us imitate the example of those who stood here two hundred and fifty-five years ago this day. As the Rev. Richard Seymour, Chaplain of the Colony was invited to perform acts of religious worship *then*, so *now* do I invite the Right Rev. George Burgess, Bishop of the Diocese of Maine, to perform acts of religious worship according to the ceremonial of the Episcopal Church of that day.

In accordance with this request, the Bishop proceeded to the religious duties of the occasion, using, as nearly as the changed circumstances of the case would allow, the same services, taken from the Prayer Book of the time of King James, as were employed by the colonists in their solemnities on the day commemorated, under the guidance of their Chaplain, the Rev. Richard Seymour. They were as follows:

AN ORDER FOR MORNING PRAYER.

At what time soever a sinner doth repent him of his sin from the bottom of his heart, I will put all his wickedness out of my remembrance, saith the Lord. *Ezekiel* XVIII.

I will go to my Father, and say to him, Father, I have sinned against heaven: and against thee, and am no more worthy to be called thy son. *Luke* XV.

Dearly beloved brethren, the Scripture moveth us in sundry places to acknowledge, and confess our manifold sins and wickedness, and that we should not dissemble nor cloke them before the face of Almighty God our heavenly Father, but confess them with an humble, lowly, penitent, and obedient heart, to the end, that we may obtain forgiveness of the same by his infinite goodness and mercy. And although we ought at all times humbly to acknowledge our sins before God, yet ought we most chiefly so to do, when we assemble and meet together, to render thanks for the great benefits that we have received at his hands, to set forth his most worthy praise, to hear his most holy word, and to ask those things which are requisite and necessary, as well for the body as the soul. Wherefore I pray and beseech you, as many as are here present, to accompany me with a pure heart and humble voice, unto the throne of the heavenly grace, saying after me.

[A general confession to be made of the whole congregation after the minister, kneeling.]

Almighty and most merciful Father: We have erred and strayed from thy ways like lost sheep. We have followed too much the devices and desires of our own hearts. We have offended against thy holy laws. We have left undone those things which we ought to have done; and we have done those things which we ought not to have done; and there is no health in us. But thou, O Lord, have mercy upon us, miserable offenders. Spare thou them, O God, which confess their faults. Restore thou them that are penitent; according to thy promises declared unto mankind in Christ Jesu our Lord. And grant, O most merciful Father, for his sake, that we may hereafter live a godly, righteous, and sober life, to the glory of thy holy Name. *Amen.*

[The absolution, or remission of sins, to be pronounced by the minister alone.]

Almighty God, the Father of our Lord Jesus Christ, who desireth not the death of a sinner, but rather, that he may turn from his wickedness, and live: and hath given power and commandment to his Ministers to declare and pronounce to his people, being penitent, the absolution and remission of their sins: He pardoneth and absolveth all them that truly repent and unfeignedly believe his holy Gospel. Wherefore let us beseech him to grant us true repentance, and his Holy Spirit, that those things may please him, which we do at this present, and that the rest of our life hereafter, may be pure, and holy, so that at the last we may come to his eternal joy, through Jesus Christ our Lord.

[The people shall answer:]

Amen.

[Then shall the minister begin the Lord's Prayer with a loud voice.]

Our Father, which art in Heaven, Hallowed be thy Name. Thy Kingdom come. Thy will be done in Earth as it is in Heaven. Give us this day our daily bread. And forgive us our trespasses, as we forgive them that trespass against us. And lead us not into temptation; But deliver us from evil. *Amen.*

[Then likewise he shall say,]

O Lord, open thou our lips.

Answer. And our mouth shall show forth thy praise.

Priest. O God, make speed to save us.

Answer. O Lord, make haste to help us.

[Then all of them standing up, the Presbyter shall say or sing.]

Priest. Glory be to the Father, and to the Son, and to the Holy Ghost.

As it was in the beginning, is now, and ever shall be, world without end. *Amen.*

Praise ye the Lord.

Answer. The Lord's name be praised.

[Then shall follow certain Psalms in order, as they are appointed in a table made for that purpose.]

PSALM 95. — VENITE EXULTEMUS.

O come, let us sing unto the Lord: let us heartily rejoice in the strength of our salvation.

Let us come before his presence with thanksgiving: and show ourselves glad in him with Psalms.

For the Lord is a great God: and a great King above all gods.

In his hand are all the corners of the earth: and the strength of the hills is his also.

The sea is his, and he made it: and his hands prepared the dry land.

O come, let us worship, and fall down: and kneel before the Lord our Maker.

For he is the Lord our God: and we are the people of his pasture, and the sheep of his hand.

To-day if ye will hear his voice, harden not your hearts: as in the provocation, and as in the day of temptation in the wilderness:

When your fathers tempted me: proved me and saw my works.

Forty years long was I grieved with this generation, and said: It is a people that do err in their hearts, for they have not known my ways.

Unto whom I sware in my wrath: that they should not enter into my rest.

Glory be to the Father, and to the Son, and to the Holy Ghost:

As it was in the beginning, is now, and ever shall be: world without end. *Amen.*

PSALM 96. — CANTATE DOMINO.

1. O sing unto the Lord a new song; sing unto the Lord, all the whole earth.

2. Sing unto the Lord, and praise his name; be telling of his salvation from day to day.

3. Declare his honor unto the heathen, and his wonders unto all people.

4. For the Lord is great, and cannot worthily be praised; he is more to be feared than all gods.

5. As for the gods of the heathen, they are but idols; but it is the Lord that made the heavens.

6. Glory and worship are before him; power and honor are in his sanctuary.

7. Ascribe unto the Lord, O ye kindreds of the people, ascribe unto the Lord worship and power.

8. Ascribe unto the Lord the honor due unto his name; bring presents, and come into his courts.

9. O worship the Lord in the beauty of holiness; let the whole earth stand in awe of him.

10. Tell it out among the heathen, that the Lord is King; and that it is he who hath made the round world so fast that it cannot be moved; and how that he shall judge the people righteously.

11. Let the heavens rejoice, and let the earth be glad; let the sea make a noise, and all that therein is.

12. Let the field be joyful, and all that is in it; then shall all the trees of the wood rejoice before the Lord.

13. For he cometh, for he cometh to judge the earth; and with righteousness to judge the world, and the people with his truth.

Glory be to the Father, and to the Son, and to the Holy Ghost;

As it was in the beginning, is now, and ever shall be, world without end. *Amen.*

PSALM 97.—DOMINUS REGNAVIT.

1. The Lord is King, the earth may be glad thereof; yea, the multitude of the isles may be glad thereof.

2. Clouds and darkness are round about him; righteousness and judgment are the habitation of his seat.

3. There shall go a fire before him, and burn up his enemies on every side.

4. His lightnings gave shine unto the world; the earth saw it, and was afraid.

5. The hills melted like wax at the presence of the Lord; at the presence of the Lord of the whole earth.

6. The heavens have declared his righteousness, and all the people have seen his glory.

7. Confounded be all they that worship carved images, and that delight in vain gods; worship him all ye gods.

8. Sion heard of it, and rejoiced; and the daughters of Juda were glad, because of thy judgments, O Lord.

9. For thou, Lord, art higher than all that are in the earth; thou art exalted far above all gods.

10. O ye that love the Lord, see that ye hate the thing which is evil; the Lord preserveth the souls of his saints; he shall deliver them from the hands of the ungodly.

11. There is sprung up a light for the righteous, and joyful gladness for such as are true-hearted.

12. Rejoice in the Lord, ye righteous, and give thanks for a remembrance of his holiness.

Glory be to the Father, and to the Son, and to the Holy Ghost;

As it was in the beginning, is now, and ever shall be, world without end. *Amen.*

[Then shall be read two lessons distinctly, with a loud voice, that the people may hear. The first of the Old Testament; the second of the New, — like as they be appointed in the Kalendar. And before every lesson the Minister shall say thus: The first, second, third, or fourth chapter of Genesis, or Exodus. Matthew, Mark, or other like, as is appointed in the Kalendar. And in the end of every chapter, he shall say, Here endeth such a chapter of such a Book.]

THE FIRST LESSON IS DANIEL I.

[Then shall be said]

Te Deum Laudamus.

We praise thee, O God; we acknowledge thee to be the Lord.

All the earth doth worship thee, the Father everlasting.

To thee all Angels cry aloud; the Heavens, and all the Powers therein.

To thee, Cherubim and Seraphim continually do cry.

Holy, Holy, Holy, Lord God of Sabaoth.

Heaven and Earth are full of the Majesty of thy Glory.

The glorious company of the Apostles praise thee.

The goodly fellowship of the Prophets praise thee.

The noble army of Martyrs praise thee.

The holy Church throughout all the world, doth acknowledge thee,

The Father, of an infinite Majesty;

Thine adorable, true, and only Son;

Also the Holy Ghost, the Comforter.

Thou art the King of Glory, O Christ.

Thou art the everlasting Son of the Father.

When thou tookest upon thee to deliver man, thou didst not abhor the Virgin's womb.

When thou hadst overcome the sharpness of death, thou didst open the kingdom of heaven to all believers.

Thou sittest at the right hand of God, in the glory of the Father.

We believe that thou shalt come to be our Judge.

We therefore pray thee, help thy servants, whom thou hast redeemed with thy precious blood.

Make them to be numbered with thy saints in glory everlasting.

O Lord, save thy people, and bless thine heritage.

Govern them, and lift them up forever.

Day by day we magnify thee;

And we worship thy Name ever, world without end.

Vouchsafe, O Lord, to keep us this day without sin.

O Lord have mercy upon us, have mercy upon us.

O Lord, let thy mercy be upon us, as our trust is in thee.

O Lord, in thee have I trusted; let me never be confounded.

THE SECOND LESSON IS ACTS XVII.

[After the second lesson shall be used and said as followeth :]

PSALM C. — JUBILATE DEO.

O be joyful in the Lord, all ye lands; serve the Lord with gladness, and come before his presence with a song.

Be ye sure that the Lord he is God, it is he that hath made us, and not we ourselves; we are his people and the sheep of his pasture.

O go your way into his gates with thanksgiving, and into his courts with praise; be thankful unto him, and speak good of his name.

For the Lord is gracious, his mercy is everlasting; and his truth endureth from generation to generation.

Glory be to the Father, and to the Son, and to the Holy Ghost;

As it was in the beginning, is now, and ever shall be, world without end. *Amen.*

[Then shall be said the Creed, by the Minister and the people, standing.]

I believe in God the Father Almighty, Maker of Heaven and Earth: And in Jesus Christ his only Son our Lord; Who was conceived by the Holy Ghost, born of the Virgin Mary, suffered under Pontius Pilate, was crucified, dead, and buried; He descended into Hell; the third day he rose again from the dead; He ascended into Heaven; and sitteth on the right hand of God the Father Almighty; from thence he shall come to judge the quick and the dead.

I believe in the Holy Ghost; The Holy Catholic Church; The communion of Saints; The forgiveness of sins; The resurrection of the body, and the life everlasting. *Amen.*

[And after that, these Prayers following, all devoutly kneeling; the Minister first pronouncing,]

The Lord be with you.

Ans. And with thy spirit.

Min. Let us pray.

Lord have mercy upon us.

Christ have mercy upon us.

Lord have mercy upon us.

Our Father who art in Heaven; Hallowed be thy Name. Thy Kingdom come. Thy Will be done in Earth, as it is in Heaven. Give us this day our daily bread. And forgive us our trespasses, as we forgive them that trespass against us. And lead us not into temptation; But deliver us from evil. *Amen.*

O Lord, show thy mercy upon us.

Ans. And grant us thy salvation.

O Lord, save thy people.

Ans. And bless thine inheritance.

Give peace in our time, O Lord.

Ans. Because there is none other that fighteth for us, but only thou, O God.

O God, make clean our hearts within us;

Ans. And take not thy Holy Spirit from us.

[Then shall follow the first Collect for the day.]

God, who declarest thy Almighty power most chiefly in showing mercy and pity, give unto us abundantly thy grace, that we, running to thy promises, may be made partakers of thy heavenly treasure, through Jesus Christ our Lord.

[The Second Collect for Peace.]

O God, who art the author of peace and lover of concord, in knowledge of whom standeth our eternal life, whose service is perfect freedom; defend us, thy humble servants, in all assaults of our enemies; that we, surely trusting in thy defense, may not fear the power of any adversaries, through the might of Jesus Christ our Lord. *Amen.*

[The Third Collect for Grace.]

O Lord, our heavenly Father, Almighty and everlasting God, who hast safely brought us to the beginning of this day; defend us in the same with thy mighty power, and grant that this day we fall into no sin, neither run into any kind of danger; but that all our doings may be ordered by thy governance, to do always that is righteous in thy sight, through Jesus Christ our Lord. *Amen.*

[A Prayer for the President of the United States, and all in Civil Authority.]

O Lord, our heavenly Father, the high and mighty Ruler of the universe, who dost from thy throne behold all the dwellers upon earth; most heartily we beseech thee, with thy favor to behold and bless thy servant, *The President of the United States*, and all others in authority; and so replenish them with the grace of thy Holy Spirit, that they may always incline to thy will, and walk in thy way: Endue them plenteously with heavenly gifts; grant them in health and prosperity long to live; and finally, after this life, to attain everlasting joy and felicity, through Jesus Christ our Lord. *Amen.*

[A Prayer in time of War.]

O Almighty God, King of all kings, and Governor of all things, whose power no creature is able to resist, to whom it belongeth justly to punish sinners, and to be merciful to those who truly repent; Save and deliver us, we humbly beseech thee, from the hands of our enemies: abate their pride, assuage their malice, and confound their devices, that we, being armed with thy defense, may be preserved evermore from all perils, to glorify thee, who art the only giver of all victory, through the merits of thy only Son, Jesus Christ, our Lord. *Amen.*

[A Prayer of *St. Chrysostom.*]

Almighty God, who hast given us grace at this time with one accord to make our common supplications unto thee; and dost promise that when two or three are gathered together in thy Name, thou wilt grant their requests; Fulfil now, O LORD, the desires and petitions of thy servants, as may be most expedient for them; granting us in this world knowledge of thy truth, and in the world to come life everlasting. *Amen.*

2 COR. XIII.

The grace of our Lord JESUS CHRIST, and the love of GOD, and the fellowship of the HOLY GHOST, be with us all evermore. *Amen.*

[Then shall be sung PSALM CXXXIX. vers. 7—10, as followeth:]

7. Yea, let me take the morning wings, and let me go and dwell
E'en in the very utmost parts, where flowing seas do swell:

8. Yet certainly there also shall thy hand me lead and guide,
And thy right hand shall hold me fast, and make me to abide.

9. Or if I say the darkness shall shroud me quite from thy sight,
E'en then the night that is most dark about me shall be light.

10. The darkness hideth not from thee, but night doth shine as day;
To thee darkness and the light are both alike alway.

This "ORDER" was distributed among the persons near the place where the worship was offered, in which many persons interested in this service, united in the responsive portions. The singing of the metrical Psalm was aided by the soft and sweet music of the Band.

When these impressive services were concluded, the Hon. William Willis, of Portland, President of the Historical Society, made the following address:

HISTORICAL STATEMENT BY THE HON. WILLIAM WILLIS.

The Maine Historical Society accepts, with great satisfaction, the honorable position assigned to it in the interesting ceremonies of this day. It is the agreeable duty of the society to explore and elucidate the sources of our history, and to trace its progress from the feeble steps of its earliest life, to the gigantic strides of the present day. We therefore welcome every occasion which gives fresh impulse to historical investigation, or awakens new interest in the antiquities of our country.

The present is one of those auspicious occasions; and we congratulate our fellow-citizens of this early discovered and renowned river, — this ancient Sagadahoc, — on the happy suggestion, to elevate into general notice, by a signal demonstration, one of the important events in the early annals of our State.

The English people, with their accustomed caution, were slow in improving the great advantage which their first discovery of the American continent, by Cabot, gave them. It was near a hundred years, before they made any attempt to plant a colony on any part of America. They took no interest in colonization, and little in commercial voyages for many years. They permitted the Spanish, the Portugese, and the French to engross maritime enterprises.

In 1524, twenty-seven years after Cabot's discovery, Verrazani, under the French, ranged the whole coast from Florida to Newfoundland. In 1534, James Cartier, with a commission from Francis I., coasted along the shores of the Gulf of St. Lawrence, and took possession of them in the name of France; and the next year, he sailed up the St. Lawrence, and laid the foundation of a colony at Hochelaga, now Montreal.

The interest of these three commercial nations was kept up by the zeal with which they pursued their *fishing* voyages on the American coast. This branch of trade was of more consequence to Europe than any other. As early as 1506, vessels visited the coast from Biscay, Brittany, and Normandy, and within twenty years from the first voyage of Cabot, 1497, fifty vessels, from Spain, Portugal, and France, were engaged in the fisheries about Newfoundland.

It was not until 1548, that the English government passed their first act for the encouragement of the fisheries, after which they became active competitors in this profitable occupation. Before the close of that century, when the English had fifty vessels on the banks, Portugal had an equal number, Spain double, and France three times as many. These large enterprises led the English people to an increasing interest in

American adventure, and to a familiarity of the coast, which induced them to take measures for the enlargement and protection of their commerce in those regions. With this view, Sir Humphrey Gilbert, in 1578, obtained a charter for "places not possessed by any Christian Prince," [1] and in 1583, he fitted out an expedition of four vessels and two hundred and fifty men, with which he entered the harbor of St. John, in Newfoundland, erected the standard of England, and took possession of the country under the English Crown. This was the first actual possession taken by that nation this side of the Atlantic. Raleigh followed the next year with a large expedition to the coast of North Carolina.

But it was not until the beginning of the 17th century, that serious attention was turned to the shores of New England. Previous to that time, the English had been beguiled by the deceitful phantom of a northwest passage, and nearly all the voyages of the 16th century were made in that fruitless search. The scales have yet hardly fallen from their eyes. It was in pursuit of this open passage, that Cabot, to his great disappointment, lighted upon this continent. He says in a desponding tone,—"I began to sail toward the northwest, not thinking to find any other land than Cathay, and from thence to turn toward India. But after certain days, I found the land run toward the North, which to me was a great displeasure." The voyages of Frobisher, (1576), Davis, (1585), Gilbert and others, were all made in the same unsuccessful pursuit. Even Weymouth, whose voyage gave an immense impulse to English colonization, was seeking the same illusive vision, when, as Gorges says, "falling short of his course, he happened into a river on the coast of America, called Pemaquid."

But the French had the start of the English on the shores

1 Gilbert's grant was dated June 23, 1579, according to Prince, but the copy in Hazard bears date June 11, in the twentieth year of Elizabeth. It was "for places not possessed by any Christian Prince."

of Maine as well as the St. Lawrence; for De Mont, the year before Weymouth made his exploration, planted a colony, in the summer of 1604, upon an island in the St. Croix, now a part of Maine, and constructed a fort, extensive buildings, and made all arrangements for a permanent settlement. But the location, like most of the early occupations, was unfortunate; the island was small, water difficult to be obtained, and no opportunity for adequate cultivation of soil. The next summer it was abandoned; and it so happened, that while Weymouth was making his examination between the Penobscot and Kennebec, De Mont was ranging the coast from St. Croix to Cape Cod, touching in at various points for a more favorable place of settlement, — all lying within his patent from Henry IV., granted November 8, 1603. He looked into the Penobscot, he touched at Sagadahoc, he spent some time in Casco Bay and Winter Harbor, and was delighted with the "Isle of Bacchus," as he called Wood Island which lies at the mouth of Saco River.

The first really sensible movement on the part of the English towards colonization of any part of New England, was the voyage of Gosnold in 1602. He was wise enough to make a direct westerly course, instead of passing through the southern latitudes as was customary; his voyage was thus very much shortened; he made the land about Cape Elizabeth; cruised along the coast, landed at York, had a conference there with the Indians, and proceeded to Vineyard Sound; landed on one of the beautiful islands there, built a store-house, and made preparations to establish a colony. But when the vessel was about to depart with their friends, and put a wide ocean between them and their dear native land and civilized life, the courage of these few colonists failed them; they hastily abandoned their design, and returned home with their companions.

The next year, 1603, Martin Prinn, at the suggestion of Richard Hakluyt, the unwearied friend and patron of colonization, made a successful *trading* voyage in two small vessels fitted out by some merchants of Bristol.

But the voyage of Weymouth, 1605, was so favorable, both in the flattering accounts which the adventurers gave of the country,—it was in the beautiful month of June they saw it,—and in the information as to the resources, furnished by the Indians, who were carried to England, that a fresh impulse was given to western adventure. It added a new patron and persevering friend, in Sir Ferdinando Gorges, then Governor of Plymouth, to whom three of the Indians were committed; who gave him such information in regard to the coast, the rivers, and other advantages which their country afforded, that he became deeply interested in making further discoveries, with a view to occupy, and improve these various sources of wealth.

For, after all, the *profit* was the grand stimulant, as Gorges himself frankly admits. He says, "I had no reason greatly to despair of means, when God should be pleased, by our ordinary frequenting that country, to make it appear that it would both profit and content, to as many as aimed thereat, these being truly the motives that all men labor, howsoever otherwise adjoined, with fair colors and goodly shadows."

In speaking of the "falling short" of Weymouth to find the N. W. Passage, and landing instead on the coast of Maine, Gorges says, "This accident must be acknowledged the means, under God, of putting on foot and giving life to all our plantations."

The first fruit of this new excitement was to secure the sanction of Government; and Sir John Popham, aided by Hakluyt, who not only promoted but recorded American enterprises, prevailed on several nobles and gentlemen to apply to the King for a charter of further privileges and immunities for the Adventurers. This was happily obtained and the grant which gave concerted, and more vigorous effort, to colonization and trade, bears date April 10, 1606, by which, the whole country lying between North latitude 34,° which is that of Cape Fear, N. C., and 45,° which is that of Passamaquoddy bay, was conceded to eight persons, who were warmly engaged in Western adventure; four of them, viz: Sir Thos. Gates, Sir George Somers, Hakluyt and Wingfield, had the Southern portion, called Southern Virginia, assigned to them, and the other four, viz: Thomas Hanham, Raleigh Gilbert, Wm. Parker, and Geo. Popham, the Northern portion, called Northern Virginia. These persons, except Hakluyt, who was a Prebendary in the church, personally engaged in the adventures which followed—Popham and Gilbert leading the Northern colony, and Gates, Somers, and Wingfield, the Southern. The King recites in the charter the object of the petitioners to be, "That wee would vouchsafe unto them our license to make habitation, plantation and deduce a colony of sundry of our people into that part of Virginia, and other parts of America."

A council of fifty-two persons was appointed by the charter to manage all its affairs, at the head of which was placed the Earl of Southampton, and among them the Earls of Pembroke, Exeter and Lincoln, and Sir Francis Bacon. It is a striking fact, that the charter does not contain the names of Chief Justice Popham, or Sir Ferdinando Gorges, although Popham, certainly, was a chief instrument in procuring it.

The Southern colony was the first to move, and on the 20th December, 1606, they dispatched three ships, one of 100 tons, one of 40, and one of 10, with their colonists, who arrived and laid the foundation of Jamestown, May 31st, 1607, the very day that the 2d, or Northern colony, sailed from Plymouth, to occupy the Sagadahoc. The Jamestown became a *permanent* colony, and was the first of that character planted on American soil, North of Florida.

But Gorges and Popham, did not wait the movements of the adventurers under the charter. The corporation was slow to move, they were unwilling to embark their funds in so precarious a speculation. Popham and Gorges would not wait upon their doubts, so in August, 1606, they fitted out a vessel at their own expense, with all needed supplies and provisions, accompanied by two of the natives taken over by Weymouth. They put this expedition under command of Capt. Henry Challong, with orders to pursue a *direct Westerly* course, as Gosnold had done in 1602. But instead of this, he put away South, and was captured by the Spaniards, to the great loss of the adventurers and the interruption of their plans; for they had instructed Challong to leave as many men as he could spare to occupy the country. It was not until the return of Prinn, who was sent after Challong with fresh supplies, and who made intelligent and encouraging reports, that the corporation was roused to action.

All the voyages hitherto made, were undertaken by individuals on private account, and had been pursued with great loss. Gorges in a letter to Challong, after his capture, says, "You knowe that the journey hath bene noe small charge to *us* that first sent to the coast, and had for our returne but the five salvadges." It was more than a year after the grant, that the Northern company were ready to commence their voyage; on the 31st of May, 1607, O. S., sailed out of old Plymouth harbor, the "Gift of God," and the "Mary and John," with one hundred landmen to plant the first English colony that ever visited the coast of Maine.[1] They were commanded by two of the patentees, the old and experienced George Popham and Raleigh Gilbert, as noble and gallant commanders as ever walked a quarter deck and worthy the command of an expedition of so grand an import. Gilbert was a son of Sir Humphrey.

These frail barks were freighted with the best hopes and anxious doubts of wise and earnest and noble men at home,

[1] Strachey says "120 men for planters." Prince says "100 landmen."

who beheld through the mist of coming time, a new world of civilization and christianity, arising out of the dark forests and rock bound shores of this wild and desolate continent. Here, on this spot, that brave and hardy crew planted the banner of St. George, and gave to *Old* England, lawful and actual possession of a *New* England, which for one hundred and fifty years was the fairest jewel of her crown. And here lie the bones of the first President, Popham, the elder brother of the learned Chief Justice of England, who died about the same time.

But, Sir, the enterprise failed; death and the stars seemed against it, and there were "no more speeches," by the Northern company, says Gorges, "of settling any other plantation in those parts for a long time after." They were in search of gain, and found it not, in peopling a rude continent. It was essentially a commercial company; the principle that moved it was adverse to generous action; it required another sentiment, the *religious* element, to give patient endurance, indomitable resolution and final success, as was signally vindicated in the renowned colony of the Pilgrims. The Northern company made no other attempt at colonization, until they obtained their charter of 1620. We must not claim too much for this unsuccessful attempt to people a continent, but regard it as *one* of the steps in the grand march of colonization.

But I leave the details of these great movements to those who come after me, while I touch briefly on one or two other topics.

The ancient and perpetual rival of England, on the other side of the channel, did not willingly yield a prize of so much worth to "perfidious Albion." France interposed her claim to the whole continent from Hudson river to the Gulf of St. Lawrence. She did not relinquish it until she was gradually driven from the soil by superior force, and conceded the territory to her rival by the peace of Paris, in 1763.

Her title was founded

1st. On the voyage of Verrazani, 1524.

2d. On the discovery and occupation of Canada, by James Cartier, 1535, and following years.

3d. The grant of Henry IV., 1603, to De Mont.

4th. The voyages and occupation of the country under Champlain and De Mont, 1603–4.

The English title is defended on the following grounds:

1st. The discovery by Cabot, 1497.

2d. The possession of Newfoundland by Gilbert, 1583.

3d. The voyages and landing by Gosnold, 1602; Prinn, 1603; Weymouth, 1605; and Popham, 1607.

4th. The Charter of 1606.

The English never denied the French title to Canada, but claimed to restrict it to what they first discovered and actually occupied. The French never had any possession of the coast, west of the Kennebec.

It is evident that these grants or *concessions*, as the French called them, could convey only a barren title, unless there was actual possession; or a well founded right to possession.

The Privy Council of England, in 1666, decided, in a question that arose under the Duke of York's grant of New York and New Jersey, That "by the law of nations if any people make discovery of any country of barbarians, the prince of that people who make the discovery, hath the right of soil and government of that place; and no people can plant there without the consent of the prince, or the persons to whom his right is conveyed."

This giving away continents by sovereigns, was ridiculed by Francis I., of France, when the Spaniards set up the right to them of the new world, by the Pope; he said, he "would fain like to see the clause in Adam's will which made the continent their inheritance."

These acts were something like the brilliant offer of the arch rebel, we read of, who offered "all the kingdoms of the earth" as a bribe to submission to him, when the rascal had not a foot of land to give.

The truth is, and that was the practical result, he who could *seize* and *hold*, had the most effectual title, notwithstanding royal seals and broad parchment deeds.

I desire to call your attention, Sir, to one fact more,— and that is, the frail vessels in which the early adventurers to America crossed our stormy seas, and advanced to high northern latitudes. Not one of them that we have any account of, went up to 200 tons, and by far the largest number were under 100 tons. They were such vessels as your hardy fishermen would scarcely venture in to the Grand Banks.

The largest ship in which Columbus made his first voyage did not much exceed 100 tons, the other two were light barks of 30 or 40 tons, and not decked, except at the bow and stern. The largest of Sir Humphrey Gilbert's fleet of four vessels in which he sailed to Newfoundland in 1533, was but 120 tons, two others were 40 tons, and the fourth, the Squirrel, but 10 tons. It was in this little pinnace of ten tons, that this most brave and noble adventurer went down, in a gale of wind, as he was returning home from his great voyage in 1584, refusing to take the large vessel, saying that he was as near Heaven on the sea as on the land. And thus perished at the early age of forty-five, one of the most experienced and worthy of the early discoverers.

Prinn's two vessels fitted out in 1603 by Hakluyt and the Bristol merchants, were but 50 and 26 tons. The Caravel of Gomez, equipped by the Emperor Charles V., in 1525, for Northern adventure, was but 60 tons. Challong's ship, sent out in 1606, by Popham and Gorges, was but 55 tons, — and lastly, the two little barks, which we see in imagination moored in yonder channel, were 60 and 40 tons. These vessels, gentlemen, fitted out by nobles and gentlemen of highest rank, to found a colony,— to lay the foundations of a new civilization in the wilderness, laden with all the supplies supposed to be needed for these great purposes, and bearing one hundred and twenty souls,— were not so large as the common coasters and fishing vessels which daily pass the mouth of this river!

And then the fort, Sir, built by these colonists, a mere stockade to repel Indian aggression, mounted by demi culverins of nine pounds, or sakers of six pounds, twelve in all.[1]

Compare these slight vessels with the noble ships of 1000 and 1500 tons, now built upon this river, larger than the largest commercial vessels which floated before the present century, and bearing burdens to all parts of the world!

And compare that humble stockade of earth and stakes, with the magnificent fortress which is now rising on the ancient site!

These glimpses at the past and present, mark the progress of our country from its feeble footsteps, two centuries and a half ago, when not a white man was to be found on its whole extensive line of coast, to the grandeur, the wealth, the resources, the dignity of the present hour. Nothing but itself, in history, is its parallel.

Gorges, in 1640, when looking upon his work in this country, triumphantly exclaimed,— "I have not sped so ill; I thank God for it; but I have a house and home there, and some necessary means of profit by my saw mills, and corn mills, besides some annual receipts, to lay the foundation of greater matters."

These greater matters have come! Since the first colonization, the Anglo Saxon race has advanced with a firm and steady step, occupying, cultivating, civilizing, until they have made

[1] Strachey says, "They fully finished the fort, trencht and fortefyed yt with 12 pieces of ordnance, and built 50 houses therein, besides a church and a store house; and the carpenters framed a pretty Pinnace of about some 30 tonne, which they called the *Virginia;* the chiefe shipwright being one Digby of London." 3 Me. Hist. Col., 308.

the craggy shores and tangled forests, the fit abode of a high civilization, the seat of commerce and the arts, and given to the ages a model of civil and religious liberty, dear to the lovers of freedom everywhere, and which the world will not let die.

Peace has its victories, and none more worthy of commemoration than those which ushered in the glorious morning of our American history and civilization.

We cannot but remember, that the ruin of empires, and the reconstruction of society, are the ever recurring problems of the past. And though clouds and shadows now hang around our horizon, and we are having our bitter experiences, we trust the day is not distant, when the full constellation of our Union shall shine forth again on the meridian sky, in its original effulgence; no pleiad lost; and our re-United States purified and strengthened by a fierce and bloody ordeal, shall again pursue its golden cycle—and the glorious old banner which shall wave on the ramparts of this fortress be the harbinger of solid peace, perpetual union and unclouded prosperity.

On the completion of this statement, the "Memorial Stone," of granite, from the Biddeford quarries, weighing about six tons, showing a front of six feet by four, and bearing the Inscription hereafter to be mentioned,—which had been placed under the platform, was rolled forward into view. The Standing Committee of the Historical Society then came forward, and through their acting Chairman, the Rev. Leonard Woods, D. D., President of Bowdoin College, solicited the consent of the State and General Governments, in the following words:

ADDRESS OF THE REV. PRESIDENT WOODS.

The Standing Committee of the Historical Society accepts the honorable service assigned to it, of causing a stone to be placed in the wall of this fort, in memory of the colony which was established here two hundred and fifty-five years ago. This earlier colony presents some claims for a grateful commemoration, as well as those more noted colonies which followed in its train, whether we regard its simple priority in the same great enterprise, or the high rank and character of its leaders, or the enlarged views of commercial policy, or the heroic spirit of adventure, or the purer motives of religion, by which they were animated. It has so happened, however, that these claims have been hitherto disregarded. While yearly honors have been rendered, and costly monuments have been erected to the later colonists of New England, not a stone has hitherto marked the spot where these earlier colonists planted themselves, and scarcely a word has been uttered in their praise. All honor to those who came over in the Mayflower and Arbella; but let justice also be done to those who came over years before them in the "Mary and John,"—that noble company of one hundred and twenty colonists, who, leaving their English homes under the auspices of the first Plymouth Company, under the charter of 1606, under the more immediate direction of George Popham, Raleigh Gilbert, and Richard Seymour, after braving the perils of the ocean, established themselves here, at the mouth of the Sagadahoc, on the 19th day of August, 1607, for the better discovery of the New World, for the enlargement of the British empire and commerce, and for the spread of the true faith. Let us not leave any longer undone the duties we owe to those who have deserved so well of their fellow-men; and to-day, after so long a time, let us perform the first act of tardy justice, in causing this stone, with its modest record, to be erected to their memory.

The commemorative act in which we are employed, performed as it is, in the name of the good people of this Commonwealth, at the same time reflects upon them no inconsiderable benefit, inasmuch as it vindicates for this State its true historic position, and affords it a new warrant for inscribing the proud motto of

"DIRIGO" upon its standard, and assigns to it a certain leadership in the course of events by which the English race was planted in this portion of the American continent, and the English title to it was asserted. It is therefore with great pleasure that we see the Government of the State represented on this occasion, and it is with great confidence that we solicit its favorable countenance on this transaction.

Hon. Abner Coburn, of Bloomfield, replied as follows:

ADDRESS OF HON. ABNER COBURN.

On behalf of His Excellency, Gov. Washburn, I appear here to-day, charged with the duty of giving the assent of the State to the placing of this memorial stone in the walls of this fort, which I now give by the direction of the Governor.

It is to me, as to all of this vast assembly, a matter of sincere regret, that our honored Chief Magistrate is detained at the Capitol, to-day, in the discharge of imperative public duties. His eloquent voice would have given an interest to this occasion which I am unable to impart to it. I rejoice, however, at the occasion, and in the opportunity of participating in these interesting services, the commencement only, as I trust, of a series of annual celebrations of the first founding of our race on these shores.

On the conclusion of Mr. Coburn's speech, President Woods, addressing Capt. T. L. Casey, of the U. S. Engineer Corps, the officer in charge, said:

REV. PRESIDENT WOODS TO CAPTAIN CASEY.

The monumental stone, which is now before us, has been provided under the direction of the Historical Society, with the design of having it placed in the wall of the new Fort now erecting by the Government of the United States, near the site of the old Fort, Saint George, erected by these early colonists. By the consent of the Federal Government, the name of Popham has already been given to the new Fort. Its consent is now respectfully asked, to place in the wall of the Fort this stone, in memory of this gallant leader and his colony.

Captain Casey replied as follows:

CAPTAIN T. L. CASEY'S REMARKS.

Mr. Chairman, and gentlemen of the Committee of the Historical Society: In the absence of Gen. Totten, Chief of the Bureau of Engineers, it is my duty as the officer in charge, to perform the duty of giving, in this public manner, the assent of the President of the United States to the insertion in the walls of this Fort, and in its appropriate place, of this memorial stone. Although holding a commission in the Engineer Corps under Gen. Totten, Chief of the Engineer Bureau, I am no less obedient to the President of the United States, who administers the Government by the aid of such departments and subordinates as by the laws are provided. The assent, therefore, which I this day give, is the assent of the President acting through the Secretary of War.

On the suggestion of the plan of placing this memorial stone in this Fort, I made known the fact, by letter, to Gen. Totten. On his arrival in Portland he took action thereon.

The following correspondence explains the official action of the Government in the matter:

PORTLAND, August 13th, 1862.

SIR:—I have the honor to place in your hands a printed circular, setting forth certain historical facts connected with the early history of New England, in which it is suggested that a MEMORIAL STONE, with a suitable inscription, should be placed in the walls of Fort Popham, now in process of construction, commemorating the facts therein set forth,—provided the approval and consent of the Government of the United States thereto can be obtained.

I am instructed by the Executive Committee in charge of these matters, most respectfully to ask permission to carry out the plan proposed, and to further request for this purpose, to occupy the grounds of Fort Popham on Friday, the 29th day of August, 1862, the 255th anniversary of the foundation of the first English Colony on the shores of New England; and such rules and regulations as may be thought proper by the Government of the United States, or the War Department.

In behalf of said Committee,
I have the honor to be your obedient servant,

CHARLES J. GILMAN, of Brunswick, Maine.

To Brig. Gen. JOS. G. TOTTEN, *Chief of Engineers of U. S. Army.*

PORTLAND, Me., August 13th, 1862.

HON. EDWIN M. STANTON, *Secretary of War, Washington.*

SIR:—I have the honor to submit herewith the copy of a letter just received from the Hon. Charles J. Gilman, writing on behalf of the Executive Committee of the Historical Society of this State, in which the approval of the General Government is asked, to the insertion in the walls of the Fort now in course of construction at the mouth of the Kennebec river, of a stone with an inscription commemorating certain historical facts connected with the early history of the State; which facts, summarily given in a printed paper, are also herewith submitted.

Mr. Gilman also requests permission for the occupation of the grounds of this Fort on the 29th day of August, in a public celebration of the event of the insertion of the "Memorial Stone."

These propositions seem to me of a nature deserving the sanction of the Government, and as no injury to the works, or material delay in their progress are at all likely to ensue, I respectfully urge them upon your approval.

Very respectfully, your obedient servant,

(Signed) JOSEPH G. TOTTEN,
Brevet Brig. General and Colonel Engineers.

PORTLAND, August 13th, 1862.

GEN. JOS. G. TOTTEN, *Chief Engineer,*

Submits and recommends to the approval of the Hon. Secretary of War, application of Chas. J. Gilman, in behalf of the Executive Committee of the Historical Society of Maine, for permission to place a monumental stone in the walls of the Fort erecting at the mouth of the Kennebec river—and to occupy the grounds of the Fort on the 29th day of August, 1862, in a public celebration of the event.

Approved.

By order of the Secretary of War,

(Signed) P. H. WATSON, *Asst. Secretary of War.*

August 19th, 1862.

PRESIDENT WOODS THEN SAID:

Under these high auspices, then, and in the presence of these honored guests who have come from a distance to participate in this celebration, and of this vast concourse of our fellow citizens, we will now proceed to cause this monumental stone to be erected. And to this end, and in order that all things may be rightly performed, we are happy that we are able to avail ourselves of the ancient rites of the Order of Free Masons, which are kindly proffered to us on this occasion. To the hands of this respected Fraternity, and to their mystic craft, the work is now committed.

MASONIC CEREMONIES.

At the completion of this portion of the assigned duties, the ceremonies proceeded under the charge of the Grand Lodge of Maine, made up as follows:

M. W. JOSIAH H. DRUMMOND,		*Grand Master.*
TIMOTHY J. MURRAY,	as	*Deputy Grand Master.*
HENRY C. LOVELL,	as	*Senior Grand Warden.*
EDWARD P. WESTON,	as	*Junior Grand Warden.*
THOMAS S. FOSTER,	as	*Grand Treasurer.*
SAMUEL KYLE,	as	*Grand Secretary.*
MARQUIS F. KING,		*Grand Marshal.*
CYRIL PEARL,		*Grand Chaplain.*
CHARLES COBB,	as	*Principal Architect.*
AUGUSTUS BAILEY, C. CUSHING, O. B. RICE,		*Bearers of vessels of corn, wine, and oil.*
CHARLES SAMPSON,		*Grand Tyler.*

This body commenced their services with the following address by the Grand Master:

GRAND MASTER. Right Worshipful Senior Grand Warden: The Grand Lodge of Maine, having been invited by the proper authorities to lay, in due and ancient Masonic form, this Memorial Stone, in this Fort here to be erected for our defense against those who would assail us, and that invitation having been accepted, I now order the Grand Lodge to assist me in the performance of this work. This, my will and pleasure, you will proclaim to the Junior Grand Warden, and he, to the brethren and others present, that all, having due notice thereof, may govern themselves accordingly.

SENIOR GRAND WARDEN. Right Worshipful Junior Grand Warden: It is the order of the Most Worshipful Grand Master, of the Grand Lodge of Maine, that this Memorial Stone be now laid with Masonic honors. This, his will and pleasure, you will proclaim to all present, that the occasion may be observed with due order and solemnity.

JUNIOR GRAND WARDEN. Brethren, and all who are present, will take notice that the Most Worshipful Grand Master will now deposit this Memorial Stone in Masonic form. You will observe the order and the decorum becoming the solemn ceremonies in which we are about to engage.

INVOCATION BY THE GRAND CHAPLAIN, REV. CYRIL PEARL.

MUSIC.

The Principal Architect then presented the working tools to the Grand Master, by whose direction the Grand Marshal distributed them to the Deputy Grand Master and Senior and Junior Grand Wardens.

During solemn music, the Square, Level, and Plumb were applied to the Stone by the proper officers.

GRAND MASTER. Right Worshipful Deputy Grand Master, What is the proper Jewel of your office?

DEPUTY GRAND MASTER. The Square.

GRAND MASTER. Have you applied the Square to those parts of the Stone that should be square?

DEPUTY GRAND MASTER. I have, Most Worshipful Grand Master, and the Craftsmen have done their duty.

GRAND MASTER. Right Worshipful Senior Grand Warden, What is the proper Jewel of your office?

SENIOR GRAND WARDEN. The Level.

GRAND MASTER. Have you applied the Level to the Stone?

SENIOR GRAND WARDEN. I have, Most Worshipful Grand Master, and the Craftsmen have done their duty.

GRAND MASTER. Right Worshipful Junior Grand Warden, What is the proper Jewel of your office?

JUNIOR GRAND WARDEN. The Plumb.

GRAND MASTER. Have you applied the Plumb to the several edges of the Stone?

JUNIOR GRAND WARDEN. I have, most Worshipful Grand Master, and the Craftsmen have done their duty.

GRAND MASTER. Having full confidence in your skill in the Royal Art, it remains with me now to finish the work.

The Grand Master then gave three knocks upon the Stone, and said:

"I find this Memorial Stone well FORMED, TRUE, and TRUSTY; and may this undertaking be conducted and completed by the Craftsmen according to the grand plan, in Peace, Love, and Harmony."

The Deputy Grand Master then received from the Grand Marshal the golden vessel, containing corn, and spread the corn upon the Stone, saying:

"May the health of the workmen employed in this undertaking be preserved to them, and may the Supreme Grand Architect bless and prosper their labors."

The Grand Marshal then took the vessel of wine and presented it to the Senior Grand Warden, who poured it upon the Stone, saying:

"May plenty be showered down upon the people of this nation, and may the blessing of the Bounteous Giver of all things attend all their laudable undertakings."

The Grand Marshal presented the vessel of oil to the Junior Grand Warden, who poured it upon the Stone, saying:

"May the Supreme Ruler of the world soon restore Peace to this people, and vouchsafe to them the enjoyment of every blessing."

GRAND MASTER. "May corn, wine, and oil, and all the necessaries of life abound among men throughout the world; and may the blessings of Almighty God be upon this undertaking, and may the structure here to be erected, stand to the latest ages as a defense to the people, and to commemorate the names of those who first planted upon these shores the seeds of religious liberty and civil freedom."

The Grand Master then returned the working tools to the Principal Architect, saying:

"To you, as the representative of the architect of this work, are confided the implements of operative masonry, with the fullest confidence that by his skill and labor a fabric will arise, which will be, at the same time an impregnable defense to these shores, and a memorial of those who first upon this spot displayed the Great Light in Masonry, and paid their adorations to the Supreme Architect of the Universe. Far distant be the day when there shall be a necessity to use this structure for the purposes for which it is designed."

FLOURISH OF MUSIC.

BENEDICTION.

The Grand Master then announced to Dr. Woods, acting Chairman of the Standing Committee of the Maine Historical Society, that the Memorial Stone was laid in due and ancient Masonic form.

When these ceremonies of the Grand Lodge were terminated, on a signal given to the Revenue Cutter, in the harbor of Adkin's Bay, a salute was fired from on board that vessel, accompanied by music from the Band.

The chief marshal of the day then introduced the orator of the occasion. Mr. Poor, advancing to the front of the platform, spoke as follows:

ADDRESS.

We commemorate to-day the great event of American history. We are assembled on the spot that witnessed the first formal act of possession of New-England, by a British colony, under the authority of a Royal Charter. We have come here, on the two hundred and fifty-fifth anniversary of that event, to rejoice in the manifold blessings that have flowed to us from that act, — to place on record a testimonial of our appreciation of the value of that day's work, — and to transmit to future generations, an expression of our regard for the illustrious men who laid the foundation of England's title to the Continent, and gave a new direction to the history of the world.

We meet under circumstances of deep and peculiar interest. The waters of the same broad Sagadahoc,* move onward in their majestic course to the ocean; the green summit of the beautiful Seguin still lifts itself in the distance — standing sentinel and breakwater to beat back the swelling surges of the sea; the flashing foam of the Atlantic still washes the rocky shores of the Peninsula of Sabino, and the secure anchorage of this open bay receives the tempest-tost bark, as on the day that the "Gift of God," the gallant flyboat of

* Sagadahoc, or *Sachedahock*, is Indian, and signifies, "The going out of the waters," or *the mouth of the river*. Eaton's Annals of Warren, p. 15.

George Popham, helped into port Raleigh Gilbert's good ship "Mary and John," freighted with the hopes of a new empire. Behind us rises the green summit of yonder mount, around whose sides soon clustered the habitations of the intrepid Popham and his devoted companions; and the same rocky rampart that then encircled this proud bay, stands unmoved amid the changes of two hundred and fifty-five years. *All else is changed.* The white sails of many a gallant ship now cover this broad expanse of water; a towering light-house rises high above the summit of Seguin, throwing the rays of its Fresnel lens far out into the darkness, and along these rocky shores; habitations of men dot every point of the surrounding landscape, while the stout steamer, unlike the ship of olden time, *gladly* encounters the rude waves of the ocean.

"Against the wind, and against the tide,
Still steady, with an upright keel." *

But the heart of man has changed less than all, in these two hundred and fifty-five years. It still bows submissive to Almighty God, and lifts its voice in prayer and praise, as when in the solemn service of his ritual their pious preacher uttered these memorable words:

"At what time soever a sinner doth repent him of his sins from the bottom of his heart, I will blot all his wickedness out of my remembrance, saith the Lord."

"I will go to my Father, and say to him, Father, I have sinned against heaven and against thee: I am no more worthy to be called thy son." †

All this was permanent and enduring. The same duty and the same dependence upon God, as then, are upon us all. We seem to see before us the faithful

* For description of the localities alluded to, see Note A, in the Appendix.

† King James's Liturgy of 1604.

Richard Seymour,* clad in the habiliments of the priesthood, as we hear the same accents of prayer and praise that he uttered,—when, before him knelt the faithful Popham and his hardy comrades, whose deep responses were borne upward to the mercy-seat. We listen to-day to the same strains of music, and to the same lessons, that first burst forth from human lips, on the shores of this great continent! That same sense of sinfulness that then found utterance in the language of the liturgy, finds expression in our hearts to-day; and may it please the Father of mercies so to mould all hearts, that these words of penitential confession shall find willing utterance from all lips, and these words of prayer and praise, raised in devout aspiration from all hearts, be continued from generation to generation through all time, till there shall be one fold and one Shepherd, and this mortal reach immortality at the final consummation of all things.

The greatness of an event is to be measured by the influence it exerts over the destinies of mankind. Acts of sublime moral grandeur, essential to the education of the race, may surpass in real magnitude the most brilliant achievements of material success, and the silent eloquence of truth, do more to conquer the fierce spirit of war, than the most imposing triumphs of warlike ambition. The ignominious execution of the Teacher of our Religion, in a remote and obscure province of the Roman Empire, was an event of so little interest at the time, as to be overlooked by the great writers of Roman history. The rise of the Christian sect in Judea, was noticed by the younger Pliny in his letter to the Emperor Trajan within the next hun-

* Who was Richard Seymour? See sketch of him by Bishop Burgess, Appendix B.

dred years;* but no human vision could then have foreseen, that their despised doctrines, would, within the next few hundred years, have become enthroned in the home of the Cæsars, and give law to the civilized world.

When Hannibal led his disciplined troops from the shores of Africa, through the perilous passes of the Pyrenees and across the Alps, into Italy, and slew more in number of the Roman youth, than the entire force of his army, we instinctively honor this sublime exhibition of martial genius and energy. When at last he failed to conquer Rome, only from the lack of succor from his own countrymen, whose jealousy of his success destroyed their country, we respect that indignant sense of justice that bequeathed his bones to a foreign resting-place, lest his unworthy countrymen should in after-times be honored, by the homage done to his remains. We weep at every fresh recital of the splendor of his achievements, and the magnitude of his misfortunes, however much we may value the superior civilization of the Roman people over that of the Carthaginians, as we reflect that the history of future times hung suspended, on the issue of that campaign. We are willing to rejoice, that at last his ungrateful nation was blotted from the earth, and Carthage lives only as a dishonor to history, while his name stands foremost, among warriors and heroes.

When the brave and accomplished Champlain returned to France after an absence of three and a half years in Acadia,† having explored all these shores, and given them the names they now bear, and placed the

* Lib. x. Epistle 99, A.D. 107.

† Champlain, with De Monts and his associates, sailed from St. Malo March 17, 1604, in two ships. They returned to St. Malo September 28, 1607. See Poor's Vindication of Gorges, and the authorities there cited, p. 20, et seq.

symbols of the authority of his sovereign, from Cape Breton to Cape Cod, confidently anticipating the future greatness of his race and nation in this their secure home in the finest portion of the new world, he found that the charter granted to De Monts under which he held and occupied the country, had been revoked,* and that the most hopeful plan of empire ever revealed to human eyes, had been marred if not destroyed. With generous valor he sought a new home amid the snows of the St. Lawrence, and in 1608 planted the flag and the power of France, upon the shores of that mighty river, where his bones now lie, in the midst of the race he there planted. But the folly of the great King Henry of Navarre, could not be overcome by any heroism on his part, for the stronger foothold of Sir Ferdinando Gorges had meanwhile been planted on the shores of this open sea, from Sagadahoc to Plymouth, and the flag of France was compelled to withdraw across the Sagadahoc, never more to return thither after 1607, and finally lay in the dust before that cross of St. George, which first floated from the rocky ramparts of Quebec on the 18th of September, 1759,† and the power of France was swept from the continent forever. But all hearts instinctively honor the immortal Champlain. The sympathy of all generous minds ever flows forth, at the utterance of his name. His monument still exists, in sight of an admiring posterity, more enduring than this stone we have this day raised in honor of another, and it shall forever remain in perpetual beauty, while the waters from the lofty summits of the Adirondac, mingling with those

* Champlain's Voyages, p. 44, 45, 99, (ed. 1632.) L'Escarbot, p. 619, 2d edition, 1612.

† The battle was fought September 13, 1759; the surrender of Quebec was agreed on in the evening of the 17th, and the English flag raised, on the morning of the 18th.

of the Green Mountains, shall fill the deep recesses of the Lake, that bears the honored name, *Champlain!**

Our duty to-day calls us to honor another, and a greater than Champlain; not greater in purpose, but in the results he achieved for humanity and his race, and more entitled to our sympathy from the blessings we owe to his labors,—the man that gave North-America to his nation, and died without even the poor reward that followed his great rival.

That colossal empire which Champlain planted on the St. Lawrence, and watched over till the close of his life,† which eventually held four fifths of the continent, was unable to regain its possession on these Atlantic shores, and from this cause alone, it finally fell beneath the power and sagacity of England's greatest war minister, Pitt, who gave to the heroic Wolfe, in his youthful prime, the noblest opportunity for fame that has yet fallen to a leader of armies. But the hero who gave the continent to England, was neither Pitt nor Wolfe, but another and greater than either, the illustrious and sagacious Knight, whose manly daring and persevering energy, upheld the drooping cause of colonization in its darkest hours, against individual jealousy and Parliamentary injustice; and saw, like Israel's great law-giver, from the top of the mountain, the goodly land that his countrymen should afterwards possess, though he was not allowed to enter it.‡ All honor, this day, to Sir Ferdinando Gorges. His praise is proclaimed by Puritan voices, after more than two hundred years of unjust reproach. His monument

* See Mrs. Sigourney's charming Sonnet to Champlain, in Note C of the Appendix.

† Champlain died in the discharge of the duties of the office of Governor-General of Canada, at Quebec, Dec. 25th, 1635.

‡ See Poor's Vindication of Gorges, p. 80, and note.

stands proudly erect among the nations, in that constitutional government of these United States which sheds blessings on the world.* His name, once perpetuated in our annals, was stricken from the records of the State, and no city, or town, or lake, or river, allowed to bear it to future times. But a returning sense of justice marks the American character, and two hundred years after his death it is heard once more in honorable renown.† Busy hands, guided by consummate skill, are now shaping into beauty and order, a work of enduring strength and national defense, that does honor to his name, and rising in sight of our chief commercial city, more beautiful in situation than any that graces the Ægean coast, or smiles from the Adriatic shore—the metropolis, too, of his ancient "Province of Mayne"—proclaims, Sir Ferdinando Gorges, *Father of English colonization in America.*‡ And in after-times,

* Gorges foresaw and predicted the independence of the colonies of North-America, of the British crown. Briefe Narration, p. 51, vol. ii. Maine Hist. Coll., also Poor's Vindication, p. 83.

† Gorges died in 1647. On the 6th of September, 1846, the Hon. George Folsom, of New-York, in an address before the Maine Historical Society, brought his claims to the public notice. See vol. ii. Maine Hist. Collections, p. 1.

‡ Fort Gorges.—The new Fort in Portland Harbor, erected by the United States Government, on Hog Island Ledge, has been named by the Secretary of War, Fort Gorges, in honor of Sir Ferdinando Gorges, "the original proprietor of the Province of Mayne and the Father of English Colonization in America."

In November last a petition was presented to the Secretary of War, as follows, namely:

To the Hon. John B. Floyd, Secretary of War:

The undersigned, citizens of Maine, respectfully ask, that the new fort now being erected in Portland Harbor by the United States Government, may be named Fort Gorges, in honor of Sir Ferdinando Gorges, "the original proprietor of the Province of Mayne, and the Father of English Colonization in America."

And as in duty bound will ever pray.

Wm. Willis,	Ether Shepley,	John A. Poor,	Jed'h Jewett,
John Mussey,	George Evans,	Ashur Ware,	Samuel Fessenden,
Samuel Jordan,	Geo. F. Emery,	Charles Q. Clapp,	Joshua Dunn,
N. Deering,	H. I. Robinson,	Samuel P. Shaw,	E. H. Elwell,
Wm. P. Preble,	P. Barnes,	Henry Willis,	Moses Macdonald,
Manasseh H. Smith,	John Neal,	Oliver Gerrish,	Jabez C. Woodman,
Geo. F. Shepley,	D. W. Fessenden,	A. W. H. Clapp,	Thomas H. Talbot,
F. A. Quinby,	Wm. Senter,	John M. Adams,	Charles A. Lord, and others.

Similar petitions were presented from Augusta, and the same were transmitted through Capt. Kurtz, of the Engineer Corps, in charge of the construction of the Fort.

when his race shall become not only masters of the continent, but of the earth, and his mother tongue the universal language, History shall perpetuate the deeds of his genius, and Song shall make his name immortal.*

The question that the European nations were called upon to solve, at the commencement of the seventeenth century, was, who should hereafter occupy and possess, the broad belt of the temperate zone of the New World, from the Atlantic to the Pacific seas. All previous explorations were preliminary efforts towards this one great object, but the question remained open and undecided. The voyages of the Northmen to these shores, interesting to the curious, are of no historic value, because not connected with the colonization of the country—unless it shall hereafter appear that Columbus obtained from them information, as to the extent of the Western Ocean. At the time of discovery by Columbus, the only races inhabiting the New World, north of Mexico, were tribes of wandering savages, incapable of accepting or acquiring habits of civilized life. An extinct race, had left their mounds in the West, and their deposits of oyster-beds along the shores of the Atlantic, and passed from traditionary story.

The adventurous Magellan in 1520 proved, by the *first* voyage round the world, the extent of the new continent, and in 1579, Sir Francis Drake, the first Englishman that circumnavigated the globe, in that daring

The Hon. John Appleton, Assistant Secretary of State, interested himself in the matter, and has forwarded us for publication the following note:

WASHINGTON, April 2d, 1860.

VERY DEAR SIR: I am much obliged for your note of this date.

You may say to your correspondent in Maine, that the Secretary of War has ordered the fortification he refers to to be named "Fort Gorges."

Yours, very truly, W. R. DRINKARD.

Hon. JOHN APPLETON, Asst. Sec'y of State.

—*Portland Advertiser* of April 10th, 1860.

* See in Note C, in Appendix, Mrs. Sigourney's admirable Poem on Gorges.

voyage which excited the admiration of his countrymen, gave the name of New-England to the Pacific shores of the continent, which name Captain John Smith afterwards, to strengthen the title to the country, affixed to the Atlantic slope.* But till the beginning of the seventeenth century, North-America, north of Florida, remained unpeopled by Europeans. The Spaniards, the Portuguese, the French, the Dutch, and the English, had all made voyages of discovery, and laid claims to the country. As early as 1542, it was parceled off to the three powers first named; Florida, belonging to Spain, extending as far north as the thirty-third parallel of latitude; Verrazzan, or New-France, from the thirty-third to the fiftieth parallel; and Terra Corterealis, northward to the Polar Ocean, thus named in honor of Gaspar Cortereal, a Portuguese, who explored the coast in the year 1500. The Spaniards were in pursuit of mines of gold and silver, the Portuguese in quest of slaves, and the French with hopes of profit in the fur trade, and crude but indefinite ideas of colonization.

Spain and Portugal originally claimed the New World by grant from the Pope.† England, practically abandoning all claim from the discoveries of Cabot on the Atlantic, and Drake on the Pacific coasts, laid down, in 1580, the broad doctrine, that prescription without occupation was of no avail; that possession of the country was essential to the maintenance of title. *Prescriptio sine possessione, haud valeat.*‡

Before this time, the attention of England had been turned to the northern parts of America, with a view to colonization. As early as March 22, 1574, the Queen

* John Smith's Description of New England, vol. ii. p. 2, Force's Tracts. Mass. Historical Coll. 3d series, vol. vi. p. 104.
† Bull of Pope Alexander VI. 1493.
‡ Camden's Eliz. Annales, 1580. See Poor's Vindication of Gorges, p. 9.

had been petitioned to allow of the *discovery* of lands in America "*fatally reserved to England, and for the honor of Her Majesty.*"* Sir Humphrey Gilbert's charter "for planting our people in America," was granted by Elizabeth, June 11, 1578, and in 1580 John Walker and his companions had discovered a silver mine in Norumbega. The explorations of Andrew Thevett, of John Barros, and John Walker, alluded to in the papers recently discovered in the British State Paper Office, under date of 1580, we find nowhere else recorded. The possession of Newfoundland by Sir Humphrey Gilbert, was abandoned on his loss at sea, and it was not till 1584, that the first charter to Sir Walter Raleigh was issued, by Elizabeth. Raleigh named the country VIRGINIA, in honor of his Queen. Of the two colonies sent out by him, one returned, the other perished in the country, leaving no trace of its history and no record of its melancholy fate.† Thus, at the period of Elizabeth's death, in 1603, England had not a colonial possession on the globe.

Sir Richard Whitbourne had made voyages to Newfoundland in his own ship in 1588,‡ and in 1600 there was a proposition to the Queen for planting a colony in *the North-west of America*,§ in which can be unmistakably traced the agency of Sir Ferdinando Gorges, who it now appears was also concerned in the voyage of Gosnold in 1602, of Pring in 1603, and of George Weymouth in 1605, the earliest ones of which we have any authentic record.‖ That eloquent passage in Gorges' *Briefe Narration*, in which he gives "the reasons and

* Calendar of Colonial State Papers, edited by Sainsbury, vol. i. page 1.
† Bancroft's History, vol. i. pp. 102, 107.
‡ Calendar of Col. State Papers, vol. i p. 82.
§ See this paper in full in Poor's Vindication of Gorges. Appendix.
‖ See Gorges' letter to Challons. Poor's Vindication, p. 34.

the means of renewing the undertaking of Plantations in America," deserves our highest praise; and it excites feelings of the warmest gratitude toward him, for it is a modest and touching statement, of his own heroic efforts, in the cause of American colonization.*

But the Hollanders and the French were equally aroused to the importance, and inflamed with the purpose, of seizing upon these shores. The vast wealth of the Dutch, their great commercial success prior to this time in both the East and West-Indies, gave them the advantage. Champlain, with greater knowledge of North-America than any of his rivals, had accompanied Pont Gravè to the St. Lawrence, by direction of the King, in 1603, when, on his return to France, he found Acadia granted to De Monts, a Protestant, and a member of the King's household, under date of November eighth, 1603, extending across the continent, between the fortieth and forty-sixth degrees of north latitude.†

In the spring of 1604, De Monts, accompanied by Champlain, Pont Gravè, Poutrincourt, and the learned and accomplished historian L'Escarbot, sailed from Dieppe for the occupation of the New World. They planted their colony at St. Croix, within the limits of our own State, in 1604,‡ and in the spring and summer of 1605, explored the coast under the lead of Champlain, from Campseau to Cape Malabar, twelve miles south of Cape Cod, "searching to the bottom of the bays," the same year that Weymouth explored this most excellent and beneficial river of Sagadahoc. To make sure of the country, Champlain, Champdore and L'Escarbot remained three and a half years, fishing, trading with the natives, and occupying at Boston, Pis-

* Gorges' Briefe Narration, p. 16.
† L'Escarbot, p. 432, 2d edition. 1612.
‡ See Poor's Vindication of Gorges, p. 23, note.

cadouet, (Piscataqua,) Marchin, (Portland,) Koskebee, (Casco Bay,) Kinnibequi, (Kennebec,) Pentagoet, (Penobscot,) and all east, to Campseau and Cape Breton. Returning to France in 1607, they found the charter of De Monts revoked,* on account of the jealousy of his rivals, and a small indemity from the King their only reward, for these four years of sacrifice and unremitting toil. This shortsightedness of the great Henry of Navarre, cost France the dominion of the New World. For on the return of Weymouth to Plymouth, in 1605, with five savages from Pemaquid, Sir Ferdinando Gorges gathered from them full particulars of this whole region, its harbors, rivers, natural characteristics and features, its people and mode of government.†

Associating with himself the Earl of Southampton,‡ Gorges, relying upon these circumstances as a means of inflaming the imagination of his countrymen, petitioned the King for a charter,§ which he obtained, under date of April tenth, 1606,‖ granting to George Popham, and seven others, the continent of North-America, from the thirty-fourth to the forty-fifth degrees of north latitude, extending one hundred miles into the mainland, and including all islands of the sea within one hundred miles of the shore. This charter is the basis on which rests the title of our race to the New World. It provided for a local government at home, intrusted to a

*L'Escarbot, p. 460, 2d edition. 1612. Champlain, pp. 44, 45, 99.

† Gorges' Briefe Narration. Maine Hist. Coll. vol. ii. p. 19.

‡ Henry Wriothesley, Earl of Southampton, the friend and patron of Shakspeare, was the *third* earl of that name, and grandson of Thomas Wriothesley, Lord High Chancellor of England, under Edward VI. Created a peer February sixteenth, 1547, he died in 1550. His son Henry, was Lord Treasurer, and grandfather of Lady Rachel Russell. His patent of nobility was declared forfeited, under Elizabeth, but restored by James in 1603. The third earl, Treasurer of the Virginia Company, and the patron of letters and of American colonization, died in command of an English regiment, in the Dutch service, in the Netherlands, in 1624. The fourth earl died in 1667, and the title became extinct.

§ Strachey's Travaile into Virginia, p. 161.

‖ See this charter in full in Poor's Vindication of Gorges. Appendix.

Council of Thirteen, with two companies, one of North, and the other of South-Virginia, for carrying into execution the plans of colonization in the country.* The venerable Sir John Popham,† Chief-Justice of England by the appointment of Elizabeth, a man of vast wealth and influence, became the patron of the Company; and his son, Sir Francis Popham, was appointed by the King, with Sir Ferdinando Gorges, one of the Council of Thirteen, under whom, as the Council of Virginia, the work of colonization was to be carried forward.‡ From the great fame of Chief-Justice Popham, and his interest in the matter, the colony sent by the North-Virginia Company was popularly known as Popham's Colony, though his name was not in the charter, or included among the Council. "The planting of New-England in the North, was by Chief-Justice POPHAM," said the Scotch adventurers, in their address to the King, September ninth, 1630, recently brought to our notice from the British State Paper Office.§ In a work entitled *Encouragement to Colonies*, by William Alexander, Knight, in 1625, he says: "Sir John Popham

* The COUNCIL OF VIRGINIA, appointed by King James, November twentieth, 1606, consisted of *fourteen* persons instead of thirteen. Their names are given in a subsequent note.

† Sir John Popham was born at Huntsworth, near Wellington, in Somersetshire, in 1531. He was at Oxford in 1547, became distinguished at the bar in 1560; was made Sergeant at Law, and Solicitor General, June twenty-sixth, 1579. He was Speaker of the Commons in 1581; became Attorney-General June first, 1581. He was knighted 1592; made Chief-Justice of the Queen's Bench June eighth, 1592. He assisted at King James's coronation in 1603. September fifth and sixth, 1604, King James and the Queen were entertained at Littlecote, the residence of the Chief-Justice. He was the richest lawyer of his time, having an income of ten thousand pounds per year. He died June first, 1607, and was buried at Wellington.

His eldest son was Sir Francis Popham, whose eldest son, John Popham, married June twenty-first, 1621, Mary, only daughter of Sebastian Harvey, at Stoke Newington, but had no children. The family of the Chief-Justice is supposed to be extinct.

The fact of his appointment as Chief-Justice by Elizabeth, in the later years of her life, proves him to have been a great lawyer. Elizabeth appointed the ablest men she could find to public office.

‡ See this charter in full in Poor's Vindication. Appendix.

§ This paper is now printed for the first time in the appendix to Poor's Vindication of Gorges.

sent the first colony that went, of purpose to inhabit there near to Sagadahoc."* But until the comparatively recent publication of Strachey, the history of this colony was almost unknown. Two unsuccessful attempts at planting a colony were made in 1606.†

On the thirty-first of May, 1607, the first colony to New-England sailed from Plymouth for the Sagadahoc, in two ships—one called the "Gift of God," whereof George Popham, brother of the Chief-Justice,‡ was commander; and the other, the "Mary and John," commanded by Raleigh Gilbert—on board which ships were one hundred and twenty persons, for planters. They came to anchor under an island, supposed to be Monhegan, the thirty-first of July. After exploring the coast and islands, on Sunday, the ninth of August, 1607, they landed on an island they called St. George, where they heard a sermon, delivered unto them by Mr. Seymour, their preacher, and so returned aboard again. On the fifteenth of August they anchored under Seguin, and on that day the "Gift of God" got into the river of Sagadahoc. On the sixteenth, after a severe storm, both ships got safely in, and came to anchor. On the seventeenth, in two boats, they sailed up the river—Captain Popham in his pinnace, with thirty persons, and Captain Gilbert in his long-boat, with eighteen persons, and "found it a very gallant river; many good islands therein, and many branches of other small rivers falling into it," and returned. On the "eighteenth, they all went ashore, and there made choice of a place for their plantation, at the mouth or entry of the river, on

* A copy of this rare work is in the possession of Gen. Peter Force, of Washington City.

† See Poor's Vindication, pp. 38, 39.

‡ Note by R. H. Major, editor of Strachey's Travaile into Virginia, p. 27. Published by the Hakluyt Society—one of the volumes of its series. Hubbard's History of Massachusetts Bay, p. 10.

the west side, (for the river bendeth itself towards the nor-east and by east,) being almost an island, of good bigness, in a province called by the Indians, 'Sabino'—so called of a Sagamo, or chief commander, under the grand bashaba." On the nineteenth, they all went ashore where they had made choice of their plantation, and where they had a sermon delivered unto them by their preacher, and after the sermon, the President's commission was read, with the patent,* and the laws to be observed and kept.†

* By the original charter, the company had the right to sell lands, work mines, coin money, transport thither colonists, expel by force all intruders, raise a revenue by imposts, carry out goods free of duty to the Crown, for seven years, with a denization of all persons born or residing in the country.

† A constituent code of laws was prepared, and signed by King James, in accordance with the provision to this effect set forth in the seventh section of the charter of April tenth, 1606. *Lucas's Charters of the Old English Colonies*, p. 4.

This constituent code is contained in two ordinances, or articles of instructions, from the King, namely:

I. Ordinance dated November twentieth, 1606, appointing

Sir William Wade,	Thomas Warr, Esq.,	Sir Henry Montague,
Sir Walter Cope,	Thomas James, Esq.,	John Doddridge, Esq.,
Sir Francis Popham,	Sir Ferdinando Gorges,	John Eldred, Esq.,
Sir John Trevor,	Sir George More,	James Bagg, Esq.,
Sir William Romney,	Sir Thomas Smith,	

as the Council of Virginia.

This ordinance provided that

1. Each colony may elect associates, and annually elect a President for one year; and assistants or councillors for the same time.
2. The Christian religion shall be preached and observed as established in the realm of England.
3. Lands shall descend to heirs as provided by law in England.
4. Trial by jury of twelve men, in all criminal cases. Tumults, rebellion, conspiracy, mutiny and sedition, murder, manslaughter, incest, rape and adultery, only, are capital offences.
5. In civil causes, the President and Council shall determine. They may punish excesses in drunkenness, vagrancy, etc.
6. All produce, or goods imported, to be stored in the magazine of the Company.
7. They shall elect a clerk and treasurer, or cape-merchant.
8. May make laws needful and proper, *consonant with the laws of England*
9. Indians to be civilized and taught the Christian religion.
10. All offenders to be tried in the colony.
11. Oath of obedience to be taken.
12. Records of all proceedings and judgments fully set forth and preserved, implying a right of appeal. In all criminal cases, magistrates to suspend sentence till opportunity of pardon is had by the king.

These were the laws "to be observed and kept."

(See Poor's Vindication of Gorges. Appendix.)

II. Ordinance, dated March 9th, 1607.

On the recommendation, or nomination, of the *Southern* company, the following additional members of the Council of Virginia were appointed, namely:

"George Popham, gent., was nominated President. Captain Raleigh Gilbert, James Davies, Richard Seymour, Preacher, Captain Richard Davies, Captain Harlowe, were all sworn assistants; and so they returned back again."*

Thus commenced the first occupation and settlement of New-England.

On a careful examination of this patent of King James, and of the articles, instructions and orders by him set down for the government of these colonies, we are struck with the sagacity and statesmanship every where evinced by the monarch. He rose superior to the notions of his times, reduced the number of capital offences to ten, and declared none should be capital but the more gross of political, and the more heinous of moral crimes. He gave them all the liberties they could desire.

In the subsequent charters for Virginia and New-England, the same broad principles of self-government were in the main reënacted.

In the contests with the King and Parliament of England, one hundred and fifty years later, the colo-

Sir Thomas Challoner, Kt., Sir George Kopping, Kt., Sir Edw'd Michilbourne, Kt.,
Sir Henry Nevil, Kt., Sir Thomas Rowe, Kt., Sir Thomas Smith, Kt.,
Sir Robert Mansfield, Kt., Sir Fulke Grevil, Kt., Sir Robert Croft, Kt.,
Sir Maurice Berkeley, Kt., Sir John Scott, Kt., Sir Edward Sandys, Kt.,
Sir Thomas Holcroft, Kt., Sir Oliver Cromwell, Kt., Sir Anthony Palmer.
Sir Robert Kelligrew, Kt.,

On the recommendation or nomination of the *Northern* Colony, the following additional members of the Council of Virginia were appointed:

Sir Edw'd Hungerford, Kt., Sir Richard Hawkins, Kt., Bernard Greenville, Esq.,
Sir John Mallett, Kt., Sir Bartholomew Mitchell, Kt., Edward Rogers, Esq.,
Sir John Gilbert, Kt.,* Edward Seamour, Esq., Rev. Matthew Sutcliff, D.D.
Sir Thomas Freake, Kt.,

These appointments made the Council of Virginia to consist of forty instead of thirteen. There was a further provision that "any twelve of them, at least for the time being, whereof six at least to be members of one of the said colonies, and six more at least to be members of the other colony," "shall have power to choose officers, call meetings," etc. (See Poor's Vindication of Gorges. Appendix.)

* Strachey, p. 301, Maine Hist. Coll. vol. iii.

* Oldmixon's History of British Empire in America, says Sir John Gilbert was President of the *Northern* Virginia Company, p. 41. Stith's History of Virginia, pp. 74, 75.

nists only demanded their *ancient rights*, as subjects of the British crown. From August 19, O. S., 1607, the title of England to the new world was maintained. At this place they opened a friendly trade with the natives, put up houses and built a small vessel, during the autumn and winter.

Richard Bloome, in his *History of the Present State of the Territories in America*, printed in London 1687, says:

"In the year 1607, Sir John Popham and others settled a plantation at the mouth of the river Sagadahoc. But Capt. James Davis chose a small place, almost an Island, to sit down in, when, having heard a sermon, read the patent and laws; and after he had built a fort, sailed further up the river. They call the fort St. George, Capt. George Popham being President; and the people (savages) seemed to be much affected with our men's devotion, and would say King James is a good King, and his God a good God; but our God, *Tanto*, is a naughty God.

"In January, in the space of seven hours, they had thunder, lightning, rain, frost and snow all in very great abundance."

On the 5th of February, 1608, George Popham died,* and his remains were deposited within the wall of his fort, which was named Fort St. George.

It is well known that the Popham Colony, or a portion of them, returned to England in 1608, with the ship they had built on this peninsula, the first specimen of naval architecture constructed on this continent, named the "Virginia of Sagadahoc."

But this possession of the Popham Colony proved

* Prince's New-England Chronology, p. 118; Brodhead's History of New-York, p. 14.

sufficient to establish the title. The revocation of the charter to De Monts gave priority to the grant of King James, covering the same territory, and this formal act of possession was ever after upheld, by an assertion of the title by Gorges. It was sufficient, effectually, to hold the country against the French and Spaniards alike.* When Argall, in 1613, destroyed the French settlement at Mount Desert, † the French Minister demanded satisfaction at the hands of the British nation. ‡ But no notice was taken of this

* The Spanish Secretary of State in 1612 and 1613 complained to King James for allowing his subjects to plant in Virginia and Bermuda, as the country belonged to Spain, by the conquest of Castile who acquired it by the discovery of Columbus, and the Pope's donation; to which Sir Dudley Carleton, Secretary of State, by order of King James made answer: "Spain has no *possessions* north of Florida. They belong to the crown of England by right of discovery and actual possession by *the two English colonies thither deducted, whereof the latter is yet there remaining.* These countries should not be given over to the Spanish."

Cal. of Col. State Papers, vol. i. p. 14, Nos. 28 and 29; also page 16, Nos. 31 and 32.

In the memorials of the English and French Commission concerning the limits of Nova-Scotia or Acadia, under the Treaty of Utrecht, the French Commissioners say: "The Court of France adjudged that they had the right to extend the western limits of Acadia as far as the River Kinnibequi," (p. 39.) On page 98 of the same Collections it says: "Chief-Justice Popham planted the colony at Sagadahoc."

† MOUNT DESERT was so named by Champlain in 1605. The English named it Mount *Mansell*, in honor of Sir Robert Mansell, the highest naval officer of England, one of the grantees of the Virginia Company of 1609, and of the New-England Company in 1620. But it has retained the name of *Mount Desert*. It has always been celebrated for the excellence of its harbor and the boldness of its shores. It is the most celebrated locality on the Atlantic coast, and one of the three great harbors of the continent. The French Jesuits, who settled there in 1613, called it St. Saviour. Their precise place of settlement is described in the Relations of the Jesuits, vol. i. p. 44, 46, and has been identified by the accurate explorations of the Hon. E. L. Hamlin, of Bangor, the present year. In Poor's Vindication of Gorges, Appendix, page 103, is a translation of the Jesuit Relation, describing this place, and of its destruction by Argall.

What is of still more interest is the fact that this was the easternmost limits of *Mavosheen*, or of the English discoveries up to 1609. See Purchase, vol. iv. p. 1873. L'Escarbot, the historian of New-France and of De Monts' expedition, says the Sagamo *Marchin* was residing at their next place west of Kinnibequi, and they named the place *Marchin*, (Portland,) in honor of him. Marchin was slain in 1607, and Bessabes was chosen captain in his place. Bessabes was slain also, and then *Asticou* was chosen in his stead. According to the statement in Purchase, vol. iv. p. 1873-4, at the easternmost part of Mavosheen, at the river of Quibiquesson, dwelt *Asticou*. In 1613, *Asticou* was dwelling at Mount Desert, and the assurance given by his followers to Fathers Biard and Masse of his being sick and desirous of baptism at their hands, led them to go thither, and finally to yield to entreaties for making their settlement there, instead of at Kadesquit, (Kenduskeag,) Bangor, on the Penobscot, as they had agreed in 1611. It would seem from these facts that the authority of Asticou extended from Mount Desert to the Saco, the river of the Sagamo Olmouchin.

‡ Calendar of Colonial State Papers, vol. i. p. 15.

demand, because the French could show no claim of title. Again in 1624, M. Tillieres, the French Ambassador, claimed the territory of New-England as a portion of New-France, and proposed to yield all claim to Virginia, and the country as far south as the Gulf of Mexico; overlooking entirely the title of Spain to Florida, which had always been recognized as extending to the thirty-third parallel of north latitude. France had at this time become aware of the importance of securing the title and possession of these shores.* King James called on Sir Ferdinando Gorges to prepare a reply to the claims of the French monarch. "Whereunto," says Gorges, "I made so full a reply (as it seems) there was no more heard of their claim." † From the abstract of this reply, recently printed in the Calendar of British State Papers, it would seem that no notice was taken of the Leyden flock, who were then at Plymouth; but Sir Ferdinando Gorges based the claim of his government on the ground of the charter of 1606, and the formal occupation of the country under it, with a continued claim of title.

In 1631, Champlain, the greatest mind of his nation, ever engaged in colonial enterprise, the boldest and most wary of all his countrymen, second only to Gorges in the results he achieved, — in his memoir to his sovereign, as to the title of the two nations, says: "King James issued his charter twenty-four years ago, for the country from the thirty-third to the forty-fifth degree. England seized the coast of New-France, where lies Acadia, on which they imposed the name of New-England." ‡

The Dutch West-India Company, in their address

* Cal. of Col. State Papers, vol. i. p. 60.
† Gorges' Briefe Narration, p. 40.
‡ Doc. Hist. of New-York, vol. ix. p. 112.

to the States General, 1632, say: "In the year 1606, his Majesty of Great Britain granted to his subjects, under the names of New-England and Virginia, north and south of the river, (Manhattoes,) on express condition that the companies should remain one hundred miles apart. Whereupon the English began, about the year 1607, to settle by the river of Sagadahoc. The English place New-England between the forty-first and forty-fifth degrees of north latitude." *

In Garneau's *History of Canada*, speaking of the destruction of Mount Desert, and Port Royal, in 1613, he says: "England claimed the territory to the forty-fifth degree of north latitude." This was seven years before the date of the New-England Charter. This claim was founded on possession; for England stoutly maintained, from the time of Elizabeth onward, that without possession there was no valid title to a newly discovered country.

This view of history is overlooked by Puritan writers, and those who follow their authority. That protection of the British nation which enabled the Puritans of Massachusetts Bay, and the humble followers of Robinson, to establish, unmolested, homes in the New World, under organized forms of government, was grudgingly acknowledged by them, and the man who secured to them these blessings, and watched over them with the same jealous care as of his own colony — they always stigmatized as their great enemy,† because, among other acts of humanity, he allowed the mild and conscientious men, who could not yield implicit obedience to their fierce doctrines, and more barbarous laws, ‡ to escape into Maine, and there remain

* Holland Doc. N. Y., p. 61.

† Winthrop, vol. ii. p. 14; Bradford's Hist. of Plymouth, p. 328.

‡ None but church members shall be allowed the privileges of freemen.—Statute of 1631, Massachusetts Colony Laws, p. 117.

unharmed. When Cromwell granted to Sir Thomas Temple the country east of the Sagadahoc, at the time that the persecution of the Quakers was at its greatest height, with the design of affording them a place of refuge beyond the limits even of the Province of Maine, * which they had just conquered by violence; the anger of Massachusetts Puritans fell upon the head of the Protector, himself a Puritan, and an Independent of the straitest sect at home. But time allows no allusion to-day to historic details, except what is essential to the vindication of the truth of history. The fact that the 19th of August, Old Style, is the true date of the foundation of England's title to the continent, is all we are called upon to establish.

It may be said, that in giving this prominence to the occupation of the country by the colony of Popham, we overlook other events of importance in establishing the English title—the possession of the Elizabeth Isles by Gosnold in 1602, and the settlement of Jamestown May 13th, 1607, prior to the landing of the Popham Colony at Sagadahoc.

In reference to the occupation of Elizabeth Isles by

Any attempt to change the form of government is punishable with death.—Statute of 1641, Col. Laws, p. 59.

Absence from meeting on Sunday, fast, or thanksgiving, subjected the offender to a fine.—Col. Laws, p. 103.

Keeping or observing Christmas was punishable by fine.—Col. Laws, p. 119.

Wages to be regulated in each town by vote of the freemen of each.—Col. Laws, p. 156.

Baptists are to be punished by banishment.—Colony Laws, 1646, p. 120.

Quakers to be imprisoned and then banished, on pain of death if they returned. —Colony Laws, 1658, p. 123.

Witches shall be put to death —Colony Laws, 1641, p. 59.

Magistrates shall issue warrants to a constable, and in his absence to any person, to cause Quakers to be stripped naked from the middle upward; tied to a cart's tail, and whipped from town to town till conveyed out of our jurisdiction.—Colony Laws, p. 125.

Under these laws Baptists had their ears cropped in Boston as late as 1658, and Quakers were put to death.

* N. Y. Doc. Hist. vol. ix. p. 71, 75.

Gosnold, it is sufficient to say, that it was prior to the date of the Royal Charter, and consequently of no legal effect in establishing title. As to the settlement of Jamestown, it was south of the fortieth parallel of latitude, and therefore did not come in conflict with the French King's prior charter to De Monts. The territory between the fortieth and the forty-fifth degrees only, was in dispute. Although the maps of the time made New-France to extend from the thirty-third to the fiftieth degree of north latitude, France practically abandoned the country south of the fortieth degree from the time of the grant of the charter to De Monts, so that below that line south, it was open to any people who might have the courage to possess it; this south line of De Monts' grant, intersecting what is now Pennsylvania, just north of the city of Philadelphia, cutting Ohio, Indiana, and Illinois very nearly in their centre. Had there been no English settlement or occupancy north of the fortieth parallel of latitude prior to 1610, when Poutrincourt obtained a new grant of Acadia, the whole country north of that line must have fallen into the hands of the French.

The reason, undoubtedly, why France at this time extended her claims no further south than the fortieth parallel was, a fear of exciting the jealousy and hostility of the Spaniards. In 1562, when Ribaut and Laudonniere planted at Port Royal, Spain looked upon it as an invasion of her just domain, and promptly expelled the French invaders. Recent discoveries show that she watched with a most jealous eye the fate of the earlier voyages of Cartier from 1534 to 1541.* Spain, at that time, was the great military and naval power of Europe. There can be no doubt that the limiting of De Monts' charter to the fortieth parallel of latitude, seven degrees

* See Historical Magazine, January, 1862, p. 14.

short of all her previous claims, was induced by a dread of Spanish interference. Spanish jealousy showed itself equally in opposition to the English occupation of the country, but their prompt assertion in 1613 of their title, averring the actual occupation of the country, and the denial, on the part of King James, of any validity in the Bull of the Pope, upheld the right of England.

It was not Spain, however, but France that became the actual competitor of England in the struggle for the new dominion. The relations of Spain and France were friendly. Between Spain and England there were many irritations, and so far had this ill-feeling grown, that the capture of English ships by Spanish cruisers was not an uncommon occurrence, as in the case of Challons, and others, bound to New-England, for purposes of colonization.

The French, therefore, made no claim to that Virginia occupied by the colony at Jamestown, while Spain claimed the whole country. French plans of empire looked northward and westward, resting their base on the great inland sea, or gulf lying inside Cape Sable and Cape Cod, where, for a whole century previous, from 1504, and onward, their fishermen had found the choicest treasures of the sea.

Whoever held this region, as all now see, must eventually become the dominant power of the New World.

The national feeling was not fully aroused in either country to the greatness of the prize at stake. Champlain comprehended the true measure of the occasion, and its importance to his country; while Sir Ferdinando Gorges, with equal grasp of intellect, rested on a more secure foundation the confidence of his sovereign.

But the people of England were incapable of estimating the value of the prize, or doing justice to the man who secured it.

In the debate in the House of Commons, in 1621 and 1622, on the bill to abrogate or annul the New-England charter, and throw open the fisheries, briefly reported in the parliamentary journals, the issue was, "*Which is of most value, fishing or plantations?*" and the result showed that the enemies of colonization were in the ascendant, and a bill to this effect passed the House. By the influence of the King acting with the Lords, it was prevented from becoming a law.*

From the time of the first conflict at Mount Desert, where Father Du Thet was killed in defending his home, in 1613—the first shedding of blood between the French and English on this continent—till the fall of Quebec, in 1759, and the Treaty of Peace consequent thereon, in 1763, surrendering New-France to Great Britain, there was a strife of races, of nationalities and of religion for the territory of New-England, while Virginia, along the Atlantic slope, was never molested by the French.

The western boundary of Virginia was the Pacific Ocean, and she came into conflict with France when she crossed the Alleghanies and descended into the Mississippi Basin, and there met the French settlers, who had seized upon the western waters, claiming a continuous possession of the entire regions drained by the waters of the Mississippi and the St. Lawrence. Had England acquired nothing in the way of title in the New

* April 19, 1621, "Mr. Neale said three hundred ships, at least, had gone this year from these ports," p. 591. Nov. 20, 1621, "Mr. Glanville moved to speed the bill," etc. "Sir Ferdinando Gorges hath exhibited patent," etc. "Friday next Sir F. G., to be heard," p. 640. Dec. 1, 1621, Bill under consideration. "Mr. Guy moves a provision; debate by Mr. Neale, Mr. Secretary, Dr. Gooch, Sir Edward Gyles, Mr. Guy, and Shewell, which is of most value, fishing or plantations? £120,000 brought in annually by fishing." "Provision lost. Bill passed, p. 654."—Extracts from the Journal of the Commons.

World north of the fortieth parallel prior to the Plymouth Plantation in 1620, there is no reason to doubt that France would have swept the British power from the continent at the first clash of arms with Great Britain.

It was this possession of the shores of the Atlantic Ocean, within the limits of the fortieth and forty-fifth degrees of north latitude, prior to 1610, that settled the future destiny of the continent of North-America. The consummation of title, therefore, perfected by the act of possession of August nineteenth, O. S. 1607, by the Popham Colony, whose two hundred and fifty-fifth anniversary we this day celebrate, must, if these premises are admitted, forever remain the great fact in the history of the New World.

The Maine Historical Society, whose duty it is made, by the charter establishing it, "to collect and preserve whatever may tend to explain and illustrate the civil, ecclesiastical, and natural history of this State and the United States," was pleased to approve of the act of two of its members, then in the service of the State, who petitioned the authorities of the General Government, that this great work of national defence, then about to be undertaken, should be named FORT POPHAM, in honor of George Popham, the Governor, who led the first British Colony into New-England, under the charter of April 10, 1606, and who, discharging the duties of his office as President, and presenting a report in the form of a letter, to the King, dated at Fort St. George, December 13, 1607,* here laid down his life—the first man of the English race whose bones were laid beneath the soil of New-England.

* Popham's Letter in the Maine Hist. Coll. vol. v. p. 341.

The venerable Chief of the Engineer Bureau of the United States Army, to whom this petition was referred, ever jealous of the honor of his country, not only as to the character of its military structures, but as to the names, to whose honor they should attest—promptly indorsed the application, and it met the ready approval of the Secretary of War.*

To mark, with greater distinctness, the event thus commemorated, the Maine Historical Society asked permission to place within the walls of this Fort a MEMORIAL STONE, bearing on its face an appropriate inscription of the event; and that a TABLET, in memory of George Popham, so honorably associated with the great event of that period, should be allowed to form a portion of its walls.

By the favor of the Government we have this day performed that duty, with appropriate form and ceremony. The learned President of the Maine Historical Society has announced the historic facts on which this somewhat novel proceeding has taken place. The accomplished and honored Chief Magistrate of the State has given to the occasion the influence of his official

* The following correspondence, copied from the files of the War Office, shows the prompt action of the Government in the matter:

TO THE HON. SIMON CAMERON, Secretary of War:

The undersigned, citizens of Maine, respectfully request that the new Fort to be erected at the mouth of the Kenebec river, in Maine, may be named FORT POPHAM, in honor of Capt. George Popham, brother of the learned Chief-Justice Popham, of England.

Capt. George Popham, as the Governor of the first English Colony in New-England, built a fort at or near the site of the proposed fort, in the year 1607, where he died February 5, 1608, and was buried, being the first person of his race whose bones were laid beneath the soil of New-England, and whose grave will be appropriately marked by the fort that rises over his place of burial.

(Signed) JOHN A. POOR,
REUEL WILLIAMS

WASHINGTON, November 18, 1861.

This proposal for a name was favorably received at the Engineer Bureau, by General Totten, who laid the matter before the Secretary of War.

On the 23d of November, General Cameron acted on the foregoing petition, and entered thereon: "Name approved.

"SIMON CAMERON, Secretary of War.

"WAR DEPARTMENT, Washington, November 23, 1861."

station, and the more acceptable service of eloquent words, proclaiming the importance of the event commemorated, upon the history of the country and the world, while the Episcopal Bishop of the Diocese of Maine and the President of our oldest Seminary of learning, as Chairman of the Standing Committee of the Maine Historical Society, have jointly participated in the appropriate services of this occasion, and that most ancient, Masonic Fraternity, has lent to the celebration whatever of dignity or grace the wisest of their Order have been able to embody in artistic form and expression. With the consent of the Government, these imposing ceremonies have proceeded, and finally the skillful hand of him who is charged with the construction of this Fort,* will place this stone in its final resting-place—for the information of those who come after us — proclaiming to future times, in the simple eloquence of truthful words, that

THE FIRST COLONY
ON THE SHORES OF NEW-ENGLAND
Was Founded Here,
August 19th, O. S. 1607,
under
GEORGE POPHAM.

It would ill comport with the dignity of this occasion to fail to speak of him, whose name is thus imperishably connected with the history of our State and Nation. To his family and the events of his life others may more appropriately refer. We allude to him as a public man, and to his claims to public gratitude and respect. His chief distinction is, that he was one of the eight persons named in the great charter of April 10th, 1606, and that he led to these shores the first colony under that charter. In it he is styled *gentleman*,

* Captain T. L. Casey, U. S. Engineers.

and he must have been a man of consequence and position, from the fact that he was one of its grantees. After his death, Gorges, in a few brief lines, thus sums up his character: "He was well stricken in years, and had long been an infirm man. Howsoever, heartened by hopes, willing he was to die in acting something that might be serviceable to God, and honorable to his country."* A glorious consummation of a long life, devoted to duty, to his country, and his God.†

Within the walls of this Fort, and as a companion-piece to the memorial stone, which records the historic fact of this day's celebration, the Maine Historical Society will place a tablet in memory of George Popham, expressing, in that sonorous Latin language which he employed in his communication to the King, and which was at that time used by all who wrote for enduring fame, these words:

In Memoriam
GEORGII POPHAM,
Angliæ qui primus ab oris
Coloniam collocavit in Nov. Angliæ terris,
Augusti mense annoque MDCVII.
Leges literasque Anglicanas
Et fidem ecclesiamque Christi
In has sylvas duxit.
Solus ex colonis atque senex obiit
Nonis Februariis sequentibus,
Et juxta hunc locum est sepultus.

Societate Historica Mainensi auspicante,
In præsidio ejus nomen ferente,
Quarto die ante calendas Septembres
Annoque MDCCCLXII.
Multis civibus intuentibus,
Hic lapis positus est.

* Gorges' Briefe Narration, p. 22, vol. ii. Maine Hist. Coll.

† Mrs. Sigourney has since embodied in song, in one of her happiest efforts, the heroic deeds of Popham. See Appendix C.

[TRANSLATION.]

IN MEMORY OF
GEORGE POPHAM
Who first from the shores of England
Founded a Colony in New-England
August, 1607.
He brought into these wilds
English laws and learning
And the faith and the Church of Christ.
He only of the colonists, and in his old age, died
On the fifth of the following February
And was buried near this spot.

Under the auspices of the Maine Historical Society
In the Fort bearing his name
August 29, 1862,
In the presence of many citizens
This stone was placed.

This fort, so conspicuously placed, bearing these appropriate testimonials, thus becomes a fitting monument to perpetuate the events of the early history of New-England, and transmit to future times, the memory of those illustrious men who laid the foundation of English colonies in America; to which the laws, the institutions and civilization of England were transferred, and from which, has sprung the glorious fabric of American Constitutional Government.

Standing here to-day, in sight of the spot where Popham, two hundred and fifty-five years ago, took upon himself the office of President, and near the place where, on the fifth of February following, he died, it seems our privilege to be admitted into his presence-chamber, as for the last time he had summoned around him his faithful assistants and companions, and gave commands for the future. The scene is worthy of a painter's pencil and a poet's pen. The ever-faithful and heroic Raleigh Gilbert, "a man," says Gorges, "worthy to be beloved of them for his industry and care for their well-being"—the future President of the colony—is by his side. The pious Richard Seymour administers to him words of comfort and consolation. Captain Richard Davies, of all his assistants, was absent in England. His devoted companions stand around their dying chief, when, in the language of Israel's great law-giver, laying the burden of the government on Joshua, he might well say to Raleigh Gilbert: "Be strong and of a good courage, for thou must go with this people into the land which the Lord hath sworn unto their fathers to give them: and thou shalt cause them to inherit it. And the Lord he it is that doth go before thee: he will be with thee, he will not fail thee, neither forsake thee: fear not, neither be dismayed."

"So Moses, the servant of the Lord, died there, in the land of Moab, according to the word of the Lord. And he buried him in a valley in the land of Moab, over against Bethpeor; but no man knoweth of his sepulchre unto this day."

In the far-distant future, not two hundred and fifty-five years from this day, the period of time that has intervened since his death, but in that period of more than three thousand years to come, like that from the death of Israel's law-giver, to that of Popham, these stones which are here builded, shall mark the place of his sepulture, and the myriads of thronging pilgrims, led by eager curiosity, to tread the soil of this peninsula of Sabino, hereafter made classic by song and story, shall pause and read, on that memorial stone, the record of his great work; and when we who are now here, shall have passed away, and beyond the reach of story or tradition, Popham's name shall live in the history of the mighty race, who have changed this continent from one vast wildernesss to a marvel of refinement and beauty, fitted for the enjoyment of civilized man.

His sagacity and ability are best evidenced by the fact, that after the experience of two hundred and fifty-five years, the highest military skill has confirmed the wisdom of his choice of a place of settlement, by the adoption of it as the proper site of the great work of defence for the Kennebec River.*

To this spot multitudes shall annually repair, for this region will continue to be, what it ever was, to the early navigators and colonists of both France and England—a chief point of interest. The French historian L'Escarbot, speaking of this river, says "*it shortened the way*" to the great river of Canada.† Gosnold's landfall, in 1602, was at Sagadahoc.‡ Pring, in 1603, made it the chief point of his discoveries; and the great voyage of Weymouth was to "the most excellent and beneficyall river of Sagadahoc."§ Here the English remained in 1608 and 1609, as related by the French Jesuits.‖ Here Vines pursued his voca-

* See Note A, with its accompanying Map.

† L'Escarbot, p. 497.

‡ Strachey, Hakluyt Society edition, p. 155; caption at the head of the chapter. See Poor's Vindication of Gorges, p. 30, note 2.

§ Much controversy and discussion have arisen as to the route of Weymouth, and as to the river he explored. Belknap's authority was generally accepted, fixing it at the Penobscot, till the critical eye and more ample knowledge of the late John McKeen, Esq., detected its errors. He maintained that the Kennebec was the true river. Mr. George Prince and Rev. Mr. Cushman have argued in favor of the river St. George. Mr. R. K. Sewall and Rev. Mr. Ballard maintain the views of Mr. McKeen. Hon. W. Willis adheres to Belknap's authority. Strachey's positive statement that it was the Sagadahoc, was unknown to Belknap.

I find in Purchase, a fact not alluded to by any of these writers, that may aid in solving the difficulty. John Stoneman, of Plymouth, who went out with Weymouth, in 1605, sailed as pilot in the ship Richard, of Plymouth, in charge of Henry Challons commander, in Gorges' employ, to found the colony at Sagadahoc, in 1606. Nicholas Hine, of Cockington, near Dartmouth, was master. Although Challons failed of his object, by disregarding his instructions, and was taken captive by the Spaniards, his purpose of going to Sagadahoc is expressly stated, and his pilot was of Weymouth's party in 1605.

This discovery of the name of *Hine*, as master under Challons, also relieves us of the difficulty in the apparent contradiction between Gorges and Strachey; the former using the name of Challons as master, the latter calling the master's name Haines, leading us to suppose there were two several voyages, instead of one in fact.

‖ Relations of the Jesuits, vol. i. p. 36.

tion,* and hither all the fishing vessels came, because the finest fish were taken in this region. The salmon of the Kennebec are to this day known in all our cities.

The Council of New-England, on the twenty-fourth of July, 1622, set apart "two great islands in the river of Sagadahoc to be reserved for the public plantation," and "a place between the branches of the two rivers" "*for a public city*."† Though the strife of races and of nationalities has kept back the settlement of this whole region, and the still more disastrous conflicts of rival grants and hostile occupation, destroyed for generations all plans of improvement, who shall dare to say that these plans shall not be realized?

When this Acadian peninsula, with its one hundred and fifty thousand square miles of territory, and its abundant resources, shall contain a population equal to that now peopling the British Isles,—this magnificent estuary, with its deep sea-soundings, discharging a larger volume of water than any river of the Atlantic coast, between the St. John and the Mississippi, may become the chief seat of wealth and power, of the mighty race who inhabit the continent,—why then *may* not the history of other lands become ours, and another Liverpool here rival the great commercial city of New-England; and Boston become to the city of the Sagadahoc, what Bristol is to the great shipping port of the Mersey?‡

We miss from our celebration to-day, one who was instrumental in creating the immediate occasion of it, and in affixing the name of Popham to this great pub-

* Gorges' Briefe Narration, p. 24.

† Minutes of the Council of New-England, July twenty-fourth, 1622. Calendar of Col. State Papers, vol. i. p. 32. This paper is given in full in Poor's Vindication of Gorges, in the Appendix.

‡ The extraordinary advantages of Bath for a naval and military dépôt, are admitted by all military engineers, but no effort adequate to such a consummation has yet been made.

lic work, and who looked forward with prophetic eye to this day's proceedings.

The propriety of associating important historic events with works of national defence, and of attesting thereby to the fame of the actors therein, met the approval of his mature judgment, and his last act of public duty was an appeal to the Secretary of War for the erection of this fort, and affixing to it the name it now bears.* His stern countenance relaxed into a smile at the first suggestion of this anniversary celebration, and the placing within the walls of this fort of this memorial stone.

Born on the banks of this river, the place of his birth continued for fourscore years to be his home; and without the aid of anything but his strong character and his indomitable will, he reached wealth and eminence early in life, and bore at the close of it, the title of "the first citizen of Maine." †

This is not the time or place to pronounce his eulogy; an abler pen at the appointed hour shall perform this pleasing duty. But among the many memorials of his enterprise and public spirit that adorn the banks of the Kennebec, this fort attests and will attest the praise of Reuel Williams, while it is made by this day's celebration a fitting monument to preserve in remembrance the greater events of an earlier time.

We must not, in this connection, forget our obligations to the people of the colony of Massachusetts, and the early settlers of Plymouth, for their share in conquering the continent for our race, though dealing harshly with Maine. ‡ These Massachusetts Puri-

* By appointment of Governor Washburn, Mr. Williams visited Washington, November first, 1861, as one of the Commissioners of Maine, in reference to the public defences of the State, his first visit after eighteen years' absence. He retired from the Senate in 1843, resigning after having been reëlected for six years. He left Washington November eighteenth, 1861, after a personal interview on that day with the Secretary of War.

† Hon. I. Washburn, Jr., Governor of Maine.

‡ See petition of Edward Godfrey and other inhabitants of Maine, to the Parliament of the Commonwealth. Cal. Col. State Papers, vol. i. p. 479.

tans of the Saxon type, inheriting all the gloomy errors of a cruel and bloody period, under the iron rule of the Tudors, were ready to demand of Elizabeth the enforcement of the Act of Uniformity against Papists, but refused obedience to it themselves. Nor would they yield to the decision of a majority of the clergy, who in 1562, in full convention, voted to retain the priestly vestments and the forms of a liturgy. While agreeing to all the doctrines of its creed, they grew restless under the forms of the church service, elevated non-essentials into the dignity of principles, and stigmatized the Prayer-Book and the priestly robes as badges of Popery.

They imagined that by a severe austerity they secured the favor of God, and became his chosen people. They mistook their hatred of others for hatred of sin. They set up their own morbid convictions as the standard of right, and rather than submit to the laws of their own land, they endured their penalties, or sought escape from them by expatriation.

Once planted on the shores of New-England, the Puritans of Massachusetts Bay endeavored to exterminate every thing that stood in the way of their ambition.* Hence, after their conquest of Maine, they

Also, Godfrey's Letters in Mr. Geo. Folsom's Catalogue of Papers in the English State Paper Office in relation to Maine, pp. 52, 54.

* The charter of the Massachusetts Company of March 4th, 1629, authorized them to make laws and ordinances for their government, "*not contrary to the laws of England.*" Notwithstanding this they proceeded at once to frame a code of laws designed for the purpose, abrogating the laws of England whenever they stood in the way of their own wishes. The obvious purpose of the charter was to allow such minor regulations to be made as might meet the peculiar wants of the local population. A similar provision is inserted in charters in modern times, designed to allow the recipients of such grants to exercise their rights in any way they choose, not infringing any of the general laws of the State. These Puritans construed their grant differently from all others, because they designed to establish a religious community on a plan of their own, discarding all portions of the English law, unless reënacted by themselves.

Their be-praised Body of Liberties enacted in 1641, but not printed till within about thirty years since, virtually abrogated the laws of England.

Equally striking was their claim to the territory of Maine. The political troubles at home, from 1637 to the restoration of Charles II., in 1660, withdrew public gloried in extirpating every trace of title granted to others, making war on whatever was opposed to them, aiming at unlimited despotism. True, they planted other men's fields, instead of devastating them, and seized upon the territory of others by the same authority and in the same spirit as the Israelites drove out the tribes, that formerly possessed the valley of the Jordan.

It is hardly necessary to remind the student of American history that, at the close of the seventeenth century, as at the beginning, the two great geographical divisions of English dominion on this continent, north of the Delaware, were "the Provinces of New-York and Sagadahoc." Such are the definitions employed in the grant of that dominion by King Charles II. to his brother, the Duke of York; and such are the titles under which the Duke of York, when he ascended the throne as James II., commissioned his Governor, Col. Thomas Dongan, afterwards Earl of Limerick, to exercise authority over these countries. In England, a country of precedents, where the law advisers of the Crown always scrupulously adhered to ancient records in the preparation of official documents, such recognition, eighty years after the death of George Popham, is another proof, if any were wanting, of the legal establishment of England's claims in these latitudes being inseparable from the foundation of the first settlement, which to-day we commemorate.

To review, in the most hurried manner, the events

attention almost entirely from America, and it was not till 1676 that the heirs of Gorges, nearly worn out in the controversy, obtained a decision in their favor against her usurpations. Thereupon March 13, 1677, for £1250 they purchased the title of Gorges' heirs.

Finally in 1684, on *scire facias*, the Court of Chancery declared their charter forfeited, and thereby put an end to the Massachusetts theocracy.

A new charter protecting all Protestant Christians in the exercise of their religion, was granted by William and Mary, in 1691, including the colony of Plymouth and of Massachusetts, the Province of Maine, and Sagadahoc, under one government, and Sir William Phipps, a native of Maine, was appointed Governor.

affecting our race, that have transpired within the two hundred and fifty-five years since it was planted here, would transcend the proper limits of this occasion. Less than five millions of people, at that time engaged in the ruder forms of labor, were shut up in the narrow limits of the British Isles,—those who speak the English language to-day in the two hemispheres, hold dominion over one fifth of the earth's surface, and govern one fourth of the human species.*

Their material greatness commenced with colonizing North-America. Slowly, patiently and in much suffering, our fathers gained possession of this soil. The title was secured by the act of possession of the Popham Colony. Others came in to help to hold it; political troubles at home favored emigration hither; and one hundred years after Popham, three hundred thousand people of the Saxo-Norman race inhabited the then eleven existing colonies. During the next sixty years they had mastered the French, and gained the Atlantic slope from the St. Lawrence to Florida. Before the end of the next one hundred years the same people had grown into the Colossal Empire of the West, embracing thirty-four States, and regions yet unpeopled of still greater extent, including, in all their dominions, a territory equal to the continent of Europe, inhabited by more than thirty millions of human beings, speaking one language; while a new power has arisen in North-America, the Colonial Empire of Great Britain, extending over a larger, but less valuable territory than the United States, and containing more than three millions of inhabitants.

Temporary differences and periods of alienated feeling, will from time to time arise, but nothing can prevent the gradual and cordial union of the English-speaking people, of this continent in every thing essen-

* See Appendix D.

tial to their highest welfare. Though divided into various governments, each pursuing its own lawful ends, in obedience to that principle of political harmony, that allows each to revolve, in its own appropriate orbit, around its common centre, an enlightened sense of justice, and obedience to the Divine law, as the highest of all good to communities and states, is the daily lesson of their life. Let, then, each returning anniversary of this day's commemoration draw closer and closer the bonds of fraternal fellowship, and strengthen those ties of lineage that shall gradually encircle the earth, and constitute all mankind of various races and nationalities, one final brotherhood of nations.

Two hundred and fifty-five years have sufficed to change this wilderness continent, as if by enchantment, into the home of a refined civilization. Cultivated fields, clustering villages, the refinements of city life, rise to our immediate view; stretching from this point eastward to Ascension Bay,—northward to the Laurentian Hills, — southward to the Gulf of Mexico, and westward to the Pacific seas, where San Francisco, at the Golden Gate, at the touch of the telegraph, sends to us kindly greetings for this hour.

The improvement in agricultural implements, the wonders of the power-loom and the spinning-jenny, the marvels of the steamship, the mysteries of the photograph, the magic of the telegraph, and the omnipotent power of the locomotive railway, have since been made our ever-willing ministers, so that man seems almost invested with ubiquity and omnipotence; yet each revolving year brings forth new marvels, till the finite mind is overwhelmed at any attempt to forecast the future.

And the historian of our race traces back this development to the two first acts in the great drama of American history by which the title of England to the Continent was established; the first, closing with the grant of the Great Charter of April 10th, 1606; the second, with the formal act of possession of the New World under it, August 19th, O. S. 1607, thereby making the title, forever clear and unquestionable.

.On that day, and upon this peninsula of Sabino, was unfurled that proud flag that had so long braved the battle and the breeze; then our fathers' flag—and now the flag of the Fatherland—and beneath its waving folds were proclaimed, for the first time, the political principles which lie at the foundation of free government, in ever memorable words.

"I give," said King James, "to my loving subjects, liberty to settle Virginia, in the north of America, between the thirty-fourth and forty-fifth degrees of north latitude. I authorize them to transport thither any of my own people, or those of other lands, and appoint over them a government of their own choice, subject to my approval, according to the laws of this kingdom. I authorize them to work mines, coin money, collect duties by imposts, and to expel all intruders therefrom by military force; and I declare, that all children born therein, and all persons residing therein, are, and shall always remain citizens, entitled to all the rights, privileges, and immunities of the loyal subjects of the British realm.

"And I do further declare, that these, my loving subjects, shall have the right annually to elect a President, and other officers; that the Christian Religion, established in this our kingdom, shall be therein preached and observed; that lands shall descend to heirs, according to the provisions of our ancient laws; that trial by jury of twelve men is established in all criminal cases, with a right of pardon by the King; that in civil causes the President and Council shall determine between party and party, keeping full records of all proceedings and judgments, with a right of appeal to the King in council; that no man shall be tried as an offender outside of the Colony where the alleged offence was committed, and no offences shall be capital except tumult, rebellion, conspiracy, mutiny, and sedition, murder, manslaughter, incest, rape, and adultery. And I do further declare, and ordain, that my loving subjects in America shall forever possess and enjoy the right to make all needful laws for their own government, provided only, that they be consonant to the laws of England. And these, my loving subjects, shall be, and forever remain, entitled to the protection of the British Crown, and I establish over them the government of the King of Great Britain, France, and Ireland."*

This charter of liberties was never revoked. It was a decree of universal emancipation, and every man of any color, from any clime, was by this act of King James redeemed, regenerated, disenthralled, the moment he touched the soil of America, between the thirty-fourth and forty-fifth degrees of north latitude; and he at once became entitled to all the rights of citizenship — one hundred and fifty years before the decree of Lord Mansfield struck off the chains and fetters from the African in England. This ordinance also established the right of the people to self-government, subject only to the paramount authority of the Crown and Laws of England.

These solemn formalities, unknown to any other of the early colonies, counselled by the Lord Chief-Justice of England, whose brother, as President of the infant commonwealth, planted on these shores the emblems of the authority of his nation,—proclaimed in no doubtful accents to all other nations, that here, the title

* See Poor's Vindication of Gorges, Appendix, for this constituent Code of Laws of King James.

of England was established. That pledge of the protection of his government, which every Englishman has always felt when he planted his foot on any portion of the empire of his sovereign, gave strength and courage to this colony,—and when the humble settlers of Plymouth, thirteen years later, impressed with their feet the sandy shores of Cape Cod, the claim of England to the country had been vindicated and established, against the asserted claims of both Spain and France.

The power of England remained undisturbed west of Sagadahoc, and southward, till it was finally yielded on the third of September, 1783—one hundred and seventy-six years from the time it was first planted—when all political connection with Great Britain was dissolved, on the conclusion of the Definitive Treaty of Peace. In announcing that fact, King George the Third said: "In thus admitting their separation from the Crown of these kingdoms, I have sacrificed every consideration of my own, to the wishes and opinions of my people. I make it my humble and earnest prayer to Almighty God, that Great Britain may not feel the evils which might result from so great a dismemberment of the empire; and that America may be free from the calamities which have formerly proved, in the mother country, how essential monarchy is to the enjoyment of constitutional liberty. Religion, language, interest, affections may, and I hope will yet prove a bond of permanent union between the two countries. To this end neither attention nor disposition on my part shall be wanting."

Memorable words, for they admit the national error.

But the repentance of the King had come too late. The loyal subjects of King James had planted on these shores the principles of civil and religious liberty, under his guidance and his express authority, and it was not in the power of King or Parliament, after one hundred and seventy-six years of the exercise of these rights, to reclaim them by force of arms.

It was in defence of rights granted by King James that our fathers took up arms, against the arbitrary enactments of King George the Third and his Parliament, under the lead of Sir George Grenville, then first Minister of the Crown. They defended a principle since made universal in its application, in every part of the British Colonial Empire. They claimed only their rights as loyal subjects of Great Britain.

Our fathers charged the acts of oppression, commencing in 1763, and ending in the Revolution of 1776, on the King, as the responsible head of the British government, but the exact truth still remains obscured, from want of public access, till a recent date, to the state papers of that period. If the odium of these acts shall justly fall on the head of the Minister rather than on the King, to what an eminence of guilt did Sir George Grenville attain, and how different the award of future over cotemporary times and opinions, as to the claims to veneration of the two men of England most intimately associated with American affairs, Sir Ferdinando Gorges, the father of English Colonization in America, a private citizen,—and Sir George Grenville, the highest officer of state, who inaugurated those measures that caused the final separation of the thirteen North-American Colonies from the British Crown,—an event, under the circumstances in which it was achieved, every day seen to have been most disastrous to humanity and our race.

The mind of each one present instinctively turns back to-day, over this long line of history, pausing to survey, in this broad sweep, the great epochs that mark its progress. It lingers longest in contemplating the initiatory steps that gave title and possession to the country,—and delights to loiter, here, around this cherished spot, and recall to present view the deeds of Gorges and Popham, and those who assisted them to transport hither the Saxo-Norman race; for that race, planted on this new continent, has favored and illustrated every thing that tends to the advancement of freedom and humanity, whatever may have been its occasional errors.

We have established our power as a people, developed the natural resources of our country, and demonstrated the ability of our government to resist foreign aggression. One further duty remains—the vindication of its principles in reference to ourselves. Can a government, resting for its strength and support on the consent of the governed, so far maintain its power as to suppress insurrection without weakening the safeguards to personal liberty? Can popular elections fill the highest offices of the state, and insure that strength and stability to the government, that can vindicate its power in times of domestic insurrection, or open rebellion, like that, now shaking it to its foundations?

Putting our trust in that power that alone can save us, invoking that arm that can alone be stretched forth for our deliverance, we bow our wills to the Divine teaching.

What though at this hour clouds and darkness hang like a thick pall over our country, and in the excess of our marvellous prosperity, we are called for a time to self-abasement and trial, the race shall survive all shocks of civil strife and of foreign invasion, and rise superior to both; this free government emerge into the full strength and measure of its giant proportions; and "the gorgeous ensign of the Republic," known and honored throughout the earth, shall once more float, full and free, as in former days, over a united and prosperous people.

At the conclusion of Mr. Poor's address, the ceremonies at the Fort were terminated with the benediction, pronounced by the Rev. Francis Norwood, Pastor of the Congregational Church in Phipsburg, within the limits of which town is the ancient province of Sabino.

AT THE PAVILION.

The next division of the commemorative acts was assigned to the Tent. In the absence of the gentleman expected to preside at this commemoration, the President of the Historical Society, the Hon. William Willis, was requested by the Executive Committee to take this office for the remainder of the day. The Chief Marshal had appointed as his assistants, the following gentlemen: Elias Thomas, 2d., John M. Brown, and Henry Willis, Esquires, of Portland; Samuel D. Bailey, John S. Elliot, David T. Stinson, and Henry W. Swanton, Esquires, of Bath; Col. Daniel Elliot, of Brunswick; Joseph McKeen, M. D., of Topsham; and Nathaniel M. Whitmore, 2d., Esq., of Gardiner.

With the aid of such of the number as were present, he organized and conducted the procession; which, preceded by the band, was led to the large and commodiously arranged tent, erected at some distance westerly from the fort, on a smooth and grassy plain, whose surroundings presented the same features as were seen from the platform at the fort. The entrance and the platform for the speakers, members of the

Historical Society, and invited guests, had been tastefully decorated, under the direction of Major C. W. King, with evergreens and the flags of the two nations, whose histories were united in this commemorative festival. Seats for twenty-five hundred persons had been provided under the broad-spreading awning, which were rapidly occupied; and a large number of persons in addition, while the doings of the occasion were continued, remained standing as listeners to the various addresses, and the cheering strains of the music interspersed at intervals.

A dinner of clam and fish chowder was supplied here for this vast assembly.

ADDRESSES.

The audience was called to order by the Chief Marshal, when the President of the Day, after a few brief remarks bearing on the event and its commemoration, announced the first sentiment in the following words:

The 19*th of August* [*O. S.*], 1607,— ever memorable as the day that witnessed the consummation of the title of England to the New World, by the formal occupation and possession of New England, under the Royal Charter of April 10, 1606.

In the absence of the gentleman whom it was hoped would respond to this sentiment, the President called upon the Right Rev. Bishop Burgess to address the assembly; who, after a few introductory remarks connecting the sentiment proposed with the name of the chaplain of the colony, read the following paper:

BISHOP BURGESS'S ADDRESS.

MR. PRESIDENT: Who was RICHARD SEYMOUR? And why should he be remembered with honor?

The house of Seymour, the second among the English nobility, first rose to eminence through the elevation of Queen Jane, the daughter of Sir John Seymour, the favorite wife of Henry the Eighth, and the mother of Edward the Sixth. Her brother, Sir Edward Seymour, became Earl of Hertford, and in the minority of his nephew, King Edward, was created Duke of Somerset, and governed the realm as Lord Protector. He was twice married, and his second wife, Anne Stanhope, being a lady of high descent, it was made a part of his patent of nobility that his titles should first be inherited in the line of her children, and only in the event of the failure of that line, should pass to his children by his first wife, Catherine Fillol, and their descendants. Accordingly, the honors, — forfeited when "the Good Duke," as the Protector was called, perished on the scaffold, — being afterwards restored, passed down in the younger line, till it expired in Algernon, Duke of Somerset, in 1750; when they reverted to the elder line, in which they continue till this day.

In the meantime, this elder branch had been seated, all along, at Berry Pomeroy, in Devonshire, a few miles from Totness, from Dartmouth, and from the sea. The eldest son of the Protector, Sir Edward, a christian name which continued in the eldest sons for eight generations, died in 1593. His son, Sir Edward, the grandson of the Protector, was married in 1576, and died in 1613, having had, according to one account, five sons; according to another, three; besides four daughters. The youngest son, according to both accounts, bore the name of Richard; and this great-grandson of the Protector Somerset, was, I suppose, the Richard Seymour who was the chaplain of the Popham Colony. The case is sustained as follows:

There is no other person of the name known in genealogical history. Among sixty-nine male descendants of the Protector, he is the only Richard.

His age corresponds with the chronology of the occasion. His father having married in 1576, the youngest of three, or even of five sons, might well have been born within ten years after, so as to have been, in 1607, a young clergyman just from the university. What more probable than that such a young man should be attracted by this noble adventure, as it happened to be in the hands of his immediate friends?

His residence corresponds with the locality of the enterprise. It was within fifteen or twenty miles of Plymouth, and amongst those gentlemen of Devonshire who chiefly formed the company with whom this undertaking originated. Of the Plymouth company, of 1620, his brother, Sir Edward Seymour, was one of the incorporated members.

This brings us to the most decisive circumstances, which are not a little interesting in the light which they cast upon the history of the colony. At Dartington, close by Berry Pomeroy, was then, and still is, the seat of the old family of Champernoun, which "came in with William the Conqueror." Francis Champernoun, who came to Maine as one of the councillors under the patent of Gorges, and settled at Kittery, was the nephew of Sir Ferdinando Gorges. Therefore, either Gorges himself, or his sister, or his sister-in-law, must have married a Champernoun. Gorges was Governor of Plymouth, and was the soul of these expeditions long after.

The mother of Sir Walter Raleigh was also a Champernoun; and as she was of course the mother also of his half-brother, the gallant Sir Humphrey Gilbert, it follows that his son, Raleigh Gilbert, the admiral of this expedition, was the grandson of a Champernoun, and had an affinity with Gorges through that family.

Sir John Popham had several children, amongst whom was a

daughter, Elizabeth, who was married to Sir Richard Champernoun; and thus there was affinity between the families of Gorges, Gilbert, and Popham, through the household at Dartington.

Sir Edward Seymour, the father of Richard Seymour, was married, as has been said, in 1576, and his wife was Elizabeth, daughter of Sir Arthur Champernoun; and thus the chain of relationship is complete between the families of Gorges, Raleigh, Gilbert, Popham, and Seymour.

Richard Seymour, therefore, the son of Edward Seymour, was related to Gorges, the projector of the colony; to Popham, its patron; to Popham, its president; and to Gilbert, its admiral, — all through the common link of the family of his mother. When they sought a chaplain, they found one in Richard Seymour; and no other Richard Seymour is known except this relative of theirs. May we not regard the identity as, I will not say demonstrated, but fairly established, to the extent of a reasonable conviction?

The connection between the families of Seymour and Popham ceased not with that generation. Sir John Popham, though Wellington, in Somersetshire, was his birth-place and burial-place, purchased from the family of Darell, to which the grandmother of the Protector belonged, the seat of Littlecote, in Wiltshire, on the borders of Berkshire, and here resided his descendants. Sir Edward Seymour, grand-nephew of Richard Seymour, married Letitia Popham, daughter of Francis Popham of Littlecote, and had a son named Popham Seymour; and the next Sir Edward, his eldest son, married another Letitia, daughter of Sir Francis Popham, also of Littlecote. This hereditary friendship accords with the association on this spot.

But Richard Seymour has his honor, this day, not from his memorable descent, but from the place assigned him by the Providence which presided over the destinies of this now Christian land. He was not the first English clergyman who ever preached the Gospel or celebrated the Holy Communion in North America: that honor fell to Wolfall, in 1578, on the shores of Newfoundland or Labrador. He was not the first English clergyman in the United States; for Hunt had already begun his pastoral office on the banks of the James. He was not even the first Christian teacher within the limits of Maine; for L'Escarbot, a Huguenot, had instructed his French associates in 1604, on an island in the St. Croix.

But Seymour was the first preacher of the Gospel in the English tongue, within the borders of New England, and of the free, loyal, and unrevolted portion of these United States. Had he inherited all the honors of his almost royal great-grandsire, they would have given him a far less noble place than this, in the history of mankind.

The Memory of Sir Ferdinando Gorges, — the Father of English Colonization in America.

As no response has been furnished to the committee in season for the present publication, it has been thought desirable to append to this account of the commemoration, in the form of a supplement, Mr. Poor's "Vindication of Gorges;" with its appendix, containing the charter of April 10, 1606; the Constituent Code of Laws publicly read at Sabino, August 19, 1607 [O. S.]; the commission of Sir Ferdinando Gorges, as Governor of New England; and many other rare documents; many of which, from the English archives, have never before been printed. A nearer approach to historical completeness will be the result of this addition. This work of Mr. Poor is given in full, as recently issued from the press of Messrs. D. Appleton & Co., New York.

Sir John Popham,— the able, learned, and upright Chief Justice of England, by the appointment of Elizabeth; under the shadow of whose great name was laid the foundation of the Colossal Empire of the Western World.

The response to this sentiment, expected in a communication from a distinguished gentleman, unable to be present, has not been received in season for publication.

Henry Wriothesley, Earl of Southampton, — patron of Letters and of American Colonization; the friend and associate of Sir Ferdinando Gorges; whose joint labors procured the Royal Charter of April 10, 1606; the basis on which rests the title of our race to the New World.

In reply to the invitation of the committee, the following letter was received from the Hon. Edward Everett:

MR. EVERETT'S LETTER.

BOSTON, 18th August, 1862.

SIR: — I have received your letter of the 14th, containing the invitation of the Executive Committee, to attend the Historical Celebration at Fort Popham on the 29th instant.

If it had been in my power to attend the celebration, I should have had much pleasure in responding to the toast enclosed in your letter, in honor of the Earl of Southampton. His services in obtaining the Royal Charter of 1606 are a just title to remembrance in America. That Shakspeare, — "the greatest name," says Hallam, "in all literature," — inscribed to him "the first heir of his invention," and, in the preface to his second poem, says, "The love I dedicate to your Lordship is without end," is a distinction enjoyed by the Earl of Southampton alone of the sons of men.

Regretting that it is not in my power to attend the celebration, and with the best wishes for its success, I remain,

Sir, very respectfully yours,

EDWARD EVERETT.

To Rev. EDWARD BALLARD,
Secretary of the Executive Committee.

The Memory of George Popham, — who led hither the first English Colony; became the head of its government by the election of his companions, and left his bones to mingle with the soil of New England, upon the Peninsula of Sabino.

The following communication, from the venerable Rev. Wm. Allen, D. D., of Northampton, Mass., formerly President of Bowdoin College, is here introduced:

PRESIDENT ALLEN'S LETTER.

NORTHAMPTON, MASS., August 26, 1862.

Rev. EDWARD BALLARD, *Secretary, &c.*

DEAR SIR: — I give my thanks to the Executive Committee for inviting me to attend, on the 29th, the proposed celebration of the 255th anniversary of the founding of Popham's Colony, at the mouth of the Sagadahoc River, the first English colony on the shores of New England. Most gladly should I meet with them on the western bank of that river, did God in his providence permit; but my ill health, now of four years' continuance, forbids the thought of such a journey, and scarcely allows me to make a reply with my pen, as you request. If any have judged that I should be likely to take a great interest in an occasion which so especially relates to the early history of Maine, they have judged rightly; for more than forty years ago I found myself an associate of many worthy and learned men, the very first members of the *Maine Historical Society*, and co-operated in their labors. Moreover, my attention had been previously long given to the history of the first settlements of our country, so that I am somewhat of an *antiquarian* in my *pursuits*, as you may well deem me to be in *years*, when I say, that I was already a graduate of old Harvard, when the first class sat down, sixty years ago, to their studies at beloved Bowdoin, the first college established in the State of Maine. With this college, during its existence of sixty years, it was my lot to be connected, during about one-third of that time, beginning with 1820, involving, in that period of nearly twenty years, great and interesting memories.

How can I forget that I became a citizen of Maine in the very year, 1820, in which Maine became one of the States of the American Union, now threatened by the most atrocious rebellion which ever sprung up in this world, — a rebellion that the vigorous, noble, patriotic sons of Maine are helping to put down, and which, in God's goodness, they will be sure to see crushed, when He shall please to give triumph to the right. How can I forget those whom I knew as the first governors of Maine, — King, Parris, Lincoln, Huntoon, Smith, Dunlap, and Fairfield, with many other of its leading men, the friends of the college?

How can I forget the beautiful village of Brunswick, the site of the college, on the banks of the *Aumaughcawgen* (or Ameriscoggin, or Androscoggin), one of the great rivers of Maine; or ever lose the recollection, that in its cemetery there sleep two of the forms most dear to me among the forms of the earth?

How can I forget my co-laborers in beloved Bowdoin nearly twenty years; namely, Cleaveland, Newman, Upham, Packard, and Smyth? And how can I overlook, without ingratitude to God, the consequences of our labors during the short period referred to, — results to spring up from a college, which the colonists at Sagadahoc would not be likely to imagine was destined to be planted, in the course of time, in the wilderness, on the banks of one of the great branches of the Sagadahoc, near Merry-Meeting Bay, and not twenty miles distant from Popham's Fort?

Those results of twenty years' labor are these, — the education of more than five hundred young men, many of whom have been lights in a multitude of our States, learned professors and teachers of various sciences in colleges scattered over our Union, and presidents of colleges; members of the House of Representatives and of the Senate of the United States; judges of courts; governors of different States, and one, John Brown Russwurm, a colored man, the governor of a free State in Africa; one the President of our whole country; one, Cyrus Hamlin, long a missionary in Turkey, now founding a college in the Mohammedan city of Constantinople; and about one hundred and fifty ministers of the gospel, of different denominations; some of whom are eminent preachers of the truth in our great cities, and all of them teachers of the way of salvation to their fellow-men, and examples of the Christian virtues, as was the solitary preacher of New England, REV. RICHARD SEYMOUR, the chaplain at Sagadahoc in 1607 and 1608. This Mr. Seymour, of the English Episcopal Church, preached the first sermon ever preached on "the main" of New England, August 19, 1607 [O. S.], when the colony was planted, although he had preached on Sunday, the 9th, a sermon to a part of the company on the shore of St. George's Island, twenty miles to the east.

It appears to me certain, beyond a doubt, that the river, at the mouth of which was Popham's Colony, was called by the early voyagers and most eminent writers, the river *Sagadahoc;* and it seems to me equally certain, that the colony was planted on the *west* side of the river, and not on Clark's Island, on the east side. The proof is as follows:

1. The very important and decisive "Account of the Northern Colonie, seated upon the river of Sachadehoc, by William Strachey," who was Secretary of the Virginia Colony about 1610: it was first published in this country in the first volume, fourth series, of the Massachusetts Historical Collections, 1852, edited by Rev. William S. Bartlett, Episcopal minister of Chelsea. This writer says: "They went early in the morning from their ship into the river *Sachadehoc*, to view the river, and to search where they might find a fitt place for their plantation." Again, he says: "They all went ashore, and there made choice

of a place for their plantation, at the mouth or entry of the river *on the west side* (for the river bendeth itself towards the northeast and by east), being almost an island of a good bigness, being in a province called by the Indians, *Sabino*, so called of a Sagamo or chief commander under the grand bassaba." This was August 18th [O. S.]. The next day, Aug. 19th, was the day of planting the colony. He says also, that September 23, " Captain Gilbert, accompanied with nineteen others, departed in his shallop to goe for the head of the river of *Sachadehoc*."

2. Captain John Smith, who was conversant with the coast of Maine immediately after this colony began, speaks of the "plantation of Sagadahoc by those noble captains, George Popham," &c. He mentions the rivers " Sagadahoc, Aumaghcawgen, and Kenabeca."

3. Prince, in his Annals, says, " that Popham and his company settled at the mouth of the Sagadehock." Dr. Belknap says that the colonists landed " at the mouth of Sagadahoc, or Kennebec River, on a peninsula ; " of course, it was on the west side and not on the east side, and on an island. It does not appear that Belknap had any authority for assigning to the river, at the site of the colony, the name of Kennebec.

William Hubbard, indeed, in his History of New England, written about 1680, speaks obscurely of " a spacious river called Kennebec," and of " a place *somewhere about* the mouth whereof was then, and is still called *Sagadahoc*," where the colony was landed. But his ignorance in this matter is obvious from his own words, and he can be of no authority. He could never have seen Strachey's decisive statement. Governor Sullivan, who wrote in the Massachusetts Historical Collection in 1792, a " Description of Georgetown," — a paper referred to by Dr. Holmes in his Annals, places the colony on Parker's Island ; but he gives no authority for his judgment.

If this matter, then, should be considered settled, I would

respectfully ask the commemorators assembled on the 29th of August, What has become of the great river *Sagadahoc?* How came it to vanish from our maps and our geographies? And will they not take into consideration the possibility of re-establishing the name of *Sagadahoc* as the name of the great river, at least as high up as twenty miles, to the junction at *Merry-Meeting Bay*, of the Kennebec from the north, and the Aumoughcawgen from the west?

Captain Smith, who made his map of New England in 1616, requested Prince Charles to change the Indian names of places and rivers on it at his pleasure. A few of the changes thus made are as follows: Smith had marked as places of note, Sagadahoc, at the mouth of the river on the west side; Aumoughcawgen, on the same side, twenty miles to the north; and Kennebec, further north about thirty miles, on the west side also. These were changed by Prince Charles, the first to Leth (or Leith), the second to Cambridge, as if by princely prediction, the beautiful site of Brunswick on the Androscoggin River would, in time, become to Maine, what Cambridge was to England, the chief seat of science. The third change is of Kennebec, near the present site of Augusta, to Edenborough; and these changes appear on the printed map. *Sagadahoc* River seems also to be changed to that of Forth, the name of a river in Scotland, where Prince Charles was born.

As you shall stand at the mouth of the *Sagadahoc* River, I trust it will not be forgotten that you stand at the very spot, where, on the day of the meeting, two hundred and fifty-five years ago, at the laying of the foundation stone of the colony, the *first sermon* ever preached in New England was preached by their chaplain, Mr. SEYMOUR, of the Episcopal Church; in giving which gospel to the people of Maine, God has given them the richest treasure on the earth. It was at a later period of thirteen years, that the gospel was first preached at Plymouth, and a few years still later, by Thomas Hooker, at old Cambridge. Most earnestly did Hooker call upon his hearers, as they would be saved, to bow their pride before the truth and authority of God; for in his view this was the great sin of man, " this pride of a man's spirit, of his mind, his reason, his will, and affections." If God's truth has come from heaven to earth, what greater guilt can there be than to deny it, and pervert it, and withhold it from dark-minded men, to whom it may be in our power to impart it?

When visited at the fort by two canoes of Indians, President Popham was careful to " carry them with him to the place of public prayer, where they were," on the first Sunday in October, " at both morning and evening, attending with great reverence and silence."

But I must close. An old and dying man must bid you farewell. The mighty God, who created the sun, moon, and stars, and who formed also this round earth; who poured out from his hand the waters that fill the oceans and the channels of mighty rivers, making also the living treasures floating in them; who framed the islands and cast up the huge rocks, and spread out and planted the fields and the forests of " the main;" and who permits us, this day, instead of a feeble, disheartened colony, to see a large province, a wide-spread State, inhabited by a hardy race of well educated and virtuous men; the God who has unfolded to us his scheme of mercy, through the death of his Son, this God, by his truth and spirit, prepare us all for the peace and joy and glory of an immortal associate abode in heaven. Yours, &c.,

WILLIAM ALLEN.

Maritime Adventure and Discovery, — illustrated by the men of Bristol and the Severne; whose Cabots and Gilberts pointed the way to the northern shores of the New World. The name of Raleigh Gilbert shall ever be honored for his fidelity in conducting to these shores the colony of Popham.

The Memory of Sieur de Champlain, — the fearless navigator and accomplished statesman; the first to explore and designate these shores; whose plans of empire, more vast and sagacious than any of his time, failed of success only through the short-sightedness of his sovereign, in allowing the Atlantic shores of New England to fall into the hands of his rivals, thereby changing the history of the New World.

The Hon. Thos. Darcy McGee, President of the Executive Council of Canada, addressed the assemblage, in response to this sentiment. He said:

ADDRESS OF THE HON. THOMAS DARCY McGEE.

I beg to assure you, Mr. President, and the gentlemen of the Maine Historical Society, who have done me the honor to invite me here, that I feel it a very great privilege to be a spectator and a participant in the instructive, retributive ceremonial of this day. This peninsula of Sabino must become, if it is not already, classic ground; and this 29th of August, the true era of the establishment of our language and race on this continent, one of the most cherished *fasti* of the English-speaking people of North America. It is, on general grounds, an occasion hardly less interesting to the colonies still English, than to the citizens of Maine; and therefore, I beg to repeat in your presence, the gratification I feel in being allowed to join in the first, of what I trust will prove, but the first, of an interminable series of such celebrations. I would be very insensible, Sir, to the character in which I have been so cordially presented to this assembly, if I did not personally acknowledge it; and I should be, I conceive, unworthy of the position I happen to occupy as a member of the Canadian government, if I did not feel still more the honor you have paid to Canada, in the remembrance you have made of her first Governor and Captain General, the Sieur de Champlain. That celebrated person was, in truth, not only in point of time, but in the comprehension of his views, the audacity of his projects, and the celebrity of his individual career, the first statesman of Canada; and no one pretending to the character of a Canadian statesman could feel otherwise than honored and gratified, when Champlain's name is invoked, publicly or privately, in his presence. We have no fear that the reputation of our great Founder will not stand the severest test of historical research; we have no fear that his true greatness will dwindle by comparison with the rest of the Atlantic leaders — the chiefs of the renowned sea-chivalry, of whom we have already heard such eloquent mention. We Canadians ardently desire that he should be better known — be well known — and, perhaps, you, Mr. President, will permit me to indicate some of the facts in the career, to point to some of the traits in the character, which haloes for us, forever, the name and memory of the Sieur de Champlain.

What we esteem most of all features in the life of our Founder, is that chief virtue of all eminent men — his indomitable fortitude; and next to that we revere the amazing versatility and resources of the man. Originally a naval officer, he had voyaged to the West Indies and to Mexico, and had written a memoir, lately discovered at Dieppe, and edited both in France and England, advocating among other things the artificial connection of the Atlantic and Pacific oceans. From the quarter deck we trace him to the counting rooms of the merchants of Rouen and Saint Malo, who first intrusted him in 1603, with the command of a commercial enterprise, of which Canada was the field. From the service of the merchants of Rouen, Dieppe, and Saint Malo, we trace him to the service of his Sovereign — Henry IV. For several successive years we find his flag glancing at all points along this rock-bound coast, on which we are now assembled, from Port Royal to Massachusetts Bay. Whenever we do not find it here, we may be certain it has advanced into the interior, that it is unfurled at Quebec, at Montreal, or towards the sources of the Hudson and the Mohawk. We will find that this versatile sailor has become in time a founder of cities, a negotiator of treaties with barbarous tribes, an author, a legislator, a discoverer. As a discoverer, he was the first European to ascend the Richelieu, which he named after the patron of his latter years — the all-powerful Cardinal. He was the first to traverse that beautiful lake, now altogether your own, which makes his name so familiar to all Americans; he was the first to ascend our great central river, the Ottawa, as far north as lake Nippising, and he was the first to discover what he very justly calls "the fresh-water sea" — of Lake Ontario. His place as an American discoverer is, therefore, among the first; while his claims as a colonizer rest on the firm foundations of Montreal and Quebec; and his project — extraordinary for the age — of uniting the Atlantic and Pacific by artificial channels of communication. As a legislator, we have not yet recovered, if we ever shall, the ordinances he is known to have promulgated; but as an author we have his narrative of transactions in New France, his voyage to Mexico, his treatise on navigation and some other papers. As a diplomat, we have the Franco-Indian alliances, which he founded, and which lasted a hundred and fifty years on this continent, and which exercised so powerful an influence, not only on American, but on European affairs. To him also it was mainly owing that Canada, Acadia, and Cape Breton were reclaimed by and restored to France, under the treaty of Saint German-en-Laye, in 1632. As to the moral qualities, our Founder was brave almost to rashness. He would cast himself with a single European follower in the midst of savage enemies, and more than once his life was endangered by the excess of his confidence and his courage. He was eminently social in his habits — as his order of "*le bon temps*" — in which every man of his associates was for one day host to all his comrades, and commanded in turn in those agreeable encounters, of which we have just had a slight skirmish here. He was sanguine as became an adventurer, and self-denying as became a hero. He served under De Monts, who for a time succeeded to his honors and office, as cheerfully as he had ever acted for himself, and in the end he made a friend of his rival. He encountered, as Columbus, and many others had done, mutiny and assassination in his own disaffected followers, but he triumphed over the bad passions of men as completely as he triumphed over the ocean and the wilderness.

He touched the extremes of human experience among diverse characters and nations. At one time, he sketched plans of civilized aggrandisement for Henry IV. and Richelieu; at another, he planned schemes of wild warfare with Huron chiefs and Algonquin braves. He united, in a most rare degree, the faculties of action and reflection, and, like all highly reflective minds, his thoughts long cherished in secret, ran often into the mould of maxims, and some of them would now form the fittest possible inscriptions to engrave upon his monument.

When the merchants of Quebec grumbled at the cost of fortifying that place, he said — "It is best not to obey the passions of men; they are but for a season; it is our duty to regard the future." With all his love of good fellowship and society, he was, what seems to some inconsistent with it, sincerely and enthusiastically religious: among his maxims are these two, — that "the salvation of one soul is of more value than the conquest of an empire;" and, "that kings ought not to think of extending their authority over idolatrous nations, except for the purpose of subjecting them to Jesus Christ."

Such, Mr. President, are, in brief, the attributes of the man you have chosen to honor, and I leave it for this company to say, whether, in all that constitutes true greatness, the first Governor and Captain General of Canada need fear comparison with any of the illustrious brotherhood who projected and founded our North American States. Count over all their honored names; enumerate their chief actions; let each community assign to its own his meed of eloquent and reverent remembrance; but among them, from north to south, there will be no secondary place assigned to the Sieur de Champlain.

Mr. President, your Excellency has added to the sentiment in honor of Champlain, an allusion and an inference as to the different results of the French and English colonial policy, on which you will probably expect me to offer an observation or two before resuming my seat. Champlain's project originally was, no doubt, to make this Atlantic coast the basis of French power in the New World. His government claimed the continent down to the fortieth parallel, which, as you know, intersects Pennsylvania, Ohio, and Illinois; while the English claimed up to the forty-fifth, which intersects Nova Scotia and Canada.

Within these five degrees of latitude the pretensions of France were long zealously maintained in diplomacy, but were never practically asserted, except in the forty-fourth and forty-fifth, by colonization. I am not prepared to dispute the inference that the practical abandonment, by France, of the coast discoveries of her early navigators, south of forty-five, may have changed, as you say, "the destiny of the New World." It may be so; it may be, also, that we have not reached the point of time in which to speak positively as to the permanent result; for Divine Providence moves in His orbit by long and insensible curves, of which even the clearest-sighted men can discern, in their time, but a very limited section. But we know, as of the past, that the French power, in the reign of Louis XIII. and XIV., was practically based on the St. Lawrence, with a southern aspect, rather than on the Atlantic, with a western aspect. All the consequences of that great change of plan and policy, I am not prepared here so much as to allude to, for that would carry me where I have no wish to go,—into international issues not yet exhausted.

I may be permitted, however, to question that French influence, as developed in its Roman Catholic religion, its Roman law, and its historical fascinations, was ever really circumscribed to Canada, or was really extinguished, as has been usually assumed, by the fall of Quebec. It is amazing to find in the colonial records of the period between the death of Champlain and the death of Montcalm, a century and a quarter, how important a part that handful of secluded French colonists played in North American affairs. In 1629, Champlain could have carried off all his colonists in "a single ship;" more than a hundred years later they were estimated at some 65,000 souls; in the Seven Years war, they were, according to Mr. Bancroft, but as "one to fourteen" of the English colonists. The part played by the Canadians in war, under the French Kings, was out of all proportion to their numbers; it was a glorious but prodigal part; it left their country exposed to periodical scarcity, without wealth, without commerce, without political liberty. They were ruled by a policy strictly martial to the very last, and though Richelieu, Colbert, De la Gallissionere, and other supreme minds, saw, in their "New France," great commercial capabilities, the prevailing policy, especially under Louis XIV. and XV., was to make and keep Canada a mere military colony. It is instructive to find a man of such high intelligence as Montcalm, justifying that policy in his dispatches to the President de Mole, on the very eve of the surrender of Quebec. The Canadians, in his opinion, ought not be allowed to manufacture, lest they should become unmanageable, like the English colonists; but, on the contrary, they should be kept to martial exercises, that they might subserve the interests of France, in her transatlantic wars with England. Such was the policy which fell at Quebec with its last French Governor and Captain General; and it is a policy, I need hardly say, which no intelligent Canadian now looks back to with any other feelings than those of regret and disapprobation. A hundred years have elapsed since the international contest to which you refer, was consummated at Quebec, and Canada today, under the mild and equitable sway of her fourth English sovereign, has to point to trophies of peaceful progress, not less glorious, and far more serviceable, than any achieved by our predecessors who were subject to the French Kings. The French speaking population, which from 1608 till 1760, had not reached 100,000, from 1760 to 1860 has multiplied to 880,000. Upper Canada, a wilderness as Champlain found it and Montcalm left it, has a population exceeding Massachusetts, of as fine a yeomanry as ever stirred the soil of the earth. If French Canada points with justifiable pride to its ancient battlefield, English Canada points, with no less pleasure, to its newly reclaimed harvest fields; if the old regime is typified by the strong walls of Quebec, the monument of the new era may be seen in the great bridge which spans the St. Lawrence, within view of the city I represent, and whose four and twenty piers may each stand for one hour, sacred to every traveler who steams through its sounding tube, on his way from the Atlantic to the far West.

In conclusion, Mr. President, allow me again to assure you that I have listened with great pleasure to the speeches of this day, — especially to the address of my old and long esteemed friend (Hon. Mr. Poor). I trust the sentiments uttered here, at the mouth of the Kennebec, in Maine, will go home to England, and show our English relatives that the American people, unmoved by any selfish motive, are capable of doing full and entire justice to the best qualities of the English character. I am sure nothing was farther from your minds than to turn this historical commemoration to any political account, — and certainly I could not have done myself the pleasure of being here, if I had imagined any such intention; — but after all the angry taunts which have been lately exchanged between England and America, I cannot but think this solemn acknowledgment of national affiliation, made on so memorable a spot as Fort Popham, and made in so cordial a spirit, must have a healing and happy effect. We have been sitting under your authority, Mr.

President, in the High Court of Posterity, — we have summoned our ancestors from their ancient graves, — we have dealt out praise and blame among them, — I trust without violence to truth or injustice to the dead: for the dead have their rights as the living have: injustice to them is one of the worst forms of all injustice, — and undue praise to the undeserving is the worst injustice to the virtuous and meritorious actors in the great events of former ages.

When we leave this place, we shall descend from the meditative world of the past to mingle in the active world of the present, where each man must bear his part and defend his post. Let me say for myself, Mr. President, and I think I may add I speak in this respect, the general, settled sentiment of my countrymen of Canada, when I say, that in the extraordinary circumstances which have arisen for you, and for us also, in North America, there is no other feeling in Canada, than a feeling of deep and sincere sympathy and friendliness towards the United States. As men loyal to our own institutions, we honor loyalty everywhere; as freemen, we are interested in all free States; as neighbors, we are especially interested in your peace, prosperity, and welfare. We are all anxious to exchange everything with you, except injustice and misrepresentation: that is a species of commerce, which, — even when followed by the fourth estate (pointing to the reporters at his right),—I trust we will alike discourage, even to the verge of prohibition. Not only as a Canadian, but as one who was originally an emigrant to these shores as an Irishman, with so many of my original countrymen resident among you, I shall never cease to pray that this kindred people may always find in the future, as they always have found in the past, brave men to lead them in battle, wise men to guide them in council, and eloquent men, like my honorable friend yonder (Hon. John A. Poor), to celebrate their exploits and their wisdom from generation to generation.

Pierre du Gas, Seigneur De Monts, — the Patentee of the first charter of Henry of Navarre, who sacrificed empire and fortune rather than his religious faith, and beheld the fairest portion of the continent, which he had apparently secured to his nation, pass into the hands of his rivals.

The following communication has been furnished by the Rev. A. D. Wheeler, D. D., of Topsham, Maine; and is given as a response to the foregoing sentiment.

THE REV. DR. WHEELER'S COMMUNICATION.

The old Province of Saintonge, the Santones and Santoni of classic history, having no more reference to the *calendar of saints* than these ancient Latin designations from which it is obviously derived, was situated upon the estuary of the Gironde, which opens, about midway of the coast, into the Bay of Biscay; and comprised, according to the more recent divisions of the empire, what is now known as the Department of Charante Inferieure. Here lived and flourished the subject of the sentiment to which these remarks are a response.

PIERRE DU GUAST, SIEUR DE MONTS.

By his natural abilities, his extensive information, his energy and integrity of character, and the favor of his sovereign, he became Governor of Pons, a small town of a few thousand inhabitants, situated in the interior of the province, on the left bank of the river, Seugne or Sevine; and likewise was made gentleman in ordinary of the royal bed-chamber. But his active disposition would not allow him to remain contentedly at home, or within the sphere of official duties already required of him; and he sought a wider field of enterprise than could be found even within the limits of France. He was desirous of obtaining distinction upon the sea as well as the land; and, actuated by the spirit of exploration and discovery that distinguished his times, he made three different voyages in three successive years, commencing in 1599, to the Gulf of St. Lawrence, the river of the same name, the country of Acadia, and the regions around. For these reasons, among others, he was regarded as the proper person to be entrusted with an enterprise of a more important kind.

The merchants of Rouen had formed an association, comprising many persons of distinction and liberal means, for the purpose of conducting their operations in the northern part of these regions. The president of this company, and the person who had taken the most active part in its organization,—Le Commandeur De Chatte,—had died. De Monts was already in possession, through a grant from Henry IV., of the exclusive privilege of trading with the natives for skins and furs between the fortieth and fifty-fourth degrees of north latitude, and of the right to dispose of lands as far as the forty-sixth; and, in addition to these, of Letters Patent, conferring upon him the offices of Vice-Admiral and Lieutentant-General in all this extent of country. In view of all these facts, and of the advantages which the company might very naturally expect to derive from one, who held such a position, enjoyed such privileges, and had already acquired so much experience in affairs of this nature, and so extensive an acquaintance with this region of country, it was almost a matter of course that he should have been the only person thought of to fill the vacancy occasioned by the death of De Chatte.

About ten years previous to this event, Henry IV. had abjured Protestantism and become a zealous Catholic. De Monts was a Huguenot, or French Calvinist, and still adhered to his opinions, notwithstanding the change in those of the king. The latter, in consideration of his acknowledged integrity and devotion to the interests of his country, for himself and his associates who adhered to the same form of faith, permitted them to enjoy the exercise of their religion in America, the same as they had done in France. In return for this concession, De Monts engaged, on his part, to colonize the country, and to establish in it the Catholic religion among the savages.

The French historian, De Charlevoix, of the company of Jesus, appends to the foregoing statement, the remark, that *in other respects* he was a very honest man, whose views were right, and who had zeal for the State, and all the capacity necessary to enable him to succeed in the enterprise with which he was charged, ("l'etoit d' ailleurs un fort honête homme," etc.) He may have referred exclusively to his Calvinism; or, he may have intended to intimate that a person who believed in one kind of religion, and labored to establish another, could hardly be honest; or, at all events, consistent in that one particular. But De Monts ought not to be judged too severely, in a matter of this kind. Doubtless he had reasons sufficient to satisfy his own conscience, at least. Men are often compelled to make a choice between evils, and perhaps this was a case in which he felt constrained to do the same. He was capable and trustworthy, and disposed to do for the interests of the company the best that he was able. But he was unfortunate, and almost always badly served. His exclusive privileges for the traffic in peltry, had excited against him men of an envious disposition, who endeavored to accomplish his ruin. He had preserved the company which had been formed by his predecessor, and had enlarged it by the addition of many merchants, from the principal ports of France, and especially that of Rochelle. Such a union of forces had placed him in a condition to prepare an out-fit more considerable than had been done by any of those whom he had succeeded. He made these preparations partly at Dieppe and partly at Havre-de-Grace.

An expedition, consisting of four vessels, was planned and got in readiness. One of these was destined to Tadoussac, at the confluence of the rivers Saguenay and St. Lawrence, for the purpose of trading in peltry. Pontgravé received orders to conduct the second to the Straits of Canseau, between Acadia and the Isle Royale, and the channel which separated it from the island of St. John, for the purpose of conveying thither those persons who were desirous of carrying on a trade with the natives, to the prejudice of the rights of De Monts, who proceeded with the other vessels to the coast of Acadia. He was accompanied by many volunteers, among whom were the Sieur de Champlain, who belonged to the same district with his commander, the province of Saintonge, and whose name has become permanently associated with the beautiful lake, whose waters wash the opposite shores of New York and Vermont; and Jean de Biencourt, Sieur de Poutrincourt, whom he had made his lieutenant in the expedition.

It was on the seventh of March, in the year 1604, that De Monts set sail from the harbor of Havre de Grace; and it was on the sixth of May, just two months after, that he entered a port of Acadia. Here he fell in with a vessel, which, in spite of the prohibitions of his patent, had been engaged in traffic along the coast. He confiscated it in virtue of his exclusive privilege. He called the harbor, however, Port Rossignol, from the name of the captain of the confiscated vessel, as if by thus immortalizing his name, he desired to make some compensation to him for the loss which he had sustained. After leaving this port, he soon entered another, which he called Port-au-Mouton, because *a sheep* had there leaped overboard and been drowned. At this place he landed all his people, provided them with tents, and remained there for more than a month, while Champlain, in a shallop, sailed along the coast in search of a place suitable for a permanent establishment. There was no necessity of his going so far for this purpose, or even of his coming to the place where he then was; for he had passed by, without deigning to enter them, two of the best harbors of Acadia, and the two, best situated for commercial objects, Canseau and La Haive; and there were many others which would have served his purpose nearly as well. But he kept on his course until he arrived at a small island, a few miles below Calais, where De Monts, arriving a short time after him, resolved to make a settlement. He gave to it the name of the "Isle of St. Croix," and as it was but half a league in circumference, it was very soon wholly cleared up. They built there a number of houses sufficient for their use, and sowed some grain which yielded them an abundant return.

But they had made a bad choice. When the winter came they found themselves destitute both of fresh water and wood; and as they were soon reduced to the necessity of living on salted meats, and as many of them, to save themselves from the trouble of going in search of water to the main land, had recourse to melted snow for their ordinary drink, the scurvy made its appearance in the new colony, and committed great ravages. Thus as soon as the navigation was open, De Monts found nothing more urgent than to seek a place having greater advantages. He took his course, at first, towards the south, ranged along the coast, which extends east and west, for the space of eighty leagues, from the river St. John as far as the "Kinibegui," or Kennebec; then north and south, to a point which Champlain, who, during the winter had occupied himself in making explorations in this direction, had named "Mallebarre," because his bark had run great risk of getting aground upon the sand. He had also taken possession of it in the name of the king, as well as of Cape Cod, at the opposite extremity of the peninsula.

In the end, De Monts having been unable, in so long a coasting voyage, to determine upon any place for establishing a colony, returned to St. Croix, where Pontgravé soon came to join him on arriving from France. They found the settlement in a very bad condition, and De Monts, convinced that it would be necessary to change the location, resolved to return to Acadia. Accordingly he embarked with Pontgravé, and, shaping his course in that direction, entered the harbor of Port Royal. He found the place so much to his mind, that he at once formed the resolution of transporting his colony to it, gave the business in charge to Pontgravé, and authorized him to act in his stead during his expected absence.

Port Royal, which owes its name to De Monts, had but one serious defect, and that was the difficulty of entering it and departing from it, to which may be added the inconvenience of frequent and dense fogs. But one vessel was able to enter at a time, and it was necessary that this one vessel should enter stern foremost, and with very great precautions, such was the force of the currents and the sea. In other respects it was regarded by De Monts as one of the finest ports in the world. The Sieur de Pontgravé, however, did not perfectly coincide in opinion respecting it with De Monts, for the advantages of the location did not appear to him sufficient to counterbalance the inconveniences. But De Poutrincourt thought differently; and, as an associate with De Monts, he had formed the design of establishing himself in America with his family, he demanded of him this port, and had no difficulty in obtaining it.

As the autumn approached, De Monts concluded to return once more to France. Upon his arrival at court he found the condition of things in regard to himself very much changed. The fishermen, at all the ports of the kingdom, had made representations to the king, that under the pretext of preventing them from trading with the natives of the country, they had been deprived of things the most necessary to their business, and that they would be obliged to abandon it altogether, if these vexatious proceedings were allowed to go on. These representations were listened to; the council comprehended the injury which would result to commerce from the interruption of the fisheries; and the "exclusive privilege" of De Monts, which, according to the terms of the patent had still two years longer to run, was revoked.

Still, under all these discouragements, he did not lose all confidence in the success of his undertaking. He entered into a new agreement with De Poutrincourt, who had followed him to France, and caused a vessel to be fitted out for him at Rochelle, which sailed on the 3d of May, 1606. The voyage was a long one, and the inhabitants of Port Royal, not wholly without reason, had begun to think that they had been abandoned. Pontgravé had neglected nothing within his power in order to reassure them; but at last, when they were absolutely in want of everything, he was constrained to embark with all his people, leaving only two men in the fort to guard the effects which they were unable to carry away; and to shape his course for France. He was scarcely out of sight of the Bay of Fundy, or "Baye Francoise," as it was then called, when he learned, from a bark which he had spoken, the arrival of Poutrincourt at Canseau. Immediately on the receipt of this intelligence, he turned back and re-entered the harbor of Port Royal, where Poutrincourt had already arrived with abundant supplies for the colony, and without having been discovered on the passage. The only thought now was to fortify the place, and to make provision against all future contingencies.

As long as Port Royal was prosperous, and afforded such good hopes, the enemies of De Monts exerted their utmost efforts to ruin him in France; and at length succeeded in causing his commission to be taken from him. As an indemnification for all his expenses and losses, he was promised the sum of six thousand livres, — dependent, however, upon the successful result of certain vessels, to be sent to America for the purpose of trading for peltry. But this in fact amounted to nothing, since the cost of collecting this money would have exceeded the amount of the compensation.

His prospects, however, appeared to be a little brighter the following year, when he succeeded in regaining the privilege of which he had been deprived, but for one year only, and on the condition that he should make an establishment upon the river St. Lawrence. The company, with which he had been associated, and over which he presided, did not abandon him in his misfortunes; but he soon ascertained that his connection with it was an injury rather than a benefit, and he, therefore, withdrew from it entirely; and, after two years of trouble and anxiety, and continual disappointments, he disposed of all his rights under the grants which he had received from the king, and thus parted with all his interest in enterprises to which he had been so long devoted, and which he had hoped would redound to his own advantage, and the glory of France. Not long after this surrender he died, a victim to the mortification of seeing his patent revoked by the royal mandate at the instance of his enemies.

As one of the pioneers of New England colonization, and as one who made the first settlement (at St. Croix) within the present limits of Maine, he is worthy of commemoration in the proceedings of this day.

NOTE. — For the foregoing facts given in relation to De Monts, consult, mainly, Charlevoix, "Histoire de la Nouvelle France;" and also "L' Histoire des Colonies Francoises, par Chrestien Le Clercq;" Haliburton's Nova Scotia; and Holmes's Annals of America.

George Weymouth,— the early explorer of the coast of New England; memorable for his description of our own coast, and his exploration of "the most excellent and beneficyall river of Sachadehoc."

In the absence of the expected speech in connection with this sentiment, remarks may be found in a subsequent portion of this volume.

The Colonization of Manhattan — by the Hollanders; whose tolerant spirit and commercial enterprise laid the foundation of the great metropolis of the New World.

The following communication was received immediately

after its date, from the Hon. John Romeyn Brodhead of New York, as a response to this sentiment.

MR. BRODHEAD'S LETTER.

NEW YORK, 8th September, 1862.

Rev. EDWARD BALLARD, *Secretary, &c.*

SIR: — On my return to town, a day or two ago, I received your letter of the 14th of August, inviting me, on behalf of "the Executive Committee," to attend the Historical Celebration at Fort Popham on the 29th of that month. I beg you to communicate to the committee my thanks for their courtesy, as well as my great regret that absence from home prevented me from knowing, until too late, the proposed arrangements, and from enjoying the pleasure of assisting at an occasion of such national interest.

Your letter also enclosed a sentiment, — "*The colonization of Manhattan, by the Hollanders, whose tolerant spirit and commercial enterprise laid the foundation of the great metropolis of the new world,*" — and requested me to respond to it at the collation in the great tent. To none of the sentiments then proposed could I have spoken more heartily. Had I been able to be with you, I should probably have said something like what, at your further suggestion, I now write.

New York certainly owes much of her present metropolitan greatness to her admirable geographical situation. Yet, I think, she owes quite as much to the magnanimous principles of the Hollanders who discovered and first occupied Manhattan and its neighboring coasts. When Jamestown was founded on the 13th of May, 1607, and George Popham read his commission at the mouth of the Sagadahoc or Kennebec on the 19th of August following, — the two hundred and fifty-fifth anniversary of which event you have so pleasantly celebrated, — the territory of New York was known only to its aboriginal owners. Excepting Verazzano, no European had visited any part of the American coast between Buzzard's Bay and the Capes of the Chesapeake. This intermediate region, although claimed by England, was a *vacant domicile*, free to the first European explorer, when Henry Hudson in the "Half Moon" of Amsterdam anchored within Sandy Hook on the third of September, 1609. That event was the birth of the Dutch State of New York. At that time Holland and the other Protestant Provinces of the Netherlands had just conquered their independence of Spain, and become a free republic, the cornerstone of which was toleration. Commercial enterprise had already placed the young nation in the van of the peoples of the earth. They had fought not less for freedom of their ships at sea than for freedom of thought and life on their low, sandy lands at home. But though the Dutch earnestly contended for their own civil and religious liberties, they were neither selfish nor bigoted. On the contrary, they were large-minded enough to make their country an asylum for refugees from the oppression of other lands.

The same autumn that Holland became the sovereign of New York by virtue of her discovery, English Puritans from Lincolnshire settled themselves quietly at Leyden, where, for eleven years, they were hospitably entertained, and where they enjoyed the opportunity of observing that growing national prosperity which was the legitimate result of the liberal religious and political principles of their Batavian hosts. At length, in December, 1620, some of those English refugees at Leyden landed at Plymouth Rock, and began the first permanent colonization of New England, which Popham and his friends had unsuccessfully attempted thirteen years before. If the pioneer settlement at New Plymouth was distinguished from the later colony of Massachusetts Bay by more tolerant ideas in civil as well as religious affairs, it may be not unjustly inferred that some, at least, of that larger liberality was derived from the lessons of Holland. Assuredly the notion of confederated States, which the New England colonies adopted in 1643, was borrowed from the United Netherlands.

Meanwhile, the Dutch colonists at Manhattan and its neighborhood had been calmly practicing those liberal principles which they learned in their fatherland. The Jesuit Father Jogues, sheltered by them from the barbarities of the Mohawks, found that eighteen different languages were spoken in the capital of the Dutch Province. There he met Protestant exiles from the persecutions of Massachusetts, Lutherans from Germany, Roman Catholics and Anabaptists, all actually enjoying, in an equal degree with the original Calvinistic settlers, the blessings of religious liberty. Without any poetical claim of seeking in America more "freedom to worship God" than they enjoyed in Holland, the colonists of Manhattan, who had early learned that commerce is the solvent of national antipathies, cordially welcomed all who came to find permanent homes among them; and thus, with large and comprehensive spirit, they laid the foundation of the attractive metropolis of the New World.

After the surrender of New Netherland to the English in 1664, New York was governed for nearly twenty years as a province, by the sole will of its proprietor, the Duke of York. As a point of special interest in the histories of two great States, I may here mention that one of the dependencies of New York was that part of Maine between the Saint Croix and the Sagadahoc, commonly known as Pemaquid. This region was granted by Charles II. to his brother on the 12th of March, 1664, in the same patent which conveyed the Dutch possessions. It was formed into a county by the name of "Cornwall," and it remained under the jurisdiction of New York until 1687. But, while the supreme political power was in other hands, the influence of the original spirit of the Dutch settlers of Manhattan continued to make itself felt. In 1681, the merchants of New York refused to pay the customs duties which the Duke exacted, as they thought, arbitrarily and illegally. This led to a demand for an assembly of the people, to be chosen by the freeholders and inhabitants of the Province. The Duke yielded to the demand; and in October, 1683, his Governor, Thomas Dongan, assented to a charter of liberties passed by the popular representatives of New York, which declared that "the people met in General Assembly" were to form a part of the supreme legislative authority. It also declared that no persons professing "faith in God by Jesus Christ," should be in any way molested for any difference in religious opinion. The tolerant spirit of the Dutch was the parent of these conspicuous clauses. At the very time that this charter of New York was enacted by the freely chosen representatives of its inhabitants, and was confirmed by its ducal proprietor, the charter which Charles the First had granted to the Corporation of Massachusetts was in process of abrogation by the judicial officers of Charles the Second. To most observers there would appear to be a strange inconsistency in these contemporaneous events. Yet I think the inconsistency is seeming rather than real. The Massachusetts charter did not grant a popular government. It established a corporate oligarchy. The corporators, as soon as they possessed the power, deliberately excluded from participation in every political and almost every civil right, all the inhabitants except the members of their own Puritan churches. The people of Massachusetts at large did not govern themselves. They were only the governed; and they were governed, not by their common sovereign in England, but by their own neighbors and fellow-subjects, who derived their authority, not from a popular election, but from the vote of a close corporation, established by a king who had expiated his arbitrary acts by death on the scaffold. The government of Massachusetts, under its old charter, was intolerant, discriminating, and unjust. Charles the Second could see no good reason why self-chosen Puritan church members alone should tyrannize over the rest of the inhabitants of that colony. In the neighboring Province of New York, a charter of liberties had just been adopted, the two cardinal ideas of which were, toleration of religious opinion and the equal and indiscriminate participation of all its multifarious population in civil rights. The charter of Massachusetts, which allowed no share of political power to the people, was therefore cancelled by the king, just as the charter of New York, which conferred a portion of the legislative authority "upon the people met in General Assembly," was signed and sealed by his brother, the Duke.

I am admonished, however, not to pursue at greater length this train of remark which might easily be extended. The history of New York, throughout its whole course, exhibits constant evidence of the liberalizing influence of her Dutch founders. That influence, I sincerely believe, has always made her more truly Democratic than perhaps any of the older colonies which formed the United States. It preserved her from that intolerant and obtrusive censoriousness which, without hesitation, assumes the privilege to rudely intermeddle with what concerns it not. While their homely Dutch maxim, "MIND YOUR OWN BUSINESS," restrained her people from interfering with the affairs of their neighbors, it taught them to tolerate no foreign dictation or inquisitorial inspection. Of this alone were Hollanders and their descendants intolerant. Surviving to the present hour, the liberality and conservatism which, at the same time, distinguished the pioneers of the "Empire State," have kept New York, for long generations, free from the blight of fanaticism, and made her the grand monument of the magnanimous principles of her Batavian founders.

I am, sir, with great regard,

your obedient servant,

JOHN ROMEYN BRODHEAD.

Captain John Smith, — the daring soldier and navigator; whose efforts in acts of government in Virginia, and of naval skill in exploring and defining the boundaries of New England, which he made known by maps and description, give his name a place among the great men of his time.

The Ancient Dominions of Maine, — Sabino, Sagadahoc, Sheepscot, Pemaquid, and Monhegan; the theater of early maritime discovery and settlement; the designed seat of empire of our colonial ancestors.

Want of time prevented the response to this sentiment intended by Rufus K. Sewall, Esq., of Wiscasset. It, therefore, now appears as a communication.

MR. SEWALL'S ADDRESS.

MAINE THE MOTHER OF NEW ENGLAND.

Claims to precedence in the History of English Colonization and European Commerce and Civilization in New England, exhibited in the developments and details of European life upon the coasts of Maine, within the Ancient Dominions.

ANCIENT DOMINIONS OF MAINE.

The popular idea of the earliest knowledge of Maine, — the idea extant in the days of Cabot, — embodied in the nomenclature of Europe, was *Baccalaos*,[1] meaning the coasts of "cod-fish."

The great feature of life in these waters, a source of wealth and commerce to the leading powers of Europe, in the significant and appropriate language of the visitors to this hyperborean Florida, gave it this name.

Succeeding ages, from more definite knowledge of the mainland, and interior and populous wilds, replaced the aboriginal name with that of the semi-mythical "Norumbega," — a series of aboriginal sounds caught from the lips of the native lords of the soil, portraying the outlines of the fame of an aboriginal

1 Folsom's address. 2 vol. M. H. Soc. *Bacalláo,* in Spanish; *Bacalháo,* in Portuguese, denotes a species of cod-fish called "ling."

empire within these unexplored wilds, — the Arambes of the geographers and voyagers of the reign of King Henry VIII.; the Arambec of later explorers, signifying, "*the place of men*,"[1] — a ruined capital of an extinct race.

During the reign of Henry VIII., of England, Robert
A. D. Thome, by eloquent descriptions of his father's voyages
1527. and discoveries in Newfoundland, moved this sovereign to dispatch two ships to these strange shores. One only escaped the perils of the ice-clad sea, by returning in more southern latitudes, along the coasts of "Arumbec, — Arambes, — or, as some call it, Norumbegua." John Rut, the chronicler of this voyage, reported to the king that the returning ship "found eleven sayle of Normans, one Briton, and two Portugal barks a fishing" there.

"SAGADAHOC," in order of time, in the visions of European enterprise, and speculations of State and Colonial adventure, appeared next, in the same latitudes, glowing in these western wilds, to absorb public interest and quicken desire, and guide the prow of the English voyager in his search for a new home.

Gosnold, in this latitude, from the decks of the Con-
A. D. cord, seeing "a land[2] full of fair trees, — the land
1602. somewhat low, — certain hummocks or hills lying into the land, and the shore full of white sand and very stoney," landed and called it "Mavooshen."[3]

But Maine, at this early date, was comprised in the territory between the Kennebec and Penobscot waters, and *was the center* of European interest and enterprise in the west, both in England and France; and "Sagadahoc" soon eclipsed all other names, and gave paramount importance to a section of the coasts of North America, whose most remarkable land-

1 Arunpeag, or Arumpik. Rev. E. Vetromile, S. J.—Purchas, p. 929.

2 Ancient Dominions of Maine. p. 55.

3 About 43° N. L. Hutchinson, vol. 1, p. 1.

marks, "*Sutquin,*[1] *and four or five isles in the mouth,*" (in the description of Capt. John Smith,) indicated the entrance "by a fair navigable river, to the so goodly a country up the most excellent and beneficial river of Sagadahoc," on the west; and "Monhegan, a round, high isle, and close by Monanis, betwixt which is a small harbor with Damarill's Isles, such another," and "mountains, them of Penobscot, together with the twinkling mountains of Ac-a-cis-co," on the east. Within the territory thus bounded and described in the early annals of colonial adventure, Monhegan, the province of Sabino, the aboriginal "Sipsa-couta,"[2] and Pemaquid, have become, in the Ancient Dominions of Maine, points of classic interest.

Monhegan, signifying an island of the main, earliest appears in the panorama of the historic scene of English life and enterprise on New England shores. Pedro Menendez, Governor of Florida, in dispatches forwarded by him to the Court of Spain, tells Philip II., "that in July of the year, the English were inhabiting an island in latitude 43°, eight leagues from land, where the Indians were very numerous." It was the story of "Carlos Morea, a Spaniard, who had learned the facts in London and communicated them to Menendez."[3] There can hardly be a doubt that Monhegan island was the spot occupied by these English dwellers in the New World. Indeed, it was only in August, three years before, that near this spot,[4] the largest ship of Sir Humphrey Gilbert struck, and was wrecked on the voyage in which he was last seen in the stern sheets of the little Squirrel, book in hand, when her lights suddenly disappeared, and he was heard to cry, "we are as neere to Heaven by water as by land."

A. D. 1586.

1 Purchas Pilgrimage, p. 215. Smith's Voyages, 1614.

2 *Aliunde* in French "Che-va-va-cotte."

3 B. Smith, Hist. Magazine, No. 9, Sept., 1859.

4 Bancroft, p. 91.

Did shipwrecked mariners first found English homes on the islands in and near Sheepscot Bay?[1]

MONHEGAN.

A. D. 1605.

The earliest description of Monhegan is from the pen of Rosier, the historian of the voyage of the "Arch-Angel, under command of Commodore George Weymouth, who on Friday, during the evening twilight, the 17th of May, made land which loomed up in bold relief against the northern sky, as some high-land of the Maine." He cast anchor under its northern and land-ward slope, a league off shore, and with his boat's crew landing for wood and water in the heart of its overgrown forests, "*discovered vestiges of human occupancy.*" A cross was set up, and in accordance with the usage of British discoverers of that day, it doubtless bore affixed thereto the armorial bearings of the Crown of England, "a St. George Cross," graven on lead; and the island[2] was called St. George.

PROVINCE OF SABINO.

There can be no doubt that the original and local center of the Norumbega of historic fame, over whatever territory it may have subsequently expanded, embraced "Our Sagadahoc" within its geographical limits, as the great center of colonial attraction, denoted by the remarkable land marks described by Captain Smith, — a river, the confluent of interior waters to the sea, upon whose margins was the territory of a river-king, known in aboriginal nomenclature, as "*Sebenoa.*"[3]

The peninsula of his province, selected as the site of Popham's town of St. George, was called "*Sabino,*" which probably is but an English abbreviation of Sebenoa, the aboriginal name of the "Lord of the river Sagadahoc."

1 Sul., pp. 160–5.

2 Palfrey's Mass. History, p. 68.

3 Cotemporary with "Sasanow," if not the same chieftain.

In its native wildness, the peninsula of Sagadahoc must have been a spot of singular beauty. An open forest of mighty towering pines below, and hill-tops of overgrown beach and oak above and on either side, fringed with a clear, broad grassy margin terminating in a sand beach, sweeping from point to point on its landward and sheltered northern point, must have commended the place as a favorite camping ground to the savages, as well as a site to the earliest English colonists of New England as a home. The indications are decisive that this peninsula was ever a place of distinguished attraction to the natives. The vestiges of the occupancy of this peninsula by them are peculiar and remarkable. Here would seem to have been the seat of aboriginal workshops and artizans, — the manufactories of their weapons of war, — the arsenals of the savage hosts on the waters of the Kennebec, where arrow-heads, stone axes, and mauls, were blocked and hewn or broken into finished shape and fitness for war or the chase. The vestiges of stone-work, chips, fragments, remains of stone-wrought tools and weapons, distinguish this peninsula, and remain as the monuments of the skill and toil of artizans and a race departed.

SAGADAHOC COLONY.

The goodly report of commander Weymouth of the Arch-Angel's voyage, confirmed Gosnold's previous observations, stimulated the highest nobility of England, led by the Lord Chief Justice, Sir John Popham, to settle "a plantation on the river of Sagadahoc."

Complex Elements of the Enterprise. — Sir John Popham operated in the west of England, and made the city of Bristol his center. From this city his colonial expeditions were fitted out.[1] There seems to have been a concert of action in the

1 Strachey, M. H. C., vol 3, p. 290.

movements at Bristol and London in the colonial adventures of the year 1606, contemplating a simultaneous occupancy of northern as well as southern Virginia, and also combining the interests of the east and west of England, centering in the cities of Bristol and London, with the design that each should be represented in the colonial enterprise at Sagadahoc.

In May, 1606, Newport, with one hundred colonists sailed for the Chesapeak; and under the supervision of Sir John Popham, a ship sailed from Bristol, under the command of Martin Prinn and Haines, for Sagadahoc. This expedition was captured by Spanish cruisers. In June, the next year, Sir John Popham fitted out a ship called the "Gift of God,"[1] in his department, placed his brother, George Popham, in command; and at London, the ship "Mary and John" was assigned to the command of Raleigh Gilbert. These ships took out one hundred and twenty men for planters. Capt. George Popham represented the interests of Sir John and the west of England men in the city of Bristol,[2] and was elected President of the colony in the Sagadahoc enterprise. Raleigh Gilbert held second rank, representing the interests of his lost uncle, Sir Humphrey Gilbert, who had sacrificed his life in his gallant endeavors to explore and colonize these shores, as well as the interests of the city of London, in the colonial adventure
then on foot. These noble pioneers embarked for the
A. D. coasts of Maine in June, under express instructions
1607. to enter the Sagadahoc, and there[3] make their planta-
tion with a view to confirm the right of England to the possession she had taken of the soil of New England. Sagadahoc became now a cardinal point of interest in the historic scene; and the peninsula of the province of "Sabino," the river-king, on the 18th of August, 1607, was selected by Cap-

1 Strachey, M. H. C., vol. 3, p. 292.

2 Strachey, M. H. C., vol. 3, p. 299.

3 Strachey, M. H. C., vol. 3, p. 289.

tain Popham of the ship "Gift of God," with thirty men, in conjunction with Captain Gilbert of the ship "Mary and John," with eighteen men. Thus London and Bristol concurred in the choice for a site for the colonial home amid the wilds of New England. A permanent establishment was contemplated, and all the elements of European civilization, under the sanction of law and religion, were here freighted and organized in the new plantation.

Ground was broken on the 20th of August, the 19th having been occupied in public acts of religious worship and service, and a body politic organized and confirmed, according to the forms and usages of English constitutional law and religion.

A fair town of fifty houses, defended by a fort mounting twelve guns, fortified and entrenched according to the arts of military science, ornamented with a church and public storehouse, at once enlivened the scene on the banks of the Sagadahoc and distinguished the peninsula of the province of "Sabino" with English homes; and the overlooking head-lands, gray old oaks, and tall pines of Arrowsic, echoed far and wide the hum and clatter of a ship-yard, from the ringing saw and maul in the hands of busy artizans led by Digby, a master-builder of London, upon the frame of the Virginia on the stocks, which was there built and launched, and was big enough to make afterwards a successful voyage to England.

The peninsula of Powhatan, in the south, and the peninsula of the province of Sabino of northern Virginia, were at this moment points of contrasted colonial enterprise; for while the plantation of Lord Popham, combining the colonial interests and energy of the Bristol and London men, gave fair promise of success at Sagadahoc, while Popham, Gilbert, Harlow, Davis, Seymour, and Digby were entrenching there to make a fort;—Wingfield, Newport, Gosnold, and Smith were having their "hearts torn and the night made hideous with outcries, sickness, and death, in every corner of their new made works at

Jamestown, in the Virginia of the south, by those to whom they could minister no relief, and whose bodies, trailed out of their cabins like dogs for burial, saddened the morning light."[1]

Such were the concurring contrasts of the 20th and 22d of August, 1607, which burdened the scenes and quickened the changes of the two days which alone separated the colonial enterprises of the London men at Jamestown, and the west of England men at Sagadahoc.

The Sagadahoc enterprise was undoubtedly the beginning proper of European colonial life with the English race, not only in Maine, but in New England.

MONHEGAN.

When the "Gift of God," the Bristol ship of Popham, and the "Mary and John," the London ship of Gilbert, discharged their living freight of English planters and shipwrights upon the banks of the Sagadahoc, the vestiges of a former occupancy alone were traceable on Monhegan, the St. George of the voyager George Weymouth. Savages held the forests of Pemaquid, whose dwellings occupied its river banks, whence emerged Nahanada and his savage bowman in battle array to repel the landing[2] of Popham and his boat's crew, who had been led there by Skidwarroes, their guide. Here, then, we take our position. Monhegan, though it may have been a transient home, had not been permanently held. There is no evidence that a white man had yet set his foot down at Pemaquid. Sagadahoc must be viewed as the point of initial movement of European life and civilization on the shores of New England. More than this, we regard the plantation there begun, as the initial step of the permanent foothold of the English race on the soil of New England. In our judgment, on a series of facts warranting the conclusion, the peninsula of the province

1 Bancroft's History, vol. 1, p. 127.

2 Strachey, M. H. C., vol. 3, p. 298.

of Sabino, and the fair English town there erected, were centers of further explorations and the sources of an emigration, which finally transferred the action of colonial life and adventure to Pemaquid and the fair and fertile meadows of the oyster-bearing waters of the "Sip-sa-couta,"[1] eastward.

As we have before observed, it would hardly have been possible for Sir Francis Popham, the representative of Sir John and of the Bristol interest in the western world, to have sustained his voyages to the Sagadahoc territory independent of main-land establishments to concentrate trade and gather furs; and *such plantations, in the insignificance of a private interest, would have been lost to the knowledge of a public recognition.* Though it does not appear in the archives of the public acts of a colonial organization, yet I repeat it as the source of our historic traditions in the premises, and supported by the facts exhibited in their natural relationship, that the Bristol interest,— the element in the Popham colonists of the Sagadahoc plantation being familiar with the fertile bottoms and prolific waters of the east, did, on the margins of Pemaquid, near the village of Nahanada and on the interior Sheepscot and Damariscotta, at the site of the early New Dartmouth, the ancient shire of the county of Cornwall of the Dukedom,—make plantations as well as at Sagadahoc,—which were permanent till Boston became the capital of New England.

What are the facts? Captain Gilbert made many discoveries,[2] we are told, into the neighboring Maine and rivers. The Sagadahoc planters wrote back to England that they found oysters "nine inches long and heard of others twice as great." They must, therefore, have been up the Sheepscot and Damariscotta, and explored the oyster-bearing waters of these rivers above Pemaquid, in a region known, in aboriginal language,

1 Aboriginal for Sheepscot; means, "little birds flock or rush;" Sipsaconte and Sipsisacoke are different forms.

2 M. H. C., vol. 3, p. 308.

as "Ped-cok-go-wake,". where the remains of the oyster nine inches long are still found. Having completed his explorations, Captain Robert Davis[1] was sent to England in the ship, the "Mary and John," of London, on the 15th of December, 1607,[2] with letters and supplies. The fort, store-house, town, and ship were not yet completed when Davis sailed; and all things were represented as promising for the colony at that date. No mention is made of the fact, and there is no probability that any of the colonists returned with Davis. Had such a fact transpired, President Popham's letter of the 13th of December would certainly have indicated it. The Bristol ship in the Popham interest, it would seem, therefore, remained at Sagadahoc. Prince in his chronology, indeed, writes "that two ships (one the Virginia, there built), sailed from Sagadahoc in early winter with all the company[3] except forty-five, for England."

The "Virginia" was not finished at the date of the first voyage from Sagadahoc, but she did sail on the final voyage with the other London ship. If then, forty-five colonists were left at all, it must have been at the date of the abandonment of Sagadahoc by Captain Gilbert and the London men. No mention is made of the return of Popham's ship, the "Gift of God," which was in the interest of the Bristol men. Indeed, it would appear to have been the London interest, in the colonial adventure at Sagadahoc, which led to the evacuation of that spot and the return to England.

A. D. 1608.

On the 5th of February,[4] the aged President Popham died. With his death the interest of the Bristol men became subordinate to that of the London men. We submit, therefore, if the company of the colonists attached to the Bristol ship, the "Gift of God," and which

[1] Strachey, M. H. C., vol. 3, p. 308.

[2] Gorges' Narrative, M. H. C., vol. 2, p. 21.

[3] Prince's Chronology, p. 117.

[4] Prince's Chronology, p. 118.

appertained to the Popham estate, were not the forty-five who, it is asserted by Prince, did not sail for England when the Virginia, and Mary and John returned?

But more than this: — Gorges tells us that the son of the Chief Justice, "could not so give it over,"[1] when Gilbert and those with him, at Sagadahoc, abandoned the enterprise of that colonial establishment; and in the annals of that day, it is further said, that upon the death of Chief Justice Popham, "*his son*[2] *and successor, Sir Francis, who was sent out, became Governor, and despatched vessels thither on his own account*," *and* "*having the ships which remained of the company and supplying what was necessary, sent divers times to the coasts for trade and fishing, of whose losses and gains he himself is best able to give an account.*"[3]

PEMAQUID.[4]

Captain John Smith, who visited Monhegan six years after, says, he found a ship of Sir Francis Popham's, which[5] had for many years past visited there, — "at the main-land opposite Monhegan, probably[6] Pemaquid." Such are the facts. Did the "Gift of God," with the Bristol fragment, embracing the Popham interest in the Sagadahoc colony, remain behind on the desertion of the London men under Gilbert? and did not this fragment take root at Pemaquid? and from thence spread to the neighboring waters of the Sheepscot? Hence, ever after we find Pemaquid the rallying point for colonial settlement,

1 Gorges, M. H. C., vol. 2, p. 28.

2 Strachey Intro. Hackluyt So. Hist. Trav. in Virginia, p. 17.

3 Plymouth Co's relations, M. H C., vol. 2, p. 33.

4 PEMAQUID. — Rev. Paul Coffin met "SABATTIS" at Carritunk, on the Kennebec, A. D. 1798, who gave him the meaning of several aboriginal words, used as names of notable localities. This native said PEMAQUID meant, "a point of land running into the sea."—Paul Coffin's Journal, M. H. Col., vol. 4, p. 397.

5 M. H. C., vol. 5, p. 161.

6 Thornton's Ancient Pemaquid.

emigration, and commercial enterprise to the Bristol men of England, who gave the name of their city to the town of Bristol, which embraces this classic ground of Maine in its territory.

The vessels of Sir Francis Popham must have had a commercial depot for trade on the main-land, at the point indicated, for import of supplies and export of furs and fish,[1] where out freight was deposited and home freight gathered. The voyages of Sir Francis could not have been sustained without the supporting nucleus of a colonial trade station. Pemaquid would be the natural and attractive coast station from the friendliness of the natives; some of whom had been in England and acquired the English tongue and a knowledge of English habits of life and civilization; and the neighboring Sheepscot meadows and waters, with their facilities for human subsistence, in fishing and planting, would be the nearest accessible inland points of attraction for interior operations.

Besides, there can be no doubt that subsequently to the decease of the aged President Popham, the Sagadahoc planters came in collision with the natives, and with doubtful results. Such has ever been the tradition of the red men of the Kennebec and of the white race in this vicinity, the occasion of which has reflected no honor upon the colonists, who excused their abandonment of Sagadahoc and their return to England on account of the savage climate of the land. The storehouse and supplies of the Sagadahoc colonists were devastated by

1 The following translation of a brief extract from the Relation of Biard, may in some degree illustrate the statement made in the text: "The English of Virginia have the custom of coming every year to the islands of Pencöit, which are about twenty-five leagues from St. Saviour, (on Mt. Desert,) to supply themselves with cod-fish for their winter. Directing their way, therefore, according to their habit, in the year of which we speak, 1613, they happened to be caught on the sea in the thick mists and fogs."—Jes. Relations, vol. 1, ch. 25, p. 46. Pencöit, like the Pemquit of Ràle, and Paincuit of Cadillac, is a representative of the present Pemaquid.

fire. Governor Sullivan, in his day, observed the remains of a fort made of earth and stones on the east side, at the mouth of the Kennebec. Seventy years after the abandonment of the Sagadahoc plantation, the ruins of a fort were shown to seamen visiting the Sagadahoc waters, by the ancient Indians there residing, with the statement, "that[1] upon some quarrel that fell out between the Indians and English, some were killed by the Indians, and the rest driven out of the fort."

The Relation of the Jesuits alleges of the natives of Arrowsick ("Ar-row-chi-quois") "that they did not appear to be bad, although they had *defeated the English who had wished to dwell* among them in the years 1608–9. They excused themselves to us," continues the Relation, "concerning that action, and recounted the outrages which they had received from the said[2] English."

Such is the historic view of the relations of the Sagadahoc plantation to the savage inhabitants of their wild home in the province of Sabino.

There can be no doubt that collisions, more or less disastrous to the colonists, aided in hastening the abandonment of Sagadahoc as the seat of a colonial home, and the breaking up of the plantation.

Although the advent of the white race to Sagadahoc had been welcomed by the aboriginal residents of Pemaquid, the bowmen and subjects and friends of Nahanada and Skidwarroes, as the harbinger of hopes of high promise to the stranger natives of Kennebec, it was a source of doubt and a prelude to perils. They greeted[3] the colonists with hostile attitudes, and tales of "Cannibals that lived near Sagadahoc armed with teeth three inches long." While the town was going up at the

1 Appendix to Hubbard's Indian Wars, p. 75; Sewall's Ancient Dominions of Maine, p. 228.

2 Jesuit Relations, vol. 1, ch. 18, p. 36.

3 Folsom's Address, M. H. C., vol. 2, p. 32.

sea side, Captain Gilbert penetrated the upper waters of the interior, and pushing his discoveries far inland, at eventide voices in broken English hailed him from the opposite shore. It turned out to be the call of certain savages; and at morning light a "canoa" came to them, and in her a Sagamo, who told them his name was "Sebenoa," "lord of the river of Sagadahoc."

The clansmen of Sebenoa were fierce and warlike men, and by stratagem, menaces, and force, sought to overpower Gilbert and his boat's crew; and, says the narrator, "these were stranger[1] Indians,— such as the like before had not been seen." The subjects of the Bashaba, the Wawennack Prince of Pemaquid, courted the acquaintance and friendship of the Sagadahoc planters while the river natives, the subjects of "the lord of the river of Sagadahoc," repelled both. It is therefore but reasonable that as a result of the changes and disturbance consequent on the decease of the President, Popham, and the accession of the London interest in the person of Captain Gilbert to the head of the management of the plantation affairs, the hostility of the Sagadahoc natives, especially the wrongs and abuses springing up under the new order of things,— that the Bristol men with the Popham ship should have extended the colonial movement and sought a new home at Pemaquid, under the protection of Nahanada and his bowmen in the Bashaba's kingdom, and near his royal abode;— and that in the breaking up of the Sagadahoc plantation under the lead of the London interest, the Bristol element, in the estate and interest of the Popham family, should have been left at Pemaquid at the departure of the London men, and there become a new center of attraction and trade supporting the subsequent private operations of Sir Francis Popham, who continued to send his ships to this point for furs and fish; whose establishment at

1 Strachey.

length grew into the city of Jamestown, and for a century nearly, was the capital of New England before Boston was. Hence, history has recorded that there were people at Pemaquid from the time Sir H. Gilbert took possession, who were strangers and did not venture south till the settlement of Plymouth.[1] And at New Dartmouth. in the county of Cornwall, (the Sip-sa-couta, or Duck River of the aborigines), there was a settlement in the early days of New England as early as in any part of the Pemaquid country.

At all events, thirteen years after the dissolution and abandonment of the plantation at Sagadahoc, history has disclosed the fact that a hamlet of "fifty families," known as the "Sheepscot farms," adorned the banks of that river, and which subsequently became the capital of the county of Cornwall in the Ducal State, into which the Sagadahoc territory was afterwards erected.

These facts warrant the conclusion, *that a fragment of the Sagadahoc plantation, embracing the west of England or city of Bristol element, and in the interest of the Popham family, on the dissolution of that enterprise, was driven off and lodged at Pemaquid, in the Popham ship "Gift of God;" while the London men in the interest of the Gilbert family, following his lead, returned with Raleigh Gilbert in the ships "Mary and John," and the "Virginia," built at Sagadahoc, to England,* 1608.

Thus we have explained, in entire consistency with historic truth, the statement[2] of Prince in his chronology, that all but forty-five planters departed from Sagadahoc for England in two ships, of which the "Virginia" was one. These, with the "Gift of God," (of whose return to England no mention is made, and which was the Popham ship), must have been left at Pemaquid, the scene of the subsequent operations of the

1 Sullivan, 160–70; Am. Statistical Soc. vol. 1, p. 1.

2 Prince's Chronology, p. 117.

Popham family, and some of these colonists, attracted to the Sheepscot meadows above, whose waters, prolific with the means of subsistence in magnificent oyster beds and shoals of fish, all within the jurisdiction of the Pemaquid sovereignty, would there have become an interior establishment for the collection of furs and freight, encouraging the annual visits of
Sir Francis Popham's ships to Pemaquid. When Capt.
A. D. Levett, sixteen years after the abandonment of Saga-
1623–4. dahoc, sailed into Boothbay harbor at the mouth of
the Sheepscot, "*Pemaquid*" *had become the great center of trade to the native hordes of Maine from the Penobscot to* "*Accacisco.*"

Therefore, if like the baseless fabric of a dream, the vision of a fair English town[1] of fifty houses, with its church and fort, mounted and entrenched, has dissolved, yet the evidence is quite conclusive that in that dissolution, English life, English homes, and English civilization did not cease to be found within the Ancient Dominions of Maine! Pemaquid took her root from the colonial plantation at Sagadahoc, and sent up fresh, vigorous, and fruitful shoots in the families of the "*Sheepscot farms,*" between the head waters of the aboriginal "SIPSA and NAAMAS COUTA," the "rivers" of abounding "fowl and fish."

SAGADAHOC A DUKEDOM. — PEMAQUID, CAPITAL OF NEW ENGLAND.

Sagadahoc[2] territory was erected into a Ducal State, it having become the patrimony of the Duke of York. The
A. D. city of New York was, at this date, the center of its
1664. civil and military authority and relationship. The rites
and services of religion were scrupulously maintained at Pemaquid; and, by royal order, "For the promotion of piety,

[1] It is said the Dutch, as early as 1607, attempted to settle Damariscotta.— Eaton's Annals, p. 17.

[2] Ancient Dominions of Maine, pp. 144–148.

it was ordered, that a person be appointed to read prayers [1] and the holy scriptures." Thus it will be seen that religion, then and there, had its support in the graced and devout ritual of the English Episcopal service. So at Sagadahoc, the historian records, that on the 5th of October,[1] 1607, it being Sunday, Nahanada and wife, Skidwarroes, Sasanow, the Bashaba's brother, and Amenquin were at Fort George; and President Popham "took them to the place of public prayers," which "they attended morning and evening with great reverence and solemnity."

In the assembly of New York, Gyles Goddard, by the freeholders of Pemaquid and dependencies, was elected as representative. The State of Maine, as a Dukedom, sur- A. D.
vived till 1687, when, by the accession of the Duke of 1684.
York to the Throne of England, and the appointment of Andros as Governor of New England by royal order, the Ducal State was merged in the civil existence of Massachusetts "as the District of Maine." This act called forth the remonstrance of the inhabitants of Pemaquid, which, for more than three quarters of a century, had worn metroplitan honors and held metropolitan relationship to New England; and on the removal of Andros to Boston, as the seat of gubernatorial authority, he was met before the government by a protest from the east,[2] "*that Pemaquid should remain still the metropolis of these parts, because it had ever been so before Boston was settled.*" But the prestige of the ancient capital of New England had gone. The plea of hoary life and honors could avail nothing. Pemaquid fell into neglect; and, on her ruins, Boston climbed into the place and power of a Metropolitan State.

PLYMOUTH A NURSLING OF MAINE.

The facts of history not only clearly assert the precedence of Maine, as the scene of the earliest developments of English

[1] Strachey, M. H. C., vol. 3, p. 307.

[2] Ancient Dominions of Maine, p. 189.

life, civilization, and commerce, but fully show that Plymouth and her Puritan refugees *owe much* to the State of Maine for their successful establishment in the New World.

About midnight of the 7th of December, 1620, an exploring party of the Mayflower emigration, who had been ranging the woods of Cape Cod in search of a suitable landing-place for a colonial home, were disturbed by "hideous cries along the shore." In the early light of morning the cries were renewed, and the sentinel had only time to cry out, "Indians! Indians![1] when the arrows came flying thick about them."

Disturbed and repelled by these menaces, the adventurers crossed over to the northern headland of the bay of Cape Cod, where was found "a harbor fit for shipping; and divers corn-fields, and little running brooks, and a place fit for a situation." It was a place of the aboriginal dead. "Many bones and skulls" were the sad mementoes of a people that had been, but now were not! In this Golgotha were reared their homes of timber, trees, and thatch, surrounded with mouldering heaps. Sometimes only six or seven sound persons were left to help the weak, the impotent, the sick and dying. "Few and very weak," the Plymouth colonists in the midst of these monuments of death and depopulation, were ready to become the prey of savages, "who were wont to be most cruel and treacherous in all these parts, and like lions." Not more than one-half of the original number survived.

Their dwelling-place with the bones of the unnumbered dead, the icy hand of winter daily laying out the corpses of their fellow pilgrims, and the wolves and tigers of mankind crouching at their doors, ready at any moment to spring upon them from their forest lair, all combined to create an emergency, in which the interposition of a friendly hand alone could save the embryo State from impending and fatal desolation.

1 Thacher's Plymouth, p. 22. Morton's Memorial.

At this juncture it was that Maine interposed, and determined the crisis; that Maine, in the person of her wild son, the savage lord of Pemaquid, a sachem of the region of the present Bristol, our Samoset, with outstretched arms and generous greetings, appeared amid the sand hills of Plymouth harbor, to welcome and introduce, under auspicious circumstances and with fostering hand, the embryo State of Massachusetts to her wild home on the shores of the New World. Great was the surprise of the Puritans at the vision of a wild man, walking boldly and alone into their streets from the depths of the environing forests, crying in a broken dialect of their own tongue, "Much welcome, Englishmen; much welcome, Englishmen;" and to find him a man "free[1] of speech and of seemly carriage."

It probably was the salvation of the Plymouth colony. "No incident," writes the chronicler of those days, "could have diffused greater joy into the hearts of the disconsolate and infirm; it seemed like an angelic herald to their sick and dying."[2] Thus was prepared the way for a peaceful fostering intercourse between the colonists and the natives, during the infancy of the Puritan State on the shores of Massachusetts. Savage fears were calmed and savage jealousies subdued, and from being foes, the neighboring and powerful savage chieftains were converted into friends; who, taking the infant State into their bosoms, cherished and warmed into new life the colony, ready to perish on the bare rock of Plymouth! Who does not read in these prefatory lines of New England history the causes determining the destinies of New England, in the opportune and kindly interposition of Maine, in the person of her humane, generous, and noble son of Pemaquid, to prepare the way for a peaceful abode among a strange and barbarous people, who had already summoned the entire force of their powows to practice their

1 Ancient Dominions, p. 102.

2 Thacher's History of Plymouth, p. 34.

incantations in a dark and dismal swamp for days together, in order to cast out the intrusive Puritans?

And it is not the only instance in which Massachusetts, from the manhood of her present proud estate, may look back to the openings of colonial life with gratitude as she beholds the fostering hand of Maine, as an elder sister, watching at the cradle of her own infancy! Aid and comfort were furnished out of the resources of Maine in her Ancient Dominions, to the Puritans famishing on Plymouth rock.

The harbor Islands of Boothbay, at this date, were the scene of commercial and fishing interests, for no less than "thirty sail[1] of vessels," and the granary of the embryo "sovereignties"[2] of New England.

The last of May, the Puritan town of Plymouth, being a year and six months old, descried from the sand hills of Plymouth harbor a vessel at sea. It proved to be a shallop from Damarin's Cove, in the eastern parts of New England, — a vision from the Ancient Dominions of Maine, — heralding the hope of relief to the famished colonists who were anxiously looking for supplies from England.

This vessel turned out to be a shallop, and to the disappointment of the Puritans landed in Plymouth harbor seven men[3] and letters, but no bread; but the sympathy and encouragement, afforded in one of these missives from the pen of John Hudson, a ship master at Boothbay, though interested in the colonial plantation of Southern Virginia, who, nevertheless, had at heart the success of the Plymouth enterprise, contributed to revive the drooping spirits of the Puritan colonists. The returning Boothbay shallop led the way of the famishing Puritans to the "Ancient Dominions of Maine," followed by Winslow, under orders of the Plymouth governor, in a Plymouth shallop, to get bread for the colony, who wrote back: — "I

1 Morton's Memorial, p. 32.

2 Thornton's Pemaquid.

3 Morton's Memorial, pp. 40-41.

found kind entertainment and good respect, with a willingness to supply our wants which were done so far as able; and would not take any bills for the same, but did what they could freely." Thus did Maine contribute of her store to sustain the infant colony of Massachusetts; and by this act of munificence on the part of the residents of the Ancient Dominions of Maine, Morton in his Memorial of Plymouth, asserts that the Plymotheans in their "plantation had a good quantity of provisions."[1]

These facts, in the historical remains of Sagadahoc, the ancient seat of colonial life of New England, warrant the position we have taken.

A summary will show that thirteen years before a Puritan foot trod the soil of New England, a fair town of fifty houses, protected by an entrenched twelve-gun fort, ornamented with a church having a stated minister of the gospel, enlivened with the hum and clatter of busy artizans in a ship-yard, had planted the colonization, the commerce and the christianity of Europe in North America on the shores of the "Ancient Dominions of Maine;" — that Maine, in the person of her wild son Samoset of Pemaquid, with out-stretched arms and generous greetings, stood on the sands of Cape Cod to welcome and introduce under favorable auspices, the embryo State of Massachusetts from the deck of the Mayflower, to her wild home on the shores of the New World; — that the Puritans, famishing on Plymouth Rock, were supplied by the charities of Maine, in the beginnings of colonial life. The "Ancient Dominions of Maine" have, therefore, been prolific of life, peace, and success to the infancy of New England.

In Sagadahoc was planted the root whose fatness has furnished New England with the strength, verdure, freshness and beauty in English life, civilization and Christian virtue.

It is a pertinent and pregnant question in the solution of the successful present of New England, what, to-day, would have

[1] Morton's Memorial, pp. 40-41.

been the history of Plymouth rock and the Puritans, — the past of Massachusetts — had it not been for Maine and her kindly offices and sisterly attentions, at the CRADLING of her existence in the wilds of the West. When Dudley and his companions found the misanthropic Blackstone, the sole occupant of the woods of Shawmut Point, the site of Boston, and who, because he had left England in disgust, "not likeing the Lords Bishops," would not welcome the new comers, because he did not like the "Lords Brethren" any better, the crisis of colonial existence and success in New England had passed. I therefore leave it for statesmen to solve what would have been the present of New England, had it not been for Maine, and the attractions and resources of her Ancient Dominions.

The Virginia of Sagadahoc, — the *first* vessel built on the North American continent; the germ of that naval architecture which has made Maine the foremost community of the world in shipbuilding.

As the Committee have received no response to this sentiment, it has been deemed proper to connect with it the following statement:

"In the year one thousand six hundred and fourteen," says De Laet, "the ship of Skipper Adrian Block took fire by accident, and he built here[1] a YACHT of thirty-eight feet keel, forty-four feet and a half on deck, and eleven feet and a half beam, with which he sailed through the HELLEGAT into the *Great Bay*, and visited all the places thereabout, and went in it as far as Cape Cod."[2] In Hazard's "Annals of Pennsylvania," the yacht is called the "*Restless*." It is also said, "In 1616, Capt. Hendricksen in the *Restless* departs for the Schuylkill," &c. With these statements is connected the assertion that this craft was "*The first vessel built in this country by Europeans*."

1 Near New York.

2 Benson's Memoir, p. 30.

This claim of priority, like some others, is clearly neutralized by the record of Strachey, that in the first year of the Popham Colony [1607–8], "the carpenters framed a pretty Pynnace of about some thirty tonne, which they called the Virginia; the chief shipwright being one Digby of London."[1]

Thus, by several years, this "pretty Pynnace" stands at the head of the list of the countless vessels for commerce and war, which have come from the forests of our country. In the great enterprise of ship-building, Maine has long taken the foremost place; and the city of Bath, near the ancient Sagadahoc, has been chief in the State. The example of Digby and the Virginia has not been neglected.

It may be proper to add, as connected with the history of our shore-line, that Capt. Hendricksen in the "*Restless*" (Onrüst), sailed along on our coast previously to "the 18th of August, 1616," and made a "figurative" map thereof as far as Pentegouet (Penobscot River), of which a fac-simile is given in 1st Colonial Document, N. Y., p. 13.

The Colony of Massachusetts' Bay, — founded in 1629, by men of the same unconquerable will as those that brought royalty to the block, and discarded prescription as heresy. Their descendants have ever shown a faithful adherence to the doctrine of "*Uniformity.*"

The following response to this sentiment was made by the Hon. Emory Washburn, of Cambridge, late Governor of the State of Massachusetts:

GOV. WASHBURN'S ADDRESS.

Mr. Washburn said, It was with something more than the ordinary awe with which one is impressed in addressing a vast assembly, that he rose to obey the call which the president had made upon him to speak of the relations between Maine and

[1] Hist. Trav. into Va., ch. x., p. 179.

Massachusetts. He seemed to stand in the conscious presence of the history of more than two centuries since Plymouth and Kennebec were embraced in a common patent, as he recalled the part which the Sons of Massachusetts had taken in helping to plant upon the virgin soil of Maine, the institutions which have changed a wilderness into the homes of a busy, prosperous and happy community.

And yet, frankness compelled him to say that he feared that like other pet children ever since the days of Solomon, this favorite child of the old Bay State had at times been inclined to take airs, even before she became of age, and had set up house-keeping for herself. And when he saw by the papers, that she was proposing to commemorate an event in her history, away back in the remote ages of the past, he felt that it was a little presuming, inasmuch as it was touching Massachusetts, and especially the old colony of Plymouth, in a tender point. He was the more impressed with this, when he recalled an excursion he had taken, less than forty years ago, along the banks of this beautiful Kennebec, over the scenes to which the romantic story of Father Râle's heroism and death had lent a charm, where as he stood and looked out upon an unbroken forest, he innocently supposed it was then a *new* country, and little dreamed that there had been a heroic age upon the banks of that river, of whose events history then knew so little.

It was therefore, with no little surprise that he received a note from his excellent friend Dr. Wheeler, enclosing an invitation to attend a celebration of the 255th anniversary of the founding of the First English Colony on the shores of New England! With the notions of a Massachusetts' man, how could he help suspecting that here was an attempt to rob her of her laurels, when he saw that it was going back to a point of time thirteen years before the genuine Puritan *hegira*. It seemed to him to be a political heresy almost equal to that of secession itself. He thereupon began to inquire what they were proposing to commemorate, and he took down from his shelves a black letter folio marked "Popham's Reports" to see if he could find something of the *Fort Popham* mentioned in his invitation. But failing in that, he hunted up his classical dictionary for the word "*Sabino*" and concluded that, after all, here must have been the spot where the early Romans are said to have got their wives, by a rather rude kind of courtship, and he looked around on his arrival at the spot, to see the veritable wolf which Romulus is said to have suckled. He came here determined, let what would happen, to protest against every thing that denied that Plymouth was the true hive of the "Universal Yankee Nation." He confessed, however, he had been utterly disarmed by the courtesies he had shared here to-day, and he would no longer protest against anything; and if anybody were to insist that Noah's ark landed on one of these hills, and would get up a celebration like this, to commemorate it, he would volunteer to come and take part in it, without doubting it was true.

He had listened with deep interest to-day, to the narrative of the sufferings and failure of the colony that was planted here. But, as a Massachusetts' Puritan, he would venture to suggest another cause of this failure, which he wished to do *sub rosa*, and in rather a confidential manner, lest some Episcopalian or Unitarian might over-hear him and take exception at his remark. And that was, that Sir George Popham, instead of bringing over with him, as we are told he did, a clergyman of the Established Church, ought to have called and settled a right-down Orthodox Congregational minister over the First Parish of Sagadahoc. And in the same spirit he would add, it might have been well if he had any Quakers or Baptists in his colony, to have made a salutary example of them, as Massachusetts afterwards did, with such signal success.

But, said Mr. W., I am wasting in remarks which may seem to be unfitted to the dignity of the occasion, the moments which ought to be devoted to more grave and serious topics.

The first thing that must suggest itself to the mind of every one, is the contrast between the motives which impelled, and the success which attended the planting of the colonies of 1607 and of 1620. Trade, commerce, worldly gain, were the incentives to the one. Free thought, and the growth and culture of pure religious sentiment were the springs of action in the other. To the one, we are told in the words of their own history, "the country was intolerably cold and sterile, and not habitable by the English nation." To the other, the terrors of an unprotected winter exposure were far less terrible than the heavy hand of a hierarchy from whose persecutions they had escaped.

> "Amidst the storm they sung,
> And the stars heard, and the sea,
> And the sounding aisles of the dim woods rung,
> To the anthems of the free."

The one, after a few months struggle, failed, and disappeared forever. The other, in spite of climate, or soil, or savage foes, planted the living germ of one of the mightiest nations on the globe. The fate of the two colonies is a lesson which should not be lost in studying the causes of human greatness, and of national success. Is it too much to say, that it was fortunate for this great and growing State, that so much of the vital germ of her present social and political existence as a body politic, was transplanted from the seed-bed of the colonies of Massachusetts Bay, rather than to have sprung directly from the adventurers who came here as the fellow colonists of President Geo. Popham? It is seen in the thriving cities and villages that are scattered over its territory. It is seen in the quiet, happy homes that skirt every wayside, and in the bold, brave, self-reliant, intelligent men, and the refined and intelligent women, that one meets with here, everywhere.

These are the fruits of institutions such as the Pilgrims

planted; and Massachusetts and Plymouth have but repeated themselves here upon a wider and broader field, which so many of their sons have helped to cultivate and people. And as their ancestors formed but one body politic in the great struggle of the Revolution, the sons of Maine and Massachusetts are now battling as brothers, side by side, in the greater struggle in which our country is this day engaged. It is a struggle whether the free thought, the manly independence, the blessings of wise laws and a good government, which our fathers purchased with their blood, shall be preserved for us and our posterity, or the iron heel of an oligarchal despotism be planted upon the necks of the down-trodden masses.

He would not pursue this thought, but he would venture to say a single word of the occasion and of this mighty gathering of the people. We need more of such meetings. We need something to bind us together, beyond the mere letter of a civil compact or the sympathy of a national name. The strongest bond of national unity among the jarring and jealous States of Greece, was found in their public gatherings and at her national games. In the eager pursuit of gain and personal advancement, there is danger of the people forgetting that they are a nation, or have a nation's history and honor to vindicate and maintain.

The sons and daughters of New England, who go out into other regions of our constantly widening republic, remember the homes and the institutions they have left, with affection and respect. But the children of the next generation have only a traditional tie in these associations, which grows weaker with each succeeding generation, where there is not something beyond the mere intercourse of business, to draw them together by feelings of a common sympathy.

The conspirators of the south understood this, and acted upon it, when they sent back to New England the schoolmasters and schoolmistresses who were teaching their children, and withdrew their sons from northern colleges, and their daughters from northern schools. They understood it, when they denied to the citizens of our State, the constitutional guaranties of protection in another; for they knew that by free intercourse and interchange of opinions between the people of the different States, the free thought and liberal training of the northern mind must ever be antagonistic to the policy which they were seeking to inaugurate. We saw here to-day, in this vast assemblage of men and women, coming up hither from no class and from no circumscribed locality, in palpable form, the fruits of that great elementary distinction there is between northern and southern institutions, in the social influence that elevates and the prosperous success which crowns free, intelligent, well paid labor. It is this great leading principle which has made the hardy soil of Massachusetts the most densely peopled spot in our whole country. It has changed the wilderness of Maine into regions of beauty and thrift and comfort. In this, as in every other good thing, Maine and Massachusetts have gone on together,—the daughter emulating the mother,—the mother, aided by the reaction of that very emulation, taking another step in a common, onward progress towards the condition of perfect commonwealths.

He would ask a moment's longer indulgence, while he followed out a single thought which pressed upon his mind as he contemplated the beautiful relation in which Maine and Massachusetts had always stood towards each other, whether under the same form of civil government, or each with its independent organization. Why, and he spoke it with pain and sorrow, did they witness such a contrast between the kindly sympathies of the once mother and the daughter, though now independent in all matters of domestic government, in the one case, and what they hear from the political leaders and read in the periodical press of the mother country of them both, towards the children of her own sons who planted English thought and

English love of freedom here on the shores of New England? The time was when they boasted a common origin, a common language, a common history, and a common sympathy of freemen. Has the mother grown alien to herself? If they could have conceived that a change so much to be lamented, were possible, they ought to believe so no longer, after listening to the eloquent language and noble sentiments of the honorable gentleman (Hon. Mr. McGee), who had preceded him. It was with pride that, while he had to speak of the politicians and the press of England, he could do justice to the heart and intellect of her noble Queen, illustrious as a sovereign, and still more illustrious as a virtuous and a high souled woman, and could say that he did not believe that the language that comes to us from the organs of public sentiment there, spoke the feelings of the great English heart. And yet he must ask why it was, that the holy cause of human liberty and human rights in America, have found so few champions in the great body of the English press? There were a few illustrious exceptions. But the press, as a power, was hostile to the cause of human freedom here. Why is the voice of Brougham no longer heard pleading the cause of down-trodden humanity? Is the mother's nature about to change? Is England to forget the scene at her own Runnymede, and is the Magna Charta becoming a dead letter? Is she going to blot out what her Milton wrote, and Hampden dared, and Chatham uttered, and to smother the silent eloquence of the history of a thousand years, beneath the cotton bales of a band of conspirators against the cause of English liberties and human rights?

If such is to be her future, let the sons of New England show to the world that if Old England is recreant to her own history, her sons here will take up that record and be true to the glorious old traditions of the past. Who, that has a drop of English blood in his veins, would not blush that the same proud nation who, through the voice of their chief justice, in

Somerset's case, proclaimed, ninety years ago, that the air of England was too pure for a slave to breathe in, could be found cheering on, by acquiesence, at least, the slaveholder in his rebellion to rear a despotism of caste, upon the corner-stone of negro slavery? If the sympathy of kindred ties are to be sacrificed to the subordinate forms of State polity, let her learn from the history of her ancient colony of the Bay, that every step made in the prosperity of the daughter, adds new strength and vigor to the mother, while it appeals to her, in the name of unborn generations, to stand up in the dignity of her better nature, to carry forward the great struggle for human freedom, in which the nations of the earth are engaged. In view of the history of States, whose names had been associated in the sentiment to which he had been called upon to respond, he would say, in closing, Beautiful mother, more beautiful daughter, honored alike in their devotion to the cause of a common country and of human rights.

The President of the United States.

Arrangements were made to secure a response to this sentiment, from a gentleman high in position in the government of our country. But his inability to be present has deprived the committee of the power to present an extended reference to our Chief Magistrate and the afflicted state of the nation, which the circumstances of that time would have rendered most appropriate, and deeply interesting, from the fearful disasters to our army under Gen. Pope on the day of this celebration.

The Queen of Great Britain.

This sentiment was responded to by John J. Day, Esq., of Montreal, on behalf of the St. George's Society of that city.

MR. DAY'S SPEECH.

Mr. Day said,—He rose under a deep sense of the responsibility which devolved upon him, and regretted it had not fallen to abler hands to respond to the sentiment proposed; but he felt consoled in the reflection that, in the peculiar relation he stood to this, as well as the mother country, his remarks might be entitled to some weight at their hands, as expressing opinions less likely to be influenced by prejudice than might be those of other gentlemen present, holding official relations to Her Majesty's Government in England. That, although an Englishman by birth, and for many years, latterly, a resident of Canada, he had for some time previously resided in the United States, and made this country, to some extent, that of his adoption. He said it was hardly necessary for him to speak of Her Majesty as an eminently virtuous and exemplary mother, one who had so fitly trained and educated her children to become the future Kings and Queens of England. That the demeanor and conduct of the Prince of Wales, some two years ago, as their guest, extolled as he was at the time for his modest bearing, consistent conduct, sound sense and good judgment, need alone be referred to as evidence of Her Majesty's maternal guidance and care in training him for the high position he is, in all probability, destined, at some future day, to fill. That, as a Sovereign Queen, her rule was universally acknowledged to be benign, righteous, and just. That, in fact, she lived in the hearts of her people. That whatever misconceptions might exist here as to the policy of Her Majesty's Ministers, with reference to the misunderstandings that have at times unhappily arisen between the United States Government and that of Great Britain, the American nation have, through their organs, the press, always expressed an implicit confidence in Her Majesty, as personally their friend and well wisher. That the time was, when tyranny and despotism were the predominant features in the reign of Kings and Queens; that happily the times had changed, and whilst we could not but admire Her Majesty, as endowed with qualities so fitted to her exalted station, it was but right to attribute those endowments, in a large measure, to the influences of the age in which we live, — to that progress in our common civilization which, under the blessings of Providence, is the peculiar characteristic of the period, — in fact, to the moral, religious, social, and political influences of that civilization to which the people of Great Britain and America, and in some respects, France, have so largely contributed in their persistent struggles, from time to time, during the last two centuries, to establish political and religious liberty, and free representative institutions.

As representing the Saint George's Society of Montreal, and as a resident of Canada and subject of Great Britain, he would tender to them, on that occasion, the warmest sympathy, and would assure them, as his honorable friend, D'Arcy McGee had done, that it is a mistake to suppose that the feeling in Canada or England, as regards their present unhappy and much to be deplored national troubles, is to any extent unfavorable to the American Union. That there would be, — there always are, — some sordid minds, actuated by the love of the "almighty dollar," who would pander to the vilest purposes, and it would be strange if either England or Canada should be entirely exempt from that foible of our common humanity. No, Mr. President, he repeated, it is with painfully sympathetic feelings that the people of England and Canada regard the devastating and ruinous internecine war now infesting our fair country, and that there did not exist amongst them, as a people, the desire to see our hitherto happy and prosperous land, composed as it is principally of the descendants of a common stock with themselves, rent asunder and destroyed in its integrity as a nation.

Mr. Day then proceeded to comment upon the remarks made

by the previous speaker, the Honorable Ex-Governor Washburn, of Massachusetts, in respect to the part which, it appeared to him (Mr. W.), England had manifested a desire to take, unfavorable to the cause of the American Union. Mr. Day said, that for a time he felt that that honorable gentleman's remarks about England, did not do her justice; but that, winding up as he did, by eulogizing Her Majesty, and expressing a doubt as to whether it was not rather a mere suspicion than a fact, rightfully attested, that the Government and people of England were adverse to the North, threw so healing a salve over the wound inflicted by that honorable gentleman's previous remarks as to England's feeling and conduct, that he (Mr. Day) felt somewhat relieved from the weight of the impressions previously made upon him by the honorable gentleman. He said the honorable gentleman had complained of England's conduct as false to her previous anti-slavery professions, — that it seemed to him (Mr. W.), that instead of desiring to aid them in their present struggle to get rid of slavery, she desired, by the policy she pursued, to perpetuate it. But he (Mr. Day) felt that England was, in that statement, unfairly accused. That England's policy would ever be the emancipation of the slave; but that in working out that policy, she would desire to have due regard to those rights of property which, under that ill-conceived institution, is here in America acknowledged, and which was unhappily found to exist at the time of the forming of the Constitution. That the question in the present struggle between the North and the South, was not really and truly whether slavery should be abolished or perpetuated, — that the President of the United States himself had but lately issued a proclamation, in which he distinctly declared that not to be the case. That it was to maintain the Constitution and restore the Union that we were fighting; not to abolish or perpetuate slavery, except as the one or the other might be necessary to the achievement of the great object of the Government in its endeavors to suppress the rebellion. Why charge England as unfriendly to the North because of her neutrality? Had not the United States Government itself pursued a similar policy on at least more than one occasion, when the deepest sympathies of a free and generous people might, to some extent, have rendered intervention less culpable? He referred more particularly to the case of "down-trodden Hungary," when their exiled patriot and leader, Kossuth, expatriated, on our shores pleaded so ably his country's wrongs? That England had thus far throughout our troubles remained firm to that policy of non-intervention, which we ourselves, under our own Constitution, deemed the right one; and this, too, in the face of the prostration of her commerce and the extremest distress amongst her working classes, occasioned by the difficulties in obtaining cotton from the South, in consequence of the blockade by our own fleets. That she had done nothing, as a Government, to aid the rebel cause.

What, therefore, he would kindly ask of us, is it that we would have her do more than she had done to convince us of her honesty and rectitude of purpose toward us, as a nation? That our answer might be, that she might evince a better feeling through her public journals. Let the fault of the "fourth estate" be atoned for by the "fourth estate." To condemn a whole nation because a part of her public press pandered to party views, would be to censure our own nation, for our press was equally at fault. A better criterion to judge by, let him suggest, would be, the feelings reciprocated by the people of the two nations in their individual intercourse with each other, here, in Canada, and in England; and he thought we might gather, even from the present occasion of our meeting together, that England and England's Queen, our common mother, and the United States, her eldest daughter, are not, after all, on such bad terms as some would have it supposed.

Why England's interference should be so much talked of,

and France, who has evinced more disposition to do so, should escape the censure of America, might, at first sight, seem strange; but he (Mr. Day) presumed it might easily be accounted for in the fact that gratitude to France for the aid she afforded this nation in her struggles for independence, and a remembrance of the wrongs which led the people of the colonies to withdraw their allegiance from Great Britain, still exerted its influence in the heart of the American nation. He said, wrongs; for while Englishmen now enjoyed the blessings of free institutions and good government, under the rule of a Queen who governs by and through her people, he (Mr. Day) was free to admit that there were periods in her history, when Englishmen, whether as colonists or otherwise, had just reason to complain of the misrule of the government.

Mr. Day then, as well on behalf of the Saint George's Society, as for himself personally, expressed his thanks to the Maine Historical Society for the invitation as their guest on this interesting occasion, and the extreme pleasure he had experienced in participating in that day's ceremonies, commemorative of the founding of the first colony on these shores, by George Popham and his companions, in 1607. He added, that to tread on the sacred soil where the bones of our common ancestors found their resting-place, after having laid the foundation on this continent of those blessed and inestimable institutions, political and religious, the fruits of which we find now so extensively scattered over these States of America, — to have had the privilege on that day of listening to the interesting speech which our talented orator of the day (John A. Poor, Esq.,) had so ably delivered to us under the auspices of our estimable society, containing so much of historical detail affecting the past and future interests of the Old as well as the New World; and to participate on that day in the performance of the solemn and original religious services of the Church of the period of the founding of this colony, so devoutly performed by the Right Reverend Bishop of the Anglican Episcopal Church; and above all, to be permitted to unite in the imposing Masonic ceremonies, with which we had that day laid the stone in memory of George Popham, as the first English colonist, as a part of the work in the erection of the fort to bear his name, and intended as a defense of our country's constitution, constituted for him that day an event in his life which would ever remain with him in pleasing remembrance.

He expressed a hope that such interchanges of good feeling as he had that day experienced at our hands, might be perpetuated between the sons of Old and New England, and never be marred by differences that would lead to hostilities against the mother country, in which the defenses of that fort, containing the memorial stone erected to George Popham, would require to be brought into exercise.

In conclusion, he asked permission to express an *impromptu* sentiment, that suggested itself to him during the interesting ceremony of laying the stone, and which he had at the moment committed to paper:

"May this fort be used rather as a shield to protect the remains of the revered George Popham, and his associates, whose bones are here deposited, than as a bulwark of defense against England as your foe; or as an instrument of destruction to England's fleets."

Richard Vines,— the faithful friend of Sir Ferdinando Gorges, whose occupation of the country, to the time of his appointment as Deputy Governor of the "Province of Mayne," in 1644, upheld the title of his nation against the French, and saved New England to his country.

The Hon. E. E. Bourne, of Kennebunk, was prepared to speak in reply to this sentiment. The want of time prevented this purpose, and his intended remarks have since been furnished, as follows:

JUDGE BOURNE'S ADDRESS.

The history of the early settlements on the coast of Maine has recently excited and received much attention. A new impetus has been given to the study of it by the arduous and efficient labors of some of the members of the Historical Society, particularly by those of its president, Mr. Willis, Mr. Sewall, of Wiscasset, Mr. Poor, and of the authors of various local histories. Our children had grown up, under the instruction of their fathers, in the belief that those who landed at Plymouth in 1620, and made an abiding habitation there, were the first settlers of New England, — the first occupants of its soil. This impression has so fastened itself on the public mind that it will take many years to remove it. Yet I have no hesitation as to the assertion, that the progress making in that direction will, in due time, come to that result. More light is yet to break out from the revelations of the archives of antiquity. These extended shores, these islands, these rivers, these mountains, are yet to impart new knowledge to the historical inquirer; knowledge, too, which will be satisfying to the candid seeker for truth. By the facilities now afforded in England, by the frequent publication of manuscripts over which the dust of ages has accumulated, and the republication of books, almost lost to the world, developments are being made, which will bring very efficient aid to every one who may choose to embark in the work of bringing to the light of day the material facts of the early occupation of our territory.

It is not to be denied that an immense field for labor and useful and interesting employment is yet before us. Amidst the conflicting claims of discoverers and occupiers of different portions of our State, much material truth has been shorn of its power, and still more has been lost from the inadequacy of any then existing agencies for its preservation. There was no printing press on these shores till 1738. The historical student will find unlimited room for the exercise of his powers of patient and discriminating research in the recovery and application of important facts, which may yet be deduced from such books, records, and documents as have survived the ravages of time. Though not pecuniarily profitable, such pursuits are wonderfully absorbing, — and any man who will give his soul to the investigation, may yet, in due time, come before the public, "bringing his sheaves with him."

There are difficulties and obstructions, much marvelous, unsatisfactory and contradictory history to be encountered, reconciled, and explained. But these perplexities and embarrassments only give zest to research and investigation. They enlarge the space for deep thought and patient and persevering examination. A work has lately fallen into my hands, published in London in 1687, entitled, "The Present State of His Majesty's Isles and Territories in America," a duodecimo of some three hundred pages. Those, who have the world of literature at hand, may be familiar with this work. But to me much of its revelations are new. Some things are stated, in relation to the events which we come here to commemorate, which I have found in no other publication. The author had some source of information other than Strachey. The following passage, while it clearly sustains this position, presents one important fact which I find nowhere else: "There being much time spent in the discovery of this country, and not without expense in the setting forth of ships, and that not without the loss of several men's lives, before it could be brought to perfection, but at length in the year 1607, Sir John Popham and others, settled a plantation at the mouth of the river Sagadahoc; but Capt. James Davis having chosen a small place, almost an island, to set down in, where, having heard a sermon, read their patent and laws, and after he had built a fort, sailed further up the river and country, where, finding an island that had a great fall of water, and having hauled their boat over with a rope, they came to another fall, which, by reason of its being very shallow and swift, proved unpassable; the head of the river lying in about forty-five degrees. They call their fort, St. George, Capt. George Popham being President; and the people seemed much affected with our men's devotion, and would say, 'King James is a good King, and his God a good God, but our God Tanto a naughty God,' which is the name of the evil spirit which haunts them every new moon, and makes them worship him for fear; he commanded them not to converse nor come near the English, threatening to kill some of them if they did, and inflict sickness upon others, if they disobeyed him, beginning with two of their Sagamores, or king's children, affirming he had power to do the like against the English, and would, the next new moon, execute it upon them. In January, in the space of seven hours, they had thunder, lightning, rain, frost, and snow, all in very great abundance. There is likewise found a bath, so hot for two miles about, they cannot drink of it. One of the Indians, for a straw hat and knife, stript himself of his cloathing, which was beaver skins worth in England 50s. or 3£, to present them to the President, only leaving himself a piece to cover his nudities." This account, though according with Strachey in some of its statements, contains other facts, of which he makes no mention. But the most material, which I have met with in no other work, is the existence of the hot water bath, "two miles about." Now where was this remarkable spring?

I have alluded to these statements merely to show that the demand for historic labor, in this immediate field, is not yet satisfied. None of these mysteries in the books make the study of true history less attractive and absorbing. They afford more cogent reasons for persevering investigation; room for useful mental exercise.

These remarks, it may be well said, have but an exceedingly remote relation to the subject of the toast to which I intended to respond. But the new occasion suggests so many interesting inquiries; so many and various thoughts rush in upon the mind, that we cannot repress the impulse to deviate from any prescribed etiquette. There can be no organism of discourse to which one can be confined.

The emigrants to the shores of New England came hither under the impulse of widely different motives. Those of Plymouth, as well as those of Massachusetts, came over "to advance the kingdom of our Lord Jesus Christ and to enjoy the liberties of the gospel in purity, with peace." I do not think that those who landed on the shores of Maine were moved in the enterprise by any such considerations. The adventurers to Sagadahoc enjoyed all such liberties in the home country. They were believers in the regime of the Church of England, and were under no necessity of self-expatriation for conscience sake. They came here for the extension of British dominion and the advancement of their pecuniary interests. Mr. Folsom's remark, that they had not "a tithe of the energy of those who landed at Plymouth," seems to me without foundation, in the fact on which he bases this charge. We all understand the obstinacy and pertinacity of religious feeling and opinion.— Many, and perhaps a large majority of Christian men, would submit to martyrdom, rather than forego their free enjoyment. The Plymouth adventurers are worthy of all honor and reverence for their fidelity to Christian principle. But there is no evidence that they were possessed of more fortitude and energy than those who landed at Sagadahoc, Saco, or any where else on the coast. The objects of the several expeditions were very unlike in their value and moral force. Popham, Vines and others landed in Maine for pecuniary and political considerations only,—and these will require no man to expose himself to the hazard which a religionist might even cheerfully encounter, to meet the demands of his spiritual convictions.

But as to courage and enterprise, RICHARD VINES, who began a settlement at Saco, in 1617, may well compare with the planters at Plymouth. It must be remembered that these planters were, in no sense, the first persons to brave the terrors and deprivations of the New World. They had been enlightened by the experience of the previous occupants at Sagadahoc and Saco. The colonists at both of these places had passed unharmed through the severities of winter, unmolested by the savage tribes, who then roamed over and claimed the whole territory. So far as previous history gave any manifestations, it had divested the expedition to New England of its most appalling terror. There was not necessarily any danger in Indian propinquity and association. In no very limited sense, the Pilgrims at Plymouth entered into the labors of others.

That much was accomplished by Vines, to open the way for a permanent settlement of the shores of Maine and to secure the territory to England, there can be no doubt; while at the same time, there is some reason for the supposition, that the occupation by him of the territory of Winter Harbor, in 1616–17, may have been continued. There is no evidence of a total abandonment of it. He made several voyages to England and transported colonists just after this time. Several of these made an abiding settlement on Little River, within the borders of Kennebunkport. Very probably some of them were his companions in their hibernation of 1616. We have every reason for thinking that he carried out the object of his mission. Gorges had sent him to secure the possession by colonization; and he makes record of the fact that he had met with good success, and that in consequence of this success, he had made another settlement at Agamenticus. Subsequently, in 1629, in consequence of the skillful and effective exertions of Vines, a grant was made to him and Oldham of a tract of land of great extent on the west side of Saco River.

It has been said that the prevalence of the plague, or whatever else may have been the character of the distemper, by which, just before the arrival of the Plymouth colonists, vast numbers of the savages were swept away, was an auspicious interposition of Providence for the safety of those emigrants. Undoubtedly it was so. But Vines and his little colony at Winter Harbor, in 1616–17, in addition to the appalling dangers from savage jealousy and vengeance, had also to encounter this most fearful and destructive enemy. They might have disembarked and escaped from the contagion; but these fearless and indomitable spirits were not moved to any such abandonment. They persevered in the grand purpose for which they were sent. If ever man had reason for abandoning an enterprise, surely Vines had at this time. He was here when this wasting disease was raging with fearful power all through the country, and sweeping off the humanity of the land with great rapidity. It seized on the adventurers. Yet, says Gorges, "Vines, and others with him, continued with the sick and dead in their cabins, and not one of them ever felt their heads ache while they stayed there."

Vines was a physician, and perhaps his professional knowledge was of essential service in this trying emergency. But whatever influences were brought to bear on their condition, the strangers survived the ravages of the disease, and placed themselves in position, so as to set about the objects of their enterprise. He visited the sea coast and traded with the French at the east, and did what was necessary to lay the foundation of title to the territory of a considerable portion of Maine. He also went into the interior, and so prudently demeaned himself everywhere, that he was kindly and hospitably received by the Indians in their wigwams, and afterwards maintained a free intercourse with them. After the base treachery, whereby some of the natives had been seized and carried away from their home in the forests to the shores of Europe, the fellowship of the Indians was to be treated with extreme delicacy and prudence. But Vines probably never lost favor with them in the area of his operations. We do not assert the permanency of the occupation of 1617, but the action of this period, undoubtedly, was the initiation of the subsequent settlement. Nothing appears in the history of their stay at Winter Harbor, which would render it probable that they left in the ensuing season. The grant to Vines a few years afterwards, in this immediate locality, must have been induced by some more beneficial services in behalf of the Lord Proprietor, and asked for by Vines from some further knowledge of its prospective value, than are exhibited in the concise account which we have of their sojourn there during one winter. But at any rate he was there a few years afterwards, — and there, too, from previous knowledge and occupancy, — making his home in Saco till his departure for Barbadoes in 1646.

In 1636, he, with five associates, was appointed a Councilor of the Province of New Somersetshire, as this territory was then denominated; and shortly after, as Gorges, in consequence of home complication, seemed to the colonists to have forgotten them, he was elected Deputy Governor, which office he held while he remained in the country. He was an energetic and enterprising man, intent on the purposes of discovery, and of using it for the security of the title of the home proprietor and the advancement of civilization. In 1642, he went up the Saco River in a birch canoe, ascended the White Mountains, making quite an accurate survey of heights and distances, considering that his pathway by water as well as by land, was through unbroken forests. On this expedition he was gone fifteen days. It is said by Winthrop that some one else from Exeter had made the ascent the year before. Whether he was the first or second adventurer on the ascent, the tour through the wilderness is indicative of a fearless and resolute spirit.

Having but a very limited knowledge of him before his embarkation to this country, I am unable to speak of him more particularly, excepting merely to add, that in his commission as Councilor he was denominated Steward General. Of the import of that denomination, or the province of the office, I am not apprised. He was evidently a man of high character and of reliable efficiency; was a staunch Episcopalian, and a friend of temperance, though not adopting the standard of the reformers of the present day. Almost the first act in the performance of his official functions, was an order restraining the use of intoxicating liquors. Much of his success was undoubtedly due to his temperate habits. I think we may well regard him as in advance of the civilization of the age.

Plymouth Plantation, — founded by men of strong faith, of earnest piety; educated under the teachings of Robinson and Brewster at Leyden, they were fitted to become pioneers in the new movement toward civil and religious liberty.

The following letter has been received from the Hon. Robert C. Winthrop of Boston, in reply to the invitation and request of the committee:

HON. MR. WINTHROP'S LETTER.

BOSTON, September 3, 1862.

MY DEAR SIR, — Absence from home prevented me from receiving your obliging communication of the 14th of August, until this late day. I am greatly honored by the invitation of the committee of arrangements for the Historical Celebration at Fort Popham; and it would have given me pleasure to respond by letter, if not by word of mouth, to the sentiment in honor of the Colony of Massachusetts Bay.

But the day has passed. The celebration is over. The public journals have already informed us of the interesting proceedings and eloquent addresses of the occasion. It only remains for me to congratulate you and the committee on the success which has attended their efforts, and to express my regrets that I was prevented from uniting in their commemoration of an event so prominently associated with the early history of New England.

With renewed acknowledgments of the compliment intended for me, I remain, Dear Sir,

Your obliged and obedient servant,

ROB'T C. WINTHROP.

Rev. EDWARD BALLARD, *Secretary.*

New Jersey, — where the Northmen of the Scandinavian Peninsula founded their first colony in the New World.

The Hon. W. A. Whitehead, of Newark, N. J., was invited to respond to this sentiment. In his inability to attend the meeting, he addressed the following letter to the committee:

HON. MR. WHITEHEAD'S LETTER.

NEW JERSEY HISTORICAL SOCIETY,
NEWARK, N. J., August 29th, 1862.

Rev. EDWARD BALLARD, Brunswick, Me.

DEAR SIR: — Not until yesterday did I receive the polite invitation of your committee to be present at the celebration *to-day*, of the "two hundred and fifty-fifth anniversary of the founding of the first English colony on the shores of New England," — an event well deserving of commemoration. The non-receipt of the invitation in season for me to avail myself of it, does not, however, preclude my acknowledging the honor conferred, and an expression of my warm sympathy in every thing calculated to revive the recollection of what "time hath blurred." It would have given me great pleasure, had circumstances allowed of my being present.

I notice that New Jersey is to be honored with a toast on the occasion, and I should be pleased to be present to hear how the gentleman from whom a response is expected will establish the fact asserted in the toast, that the Scandinavians founded their first colony within the limits of the State. I fear that he will find it a difficult subject. It is presumed that the colony referred to is the settlement of the Swedes on the Delaware in 1638, leading to the occupation of the soil within what is now New Jersey, and the erection of Fort Elsenburgh in 1643, — an interesting episode in the history of the State, which has been less studied than it deserves. But to assert that this was the first establishment of the Scandinavians in the New World, seems to ignore what we have thought to have been for some years acknowledged to be beyond doubt, the visit of the Northmen to the shores of Massachusetts and Rhode Island in 1607, and their residence there for three years thereafter. The settlers on the Delaware certainly made a more permanent lodgment than those who located in "Vinland;" but even if priority is to be given to them on this account, New Jersey cannot properly lay claim to them, as their settlements in Delaware and Pennsylvania ante-date the erection of Fort Elsenburgh full five years.

In this connection it may be remarked, that a supposition of a settlement of Scandinavians in the northern part of the State at an earlier period than that named for their establishment on the Delaware, has found admission into many of our general and local histories, based upon the name given to the settlement at Bergen, — corresponding to that of the capital of Norway; — but there are no good grounds therefor. Smith, the Provincial historian, is generally referred to as the authority; but all that he says is, that "a few *Danes were probably* concerned in the original settlement of this county, whence came Bergen, after the capital of Norway." Gordon, following, and as he thought, improving upon Smith, says, "The Hollanders were here the pioneers of civilization, aided, probably, by some Danes *or Norwegians*, who adopted the name of

Bergen, from the capital of Norway;"—and others have presented similar suggestions.

The supposition seems to have originated with Oldmixon, who, in his "British Empire in America," written some twenty years before Smith published his History of New Jersey, describes Bergen County, and adds, "The chief town is Berghen, the name of the capital city of Norway, which gives me reason *to doubt whether it was not rather Danes than Swedes that first planted here;*" his sources of information leading him to give to the Swedes the priority over all other Europeans in settling New Jersey. "The Dutch," he says, "always industrious in trade, worked them so far out of it that Berghen, the northern part of New Jersey, was almost entirely planted by Hollanders."

I am not aware that any peculiarly Danish or Norwegian family names are to be found in Bergen County; and it may be safely assumed that the name was adopted, as others were with which they were familiar in the "Faderlandt," because of the home reminiscences it awakened; *Bergen*, — like "Amsterdam," "Haarlem," "Utrecht," "Bevervyck," &c., — being one of the towns of North Holland. It has, however, been suggested, that the name had reference to the high ground upon which the settlement was made.

I think, therefore, that the claim set up for New Jersey, as the fostering parent of the first Scandinavians, is untenable.

With thanks for the courtesy extended to me, I remain,

Very respectfully, your ob't serv't,

W. A. WHITEHEAD.

New Brunswick, — cotemporaneous with Maine in origin and neighboring in territory; may their bonds of good fellowship never be broken.

The following letter from the Hon. S. L. Tilley of Fredericton, N. B., having reference to the spirit of this sentiment, is here inserted:

HON. MR. TILLEY'S LETTER.

PROVINCIAL SECRETARY'S OFFICE,
FREDERICTON, N. B., August 22d, 1863.

SIR,—I have delayed answering the invitation from the Executive Committee of the public Historical Celebration to commemorate the two hundred and fifty-fifth anniversary of the founding of the first English colony on the shores of New England, in the hope that I could make such arrangements as would enable me to accept it.

I will be compelled to be at Quebec on the tenth of September as a delegate from the Government of this Province to confer with delegates from the Governments of Canada and Nova Scotia in relation to the construction of an Inter-colonial Railway; and were I to go to "Fort Popham" on the 29th inst., the two engagements would cause an absence from the Province of more than three weeks,—more time than I can possibly spare.

Please present to the committee my sincere thanks for their invitation.

Not to be able to meet with you I consider a great privation. I hope to prevail upon some member of our government to go on. Apart from the special object for which the celebration was agreed upon, I trust it will create and strengthen friendly relations between the English race on both sides of our lines; and that no other feelings should ever exist is the sincere desire of Your obedient servant,

S. L. TILLEY.

REV. EDWARD BALLARD, *Secretary.*

Sir William Phips, — the ship carpenter of Woolwich, — the bold seaman and adventurer, the Baronet, the successful General and Governor. His life and character illustrated the spirit and genius of New England.

The Rev. Francis Norwood, pastor of the Congregational Church in Phipsburg, in which town is embraced the Peninsula of Sabino, has furnished the following communication:

THE REV. MR. NORWOOD'S SKETCH OF THE LIFE AND CHARACTER OF SIR WILLIAM PHIPS.

Sir William Phips, Governor of Massachusetts, was born in the southern part of Woolwich, near a little bay, still called Phips's Bay, February 2, 1650, thirty years after the landing of the Pilgrims at Plymouth, and forty-three after the English settlement at the mouth of the Kennebec.

He was the son of James Phips, a native of Bristol, England, and one of a family of twenty-six children and twenty-one sons. His father dying when he was young, he spent the first eighteen years of his life with his mother, engaged in agricultural employments. At the end of this time he served an apprenticeship of four years with a ship carpenter, and became master of the trade. Whereupon, at the age of twenty-two, he removed to Boston, influenced by the greater advantages there furnished for the prosecution of his business.

Surprising as it may now seem, it was during his first year's residence in Boston, and while engaged in the business of his trade, that he learned to *read and write.* He pursued his trade of ship carpenter one year in Boston, at the end of which, having established a good name and character, he marries an estimable lady, the widow of one John Hall, a Boston merchant. Shortly after this, he contracts with persons in Boston to build them a ship in his native village, two leagues from the Kennebec.

Just as this was completed, and he was about to take in a

load of lumber, the Indians made a murderous assault upon the inhabitants; and he, to save them, left his lading, took them on board and gave them a free passage to Boston.

Notwithstanding, however, the partial failure of this enterprise by reason of the loss of his lumber, he was not *discouraged*, but would frequently tell his wife that he should yet be captain of a king's ship, and owner of a fair brick house in the Green Lane of North Boston. Such were the visions that floated before his mind, like the dreams of Joseph in his youthful days; a common indication and accompaniment of aspiring genius.

Hearing, about this time, of a Spanish wreck on the coast of the Bahamas, he sails there to make explorations, and from thence to England, where he made such representations at White Hall, that in the year, 1683, he became the captain of a king's ship, Algier Rose, a frigate of eighteen guns and ninety-five men.

In this ship he sails to the Bahamas in search of the buried treasures. But after long delays and the experience of many hardships and dangers, the crew mutinied once and again, compelling him to return to England, that he might make the necessary preparation for another voyage of discovery. Arriving there, his wishes are again seconded; another ship is furnished and he returns to prosecute his enterprise.

While at the supposed place of the buried wreck; viz., a reef of shoals a few leagues to the northward of Port de la Plata, upon Hispaniola, and in the very act of exploration, a sea feather is spied, and one of the Indian divers was ordered to bring it up. The diver bringing up the feather, brought with it a surprising story that he saw a number of *great guns* in the watery world below. This led to renewed and enlivened activity, till at length they secured thirty-two tons of silver, with much gold, pearls, and jewels, all drawn up forty feet from the sunken wreck, and that without the loss of a man's life.

But by this sudden and unexampled prosperity, Capt. Phips was greatly embarrassed and perplexed. His crew had been hired on seamen's wages, at so much a month. When, therefore, they saw such vast litters of silver sows and pigs, as they called them, come on board at the captain's call, they were dissatisfied and threatened to rise and take the ship and divide the treasures among themselves.

In this terrible distress, Captain Phips made a *vow* unto Almighty God, "that if he would carry him safely home to England with what he had now given him, he would forever devote himself to the interests of the Lord Jesus Christ and of his people in New England." At the same time he sought to conciliate his men by kindness of deportment and by assuring them that they should be amply remunerated, though obliged himself to distribute his own share among them. Thus quiet and confidence were restored, and he, returning to England, came up to London in the year 1687, with nearly 300,000 pounds sterling aboard, in our money, $1,500,000.

Such, however, was his *honesty* in fulfilling his promises to his seamen and in making *exact returns* to his employers, that he received as his part only about 16,000 pounds, in our money, $80,000. At the same time the Duke of Albemarle made his wife, whom he had never seen, the present of a golden cup, worth 1000 pounds, in our money, $5000. The King, also, King James II., in consideration of the skill, energy, and enterprise displayed in this undertaking, and of the service done by him in bringing such a treasure into the nation, conferred on him the *honor of Knighthood;* the first honor, it is believed, conferred on a *native American.*

In the next year, 1688, he was appointed by the King, *High Sheriff of the country;* and having made a second visit to the wreck, though with little pecuniary benefit, he returned to New England to fulfil the promise made to his wife of building a fair *brick house* in the Green Lane of North Boston.

Two years after, having now passed through varied scenes of self-discipline and prosperity, at the age of forty, he felt himself called upon to make a profession of his faith in Christ and to unite with the North Congregational Church in Boston, of which the Rev. Cotton Mather was pastor.

As it may be instructive and profitable to know and remember what were the *views and practices* of the Congregational churches of this country at that time, 1690, these, with few exceptions, being the only churches then in existence in New England, I give the following statements in the very words of the Rev. Cotton Mather, the distinguished minister of Sir Wm. Phips:

"It has been ever the custom in the churches of New England to expect from such persons, as they admit into constant communion with them, that they do, not only publicly and solemnly declare their consent unto the covenant of grace, and particularly to those duties of it wherein a church state is more immediately concerned, but also *first relate* unto the *pastors*, and by them unto the brethren, the special impressions which the grace of God has made upon their souls in bringing them to this consent. By this custom and caution, though they cannot keep hypocrites from their fellowship, yet they go, as far as they can, to render and preserve themselves churches of saints, and edify one another.

"When Sir William Phips was now returned to his own house he began to think himself, like David, concerning the house of God; and accordingly applied unto the North Church in Boston, that by an open profession of the Lord Jesus, he might have the ordinances and privileges of the gospel added to his other enjoyments. One thing that quickened his resolution in this matter, was a passage heard from a minister, preaching from the fifty-first Psalm; viz., this, 'to make a public and open profession of repentance, is a thing not misbecoming the greatest man alive. It is an honor to be found among the repenting people of God, though they be in circumstances never so full of suffering.' "

"Upon this excitation Sir William Phips made his address unto a Congregational Church, and had therein one thing to propound unto himself, which few persons of his age so well satisfied of infant baptism as he was, have then to ask for. Indeed, in the primitive times, although the lawfulness of infant baptism was never so much as made a question, yet we find baptism was frequently delayed by persons for superstitious reasons. But Sir William Phips had hitherto delayed his baptism because the years of his childhood were spent where there was no settled minister; and therefore he was now not only willing to attain a good satisfaction of his own internal and practical christianity, before he received the mark of it, but he was willing to receive it among those Christians that seemed most sensible of the *bonds* which it laid them under.

"Offering himself, therefore, first unto the *baptism*, and then unto the Supper of the Lord, he presented unto the pastor of the church, in his own hand-writing the following instrument; which, because of the exemplary devotion therein expressed, and the remarkable history which it gives of several occurrences in his life, I shall herewith faithfully transcribe, without *adding* to it so much as *one word*." Here, then, we have an account of Sir William Phips's religious experience in his own words:

"The first of God's making me sensible of my sins was in the year 1674," (in his twenty-fourth year), "by hearing your father, (Dr. Increase Mather, President of Harvard College), preach concerning 'The day of trouble near.'

"It pleased Almighty God to smite me with a deep sense of my miserable condition, who had lived until then in the world, and had done nothing for God. I did then begin to think *what I should do to be saved?* and did bewail my youthful days, which I had spent in vain. I did think I would begin to mind the things of God.

"Being then sometime under your father's ministry, much troubled with my burden, but thinking on that scripture, 'Come unto me, ye that are weary and heavy laden, and I will give you rest,' I had some thought of drawing as near to the communion of the Lord's table as I could. But the ruins which the *Indian* wars brought on my affairs, and the entanglements which my following the sea laid upon me, hindered my pursuing the welfare of my own soul as I ought to have done. At length God was pleased to smile upon my outward concerns.

"The various providences, both merciful and afflictive, which attended me in my travels, were sanctified unto me, to make me acknowledge God in all my ways. I have divers times been in danger of my *life*, and have been brought to see that I owed my *life* to Him that hath given a *life* so often to me. I thank God, he hath brought me to see myself altogether *unhappy*, without any interest in the Lord Jesus Christ, and to close heartily with him, desiring him to execute all his offices on my behalf.

"I have now, for sometime, been under serious resolutions, that I would avoid whatever I should know to be displeasing to God, and that I would serve him all the days of my life. I believe no man will repent of the service of such a master. I find myself unable to keep such resolutions; but my serious prayers are to the Most High, that he would *enable* me. God hath done so much for me that I am sensible I owe myself to him. To *him would I give* myself and all that he has given me. I can't express his mercies to me. But as soon as God had smiled upon me with a turn of my affairs, I had laid myself under the vows of the Lord that I would set myself to serve his people and churches here, unto the utmost of my capacity.

"I have had great offers made to me in England, but the churches of New England were those my heart was most set upon. I knew that if God had a people anywhere, it was *here*. And I resolved to *rise* or *fall* with them; neglecting very great advantages for my worldly interest, that I might come to enjoy the ordinances of the Lord Jesus here.

"It has been my trouble that since I came home, I have made no more haste to get into the house of God, where I desire to be; especially having heard so much about the *evil* of that omission. I can do little for God, but I desire to wait upon him in his ordinances, and to live to his honor and glory.

"'My being born in a part of the country where I had not, in my infancy, enjoyed the first sacrament of the New Testament, has been something of a stumbling block to me. But though I have had proffers elsewhere made to me, I resolved rather to defer it, until I might enjoy it in the communion of these churches. And I have had awful impressions from those words of the Lord Jesus in Matthew viii. 38: 'Whosoever shall be ashamed of me and of my words, of him shall the Son of Man be ashamed.' When God hath blessed me with something of the world, I had no trouble so great as this, lest it should not be in mercy, and I tremble at nothing more than being put off with a portion here.

"That I may make sure of better things, I now offer myself unto the communion of this church of the Lord Jesus."

"Accordingly on March 23, 1690, after he had given himself up, first unto the Lord, and then unto his people, he was baptised, and so received into the communion of the faithful there."

Most men, situated as he was, possessed of abundant wealth and the recipient of distinguished honor, would have sought exemption from the cares and responsibilities of *public life*. But a desire for personal ease and aggrandisement was not the feeling which possessed and ruled his breast. His aim was to do good and be useful while he lived in the world.

"Often," says his pastor, "*about*, *before*, and *after* this time, have I heard him express himself after this manner: 'I have no need at all to look after any further advantages for myself in this world. I may sit still at home, if I will, and enjoy my ease for the rest of my life. But I believe I should *offend God* in doing so. For I am now in the prime of my age and strength, and I thank God, I can undergo hardship. He only knows how long I have to live; but I think 'tis my duty to venture my life in doing good, before a useless old age comes upon me. Wherefore I shall now expose myself, while I am able and as far as I am able, for the service of my country, I was born for *others*, as well as myself.'"

Accordingly, in the spirit of these remarks, he made to the General Court of Massachusetts the offer of his own person and estate in invading Canada; believing that the Indians, in their frequent murderous assaults, were set on by the inhabitants of that country; that we could have no peace with the Indians till Canada was conquered.

Hence a naval expedition against the French, with about seven hundred men, under the conduct of Sir William Phips, was entered upon, and proved victorious in the capture and subjugation of Nova Scotia.

This led on to a *second* expedition against Quebec, with a fleet of thirty-two ships and two thousand men, all under Sir William Phips, as general and commander-in-chief in and over their Majesty's forces of New England by sea and land. If success did not attend this expedition, it was not owing to any want of ability in the commander, but mainly to the lateness of the season, and the want of coöperation by troops ordered to come down from the lakes. To pay the soldiers and seamen engaged in this invasion of Quebec, the General Court issued *bills* of *credit*, and thus originated that *system* of *credit* and *bills* of *credit*, which has ever since been in use in this country.

About this time James II., hated by the English nation, on account of his Romanism and tyranny, was driven from his throne by William of Orange, and that despotic governor, Edmund Andros, who had long been the scourge of New England, was *deposed.* Dr. Increase Mather being then in England to obtain redress for the grievances of his country, and being requested by the king to nominate a worthy person for governor, presented the name of Sir William Phips, saying in his address to the king, — "he hath done a good service for the crown by enlarging your dominions, and reducing Nova Scotia to your obedience. I know he will faithfully serve your Majesty to the utmost of his capacity; and if your Majesty see fit to confirm him in that place, it will confer a great favor on your subjects there."

The effect of this was, that Sir William Phips was invested with a commission under the king's broad seal to be Captain-General and Governor-in-Chief over the Province of Massachusetts Bay. Accordingly, having with Mr. Mather kissed the king's hand, on January 3d, 1691, he departed, and arrived in New England the May following, welcomed with the loud exclamations of that long shaken and shattered country. On his arrival, the Great and General Court of the Province appointed a day of solemn *thanksgiving* to Almighty God for the safe return of his excellency the Governor.

Suffice it to say, that for three years he faithfully and successfully discharged the duties of this high office, in a way that greatly promoted the prosperity of the people, and secured their highest commendation.

At the end of this time, by request of the king, he visited England, and while in London was seized with a cold, which proved a sort of malignant fever, terminating in his death, after a few days, on the 18th of February, 1694, in the forty-fourth year of his age. With due honor, his remains were buried in the Church of St. Mary Woolnoth, London, — New England mourning over his early departure as a public calamity, and embalming in grateful affection his virtues and his deeds.

In personal appearance, he was tall and commanding, of features comely and symmetrical, courteous and dignified in manners, and of amiable and generous disposition. He was characterized by *indomitable perseverance*, evinced in overcoming the difficulties of his neglected education, in pressing his way from humble mediocrity to elevated positions in society, in the prosecution of his voyages against great obstacles, and in the resolute discharge of high official duty.

His capacity for business is shown in the *success* which attended his enterprises, as ship-carpenter, sea-captain, commander-in-chief of His Majesty's forces by land and sea, high sheriff, and governor. As evidence of his courage, it is related of him, that when he was captain of the Algier Rose, his men mutinied, and approached him on the quarter deck with drawn swords in hand, demanding that he should join them in prosecuting a voyage of piracy. Whereupon Capt. Phips, though wholly unarmed, yet with most undaunted courage, rushed in among them, and, with blows of his bare hands, felled many of them, and quelled all the rest. When asked what made him so little afraid of dying, his answer was, "I do humbly believe the Lord Jesus Christ shed his blood for me to procure my peace with God. Why, then, should I be afraid of dying?" At the same time, he was a man of real, unsophisticated *modesty* and *humility*. Though springing from a low condition, he never seemed *proud* and *haughty*, and would very gladly have dispensed with many of the *official forms* and *ceremonies*, which custom had sanctioned.

On his return to this country, loaded with wealth and honor, he made a splendid feast to the ship-carpenters of Boston, in commemoration of God's favor to him, who had been himself a ship-carpenter. When sailing in sight of Kennebec, with armies under his command, he would call the young soldiers and sailors upon deck, and speak to them after this fashion: "Young men, it was upon that hill I kept sheep a few years ago; and since you see Almighty God has brought me to something, do *you* learn to *fear God*, and be honest, and mind your business, and follow no bad courses, and you don't know what you may come to."

The Christian temper of *forgiveness* was remarkably displayed in his life. Says his pastor: "I never saw three men in this world that equalled him in his wonderfully *forgiving* spirit. In the vast variety of his business, he met with many and mighty *injuries;* but I never did hear unto this hour, that he did ever once deliberately *revenge* an *injury*. Under great provocations, he would commonly say, ''tis no matter, let them alone. Some time or other they'll see their weakness and rashness, and give me occasion to do them a *kindness*. And they shall see that I have quite forgotten all their ill-treatment of me.' And in his life there were frequent verifications of this remark."

It was, indeed, the *moral elements* which laid the foundation of all his greatness, and was the *crowning excellence* of his character. I mean his *piety*, so *humble*, *experimental*, *solid*, *practical*. Not indeed that he made any great *display* of religion, or had any sympathy with those who did, especially if they were delinquent in private duties, or wanting in outward moralities.

Still he was *honest*, *faithful*, *steadfast* in his profession; striving to walk in all God's commandments and ordinances blameless; conscientiously attending upon the exercises of devotion and worship; upon the weekly lectures, as well as the Sabbath solemnities; upon the daily service of morning and evening prayer in his own family; as also upon private meetings of devout people, held every fortnight in the neighborhood.

"Besides all this," says his pastor, "when he had any great works before him, he would invite good men to come and *fast and pray* with him at his house for success; and when he had succeeded in what he had undertaken, he would prevail with them to come and keep a day of solemn *thanksgiving* with him. His love to Almighty God was indeed manifest by nothing more than his love to those who had the image of God upon them. He heartily loved and honored all godly men; and in so doing he did not confine *godliness* to *this* or *that party*. But wherever he saw the *fear of God* in one, of Congregational, Presbyterian, Baptist, or Episcopal persuasion, he did without any difference express towards them a *reverend affection*."

But, most of all, he loved and honored Christ's ministers, and in proportion as they were faithful and devoted to their holy calling.

Happy were it for our land, if this religion of apostles, reformers, martyrs, prelates, puritans, had been universally prevalent and predominant in the hearts of ministers and people, rulers and ruled, in this our day and in this our land. Then had not occurred this *civil war* which is now dividing and desolating this once happy land, and putting forever in jeopardy the cause of free institutions and republican government.

By our *transgressions* and *our sins* we have brought upon us the terrible judgments which we suffer. Let us, then, humble ourselves before God and *repent*, each individual and family and tribe by itself, and let us return to the good old ways of God's Word, as the prophet exhorts, "Stand ye in the ways and see, and ask for the old paths, where is the good way, and walk therein, and ye shall find *rest* to your souls."

The Eastern Coast of New England, — the arena of the conflict of the races, where alternated the fortunes of the French and English.

The following communication has been furnished by the Hon. George F. Talbot, of Machias, United States Attorney for the District of Maine.

THE HON. MR. TALBOT'S COMMUNICATION.

INFLUENCE OF THE PEOPLE OF THE EASTERN SETTLEMENTS IN FIXING THE BOUNDARIES OF THE REPUBLIC.

That Maine is not now a provincial dependency of Great Britain, instead of an important and influential State in the American Republic, is due to causes running back to its earliest settlement. It would seem to have been sound policy for the British Government, as soon as it became certain that the Canadian and Acadian provinces would not join the other provinces in the revolt against the mother country, to push its frontiers from its assured possessions on the St. Lawrence and Bay of Fundy as far southward and westward as possible. It would have been comparatively easy to achieve the permanent conquest of the greater portion of our State, then held by a feeble and scattered population, and also of the unsettled portions of New England and New York, in which remained considerable bodies of Indians, hostile to the frontier settlers. Great Britain has long since come to see the advantages to her of the possession of a territory now thrust, for three hundred miles almost, as a barrier of separation between her upper and lower provinces. Nor need we wonder that she clung so pertinaciously to the argument, which a possible construction of an uncertain clause of the treaty of 1783 furnished, to recover a portion of the territorial advantages which, as we claimed, she had surrendered in that treaty. Why then, with such strong interest to possess and such ease of acquiring this frontier State, was it suffered to pass under the dominion and fortunes of the American Republic?

History furnishes three causes of this result; a brief exposition of which may not be inappropriate to this occasion. They are: First, the influence of the nationality of the settlers of the frontiers of the countries now foreign to each other; second, the policy under which the war of the Revolution was conducted by the British ministry; and third, the active participation by the settlers of the coast of Maine in the resistance to the British arms.

It would have been supposed that when, by the treaty of 1762, all the colonies on the North Atlantic coast passed under the sovereignty of the British crown, that the general system of colonial taxation would have been met by a common resistance in all the provinces to which it was applied. The Continental Congress had strong hopes of inducing both Canada and Nova Scotia to make common cause with them in the war. The invasions of Arnold and Montgomery were undertaken, rather with the expectation of rousing allies among the French settlers, than of effecting the conquest of the province. Expeditions, with similar objects, set forth from Maine and Massachusetts to rouse the whig spirit in the eastern provinces. All these enterprises, however, ultimately failed. The provincial government, feebly supported by royal troops, resisted, and the mass of the people remained neutral and indifferent. But the invasions failed on account of the rigor of the climate and the breadth of wilderness that separated the continental army from its source of supplies.

The French race had not been electrified with the revolutionary spirit of a later age. All the instincts of their nationality, all the principles of their religious faith made them loyal and monarchical. If they had participated in a quarrel between a king and his revolted subjects, it could scarcely be on the side of the revolt. Besides the long and cruel controversy for dominion on this continent, a controversy embittered by the alliance of fierce savages, had been between them and the colonies, rather than between them and the British nation. There had been a chronic hatred and hostility begotten of religious antipathy betwixt the Puritan settlers of New England and the allied French and Indian Catholics to the east and north of them, from the time that Argal broke up the French settlement at Mount

Desert, in 1613. The colonial authorities had always been ready for invasions and expeditions against the French. If the wars between France and England were not provoked and fomented by them, they entered joyfully into them and furnished from their scanty population and treasures, men and money without stint or complaint; nor did they always wait for actual war, when an opportunity offered to strike a fatal blow at an unprotected rival settlement. Indeed, the love of territorial aggrandizement and the propagandism of the English name and faith, was far stronger in the town meeting of New England than in the British parliament or court. The colonies had borne the brunt of the conquest of Canada, and exulted over its result far more than the home government, which hardly seemed to appreciate its vast advantage to the British power. When, then, only twelve years after, a treaty had terminated these border wars and feuds, the very people most active in the violence, appealed to the conquered provinces, still smarting from defeat, for alliance and aid, it is no wonder they were received with profound indifference. Thus the spontaneous influence of the Revolution extended no farther than the animosity and passions out of which it grew, and religious and political propagandism extended no farther eastward than Massachusetts.

Ideas and not interests, ideas and not military or commercial necessities, shaped our territorial limits, and gave us our boundaries. The British crown succeeding to the French title, and, though quite unnaturally, to the French antipathies, revived as against us the old controversy of boundary. It was not settled by the treaty of 1783, because the limits of Nova Scotia itself were not determined; and not until our own time, and by the treaty of 1842, was the line, separating two forms of government and two races of people, over which two great nations had quarrelled for more than two centuries, definitively settled, — a line of more political importance on this continent than any other, unless the intense domestic agitation that has raged over *Mason and Dixon's* may have given that a preëminence.

But though the line between our possessions and the English has fallen precisely where the separating line between hostile political ideas would determine it, it might have been changed by military force. As soon as it became settled that the people of Canada and Nova Scotia could not be roused to sympathy with the revolt, British armies might have been massed in those provinces as bases of support, and have pushed their frontiers westward and southward towards the centers of the continental population. It would seem to have been easy to have driven out or subdued the entire population of Maine, sparse as it was in 1776. With the possession of Canada on the north and Nova Scotia on the east, and an absolute control of the sea, resistance to a concerted invasion could scarcely have been supported. But the policy of the war as conducted by the British ministry, never contemplated the question of boundaries. It never contemplated a treaty of separation with a part of the colonies, but aimed at the absolute subjection of the whole. The English government treated our Revolution much the same as we are now treating our own rebellion. Accordingly its first campaign was directed against Boston and Massachusetts as the head and front of the disaffection, and failed on account of the obdurate courage and united hostility of New England, which sent enormous *quotas* to the Revolutionary armies, while nearly all the people left at home were ready to serve as soldiers to resist domestic invasion. Failing to crush New England, they next tried to isolate it, to *leave it out in the cold,* and seizing the commercial and political capital to break in two the revolutionary confederation. This was the second campaign, terminating disastrously in the defeat at Saratoga. The last policy was to assault the colonies where they were weakest, both in the large percentage of loyalists and the presumed enmity of the slaves, while, though it came nearer to success than either of the others, broke down at length on account of the languid co-operation of Clinton, and the superior strategy of Washington; and with it failed all hope of preventing American independence.

Disdaining to contend for favorable boundaries, and occupied with the vast military plans, only transient and inadequate efforts were applied to make conquests upon the coasts of Maine. Even these, however, came very near success, and in addition to the influences I have already considered, it is due to the heroic courage and devoted attachment to the cause of independence by the pioneers of eastern Maine, that these remote frontiers were preserved to the American Union. The burning of Falmouth early in the war gave the inhabitants of the coast of Maine notice of what their attachment to the Revolution would be likely to cost them. The occupation for two years, by the royal forces, of the region of Penobscot, would have made that the most favorable limit at which a boundary could have been established on the return of peace, but for the spirited defense which had secured Machias and the eastern settlements to the Continental Congress.

Machias was first settled by Englishmen in May 1763. So uncertain at that period were the boundaries between Massachusetts and Nova Scotia, that the petition for an incorporation as a town was addressed to the legislature of the latter province by the people, who supposed themselves within its jurisdiction. Nova Scotia disclaimed the jurisdiction, and the act of incorporation, sent out for the king's sanction before the Revolution, was not finally passed till after the peace which established our national independence in 1784.

At the breaking out of the war in 1775, less than five hundred people, one-fifth of them, perhaps, capable of bearing arms, held this remote frontier settlement, separated from the great mass of their countrymen by hundreds of miles of forest, through which were no roads, and by several navigable rivers, over which there were no bridges. Their only channel of communication with their government and fellow-citizens was across three hundred miles of ocean, swept by the irresistible navies of the British king. Their country was not a grain producing country; and turning their attention exclusively to lumbering, they depended for subsistence upon the returns of shipments of cargoes of boards to the Boston market. If the ocean was open and lumber saleable, they lived and throve. If the ocean was shut or lumber unsaleable, they descended to the clam beds to ward off instant starvation. "When the war commenced that prostrated this commerce by which they lived, there were," as Judge Jones says in a memorial addressed in 1784 to the Massachusetts General Court, "but three weeks' provisions in the place."

It would be thought, that a people thus isolated and distressed would have had the least interest in the political questions, upon which king and colonies were about to go to war, — that their only thought would have been for their own prosperity and preservation, and that they would gladly have accepted the powerful protection of the British government for immunity for their trade or subsistence for their families. But all such pusillanimous considerations were the farthest from their thoughts. Instead of being dismayed at the fear of falling the first victims to the rage of their incensed sovereign, or apprehensive of suffering or losses to themselves, they were planning with patriotic zeal quite disproportionate to their power, how to extend the dominions of the Continental Union, and to add new provinces to the American Republic. Just after the battle of Bunker Hill they suddenly planned and splendidly executed an attack upon a British armed vessel, pursued down the harbor, thus winning the first naval battle of the Revolution.

The second year of the war, the people of Machias engaged with Jonathan Eddy, who had brought them supplies from Boston, to invade Nova Scotia.[1] A mere handful of them started eastward, passed the St. John River, and attacked the enemy at the head of the Bay of Fundy, but being repulsed were obliged to retreat through the wilderness a distance of more than three hundred miles. Nothing daunted by this reverse, they planned a new invasion the next year on a larger scale, and were expecting the arrival of stores and continental troops, who were to rendezvous at Machias, when the place was attacked by a British fleet. Sir George Collier commanded the expedition, which consisted of two forty-four and one twenty-eight gun frigates and an armed brig, and arrived in the harbor August 13th, 1777. The inhabitants raised earth works at the junction of the two rivers, stretched a boom across the channel, and stationing Indians and musket-men upon the banks, gave the invaders so warm a reception that after a two days fight they were compelled to retire. Although repeated alarms of invásion occurred afterwards, the settlers were left in peace for the rest of the war, guarding this frontier post and securing our good State for the good cause, while many people farther west, who had not even been subjected to invasion, were circulating petitions to procure British protection on the promise of neutrality. These petitions were sent to Machias for signature; and as Judge Jones's memorial states, "We re-

1 The spirit of the Machias people is well disclosed in the admirable and patriotic letter of Rev. James Lyon, the first minister of the place, to Gen. Washington, proposing an invasion of Nova Scotia with a thousand men. The learned and pious minister naively expresses himself thus: "I should be more at a loss for an able person to conduct the enterprise. I know of fitter persons than myself in many respects, but they are strangers to the province and the people. But I have dwelt there for many years, and have a personal acquaintance with almost all the principal men, and know the country well. I should rejoice, therefore, in the appointment to the necessary business, and if your excellency, together with those only who must necessarily be acquainted with the appointment, in your great wisdom should see fit to appoint me, I will conduct the expedition with the utmost secrecy, and (Deo adj.) will add to the dominions of the Continental Congress another province, before our enemies are able to defend it."

fusing, the steps we took prevented those places, who were in favor of it, from falling in, whereby the whole of the country, east of Bagaduce,[1] was preserved."

If it be asked, why these poor eastern settlers entered so zealously into a cause, which only promised them sufferings and losses; the answer is, that they were of Puritan ancestry, and looked upon Masschusetts, the leading colony of the Revolution, as their father-land. They were *republican;* and in a controversy betwixt the king and his people, their sympathies were all with the people. In taking this stand they surrendered no ancient attachments. For the wars with the French, through which their national feelings had become aroused, were quite as much wars of the American Colonies as of the British government. Some of the eastern settlers had partaken in the invasion of Cape Breton and of Canada. When, then, the controversy arose with their own sovereign about independence, these people cast their fortunes unhesitatingly with the cause of the revolutionists, without a thought of its desperation or of their own almost assured loss. In revolution, masses of men act from passion rather than from interest, nor can any conquests be permanent, that do not carry with them the ideas and principles of the conquerors. The *Yankee*, whether in eastern Maine or in Nova Scotia, was a natural rebel; and when hostilities broke out against the home government, without much regard to his personal safety, he began to plot resistance and invasion. It thus happened that the Revolution, and with it the boundaries of our republic, extended as far eastward as Massachusetts influence and culture extended, and there stopped, in spite of strenuous efforts to push it farther.

Nova Scotia,—the earliest battle ground of the races upon this continent; the home of the loyalist in Revolutionary times. Distinguished for the fascinations of its scenery and its treasures of mineral wealth, but still more distinguished for the intelligence of its people and the ability of its public men.

[1] Now Castine.

The following letter was received from the gentleman invited to make a speech in response to this sentiment:

LETTER FROM THE HON. JOSEPH HOWE.

HALIFAX, NOVA SCOTIA, 26th August, 1862.

DEAR SIR, — I have delayed till the last moment replying to the committee's kind invitation to their proposed celebration, in the hope that I might be able to accept it; and it is with great reluctance that I am compelled to decline. Lord Mulgrave is absent and I am surrounded by public duties, from which I cannot escape for some days, and am then under engagement to go to Quebec on an inter-colonial conference. Few things would afford me more pleasure than to see and hear the leading men of Maine, and to exchange thoughts with them on the day, when they meet to decorate the head waters of that mighty stream of population, which, it may be under different banners, is destined to overflow the continent.

As I cannot come, I would gladly send a sentiment, and with all my heart I say, "May PEACE be with you."

Believe me, my dear sir,

Very truly yours,

JOSEPH HOWE.

The Saco, — the home of Vines and companions in 1616, and the first seat of justice, in which the forms of the common law were put into practice.

The Fall of Quebec, — under the leadership of the heroic Wolfe, in 1759, which gave peace, security, and progress to the frontier settlements of the colonies, and supremacy to English power in North America.

Pennsylvania, — to whose archives we are indebted for the only exact account of Arnold's expedition to Canada.

The following note from the Right Rev. Dr. Stevens, a native of Bath, now Bishop of Pennsylvania, explains why a communication on this sentiment could not be furnished:

BISHOP STEVENS'S LETTER.

HOUSE OF BISHOPS, N. Y.,
October 4, 1862.

MY DEAR SIR, — Yours of the 2d inst. has just been received. Under the duties which now press upon me, and those which will devolve on me in the process of an Episcopal visitation immediately after our adjournment here, I shall be unable to prepare the desired paper for the interesting volume on the Popham Celebration.

I remain, very truly yours,
WM. BACON STEVENS.

REV. EDWARD BALLARD.

The Memory of Governor Sullivan, — the earliest Historian of his native State, and the honored Chief Magistrate of the Commonwealth of Massachusetts, of which Maine then constituted a part; his residence on the banks of the Kennebec fitted him for the study of the earliest annals of our State, and made him eminent not only in the department of law and of statesmanship, but of history.

The following letter from the Hon. Thomas C. Amory, Jr., of Boston, was prepared in reply to the request of the committee:

LETTER OF THE HON. MR. AMORY.

BOSTON, August 25th, 1862.

DEAR SIR, — I regret exceedingly that my engagements must prevent my attending the celebration of the first settlement of Maine, and responding to the sentiment in honor of James Sullivan, its earliest historian.

The preservation of whatever related to its ancient annals, was with him a constant thought; and his first contribution to the collections of the Massachusetts Historical Society, of which he was the first President, was an account of Georgetown, prepared from what he had been able to collect of its history from his neighbors, when he there commenced, about the year 1768, his professional career.[1]

He selected it as a spot peculiarly favorable to fresh efforts, possibly bearing in mind that the flourishing settlements, which in his day not only lined the shore but penetrated inland, had there their beginning.

The colony at Georgetown, and also that of Jamestown, in Virginia, nine months earlier, experienced gloomy days, overwhelming the one and darkening both with disaster. This but nerved an enterprising race to more strenuous efforts, which eventually were marked with signal success. Maine has now a larger population than the whole Commonwealth, when seventy years ago, my grandfather published his history of the District, and nearly equal to that of the Old Dominion, out of servitude. In her material prosperity, as in the character, courage, and intelligence of her people, she compares favorably with her twin sister, while in attachment to the principles of Washington and Jefferson, she has immeasurably the advantage over her.

For the practical application of those principles we have been favorably placed, and also fortunate in the character of the statesmen who have moulded our opinions and shaped our destiny. We were peculiarly fortunate in the influence exercised over public sentiment by Governor Sullivan and his cotemporaries, who, whether republican or federalist, never lost faith in the value of free institutions as the greatest of earthly blessings. If in his published writings, he attaches more than ordinary importance to an unswerving fidelity to constitutional obligations, and carries respect for State rights beyond the measure of modern politics, if he regarded the harmony and union of the States as paramount to all other political considerations, it was from a faith that the maintenance of our liberties depended upon union, and from an apprehension that in

[1] Mass. H. C., vol. 1, p. 251.

some moment of irritation we might fatally disarrange that excellent system of government, which had been established for us by our fathers on mutual compromises. No one abhorred slavery more than he did. It is a matter of historical record, that when on the bench he mainly contributed to putting an end to its existence in Massachusetts. But he recognized, both in the constitutional compact and in the national law, a limit to individual responsibility not to be overlooked.

It might be pleasant to divest the mind of present anxieties, in contemplating the interesting events of the long distant past, which it is your purpose to commemorate. But this is hardly to be hoped. No one that loves his country can, for one moment, be unmindful of her peril. And if any modern subject is to be discussed at your table, I cannot but believe that the spirit of my grandfather, Governor Sullivan, would present views of the present great issue, that might, if generally received, go far to bring about a restoration of our Union, and of our national prosperity and independence. I should have been glad for this and for the many ways in which he was connected with the history of Maine, to have been permitted, before the distinguished assemblage this occasion is sure to attract, to respond to a sentiment in honor of an ancestor, whose memory I so deeply revere. It was precisely such an occasion as he thought most favorable to the encouragement of historical tastes. At the close of the third century from the discovery of America, in 1792, after an oration, he entertained the Historical Society and all the historical characters of that day at his house, opposite the Revere on Bowdoin Square, in Boston. This celebration of the first plantation at the north, so near in time to that of Virginia, offers fruitful themes for the suggestion of associations of common origin and future fellowship, which he would have gladly improved if presented in his day. Let me hope that some one more able to do justice to his memory will be found willing to assume the task which you have assigned to me.

I remain, very respectfully,
Your obedient servant,
THOMAS C. AMORY, JR.

Rev. A. D. WHEELER, D. D., for the Executive Committee.

Change and Progress, — these make up the history of the world, mental, moral, and physical. Slowly were they written upon its pages, till Fulton, Stephenson, Henry, and Morse, solved the problem of intercommunication by steam and lightning.

No report of the speech made by the Hon. Francis O. J. Smith, of Westbrook, has been received by the committee.

The Heroes of 1776, — may the men of to-day prove themselves worthy to be called their sons.

The Memory of Ex-Governor King, — the first Governor of Maine after she ceased to be a Province of Massachusetts, and became one of the States of the Union.

The pressure of the time prevented the reverend gentleman invited, from making a speech in response, and it is now presented as a communication.

WILLIAM KING: FIRST GOVERNOR OF MAINE.

BY THE REV. JOHN O. FISKE, OF BATH.

Some of us have had the privilege of learning to-day, more than we ever knew before of the character and history of eminent men connected with the early settlement of our State. It is an honor to have descended from worthy ancestors, and to tread in the footsteps of illustrious pioneers; but it would be no credit to a people to resemble Dr. South's apple tree, whose *fruit* was intensely sour and bad, but in behalf of which it was charitably argued that it had rare excellencies in its *roots!* The inhabitants of the Pine-tree State are driven to no such lame methods of vindicating for themselves an honorable position among the other inhabitants of the country. The great man, whose memory it has fallen to my lot to recall to-day, is a signal proof that whatever of natural worth or official dignity may have been concerned in our early colonial history, nature has not failed to place her broad seal of the truest nobility on some of the sons of Maine in later days.

WILLIAM KING, the first Governor of Maine, was a product of the State, and shared the blood of a family whose abilities and public services have added historic honor to the annals of our country. His father, Richard King, was an eminent merchant in Scarboro'. His oldest brother, Rufus, was one of those great men, who laid deep and strong the foundations of our Republic, and the whole of his long career is a bright page in the records of our far-seeing and patriotic statesmen. Another brother, Cyrus, was also endowed with superior powers of eloquence and wisdom; but after a shorter public course, which afforded large promise for the future, he died at an early age, and sleeps in peace on the banks of the Saco.

William King was born in Scarboro', February 9, 1768. His early education, unlike that of his brothers to whom I have referred, was quite limited, and this deficiency was sensibly felt through his life. He resided for a few years in Topsham, where he was concerned with his brother-in-law, Dr. Porter, in a store, and was engaged, laboring with his own hands, in the manufacture of lumber. About the year 1800, he removed to Bath, where he resided until his death, which took place June 17, 1852.

He was a man whose whole presence and bearing attracted attention. His frame was large and well-proportioned, his hair and beard black, his eyebrows remarkably heavy and overhanging, his eyes keen and burning, his voice deep and agreeable. No once could receive his cordial welcome at his house, or mark his eagle eye, fixed on the preacher in the house of

God, as it was for years my privilege to do, or see him rise to address a public meeting, or listen to his ordinary conversation, or hardly pass him in the street, without being impressed that his was one of those princely and uncommon natures, which are formed for great influence in the world. He became mature in his intellectual powers at an early age, and from the first took his place as an acknowledged superior or equal in whatever society he was found.

He was chosen for some successive years a member of the Massachusetts Senate and House of Representatives, and in the midst of the eminent men of that day was felt to be one of the commanding minds of the State. One of his speeches, in reply to what he regarded as an unhandsome personal attack on him by a gentleman of high position and ability, was widely commented on at the time for its impressive power.

Indeed, *power* was the prominent attribute of the man. He never made long speeches; and without the advantages of a thorough and polished education, writing was not easy to him. He carried his points, not by *arts*, but by main strength; not by long drawn arguments, nor sonorous periods of eloquence, but by a sort of irresistible rush and crushing stroke. He was terrible and severe, sometimes rough and uncourteous, in his encounters with other men in debate. What he believed was very clear to his own mind, and he threw himself on an opponent with a fiery indignation, or sought to trample him down with a withering contempt. His views of any business in hand on which he spoke, were well-considered and usually just, and he had so fair and plausible a method of statement, and such an oracular impressiveness of manner, as if he were closing up all that could possibly be said upon the subject, as gave to his remarks great influence.

While in the Legislature he took a prominent part in securing the passage of what was called the "Religious Freedom Act;" a measure which afforded more complete religious toleration than had been enjoyed before. He was also equally conspicuous in the origination and enactment of the "Betterment Act," which contributed very successfully to the settlement of conflicting land claims, and much promoted the interests of the people. Although this Act involved a pecuniary loss to Governor King, he zealously favored it, and was accustomed through his life to refer with manifest gratification to his agency in accomplishing these measures for the public welfare.

He was by far the most prominent citizen of Maine in effecting the political separation of this State from Massachusetts. After having been almost unanimously chosen president of the convention for forming our constitution, he was elected with similar cordiality our first governor, in 1820. His appointments, while governor, were made with great impartiality and wisdom; and such were the skill and good temper, with which he put the wheels of government in motion, and touched all the springs of affairs, that as he was the *first*, he has often been called the *best* of all our governors. Such testimony concerning him has been repeatedly given by men who themselves have occupied the gubernatorial chair with honor, as well as by others well qualified to judge.

While governor, and afterwards, he strenuously urged the purchase by Maine of all the public lands, then held in common by her and Massachusetts. This measure, which then could have been executed at a comparatively small expense, would have added very greatly to our wealth, would have promoted the rapid settlement of the State, and the development of its resources, and is one of the striking testimonials to Gov. King's sagacity.

He resigned his office of governor in 1821, to accept the place of one of the commissioners on Spanish claims, a trust which he executed with faithfulness and success. He was major-general of the militia during the war of 1812–14, and in that capacity rendered valuable service. He held various other responsible offices under the general and State governments; he was a successful merchant, a generous and intelligent patron of institutions of learning, a firm friend of the interests of morality, and ever ready to contribute his large influence to purposes of public advantage.

He mingled largely with political affairs until late in life, when his great powers of mind began to falter. He corresponded extensively with public men; often entertaining them with a grateful hospitality, and with a racy and animating conversation at his home. There was a charm in that home, in the beauty, the refinement, the courtesy, the sweetness of temper, and piety of his wife, which threw around it all the attractions which he, or any others who resorted to it, could possibly desire. Her maiden name was Ann Frazier, and she was born, I believe, in Boston. He loved her with an almost idolatrous affection. Her amiability and love held her husband with a strong and instantly subduing power, whenever she approached him, though in the stormiest moments of his life.

He died full of years and honors. His funeral was attended by the chief executive of the State, and by others who had occupied the same high position; the president and professors of Bowdoin College, of which he had been for twenty-eight years an influential trustee; large numbers of other gentlemen from abroad, and of his fellow-citizens at home, attended his remains to the narrow house appointed for *all* living. With military honors, with tolling of bells, and discharge of cannon, through the streets which he used to walk in manly pride, now draped in black and hung with flags, his venerable form was borne to its last resting-place, where now it sleeps under a monument erected by the authority of the State. A greater son, in native intellectual strength, Maine has never yet produced.

His wife survived him about five years ; and his only living representative, — present on this occasion,— his son, Major Cyrus W. King, has laid our Historical Society under lasting obligations by depositing in its charge a large body of papers and correspondence belonging to his honored father, which will shed valuable light on the history of our State and the lives of many important public men.

I have said he was a man of large and comprehensive designs, and the truth is, he was often impatient of those minute details of arrangement, on which the success of the greatest purposes often depends. His great purchase of lands, now included in Kingfield, New Portland and adjacent towns, was designed for an estate and a general style of life, which would have done honor to the most lordly baron in the middle ages. His large farm in Bath, with its orchard, which, at the time it was set out, was probably the largest in the State, and its stone farm-house, with its long Gothic windows, was quite in keeping with the general character of the man. But the pecuniary profit of these investments was much diminished by a want of attention to, and economy in the little details of affairs. Indeed, he could hardly bear to look at these smaller matters. He was, for a considerable time, the largest ship owner in Bath. But I have heard that when some worthy shipmaster, on returning from a voyage, would begin to unroll before him the long columns of his accounts, the restless governor would interrupt the whole by the exclamation, "Ah! that will do. We will just lay these two accounts of debt and credit on the floor, and find the difference by pacing them off!"

A similar anecdote, illustrating this trait of his character, is told of him, when he was engaged in the saw-mill in Topsham. Happening to be in the store one day with the business of which he was not very familiar, a woman came in to buy some needles. The general handed her some, and she asked the price. "Ah!" said he, "I suppose about a cent apiece." The thrifty housewife rejoined that she could buy enough elsewhere at the rate of three or four for a cent. "Ah!" said he, "if that is the case, take the whole; throw them out; I will have nothing in my store that is not worth a cent!"

There are many stories of his methods of confounding an opponent with some sharp thrust in debate. As I have said, his mind grasped strongly the great main features of a question; and then he could have little patience with hair-splitting and verbal quibbles about details. Some discussion having arisen between him and another of the citizens of Bath in a town meeting, upon a measure of public interest, his opponent seemed to Gov. King to be unduly magnifying trifling things, and to be ingeniously and tediously dwelling on what was not at all material to the case. When he sat down, Gov. King arose, and said that the fine-spun and irrelevant talk, which had just been given off with so much of the appearance of wisdom, reminded him very much of a sort of wooden-headed, ignorant justice of the peace in some obscure town, who was once sitting, with his cocked hat, gravely listening to the arguments of two lawyers, in a case of assault and battery, which he very poorly understood. His confused perceptions had been thoroughly darkened by the quibbling of the lawyers, but with a most portentous solemnity he finally gave his judgment in these words: "The whole question here seems to depend on the words which the defendant used. It might seem to a *common mind* very immaterial, whether he said, 'Come out here, McCartee, or McCartee, come out here;' but in *point of law*, *in a high court of justice*, the terms are as wide apart as the poles of the earth!" The laugh of the assembly and the manifest confusion of his opponent, a man not easily disconcerted, told how effectually the apposite story had done its designed work.

To another, who was reflecting on him for having changed his political associations, and boasting at the same time that *he* had never varied from an opinion, which he had once formed and declared; "I perceive then," said the general, "you are one of the most extraordinary and confounded fools whom I have ever met. It is a wise man who, for good reasons, changes his opinions. A fool only never alters."

He often told me with an obvious pride, how, accompanied by a large number of personal friends, he abruptly and publicly took his departure from a convention of his former political associates, because they refused to coöperate with him in measures which he deemed very important to adopt. Party lines were nothing to him in comparison with measures, the success of which lay near his heart. This change was made from the Federalist to the Republican party, sometime previous to the war of 1812. He continued to be associated with the Republicans or Democrats, until about the year 1832, when he joined the Whigs with whom he sympathized until their party was practically annihilated, the very year of his death.

He became a member of a church soon after he removed to Bath. The organization of this church was on so liberal a basis, that evidence of true piety was not a condition of membership, and it was not understood that any very rigid discipline and inquiry were to be instituted in regard to the private affairs of the members. A zealous brother however, felt it his duty to labor with the governor on account of his occasionally allowing the use of cards in his house. In his efforts to convince Gov. King of the evil influences of such amusements, his fellow-member remarked that it led to cheating, and that he always used to *cheat himself* whenever he played. "Ah!" said the general, "I dare say this is true, but you need have no such fear for me; I never allow myself to play in such company as yours!"

He always had a great jealousy of the continuance of the black race in this country. He believed that if they remained, amalgamation would continue to go on, until the white race at last would become completely depreciated and displaced. He often referred to the significant lessons, presented in Anquetil's Universal History, of the inevitableness in any country, which tolerates the continued existence of two distinct races, of the destruction of both by the mixed race which will take their place. "I am in favor," he used humorously to say, "of removing the blacks to some distant part of our continent. There I would build a high wall between them and ourselves, and then would hang every one who should attempt to return." We should not, of course, precisely concur in just these features of his plan. But in regard to the desirableness and great importance of the colonization of the negro race, he was sustained by the concurrent opinions of the most profound statesmen, philanthropists, and divines our country has ever produced.

The memory of William King is a valued inheritance of the State of Maine. He lived, and his commanding form now peacefully reposes on the banks of that river, at whose mouth the first formal, chartered settlement of white men was made in New England. As long as Gorges shall be honored for schemes of colonial improvement, and Popham be known as an explorer, and the placid waters of the Kennebec continue to gladden an intelligent and prosperous population, the State of Maine will hold in reverential regard her first governor as one of her noblest sons.

The Art of War, — the only guarantee of the blessings of peace. For the vast improvements in the means of attack and defense of the present day, our country is mainly indebted to the ability, caution, and consummate skill of the distinguished Chief of the Bureau of Engineers of the Army of the United States.

The following letter from Gen. Totten, of the Engineer Department of the United States, was received in reply to the invitation of the committee:

LETTER FROM GEN. J. G. TOTTEN.

BANGOR, ME., August 17, 1862.

Rev. EDWARD BALLARD, Brunswick, Me.

SIR, — I have had the honor to receive your letter of the 11th instant, inviting me to the "Historical Celebration," to be held on the 29th instant, in the fort at the mouth of the Kennebec.

Your letter encloses a toast to be given on that occasion, to which I am invited to respond.

I beg you to be assured that I feel highly complimented by these attentions, and am very grateful for them; at the same time, I am obliged to add, that very pressing public duties will keep me at a great distance from a meeting which, in all that shall transpire, will, I hope, satisfy the desires of the projectors and patrons of the celebration, and mark the day as a bright and memorable one in the annals of New England.

I am very respectfully,

Your obedient servant,

JOS. G. TOTTEN.

The Coast Line of Maine, — the nursery of seamen; affording the highest advantages for maritime and commercial pursuits; more deeply indented than any on the globe. The efforts and skill of modern science have laid open its most secret recesses to the uses of commerce.

Professor Bache, of the United States Coast Survey, sent the following letter in partial response to this sentiment. It is to be regretted that he has not been at leisure to complete his purpose of furnishing the proposed communication, as indicated in a letter from Washington of last January, by reason of the increasing demands upon his time and labors in the public service. As he had made a commencement of his effort in this direction, it is hoped that his paper may still be published for the benefit of the citizens of Maine.

LETTER OF PROFESSOR A. D. BACHE.

BANGOR, ME., August 17, 1862.

SIR,— I beg leave to acknowledge the honors done me by the Executive Committee of the Historical Society, in their invitation to attend the celebration at Fort Popham. The special interest which I take in the coast of Maine makes it a source of much regret to be obliged to decline the invitation. I have been requested by the Navy Department to take part in a commission in reference to the site of a navy yard for iron clad vessels, which is to meet in New London on the 26th, and which must prevent my attendance at the mouth of the Kennebec, on the day of your celebration. I shall have a few words to say on the "Coast Line of Maine," which I shall send you soon. With great respect,

Truly yours,

A. D. BACHE.

Rev. EDWARD BALLARD, *Secretary, &c.*

Rhode Island, — the early home of toleration, and of civil and religious freedom, — the greatness of whose example is in inverse proportion to the extent of her territory.

The letter of the Hon. Mr. Arnold, here given, assigns the reason for his inability to comply with the request of the committee:

HON. MR. ARNOLD'S LETTER.

PROVIDENCE, R. I., August 28, 1862.

SIR, — By some delay of the mails, your favor, with invitation to be present at the celebration at Fort Popham to-morrow, did not reach me till last evening.

I regret very much that public duties will prevent my acceptance of the same. Our Legislature is now in session, otherwise it would afford me much pleasure to be with you on so interesting an occasion, and to reply to the complimentary toast in behalf of Rhode Island.

Respectfully yours,

S. G. ARNOLD.

Rev. EDWARD BALLARD, Brunswick, Me.

The West, — the proudest achievement of modern civilization. The march of empire Westward, — unlike the conquering hordes of Attila, or the advance of the Tartar tribes of Tamerlane, — diffuses peace, plenty, and content among the teeming millions, that throng the vast domain of the Mississippi valley.

The following letter was received in reply to the invitation of the committee from the Hon. S. P. Chase, Secretary of the Treasury:

HON. MR. CHASE'S LETTER.

WASHINGTON, D. C., August 21, 1862.

MY DEAR SIR, — I have received your card. Accept the urgency of indispensable public duties here, as an adequate apology for my omission to reply in due season to your very kind note, inviting me to attend the Historical Celebration at Fort Popham on the 29th instant, and for my necessary absence.

Yours truly,

S. P. CHASE.

Rev. EDWARD BALLARD, Brunswick, Me.

The Clergy of New England, — who, by their early and assiduous devotion to popular education, became the architects of our civilization. Their teachings and influence have saved our prosperity from degenerating into luxury, and have helped to preserve in our children the fidelity to principle and the fear of God, which characterized the fathers and founders of the New England colonies.

The Rights of New England Citizenship, — Hard Work with Freedom; Hard Thought with Generosity; Hard Fighting with Patience unto Victory.

Poetry and Art, — twin products of civilization, at once the loftiest expressions of human genius and the most elevating in their influence on mankind, — the works of a Longfellow and an Akers attest that their growth is native to our soil, and that after the lapse of two centuries and a half, the wilderness, in this highest efflorescence of humanity, has indeed been made "to blossom as the rose."

Diplomacy: the Instrument of International Conciliation, — wisely used by the Master's hand; may it guide us as it has guided our imperiled ship of State past the threatened dangers of foreign intervention, and while restoring our own, preserve the world's peace.

The Mountains and the Seas, — Hindrances to the sluggish, — helps to the adventurous.

The Valley of the Mississippi, — the garden of the world. Its development in population, wealth, and power, — in all that constitutes progress in the highest civilization, finds no parallel in history.

The Brotherhood of Nations, — the holiest of all brotherhoods; requiring only that mankind should remember their parentage, their relationship, and their inheritance.

The letter here given, from Walter Shanley, Esq., of Montreal, was sent without special reference to the sentiment with which it is now connected. But as it embodies the spirit of that sentiment, it has been deemed proper to add it in this place.[1]

MR. SHANLEY'S LETTER.

MONTREAL, C. E., 2d Sept., 1862.

DEAR SIR, — On my return from New Brunswick this morning, I found among the letters awaiting me, your printed note of the 12th ult., in relation to the two hundred and fifty-fifth anniversary celebration at Fort Popham, of the founding of the first English colony on the shores of New England; and I regret very much that my inopportune absence from home should have prevented my receiving your kind and thoughtful invita-

1 Communications on "Pemaquid," "Weymouth," "The Lost Augusta," and others, not received in season for insertion in the "Proceedings" at the Pavilion, will be found after the LETTERS."

tion in time to have allowed of my availing myself of it; for it would, I assure you sir, have afforded me the highest pleasure to have been with you on that most interesting occasion,— one so well calculated to remind us, — us of OLD and you of NEW England, — that we are of the same hearth, and to inculcate the lesson that being brethren, we should "dwell together in unity."

Trusting that your meeting of the 29th of August was a happy and joyous one for all present, and thanking you for your mindfulness of me, I remain,

Dear sir,

Faithfully yours,

W. SHANLEY.

REV. EDWARD BALLARD, *Secretary, &c.*

THE CONCLUSION.

At the close of the several addresses, the Chief Marshal read in order the sentiments already given in this account, to which no response was made in the Pavilion; thus intimating to the large assemblage the design of the commemoration, and imprinting on the public mind its true historic purport. He then announced that the proceedings, for which preparation had been made by the committee, were now terminated; and the immense gathering separated for their return to their homes, whether distant or near.

It was a remarkable incident in the history of our State, that this large number of people should turn aside from the ordinary avocations of life, in devotion to the memory of by-gone days; at a time, too, when the public mind was absorbed in events of the greatest magnitude, growing out of the civil war. And it was a subject of gratitude to a kind Providence that no personal injury was sustained by any individual among the thousands, whose interest, whether social or historical, had led them to the place and occasion. To this safety, as well as to the historical information imparted, was added the enjoyment, new to a large portion of the number, of the attractive views on the shores of the Kennebec, and the grandeur of its opening into the broad expanse of the ocean: — scenes which had been beheld with interest more than two centuries and a half before this day of anniversary remembrances, by the most distinguished navigators to these western shores. No event greater than adverse tides occurred to mar the festive spirit of the day. No violation of the proprieties of the occasion occurred in the vast assemblage in presence of the speakers to interrupt, for a moment, the course of their remarks. The interest was fully sustained to the close; and both old and young left the scene and the occasion, rejoicing in the opportunity of recalling the events of the distant past, and associating the "Ancient Province of Sabino" with one of the most memorable events in the history of New England.

LETTERS.

PRESIDENT POPHAM'S LETTER TO THE KING.

The following letter, in the Latin of his day, was written by the leader of the colony at Sabino, after an experience of about four months in the affairs of the new enterprise, and is dated two days before "the ships were to be despatched away for England,"[1] under "Capt. Robert Davies in the Mary and John."[2] It is addressed to his sovereign, whose divine right to rule he carefully recognized, in the adoption of language employed by writers in his own and a former age.[3] A certified copy of the original, from the English archives, was furnished to the Maine Historical Society, by the attention of the Hon. George Bancroft, and has been published in the fifth volume of their transactions. Its importance, and the many errors in the printing of the document, make its reproduction a suitable addition to the present volume. The orthography and punctuation are here made to conform to common usage, and therefore it is not presented as a *fac simile*, and the paragraphs are separated for greater convenience.

1 Gorges, in Me. H. C., vol. 2, p. 21.

2 Strachey.

3 Buchanan, one of the purest scholars of his time, says of Henry VIII., whose virtues certainly did not entitle him to the eminence: "Te dîs immortalibus æquum;" and Parmenius, the companion of Sir Humphrey Gilbert in his voyage to America (1583), speaks poetically of Queen Elizabeth as "diva" and "divina," to represent, perhaps, even more than here, "Her Most Sacred Majesty." Mass. H. C., vol. 9, p. 51.

A few explanatory notes are added. They will show that the venerable writer, — like many of his own and the earlier time, from Columbus onward, — had his mind filled with the expectation of finding here the productions of the east, while they were hoping to reach the country of spices and fragrance, by sailing to the west. This spirit is well described in the following extract from a distinguished scholar of our own country: "The discoverers expected to find the same animals, vegetables, minerals, and even arts, with which observation had made them familiar in corresponding latitudes of the eastern hemisphere. They came prepared to recognize resemblances, not to detect differences; * * * and naturally saw what they expected. Their early reports make constant mention of plants, animals, and mechanical processes, as of common occurrence in America, but which we now know never to have existed on this continent."[1]

The chart in Irving's Life of Columbus, places the present Isles of Japan and the country of China in a position westerly from Spain, scarcely more distant than the Atlantic shore of North America. Strachey, too, says that in Virginia, "from the topps of high hills afar off within the land, the people saie they see another sea, and that the water is there salt."[2] Mr. Major adds, "that this delusion was entertained for many years; for in a Map of 1651, *The Sea of China and the Indies* is brought close under the Alleghany Mountains," and the distance about a hundred and sixty miles. It is not to be wondered at, then, that Popham should have listened to the Indians, describing rudely or extravagantly, perhaps Lake Champlain or Ontario, in the conviction that they spoke of the Austral Sea "reaching to the regions of China."

George Popham to King James I.

13 December, 1607.

Ad pedes serenissimi regis sui humillimè se projecit Georgius Pophamus, Præsidens secundæ Coloniæ Virginiæ.

Si divinæ Majestatis Tuæ placuerit patientiæ, a servo obser-

1 Marsh's Lect. p. 243.

2 Hist. Trav. p. 31.

vantissimo ac devotissimo, quamvis indigno, pauca recipere, ab Altitudinis Tuæ claritate vel minimum alienare arbitror; quoniam in Dei gloriam, Sublimitatis Vestræ amplitudinem, et Britannorum utilitatem redùndare videantur. Peræquum igitur judicavi Majestati Tuæ notum fieri, quod apud Virginios et Moassones, nullus in orbe terrarum magis admiratur, quam Dominus Jacobus, Britannorum Imperator, propter admirabilem justitiam ac incredibilem constantiam, quæ istarum provinciarum nativis non mediocrem perfert lætitiam; dicentibus insuper nullum esse Deum verè adorandum, præter illum Domini Jacobi; sub cujus ditione atque imperio libenter militare voluerint. Tahanida, unus ex nativis qui Britanniæ adfuit, Vestras laudes ac virtutes hic illis illustravit.

Quid et quantum, in his negotiis subeundis et illorum animis confirmandis, valerem, eorum sit judicium, qui domi volutarunt scienter; agnoscens omnes conatus meos perire, cum in comparatione officii debiti erga Principem habeantur. Optima me tenet opinio, Dei gloriam facile in his regionibus elucescere, Vestræ Majestatis imperium amplificari, et Britannorum rempublicam breviter augmentari.

Quod ad mercimonium attinet, omnes indigenæ constanter affirmant, hiś inessse provinciis nuces amisticas, maciam et cinnamomum; præterea bitumen, lignum Brasiliæ, cochinelam et ambergetie, cum multis aliis magni momenti et valoris; eaque maximâ quidem in abundantiâ.

Insuper affirmativè mecum agunt, esse mare aliquod, in adversâ vel occidentali hujus provinciæ parte, non plus[quam] septem dierum itineris spatium à præsidio nostro Sancti Georgii in Sagadahoc, amplum, latum et profundum; cujus terminos prorsus ignorant: quod aliud esse non potest nisi Australe, tendens ad regiones Chinæ, quæ longè ab his partibus procul dubio esse non possunt.

Si igitur placuerit divinos habere oculos Tuos apertos in subjecto certificationis meæ, non dubito quin Celsitudo Vestra absolvet opus Deo gratissimum, magnificentiæ Vestræ honorificum, et reipublicæ Tuæ maximè conducibile, quod ardentissimis precibus vehementer exopto; et à Deo Optimo, Maximo, contendo ut regis mei Domini Jacobi Majestatem quam diutissimè servet gloriosam.

In præsidio Sancti Georgii, in Sagadahoc de Virginiâ, 13° Decembris 1607.

Servus Vestræ Majestatis omnimodis devotissimus,

GEORGIUS POPHAMUS."

The following indorsement is on the original:

"To the most heigh and mightie my gratious Sovereign Lord James of Great Brittain, France, and Ireland, Virginia and Moasson, Kinge."

The translation of this document, as it appeared in the fifth volume of the Maine Historical Society's Collections, is here adopted, with a few verbal alterations approved by the translator:

[TRANSLATION.]

At the feet of his most serene King, humbly prostrates himself George Popham, President of the second Colony of Virginia.

If it may please the patience of your divine Majesty to receive a few things from your most observant and devoted, though unworthy servant, I trust it will derogate nothing from the lustre of your Highness, since they seem to redound to the glory of God, the greatness of your Majesty, and the utility of the Britons. I have thought it, therefore, very just that it should be made known to your Majesty, that among the Virginians and Moassons,[1] there is no one in the world more admired than King James, sovereign Lord of the Britons, on account of his admirable justice and incredible constancy, which gives no small pleasure to the natives of these regions; who say, moreover, that there is no God to be truly worshipped, but the God of King James; under whose rule and reign they would gladly fight. Tahanida,[2] one of the natives who was in Britain, has here proclaimed to them your praises and virtues.

What and how much I may avail in transacting these affairs and in confirming their minds, let those judge who are well versed in these matters at home; while I wittingly avow that all my endeavors are as nothing when considered in comparison with my duty towards my Prince. My well considered opinion is, that in these regions the glory of God may be easily evidenced, the empire of your Majesty enlarged, and the public welfare of the Britons speedily augmented.

So far as relates to commerce, all the natives constantly affirm that in these parts there are nutmegs,[3] mace,[4] and cinna-

1 The people of the Bashaba's country, called "Moasham" by Gorges, 2d Book, in Maine Hist. Coll., vol. 2, p. 62. Probably it was another mode of writing the word, "Mavooshen," the name for the territory between the Kennebec and the Penobscot, given by the English, and adopted from the Indian name of some locality within the region thus denoted. The word, "Norumbega," the name of a place, was used in the same way, and embraced a large extent of country east and west of the Penobscot; to a part alone of which it was originally applied.

2 Usually called Nahan'ada.

3 *Nuces amisticas;* The last word is not found. The nearest to it is *myristicas*, which harmonizes with the expectations of the primitive voyagers, inasmuch as it indicates that these fruits were "nutmegs;" the kernel or seed of the *myristica moschata.* The *hazel-nut* was probably described by the natives. The next word makes this opinion probable.

4 *Maciam;* The *husk* of the hazel-nut; which the writer, from the words of his informers, took to be "mace;" a natural sequel to the nutmegs.

mon,[1] besides pitch,[2] Brazil wood,[3] cochineal,[4] and ambergris,[5] with many other products of great importance and value; and these, too, in the greatest abundance.

Besides, they positively assure me, that there is a certain sea in the opposite or western part of this province, distant not more than seven days' journey from our fort of St. George in Sagadahoc: a sea large, wide, and deep, of the boundaries of which they are wholly ignorant; which cannot be any other than the Southern Ocean, reaching to the regions of China, which unquestionably cannot be far from these parts.

1 *Cinnamomum;* Williamson, (I. p. 111), quoting Bigelow, (2, 146) says that "*Cinnamon*, *cassia*, the *camphor-tree* and *sassafras* belong to the same family." It, therefore, was proper for the writer, in mentioning from the natives the *sassafras*, to use a word for description from the same group, when he had no knowledge of the specific term in the language of his letter.

2 *Bitumen;* Pitch of the Pine; an early indication of the resources of the "Pine-Tree State."

3 *Lignum Brasiliæ;* The word *brasil* was in use before the discovery of America, in the sense of bright red, the color of "*braise*, or hot coals." It is found "in the Catalonian tariffs of 1221;" perhaps the African *Camwood*. "The province of Brazil was certainly so named because of a dye-wood, which gave a color, similar to that already known as *brasil*, was found there." (Marsh's Wedgewood's Etymol. Art. *Brase*, *Brasil*). The wood of the *Red-cedar* corresponds in appearance to the well known Brazil dye-wood. As its bark was deemed to have medical properties, the natives would be ready to give a good account of it to willing listeners, and speak of its *red* wood as a means of description.

4 *Cochinelam;* Capt. John Smith (Mass. H. C., 3d series, vol. 6, pp. 115, 120), speaks "of certain red berries called Kermes or Alkermes found on the coast, like those in the south of Europe used in dyeing." Josselyn refers to Smith, and quoting from Gerard's Herbal, says, "Kermes is Cutchinele," (Id. III., p. 254). Harris (Voy. vol. 2, p. 871), says, "The Persians call Cochineal, Kermes or Kerm;" which is found on a kind of oak in eastern countries. But now they are regarded as different.

5 *Ambeg*[*r*]*eti*[*m*]; "Ambergris." As formerly whales were frequent on our coast, Josselyn, also, (Id. p. 265), deemed himself authorized to speak of this, their reputed product, as having been found on our shores.

If, therefore, it may please you to keep open your divine eyes on this matter of my report, I doubt not but your Highness will perform a work most pleasing to God, honorable to your greatness, and most conducive to the weal of your kingdom, which with most ardent prayers I vehemently desire; and I beg of God, the best and the greatest, that he will preserve the glorious majesty of my Sovereign James for ages to come.

At the Fort of St. George, in Sagadahoc of Virginia, the thirteenth of December, 1607.

In all things your Majesty's most devoted servant,

GEORGE POPHAM.

The following letter from the venerable Dr. Jenks, formerly a resident of Bath, to which reference is made in his reply to the committee, expressing his inability to comply with their invitation, is here added, as in proper connection with the letter of President Popham.

REV. DR. JENKS'S LETTER.

BOSTON, Aug. 27th, 1862.

REV. AND DEAR SIR: — I have unhappily failed to find the memoranda which I mentioned, and which I was expecting to see in my Diary of 1807. And I have been equally unfortunate in regard to the volume containing the family coat of arms of Lord Chief Justice Popham. However, I have found a sufficient authority in "Burke's Armory," which I copy.

"Popham." Of "Popham, county of Hants [or Hampshire], *tempore* King John [1199—1216]; also of Huntworth, county of Somerset, and of Bagborough in the same county, as likewise of Littlecott, county of Wilts, and Shanklin, Isle of

Wight; — all bearing Argent, on a chief, Gules, two bucks' heads cabossed [fronting], Or." (Crest a stag's head erased.)

These arms are traced to "Sir John Popham, Lord Chief Justice of England, *tempore* Queen Elizabeth, second son of Alexander Popham, of Huntworth, Esq., by Jane his wife, daughter of Sir Edward Stradling, of St. Donat's Castle, county of Glamorgan." As George Popham was younger brother of the chief Justice, then probably head of the family, it would be proper to place on his coat of arms "a crescent for difference."

Though I have found no record of the visit paid to Point Popham in 1807, yet I feel certain of having been there, and at a bi-centennary celebration, — such as it was.[1] For indeed it was mostly confined to the family of Major Joshua Shaw. His son, Charles, had been a member of my family at Cambridge, and was author of the "Monody on President Willard," contained in Prof. Willard's "Memoirs," a scholar and man of taste. He wrote and published a brief "History of Boston," and we had many conversations respecting Maine. But our authorities concerning the first European colonization of the Sagadahoc region, consisted of Prince's Chronology and Sullivan's History of Maine only.

The Rev. Mr. Bartlett, in his Life of Rev. Mr. Bailey, "Frontier Missionary," has given some notices taken from publications of the "Hakluyt Society," which are, I think, additional to the quotations cited by Williamson.

[1] A notice of this visit will be found in Me. H. C., vol. 3, p. 285, and is cited on the introductory pages in reference to the Map.

I hope the result of this celebration will be a copious, well-digested, thorough exhibition of the history of the enterprise, from its design and inception to its close, — including what Prince had denominated the *branding* of the country as over-cold, and not inhabitable by men of European constitutions,— for this has long since been proved a calumny.

I am fearful my letter will not reach you in due time; and must be content if it may only show an intention to comply with my promise, had it been practicable, and that I am,

Yours truly,

WILLIAM JENKS.

Rev. PRESIDENT WOODS.

The letter here annexed, from a lineal descendant in the Popham family, introduces an extended account of its genealogy, and comes in fitting connection with the letter of the Rev. Dr. Jenks.

MR. POPHAM'S LETTER.

SCARSDALE, N. Y., Aug. 1, 1862.

REV. AND DEAR SIR: — Your very welcome and interesting letter of the 24th of July came safe to hand. I have endeavored to collect all the information in my power relative to the subject of the genealogy of our family, which I herewith enclose, hoping it may be acceptable.

I regret very much that it will not be in my power to accept your kind invitation to visit Brunswick and be present at the interesting celebration, which I assure you I should enjoy most heartily. With kind regards,

Yours very truly,

WM. S. POPHAM.

Rev. EDWARD BALLARD.

THE POPHAM GENEALOGY.

The Popham family were originally from Popham, in the county of Hampshire, England, and sprung from Gilbert Popham, of Popham, who, in the year 1200, married Jane, daughter and heiress of Robert Clarke, a feofee in trust for the manor of Popham. They were greatly distinguished by the favor of the Empress Maud, A. D. 1140, and held high and honorable stations in the reign of Henry III. To Hampshire County they gave several sheriffs; viz., Robertus de Popham, 1227; Stephanus de Popham, cir., 1428. Sixth in descent from Gilbert, was Sir John Popham, Knight of the Bath, Lord Chief Justice of the Queen's Bench, purchaser of the Littlecott estate, Wiltshire, England. This individual died A. D. 1607, and his remains repose under a magnificent tomb in the church of Wellington, surrounded by a palisade, and on a tablet are the effigies of himself and lady Popham. His only son was Sir Francis Popham, Knight of Littlecott. This gentleman, together with his son Alexander, became so obnoxious to King Charles I., that he excepted them both out of the general pardon. John Popham, eldest son of Sir Francis, was, for many years, a gentleman of the household to King James I. On the restoration of Charles II., he removed to Ireland and there purchased the Bandon estate, county of Cork. His only son he significantly named Ichabod, "the glory is departed." Ichabod left one son, John, the father of James and grandfather of William Popham, of Bandon, whose son was the late Major Wm. Popham, of Scarsdale, N. Y., who was born in the town of Bandon, Cork County, Ireland, September 19, 1752. He was brought to this country at the early age of nine years, and his parents settled in the town of Newark, Delaware. It was his intention to enter upon the holy office of the ministry; but on the breaking out of the Revolutionary war he was fired with military zeal, and accepting a commission in the army, immediately raised a company in the defense of his country. He afterwards settled in the legal profession in the city of New York. Late in life he was chosen President General of the Society of the Cincinnati, and held the office at the time of his decease at the age of about a hundred years.

The writer of the foregoing letter is the oldest living representative of the family in this country. In Canada, John Popham, Esq., Advocate, Montreal, bearing the name of the Chief Justice, is a lineal descendant of the Somersetshire family.

REPLY FROM THE PRESIDENT OF THE UNITED STATES.

EXECUTIVE MANSION,
WASHINGTON, Aug. 23, 1862.

MY DEAR SIR:—The President has received your kind letter of the 12th of August, inviting him to join in the celebration of the anniversary of the founding of the first English Colony on the shores of New England. He directs me to thank you for the courtesy of the invitation, and to express his regret that his engagements will not permit him to avail himself of it.

Very truly,
Your ob't servant,
JOHN HAY.

Rev. EDWARD BALLARD.

REPLY FROM LORD MULGRAVE, GOVERNOR OF NOVA SCOTIA.

GOVERNMENT HOUSE,
HALIFAX, N. S., 20th Aug. 1862.

SIR:—I am directed by His Excellency the Earl of Mulgrave, to express his regret that he is unable, in consequence of other engagements, to accept the kind invitation of the Committee of Management to be present at the celebration of the two hundred and fifty-fifth anniversary of the founding of Maine. I have the honor to be, sir,

Your obedient servant,

WILLIAM HICKMAN, R. S.

FROM THE GOVERNOR OF MAINE.

STATE OF MAINE, EXECUTIVE DEPARTMENT,
AUGUSTA, August 16th, 1862.

EDWARD BALLARD, ESQ., *Sec'y of Executive Committee.*

DEAR SIR, — I have the honor to acknowledge the receipt of your invitation of the 12th inst., to attend the public celebration on "the two hundred and fifty-fifth Anniversary of the Founding of the First English Colony on the shores of New England," and shall be pleased to be present.

Respectfully yours,

I. WASHBURN, JR.

FROM GOVERNOR ANDREW.

COMMONWEALTH OF MASSACHUSETTS,
EXECUTIVE DEPARTMENT, BOSTON, Aug. 21st, 1862.

Rev. EDWARD BALLARD, *Secretary, &c.*

DEAR SIR: — I regret that my official engagements will prevent me from accepting the invitation, with which I am favored, to attend at the celebration of the anniversary of the first British colonial settlement on the shore of New England. Although there are not such immortal associations of great religious and political ideas, with the landing of Popham and Gilbert on the Kennebec, as are inseparable from the memory of Plymouth, yet in these times there is no truer source of inspiration for the needs of the present hour, than in recollection of the faith, the courage, and the principles of our forefathers. I have the honor to remain,

Respectfully, your obedient servant,

JOHN A. ANDREW.

FROM THE HON. MR. BANCROFT.

NEWPORT, R. I., 27th Aug. 1862.

MY DEAR SIR: — Absence from New York prevented my duly receiving your favor of the 14th, which was addressed to me at that city, while I have been passing the month of August here. Various causes combine, at this late moment, to prevent my joining your party; a celebration which otherwise it would have been most agreeable to me to have shared.

I am glad to see that in reckoning O. S. you have avoided the blunder made respecting the landing at Plymouth.

Very truly your obliged,

GEORGE BANCROFT.

REV. EDWARD BALLARD.

FROM PRESIDENT SPARKS.

CAMBRIDGE, MASS., 21st August, 1862.

DEAR SIR: — I have received your note inviting me to attend the public celebration proposed for the 29th instant. It would give me great pleasure to be present on so interesting an occasion, and if nothing should intervene to prevent it, I shall endeavor to be there. With thanks to the Committee for this mark of their attention,

Very respectfully yours,

JARED SPARKS.

REV. EDWARD BALLARD.

FROM HON. MR. CUSHING.

NEWBURYPORT, MASS., 8th Nov., 1862.

DEAR SIR: — I have just received your favor of the 1st of October, which reminds me also of the invitation addressed to me during my absence from home. It will afford me pleasure to send you some remarks on the subject of Chief Justice Popham and his connection with America, if there be time for your purposes, in the midst of my own professional engagements.

I beg you to let me know the progress of your work, and the period of its probable completion, by a line in return; and I remain meanwhile,

Your ob't servant,

C. CUSHING.

Rev. EDWARD BALLARD.

FROM HON. MR. PALFREY.

BOSTON, MASS., August 22d, 1862.

GENTLEMEN: — It would give me very great pleasure, if it were in my power, to accept the invitation with which you honor me, to be present at your commemoration of the arrival of the English company, part of which passed the winter of 1607–8 at the mouth of the Kennebec. But I had made engagements for the last week of this month in another direction, before I received your note.

I found it yesterday awaiting me on my return from an absence of several days. But for this, your obliging attention would have been earlier acknowledged.

Be pleased to accept my best thanks for it and the assurance of my wish for the successful result of your arrangements.

I have the honor to be, gentlemen,

With high regard, your ob't servant,

JOHN G. PALFREY.

Messrs. B. C. BAILEY and others, *Executive Committee, &c.*

FROM HON. MR. GOODWIN, LATE GOV. OF. NEW HAMPSHIRE.

PORTSMOUTH, N. H., Aug. 26, 1862.

GENTLEMEN: — It is with great regret that I am obliged to decline the kind invitation I have received from you, on account of pressing engagements.

There is no place that ever gives me so much pleasure to visit as my native State; and no place in that State would be more agreeable to me than the one to which I am invited, hallowed, *as it is*, by so many pleasant historical recollections of our forefathers. I am, gentlemen, with much respect,

Your obedient servant,

ICHABOD GOODWIN.

Messrs. B. C. BAILEY, and others, *Executive Committee.*

FROM JUDGE TANEY.

WASHINGTON, D. C., August 28, 1862.

SIR: — The letter of the Executive Committee, inviting me and the ladies of my family to the public celebration on the 29th inst., of the two hundred and fifty-fifth anniversary of the founding of the first English colony on the shores of New England, has been forwarded to me from Baltimore, but unfortunately, not in time to enable me to reply before the day appointed for the celebration. But it is not too late to return my thanks to the Executive Committee for the honor they have done me, and to express my regret that I cannot be present upon an occasion so full of historical interest. My advanced age and the length of the journey would have put it out of my power to attend, even if the invitation had been received in time. Accept for yourself and for the Executive Committee the high respect of

Your obedient servant,

R. B. TANEY.

Rev. EDWARD BALLARD, Brunswick, Me.

FROM HON. L. BRADISH.

SARATOGA SPRINGS, N. Y.,
August 25th, 1862.

Rev. EDWARD BALLARD, *Secretary, &c.*

DEAR SIR: — I am this morning honored by the receipt of your communication, inviting me individually, and officially as President of the New York Historical Society, to be present at "the Public Historical Celebration," on the 29th inst., at the site of Fort Popham, near the place of the original Fort St. George, at the mouth of the Kennebec River, in the ancient Province of Sabino, of the two hundred and fifty-fifth anniversary of the founding of the first English Colony on the shores of New England, August 19, 1607, O. S.

I regret exceedingly that neither my engagements, nor the present state of my health will permit me the high gratification thus politely offered in your invitation. With the expression of my regrets, therefore, it only remains for me to request that you will be pleased to receive, for yourself, and to communicate to the Committee and Society you represent, my cordial and due acknowledgments for your kind recollection of me, on an occasion of so great interest, as the one in question; an occasion on which will be worthily commemorated one of the most important eras, and one of the most interesting events in the chronicles of our country,— an era and event which form one of the first chapters in the history of a great people.

I have the honor to remain,
Dear sir, very respectfully,
Your obedient servant,
L. BRADISH,
President of the N. Y. Historical Society.

FROM THE NEW YORK HISTORICAL SOCIETY.

At a stated meeting of the New York Historical Society, held at its hall, on Tuesday evening, October 7, 1862, the following resolution was adopted:

Resolved, That this Society has observed with pleasure the efforts of the Historical Society of Maine to perpetuate the earliest history of their State, by associating important historic events with the great works of national defense of the United States Government; that they acknowledge with satisfaction the courtesy extended by the Historical Society and the citizens of Maine, in inviting the Society and its officers to participate in the commemorative celebration of the founding of the first colony on the shores of New England on the two hundred and fifty-fifth anniversary of that event, on the 29th of August, 1862, at which time a Memorial Stone was placed in the walls of Fort Popham, commemorating the establishment of the first Protestant civil government on the shores of New England; and that this Society cordially approves the act of its President, in his acknowledgment and reply to the invitation to participate in that celebration.

Extract from the Minutes,

ANDREW WARNER,
Recording Secretary.

FROM THE PRESIDENT OF THE N. E. SOCIETY OF MONTREAL.

MONTREAL, 26th August, 1862.

Rev. EDWARD BALLARD, *Secretary Public Historical Celebration.*

DEAR SIR:—I regret that business engagements will not allow me the pleasure of accepting your kind invitation to be present at the public celebration of the two hundred and fifty-fifth anniversary of the founding of the first English Colony on the shores of New England; but I beg to say that the New

England Society of Montreal deeply sympathize with their New England brothers in this dark hour of their country's history, and believe that the same kind Providence that led the Popham Colony to the shores of New England in 1607, is still the God of her children, and will safely guide them through the conflict that they are now engaged in; that the principle of civil and religious liberty will be still maintained; and "free thought, free speech, and a free press," will yet be enjoyed in the whole United States.

Yours very respectfully,

H. A. NELSON, *Pres. N. E. Society.*

FROM CHIEF JUSTICE HORNBLOWER.

NEWARK, N. J., August 29th, 1862.

Messrs. B. C. BAILEY and others, *Executive Committee on Celebration of First English Colony in New England.*

GENTLEMEN:—Your kind invitation to attend the public celebration of the two hundred and fifty-fifth anniversary of the founding of the first English Colony on the shores of New England, at Fort Popham, was duly received, and would have been sooner answered had not my increasing infirmities prevented me from writing. I thank you for this mark of attention, and I would have been pleased to attend the celebration had my health and strength and other circumstances permitted. But having myself lived through just one-third of the period which has elapsed since the founding of the colony referred to (viz. 85 years), I do not possess sufficient vigor to make such a long journey. And, then, the present torn and bleeding condition of my native country, and the disasters which threaten its cherished system of government, affects with sadness all the once glorious and animating associations of its history. I feel, therefore, that I should have but illy enjoyed the festivities of your anniversary, had I been able to attend.

Respectfully, your obedient servant,

Jos. C. Hornblower.

FROM HON. W. H. Y. HACKETT.

Portsmouth, N. H., August 22d, 1862.

My Dear Sir:—I have received your favor of yesterday's date inviting me in behalf of the Executive Committee to attend the Popham celebration on the 29th inst., and to respond to a sentiment on the early Piscataqua settlement.

I regret to say that I am so circumstanced that it will be out of my power to be with you on that occasion. I thank you and the committee for an invitation which I would gladly accept.

If able to participate in your festivities the substance of my response would be: "If the Kennebec was colonized before the Piscataqua, the people on the banks of the Piscataqua will not be behind those on the banks of the Kennebec, in defending those principles which led to the settlement and colonization of both."

I hope you will not deem it impertinent in me to suggest that the Rev. Charles Burroughs, D. D.,—one of my predecessors in the Presidency of the N. H. Historical Society,—resides in this city, and if the committee should think it proper to invite him, he would be likely to attend.

I am, very respectfully, your obedient servant,

W. H. Y. Hackett.

Rev. A. D. Wheeler, D. D., Topsham, Me.

FROM WILLIAM TURNER, ESQ.

St. George's Society,
Montreal, C. E., August 22d, 1862.

Rev. Edward Ballard,

Sir:—I am instructed by the President of this Society, (the Hon. George Moffatt), to acknowledge the receipt of a circular handed to him by John Lewis, Esq., the late President, inviting him to assist at a public celebration on the two hundred and fifty-fifth anniversary of the founding of the first English Colony on the shores of New England, Aug. 19th, 1607, &c.

The President desires me to express his thanks for the kind invitation and his regret that other engagements will not allow him to be present on an occasion so interesting.

The invitation has, however, been forwarded to the First Vice President, J. J. Day, Esq., who is sojourning at Portland, or the vicinity, and who should it come to his hands in time, will doubtless do himself the pleasure of representing this Society on the occasion.

I have the honor to be, Sir,
Your very obedient servant,
Wm. Turner, *Secretary.*

FROM REV. DR. HEDGE.

Brookline, Mass., Aug. 20th, 1862.

To the Executive Committee for the celebration of the Anniversary of the Settlement of Fort St. George.

Gentlemen:—I acknowledge with many thanks your favor of the 12th inst., inviting me to be present at the celebration of the two hundred and fifty-fifth anniversary of the first settlement of the English in New England.

The occasion is one of great interest, and like all attempts to uncover and illustrate the antiquities of our country, it has my warmest sympathy. I was too long a citizen of Maine not to feel a personal pride in her past, as well as in her present and her future. I glory in her historical memorials as well as in her industrial and civil promise.

That early settlement at the mouth of the Kennebec carrying the history of New England farther back by several years than the landing of the Pilgrims of Plymouth Colony, and bringing it near to the beginning of the 17th century, is a fact well worthy of commemoration as the first act in the annals of Maine. I rejoice to know that historical interest and patriotic feeling have combined to give it the prominence it deserves.

Nothing would give me greater pleasure than to be present with you on that occasion, but circumstances beyond my control will oblige me to forego that privilege.

Hoping that the celebration proposed may prove every way successful and satisfactory to all concerned in it,

I am, gentlemen, your obliged servant,

FRED. H. HEDGE.

Messrs. B. C. BAILEY, J. O. FISKE, OLIVER MOSES, &c., &c.

FROM PRESIDENT KING.

COLUMBIA COLLEGE, N. Y.
PRESIDENT'S ROOM, 25th Aug., 1862.

GENTLEMEN:—Your invitation to be present at the public celebration "of the two hundred and fifty-fifth anniversary of the founding of the first English Colony on the shores of New England," on the 29th inst., finds me and my household in deep affliction at the loss, within a few days, of my youngest son, who had just reached the age of manhood, with every promise of a vigorous, useful, and honorable life.

Under other circumstances the opportunity thus offered to me would have been eagerly embraced to show my affection and respect for those founders; and to claim, in right of my father's blood and birthright, some share in the inherited glories of such an ancestry.

May that star which has thus far directed the progress of your great Commonwealth, which on every ocean has guided in safety your multitudinous shipping, and which now burns anew with undimmed lustre in the van of the great battle waging by the freemen of our land for the preservation of its liberties and Union, continue to shed its heavenly light and life over the strong-handed and high-hearted race, whose beginnings you meet to commemorate.

In the bonds of a common fellowship,

I remain, very truly yours,

CHAS. KING.

REV. EDWARD BALLARD, *Secretary, &c.*

FROM REV. DR. BEARDSLEY.

SECRETARY OF NEW HAVEN HISTORICAL SOCIETY.

NEW HAVEN, CONN., August 26th, 1862.

REV. AND DEAR SIR:—My engagements will not allow me the pleasure of being present at the "public celebration on the two hundred and fifty-fifth anniversary of the founding of the first English Colony on the shores of New England."

I regret this the more as I take special interest in all historical researches, and in all gatherings designed to perpetuate the memory and the deeds of the first settlers of our country. Although the colony of Popham, which sought to transfer the religion and civilization of England to the wilds of North America, met with disaster and became disheartened,—still I am glad that the enterprise is to be commemorated at this late day; and that henceforth it will be more widely known how that the shores of the Kennebec thirteen years before the landing of the Pilgrims at Plymouth Rock, echoed to the voice of a

Protestant faith, and to the sound of the pure and fervent Liturgy of the Church of England.

Maine, within my recollection, has risen from a province in the Commonwealth of Massachusetts to the dignity of a great State, and while there may be no descendants of those who belonged to the colony at Sagadahoc, you have the descendants of noble men who shared in the earlier perils of our government, as their sons share in the later.

In looking over the names of your "Executive Committee," I thought of Jacob Bailey at Pownalborough — a man of many trials and persecutions — and of Wheeler at Georgetown, for several years his only counselor and co-worker in the missions of the Church of England in Maine. I am not aware that your State contains persons of my own name — but I know that just over the line, in the British territory, there *were* branches that shot off from the parent tree in the storms of the revolution; and if they have since sprung up and had a comely growth, it will redound to the credit of an honored ancestor; but if otherwise, it will not be the first time in history that the branch has so degenerated as to yield no wholesome fruit.

Thanking you for your invitation and wishing you a pleasant and successful gathering,

I remain,

Very truly your friend and brother,

E. E. Beardsley.

Rev. Edward Ballard, *Secretary, &c.*

FROM HON. MR. STEWART OF THE BRITISH EMBASSY.

Washington, D. C., August 19th, 1862.

Sir: — I regret that my engagements here will prevent my being able to avail myself of the invitation which you have done me the honor to address to me, in the name of the Executive Committee, who have undertaken to manage the approaching public celebration of the founding of the first English Colony on the shores of New England.

I may also mention that Lord Lyons' absence in England, renders it impossible for him to be present upon that interesting occasion.

Begging that while you express my regret to the Committee, you will, at the same time, convey to them my thanks for their courteous invitation,

I am, sir, your most obedient,
Humble servant,
W. STUART.

Rev. EDWARD BALLARD, Brunswick, Me.

FROM THE LATE DR. FRANCIS.

CAMBRIDGE, MASS., Aug. 20, 1862.

GENTLEMEN: — Accept, I beg you, my very grateful acknowledgments for the honor you have done me in extending to me an invitation to attend the "public celebration of the founding of the first English Colony," &c., on the 29th of August. Few things, I assure you, would gratify me so much as to be with you in the enjoyment of an occasion so full of important historical interest. I regret, however, that in all probability I shall be obliged to deny myself this pleasure, as the time when the celebration is to take place coincides with the commencement of the next term in our Divinity School, the duties of which will require my presence here. I hope, I doubt not, that you, and all who may be with you, will enjoy highly the reminiscences and the grateful excitement of the day.

Most respectfully yours,
CONVERS FRANCIS.

Messrs. B. C. BAILEY, J. O. FISKE, &c.

FROM THE REV. H. G. STORER.

OAK HILL, SCARBOROUGH, Aug. 25, 1862.

DEAR SIR: — Please accept my thanks for the honor done me by your invitation of the 12th inst. Twenty-five years since, I was pleasantly attacked by what is sometimes styled "the Antiquarian Fever;" and in its earliest stages became deeply interested in the Popham settlement at the mouth of the Kennebec, — *painfully* interested in it, because *Maine* came so near to being "the mother of New England," and as old as "the old Dominion" itself, and yet *lost* that honor by a sad mishap. From that day to this I have never ceased to regret that lost wreath of laurel, which should have hung on the trunk of our Pine; and have been so long waiting for an auspicious day on which to visit the spot where *our* "Plymouth Rock" first appeared for one dreary winter, and then reappeared elsewhere. Great is my regret that I cannot visit it on the day, when its attractions will be so greatly multiplied by the presence of so much learning, wisdom, wit, and beauty; but the loss is all my *own*, exclusively, and may the sun shine brightly on the more favored ones who shall be there.

Gratefully yours,

H. G. STORER.

Rev. EDWARD BALLARD, *Secretary, &c.*

FROM JOS. DOW, ESQ., PRESIDENT, OF N. H. HISTORICAL SOCIETY.

HAMPTON, N. H., Aug. 23, 1862.

Rev. EDWARD BALLARD,

DEAR SIR: — Your circular, of the 12th inst., has been received. I am very much obliged to the Executive Committee and yourself, for the honor of an invitation to be present "at the public celebration on the two hundred and fifty-fifth anniversary of the founding of the first English Colony on the shores of New England," to take place on the 29th instant.

The settlement at the mouth of the Kennebec, near the close of the summer of 1607, although it failed to be permanent, is, nevertheless important *as a historical event.* It is well, therefore, that it should be remembered; and I am glad that now, after the lapse of so many years, measures have been taken for having it celebrated in an appropriate manner. I feel assured that the occasion will be one of interest and pleasure to all who may enjoy the rich privilege of joining in the celebration. It would afford me a great deal of pleasure to be with you on this occasion, but a previous engagement at Concord, N. H., will compel me to forego this pleasure.

Yours sincerely,

JOSEPH DOW.

FROM JOHN E. GODFREY, ESQ.

BANGOR, Aug. 25th, 1862.

GENTLEMEN: — I regret that my engagements at the time, will prevent my accepting your kind invitation to be present at the "Celebration on the two hundred and fifty-fifth anniversary of the founding of the first English Colony on the shores of New England, at the site of Fort Popham," on the 29th inst.

I well remember the feeling of regret I experienced, when first reading the history of this colony, many years ago, that it had not succeeded, and given to our good State the advantages of the first permanent settlement of New England, which afterward accrued to Massachusetts. And I was disappointed at the want of pluck and perseverance in the colonists. But when I examined further, and became satisfied of the character and objects of the patrons of the colony, I was not surprised at its failure.

The principal individuals of the projectors of this enterprise were Lord John Popham and Sir Ferdinando Gorges. The former was an individual whose varied life had given him, at the age of seventy, a singularly marked character. He was of gentle parentage. In childhood he was sickly, but, having been stolen by gipsies, the life he led with them invigorated his constitution, and he was afterward strong and athletic. He was educated at Oxford in classical and theological lore, then put to the study of the law, when he became a drunkard, a gambler, and a highwayman. At thirty he changed his course of life, and applied himself so closely to study, that he became, in the estimation of Lord Coke, a "consummate lawyer." Many important offices were conferred upon him, and finally that of Lord Chief Justice of England. In the discharge of the duties of this office he exercised so great severity, that he acquired the title of the "hanging judge;" and he had such regard for the emoluments, that he accumulated an immense fortune. His coadjutor, Sir Ferdinando, was an adventurer.

Under the auspices of such men, it was not difficult to understand the objects of the enterprise. Nor was it difficult to believe that the forty-five of the hundred colonists who passed the winter near the "site of Fort Popham," were actuated by no higher motive, such as influenced the Plymouth colonists. Had they been men of strong character and high principle, like the Massachusetts men, and come here for "conscience sake," the fate of the colony would have been very different, notwithstanding the death of Sir John Popham and his brother George, the President of the colony, and the return of the second in command, Sir Raleigh Gilbert, to look after a fortune that had fallen to him; and, notwithstanding the destruction of their store-house and provisions by fire, the supposed "sterility and inhospitality of the climate," and the fear of the savages. And its fate would probably have been different, if the colonists had had even the enterprise of Gorges, who declared that, "as to the coldness of the clime, he had too much experience in the world to be frighted by such a blast, as knowing many great kingdoms and large territories more northerly seated, and by many degrees colder, were plentifully inhabited, and divers of them stored with no better commodities than these parts afford."

States must be founded by the right men in order to succeed. Had these been the right men, Maine, instead of becoming for a time an appendage to the mother State, would have been itself the mother State with all its glorious traditions.

It is well to celebrate important epochs in the history of our State. There are some such. We could wish that her history were more glorious. She is, however, destined to have a glorious history. With such inexhaustible resources, with such a vigorous, enterprising, intelligent, and virtuous population as she possesses, she must, at some future day, become a leading State upon this continent, and, perhaps, *the* leading State of our great galaxy, again to be united, and to be restored to its former splendor. In the meantime, let us do justice to the history she possesses;

> "Nothing extenuate,
> Nor set down aught in malice."

I am, very respectfully,
Your obedient servant,
JOHN E. GODFREY.

Messrs. B. C. BAILEY and others, *Executive Committee.*

FROM HON. MR. HALL, PRESIDENT VT. HISTORICAL SOCIETY.

NORTH BENNINGTON, VT., Aug. 23d, 1862.

DEAR SIR: — It would afford me much gratification to attend your celebration of the two hundred and fifty-fifth anniversary of the first decided English attempt to establish a permanent colony on the shores of New England, but other engagements with which I cannot dispense, must prevent it. Trusting that the efforts of your people and their committee to call to mind, and to cause to be duly appreciated, the merits and sufferings of the Pophams and Gilberts and their associates of the ancient time, will be entirely and agreeably successful.

I am, dear sir,

Very respectfully yours,

HILAND HALL.

Rev. EDWARD BALLARD, *Secretary, &c.*

FROM RIGHT REV. BISHOP McILVAINE.

CINCINNATI, OHIO, Aug. 26, 1862.

DEAR SIR: — It was only yesterday that I received the note of the Executive Committee, inviting me to the approaching celebration of the founding of the first English Colony on the shores of New England. I know well with what pleasure I should meet the thousands whom that interesting occasion will call together. But circumstances do not allow me to do more than express my kindest wishes for their mutual enjoyment, and my hope that, gathered around that birth-place of New England population and of the influences which have contributed so powerfully to form the character and promote the prosperity of our whole country, they may depart thence animated with new zeal to put down and destroy the wicked rebellion by which the very being of our country is now so imminently endangered. I remain, very truly yours,

CHARLES P. McILVAINE.

FROM G. F. HOUGHTON, ESQ., SEC'Y OF VT. HISTORICAL SOCIETY.

ST. ALBANS, VT., 20th Aug., 1862.

Rev. EDWARD BALLARD, *Secretary, &c.*

REV. AND DEAR SIR:—For the courteous invitation extended

through you to me to attend the public celebration of the founding of the first English Colony on the shores of New England, I desire to return my grateful acknowledgments. I regard the invitation as a compliment to the Vermont Historical Society, whose Recording Secretary it is my good fortune to be. That Society as well as the Maine Historical Society, which has the advantage of your services as Recording Secretary, is actively engaged in "bringing from darkness into light," such facts as may tend to illustrate her earliest and most interesting history. The result of the action of the Historical Societies in New England in those departments of knowledge, which have but few attractions to the general student and common reader, can hardly be over-estimated. It is highly gratifying to perceive daily proofs that a taste for historical research is increasing throughout the country ; and perhaps, no better mode for awakening a love for antiquity can be devised than to celebrate in a fit manner, such events in American history, as the one you propose to celebrate on the 29th day of August, 1862, at the mouth of the old Sagadahoc.

As prior engagements will preclude the possibility of my being present on this interesting occasion, will you pardon me for expressing a hope that a full and detailed report of this celebration will be prepared and suitably published and be distributed far and near, that the pleasure to which the occasion gives birth may be enjoyed, in a modified manner, by those unable to be present ?

Cherishing a lively remembrance of your past courtesy, and thanking your Executive Committee anew for their polite invitation, I am, Rev. and dear sir,

Your friend and ob't servant,

GEORGE F. HOUGHTON.

FROM GEORGE POPHAM SEWALL, ESQ.

BANGOR, 27th August, 1862.

SIR:—I regret to inform you that the discharge of public duties preclude the possibility of my being present at the Fort Popham celebration.

I regret it the more, as my first recollection of life was at the spot on which you will gather, and I have the honor to bear the name of its first great and distinguished tenant.

I am, very respectfully,
Your most obedient,
G. P. SEWALL.

Hon. J. A. POOR, Portland.

FROM MR. EZRA ABBOT.

CAMBRIDGE, MASS., August 21, 1862.

DEAR SIR:—I have had the honor to receive from you an invitation to attend the public celebration, to take place on the 29th inst., of the two hundred and fifty-fifth anniversary of the founding of the first English Colony on the shores of New England. Begging you to accept my thanks for your polite invitation, I regret to say that my engagements are such that it will be out of my power to be present on this interesting occasion.

The historical event which you propose to commemorate, might justify the proud motto on the shield of our native State; but the promptitude of her response to the call of the country in its hour of peril, the gallantry of her sons on the field of battle, and the noble spirit of patriotism which everywhere stirs the hearts of her men and women, show that she is still determined to be found in the van. Let us not doubt that the upas of treason shall fall, when the lumbermen of Maine lay their axes at the root of the tree!

With great respect, I am,

Yours truly,

EZRA ABBOT.

Rev. EDWARD BALLARD, *Secretary, &c.*

FROM CAPT. GEORGE PRINCE.

WASHINGTON, D. C., August 25th, 1862.

Rev. EDWARD BALLARD, *Secretary, &c.*

DEAR SIR:—I have this day received your invitation to attend the public celebration of the two hundred and fifty-fifth anniversary of the founding of the first English Colony on the shores of New England.

Circumstances beyond my control, will forbid me the pleasure of being present on that highly interesting occasion; but I may be permitted to say that I fully believe that the site of Fort Popham, is near the place of the original Fort St. George, constructed more than two centuries and a half ago, by the Popham and Gilbert colony. They entered the mouth of the "Sachadahoc," passing in by the island of "Satquin," names yet retained, and familiar to us all. They landed on the west side of the river near its mouth, on what is described as "almost an island."

Hunnewell's Point seems to answer to the description better than any other locality; and the antiquarians, who, in the beginning of the present century, or earlier, made observations, and thought they found evidences that the colony was located on Stage Island, must have been deceived by the remains of some ancient fishing station, but of a more recent date than the Popham colony.

Two hundred and fifty-five years have hidden all traces of

this little pioneer band, as effectually as the tide waters cover the anchoring ground of their gallant ships, the "Gift of God," and the "Mary and John."

The discovery of the river the year before by Martin Prinn, bid fair to turn the tide of emigration northward, so flattering was the account he gave of it; and Capt. Popham's letter to the king speaking of the nutmeg and cinnamon trees abounding in the region, was calculated to increase the excitement, until the voluntary return of the whole colony in 1608, again turned the current southward.

I remain, very respectfully,
Your obedient servant,

GEO. PRINCE.

FROM THE HON. JUDGE HARVEY.

CONCORD, N. H., August 27th, 1862.

DEAR SIR:—I must thank you and the Executive Committee for an invitation to be present at the anniversary of the celebration of an important event in the history of the early settlement of the country on the 29th of this month.

I am sorry to say that I am prevented from availing myself of the pleasure it would give me to be present.

It is well for us, I imagine, to keep in remembrance events connected with the early settlement of our country, though they be in times gone by; for amidst the gloom that now hangs over us, it is impossible to say, what, of the future, we may wish to remember.

Your obedient servant,

MATTHEW HARVEY.

REV. EDWARD BALLARD, *Secretary, &c.*

FROM THE REV. DR. HALLAM.

NEW LONDON, Ct., August 22, 1862.

REV. AND DEAR SIR:—It would give me great pleasure to join your celebration at the mouth of the Kennebec, and help you convince the world that there are other people deserving to be remembered besides the "Pilgrim Fathers." It is just the thing I should like, but I fear it is quite out of my power.

You must, therefore, accept the assurance of my thanks for your courteous invitation, and of my sympathy in the object you contemplate.

I trust the occasion will be altogether a success, and prove alike pleasant and useful.

Very truly yours,

ROB. A. HALLAM.

REV. EDWARD BALLARD, *Secretary, &c.*

FROM PRINCIPAL DAWSON.

MCGILL COLLEGE,
MONTREAL, August 19th, 1862.

MY DEAR SIR:—I beg to thank you for the kind invitation extended to me in yours of the 12th inst., and also for the interesting pamphlet by which it was accompanied.

I regret, however, that my engagements here will not permit me to avail myself of your kindness.

Trusting that your celebration may be eminently successful, and that it may tend to revive and perpetuate the memory of those old glories of the English race, which unite the hearts of Americans and Englishmen, through the bonds of their common ancestry,

I am, truly yours,

J. W. DAWSON.

Rev. EDWARD BALLARD, *Secretary, &c.*

FROM THE HON. WM. WRIGHT.

ADVOCATE GENERAL OF THE PROVINCE OF NEW BRUNSWICK.

ST. JOHN, N. B., August 25th, 1862.

SIR:—I have postponed until now acknowledging the receipt of your favor of the 12th inst., in hopes that I might so have arranged my affairs as to have enabled me to accept the very kind invitation of the Executive Committee of the public historical celebration to take place at the site of Fort Popham on the 29th instant.

To a native born Englishman and one sincerely desirous of cultivating the most friendly relations with the people of the United States, and those of Maine in particular, the intended celebration is pregnant with lively interest. It is, therefore, with profound regret that I find myself unable to take part in it.

I have the honor to be, Sir,
Your obedient servant,
WM. WRIGHT.

Rev. EDWARD BALLARD, *Secretary, &c.*

FROM GEN. WALBRIDGE.

NEW YORK, August 25th, 1862.

Rev. EDWARD BALLARD, *Secretary, &c., Brunswick, Me.*

MY DEAR SIR: — No greater pleasure could be afforded me, than to witness the interesting ceremonies to transpire at Fort St. George, on the 29th inst., under the guardianship of the committee you represent, and whose generous invitation I take the earliest moment to acknowledge.

I, however, regret that other prior engagements will prevent my going and pressing, for the first time, my feet upon a soil that has reared so many illustrious sons, who have adorned every department in government, art, trade, science, learning, and business, wherever genius, energy, capacity, industry, and fidelity have secured their legitimate reward.

I the more regret it, that I shall not enjoy the intellectual inspiration of your eminent fellow-citizen, whose learning and devotion to the interests of his native State, have made him the worthy orator of your patriotic anniversary.

With sentiments of respect,

Yours sincerely,

HIRAM WALBRIDGE.

FROM RUFUS McINTIRE, ESQ.

PARSONSFIELD, August 19th, 1862.

Rev. EDWARD BALLARD, *Secretary, &c.*

SIR: — Your note inviting me to attend the two hundred and fifty-fifth anniversary of the founding of the first English colony in New England, on the 29th inst., is received.

I regret that I shall not be able to be present and take part in the celebration on the interesting occasion proposed in your note. I rejoice to witness a wakening sense to the facts of our early history, too long neglected. Many memorials of the enterprise of European adventurers to these shores, might and should now be gathered, as they are fast fading into forgetfulness, and unless rescued will soon be lost. My health is not very firm, and makes it inconvenient to attend on this occasion.

Yours respectfully, &c.,

RUFUS McINTIRE.

FROM REV. J. S. C. ABBOT.

NEW HAVEN, CONN., August 18th, 1862.

Rev. EDWARD BALLARD,

MY DEAR SIR: — It is with deep regret that I am obliged to decline the invitation to join in your interesting celebration on the 29th proximo. I should very much enjoy meeting my friends in a place of so much historic interest, to review those scenes which have been so carefully collected by our beloved and so much lamented friend, Mr. McKeen. My own duties are now so pressing at home, that every hour comes freighted with double duty; and inclination must be laid aside for home employments.

Please present my acknowledgments to the gentlemen associated with you for your polite invitation, which I would have been only too happy to have accepted had it been in my power. With the hope of a very pleasant occasion for all who may assemble at Fort Popham,

I am, my dear sir,
Yours very truly,
JOHN S. C. ABBOT,
per J. W. ABBOT.

FROM H. B. DAWSON, ESQ.

MORRISANIA, N. Y., October 4th, 1862.

MY DEAR SIR: — I have just received your circular, dated August 12th, 1862, inviting me to attend the public celebration of the two hundred and fifty-fifth anniversary of the founding of the first English Colony on the shores of New England, and I beg you will accept, for yourself and for the committee, my thanks therefor.

The mis-direction of your note (to New York city), has prevented me from enjoying the privilege of meeting with you on the occasion referred to; but I have been much gratified with a careful report of the ceremonies in one of your papers, as well as with a verbal description by one of your members,—my friend Mr. Poor,—and I congratulate you and the Society on the result of its judicious efforts.

Trusting that the cause of Historical Literature will be benefited, and the claims of the Society advanced among the people of Maine, from this recognition of one of her holidays,

I remain, dear sir,

Very truly yours,

HENRY B. DAWSON.

Rev. EDWARD BALLARD.

FROM C. J. PETERSON, ESQ., PHILADELPHIA.

RIDGEWOOD, NEAR READING, PA.

DEAR SIR:—I have just received your polite invitation for the celebration of the two hundred and fifty-fifth anniversary of the first English colony in New England. Had it come to hand earlier, I should have been able, probably, to be with you; for I have been in New England for several weeks, and would have liked to have protracted my stay for such a purpose. I found your letter on my table last night,—it having been forwarded to me here from my office in Philadelphia, to await my return home.

I feel the more interest in your celebration, because I am, on my maternal side, descended from a New England stock,—my ancestors having removed to Massachusetts as early as A. D. 1632. We Pennsylvanians, even when not of New England blood, are proud of our "Yankee cousins," and send greeting, now as in '76, from Independence Hall to "old Faneuil," in the words of Webster, — "Union and Liberty, now and forever, one and inseparable."

Very sincerely,

CHAS. J. PETERSON.

REV. E. BALLARD, *Secretary Public Historical Celebration.*

FROM J. LIPPINCOTT, ESQ.

COLUMBIA, PA., August 16, 1862.

To REV. EDWARD BALLARD, *Secretary of the Public Historical Celebration.*

DEAR SIR: — It is with pleasure I acknowledge the honor of your invitation to be present at the celebration at Fort Popham on the 29th inst.; but with deep regret that circumstances will not permit me to share in the festivities of the occasion.

I can but contemplate with pride the generous spirit that will not suffer these historic memories to fade, — the persistence, which in conflict with circumstances, will continue to draw from the "lap of ages," and give to them tangible expression, — and those considerations which are our richest legacies; and which, at all times, it is eminently fit that we should entertain.

Especially does the event, the anniversary of which gives rise to this proposed celebration, deserve our attention, — an event, which though born amid discouragements, and fostered in doubt, has nevertheless ripened into character so potent, into results so glorious.

May we never fail to perpetuate the memory of our humble beginning, nor prove recreant to the earnest faith of our fathers; but like them, ever rely on Liberty, Justice, and Truth. Then will the principles which have so gloriously developed the resources of our strength *never* fail us. For from their adequate might, victories come. And though Justice briefly slumbers, yet from her latent fires there shall flash out the lightnings of inherent power, till Liberty, again enthroned, shall raise *our* banner, the emblem of her life, over a chastened but a better nation.

Hoping the occasion may prove one of eminent success, I remain with considerations of esteem,

Your humble servant and fellow-citizen,

JOTHAM LIPPINCOTT.

FROM AARON HAYDEN, ESQ.

EASTPORT, August 28, 1862.

GENTLEMEN: — I regret that an absence from home prevented a seasonable answer to your note of August 12th, inviting me to act as a vice-president at the Historical Celebration on the 29th inst. I regret still more that I am unable to accept an invitation by which I am so much honored.

In a contest of priority between Kennebec and Plymouth, I may well stand neutral, being a native of Maine, and at the same time one of the legitimate results of the "Courtship of John Alden."

If I am allowed to offer a sentiment, I should say:

"If the sons of the Northern Colonists do not preserve and perpetuate the Union and Constitution made with the Southern Colonists, Fort St. George and Plymouth Rock are not a full success."

Very respectfully,

AARON HAYDEN.

HON. B. C. BAILEY, and others, *Executive Committee.*

FROM REV. W. S. BARTLETT.

CHELSEA, MASS., August 19th, 1862.

REV. AND DEAR BRO.: — In answer to your invitation as Secretary, &c., to be present at the celebration on the 29th inst., I would say, that I anticipate much pleasure from sharing in these ceremonies.

Allow me to make one or two suggestions, which, it may be, have already occurred to you.

1. That a full and accurate narration of this celebration, with the names of those who may take part in it, be preserved, as of interest to those now on the stage, and of much more interest to those who shall come after us.

2. That a competent artist be invited to take one or more photographic views of the company when assembled. Similar views were taken of the members of the Massachusetts Historical Society when they visited Frederic Tudor, Esq., at Nahant, some three years since. A number of those then present have since passed away, and the picture will probably increase in interest by the lapse of time.

The artist who would be at Fort Popham on the 29th would probably be remunerated for his trouble and expense by the sale of his pictures, as most of those present would be likely to purchase copies.

Trusting that I may meet you at the mouth of the Sagadahoc next week, I remain,

Very truly yours, &c.,

Wm. S. Bartlett.

The Rev. Edward Ballard.

FROM HON. JUDGE RICE.

Augusta, August 22d, 1862.

Rev. Edward Ballard.

Dear Sir: — Your note of the 12th inst., inviting myself and ladies to be present at the public celebration on the two hundred and fifty-fifth anniversary of the founding of the first English colony on the shores of New England, has been received. Official duties may prevent my personal attendance; if so, I shall endeavor to be duly represented by "the ladies." Trusting that this celebration will bring out distinctly this *initial point* in the history of the settlement of New England,

I am, truly yours,

R. D. RICE.

FROM J. MAXWELL, ESQ.

BANGOR, August 16, 1862.

Rev. EDWARD BALLARD.

DEAR SIR: — Owing to urgent business, I am obliged to decline the invitation you have so kindly tendered me, to be present at the two hundred and fifty-fifth anniversary of the founding of the English colony on the New England shores.

Although I cannot be there in person, yet when the 29th of August arrives, I shall feel that I am losing an opportunity to witness the anniversary of an event, which I look back upon as the era of that prosperity and Union-loving happiness which fully showed itself in the struggle for Independence, in 1776; and again, for the maintenance of that Independence so nobly gained by the Forefathers, by the valor and bravery of *our* sons in the army of the Union.

Hoping that the day may be pleasant, and everything pass off as well as any could wish for, I remain,

Yours truly,

JERE. MAXWELL.

The foregoing letters, selected out of some hundreds received by the committee, have had a place given to them in this volume, to show the wide-spread interest in this commemoration of the "initial point in the history of the settlement of New England," and in the cultivation of historical pursuits in general; as well as the deep sympathy expressed in many of them with the sufferings of our common country, and love for the Union.

ADDITIONAL COMMUNICATIONS.

The following communications have been prepared and received while this volume was going through the press. Their subjects would have entitled them to an earlier position, if that had been possible; but it is believed they will make a valuable and interesting addition to the papers already presented. As intimated on a previous page,[1] they are now given here.

PEMAQUID.

BY JOHN JOHNSTON, LL. D.,

PROF. OF NATURAL SCIENCE IN THE WESLEYAN UNIVERSITY, MIDDLETOWN, CONN.

It is proposed in this paper to give briefly a description of the place, called by the Anglo-Indian name of Pemaquid; and also of the ancient ruins yet to be found there, — to notice some of the more important points in its early history, the effects of which have come down to our own times, — and then to trace the history of the four forts which were successively erected very nearly on the same site. To this will be added brief notices of two of the native Indians, — Sagamores of the place.

DESCRIPTION OF THE PLACE.

The island of Monhegan is one of the most prominent landmarks on the coast of New England east of Cape Cod, and could not have failed to attract the attention of the early navi-

1 Page 217.

gators, especially when they approached this part of the coast from the east, as most of them did. But the same remark would be true if they approached from the west, as was the case with Capt. Weymouth in 1605. In plain view from this island, and about ten miles distant, in a northwest direction, is Pemaquid Point; which, as it is the nearest point of the main land, could not fail to be early visited.

Just at the point, boats could not land safely, except in the finest weather; but three miles north of the extreme point, on the east side, is New Harbor, which is only a small cove, but still affords a good landing place for boats, and a tolerably good harbor for small vessels at all times. On the west side, between three and four miles from the extreme point, is Pemaquid Harbor, which was destined to be the scene of most of the important transactions here during the first century of its occupation by civilized man. This harbor, though the entrance is rather narrow, is perfectly protected from the sea on every side, and is one of the safest havens on the coast at all seasons of the year.

This is the precise locality generally known in modern times by the name of Pemaquid; but by the early writers, it is believed, the name was often used to designate the whole coast from George's Islands west to the mouth of the Kennebec. The Indian name probably was Pemaquideag,[1] and signified "*long point* or *promontory*."

The peculiar formation of the harbor of Pemaquid is very interesting to the geologist, as being separated from the sea on the south side by an immense trap dyke; which, like an artificial breakwater, protects it from the waves, but allows a sufficient space for the passage of ships. The rocks of this whole

1 The more important variations in the orthography of this name are the following: Pencöit, (Biard); Penaquid, (Smith); Pemquit, (Râle); Paincuit, (Cadillac); Pemaquin, (N. Y. Col. Doc.); Pemicuit, (Bowen Geog.); Pemkueag, Pemakeag, Pemmaquideag, and a few other modes by other writers.

region are of the kind called by geologists, *metamorphic*, with frequent masses and veins of granite and quartz, and occasional veins or dykes of trap or basalt. The shores in all the vicinity, denuded as they have been by the long dashing of the waves, afford an excellent opportunity for the study of these rocks; and in many places the peculiar relationship of the stratified gneiss and the intruded granite, quartz, and trap is beautifully exhibited. The upheaval of the stratified gneiss and mica slate, has been in lines nearly north and south, the axial lines being continued down into the promontories; and between these the tide flows up a greater or less distance. Pemaquid Point is the extreme point of one of these promontories, having the Muscongus Bay on the east, and John's Bay and the Damariscotta River on the west.

The dyke of trap or basalt, alluded to above, makes its appearance on the west side of the harbor, just at the head of John's Bay, and extends a distance of several rods nearly east towards the site of the old fort; but is suddenly broken off, as if to allow a sufficient space for an entrance to the harbor. This rock is very hard, and less liable to be worn away by the action of the elements than the adjacent metamorphic rocks; and it is to this cause, probably, we are to attribute the existence of this curious sea-wall.

It is familiar to geologists, that these dykes of trap may often be traced, usually in straight lines, to a distance of many miles; but this one has not been sufficiently explored to enable us to determine its extent. Evidences of its existence a few rods west from the harbor are readily seen; and probably it might be discovered at other places farther west or southwest. About three miles to the northeast, near the head of Long Cove, a narrow trap dyke is found, which is probably a continuation of the same one; and again it is seen at a place on the shore, half a mile north of the extremity of Long Cove Point. An old man, who formerly lived in the vicinity, though knowing nothing of the science of geology, recognized the peculiarities of the trap rocks in this place last mentioned, calling them the "Indigo Rocks." Those who have noticed the peculiar form and appearance of blocks of indigo, as the article is imported, would not fail to observe the resemblance.

This projecting sea-wall of basalt at Pemaquid Harbor, the early writers often call the "Barbacan," from its supposed resemblance to certain walls or watch-towers, which in ancient times were erected in connection with fortifications, and called by this name. A particular locality in the city of London was long known as the "Barbacan," and a place of worship was maintained there by some of the early dissenters. It may be that the name is still applied to the place.

The several forts, — not less than four, — which were successively erected here, it is believed, were all on the east side of the entrance to the harbor, and nearly opposite to the trap dyke or sea-wall just described, but rather south of it, as was required by the peculiar conformation of the surface. This point of land, which has been the scene of so many important events, including a number of bloody conflicts, is really a small promontory, made so by an indentation from John's Bay on the south, and a small cove on the north, connected with the harbor. This was formerly called Cox's Cove, from the circumstance that a descendant, probably a son of William Cox, one of the witnesses to John Brown's deed from the Indian Sagamores, long lived there. The name is not often heard now, and does not appear on the recent map of Lincoln County. Between this cove and the indentation from John's Bay, alluded to above, the land is quite low, and no very considerable rise of the water would be required to cause it to flow over at this point, and change the peninsula into an island.

Mr. Sewall describes the "peninsula, which was the site of the ancient town and fort of Pemaquid," as having obviously been made by "the sands and debris of the river, brought down and accumulated by the tides, in the rotary motion given by the interposing and curved shores of the Barbacan point on the west, and the immense projecting strata of inclined granite forming the eastern shore." He also speaks of the peninsula as having once been an island, and connected with the main land by an "artificial way." But such speculations, in regard to the forces by which the present conformation of any portion of the earth's surface was produced, amount to little; for the reason, that on such points we really know, and can know but very little. And, besides, geologists would probably tell us, if this peninsula ever was an island, as supposed, it could only have been in that distant pre-Adamite time, known as the "drift period," and then the theory of an "artificial way" becomes unnecessary.[1]

FIRST VISITS OF THE WHITE MEN.

The Anglicised Indian name, Pemaquid, occurs first in the writings of Strachey, who, in his account of the Popham expedition, informs us that "about midnight (August 7th, 1607, O. S.) Capt. Gilbert caused his shipp's boat to be mannde with fourteen persons, and the Indian Skidwares, (brought into England by Capt. Wayman,) and rowed to the westward from their shipp, to the river of Pemaquid, which they found to be four leagues distant from the shipp, where she road. The Indian brought them to the salvadges' houses, where they found a hundred men, women, and children; and their commander, or sagamo, amongst them, named Nahanada, who had been brought likewise into England by Capt. Wayman, and returned thither by Capt. Hanam, setting forth for those parts and some part of Canada the year before. At their first comyng, the Indians betooke them to their armes, their bowes and arrowes;

1 Ancient Dominions of Maine, pp. 114, 115.

but after Nahanada had talked with Skidwares, and perceaved that they were Englishmen, he himself came unto them and ymbraced them, and made them much welcome, and entertayned them with much chierfulness, and did they likewise him; and after two howers thus enterchangeably spent, they returned abourd againe." This was Saturday, August 8th.

The Monday following, Capt. Popham, Capt. Gilbert, and fifty others, in two boats, made another excursion from the ships to "the river of Pemaquid," taking with them Skidwares a second time, who it seems, on the previous visit, made no attempt to escape from them. On their arrival, "Nahanada, with all his company of Indians," with arms in their hands, came out to greet them, but not without some shyness; for, after an hour's intercourse, himself and company suddenly withdrew, taking with them Skidwares, who now chose to remain with his old friends. The Englishmen spent the following night in the vicinity, and the next day returned to their ships, which "still road under St. George's Island."

But we are not to suppose, that we have in this interesting account of Strachey, a description of the very earliest visit of Europeans to this place; the language used plainly implies that the situation of places here, and in the vicinity was well understood by the leaders of the expedition; and further, that the excursions of the boats to Pemaquid were only incidental to the principal object, which was to find their way to the "river Sachadehoc."

To go back a little, it is altogether probable, that Capt. Hanam, by whom Nahanada was restored to his home, was at Pemaquid in 1606; Capt. Weymouth, in 1605; and De Mont, also, in 1605. And we are informed by Purchas, (as is well-known,) that a French seaman, named Savalet, previous to the year 1609, had made no less than forty-two voyages to this region. May we not, then, conclude that Pemaquid and other prominent places on the coast were known, at least to the fishermen of western Europe some time before the close of the sixteenth century; and perhaps as early as the beginning of the reign of Elizabeth.

But while there seems to be sufficient evidence to warrant the above conclusion, there is also reason to believe that previous to the voyage of Weymouth, in 1605, there had been comparatively little intercourse between the natives and the strangers who annually made their appearance on the coast. As a good reason for this opinion, the fact may be mentioned, that up to this period, we have no information that any one had made any progress in learning the language of the natives. When Weymouth's ship rode at anchor in "Pentecost Harbor," (George's Island Harbor,) the natives visited him freely; but no one, of either party, so far as we can learn, understood a word of the language of the other party.

Soon after this period, we begin to have more full accounts of events transpiring on this coast; as in the voluminous writings of Capt. John Smith, and the less pretending and simple narrative of Capt. Levett; but it is not our object here to enter into details. Capt. Levett made his voyage to this country late in the year 1623, first making the coast at the Isle of Shoals. From this place he cruised eastward as far as Cape Newagen, now Boothbay, where he saw many of the natives from Pemaquid, and learned that the place "had been granted to others;" and determined, in consequence, to prosecute his voyage no further in this direction.

By this he meant that a settlement of Europeans had already been commenced here; but how old it was, we have no means of knowing. Capt. Dermer, in pursuit of Rocroft, came to Monhegan in the spring of the year 1619, and found there two seamen who had spent a miserable winter on the island. They had been left at Saco the year before by Rocroft, and had, by some means not now known, found their way here. From these circumstances, we may, without question, fix the first permanent occupation, of both Monhegan and Pemaquid, as between the two dates of 1619 and 1623.

In the summer of 1619, business was active at Monhegan; and Dermer made preparations for his voyage from the island to Virginia, which he made in the latter part of the season, by way of Long Island Sound and Sandy Hook.

ANCIENT RUINS.

The remains of the early settlements at Pemaquid Harbor and vicinity, still to be seen, are of considerable interest and importance. Many old cellars yet remain to indicate something of the populousness of the place; but many more, it is believed, have been entirely obliterated by the hand of improvement. The old burying-ground, where the dust of many of the early inhabitants reposes, is about forty rods northeast of the fort; but, most unfortunately, the stones used to mark the places of the graves were only rough pieces found in the vicinity, and are without any inscriptions. And it is believed that very many of this kind have been from time to time removed, so that the very places of the graves are lost. The oldest grave that can now be determined, is entirely alone in a cultivated field, at a distance of several rods from the present cemetery; and it is believed that the graves by which it was once surrounded have been leveled down by the plow. The stone which marks the place of this grave, is of the kind just described, and has rudely cut upon it, the letters H and M, (but they are cut together, thus, HM,) and the date of the year, which some read 1625, but probably it should be read 1695. All the other inscriptions are of a date subsequent to the last rebuilding of the fort, and the revival of the settlement by the English.

A few rods southeast of the fort, but entirely concealed from view by several inches of loose earth and gravel, the supposed ancient pavements are found. This is a subject upon which we cannot proceed too cautiously; and it is a question whether sufficient explorations have yet been made to enable us to decide satisfactorily whether they are to be considered real artificial pavements, and still less to determine their age and the purpose for which they were laid. It is certain, however, that at several points in the locality mentioned, by removing some six or ten inches of very loose black earth and gravel, a regular layer of stones is brought to view, wonderfully like modern pavements, except that the stones are smaller than those now generally used. They are very uniform in size, and present the appearance of water-worn pebbles, like those found upon the shore. How extensive the pavement is, and whether it would be found to indicate the existence, at some former time, of regular streets, or whether it may have served some purpose in connection with the fort, are questions which must be left until further and more accurate investigations have been made.[1]

1 The "Ex-Editor" of the Eastern Times, who explored the place in 1858, (see number for Sept. 17, 1858,) expresses himself as fully satisfied that these are the remains of ancient streets, the direction of which he can determine. But the writer has not been able to satisfy himself so fully. Certain it is that in two or three places seen by the writer, the pavement looked wonderfully like a real artificial work; but the existence and direction of regular streets could not be so well made out. It is proper, however, to say that the field at the time was covered with growing corn, so that extensive explorations could not well be made, even if the party had gone there properly prepared for the purpose.

But the "Ex-Editor," is mistaken in saying, as he does in substance, that "the traditions of the oldest inhabitants," say nothing on the subject. Sullivan (Hist. of Maine, p. 161) alludes to it; and the writer well remembers often to have heard several of the old inhabitants speak of the supposed pavements; and during the winter of 1828–9, while boarding for a time in the family of the late Capt. John Nickels, who was born and spent nearly his whole life almost on the very site of the old fort, had several conversations with him concerning the history and traditions of the place. On the subject of these pavements, he always was careful to speak very hypothetically, indicating considerable doubt in his mind in regard to them. He expressed the opinion that the date on the gravestone above described should be read 1695, and not 1625.

At the place where these supposed pavements are found, the surface of the ground is a little lower than in the immediate vicinity; and it is easy to conceive that the loose material now covering the pavements may have been washed there by the rains, but this cannot be said of the street which, it is claimed, began "near the easterly bastion of the old fort," and ran in a north-easterly direction towards the old burying ground. This, if a street, passed directly on the crest of the ridge, and the rains would constantly wash all loose material away from it rather than to it; yet for a distance of more than forty rods in the direction mentioned, by the use of a crow-bar, we can feel that there are many loose stones a little distance beneath the surface, arranged in such a manner as to indicate the existence of a street or road. But it is to be kept in mind that the soil here is stony; and we are, therefore, specially liable to be deceived in these explorations.

On the west side of the harbor, and a mile or so northerly from the fort, we find the remains of an old structure, the character of which we cannot now determine. It may have been nothing more than a dwelling house; but among the rubbish some pieces of a kind of freestone occur, which are of a character not to be found among the metamorphic rocks of this region. They were, without question, brought here from abroad, and very possibly from Europe.

It is said that several copper coins were found here some years ago; but they have not been preserved. Common report says that the superscriptions upon them were not in English.

Fragments of tobacco-pipes are abundant among the rubbish here, as at other places in the vicinity, giving us some indications in regard to the habits of the people here in the olden time.

Near by, portions of the soil, which, it is believed, have not been disturbed in modern times, give evidence of having been cultivated by the early settlers; and it has been suggested, that the mode of tillage suggests a Dutch rather than English origin.

In the same field, in a low, wet place, are the remains of an ancient tannery; and pieces of plank forming the vats, and even pieces of leather, well preserved, were found there a few years ago.

Going another mile northeast from this place, we come to "The Falls," so called, because of the water-power that occurs there. It was a place of no little importance to the early inhabitants, both because it offered a good site for the erection of mills, and also for its excellent shad and alewive fisheries at the proper season of the year.

As an object of special interest to the antiquarian, we find here the remains of an ancient canal or water-course, which begins near the present road on the east side of the stream, and extends down some twenty rods, curving considerably at places so as to follow along the bank at about the same level. It was, probably, about ten feet wide and six or eight feet deep; and evidently was constructed for the purpose of carrying water to mills that were situated below. On the side next to the stream, were several side-cuts to draw off the water for the use of the mills. Only a short and low dam was required exactly where the bridge now stands, for the purpose of turning the water into the canal, or, in time of freshets, as much of it as was needed for the mills.

Tradition informs us, that when the ancestors of the present inhabitants came here, nearly a century and a half ago, forest trees a foot in diameter were found growing in the bed of the canal and on its banks; but no information concerning its origin or use, from any source whatever, has come down to us, except what we may derive from the appearance of the thing itself.

Were these ruins, which we have now briefly described, the

work of the early English settlers; or are we to attribute them to a period still more distant in the past, and to a people of whom no other information has come down to us? This question was discussed by the ancestors of the present inhabitants of the place; and some of them who saw these ruins in a better condition than they now present, it is certain, entertained the opinion that they could not have been constructed by the English. The very judicious writer in the Eastern Times, before referred to, also adopts the same view; and inclines to attribute them to the famous Northmen, who are supposed to have visited the shores of New England at a very early period. It has also been conjectured, that a Dutch colony was established here, before the earliest English settlement was begun, but was destroyed by the Indians; and certain very indefinite traditions to this effect were said to have been derived from the natives.

But while the writer supposes these circumstances, trifling as they may seem, of sufficient importance to be noticed here, it is not with the view of giving them any special prominence. They are mentioned rather by way of suggestion to future inquirers, than as indicating an opinion in regard to them.

As it regards the canal or water-course at "The Falls," may we not consider it as affording good evidence that mills, or at least a grist-mill, was erected here by the very first English settlers, being perhaps the first erected in New England?

How did the early colonists in different places supply themselves with bread? At the very first, much meal and bread were brought from the mother country; but as soon as the soil began to be cultivated, mills for grinding were indispensable. When and where was the first grist-mill erected in the Plymouth Colony? A pounding-mill, for preparing samp, (*nawsaump, Indian,*) was erected near Billington Sea in 1633, from which fact it may be inferred that there was then no mill for grinding. Probably it was several years after this that their first grinding-mill was built. It is certain they had a grist-mill in 1638, as John Jenney was that year prosecuted "for not grinding well and seasonably." [1]

The first grist-mill in the Massachusetts Colony, was erected at Cambridge in 1632, nearly two years after the founding of the colony; but in a few months it was taken down and removed to Copp's Hill, in Boston, for the reason, that, in the former place, "it would not grind but with a westerly wind." Of course it was a wind-mill.

Mason's colony at Piscataqua was begun in 1623, but for nine years, at least, they had no mill for grinding. This appears from the fact, that they brought their corn to the wind-mill in Boston to be ground at a period as late as October, 1632.

At the Casco settlement, according to Mr. Willis, there was a mill on the Presumpscot in 1646; but we have no information as to the time when it was erected. [2]

Mr. Thornton suggests that the early settlers at Pemaquid probably sent their corn to Boston to be ground; [3] but is it not more probable that they early erected mills of their own at the place before described? Considering that the settlement here had become of sufficient importance, as early as 1630, to justify the building of a fort, and that it was the chief place of resort for the multitude of fishing vessels annually visiting the coast, giving rise necessarily to considerable business,—that of agriculture we know not being neglected,—the absolute necessity for the early erection of a grist-mill is apparent. And as we know there was none nearer than Boston for some time after 1632, when the first one was erected there, is there not good reason for concluding that these remains which have come down to us, are the silent mementos of the industry and

1 Thacher's History, p. 74.

2 History of Portland, vol. 1, p. 47.

3 Maine Hist. Col., vol. 5, p. 204.

enterprise of the people of that day, employed in this manner in order to provide a great public benefit?

The water-power here is not very considerable, but for a large part of the year, was probably sufficient, at this period, for all purposes. The site was an excellent one for this purpose, only about two miles distant from the fort, which was the center of operations, and accessible by water. The method adopted for constructing the works was probably the least expensive that could be devised; only a short, and comparatively low dam being required, little liable to be carried away, or to suffer serious damage by freshets.

IMPORTANT EVENTS AS AFFECTING LAND TITLES.

At the very beginning of the settlement here, we notice two important events, which, as they laid the foundation for two sets of claims to the soil, could not be without important results in the subsequent history of the place. The first of these, in the order of time, was the purchase from two Indian Sagamores of a large tract of land here by John Brown, a gentleman of Bristol, England; and the second was the issuing of the "Pemaquid Patent" by the "Council of Plymouth," to Robert Aldsworth and Gyles Elbridge, also of Bristol.

Brown's deed, which was dated July 25th, 1625, is to be found in that most important, but now very rare document, entitled an "Order of both Branches of the Legislature of Massachusetts, to appoint Commissioners to investigate the Causes of the Difficulties in the County of Lincoln, and the Report of the Commisioners thereon, with the documents in support thereof, Boston, 1811," and in Mr. Thornton's "Ancient Pemaquid."

The tract of land conveyed by this deed, as was claimed by those who held it, included the whole peninsula between Muscongus Sound on the east, and Damariscotta River on the west, extending north several miles beyond the head of the tide which flows on both sides; and the consideration mentioned in it is "fifty skins." The deed is a curiosity of its kind, and, at the present day, would not probably be considered by the courts as of any worth.

Brown subsequently conveyed to others a part of this tract; and his heirs, many years later gave deeds of undivided parts, which they supposed of right belonged to them, until near the close of the last century, when it became necessary to take legal measures to confirm the title. At that time, the "proprietors" under this claim formed a numerous body and were living in nearly all the New England States.

For many years, and until driven off by the Indians, Brown himself and many of his descendants lived within the limits of the claim; and after this time occasional acts of ownership, as the making of surveys of some part of the tract, were performed by one or more of the claimants; but the whole claim was ultimately set aside as worthless, as will be more fully described further on.

The other important event, alluded to above, was the issuing of the "Pemaquid Patent," February 29th, 1631, as already stated. This patent, which, in its terms, was in part conditional, conveyed twelve thousand acres of land; and when possession was given, May 27th, 1633, according to the legal forms then practiced, it was agreed to bound it "from the head of the river of Damariscotta to the head of the river of Muscongus, and between it to the sea." Of course the claim covered very nearly the same land as the Indian deed to Brown, but did not extend quite as far to the north.

Aldsworth died not long after the date of the patent, leaving Elbridge, as was claimed, sole owner of the patent; and on the death of Elbridge, his oldest son, Thomas, came over and took possession of the patent as sole heir to his father. He resided many years at Pemaquid; and, in accordance with the usage of the time, it is said he "held a court" here, and performed many acts of ownership. In 1651, he, by deed, conveyed one-half of the patent to Paul White, a gentleman of Charlestown, Massachusetts; and subsequently other deeds were given until 1657, when Nicholas Davison, also of Charlestown, became sole owner.

From Davison, the claim passed by will to several relatives of his; and their heirs, by the names of Savage, Alford, Clarke, Winslow, Ruck, Parrott, Sweetser, Phillips, Mousell, Paine, Fitch, Kneeland, and others, who lived mostly in Boston and the immediate vicinity, became the hated "proprietors" under the "Drowne claim" so much dreaded by the inhabitants three-quarters of a century ago.

Among the heirs of Davison was a Miss Russell, who married a man by the name of Shem Drowne, a citizen of Boston of some distinction, by reason of his being often engaged in the public affairs of the town. He was a man of great energy and enterprise, and an enthusiast in the matter of this eastern property belonging to the family and supposed to be very valuable; and it was because of his being long identified as the leader in prosecuting the claim, that it became known as the "Drowne claim."

Drowne began his labors in 1743, by procuring a call for a legal meeting of the claimants under the patent, which was held at the "Orange Tree" Tavern in Boston, August 31st, of the year just mentioned. Here measures were taken to have a survey of the lands made, and a division into lots of about a hundred acres each; and plans laid for the recovery and appropriation of the property.

This survey and division was in due time made, and the land distributed by lot among the claimants at several different meetings. Every thing was done according to legal form, and all the necessary signatures obtained, which, as the parties were somewhat scattered, required considerable time and expense. It was not until 1763, more than twenty years after the first meeting was held, that the last required signature was obtained. The documents were put on record in 1768, and in 1774 Drowne died.

He was by trade a "tin plate worker," and had his place of business in Boston. A few years ago, the grasshopper vane, which had long faithfully indicated the direction of the wind over Faneuil Hall, was blown down, and in it was found concealed a fragment of a paper much weather worn and difficult to read; but enough was made out to determine that Shem Drowne was the maker of the vane. Thomas Drowne, a brother of Shem, lived many years at New Harbor, and married his wife there. Her maiden name was McFarland.

Besides these two claims to the soil at Pemaquid, there were other claims to some parts of it, but they were of secondary importance and will not be further noticed.

These claims, after producing no little trouble, and much bitterness among the inhabitants of the place, who regarded the "proprietors" as much their enemies as they did the native savages, were at length put to rest by the interference of the Legislature of Massachusetts, early in the present century.

About the beginning of the century, in consequence of the law limiting the time in which actions in certain cases could be brought for the recovery of real estate, it became necessary for these non-resident claimants to bring actions to establish their supposed titles. Several actions against citizens of the place were begun in the Supreme Judicial Court; and in the prosecution of them it became necessary that surveys should be made, and certain lines indicated by ancient deeds re-determined. This was ordered to be done by the court, and a surveyor appointed for the purpose, who, however, met with so much opposition from the people, that he retired from the contest and reported the facts to the court. Subsequently, in the autumn of the year 1810, a part of the militia from a neighboring town was ordered out by the court to support the surveyor; but as many of the men who were drafted were known to sympathize strongly with the settlers, the difficulty and danger of such a movement became apparent. Wiser counsels now began to prevail; immediate action was postponed, and the whole matter was again brought by petition before the Legislature of the State.

It is not proposed to enter further into the details of this subject here; and it will be sufficient to say that the decision finally arrived at, seemed to establish the principle that grants of land on this continent made by a sovereign of Europe were good and valid, while grants made by the natives of the country were void and of no effect!

The commissioners to whom the subject was referred, awarded to the Drowne claimants eleven thousand five hundred and twenty acres of wild land, to be selected from the public lands of Maine, as a proper compensation for their claim at Pemaquid; but rejected the Brown claim as worthless. The Kennebec Company at the same time received a township of wild land as a compensation for their claim to lands in Boothbay and Edgecomb, which were in dispute at the same time as those at Pemaquid.

THE FORTS AT PEMAQUID.

The exact site of the last fort erected at Pemaquid Harbor is well known, as the foundations can still be traced very satisfactorily; and a small part of the wall in one place yet remains; and it is very certain that all the others of more ancient date, of which there were three, occupied very nearly the same spot. As before stated, the place is a little south of the narrowest part of the entrance to the harbor, some fifteen or twenty rods from the water. The shore is rocky and very bold, so that ships of considerable size may approach very near. Just at this place is the highest point of the peninsula; but the surface, probably, is not elevated more than thirty or forty feet above the water of the bay and harbor.

The first fort at Pemaquid, which was erected in 1630, it is believed, occupied this spot, but no positive evidence of the fact has come down to us; nor is there any description of it known to be in existence. Very probably it was merely an earthwork, surmounted with a stockade. Only two years after it was built, it was taken and sacked by some pirates, led by a daring desperado by the name of Dixy Bull. As the object of these freebooters was only to obtain all the plunder they could, it is believed that the fort itself was not destroyed. After this, for thirty years or more, the place enjoyed almost uninterrupted peace, and no mention is made of the fort. We may, therefore, conclude that it had been allowed to fall into decay; and when the troubles connected with King Philip's War began, we do not learn that the inhabitants had any place of protection to which they could fly.

As the difficulties with the natives, which preceded this war, were gradually increasing in Massachusetts, Rhode Island, and Connecticut, the changing conduct and temper of the Indians in the east plainly showed, that, though destitute of telegraph or post, the people of the two sections were not without means of communication with each other. Matters proceeded less rapidly in Maine than in the region of Mount Hope, but there was the most perfect sympathy between the people of the two sections.

For some time after the war actually broke out in Massachusetts, the natives about Pemaquid, though very uneasy, and much disposed to complain of the encroachments of the English, were kept comparatively quiet, chiefly by the exertions of

Mr. Abraham Shurte, a leading citizen of the place, who had ever maintained towards them a kind and conciliatory course, and thereby secured their confidence. But for the injudicious and altogether unjustifiable conduct of others, it is quite possible that the settlement might have passed uninjured through that perilous period of its history. But this was not to be; and if the savages, stung with a sense of their wrongs, burned for revenge upon those whom they considered their enemies; there were among the English those, who, judged by their conduct, were actuated by a spirit no more justifiable.

King Philip himself was slain August 12th, 1676; but the war in the east was then only just begun, and a few days later all the settlements in Maine, east of Casco,—Pemaquid included,—were utterly destroyed. Fortunately, the inhabitants of Pemaquid received timely warning, and made their escape,—first to Damariscove Island, and then to Monhegan; but before winter all removed to the west.

The second fort at Pemaquid was, like the first, only an earthwork, surmounted with heavy timber. The territory of Sagadahock, including substantially all that part of Maine east of the Kennebec, had been granted, a few years before, to the Duke of York; and it was for the protection of this interest, that the expense was incurred. June 9th, 1677, Sir Edmund Andros being then Ducal Governor of New York and Sagadahock, it was determined in Council, "to send and take Possession and assert the Duke's Interest at Pemaquid, and parts adjacent Eastward;" and immediately a force was dispatched from New York for this purpose, under the direction of Captain Cæsar Knapton. It was also magnanimously decided if they "made Peace with the Indyans there, the Massachusetts to bee comprised if they Pleased."

The thing having been determined on, no time was lost; and in the archives at the State House in Albany, are still preserved original letters from Capt. Brockholes, who had sailed there on this business, dated Pemaquid, July 12th and 13th of the same year. The fort which was erected in a little time, was named Fort Charles, and received a "considerable number of soldiers," as a proper garrison for the place. A custom-house was also established in connection with the fort; and a stringent system of rules laid down for the regulation of trade with the natives and others, and for the government of the place. This garrison was ever afterwards maintained there at the expense of the Duke's government, until the surrender of the place to Massachusetts by a royal order, dated September 19th, 1686. The heavy guns were removed, first to Boston, but afterwards to New York.

It would seem that the order for its surrender was not very promptly obeyed, for a year and a half afterwards, (March 28, 1688,) at a Council held at Fort James in New York, it was agreed to send a remonstrance to His Majesty against the measure. The language of the document, however, implies that the thing had been done; and the remonstrance, or address, if actually sent, amounted to nothing more than an exhibition of the signers' personal feelings and mortification.

After the surrender of the place to Massachusetts, only a small garrison was kept at Fort Charles, although it was known to be a special object of vengeance on the part of the Indians. Even the destruction of Cocheco, (Dover, N. H.,) in June, 1689, was not taken as a sufficient warning to induce them to increase their means of defense. The consequence was, that, being attacked furiously by a body of Indians under "old Moxus," August 2d, of this year, the fort was obliged to surrender, and, with all the houses in the vicinity, was given to the flames.

This attack upon the place appears to have been devised and carried into effect entirely by the Penobscot Indians, who, about one hundred in number, came in canoes, and landed at New Harbor. They had sent before them several of their number as spies, to learn all they could of the condition of the garrison. How successful these were, we are not informed; but it is certain that the English people saw nothing of them; or, at least, had not had their suspicions excited by anything that occurred. When the savages landed, they were so fortunate as to make a prisoner of an Englishman, by the name of Starkey, whom they met entirely alone, and compelled him to give them information in regard to the condition of affairs in the place. Learning that Mr. Gyles, one of the chief men of the place, had gone with his men to make hay at "The Falls," and that there were only a few able men at the fort, they separated in two parties, one going directly to the fort, and the other turning to the right so as to intercept Mr. Gyles and his party. Both parties succeeded only too well; Gyles and several of his men were killed, and nearly all the others, with two of his sons, were taken captives; all the houses in the place were burned, and the fort taken and destroyed, after a contest that lasted until sometime the next day.

The "weak old fort," as Gyles calls it, was commanded by Capt. Weems, who made a resolute defense; but being himself wounded, and several of his ablest men killed, he at length capitulated, on condition that all in the fort, with three of the captives whom the Indians had taken, should be allowed to depart unmolested from the place in a sloop, which they had also seized, and that they should be allowed to take from the fort whatever they could carry in their hands.[1]

Dr. Mather says that the Indians afterwards violated the agreement by "butchering and captivating many" of the

1 This last condition was, a few years ago, made the basis of a pleasant story, by Mr. Thomas McClure, which attracted some attention at the time.

prisoners; but as Gyles, who was one of the prisoners, does not mention the fact, it must be considered doubtful.

Charlevoix says, that after the capitulation, Capt. Weems "came out at the head of fourteen men, who alone remained of the garrison, with some women, all of them with packs upon their backs. The Indians allowed them to pass unmolested, only saying to them, if they were wise they would never return; for the Abenaki nation had learned so much of their perfidy, that they would never again allow them to live there in peace; that they were masters of the country, and would not endure the presence of a people so officious and disposed to trouble them in the exercise of their religion." The same writer affirms further, that the savages committed no disorder, either in the fort or in the houses, — even destroying, without tasting, some barrels of spirituous liquors (l' eau de vie) which they found. According to Charlevoix, Capt. Weems, after his surrender, affirmed that seven men of the garrison were killed during the fight; but he intimates that in his own opinion, the number was much greater. Only one of the attacking party was badly wounded.

A point of some importance in connection with this fight is to be noted. A large rock which lay between the fort and the shore, aided the Indians very considerably in their attacks, — affording them great protection from the guns of the fort, and enabling them, by climbing its sides at fit opportunities, to annoy those within the walls more effectually. This same rock still remains in its place, but is now found within the walls of the fort. We are informed by Cadillac, that, in building the next fort, in 1692, this rock was inclosed because of the advantage it afforded the enemy at this time.[1] This circumstance enables us to fix very satisfactorily the exact site of Fort Charles, which we thus find stood a little to

1 Maine His. Col., vol. 6, p. 283.

the east of the one that succeeded it, called Fort William Henry.

The feelings of the savages, on their return, are well indicated by their assurances to the Catholic priest, M. Thury, that "with two hundred Frenchmen, acquainted with the places and earnest to follow, they could lead them even to Boston." The whole country east of Casco was now made desolate, and the Indians roved everywhere undisputed; and the next spring, Casco also suffered the same fate.

The next and third fort at Pemaquid, was constructed under the direction of Governor Phips, in 1692. Sir William Phips, whose romantic history is familiar with most persons, was appointed Governor of Massachusetts early in this year; and being well acquainted with the eastern country, he very soon, in accordance with instructions from the English Government, determined upon building here a strong fort for the protection of the country from the further incursions of the Indians, and also to serve as a check against the increasing influence of the French in this region. Repairing here with four hundred and fifty men, a substantial stone fort was soon erected, and called Fort William Henry. According to Mather, it was of a "quadrangular figure, being about 737 feet in compass, without the outer walls, and 108 feet square, within the inner ones." "The wall on the south line, fronting to the sea, was 22 feet high, and more than 6 feet thick at the ports, which were 8 feet from the ground. The greater flanker, or round tower, at the western end of this line, was 29 feet high. The wall on the east line was 12 feet high; on the north it was 10; on the west it was 18. It was computed that in the whole there were laid above 2000 cart-loads of stone."[1] A force of sixty

1 This description is very obscure. The language would seem to imply that the walls were double; but this we know could not be the case. And if the fort was only one hundred and eight feet square inside the walls, — supposing this to be the meaning, — how could it be seven hundred and thirty-seven feet

men was left to garrison the place, commanded at first by Capt. March, and afterwards by Capt. Chubb.

This fort, in elegance and strength, far surpassed anything that had been erected in that region; and a decidedly favorable impression was produced upon the minds of the natives, who were soon disposed to enter upon negotiations of peace. Accordingly, the next summer, many chiefs of different tribes assembled at Fort William Henry, and agreed with Gov. Phips upon terms of peace and submission to the English authority, delivering up three of their number as hostages, and promising at once to forsake their former allies, the French.

But the peace was of short continuance: the natives had become so deeply exasperated with the English, that they could not be controlled by the promises of their leaders; and, as a consequence, the robbery and murder of the English continued whenever a favorable opportunity occurred. So the English, on the other hand, finding that no faith could be put in the promises of the savages, often committed acts of revenge upon the Indians altogether unjustifiable.

The result of this was, that, early in the season of 1696, preparations began to be made by the French and Indians, for an attack upon the fort at Pemaquid, which actually took place in the month of July following. For this purpose, Iberville started from Quebec with two companies of soldiers in two war vessels; and at St. Johns he was joined by Villebon with a company of Indians, all of them eager for the destruction of the hated strong-hold, Fort William Henry, at Pemaquid. From the mouth of the Penobscot, Castine, with two

"in compass." The "greater flanker," or round tower, of the next and last fort built there, — the foundations of which still remain, was one hundred and thirty feet "in compass;" but, including this, we cannot make the distance around the walls so much as is given. May there not have been at the eastern angle, diagonally opposite to the "greater flanker," a large bastion, or lesser "flanker," which increased the distance around so as to make it as stated.

hundred Indians, in canoes, proceeded to join the expedition, which now became of a formidable character.

On their way to Pemaquid, the French ships were so fortunate as to capture the English ship Newport, which, with some others, was bound for the Penobscot; and, with their prize, made their appearance before the fort on the 14th of July. After a summons from the French commander, Iberville, to surrender, which was refused by Capt. Chubb, the attack commenced late in the afternoon. During the night, the French were very active, and so prepared their means of assaulting the place, that Chubb was induced to surrender. He was much alarmed by a threat of Castine, which by some mode was sent into the fort, that if they continued the defense, when the fort should be taken, they would have to deal with the savages who would show no quarter.

The surrender was made on the conditions, that all persons in the fort should be sent to Boston, and exchanged for an equal number of French and Indians. On entering the fort, the French found there an Indian in irons, which greatly exasperated the savages; and the English account of the transaction says, that several of the soldiers were murdered on the spot. The rest were taken to an island in the vicinity, to protect them from the savages. The loss of this fort put an end, for the time, to the English influence in these parts; and for more than thirty years this whole region, between the rivers Kennebec and Penobscot, was utterly desolate.

The fourth, and last fort at Pemaquid, was erected by Col. Dunbar, in 1729; and it is the remains of this which we now find there. The settlements west of the Kennebec were revived in a few years; but east of this river little progress was made; and at Pemaquid nothing was done until the rebuilding of the fort, at the date above given. And the cause of the delay is easily understood: Gov. Phips being well acquainted with the eastern country, was prepared to appreciate the importance of holding Pemaquid; not to Massachusetts only, but to the whole English people, as being the extreme eastern outpost which they could then expect to hold. But it was not so with the British Government, by whom the governors of Massachusetts were now appointed. Gov. Phips died in 1695, nearly a year before the destruction of the fort he had built at Pemaquid; and his successors being in the interest of the home government, claimed that the expense of protecting this eastern territory, including the rebuilding of the fort, was properly chargeable to the people of Massachusetts, and not to the royal treasury. Peremptory orders were sent from the government to the legislature, to make provision for the rebuilding of the fort; but they were disobeyed. From year to year, the contest was kept up, and the place remained desolate.

Considering the persevering audacity of Massachusetts, for some time before this, in extending her jurisdiction over the soil of Maine, in spite of all opposition, and almost in open defiance of the British Government, it cannot be thought strange that the latter should hesitate to build and support a fort in those parts. In fact, the conduct of Massachusetts in this matter was most extraordinary. By a new interpretation of her charter, she had extended her borders so far north as to include the southern part of both New Hampshire and Maine, including most of the Pemaquid settlement; and, almost by force of arms, actually extended her jurisdiction over the territory; but, at the same time, refused to rebuild the fort which was absolutely necessary for the protection of this same territory. But Massachusetts had been made to feel her dependence upon the mother country in a way she disliked; and in this particular contest, she had the advantage to understand, in all its relations, the question at issue. She knew well, that, sooner or later, the power of England must be used for the protection of this part of the empire from the

French, whatever other collateral issues might arise. And so it proved, after a contest between the royal governors and the legislature of the colony for nearly a quarter of a century. The ministry at length determined to rebuild the fort, and sent their agent, Col. David Dunbar, a reduced colonel of the army, to the place for the purpose.

As the shrewd men of Massachusetts had foreseen, they were obliged to this course, to prevent the country from falling under the dominion of France; but, as Massachusetts had not foreseen, a claim was now put forth in regard both to right of jurisdiction and the ownership of the soil, which was a little extraordinary.

The territory of Acadia, without any definition of boundaries, was ceded to France by England by the treaty of Breda, in 1668; but was again restored to England "with all its ancient boundaries" by the treaty of Utrecht, in 1713. Whether Pemaquid was within this territory, was a question that had not been decided. But the French, while in possession, claimed the country as far west as the Kennebec. What an excellent foundation there was then for the claim now brought forward; that, whatever rights Massachusetts, or other parties, may have had to the soil here, were lost by the treaty first mentioned; that the country being now recovered by conquest, not only the civil jurisdiction, but also the right to the soil, was vested in the crown.

When, therefore, it was resolved by the British Government to rebuild the fort, it was also determined to claim the ownership of the soil, and to assume the civil jurisdiction. Dunbar, therefore, only acted in accordance with the design with which he was sent to the country, when he proceeded to introduce settlers and to make grants of the land.

It is a question, whether Dunbar erected a new fort altogether, or whether he only repaired the old one built by Gov. Phips. But there are some reasons for believing that the old foundations at least were preserved. Probably little more than the mere foundations, which would in a great measure be protected from the weather, after the lapse of a third of a century, would be worth preserving.

The foundations of the last fort, whether they be the same as laid by Phips or not, can still be easily traced. By this, we learn that the fort was quadrangular in form, but not perfectly square. The four sides faced towards the southeast, southwest, northwest, and northeast; the four corners or angles being of course towards the four cardinal points. At the west angle was the round tower, or "greater flanker," which inclosed the large rock before mentioned, and was in form perfectly circular, the distance around being one hundred and thirty feet. The southeast and northeast sides were one hundred and forty-eight feet, and the southwest and northwest sides, each one hundred and thirty feet in length. The entrance was in the northeast side; and at the eastern angle, diagonally opposite the "greater flanker," was a proper bastion, and probably the magazine.

The walls were built of small stones, which were evidently collected from the shores in the immediate vicinity. These stones, though small, were well laid in mortar; and the walls, several feet above the foundations, were probably two feet thick.[1] But, however formidable they may have appeared to the Indians in those days, they would afford little protection against the ponderous missiles now used, hurled from ships that could approach within a few hundred yards. It was evidently designed rather as a means of defense against the native savages than against ships of war, which could easily

[1] The writer's personal recollections of the place go back to the year 1816, at which time the remains of the walls, at the lowest places, were two or three feet high, and not less than ten or fifteen feet in some places, and especially around the "greater flanker" next the bay.

batter down walls thus made. Dunbar called his new fortification "Fort Frederic."

Dunbar was dismissed in 1732; but during the three years of his administration, he conducted affairs with the greatest energy. As a matter of course, a violent opposition was waked up against him, not only from Massachusetts, which still claimed jurisdiction by right of her charter, but also from all persons claiming to be proprietors of the soil, including both sets of claimants to the soil at Pemaquid. This opposition soon became too strong for him, and effected his removal as just stated.

The fort was afterwards kept in tolerable repair, and a small garrison maintained there most of the time, until a few years after the taking of Quebec, in 1759. Persons now living in the place, have heard the old people describe the scene at the time it was dismantled, and the "big guns" removed by passing them through the gate in the northeast side.

The wood-work about it, of course soon decayed, but the stone walls remained in good condition until the beginning of the war of the Revolution. At a "regular town meeting," May 2d, 1774, a vote was passed to "pull down Pemaquid Fort; and that Tuesday next be appointed for the purpose."

Tradition says, that, at the time appointed, many of the citizens assembled, and actually "pulled down" the walls in accordance with this vote; and it also adds, that the reason for the proceeding was a fear that it might be seized by the British and used to the disadvantage of the cause of liberty.

TWO SAGAMORES OF PEMAQUID.

It is scarcely possible to hear the name of an American Indian without associating with it thoughts of treachery, cruelty, and bloodshed. But, whatever occasion there has been for this, it is pleasing to know, that, among those whose names have come down to us, there have been some whose fair fame is entirely unsullied by any such aspersions. Such were NAHANADA and SAMOSET, two sagamores of Pemaquid, of whose history, so far as known to us, it is proposed to give a brief sketch.

SKETCH OF NAHANADA.

NAHANADA. This man, whose name we find occasionally written *Tahaneda* and *Dehamida*,[1] was sagamore of one of the tribes at or near Pemaquid, probably the Wawenocks, at the time of Weymouth's famous voyage to the coast of Maine, in the summer of 1605. When he was at anchor in Pentecost (George's Island) Harbor, his ship was visited freely by the natives, who manifested the most friendly disposition; and a considerable intercourse took place, although they could converse only by signs. Mutual confidence seemed to be established between them; until at length Weymouth and his company began to inquire among themselves, how they could best secure a number of their confiding friends, to be taken with them to England. Few natives of America had then been seen in Europe, and they attracted much attention.

Having decided that they could best accomplish their object, not by the manly way of a mutual agreement, but by stratagem and violence, it was natural that they should very soon begin to see indications of treachery and lack of good faith on the part of the Indians. They, therefore, justified themselves, as soon as a favorable opportunity occurred, in seizing upon five of the natives, and securing them on board, with their

1 The different modes of writing this name appear to have proceeded from the way in which the native word, "N'tahánada," was caught by the English ear, by losing the first consonant and taking the second; or, *vice versâ*. The name is written in other forms besides those given in the text, which are easily resolvable into the original name.

canoes and whatever else they had. Their names, as given by Rosier, the apparently faithful chronicler of the voyage, were Tahanedo, a sagamore, or commander, Amoret, Skicowaros, and Maneddo, gentlemen; and Saffacamoit,[1] a servant.

When, a few weeks afterwards, the ship arrived in Portsmouth, where Sir Ferdinando Gorges then had command, three of them were given to him, (probably considered as slaves,) and the other two, it is believed, were sent to Sir John Popham, Lord Chief Justice of England, who was deeply interested in the projects then under discussion for the colonizing of North America. One of these last mentioned was undoubtedly Nahanada, the subject of our notice; who was thus favored with an opportunity to become acquainted with the English and English society. After about a year's residence with the Lord Chief Justice, he was restored to his native country, by Capt. Hanam, according to Strachey; but by Capt. Prin or Pring, according to Gorges.[2] This was in 1606.

Sir Ferdinando Gorges, writing many years afterwards, gives the names of the three "whom he seized upon," as Manida, Skettwarroes, and Tasquantum; but it is plain there is some mistake as to the last name.[3] Two of the five, — names not given, — were, in 1606, put on board of a ship commanded by Capt. Henry Challong, to be restored to their homes; but he was captured by a Spanish ship and taken to Spain, and it is not known whether the Indians ever again reached their native land. Skidwares[4] returned to America with the Popham expedition in 1607, and one of the five is unaccounted for.

1 This is a misprint in Rosier for Sassecomoit. The Abnaki Indians never use the letter *f*.

2 It is probable that these two men were officers of the same ship, but of different grades. See *ante*, p. 87, *note*, where Hine or Haines was "master under Challons," the "commandor."

3 Tasquantum is the name of an Indian taken by Hunt. Perhaps he had come into the hands of Gorges.

4 The same as Skettwarroes.

Gorges says that Skidwares accompanied Nahanada with Pring in his voyage to this coast in 1606, but if he did (which is doubtful), he certainly returned again to England before the sailing of the Popham expedition in the spring of 1607; as he was with them when they arrived, and made one of the first company that landed at Pemaquid. When the boat landed, "he brought them to the salvadges' homes, where they found a hundred men, women, and childrene, and their commander or Sagamo amongst them, named Nahanada." * * * * * "At their first comyng the Indians betook them to their armes, their bowes, and arrowes; but after Nahanada had talked with Skidwares, and perceaved that they were Englishmen, they caused them to lay aside their bowes and arrowes, and he himself come unto them and ymbraced, and made them much welcome, and entertayned them, and did they likewise him; and after two howers thus enterchangeably spent, they returned abourd againe."[1]

Another excursion to Pemaquid, by a larger company, was made a few days afterwards, who were kindly received by Nahanada at the head of a large body of Indians, all armed with bows and arrows. In their intercourse both parties manifested a little shyness, but no act indicated any unfriendliness.

The country between the St. George's and Kennebec Rivers was inhabited by the Wawenocks; and it is probable that Nahanada was sagamore of this tribe. Little is known of him during his residence in England, but it is believed that his character as a chief was recognized from the first. Though made an unwilling exile from his native country, we do not learn that he yielded to unmanly regrets on the one hand, or indulged in vain vituperations against his captors, on the other. And when the next year the English made their appearance in his country, though a little cautious, he received them with a

[1] Strachey.

degree of respect and confidence which they themselves felt they did not deserve.

After Popham's company had located themselves at Sabino, near the mouth of the Kennebec, Nahanada with Skidwares and numerous other attendants soon made them a friendly visit, as if to cultivate feelings of mutual friendship and confidence. Before leaving, it was agreed that Captain Gilbert, as representative of the colony, should make a visit to the great Bashaba at Penobscot, and that they should be accompanied from Pemaquid by Nahanada and a suitable number of attendants. Unfortunate circumstances prevented the full accomplishment of the plan, which is greatly to be regretted, as we should then have learned something worthy of our confidence of this now quite mysterious personage, "the grand Bashaba."

In the course of the autumn, Nahanada and his wife, attended by a brother of the Bashaba, and others, came again in two canoes to visit the new colony at Sabino, where they were kindly entertained by the English. As they remained there over the Sabbath they were invited to attend the religious services, which they did, "both morning and evening," behaving in all respects with propriety and reverence. Having spent as much time with their English friends as they desired, they returned home, having deported themselves in all respects in a becoming and friendly manner; and this although at the same time they were having some difficulty with the Indians living above them on the river.

Popham's colony, as is well known, was broken up the next spring and returned to England; and we hear no more of Nahanada until the time of Captain Smith's visit here in the summer of 1614. Smith speaks of the visit he received from him in terms that appear almost extravagant. He says that he was the main assistance to him, under God, and calls him one of the "greatest lords of the country," "who had lived long in England."

This noble testimony to the character of Nahanada is the last we hear of him; and his name passes from history without a reproach resting upon it.[1] Soon after this, those two worst scourges of the human race, pestilence and war, fell upon the natives of New England, and it is quite probable that by one or the other our Indian friend was swept away. Certain it is, that when, eight or nine years after the visit of Smith, we again get a glimpse of affairs at Pemaquid, the names of Nahanada and Skidwares are no more heard, — all is changed, and their places are filled by others.

SKETCH OF SAMOSET.

Samoset. This is the name[2] of another sagamore of Pemaquid which has been preserved to us, and the history we have of him is every way honorable and interesting. The first we hear of him is at Plymouth, March 16th, 1621, where he introduced himself to the "pilgrim fathers" by that generous salutation, "Welcome, Englishmen, Welcome, Englishmen," which was so grateful to their ears.

The passengers from the May Flower, we know, landed Dec. 21st, but the natives feared and avoided them; and until this time not a word of communication had passed between them. Indeed, few Indians had been seen, all of whom manifested feelings of hostility. In "Mourt's Relation," the account of Samoset's appearing among them is as follows: "And whilest we were busied hunting about, we were interrupted again; for there presented himself a savage, which caused alarm. He very boldly come all alone, and along the houses, straight to

1 There is, however, a probability that he was alive in 1648. A deed was then given to William Bradford and others, of land "from Cusenock up to Wesserunskick," by "Natahanada, son of old Natawormett, Sagamore of Kennebec." Copies of this instrument are preserved in the Pejepscot Papers, and in the records of Lincoln County.

2 Written also Summuset, Somerset, Sameset, and Sommarset.

the rendezvous, where we intercepted him, not suffering him to go in, as undoubtedly he would out of his boldness. He saluted us in English, and bade us 'welcome,' for he had learned some broken English among the Englishmen that came to fish at Monhiggon (Monhegan), and knew by name most of the captains, commanders, and masters that usually come. He was a man of free speech, as far as he could express his mind, and of a seemly carriage. We questioned him of many things; he was the first savage we could meet withal. He said he was not of these parts, but of Monattiggon (Monhegan), and one of the Sagamores, or lords thereof, and had been eight months in these parts, it lying hence a day's sail with a great wind, and five days by land. He discoursed of the whole country, and of every province, and of the Sagamores and their number and strength. The wind beginning to rise a little, we cast a horseman's coat about him, for he was nearly naked. * * He had a bow and two arrows, the one headed, and the other unheaded. He was a tall, straight man, the hair of his head black, and long behind, only short before, none on his face at all. He asked for some beer, but we gave him strong water, and biscuit, and butter, and cheese, and pudding, and a piece of mallard; all of which he liked well, and had been acquainted with such amongst the English." * * * "We would gladly have been rid of him at night, but he was not willing to go this night." At length it was arranged that he should sleep on board the May Flower, which still lay in the harbor; but the wind and tide being unfavorable for the shallop to go to her and return, they finally concluded to lodge him at the house of Mr. Stephen Hopkins, of course keeping a watch over him. The next morning he left them, promising to return again, which he did in a day or two, bringing "five other tall and proper men" with him.

Thus commenced the first acquaintance of the Plymouth colonists with the natives, by the kind services of this native of

Pemaquid, who for some time before returning to his own country, continued to make himself useful to them in giving them important information concerning the feelings of the neighboring Indians, the best places for fishing, the productions of the country, &c.

He introduced to them his friend Squanto, or Tisquantum, a native of the place, who could speak English, as he said, better than himself. This man was one of the twenty whom Hunt seized and undertook to sell into slavery six or seven years before this, and had resided some time in England. He afterwards proved himself a real friend, and Bradford says of him that he "became a spetiall instrument sent of God for their good beyond their expectation."

While Samoset remained in Plymouth both he and Squanto manifested a more friendly spirit towards the colonists; and sought always to promote good feeling between them and the Indians. Through their instrumentality a treaty of peace and friendship was established between them and Massasoit, sagamore of a neighboring tribe, which was kept inviolate between them for more than fifty years, or until King Philip's war, as it has been called, which broke out in 1675. Philip was the youngest son of Massasoit, and succeeded an older brother as sagamore of the same tribe.

Many other services of Samoset to the Plymouth Colony cannot be here given in detail. When or by what means Samoset returned to his native Pemaquid we are not informed; but we hear of him next at "Capmanwagan" (Southport) at the time of Levett's visit there in the winter of 1623–4. Levett introduces him to us as a "sagamore that hath been found very faithful to the English, and hath saved the lives of many of our natives, some from starving and some from killing." He met Levett and his company with the same generous confidence he had ever before shown in his intercourse with the English, and proposed that perpetual friendship should be maintained between them "until Tanto carried them to his wigwam, that is, until they died." He had with him, at this time, his wife and son, and several other attendants; and all are placed before us in an interesting light by the simple narrative of Levett. Samoset's wife, in particular, conducted herself in truly royal style. "When we came to York," he says, "the masters of the ships came to bid me welcome, and asked what savages they were. I told them and thanked them, they used them kindly, and gave them meat, drink, and tobacco. The woman, or reported queen, asked me if they were my friends. I told them they were; then she drank to them, and told them they were welcome to her country, and so should all my friends be at any time; she drank also to her husband, and bid him welcome to her country too; for you must understand that her father was the sagamore of the place,[1] and left it to her at his death, having no more children."

This, it will be observed, was only a little more than a year before the date of the celebrated Indian deed to John Brown, of which an account has already been given. This deed was given by Samoset and Werongait, sagamores of the place. We have no information as to the second signer of the deed, as his name does not again occur; but Samoset lived many years after this at Pemaquid, in quiet and peaceful intercourse with the settlement, so far as we know. In 1641, and again in 1653, his name is mentioned. At the last date it is probable that he was an old man, and we may suppose soon passed away. It is very certain that he was not living at the time of King Philip's war.

Though only an "untutored savage," he has left behind him acts highly creditable to him as a man of elevated rank among his countrymen. He appears not only to have been entirely free from the jealousies and petty vices of his race, but on all

1 It must be noticed that they were now at York, which it seems was her native place, but she had married a man out of her own tribe.

occasions manifested a love of truth and justice, and a generous confidence in others, quite superior to many of the Europeans with whom he came in contact. And the fact, that seventy years after the last date above mentioned, his name was still remembered among the natives as that of a "famous sachem," shows that his manly character was not unappreciated by his countrymen.

GEORGE WEYMOUTH AND THE KENNEBEC.

BY THE REV. EDWARD BALLARD, OF BRUNSWICK.

The following notice of this early navigator [1] and his discoveries has been prepared by the editor, to supply in part a connection in the events, which led to the founding of the colony under President George Popham. In past times, the "most excellent river," entered and explored by him without his giving its name to the public of his day, has been claimed, more as the opinions of the different writers have chosen to regard it, than as proved by an examination of all the evidence. The Penobscot, the Kennebec, the Saco, the Hudson, the James, and more recently, the George's, have each had their defenders, as the one which Weymouth examined and Rosier described. The purposed obscurity of the account naturally led to these disagreements. But fuller information and more accurate investigations, leave no uncertainty in determining the truth involved in the inquiry.

Little is known of George Weymouth before he engaged in his voyage to the Arctic regions, in search of a Northwest passage, from which he returned in 1603. His experience "by employments in discoveries and travels from his childhood,"

[1] The sentiment in his honor will be found on page 127.

and specially in this last effort in exploring, as well as his active fidelity to the duties of his commission, made him a suitable person to be employed by the Earl of Southampton and Lord Arundel of Wardour, in a new enterprise to the American shores. The fear, that the neighboring nations of Europe might be stimulated to the like efforts in the same direction, if the expectations connected with the voyage were known, caused its patrons to conceal its destination and hopes from general knowledge; and the public mind was allowed to believe that this second attempt was to be directed to the same northern quarter as its predecessor. But in reality, it was sent to explore the coast of New England, then known as North Virginia, for the purpose of colonization and the benefits to accrue therefrom. With a partial equipment of men, with provisions more than enough for the time occupied, and articles for traffic with the natives, he sailed in the ship "Archangel" from Ratcliffe, England, March 5, 1605, "upon a right line"[1] to the new world. He first went to Dartmouth Haven to complete his crew, where he was detained by opposing winds. But on the thirty-first day he put to sea, with "the whole company, being but twenty-nine persons." The narrator of the voyage was JAMES ROSIER; who says that the obscurity of his narration, by omitting to give the latitude, longitude, and names of places, was intended, so as to prevent foreign nations from gaining an advantage from the success of the English.

But this account, now read with the light thrown upon it from other sources, tells us that Weymouth came to the coast of New England in the neighborhood of Cape Cod, on the 13th of May; and that afterwards, in turning his course away from the perils of that shore, he was misled in seeking land, "and much marveled that we descried it not, wherein we found our sea-charts[2] very false, putting land where none is."

1 Formerly the course had been by the West Indies.

2 Prepared by former navigators, perhaps Gosnold.

Four days afterwards, he came to an island, which he called St. George's,—but by the Indians it was named Monhegan,—and anchored about a league from its northern side. From this anchorage, "the captain with twelve men rowed in his ship boat to the shore," where he erected a cross;[1] and from the island itself, and probably its high part, "a great way (as it then seemed, and we after found it) up into the main we might discern [i. e. dimly see] high mountains, though the main seemed but low land."[2] The evidence, drawn from several circumstances in the account, leads to the belief that these distant elevations were the White Mountains; which Levett calls "the Crystal Hill," and says it can be "seen to the east so far as Monhegan."[3] The present residents say the same.[4] The Camden Hills can hardly be said to be "a *great* way up into *the main*," as they are not much more than twenty miles from the southern point of the peninsula nearest to Monhegan, and scarcely more than half that distance from "the main," whence the peninsula projects into the ocean.

The next day he sailed in the direction of these "mountains," towards the islands lying outside of the broad expanse of water, now known as Boothbay Harbor, some of which lie about twelve miles from Monhegan; and which he says were about three leagues from it: a league being three geographical miles, or 3.45 English or statute miles. This place he called "Pentecost Harbor," in memory of the day of his arrival there. On one of its shores he set up another cross, and "dug wells, to receive the fresh water, which they found issuing down out of the land in many places."

The reasons for this opinion are, that this sheltering place then, as now, could be reached by "four several passages;"

1 Strachey in Maine His. Col., p. 296.

2 Rosier in 3d ser. Mass. His. Col., vol. 8, p. 132.

3 Maine His. Col., vol. 2, p. 84.

4 Maine His. Col., vol. 6, pp. 309, 310. See also Id., vol. 5., p. 314.

and also that the general description of the water, and the land, bating the changes by settlement and cultivation, will answer well for the present day. But a *special* reason for this claim is found in the following fact: that in going to explore the "great river," they sailed DOWN to "the islands[1] adjoining to the mouth thereof." This course is proved by the fact, that after the captain "had searched the soundings all about the mouth and coming to the river," "with a breeze from the land," they "sailed [from these islands at the mouth] UP to their watering place, where they filled their casks with the fresh water from their wells," and there stopped[2] in the harbor. This description suits the passage from the mouth of the Kennebec, — the real Sagadahoc, — and not the Penobscot or the George's. For sailing *up* from the islands at the mouth of either of these rivers, would have carried them away from their supposed harbor, amid the islands of the ocean, whether at Monhegan[3] or the George's,[4] and of course farther inland on the river, which they had just before left.

Here the expedition made its chief tarrying place; cultivated acquaintance with the Indians, and collected a vocabulary of four or five hundred words and phrases. Of these the narrative gives but two, which show that the language was the same as has been preserved in part by Ràle. From hence parties went out to explore "the river," which is described in terms of the highest commendation.

The question here arises: Was the Kennebec the river which Weymouth entered, and from the mouth and island of which he sailed *up* to his anchorage in Pentecost Harbor, "with a breeze from the land?"

Belknap, who had not seen Rosier's account, but guided by Purchas, who made additions to the portions extracted,— un-

1 Ros., pp. 146, 148.

2 Ros., p. 153.

3 Me. Hist. Col., vol. 5, p. 348.

4 Me. Hist. Col., vol. 6, p. 296.

less his N. N. E. is a misprint for N. N. W., in which last letter lies the complete correction of Belknap's error, — decided for the Penobscot.[1] The late John McKeen, Esq., of Brunswick, in his long and accurate investigations in historical pursuits, discovered the error, and communicated his views in behalf of the Kennebec, in a paper published in the Maine Historical Collections, volume fifth. Writers since have ingeniously adopted the George's. But it will be a sufficient answer to these claims, to show that the Kennebec was the river that drew forth the eulogy of Rosier. The few statements to be made are mostly those which Mr. McKeen either proposed in writing and conversation, or approved when presented for his consideration. It is a pleasant duty of friendship to reproduce the thoughts of this honest and industrious investigator in regard to the path of Weymouth, as it would be to do the same for Popham's Colony and Gilbert's exploration on the Androscoggin.

1. The first of these statements, in addition to the *upward* course from the river to their watering place is drawn from an *exploring march*, made by Weymouth from its western shore.

Having left his harbor for this purpose on the 12th of June, from his "ship riding in the river," and in his pinnace with seventeen men, he ran "up to the codde thereof,"[2] where they landed, leaving six men to guard the boat.

The Saxon word "codde," in this ancient orthography and application, denotes a small creek-like opening of inland water, with a narrow entrance where it is connected with the larger body. A little bay or creek of this kind, about twelve rods wide, is known to have existed, and indeed in large part still

[1] So does the editor of Rosier, p. 154, note; and also of Gorges' Brief Narration, Maine His. Col., vol. 2, p. 17; and writers generally following Belknap, till Mr. McKeen.

[2] Rosier, p. 149.

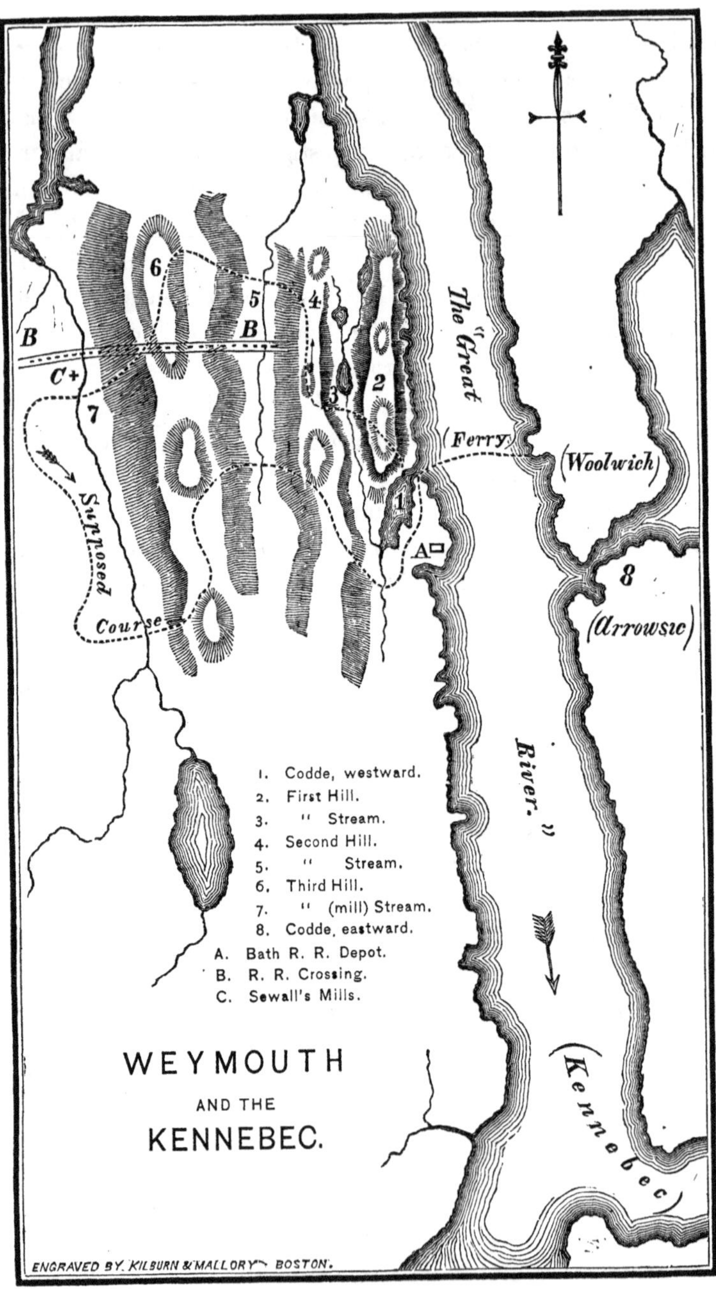
The "Great
(Ferry)
(Woolwich)
8
(Arrowsic)
River."
(Kennebec)
Supposed
Course
B
B
C+
A
1
2
3
4
5
6
7
1. Codde, westward.
2. First Hill.
3. " Stream.
4. Second Hill.
5. " Stream.
6. Third Hill.
7. " (mill) Stream.
8. Codde, eastward.
A. Bath R. R. Depot.
B. R. R. Crossing.
C. Sewall's Mills.
WEYMOUTH
AND THE
KENNEBEC.
ENGRAVED BY KILBURN & MALLORY BOSTON.

remains, in the place now occupied by the city of Bath, and is shown on the accompanying map, having its narrow channel opening near the steamboat wharf.[1] It has been sufficiently deep, within the memory of persons now living, to admit a vessel much larger than the "pinnace" is supposed to have been, and indeed could do the same now, if the entrance was not covered with a low culvert in the principal business street. It ran back in a south-westerly direction for fifty or sixty rods, and then abruptly turned to the north, where it received into the tide a small stream of fresh water, from the two abrupt bordering ridges between which it flowed, and little ponds at its head.

From this inlet, ten of the men "with shot and some armed, with a boy to carry the powder and match, marched up into the country towards the mountains," which they had seen from the heights of Monhegan.[2] The account does not say that they now saw the distant summit; but that they proceeded in that direction as they saw it at first. As they came up the river they were so near "some of them," as the group appeared in the distance, that they deemed themselves "when they landed, to have been within a league of them," and this distance accords well with their ascribed position in "the codde." It is worthy of note in this connection, that in Strachey's account of Popham's arrival off Seguin, he gives a sketch representing the highlands on the western side of the Kennebec, looking north, and calls these same elevations, "The high mountains;"[3] which, from a right point of view, would make a part

[1] Its outlines in its primitive state are given in Hammatt's Map of the "Town of Bath," 1833.

[2] Here Purchas perplexes by adding that they were "continually in our view." This is true of the highlands in Phipsburg and Bath, near which they passed on the river, and which make the foreground of the "clump." There are, however, several places in Bath where the White Mountains can be seen.

[3] Maine Hist. Col., vol. 3, p. 298.

of the foreground, in which "the twinkling mount of Aucocisco,"[1] would appear as the crowning ridge.

The party marched up into the country in the direction indicated, "about four miles in the main;[2] passed over three hills; at the bottom of every hill a little run of fresh water; and the last ran with a great stream, able to drive a mill."

All this is true now. Going diagonally to the right from the north side of the little bay still partly open, as indicated on the accompanying map, the pedestrian passes over a steep hill, now at one place ascended by stairs. On the other side at the bottom, formerly several feet lower than now, where the railroad track is laid, is a "little run of fresh water," flowing toward the tide of the ancient "codde," with its original course somewhat diverted by the filling up for the railroad. Thence he ascends another hill, and in descending the slope beyond the summit, comes to a second rivulet of "fresh water," flowing in the opposite direction; and at a longer distance across the third rise to the "Waskeag,"[3] which has been able "to drive a mill" for centuries, and does now. The rambling nature of the excursion will account for the estimated distance. The kind of trees and other vegetation, and the character of

1 This is Smith's description of the White Mountains, which he places on his map less than five leagues from the salt water in Casco Bay. Perhaps to such a foreground as is mentioned above, he applied on his map the name "The Base." May not "Casco" be the same as "Aucoc'isco," with its first syllable sounded as an Indian guttural, and the accent on the second, as if pronounced "Uh-cos'-is-co?" The name "Koskebee" occurs in Mr. Poor's Address. [p. 68, *ante*], denoting the inner portion of Portland Harbor, and meaning "Crane-Water." [Me. Hist. Col., vol. 6, pp. 146, 147]. It was easy for the English to change the native word to "Casco Bay," and make it embrace the waters, with their multitudinous isles of beauty and value, between Cape Elizabeth and Small Point.

2 i. e. "For the most part; or about;" afterwards he speaks of "the space of about three miles."

3 Commonly pronounced Whiskeag.

the soil, harmonizes with the description given, even at the present day.

As they were returning to the ship in the pinnace, they "espied a canoe, coming from the further part of the codde of the river eastward, which hasted to us,"[1] bearing an Indian, whom they had a special reason for knowing in Boothbay Harbor, and who had come west through a well known inland passage with a message to the captain from the Bashaba. This accuracy of expression, — "the codde of the river eastward," was used in opposition to the "codde" *westward*, which the explorers had just left. This *eastward* passage, appearing to these strangers like a narrow and receding bay, is the strait between Arrowsic and Woolwich, which spreads out broadly at a short distance within, and affords a passage through the "Gates" to the Sheepscote, through which the Jesuits came to the Kennebec for grain in 1611,[2] and also a southerly one to the ocean.

It is here believed that these striking circumstances respecting the western "codde," the "march," the "three hills," and as many "fresh water streams," with "the codde of the river eastward," and the return "up" to their harbor, have never been fully noticed or explained in their relation to the other rivers mentioned.

2. A second exploring excursion was made the next day, further "up to that part of the river which trended westward into the main, to search that," where Weymouth had probably been to discover on the 30th of May."

The company started "by two o'clock in the morning" by reason of the favoring tide. They "carried with them a cross to be erected at that point" where the waters turn to the

1 Rosier, p. 150.

2 Biard's Rel., p. 36.

west;[1] which, because they reached the place before daylight, they left there until their return, when they "set it up in manner as the former" on Monhegan, afterwards found by Popham. On the waters of the Merrymeeting "trending westward," they sailed up into the Androscoggin, "towards the great mountains," and found the "profit and pleasure, described in the former part of the river, wholly doubled in this."

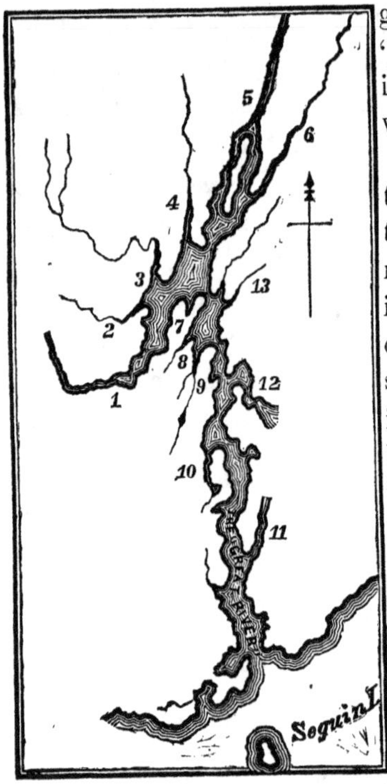

THE "BRANCHING STREAMS" OF THE "GREAT RIVER," (KENNEBEC.)

1. Androscoggin. 2. Psazeské, or Muddy. 3. Cathance. 4. Abagadusset. 5. Kennebec. 6. Mundooscotook, or Eastern. 7. Butler's Cove. 8. Whisby. 9. Waskeag. 10. Winnegance Creek. 11. Back River. 12. do. 13. Towessuc, or Trott's Creek, and Chops' Creek.

But the particular feature in these waters, bearing convincing testimony to the identity of the river, is contained in the following extract: "From each bank of the river are divers branching streams into the main, whereby is afforded an unspeakable profit by the conveniency of transportation from place to place, which, in some countries, is both chargeable, and not to be fit by carriages, or wain, or horseback."[2]

In no part of the account is the description more matchable with the unchangeable facts.— Personal acquaintance with these waters, or the map of Sagadahoc County, of which a section is here given, shows that these "branching streams," — which in the next paragraph are called "arms running up into the

1 The aboriginal name of this point was "Acquehadongonock," "Smoked-Fish-Point;" now called "Chops' Point," from the narrowness of the opening out of Merrymeeting Bay into the lower Kennebec.

2 Rosier, p. 151.

main," — are the Androscoggin, the Psazeské or Muddy, Cathance, Abagadusset, and the Kennebec; all of them opening into the expanse of the "great river," and the smallest large enough to bear heavy boatable burdens for several miles inland, and all of them actually used for that purpose. Butler's Cove, more "arm"-like when its sides were clad with trees; the Whisby, from which a canal was dug in later years to the New Meadows River, opening into Casco Bay; the Waskeag, both on the western side of the Kennebec just below the Point; the Towessuc and its neighbor stream, Chops' Creek, with their cove-like mouths, nearly opposite; Back River, over against Bath; the Winnegance inlet, and the river-like passage, dividing Arrowsic from Georgetown, all boatable, with others of smaller note, may be added; as also at a short distance above the Bay, the Mundooscotook, or Eastern River, equally used for transportation by sailing vessels for miles upward.[1]

The like confluence of navigable streams within so narrow a compass, is not to be found in either of the rivers into which it has been argued that Weymouth entered; and we need not wonder that these advantages for commercial pursuits filled the mind of Rosier, beholding the whole with the admiring eyes and vivid impressions of a first voyager;[2] and that he should celebrate its praises in terms little short of extravagant. The distances were given by estimation, and are not probably too long, if compared with the shore line, along which he must have gone to see the branching rivers and their shores covered with "clear grass."

This remarkable fact of these several confluent streams has

1 Lescarbot gives the results of De Monts' researches the same year. His Map shows the Androscoggin, Merrymeeting Bay, the Kennebec, and Swan Island.

2 He says: "It floweth eighteen or twenty feet at high water." This mention of its depth has been strangely taken to mean the rise of the *tide*. But the connection shows it to have been the depth of the *river* at flood tide, which is true now.

not received merited attention from the advocates of the Penobscot and George's theory. As no similar fact is there known, this evidence alone may be deemed conclusive ; and the various incidents of the exploration, as well as the distances, can be shown to be in agreement with Weymouth's entrance into the Kennebec.

3. The testimony from ancient maps may be here introduced.

Smith's map (1614), gives the Kennebec with the two "coddes," as far as Richmond, and in Merrymeeting Bay places five intimations of the entrances of the "branching streams." It gives but little space to George's Bay, and less still to its river, and none to the Penobscot above its broad bay; thus showing the value he put on the Kennebec as *the* river for trade and profit. The Dutch maps of 1616[1] and 1621 give no indication of the George's, which they could hardly have failed to do if it had been deemed of great commercial promise. It is the same on the maps of Lescarbot, La Hontan, and Charlevoix, though they all give the Kennebec and Penobscot. A map in "Heylin's Cosmography" (1663), shows two large rivers. The easternmost is "Pentoget," an ancient name applied to the Penobscot. The other with two large branches, and the only one on the New England coast thus depicted, bears the name of "Weymouth." But the George's has no place.

4. But in addition to these testimonies there are statements in early writers to show that Mr. McKeen entertained no new theory, when he disclosed the unintended error of Belknap. In this country Hubbard had said, long before any controversy had arisen on the point, that "Att this time they discovered a great river in those parts, supposed to be Kennibecke, neare unto

1 *Ante*, p. 155.

Pemmaquid, which he found navigable 40 miles up into the country, 7, 8, 9, or 10 fathome deepe, as Capt. Weymouth reports."[1] Prince, at a later date (1732), records of the river that Weymouth entered, "this seems to be Sagadahoc."[2] He adds, that "Sir F. Gorges doubtless mistakes in calling it Pemaquid River." It is not here known from what part of Gorges' "Narration" this was taken. But it is probable that he meant the *region*, not the river of Pemaquid, a stream of no commercial importance. He says, "Weymouth happened into a river on the coast of America, called Pemaquid." (ch. II). It would seem that by this name he meant the *coast;* and the river might then be the "great river" on this *coast.* Smith[3] says that Weymouth's "Relation" described "Pemaquid," which surely must denote the "coast."[4] Belknap stands alone in saying that the "Penobscot was sometimes called Pemaquid."[5]

In England we have the clear and explicit testimony of Strachey. As Secretary under the charge of the Virginia Company, he had access to papers in their possession, and was also in the way of hearing the verbal reports of persons engaged in the discovery; and therefore his record of facts must be regarded as ample evidence touching "the most excellent and beneficyall river of Sagadahoc;"[6] He quotes largely the very language of Rosier; gives to the world the *name* which Rosier studiously concealed, and adds to his description but little else. In immediate connection with these statements, he describes the colony of Popham as coming directly to the same river, doubtless chosen for occupancy from Weymouth's information.

1 Hist. N. E., p. 12.

2 Chron. p. 109.

3 3d series Mass. H. C., vol. 6, p. 105.

4 *Ante*, p. 264, see a similar opinion expressed.

5 Biog., p. 150.

6 In Me. H. C., vol. 5, p. 300, it is asserted that "Sagadahoc" may be applied to any river. But universal Indian and English usage restrict it to the Kennebec when employed as a local name.—*Ante*, p. 9, note.

For he says: "That upon his (Weymouth's) returne, his goodly report with Capt. Gosnolls cawsed the business with so prosperous and faire starrs to be accompanied," that new enterprises were commenced; in which was actively engaged, — under "the letters patents, the tenth of April, 1606," — "the upright and noble gentleman,[1] late Lord Chief Justice of England, chief patron of the same, Sir John Popham, knight."[2]

Among these enterprises were the voyages of Chalons and Prynn, destined to the Sagadahoc, but without success for settlement. Then came the colony of Popham and Gilbert, who sailed for the same river, and settled within it, because, as in the two previous expeditions, it had been recommended by Weymouth. For it would have been strange indeed, that if either the Penobscot or George's had been so eulogized, they should have sailed past both in good weather, and purposely have sought "Satquin" as a landmark, and the neighborhood of Sagadahoc in a storm, into which so strong was the wind, that on the first attempt, only "the fly-boat gott in." But their perseverance effected their intention, and they thus illustrated a chief motive, which Williamson ascribes to the promoters of Weymouth's voyage; namely, the advantages of *prior possession* and *continued claim.*[3]

The advocates of the other theories fail to allow Strachey a fair hearing. As a competent witness both in opportunity and knowledge, as well as fidelity in narration, his testimony, corroborated by the facts that the first attempts at colonization were directed to the mouth of the Kennebec, is sufficient to gain a verdict in favor of this river.

If the foregoing positions are true as to the geographical relations of Pentecost Harbor to "the islands adjoining to the

1 Smith had the like opinion of the Chief Justice, whom he styles "that honorable patron of virtue."—3d Series Mass. H. C., vol. 6, p. 105.

2 Me. H. C., vol. 3, pp. 289, 290. Gorges also laments of him that he "had lost so noble a friend, and his nation so worthy a subject."—Nar., ch. 9.

3 Williamson, vol. 1, p. 191.

mouth of the 'great river,'" as well as to the discoveries made therein; if maps of the olden time can speak evidence; and if the affirmation of American and English historians, made before any doubt or controversy had arisen on the subject, be of value in determining facts, then is it plain that the Kennebec was "Weymouth River;"[1] Boothbay was Pentecost Harbor; and the course from Monhegan to the outlying islands at its opening, was "in the road directly with the mountains;" which, by a line drawn according to this indication, a little north of "Fisherman's Island," in the Damariscove group, are shown to be the White Mountains, and which, on a nearer approach, would have the smaller coast elevations in range, forming the foreground of the landscape.[2]

In reading the narrative of Rosier, it is a pleasure to witness the devout spirit of the writer in his frequent recognition of divine Providence in protecting the company of explorers, and the benevolent purpose for which the voyage was made. "For," he writes, "we supposed not a little present profit, but a public good and true zeal of promulgating God's holy church, by

1 Heylin says, "Weymouth Rio." In Ogilby's Map of New England, etc., the word "Rio" is applied to several well-known rivers. This use of a Spanish word implies that the map makers consulted Spanish authorities. Ships of this nation were on the North American coast as early as 1578, and continued afterwards engaged in fishing. It is not improbable that Weymouth's discoveries on the Kennebec were known to them, which might have been learned from Chalons while their prisoner.

2 While these pages were in press, an intelligent gentleman, familiar with coast and ocean voyages, states, "that on two occasions, and early in the summer, he saw the White Mountains distinctly, when about ten miles southwest of Monhegan. On one occasion the mountains were very white, the snow not having entirely melted. On both occasions no land was in sight in the direction of the mountains. They seemed to rise out of the sea." A line, drawn from the point thus indicated, to the White Mountains, shows a distance but little greater than from the supposed point of Weymouth's anchorage north of Monhegan. Another gentleman, of the like experience, once saw them clearly for several hours from the neighborhood of Nantucket, a distance perhaps even greater. The sight might have been aided by a high state of refraction.

planting Christianity, to be the sole interest of the honorable setters forth of this discovery."[1] Weymouth, whose care and activity as a commander is favorably presented, appears to have been actuated by a similar spirit. The fact of his having "service" on ship-board on Saturday evening, at which two Indians, invited to supper, afterwards attended, and "behaved themselves very civilly;" and the strictness of his observance of "the Sabbath day" following, are indications of regularity in the duties of religious worship, such as is known to have been observed by many Arctic navigators, reminding us of Smith's account of "daily common Prayer morning and evening," besides the services "on Sundaies," in Virginia. It is not improbable that a chaplain made a part of the complement of men in the Archangel.

In opposition, may be placed his capture of five Indians, of whom "Tahánedo" was a "sagamore or commander,"[2] to carry them to England. Of these only two appear to have been taken against their will. But while this action may not be easy to be justified by present views, it may be said, that he regarded them as natural curiosities, — wild men, — to be taken as wild animals and shown to his friends at home, and thus advance the interests of the enterprise. They all received kind usage. One was specially "delighted with their company;" and the two, that were at the first surprised, never seemed discontented, "but very tractable, loving and willing by their best means to satisfy us in any thing we demand of them." On their arrival in England, three of them were taken by Gorges, who regarded their coming as most auspicious for the colonizing interests of the country, in which he was the leader, giving to them his time, venturing[3] his estate in their promotion, and suffering great losses. For he says, "This accident (of the Indians coming into his hands) must be

1 Rosier, p. 153.

2 *Ante*, p. 224, note 2.

3 Narration, chapter 2.

acknowledged the means under God of putting on foot and giving life to all our plantations." [1] And thus this act of Weymouth and his kind treatment of the captives, became one of the connecting links between English civilization and American colonization. Nahanada prepared the way for Popham, who followed the intimations of Weymouth, and placed his colony at the mouth of the Kennebec.

THE CHURCH OF ENGLAND AND EARLY AMERICAN DISCOVERY AND COLONIZATION.

BY REV. WILLIAM STEVENS PERRY, OF PORTLAND.

The deep religious character of the colonists, preceding those of Plymouth and Massachusetts Bay, has been little noticed by historians, and rarely if ever alluded to in the more popular compends whence most of our countrymen gain their acquaintance with the discovery and settlement of our shores.

1 From the great risks and losses sustained by Gorges, he may well be called, as he sometimes has been, "an adventurer." But it must be in accordance with the usage of his times; and in the same sense as Hubbard describes the members of the joint stock company, which was formed by the London merchants, "the adventurers," with "those of Leyden," before sailing to Plymouth, "the poor people, who were to adventure their persons as well as estates." All persons engaging to go, above sixteen years old, are named "adventurers and planters," as members of this "joint stock and partnership for the space of seven years," when the capital and profits were to be divided. [Hubbard, Appendix to Morton's Memorial, pp. 279, 280.] But "the company of adventurers broke in pieces" in 1625. [Prince Chron.] It was no discredit to the early and constant patron of the discoverers and colonists to our shores to bear that name; nor others to engage the services of men at a price, as did the persevering settlers at Plymouth, when they "hired the master and his company (in one of the ships engaged) to stay a whole year in the country;" and not wasting their toil in a hopeless exploring for mines, which were a common expectation, sought and found their profit in support of the settlement, from the "fishes of the sea." [Morton's Memorial, pp. 20, 29.]

And yet, as might have been inferred from the condition of both Church and State in England, — at a time not very far removed from the purifying of the Reformation and the Marian fires, and when, in the ceaseless and embittered struggle with France and Spain for the Empire of the West, it was a *religious* war that was waged, in which Raleigh, Gilbert, Drake, and their compeers, were champions of the Protestant faith of the English Church, against the Papacy and its allies, — the leaders of colonization at home, the earliest voyagers to our shores, and the settlers here, were men influenced as much by the desire for the salvation of souls, the good of the Church of Christ, and the wide extension of the limits of a common christianity, as any that followed them. Perhaps a few references to the well-established facts of history, will fittingly preface and confirm the statements I propose to make, with reference to the piety and faith of the little colony at Fort St. George in Maine in 1607–8, the anniversary of whose landing day has of late received, for the first time, appropriate attention.

Even at the early date of A. D. 1578, had the wilds of North America echoed with the solemn words of the service of the English Church, — words fitting, from their scripturalness and their spirituality, to be the vehicle of the first act of public Protestant devotion in a new world. Martin Frobisher, who first led an English colony to our shores, and among whose "Articles and Orders to be observed for the Fleete," was "Imprimis, to banish swearing, dice, and card-playing, and filthy communication, and to serue God twice a day with the ordinary seruice as usuall in the churches of England,"[1] was wont thus to set sail on his expeditions of discovery and colonization:

"On Monday morning, the 27th of May, aboored the *Ayde*, we received all the Communion by the Minister of Grauesend, and prepared us as good Chris-

[1] Hakluyt 3, 74, in Prot. Ep. Hist. Col. 2, 244.

tians towards God, and resolute men for all fortunes. And towards night we departed for Tilberry Hope."[1]

And so when on his third voyage, Frobisher took with him a hundred colonists to settle on the lands he had discovered, the narrative of his Expedition tells of the services and character of Wolfall, their Chaplain, who was certainly the first Protestant missionary as well as minister on our continent. It was after the recital of a marked deliverance that the old annalist proceeds to tell that,

"They highly praysed God, and altogether vnpon their knees gave Him due, humble and hearty thanks; and Maister Wolfall, a learned man, appointed by her Majestie's Councell to be their Minister and Preacher, made vnto them a godley sermon, exhorting them especially to be thankeful to God for their strange and miraculous deliuerance in those so dangerous places and putting them in mind of the vncertaintie of man's life, willed them to make themselves alwayes readie as resolute men to enjoy and accept thankfully whatsoeuer aduenture His diuine Providence should appoint. This Maister Wolfall, being well seated and settled at home in his owne countrey, with a good and large liuing, having a good honest woman to wife and very towardly children, being of good reputation among the best, refused not to take in hand this paineful voyage, for the onely care he had to saue soules, and to reforme these infidels if it were possible to Christianitie: and also partly for the great desire that he had that this notable voyage so well begunne, might be brought to perfection: and therefore he was contented to stay the whole yeare, if occasion had serued, being in euery necessary action, as forward as the resolutest men of them all. Wherefore, in this behalfe, he may rightly be called a true Pastor and Minister of God's Word, which for the profite of his flocke spared not to venture his own life."

The pious faith of these brave discoverers, and the source whence their strength for endurance came, appears in further extracts such as this, under date of August 20th, 1578:

"Maister Wolfall on Winter's Fornace, preached a godly sermon, which being ended, he celebrated also a Communion upon the land, at the partaking whereof was the Captain of the *Anne Francis*, and many other Gentlemen and Souldiers, Mariners and Miners with him. The celebration of the diuine mys-

1 Id. in Anderson's Hist. Colon. Ch. 1, 81.

tery was the first signe, seale, and confirmation of Christ's name, death, and passion, euer knowen in these quarters. The said Mr. Wolfall made sermons, and celebrated the Communion at sundry other times, in seuerall and sundry ships, because the whole company could neuer meet together in any one place."[1]

The same year Sir Humphrey Gilbert obtained his patent for discovery, which, as his son Raleigh Gilbert was connected with the "Popham" Colony, stands in close relationship with that later movement we are about to notice. This Patent conferred upon the worthy Knight full power and authority over the lands he should discover, and established in the Colonies to be settled under his leadership, "the true Christian faith or religion now professed in the Church of England."[2] In pursuance of these designs, after one unsuccessful attempt, Gilbert and his company landed on the shores of Newfoundland on Sunday, August 4, 1583, and on the following day, with "twig and turf," took formal possession of the island. This done, the first of all the laws which he enacted, enjoined that the services of religion should be "in publique exercise according to the Church of England."[3] Lost at sea in a fearful storm on his return voyage, Gilbert died as a Christian hero should die. Choosing the weakest vessel as his own, he was last seen "sitting abaft with a booke in his hand," and his last words were, "we are as neare to heaven by *sea as by land*." The sea swallowed him up; but his faith and his example were the encouragements of those who, a few years later, settled on the coast of Maine.

1 Anderson's Colon. Ch. 1, pp. 81, 82. It is an interesting fact, that the place where Frobisher made his tarrying place in the strait, or rather bay, as it now appears, bearing his name, has recently been visited; and undoubted traces discovered of the men, who were lost by him among the Esquimaux. [C. F. Hall, in American Geog. and Statistical Soc., N. Y., Nov. 6, 1862.]

2 Id. p. 48. Hazard's State Papers. vol. 1, p 24. The early charters, as contained in Hazard, are full of proof of this design of Christianizing the Indians.

3 Id. 1, p. 53. Palfrey's Hist. N. E., 1, p. 68.

The close connection of the English Church with these early efforts for maritime discovery and colonization, is seen in the aid given by the Rev. Richard Hakluyt, the excellent prebendary of Westminster, in the early expeditions following Gosnold's return in 1602. The expedition of Martin Pring, in 1603, was undertaken by the chief merchants and inhabitants of Bristol, mainly at the solicitation and through the influence of this noble Churchman, whose name is not only inseparably connected with the efforts for settlement, but is also illustrious for the pious care with which he has preserved for posterity the quaint narratives of the old voyages. Hakluyt had earlier incited Raleigh to the work to which this nobleman afterwards gave so many of his best years, on the ground that "no greater monument could he raise; no brighter name could he leave to future generations, than the evidence that he had therein sought to restrain the fierceness of the barbarian, and enlighten his darkened mind to the knowledge of the true God."[1] And now that Raleigh's efforts to the Southward had failed of permanence, — though there had been gained at Raleigh's colony at Roanoke, in 1587, the baptism into the English Church of the first aboriginal convert to Christianity,[2] — Hakluyt sought in other quarters to encourage that spirit of adventure and colonization which should result in the gain of lands and nations to the service of Christ and His Church.[3]

The expedition which Hakluyt had aided in sending to the Northeast coast of America in 1603, was followed by another, also dispatched from Bristol, under the command of George Weymouth, in 1605, fitted out by Henry Wriothesley, Earl of Southampton, the friend and patron of Shakspeare, and Thomas,

1 Latin Epist. Dedic. to Peter Martyr's Hist. New World.

2 Anderson, vol. 1, p. 75. Bancroft, vol. 1, on Early Settlements.

3 In Anderson, 1, pp. 156–162.

Lord Arundel,[1] who had earlier been concerned in Gosnold's expedition. We have no certain knowledge that this expedition was accompanied by a chaplain, other than the fact that voyagers rarely went on such undertakings without the presence of a clergyman, and the inference we may draw from Rosier's own words in his account of the voyage, where he says they had two of the Indians " in presence at service, who behaved themselves very civilly, neither laughing nor talking all the time."[2] This whole account, to quote the fitting language of Anderson,[3] " bears evident marks of having been written by one who, whilst he recorded fresh discoveries and opportunities of extending temporal dominion, sought thereby to enlarge the borders of Christ's spiritual kingdom." An instance of this we may cite where the true objects of the expedition are announced, by Rosier: " We supposing not a little present profit, but a public good and true zeal of promulgating God's holy Church by planting Christianity, to be the sole interest of the honorable setters forth of this discovery," &c.

It was on the receipt of the cheering intelligence gained by these voyages, that there appeared the first Letters Patent, dated April 10, 1606, granted by King James I. for the plantation of Virginia, lying between the 34th and 45th degrees of north latitude, and divided into two parts, called South and North Virginia. The religious character of those who sought these grants is apparent from the professed object of their efforts for Colonization as set forth in the Patent itself, where it is expressly stated that the desire of the Patentees was granted by the King, that

" So noble a worke may by the Providence of Almighty God hereafter tend to the glorie of his Divine Majesty, in propagating of Christian religion to such

1 Strachey, Hist. Trav. p. 158. Williamson, 1, p. 191.

2 3d ser. Mass. H. C., vol. 8, p. 139.

3 Col. Ch., 1, p. 162.

people as yet live in darkness and miserable ignorance of the true knowledge and worship of God, and may in time bring the infidels and savages (living in those parts) to human civility and to a settled and quiet government." [1]

An ordinance under the sign-manual of the King, and the Privy Seal, explanatory of these Letters Patent, and passed November 20, 1606, before any expedition under either of these grants had sailed, further declares,

"That the said presidents, councils, and the ministers, should provide that the Word and service of God be preached, planted, and used, not only in the said colonies, but also, as much as might be, among them, according to the rites and doctrine of the Church of England." [2]

Under this Royal Patent the first expedition to Virginia sailed December 19, 1606, and landed at Jamestown, May 13, 1607. This colony had for its chaplain the saintly Robert Hunt, an English clergyman chosen for this work by the celebrated Hakluyt, with the concurrence of Archbishop Bancroft, the Primate of all England. Of his pious labors, and of the godly men who followed him, Bucke, Whittáker, and Copeland, and others like them, devoted Presbyters of the English Church, we have not time to speak. They labored not alone for the white colonists, but for the aborigines. Their efforts were not unsuccessful, and their record is on high.

A little later the same year, May 31, 1607, — the expeditions thither of the preceding year having proved unsuccessful, — the first colony to the Northern Virginia, or, as afterwards called, New England, set sail from Plymouth, under the patronage of Sir John Popham, Lord Chief Justice of England, and Sir Ferdinando Gorges. This expedition, as was the case with that to the Chesapeake, had its chaplain. It is but recently that his name has been discovered. That honored name is

1 Anderson, 1, p. 165.

2 Id. 1, p. 166. Stith's Va., p. 37. Chalmers's Polit. Annals, p. 16.

Richard Seymour. An ingenious conjecture has been lately advanced by one of our most exact and well-informed historical investigators, that this clergyman was connected with the Ducal house of Somerset, the family name of which house being the same as that of our first New England missionary clergyman, and that he was possibly a younger son of the first Duke, who was himself, but a few days afterwards, a Patentee in the company which succeeded that of which we have been speaking. Be this as it may, that Richard Seymour was a Presbyter of the English Church, has been acknowledged by our most painstaking and accurate historical writers,[1] and the language of Strachey, the historian of the expedition, in which the services of the Church and the "publike prayers" themselves, are referred to in language which is conclusive on this point.

This colony, brought to our coast in a fly-boat called the *Gift of God*, under Popham's command, and the good ship *Mary and John*, of London, of which Raleigh Gilbert, son of Sir Humphrey, was the captain, came in August 7, to an island where "they found a crosse set up, one of the same which Captain George Weyman, in his discovery, for all after occasions, left," and on "Sonday, the chief of both the shipps, with the greatest part of all the company, landed on the island where the crosse stood, the which they called St. George's Island, and heard a sermon delivered unto them by Mr. Seymour, his preacher, and soe returned abourd againe." Having chosen a fitting place for their settlement, near the mouth of the river, on the 19th of August, 1707, as Strachey informs us,—

> "They all went ashoare where they had made choise of their plantation, and where they had a sermon delivered unto them by their preacher; and after the sermon, the president's commission was read, with the lawes to be observed and kept."

1 *Ante*, p. 101. Bartlett in Ch. Monthly, 1, p. 56.

Mindful of their professed designs for the instruction of the Indians, after several explorations, in which, though under much provocation, they abstained from firing their guns at the crafty natives, they sought to bring them to their humble church, and there acquaint them with the worship of the Englishman's God. Under date of October 4th, the narrative thus details one of these efforts:

> "There came two canoas to the fort, in which were Nahanada and his wife, and Skidwares, and the Basshabaes brother, and one other called Amenquin, a Sagamo; all of whome the president feasted and entertayned with all kindness, both that day and the next, which being Sondaye, the president carried them with him to the place of publike prayers, which they were at both morning and evening, attending yt with great reverence and silence."[1]

Thus cultivating amity with the natives, and thus mindful of their God and Church, this little colony proceeded to establish themselves upon our soil, with success for a season.

The church thus inaugurated in Maine, reappeared twenty-eight years afterwards, when first Richard Gibson, and then Robert Jordan came to minister to the settlements on the coast. They were checked in their labors by the restrictions of the Massachusetts government, even so far as by imprisonment for clerical duties; and after that colony, "under pretence of an imaginary patent line, did invade our rights and privileges, erecting their own authority,"[2] at length the Church was compelled to yield to that power, and depart from the place, leaving her members without the ministrations of their affections and choice.

The question has been presented, how do we know that the Common Prayer prefaced the sermon given on that memorable August 19, 1607, thus giving it claim to the honor of having been the first form of worship in the English tongue

[1] Strachey, pp. 168, 172, 178.

[2] Me. Hist. Col., vol. 1, p. 302.

sounded on the crisp air of New England? The subsequent language of Strachey, where he refers to the "morning and evening" and "publike prayers," is certainly conclusive, when we remember that the use of the Book of Common Prayer was then obligatory by the terms of the very patent under which these men had sailed. The nature of the service in which they were engaged confirms this statement. It was the public induction into office of the magistrates of the new plantation; and the statute law of England then, as was the case for many subsequent years, required the reception of the sacrament from the hands of a clergyman of the Established Church, either at the time or immediately after such formal institution. This was the case in the sister colony of Virginia, where, on June 21st, of this same year, the day after the members of the council had been fully sworn in, and the organization of the government happily accomplished, the Holy Sacrament was duly celebrated for the first time within the limits of the United States.[1] That a similar observance marked these inaugural rites on our Northern coast, it is hardly possible to doubt; and the fact that special mention is not made of it by Strachey, who received his knowledge of the fortunes of the Sagadahoc Colony at second hand, and who has condensed his account of their proceedings into the briefest possible space, is easily explained on the ground that such a procedure was the ordinary rule, and that only the exception would be likely to receive direct notice. Surely to convince us that the Episcopal Liturgy was used in connection with this sermon, it were enough to cite, in addition to the positive injunction of the Patent, the "laws of uniformity" and "canons ecclesiastical" of England then enforced by the court of High Commission. The *disuse* of this service would have perilled the very existence of the company, had they desired it; while the fact that they sent out in every subsequent case none but clergymen

1 Anderson, vol. 1, pp. 174, 175.

well affected toward the Church of England,[1] proves that no such wish was ever entertained by them. The connection of the principal men of the colony with England's highest noblemen as well as with her Christian worthies of an earlier day, goes to confirm the fact of the Episcopal character of both preacher and people; and Popham's brother, holding office under the Crown, and Raleigh's nephew, and Gilbert's son, would hardly be found linked in with the "separatists" from the English Church at so early a date as this. In fact, the "separation" from the Church of England had not as yet begun; for, if we may credit Neal, the first actual instance of "Independency" or "Congregationalism" in England was not till the year 1616, when Henry Jacob gathered his "Church," and openly separated from the Establishment.[2]

And now, to sum up all this matter in the language of one, the weight of whose authority has secured these words of his a place in the Historical Collections of Maine, these facts are established: "That the first religious services [in the English language] of which any knowledge has been preserved, as having taken place in New England, were performed by the chaplain of this colony; that these services were held in accordance with the ritual of the Church of England; that the minister who celebrated this worship and preached these sermons was a clergyman of that Church, deriving his authority for his sacred office from ordination by the hands of a Bishop of the same Church; and that these acts were performed at first on an island, and in the open air, and afterwards continuously in a church near the Kennebec River, on the west side of one of the peninsulas of the coast, in the year 1607, *thirteen years before the landing of the colony on Plymouth Rock*, and some time before the Puritans left England to reside for a season in Holland."[3]

[1] The Rev. William Morrell in Massachusetts, and Gibson and Jordan in Maine, were pioneer clergymen of this Church.

[2] Neal's History, Pt. 2, ch. 2.

[3] Maine His. Col., vol. 6, pp. 177, 178.

The celebration of this interesting event, the first real occupation and settlement of New England, from which the title of England to a most important share of the northern coast of America dates, would have been confessedly imperfect, and certainly unworthy of the high and holy faith of the adventurers whom it would commemorate, without suitable religious services. It was but just that this commemoration should reproduce the words of prayer and praise first echoed on the still air of New England in August, 1607.

These *very words*, made use of two hundred and fifty-five years ago by Richard Seymour, Presbyter of the Church of England, are still preserved. Popham's colony bore to our shores the revised Prayer Book of the reign of James I. The *old words themselves*, identical, unchanged, are accessible both in the few copies of the original edition of 1604 in our public libraries, and in the reprint issued by Mr. William Pickering of London, a few years since.

The words "preacher" and "sermon," employed by Strachey in his narrative, are indicative of the same facts, and are sustained by the recorded formularies and documents of that Church. In the "injunctions" of King Edward VI., A. D. 1547, the whole body of the English Clergy of the Establishment is spoken of as "preachers."[1] In the record of Purchas, speaking of "true preachers," we find in the same relation, "every Sunday, sermons twice a day, and every Thursday, a sermon."[2] Indeed, quotations might be multiplied to the largest extent, to prove the existence of these names and esteem for the men who bore the office and did its duties, in the Church, which sent out Richard Seymour as the first Protestant minister and missionary to our northern coasts of New England.

1 Sparrow's Collection of Articles, p. 8, seq.

2 In Anderson, vol. 1, pp. 216, 217.

FROM THE HON. MR. BANCROFT.

The following letter would have been assigned an earlier place,[1] if it had been received at an earlier date.

NEW YORK, June 13, 1863.

MY DEAR SIR: — I regret that it was not in my power to be present at the celebration of the landing of the first colony in Maine. I am very glad to find that the citizens of Maine are determined to set in a distinct light, the relation of that region to the general colonization of the country. It was the noble harbors along your coast which first raised the hope of planting a nation on your soil; and the effort of Gorges was a sort of prophecy of the future commercial greatness of your State.

I have not perhaps formed so high an idea of the importance of the essay at Fort Popham, as some others may have done; but the charter under which it took place, was undoubtedly one of the means which reserved that part of New England, and indeed all New England, to the enterprise of Englishmen. I hope your historical students will not only renew attention to the various patents which covered their territory, but also be unremitting in their zeal to trace with distinctness the various places which successively became occupied by men of English descent.

It is the fashion of the world to speak of all New England as if it were homogeneous; and so in one sense it is; but more careful discrimination will show marked points of difference between the several New England States. To register these differences with impartiality, and to deduce them from their causes is the duty of the historian.

Time sweeps away all the influences which have interfered with just and candid judgments. Now-a-days, it will be

[1] *Ante*, pp. 100, 232.

admitted that the English Government did not sin against fairness, when it claimed that the Anglican Church should at least be tolerated in an English colony; and had the advisers of the Stuarts demanded no more than equality, impartial history must have qualified its censure of their tyranny. But it was with New England, as it was so often in the world's history; it needed intense suffering to induce the best men of England to exchange their native country for the wilderness; and however interesting it is now to define the action of English royalists in founding colonies, the great result was certainly accomplished by men who were driven from their homes for conscience' sake.

But the self-defending energy of the founders of Massachusetts does not in the least degree take from the interest that attaches to the efforts at planting colonies in Maine; and the country will look to your historical inquirers to persevere in collecting and analyzing all the facts which illustrate its origin, and so to explain the shades of difference that mark its character. I remain, my dear sir,

Very faithfully yours,

GEO. BANCROFT.

GOVERNOR WASHBURN.

His Excellency, Israel Washburn, Jr., of Orono, Governor of Maine, accepted the invitation of the committee of arrangements, for the purpose of giving his assent in person, as the Chief Magistrate of the State, to the placing of the "Memorial Stone" in the walls of Fort Popham. But the imperative calls of the Federal Government, at this trying moment in its history, upon his time and thoughts, in connection with military affairs, rendered it impossible for him to attend the commemoration, consistently with his convictions of public duty. At the last moment, therefore, he was compelled to devolve upon the Hon. Abner Coburn, soon to be his successor in office, the service assigned to the Governor, of which an account is given in the early part of the volume.[1]

Governor Washburn has, however, at the request of the committee, favored them, for publication, with the notes of his speech as prepared for the occasion, which they are pleased to be able now to present.

SPEECH OF GOVERNOR WASHBURN.

We celebrate to-day, on the soil of Maine, and on the spot of the first settlement made by Englishmen in New England, and coincident with the first in America, an event the most significant and auspicious in the history of the continent, and of modern civilization. This occasion implies a retrospection and a prophecy. We shall bring before our minds the circumstances of Popham's Colony; its landing here, two hundred and fifty-five years ago; its various fortunes and its fate; the thought which created it; its connection with, and its influence upon, the permanent occupation of the country by the Saxo-Norman race; and the great and wise men, Sir Ferdinando Gorges and others, by whom it was originated and conducted. But our highest concern is with the future which it postulated; with the principles of civil and religious liberty which it represented; for the final expression and embodiment of which, this continent, as I believe, had been reserved.

The recorded object of Gorges, was to lay the foundations of a State, in which the rights of human nature should be adequately recognized, and the progress of mankind assured.

[1] *Ante, p.* 50.

As stated in his own simple yet grand words, his purpose was to promote "THE ENLARGEMENT OF THE CHRISTIAN FAITH, THE SUPPORTATION OF JUSTICE AND LOVE OF PEACE." Not so much for the protection and upbuilding of a religious party or sect, as for that freedom of thought in religious matters, which is the condition of a healthy and saving faith; not for outward prosperity mainly, but for equal and exact justice among men; not that the ambitions and strifes of the old world should be repeated in the new, but that the reign of peace and good will might be established; not for the transfer hither of old principles and policies, but for the development of what has come to be known throughout the world as the "*American idea*," did the illustrious founder of Maine give his fortune, his thoughts and his heart. And the plant which he caused to be set in our soil, has grown to the proportions of a noble tree. It blossomed in the Declaration of Independence, and its consummate fruit is the American Union.

It was a happy thought that suggested the commemoration of his great work at this time, that we, who have profited by it, might testify our appreciation of the noble objects for which it was begun, and our unshaken faith in the perpetuity of the Government established to promote them. For in this mad revolt of barbarism and violence against that government, it is well for us to come here that we may examine the foundations upon which it rests; that we may consider how well it is worth preserving, and how recreant we shall be if we permit it to be destroyed.

And standing on this ground, fitly chosen of all spots from ocean to ocean, how clearly do we see that the old principles of bigotry and intolerance, of despotism and oppression, of hatred and war, are not to prevail against the nobler, more catholic, more humane, more Christian ideas to which this continent was dedicated so long ago; and that the government which represents them so well now, shall be preserved to be their fuller representative hereafter; as under its protection and influence, "Christian Faith" shall be increased to the stature of that Charity which "casteth out fear;" and "Justice" shall be practiced more and more until oppression shall cease, and the last fetter be struck from the last slave in the land, and the "love of Peace," filling the hearts of men, shall herald the golden period foretold by our greatest poet, when

"No longer from its brazen portals,
The blast of war's great organ fills the skies;
But beautiful as songs of the immortals,
The holy melodies of love arise!"

FROM E. F. JOHNSON, ESQ., MIDDLETOWN, CONN.

This letter was not received from the writer until too late for insertion in connection with the appropriate sentiment in its order; which, being prolific in the materials for a speech or an essay, is here repeated[1] as the proper introduction to the remarks which follow.

Maritime Adventure and Discovery, — illustrated by men of Bristol and the Severn; whose Cabots and Gilberts pointed the way to the northern shores of the New World. The name of Raleigh Gilbert shall ever be honored, for his fidelity in conducting to these shores the Colony of Popham.

DEAR SIR: — Had it been possible for me to have attended your late celebration, on the anniversary of the founding of the first English Colony in New England, I could have contributed nothing to the interest of the occasion, so far as knowledge connected with that settlement was concerned.

But the several expeditions which came to these shores at

1 *Ante,* p. 111.

the close of the sixteenth and beginning of the seventeenth centuries, were a natural sequence to the fact of the prior numerous visitations to the Banks of Newfoundland for fishing purposes.

That this continent was visited long anterior to this time by Europeans the evidence is now too strong to be questioned. The fleet that annually congregated in the Thames and other British ports to convey grain to the continent in the time of the Romans, is evidence that the art of navigation was then sufficiently advanced to justify the belief that a trans-atlantic voyage was practicable. It was indeed not only practicable, but it was possible to make it with less difficulty and danger, than was incurred in making the passage of Behring's Straits in such crafts and with such means as the natives of the eastern coast of Asia were supposed to possess.

We know that Iceland, which is an American island, was visited and settled by Europeans at a very early date. We know, also, that from the fourth to the seventh century, Christianity and civilization had made great advances in Iceland; and that from this time, and for a long period after, the British Isles were exposed to Scandinavian raids and invasions from the north; and it is not unreasonable to infer, that during this period many expeditions may have left those islands and landed on the American coast never to return.

The superior intelligence of those thus migrating would give them, in mingling with the natives, rank and importance. Intermarriages with the families of chieftains would be the consequence. Their children would inherit their honors, and to a certain degree their intelligence, and the result would be a marked difference in the intelligence of the chieftains and their families compared with the natives generally.

Indian history, so far as we have knowledge of it, confirms the superior intelligence of their chief men; and the portraits of such of them as have come down to us, show, I think, unmistakably the European lineaments. The mounds in the valley of the Mississippi afford important evidence in support of this hypothesis.

These mounds, as they appear in northern Wisconsin, are very rude and imperfect in form compared with those in the valley of the Ohio. The latter possess a magnitude and accuracy of outline which indicates such a knowledge of Geometry as might have been communicated by the early navigators in question.

This reasonable supposition may be said to be confirmed as truth by the discovery of the stone tablets in the mounds of "Grave Creek," in western Virginia, having inscriptions in the old Celtic and Manks characters; mounds upon which trees of six hundred to seven hundred years old were found growing on the first settlement of the country.

In the center of the largest of these mounds at Grave Creek, which was seventy feet high and over three hundred feet in circumference, was found the smaller of the two tablets and a human skull, which answers well to that of a European. These inscriptions have recently been deciphered, and prove, beyond a doubt, that the bodies there deposited once spoke the language of the British Isles. The translation of these inscriptions, which have been made by a friend at my request, I will endeavor to procure for you, if you desire it, in time for insertion in the published proceedings of your celebration.

The question will naturally be asked, Why, if all that I have stated is true, was there not some traditional knowledge of it in possession of the Indians? The answer is this, that from the twelfth century to the voyage of Columbus in 1492, intercourse between the continents was probably wholly suspended, and in that period the knowledge of the early visitations had faded from the Indian mind, as had also the European complexion from their bodies.

That this is a very proper conclusion is proved by the fact, that traditionary knowledge, unsupported by a written language, is unreliable after a few generations. A writer, who lately visited the Auracanian Indians in South America, a people whose ancestors fought the Spaniards in many pitched and bloody battles and were never subdued, states that those Indians have, at the present time, no traditionary knowledge of those battles; and this knowledge would have passed into oblivion had it not been preserved in Spanish history.

The researches of antiquarians and others, during the last thirty years, tend very clearly to establish the fact of the early visits of the so called Papæ and of the Norsemen to this continent, and it is not unreasonable to suppose that Columbus derived, on his visit to Iceland, certain evidence of our Atlantic coast, which he supposed to be the eastern coast of Cathay,[1] and of its general direction, as far south as the Gulf of Mexico.

Preparatory to his voyage thither, he had gone to the northern shores of Europe and sought out the results of the daring sea expeditions of the Danes and Norwegians. With the ruling desire to learn all that had been known of the Atlantic waters, he would not be likely to omit to visit the most eligible point in the British Isles for obtaining a knowledge of what had been more recently done or learned in relation to discoveries in the western seas; and hence the city of Bristol and the waters of the Severn would receive from him particular attention.

Bristol was at that time the principal seat upon the Atlantic for maritime adventure and enterprise; and it was from thence that John Cabot sailed in 1497, and Sebastian Cabot in 1798; the former reaching this continent on the coast of Labrador in June, 1497, and the latter the coast of Maryland in 1799.

Lord Bacon, in his life of Henry VII., says: "And there had been before that time a discovery of some lands which they took to be islands, and were indeed the continent of America to the northwest."

[1] China and Japan. *Ante*, p. 221.

This "discovery of some lands" had reference, evidently to voyages prior to those made by the Cabots. The voyages of the latter, made in the years named, resulted in the re-discovery or confirmation of what was probably previously known in respect to the northern portion of this continent.

The discovery by Columbus was at a later date. He accomplished no more on his first visit to San Salvador than did Nadod when he discovered Iceland in A. D. 860; nor as much as was effected by those who founded a colony on the same island in 874; or as did Eric the Red, when he discovered and founded a colony in Greenland in A. D. 982.

Columbus landed in 1492 on the island of San Salvador, but did not see the continent until his second voyage several years later, after the Cabots had actually set foot upon it at two different and distant points, and explored much of its coast. San Salvador and Iceland are both American islands, the former being farther from the main land than the latter from Greenland. Hence the credit of the discovery of the American continent cannot with propriety be given to Columbus. It must be given either to John Cabot or the Norsemen who preceded him.

That Columbus is entitled to very great credit for enterprise and an indomitable perseverance, all must admit; but neither his discoveries or the difficulties he surmounted should be unduly magnified at the expense of truth or the just claims of others equally deserving.

In his journal of his visit to Iceland, prior to his voyage made in 1492, he distinctly states that he sailed three hundred miles to the north of that island; which distance, as we now understand the Geography of that region, would bring him in close proximity to the coast of Greenland, near Cape Brewster. This view receives support from the fact of the readiness with which he pledged himself to his mutinous crew to return to

Spain if he did not find land within three days. This does not detract from his great merit in being the first to traverse the widest and previously unexplored portion of the Atlantic, and as the leader of an expedition, which only his superior intelligence and indomitable perseverance could have organized at that period of the world.

It may be asked, why, if all that is here suggested is true, there are not to be found in Iceland and elsewhere, records more complete and authentic than the meager collections already made of the first visits of the Norse navigators to this continent? The absence of such records will cause less surprise when it is remembered, that records of that description, at that period, were made and kept by persons who had an interest in maintaining the claim of the head of the Roman Church to the ownership of all lands discovered by Columbus. At that day the doctrine that "the end justified the means," was boldly avowed by the highest ecclesiastical authority; and the search, should one be made for the desired evidence, if that evidence still exists, will be quite as likely to be crowned with success, if made in the cloisters and convents of Spain and Italy, as if made in Iceland or the British islands.

Columbus, in his journal of his voyage to Iceland, speaks of the trade carried on with that island by the merchants of Bristol. I have stated my conviction of the value of the information which he must have derived from the English navigators who frequented the waters of the Severn. In those waters, it may be said, was cradled the maritime policy and power of England; and there is paid no more than a just tribute to the memory of the Cabots and the Gilberts in the sentiment, in which they are so honorably mentioned, and which connects the name of the latter with Popham and the Sagadahoc. They were, indeed, bright stars in the galaxy of nautical skill and enterprise, which has shed its luster upon the British Isles from their first appearance in history, and which, for many centuries, has placed England in the front rank of European civilization.

Yours respectfully,

EDWIN F. JOHNSON.

Middletown, Conn., June, 1863.

THE LOST AUGUSTA.

BY R. K. SEWALL, ESQ., OF WISCASSET.

At the request of the committee, while this volume was passing through the press, an account of a once thriving town within the limits of the "Province of Sabino," has been cheerfully prepared by the historian of the "Ancient Dominions of Maine." It is here presented to the reader.

Between the city of Bath and the town of Brunswick, an arm of the sea pushes up and in toward Merrymeeting Bay, called "New Meadows River," the upper portion of which was the ancient "Stevens River," on the margin of which an Indian truck-master or trader of this name, had his station; and near which in later years a canal, eight feet wide and deep enough to float lumber[1] to the sea, opened into the waters of the Kennebec, one and a half miles distant, at or near the ancient dwelling-place of Thomas Purchas, an early settler on this part of the river.[2] The remains of this canal are yet traceable.

[1] Williamson, vol. 1, p. 47. In some places "thirty feet wide."—Id. p. 33.

[2] Williamson, vol. 1, p. 266. On the Kennebec the outlet through Whisby Creek was near the residence of Christopher Lawson, the first settler on that part of the river. [Old Map in Pejepscot Papers.]

The point around which the "Stevens and New Meadows River" join the waters of Casco Bay, and enter the sea by way of Sagadahoc Beach, is termed "Cape Small Point;" which, terminating the Peninsula of Phipsburg on the west and south, is broken into sundry headlands and rocky islets, indentations and eminences, where the tides of "Casco" and "New Meadows" embrace each other in pools of deep sheltered waters, forming a small but convenient harbor, behind the islets and under the headlands of the cape. The Peninsula of Phipsburg, from which, on its eastern shore, the famous "PENINSULA OF SABINO" strikes out into the sea as a lateral spur, — Sagadahoc Island of the ancients forming its prominent feature, — makes what is now known as "SMALL POINT HARBOR," some three miles distant from the margins of "Atkins Bay," southwesterly.

JOHN PARKER'S OWNERSHIP.

June 14, A. D. 1659.

Mohotiwormet, or "Robin-Hood,"[1] the great Sachem of Nequasset, in consideration "of one Beaver skin and a yearly rent of one bushel of corn," and a "*quart of liquor*," to be unto him paid, or to his heirs forever, by John Parker, at or before the 25th day of December, being Christmas day, at the dwelling-house of the said Parker, "let, set and sold" out to the said John Parker the aforesaid peninsula, including the site of "Small Point Harbor;" but which was then known only as "Parker's Plantation," within the jurisdiction of "Sebenoa," the ancient Lord of Sagadahoc.[2]

1 Mss. Indenture, Robin-Hood to Parker.

2 Strachey quoted in Ancient Dominions of Maine, p. 90.

FRANCIS SMALL'S TRADING-POST.

Francis Small, an Indian trader, owned and occupied
the lands at the mouth of New Meadows River; and A. D.
from this man's relations to this point, the locality ob- 1664.
viously derived its existing name, and which the said "Small" must have held under Parker, who, by certain stipulations with "Richard Wharton," in the reign of Charles II., A. D. 1684, engaged to "*settle a town on the premises*," as well as pay an annual quit rent of "*two dried cusk, or two cod-fish*," if demanded by the said Wharton or his heirs, as the conditions of peaceable and quiet possession of his purchase of Robin Hood, to himself, his heirs and assigns. The indenture recites as an additional consideration in the premises, that the said "John Parker *was the first of the English nation that began to subdue the land there and undertook the fishing trade;*" and the town to be settled was required (as a further condition of title in homesteads) "*to submit its regulations and affairs to such persons as the major part of the free-holders or inhabitants should annually choose.*"[1] Thus were laid the foundations of a commercial depot at the mouth of New Meadows, for the trade of the interior waters of the Androscoggin and Kennebec.

DEATH OF JOHN PARKER.

But the ruthless savage soon invaded the peaceful homes of these enterprising frontiers-men, and the torch of barbarian hordes, preceded by the horrors of the tomahawk and scalping knife, forced all to fly. John Parker and his son James reached "Casco[2] Bay," (now Portland,) and were there

1 Wharton's Mss. papers, Indenture to John Parker.

2 Ancient "Aucocisco."

slain[1] at the taking of the Fort Loyal, 20th of May, 1690, when Falmouth was sacked by the French and Indians.

REVIVAL OF SETTLEMENTS.

A. D. 1713.

The peace, a result of the treaty at Portsmouth, the 13th of July, so far restored confidence, that the re-settlement of the "eastern frontiers," in the occupation of the depopulated plantations, began with marked promise and unusual energy. The titles of the former inhabitants, by purchase and inheritance, in many cases had passed into fresh hands. The Parker estate changed possessors.

The estate of the ancient Thomas Purchas, near the head of Stevens River, and its improvements, together with that of John Parker, on the Peninsula of Phipsburg, became the property of Richard Wharton's assigns. Although the Plymouth Company first located on the site of Fort George in the Province of Sabino, where the Popham Colony[2] had landed, supposing and intending it to be embraced in their purchase at Kennebec, the subsequent removal of their trading station to "Cushnoc," (Augusta, the site of the present capital of Maine,) and the determination of their rights at law, limiting their boundaries on the south above Merry-meeting Bay, admitted the rights of the Pejepscot proprietors, under the titles of Wharton, to the settlements of John Parker and his assigns.

Belcher Noyes, of Boston,[3] a physician, and secretary, or clerk, of the Pejepscot Company, became interested in the Parker estate, and located himself at Small Point Harbor, and concentrated his means and energies to the execution of Wharton's designs, in reviving the town attempted by Parker and Davis prior to the catastrophe of the late war. The Pejepscot

1 Deposition, Mss. John Philips, Williamson, vol. 1, page 621.

2 Williamson, vol. 1, p. 52. *Ante*, 108, 109.

3 Mss. Certificate, John Parker's Deed.

Company sanctioned the effort, as coming within the limits of their jurisdiction; and at a meeting of the Proprietors, May 24, 1716, passed a vote "that there be a Town laid out at Small Point Harbour." At the same time fifty acres of land were granted to each of the first fifty families, who should build a house and occupy it for three years. A town-meeting was held for action under this vote, "Augusta, Nov'r 6th, 1717."

The trading post of Francis Small, at the cape harbor at the mouth of New Meadows River, the opening of the direct trade with Merry-meeting and the Kennebec at the sea, was re-occupied. Capt. John Penhallow, — the military leader of the inhabitants, — took up his residence here with Dr. Noyes; and to Mr. Mountfort was set off and assigned within that town two hundred and fifty acres of land, adjoining Dr. Noyes' harbor farms;[1] and the newly revived town was called "Augusta," which now arose to adorn the margins of Casco Bay, at the mouth of New Meadows River, in the present town of Phipsburg. Emigration was stimulated; the Halls, the Springs, the Rideouts, and the Owens, were landed here from the western emigration; two streets were laid out on which the house lots abutted; a road eight rods wide was opened to the Sagadahoc from "Augusta Harbor;" and Edmund Mountfort[2] who acted as clerk of "the Inhabitants of Augusta," was authorized to lay out farms of ninety-five acres each for the settlers newly arrived; "Lots," seventy to one hundred feet wide were surveyed and laid out at the harbor;[3] and a cart-way was cut across the Peninsula of Phipsburg opposite "Arrowsic." A stone fort was also reared, — esteemed the best military de-

[1] Ancient Dominions of Maine, pp. 225–6.

[2] N. H. Historical Collections. Pejepscot Records, vol. 1, p. 113.

[3] A special grant of land was made to "Benj[a] Purrington" because "his wife was of forwardness in promoting said settlement." Pejepscot Records, vol. 1, p. 97.

fense in the east, — and maintained[1] at the public cost. The sloop "Pejepscot" regularly plied between Boston and the "Augusta" of the ancients;[2] foreign commerce here started, and it became the point of an export trade for vast quantities of pipe staves, boards, plank, and timber; agriculture also throve; and the fisheries were re-established by Dr. Noyes, in which some twenty vessels were by him engaged, — particularly the sturgeon fishery near Brunswick which, nearly a century before, had been carried on by Thomas Purchas, and many thousand kegs cured for export every season. Fine buildings were erected; saw mills put up; a convenient mansion-house was built; lots for a "Meeting House and Burying place"[3] were set apart for public use.

To carry out the intention of increasing the settlement, an agreement, signed and sealed by the leaders in the enterprise, was made March 7, 1719, with "the Rev. James Hillhouse of Boston, New England," to grant him six hundred acres of uninhabited land in two lots, to be chosen in Topsham, Brunswick, or Augusta, each lot having a frontage of half an English mile on navigable water, in consideration of his going to Ireland to induce settlers to remove to these new towns. The allotment was to be made after his return; and if he settled in any of these three places himself, he was promised suitable encouragement.[4]

Such were the site and prospects of the Augusta of the ancients, which, by the energy and skill of its founders, had contrived to concentrate the trade of the Kennebec and Androscoggin at Small Point Harbor, as the nursery of the new town aspiring to the honors of commercial eminence.

1 Penhallow, p. 88.

2 Ancient Dominions of Maine, p. 225.

3 Augusta Town Records.

4 Penhallow says that a minister was supported in these eastern towns by the Pejepscot Company. p. 88.

But the desolations of savage warfare [1] against which Penhallow had been a leader, subsequently swept over this fair and promising establishment. The fort for a while was kept at public cost. But it was afterwards neglected by the government, and the inhabitants, unprotected by military force within its shelter, withdrew from the settlement, and left all to the Indians, who burnt the combustible part of the structure, and with it several houses. Thus its fisheries were broken up; its inhabitants scattered; its fort ruined; and its trade destroyed. The benefits of an inland water-way, devised, completed, and used in years long after, from Casco Bay as an outlet to the resources of the interior waters of the mighty Kennebec, would have added to its prosperity and wealth, if it had been protected or left undisturbed by the onsets of the savages. Its reminiscences even, are buried under its ruins, now overgrown and nearly lost amid the decay of almost a century and a half. [2]

The importance of this ancient town to one of the most fertile and populous sections of Maine, had it survived to this day, can hardly be estimated. In all probability, it would have rivalled both Bath and Portland, in extent of facilities for trade and commerce. The location of the ancient "Augusta" [3] was most eligible for commercial enterprise; and had it remained in its incipient prosperity, until the Merry-meeting waters, by navigable communication with the sea by the way of Stevens River, had been laid open, a city of important relations and extent would now, doubtless, have distinguished this early appreciated spot, as a center of trade to the Androscoggin and Kennebec valleys, of which Brunswick would have been the great interior depot.

1 The "Four Years' War," beginning 1722.—Williamson, vol. 2, pp. 111, 119.

2 Ancient Dominions of Maine, p. 225.

3 The knowledge of this lost town was recovered by the investigations of the late John McKeen, Esq.

The following addition is to be made to Mr. Sewall's communication, under the caption, "Pemaquid," on page 143, and at the end of the first sentence, after the words "probably Pemaquid."

The "Gift of God" was the Popham ship. The writer of "Ancient Pemaquid" tells us that Capt. John Smith,—who visited Sagadahoc in 1614, six years after the abandonment of the Peninsula of Sabino by the London men under Raleigh Gilbert,—projected a map from point to point and harbor to harbor, as he had coasted along shore. "This map he presented to Prince Charles, who gave Pemaquid the name of 'John's town,' and to Monhegan, 'Barties' Isles.'"[1] It is obvious, therefore, that at this date the Peninsula of Pemaquid exhibited such rudiments of English occupancy, or had grown into *a fair English town of such extent and importance as to entitle it to receive, by Royal donation, an English name and place on the charts of English authority!*

The "St. John's town" of Pemaquid must, therefore, have been nearly cotemporaneous with the "Georgetown" of Sabino and the Popham colony; and there cannot be a reasonable doubt, that both had a common origin from the Popham enterprise; and that this "St. John's town" of Pemaquid, as found and described by Capt. Smith, was a fruit of Sir John Popham's colonial adventure at Sagadahoc.

REV. MR. NORWOOD'S SERMON.

On the Sunday following this celebration, the Rev. Francis Norwood, the Congregational minister of Phipsburg, "the ancient Sabino,"—within the limits of which town the celebration was held,—preached a sermon, having special reference to the occurrence. The

[1] Ancient Pemaquid in Me. H. C., p. 162. 3d Series Mass. H. C., vol. 6, pp. 97, 105. May not this name, "St. John's town," be the origin of the "Jamestown" of a later period, which appears in the annals of Pemaquid? The John's River may have derived its name from this early gift.

following extract from this discourse is worthy of being reproduced in this volume; as well to show the kindly feelings of the author towards the Episcopal Church, as the reasons why the services of that Church should have been used on the occasion.

EXTRACT FROM SERMON.

"The day was indeed auspicious, the assemblage vast, the scene imposing. But why this grand preparation and splendid array? It was to commemorate a historic fact; viz., the settlement on this spot of an English colony under George Popham, in August, 1607. Certainly this was a memorable event, that should be known, cherished and transmitted to posterity. And it was natural that the Episcopal Church should lead in this commemoration, since the colony was planted under their auspices; and on their first landing, as was most appropriate, worship was conducted according to the forms and rites of that Church.

I venerate this ancient Christian Church; the good and learned men who have ministered at its altars; who have vindicated God's word against Romish assumptions and despotism; and who, by the light of holy doctrine and example, have guided thousands on in the path to glory. I subscribe to the Apostles' Creed embodied in its Liturgy; to its Thirty-Nine Articles, with slight exceptions; and especially and emphatically to that one which declares that "Holy Scripture containeth all things necessary to salvation, so that whatsoever is not read therein, nor may be proved thereby, is not to be required of any man, that it should be believed as an article of the faith or be thought requisite or necessary to salvation." And I rejoice in the present prosperity of that Church in the old world and new; and pray God, that, divested of all error in doctrine and practice, she may live on for ages to bless the world."

SHIP-BUILDING IN THE DISTRICT OF BATH.

The following statement has been made in reply to the request of the Chairman of the Executive Committee, and should be connected with the remarks made on page 155.

CUSTOM HOUSE, BATH,
June 9, 1863.

Statement of number of vessels built in the District of Bath, from January 1, 1832 to January 1, 1862, and amount of tonnage of the same:

Number of vessels, - - - - - 1170.
Tonnage, - - - - - - - - 505,293 tons.

ROLAND FISHER, *Collector.*

HYMN:

BY THE REV. DR. WHEELER, OF TOPSHAM.

The following Hymn, written with reference to the celebration, and given for this publication at the request of the Editor, is here inserted, as an appropriate termination to the various communications appearing in this volume.

I.

God of the firm and solid land!
God of the deep and restless sea!
Here, on this wild, surf-beaten strand,
We raise our willing thoughts to Thee.

II.

Where once the wily red man stood,
Where oft he dipped the plashing oar;
By river's brink, and briny flood,
We bow before Thee, and adore.

III.

Where men of wit, and men of toil,
  And Christian heroes, brave and true,
First planted on New England's soil
  The sturdy stock from which we grew, —

IV.

Where first the song of praise was heard,
  And first the solemn voice of prayer;
And first the reconciling word
  Was borne upon the summer air, —

V.

And where the first low grave was made
  Beneath New England's wintry snows;
And the first Christian relics laid,
  To slumber in their long repose; —

VI.

We meet and bend the knee to day;
  Those early times bring back to view:
We sing again the sacred lay,
  Again those ancient rites renew.

VII.

Lord! Hear us in this solemn hour;
  Accept our thanks for mercies given;
Dispel the storms that darkly lower,
  And be our Guide to peace and Heaven.

It is proper to add, as supplying an omission, that in the closing exercises at the Fort, after the address, the doxology

"From all that dwell below the skies,"

was sung by the assemblage, before the Benediction.

ADDENDA.

It will be noticed, that the papers appearing in this volume relate to other subjects than the first English settlement on the wild shores of New England. The celebration had another purpose added to the memory of this leading event: that of awakening in the citizens of Maine an interest in historical research within our own territory. Reasons there may have been why, except in rare instances, these studies have not received the attention that might well be claimed for this State; which, while nearest of the States in position to the Mother Country, was among the first to be occupied by her colonists; furnishing a field for explorers and men of enterprise in commercial pursuits, and beholding the first blood shed on her soil in the long contest for supremacy with France. It can now hardly be doubted that the acquaintance with this North Eastern Shore, and the occupancy of its land and waters by the perseverance of English navigators and settlers, had a special influence, permanently acting on the settlements farther west, — protected as they were by the charter, procured by the labors of Gorges, for the region then known as North Virginia. As auxiliary to the true understanding of this influence, useful study might be expended on the character, purposes, and motives of the men, who were prominent in counsel and action, for exploring the coast and in its occupation.

The State of Maine has not yet had her true position in the written history of our nation ; and the researches of her sons are needed to bring to light full information as to her claims, now locked up in archives, or perpetuated in unwritten traditions. Every year is adding to the results of investigations, already commenced ; and as they proceed under the auspices of the Historical Society, local celebrations, and the Histories of Towns, erroneous impressions will be corrected, and true ones produced out of these recovered events of the past.

It has not been the purpose of the directors of this celebration to detract from the merits of the earlier settlement at Jamestown, or the later one at Plymouth. Each has its own history, as has also the first settlement in Maine, made from the same nation. The leading desire in promoting its commemoration, was to bring to view facts not generally known, and to excite inquiry into the treasures of the past. The result of this gathering will be most cheering, if it become the starting point of new labors in the department of our own history. The act of the Legislature of the State in granting funds to procure papers of importance from the English archives, which have been beyond reach until the present day, will be of great aid in showing the value and effects of the early occupation and civilization of this portion of the hemisphere. It was a generous act of that body, representing the interests of the State, thus nobly sustaining the efforts of her citizens to develope her own historical resources.

In the retrospect of these facts and considerations, we have learned to say that Maine has her EPOCH and her GATHERING-PLACE, which untoward circumstances have heretofore kept concealed from her own observation. When the true bearings of the commemorated event are properly applied and rightly appreciated, it will be seen to have had no small directing influence on subsequent efforts for settlements, under the guidance of Sir Ferdinando Gorges, the great Patron of Colonization on the Shores of New England.

APPENDIX.

NOTE A.

To enable those not familiar with the localities of Sabino, to understand the allusions made to them, a map and a brief description are given.

The Sagadahoc river, so famous in the early history of the country, is formed by the junction of two large rivers, the Androscoggin and the Kennebec, at Merrymeeting Bay,* twenty-five miles from the sea, from which junction the Sagadahoc is a deep estuary of very irregular width, often contracted into narrow limits, but carrying a large volume of water to the ocean.

At its mouth, between Stage Island on the eastern shore, and the lower end of the Peninsula of Sabino on the west, it is about a mile and a half in width. One mile above this, is its narrowest point, where the north-east point of the Sabino Peninsula projects far out into the channel, nearly opposite which point, only a few rods higher up the river, the lower end of a sharp rocky isle, called Long Island, narrows the main channel to less than a third of a mile. There is no navigable passage on the eastern side of this island. This outermost north-eastern point of the Sabino Peninsula is the site of Fort Popham. It was occupied by a small fort in the war of 1812. Above this point opens out Adkins Bay, extending south-west for a mile or more, where formerly it evidently connected with the ocean. In De Barre's chart, made for the British government between 1764 and 1774, it is laid down as flats, subject to the overflow of the tide, between this Bay and the ocean. At the present time, there is enough of earth formed by action of the sea, to afford a good road-bed, free from overflow, connecting Sabino with the mainland.

From Merrymeeting Bay south to the ocean, there is a constant succession of narrows, formed by high, sharp, projecting points of rock, alternating into broad reaches or bays. A reach of some miles in front of the city of Bath, varying from one half to a mile in width, having abundant depth of water, forms one of the noblest landlocked harbors in the world, when the river turns, first east, at right angles, then again south, between high, rocky shores, with great depths of water. Nothing can be more beautiful or picturesque than the sail between Merrymeeting Bay and the sea.

As you descend towards the mouth of the river, the Island of Seguin, a high, rounded, rocky ridge, rising one hundred and forty feet above the sea-level, stands directly in front, apparently closing the mouth of the river, though three miles distant from it, clothed with a native growth of evergreen to its summit. Above this, rises a first-class lighthouse, holding in its spacious iron lantern a Fresnel lens of the largest size, seen for more than twenty miles at sea, and for a very great distance from the high lands of the interior.

The Peninsula of Sabino is the outer point of the mainland, on the right

* Marimitin. See Father Dreuilletts' Journal of an Embassy from Canada to New-England, in 1650, published from a translation of John G. Shea, with valuable notes, in the Collections of the New-York Historical Society, 1857, vol. iii. Second Series, part i. page 303. The country was then occupied from Cushnoc (Augusta) to Merrymeeting Bay.

or west bank of the river, three miles from Seguin. It is very nearly an irregular triangle in shape, its shortest line fronting the Sagadahoc—the other two side-lines formed, one by Adkins Bay, and the other by the ocean. It rises into two rocky ridges, lying nearly east and west of each other, with a deep depression running north and south the bulk of the land, lying west of it, where it rises from two to three hundred feet into two considerable peaks in a ridge running north and south. In the valley, or narrow depression running north and south, the land is free from stones, and the soil is made up chiefly of sand. Toward its southern end there is a beautifully clear lake or pond of fresh water sufficient for the wants of the Peninsula. The level of this lake is only about thirty or forty feet above the sea, and is said at times to be reached by the flashing spray which is dashed with prodigious force at times upon this rocky shore.

Near the shore of Adkins Bay is a spring of water half a mile from the site of Fort Popham, near which, are remains of ancient habitations; and those who have explored the localities profess their belief that the principal fort was in the "vicinity of this spring." There is an old gentleman still living, more than ninety years of age, who was present at the celebration, who testifies to the ploughing across a covered way between the ruins of an old fort and this spring of water, in his early days.

The whole Peninsula was originally covered with a forest growth, and materials would have been abundant for the building of houses and a stockade fort.

As to the probable site of their fort, that must depend upon the purpose of its construction. If an European foe, Spaniard or French, was dreaded, the site of the present fort would naturally be chosen. If, on the other hand, the enemy they feared was the Indian, they would naturally select a spot convenient to fresh water, where they could best guard the approach of the foe, coming across the neck, that alone connected the peninsula with the main. The site pointed out as that of their fort, would, in that view of the case, be at once determined on the southern shore of Adkins Bay, near to the neck, in the vicinity of this spring.

No one can fail to perceive the wonderful foresight of the men who selected this spot for their plantation. Easily approached at all times by water, capable of being defended at all points, those in possession of this peninsula hold complete control of the country and the rivers above, one of the finest agricultural districts in New-England. It was also the finest river for fish on the coast. When the Pilgrims of Plymouth were considering the question of abandoning their home, from the poverty of the soil and the want of means of subsistence, Sir Ferdinando Gorges gave them a valuable tract of land on the Kennebec in 1629, at the time he established their boundaries at Plymouth, which they farmed out to advantage, deriving thence, and from the fisheries their chief means of support. The facts stated by Father Dreuilletts, at the time of his visit in 1650 and 1651, are of great historic interest.

At the time of the celebration, the level floor or parade of the fort was occupied by the large assemblage of people. A platform facing east, overlooked the fort and the Sagadahoc river, resting for its background against the end of the large shed occupied for dressing stone. This platform was occupied by the distinguished guests from abroad, the members of the Historical Society, the Masonic fraternity, and those taking part in the celebration. The various steamers and barges in attendance, the United States revenue cutter, and a large fleet of smaller craft, all gaily dressed in flags, lay at anchor in Adkins Bay. A strong tidal current swept past the fort, aided by a stiff north-west wind. The speaker's stand commanded a complete view of all the localities alluded to.

NOTE C.

THE SETTLEMENT OF MAINE BY GOVERNOR GEORGE POPHAM, AUGUST, 1607.

Before the Mayflower's lonely sail
  Our northern billows spanned,
And left on Plymouth's ice-bound rock
  A sad-eyed pilgrim band;

Ere scarce Virginia's forest proud
  The earliest woodman hewed,
Or gray Powhatan's wondering eyes
  The pale-browed strangers viewed;

The noble Popham's fearless prow
  Essayed adventurous deed;
He cast upon New-England's coast
  The first colonial seed;

And bade the holy dews of prayer
  Baptize a heathen sod;
And 'mid the groves a church arose
  Unto the Christian's God.

And here, on Sabino's green marge,
  He closed his mortal trust,
And gave this savage-peopled world
  Its first rich Saxon dust.

So, where beneath the drifted snows
  He took his latest sleep,
A faithful sentinel of stone
  Due watch and ward shall keep;

A lofty fort, to men unborn,
  In thunder speak his name,
And Maine, amid her thousand hills,
  New-England's founder claim.

L. H. Sigourney.

Hartford, Ct., Sept. 3, 1862.

LE SIEUR DE CHAMPLAIN.

Onward o'er waters which no keel had trod,
  No plummet sounded in their depths below,
No heaving anchor grappled to the sod
  Where flowers of ocean in seclusion glow;
From isle to isle, from coast to coast he prest
  With patient zeal and chivalry sublime,
Folding o'er Terra Incognita's breast
  The lilied vassalage of Gallia's clime.
Though Henry of Navarre's profound mistake
  Montcalm must expiate and France regret;
Yet yonder tranquil and heaven-mirrored lake,
  Like diamond in a marge of emerald set,
Bears on its freshening wave, from shore to shore,
The baptism of his name till time shall be no more.

Hartford, Ct., Oct. 1, 1862. L. Huntley Sigourney.

SIR FERDINANDO GORGES.

NOT 'mid Ambition's sterner sons, inspired with restless rage,
Whose wreaths of laurel stain with blood the snow of History's page,
Nor 'mid those sordid hordes who wrap their souls in cloth of gold,
And smother every generous aim in that Laocoon fold;
But with the men whom age on age complacently shall view
Unostentatious in their course, and like the pole-star true,
Who nobly plan, and boldly aid the welfare of their race—
Sir Ferdinando Gorges' name shall find an honored place.

On the new Western Continent, his earnest eye was bent,
Nor rising cloud, nor rolling storm obscured his large intent;
Though Raleigh, that chivalrous friend, upon the scaffold bled,
And many an unexpected foe upreared the hydra head;
Though adverse fortune ruled, and loss his flowing coffers drained,
And monarchs vacillated sore, and parliaments complained;
Yet with a persevering zeal that no defeat impaired,
When others failed, he onward pressed—where others shrank, he dared.

Then colonizing ships went down beneath the engulfing main,
Or on their cargoes fiercely fed the pirate power of Spain,
And homeward from their rude abodes the baffled planters steer,
Discouraged at the hardships dire that vex the pioneer;
The wily Aborigines* his proffered kindness grieved,
And the great Bashaba himself all Christian trust deceived:
Still as the beacon rises brave o'er desolation's flood
Sir Ferdinando Gorges, firm in faith's endurance stood.

He ne'er beheld New-England's face that woke such life-long toil,
Nor traversed with exploring foot his own manorial soil,
Nor gazed upon those crested hills where misty shadows glide,
Nor heard her thundering rivers rush to swell old ocean's tide,
Nor like the seer on Pisgah's cliff one distant glance enjoyed
Of those delightful vales that oft his nightly dreams employed;
Yet still with deep indwelling thought and fancy's graphic art
He bore her strongly-featured scenes depictured on his heart.

She gave him no memorial stone 'mid all her mountains hoar,
Nor bade one islet speak his name along her sounding shore,
Nor charged a single mirrored lake that o'er her surface spread
To keep his image on its wave till gratitude was dead:
The woodman in the forest hews, the kingly mast to rear,
And forth the fearless vessel goes to earth's remotest sphere;
But who of all the mariners upon the watery plain
Gives praise to that unswerving knight, who loved the hills of Maine?

HARTFORD, CT., Nov. 5, 1862. L. H. S.

* Some native Indians being brought to England, were kindly received by Sir Ferdinando Gorges into his family, from whom he acquired much information of their country, its scenery and productions. One of them, a native of Martha's Vineyard, named Epinow, artfully invented a story of a mine of gold in that region.

A vessel having been fitted out for the coast of New-England by Sir Ferdinando Gorges and the Earl of Southampton, Epinow went in it, and when it approached his native island leaped into the sea and swam ashore. Soon a shower of arrows from about twenty canoes was discharged on deck, much disconcerting the crew. This expedition, like several other unsuccessful ones, returned without having performed any service adequate to the equipment.

NOTE D.

ESTIMATED TERRITORY AND POPULATION OF THE GLOBE.

	Square miles.	Population.
Europe,	3,500,000	275,000,000
Asia,	16,800,000	720,000,000
Africa,	11,700,000	100,000,000
America,	16,000,000	70,000,000
Oceanica,	4,000,000	35,000,000
	52,000,000	1,200,000,000

ENGLISH SPEAKING OR ENGLISH GOVERNED.

	Square miles.	Inhabitants.
United States of America,	3,250,000	31,445,080
United Kingdom of Great Britain and Ireland,	122,556	29,334,788
British Colonies and Dependencies,	8,124,528	189,610,665
Total,	11,497,084	250,390,533

THE FOLLOWING TABLE GIVES IN DETAIL THE

BRITISH TERRITORY AND POPULATION IN 1861.

COUNTRIES, ETC.	AREA. SQ. M.	POPULATION.
Europe.		
England,	50,922	18,949,930
Wales,	7,398	1,111,795
Scotland,	31,324	3,061,251
Ireland,	32,518	5,764,542
Channel Islands:		
Man,	282	52,339
Jersey,	62	56,078
Guernsey, with adjacent Islands,	42	29,846
Alderney,	6	4,933
Sark,	2	583
Army, Navy, and Sailors,	..	303,491
United Kingdom,	122,556	29,334,788
Gibraltar,	2	17,750
Maltese Islands,	115	136,271
Ionian Islands,	1,045	229,726
Heligoland,	5	2,800
Total in Europe,	123,723	29,721,355
Asia.		
Bengal Presidency,	221,969	40,852,397
Madras "	132,090	22,437,297
Bombay "	131,544	11,790,042
North-West Provinces,	105,759	33,655,193
Punjab,	73,535	10,435,710
As-Sutlej States,	8,090	2,282,111
Oude,	25,000	5,000,000
Nagpore or Berar,	76,432	4,650,000
Pegu,	32,250	570,180
Tenasserim Provinces,	29,168	115,431
East'n Straits Settlem'ts:		
Penang and Wellesley,	251	90,688
Malacca and Naning,	1,049	19,103
Singapore,	275	92,749
Native States subordinate		
to Bengal,	515,535	38,702,206
to Madras,	51,809	5,213,671
to Bombay,	60,575	4,470,370
British India,	1,465,331	180,377,148
Ceylon,	24,700	1,759,528
Labuan,	50	1,163
Hong-Kong,	29	75,503
Aden,	10	80,000
Total in Asia,	1,490,120	182,293,342
Africa.		
Gambia,	2,000	5,693
Sierra Leone,	3,000	38,318
Gold Coast,	6,000	151,346
Cape Colony,	104,921	267,096
Caffraria,	22,000	120,000
Natal,	18,000	121,068
St. Helena,	47	5,490
Mauritius,	708	238,363
Seychelles,	200	8,276
Total in Africa,	156,876	955,650
Oceanica.		
New South-Wales,	356,480	350,553
Victoria,	86,940	544,677
South-Australia,	398,830	117,967
Western Australia,	988,980	14,823
Queensland,	450,780	30,115
North-Australia,	698,770	6,987
Australia,	2,980,780	1,065,122

BRITISH TERRITORY AND POPULATION IN 1861.—Continued.

COUNTRIES.	AREA. SQ. M.	POPULATION.	COUNTRIES.	AREA. SQ. M.	POPULATION.
Tasmania,..............	22,629	89,977	St. Vincent,.............	132	30,128
New-Zealand,...........	95,500	129,477	Tobago,..................	144	16,363
Norfolk Island,..........	18	600	St. Lucia,...............	296	26,471
Auckland Island,........	500	100	Nevis,..................	21	9,601
Feejee Islands,..........	8,034	133,500	St. Christopher,.........	68	23,177
			Antigua,................	108	37,757
Total in Oceanica,...	3,107,461	1,418,776	Montserrat,.............	47	7,653
			Virgin Islands,..........	92	6,689
America.			Dominica,...............	274	25,230
Vancouver,..............	12,756	25,000	Barbuda,................	72	1,707
British Columbia,........	237,250	64,000	Anguilla,...............	34	3,052
Hudson Bay Co.'s Ter....	2,250,000	71,000			
Labrador,...............	170,000	1,650	West-Indies,........	15,663	942,245
Canada West,...........	147,832	1,396,091			
Canada East,............	209,990	1,111,566	Guayana:		
New-Brunswick,.........	27,704	252,047	Essequibo,............	44,000	22,925
Nova Scotia, etc.,........	18,746	330,699	Berbice,..............	25,000	29,003
Prince Edward,..........	2,134	80,648	Demerara,............	27,000	75,767
Newfoundland,..........	35,913	122,958	Falkland Islands,........	6,297	539
Bermuda Islands,........	19	11,612			
Balize, (Honduras,)......	18,600	18,600	South-America,......	102,297	128,234
North-America,......	3,250,944	3,485,871	Total in America,....	3,368,904	4,556,350
Bahama Islands,.........	5,094	31,402	European,...............	123,723	29,721,355
Turk's Isl. and the Caicos,	430	4,428	Asiatic,................	1,490,120	182,293,342
Jamaica,...............	6,250	441,264	African,................	156,876	955,650
Cayman Islands,.........	260	1,760	Oceanic,................	3,107,461	1,418,776
Trinidad,...............	2,020	78,845	American,...............	3,368,904	4,556,350
Barbadoes,..............	166	161,201			
Grenada,...............	155	35,517	GRAND TOTAL,.......	8,247,084	218,945,453

The oldest of the present Colonies of Great Britain is Newfoundland, obtained by settlement in 1608; Bermuda was obtained in 1609; St. Christopher, in 1623; Barbadoes, in 1625; Nevis, in 1628; Bahamas, in 1629; Gambia, in 1631; and Antigua, in 1632. There are fifty distinct colonial governments over the British possessions.

NOTE E.

From the N. Y. Christian Times of Nov. 20, 1862.

THE POPHAM CELEBRATION.

ACTION OF THE NEW-YORK HISTORICAL SOCIETY.

AMONG the pleasing incidents not remotely connected with the meeting of the General Convention, was the gathering of a number of the members of that body, both clerical and lay, of acknowledged interest in historical pursuits, at the October meeting of the New-York Historical Society, to notice appropriately the late celebration of the Popham settlement at the mouth of the Kennebec. Invitations were extended by the courtly and accomplished President of the New-York Historical Society, the Hon. Luther Bradish, in behalf of the Society, to a number of the Bishops, to the delegation from the Diocese of Maine, and to several prominent members of the Maine and Massachusetts Historical Societies at that time in New-York, to be present on this interesting occasion. The invitation was very generally responded to; and, among others, the Rev. James Craik, D.D., of Kentucky, President of the House of Clerical and Lay Deputies; the Hon. R. C. Winthrop, President of the Massachusetts Historical Society; Prof.

Shattuck, of Boston; the Rev. Dr. Edson, of Lowell; the Hon. John A. Poor, and the Rev. William Stevens Perry, of Portland, members of the Maine Historical Society, were received by a large and brilliant assembly, consisting of prominent historical and literary characters of New-York and vicinity, in the elegant hall of the Society, on Second Avenue.

After the paper of the evening was read, the Hon. Luther Bradish, President of the Society, said, that in reporting upon the miscellaneous business of the Society, it was his pleasing duty to refer to an interesting event that had taken place during the vacation—the celebration in Maine of the founding of the English race in the New World. In many particulars, this celebration was one of the most memorable and successful historical commemorations that had yet taken place. On the Peninsula of Sabino, at the mouth of the ancient Sagadahoc, the modern Kennebec river, in the State of Maine, the two hundred and fifty-fifth anniversary of the founding of the first English colony on the shores of New-England was celebrated on the 29th of August, 1862, at which, after the use of the old words of prayer and praise of the English Prayer-Book of that time, an eloquent and appropriate oration, with speeches, was delivered, and other proceedings took place, at the erection of a monumental stone in the walls of Fort Popham. The New-York Historical Society, through its President, was honored with an invitation to participate in that celebration. Absence from home prevented his receiving the invitation in time to be present, had his health permitted. He had replied in what he trusted were appropriate terms. He was glad to know that other members of this Society had responded for our city and State. He regretted that we had not been able to do full justice to our sense of obligation to our sister Society in Maine. He trusted the Society would in some form take notice of it in an appropriate manner.

The Hon. George Folsom, a son of Maine, and well known as the learned historian of one of Maine's cradle homes of civilization and Episcopacy, rose, and said he fully sympathized in all that had fallen from the President; he regretted that absence in Canada, with his family, prevented his acceptance, in person, of the honor done him by an invitation. He asked leave to introduce the following resolution:

"*Resolved*, That the New-York Historical Society has observed with pleasure the efforts of the Historical Society of Maine to perpetuate the earliest history of their State, by associating important historic events with the great works of national defence of the United States Government; that they acknowledge with satisfaction the courtesy extended by the Historical Society and citizens of Maine, inviting the Society and its officers to participate in the commemorative celebration of the founding of the first colony on the shores of New-England, on the two hundred and fifty-fifth anniversary of that event, on the 29th of August, 1862, at which time a memorial stone was placed in the walls of Fort Popham commemorating the establishment of the first Protestant civil government on the shores of New-England; that this Society cordially approves the act of its President, in his reply to the invitation to participate in that celebration, and the good-will therein expressed; that all such efforts to preserve and illustrate the history of our race in the new world are worthy of general notice."

The Hon. J. Romeyn Brodhead said he seconded the resolution with great pleasure. He was pleased further to learn that several members of the Maine Historical Society had honored our meeting by their presence this evening, as had the President of the Historical Society of Massachusetts. Among others from Maine, the orator of the Popham Celebration, the Hon. Mr. Poor, was present, and he trusted this resolution would be adopted and that Mr. Poor would be called on to favor us with some reply thereto.

The resolution was unanimously adopted. In reply to a call from the

President, Mr. Poor said his associates of the Maine Historical Society and other friends from Maine present, with himself, felt personally complimented by the action here taken, in reference to the Popham Celebration. He rose with a feeling of embarrassment to return thanks for this cordial and unlooked for compliment. He doubted not that the Historical Society of Maine would, in its own befitting manner, return appropriate acknowledgments for this generous courtesy on the part of the New-York Historical Society.

The Popham Celebration, so courteously alluded to, had already borne fruits, in awakened attention to the study of the early history of the country, and we are largely indebted to eminent historical minds of New-York for much of the interest already attached to it. The fact so happily alluded to by your own historian, Mr. Brodhead, the political connection between New-York and Maine under the charter of Charles II., in his most interesting and appropriate reply to the invitation to speak for *the great metropolis of the New World*, cannot fail to excite a feeling of mutual sympathy, at this day, with the more recent but increasing commercial intimacy of the two States. It is certainly refreshing to revive and recall, for this brief hour, the kindly intercourse of other days. It is a fact, almost forgotten, even by the active men of this time, that much the largest portion of Maine was at one time under the same government as that of New-York, and that Gyles Goddard, the renowned representative from *Pemaquid*, sat in the Legislature of New-York in 1684, chosen by the free-holders of the county of Cornwall, in ancient Sagadahoc. This letter of Mr. Brodhead, already published in the Maine papers, will be preserved in our memorial volume as one of the choicest of the many interesting contributions to its pages. The courteous and appropriate letter of your President is already published in the papers of Maine.

One from the Hon. Mr. Bancroft, the most eminent of living American historians, and another from one of Maine's honored sons, Mr. Folsom, are promised for this volume. Mr. Folsom's invaluable labors in bringing to light and preserving the earliest history of his native State, have been publicly acknowledged by formal resolutions of the Maine Historical Society.

New-York, therefore, will have a foremost position, if not, in fact, the post of honor, in the records of that commemorative festival.

That celebration was well calculated to attract attention, for in its purpose it appeals at once to the sympathy of all who speak the English language, or share in any proper measure a feeling of pride at the achievements of our race. It had for its object the due observance of the great fact, the planting of our race in North-America, with the language, literature, laws, and religion of England, an event, if rightly comprehended in its relations and consequences, of as much importance as any one that has taken place since the establishment of the Roman Empire.

Eight years before the Leyden Church had been gathered in Holland, under the charge of the pious Robinson, twenty years before they set foot on Plymouth sands, the purpose of "planting colonies in the north-west of North-America" had been set forth in a paper on file in the British State Paper Office. More than thirteen years prior to the voyage of the May Flower, the title of Old England to New England had been secured by a formal act of possession and occupation at the mouth of the Sagadahoc by Governor Popham's colony.* No Frenchman ever set foot on the Atlantic

* The Seven Articles of the Leyden Flock, signed by Robinson and Brewster, sent to King James before their departure from Holland, signifying their full assent to the authority of the English Church, form a striking contrast to their subsequent pretensions, under the guidance of such men as Bradford and Winslow. See Poor's Vindication of Gorges, p. 108, for this remarkable document in full.

shore, claiming title west of the Kennebec, after the planting of Popham's colony in 1607.

The Colonial Empire of Great Britain, the wonder of this age, had its root in the charter of April tenth, 1606, and its development in the New-England charter of 1620, both granted on the petitions of Sir Ferdinando Gorges. The great idea of a strong central government, having extended dominions in distant lands, divided into separate provinces, communities, and states, each enjoying equal and just laws, suited to the local wants of each, fully developed in action under the rule of Cromwell, originated in an earlier day, and in the mind of him who secured those great charters, and maintained them till the soil of the New World was planted with our race, where it has gradually advanced toward universal dominion.

The failure of Sir Humphrey Gilbert, of Sir Walter Raleigh, and of Sir Richard Grenville to comprehend the geographical and commercial laws that control the destiny of races and of empires, imposed on Sir Ferdinando Gorges, or rather left to him, the task of occupying the continent of North-America, from the fortieth to the forty-eighth parallel of north latitude, in which limits, in spite of individual jealousy and parliamentary injustice, he achieved the great work of English colonization in America. In their zeal against monopolies, in 1621 and 1622, the Commons of England declared "*fishing is of more value than plantations in America*," and would have abandoned the continent to the French but for the pertinacity, foresight, and enlightened views of Gorges, and his favor with the King, from the possession of these great qualities.

But the chief significance of the Popham Celebration, undoubtedly, is the introduction of a new principle in the naming of our forts, making them serve the double purpose of national defence and of preserving the memory of the great events in our history.

We have seen the national honor tarnished, and the moral sense of the nation shocked, by the bestowal of unworthy names—names of mere partisan leaders — upon national vessels, forts, and other public works. This form of coarse flattery panders to the lower tastes of men and destroys the independence of official men, who are made the recipients of it.

It was, therefore, with a feeling of relief that Gen. Totten was pleased to accept the proposal of affixing to the great work in Portland harbor the name of Fort Gorges, in honor of Sir Ferdinando Gorges, the father of English colonization in America, and naming the new work at the mouth of the Sagadahoc or Kennebec Fort Popham, in a similar spirit, and we hope to see this rule made universal. Especially do we look forward to the construction of a new fort, to guard the entrance to Portland harbor, to be named Fort Gosnold, and placed on the shore of Cape Elizabeth, the first point of the northern main of New-England, touched by that great English navigator, who has left on record the details of his discovery of the New-England coast in 1602.

The fitness of the policy proposed will be readily appreciated by all men endowed with any share of that quality we call the historic sense; for all know that the reputation of no public man is secure within the first hundred years after his death. Personal ambition, partisan motives, and narrow views characterize the popular movements of every age—our own as of all past ones—and the value of no man's life can be justly measured in his own time. We build monuments, we name towns, cities, and counties, for men that a future age will hold in disfavor. We almost execrate the memory of men to-day, that a later time shall honor. We rear in affected grandeur an obelisk in devotion to the demon of war, that the calmer reason of the coming centuries will demolish or condemn. We do homage to popular partisan leaders to-day, whose doctrines have undermined the foundations of our Government and brought upon us civil war.

Thanks to the good sense of the people of the Empire State, they have preserved the name of their great navigator, Hudson, from any possibility of forgetfulness or decay, by affixing it to the great *river of the mountains* that must forever bear to this great metropolis the treasures of an expanding commerce with the interior.

Looking back to the first dawnings of American history, we are beginning to discover the superior lustre of the great lights that guided hitherward the adventurous and heroic spirits of that great age. Under their benignant glow we revisit the spots made sacred by self-denying labors. We hope to strengthen our love of what is noble and heroic by an annual pilgrimage to that spot where, in prayer and faith, the foundations of empire in the New World were laid.

Associating the history of Maine with New-York, so appropriately done by Mr. Brodhead, may serve to increase your interest in our State. Maine — so rich in historic interest, so full of legendary romance, so marked by the fascinations of its scenery;* the territory claimed by the great European powers, Spain, Holland, France, and England; the home of the earliest French settlers and of the first English colonists; the *Norumbega* of Milton's *Paradise Lost*, the *Mavosheen* of Purchase's strange narration; "discovered by the English in 1602, '3, '5, '6, '7, '8, and '9;" the *New-England* of John Smith in 1614, and of later times—obeys the law of historic as of commercial gravitation and gladly finds sympathy, "without reservation," in the great metropolis of the Western World.

Maine, too, builds the ships that fill the docks of the East River and the Hudson. She lifts from her quarries the granite columns that form the ornaments and support of your public edifices, and the rich colonnades and solid walls of the Treasury Extension at Washington. She needs, most of all, the pen of the historian and the pencil of the painter, to be made as familiar as household words in the private residences of the Fifth Avenue and Madison Square, by means of landscapes that shall equal in beauty the richest scenery of the Rhine and the Alps; true to nature from the seashores, the valleys, and the mountains of Maine. With her summer retreats thus laid open, she shall annually attract pleasure tourists of other lands than our own.

Rejoicing in the success of your Society, and grateful for your generous courtesy, I may be allowed to close, as I began, by expressing for our Society and its members, here present, the assurance of our hearty thanks.

* "We, Americans, neglecting both the surpassing magnificence—nay, often sublimity—and the rare loveliness of various districts of our own Continent, wander forth across the seas, to seek, at great expense, and amid physical and moral dangers, scenery in foreign lands, which falls short of the attractions of much we possess at home. Thus, how few are alive to the glorious and varied beauty of that zone of islands, which, commencing with the perfection of Casco Bay, terminates with the precipitous, seal-frequented shores of Grand-Menan, at the entrance of the Bay of Fundy. Of all the Archipelagoes sung by the poet, described by the historian, and depicted by the painter, there is none which can exceed, in its union of charms, those two hundred miles of intermingling land and ocean, where, lost in each other's embrace, the sea seems in love with the land, and the shore with the foam-frosted waves!"—*General J. Watts de Peyster's Dutch in Maine*, p. 44.

LIST OF SUBSCRIBERS TO THE MEMORIAL VOLUME.

ANDREW, Hon. JOHN A., Gov. of Mass.,	Boston, Mass.,	1
ALDEN, HIRAM O.,	Belfast, Maine,	1
ANDERSON, JOHN F.,	Windham, "	1
ANDREWS, Hon. LEONARD,	Biddeford, "	1
ANTHONY, C. J.,	Worcester, Mass.,	1
BANCROFT, Hon. GEORGE,	New York City,	1
BACHE, Prof. ALEX D.,	Washington, D. C.,	1
BALLARD, Rev. EDWARD,	Brunswick, Maine,	1
BURGESS, Rt. Rev. GEORGE,	Gardiner, "	1
BRODHEAD, Hon. J. ROMEYN,	New York City,	1
BOLLES, Rev. E. C.,	Portland, Maine,	1
BURGESS, Rev. ALEXANDER,	" "	1
BARRETT, F. R.,	" "	1
BROWN, Hon. J. B.,	" "	1
BROWN, J. M.,	" "	1
BUZZELL, Dr. J.,	" "	1
BROWN, J. OLCOTT,	" "	1
BRYANT, HUBBARD W.,	" "	2
BRADLEY, ROBERT,	" "	1
BRACKETT, H. S.,	" "	1
BEAL, GEO., W.,	" "	1
BAILEY, FREDERICK WILLIAM,	" "	1
BROWN, Hon. JAMES S.,	Milwaukee, Wis.,	1
BARKER, C. H.,	Wayne, Maine,	1
BOURNE, Hon. E. E.,	Kennebunk, Maine,	1
BUFFUM, J. N.,	Lynn, Mass.,	1
BELL, SAMUEL D.,	Manchester, N. H.,	1
BOWDOIN COLLEGE LIBRARY,	Brunswick, Maine,	1
BEARDSLEY, Rev. E. E., D. D.,	Hartford, Conn.,	1
BREVOORT, J. C.,	New York City,	1

COBURN, Hon. ABNER, Gov. of Maine,	Skowhegan, Maine,	5
CHANDLER, Hon. P. W.,	Boston, Mass.,	1
COAST SURVEY OFFICE,	Washington, D. C.,	1
CLARK, Dr. E.,	Portland, Maine,	1
CUMMINGS, Dr. HENRY T.,	" "	1
CUTLER, OTIS,	" "	1
COREY, WALTER,	" "	1
CLARK, CHARLES,	" "	1
CHADWICK, Dr. GEO. H.,	" "	1
CARTER, J. E,	" "	1
CONEY, Hon. SAMUEL,	Augusta, "	2
CLARK, ISAAC R.,	Bangor, "	1
COBB, FRANCIS,	Rockland, "	1
CHAPMAN, R. M.,	Biddeford, "	1
DRUMMOND, JAMES,	Bath, Maine,	5
DRUMMOND, Hon. J. H.,	Portland, Maine,	2
DRUMMOND, Hon. THOMAS, U. S. Judge,	Chicago, Illinois,	1
DRAKE, S. G.,	Boston, Mass.,	3
DOLE, ANDREW T.,	Portland, Maine,	1
DOW, JOHN E.,	" "	1
DIX, GEO L.,	Boston, Mass.,	1
DOANE, WM. C., Rector St. John's Ch.,	Hartford, Conn.,	1
DAVIS, W. J.,	New York City,	1
DANE, J.,	Kennebunk, Maine,	1
DAY, HORACE H.,	New York City,	1
DONNELL, WM. E.,	Portland, Maine,	1
DOW, JOHN E., Jr.,	" "	1
DAWSON, H. B.,	Morrisania, N. Y.,	1
DAY, JOHN J.,	Montreal, C. E.,	2
DANFORTH, F. A.,	Mechanic Falls, Me.,	1
DWIGHT, T. B.,	Philadelphia, Pa.,	1
ELIOT, SAMUEL, Pres. Trinity College,	Hartford, Conn.,	1
EASTMAN, Hon. PHILIP,	Saco, Maine,	2
EATON, L. H.,	Bucksport, Maine,	1

Emery, Joshua T.,	Portland, "	1
Elliott, Daniel,	Brunswick, "	1
Everett, Hon. Ebenezer,	" "	1
Elwell, Edward H.,	Portland, "	1
Folsom, Hon. Geo.,	New York City,	1
Fessenden, D. W.,	Portland, Maine,	1
Furbish, Henry H.,	" "	1
Farwell, N. A.,	Rockland, "	1
Fisher, Roland,	Bath, "	1
Fletcher, H. A.,	Lancaster, N. H.,	1
Fogg, O. S.,	Portland, Maine,	1
Fowler, John, Jr.,	New York City,	1
Fellowe, R. S.,	New Haven, Conn.,	1
Gardiner, Hon. R. H.,	Gardiner, Maine,	1
Gilman, Hon. Charles J.,	Brunswick, "	5
Gilman, Dr. John T.,	Portland, "	1
Goodenow, Hon. John H.,	Alfred, "	1
Greene, Hon. J. D.,	Cambridge, Mass.,	1
Goddard, John,	Cape Elizabeth, Me.,	1
Griffin, C. S. D.,	Portland, Maine,	1
Gibson, E. T. H.,	New York City,	1
Griffin, Joseph,	Brunswick, Maine,	1
Howe, Hon. Joseph,	Halifax, N. S.,	2
Hillard, Hon. Geo. S.,	Boston, Mass.,	1
Hedge, Rev. F. H., D. D.,	Brookline, "	1
Hodsdon, Gen. J. L.,	Bangor, Maine,	1
Hall, Hon. Joseph B.,	Portland, "	1
Hammond, Geo. W.,	Westbrook, "	1
Heald, J. S.,	Portland, "	1
Howard, Hon. Joseph,	" "	1
Haines, Allen,	" "	1
Hall, Edward W.,	Washington, D. C.,	1
Hull, John T.,	Portland, Maine,	1

HARMON, C. C.,	Portland, Maine,	1
HUBBARD, T. H.,	North Berwick, Me.,	1
HANSON, CHAS. V.,	Portland, Maine,	1
INMAN, HENRY, U. S. A.,	Portland, Maine,	1
JEWETT, Hon. JEDEDIAH,	Portland, Maine,	2
JACKSON, GEO. E. B.,	" "	1
JONES, T. R.,	" "	1
KINGSBURY, BENJ., Jr.,	Portland, Maine,	1
LOMAX, J.,	Kalamazoo, Mich.,	1
LARRABEE, W. H.,	7th Reg. Me. V. M.,	1
LIBRARY, NEW YORK STATE,	New York,	1
LIBRARY, NEW YORK SOCIETY,	New York City,	1
LIBRARY, NEW YORK MERCANTILE,	" " "	1
LIBRARY, BOSTON PUBLIC,	Boston, Mass.,	1
LIBRARY, STATE,	" "	1
MAINE HISTORICAL SOCIETY,		150
MAINE, STATE OF,		50
MCCRILLIS, WM. H.,	Bangor, Maine,	2
MORRIS, E. S.,	Portland, "	1
MOORE, Rev. H. D.,	" "	1
MORRISON, J. B.,	Farmington, Maine,	1
MOSHER, A. J.,	Westbrook, "	1
MERRILL, A. R.,	Buckfield, "	1
MURRAY, H. J.,	Portland, Maine,	1
MUNSELL JOEL,	Albany, N. Y.,	2
MERCANTILE LIBRARY ASSOCIATION,	Portland, Maine,	1
NORRIS, B. W.,	Skowhegan, Maine,	1
NOYES, JAMES,	Portland, "	1
NICHOLS, F. W.,	" "	1
OSGOOD, J. R.,	Boston, Mass.,	1
PIERCE, Hon. JOSIAH,	Gorham, Maine,	2
PERRY, Rev. WM. S.,	Portland, "	1

Patten, James T.,	Bath, Maine,	3
Poor, Henry V.,	New York City,	1
Peabody Institute,	Boston, Mass.,	1
Pelton, F. W.,	" "	1
Poor, John A.,	Portland, Maine,	5
Page, Moses B.,	Great Falls, N. H.,	1
Pierce, Lewis,	Portland, Maine,	1
Pennell, Thos.,	" "	1
Poor, Fred. A.,	" "	1
Page, Benj. V.,	Chicago, Illinois,	1
Purington, George E.,	" "	1
Richardson, C. B.,	New York City,	10
Robinson, Dr. W. C.,	Portland, Maine,	1
Richardson, Thomas,	" "	1
Rogers, Charles B.,	" "	1
Ross, George E.,	" "	1
Robinson, R. I.,	" "	1
Robinson, A.,	" "	1
Robinson, R. L.,	" "	1
Shaw, Abner O.,	Portland, Maine,	1
Shaw, Samuel P.,	Cambridge, Mass.,	1
Smith, Hon. F. O. J.,	Westbrook, Maine,	5
Sparrow, John,	Portland, Maine,	1
Sweat, Hon. L. D. M.,	" "	1
Sewall, R. K.,	Wiscasset, "	1
Smith, Jacob,	Bath, "	1
Stevens, Rev. W. B.,	Philadelphia, Pa.,	1
Sewall, W. B.,	Kennebunk, Maine,	1
Swan, Rev. J. A.,	" "	1
Souther, Rev. Samuel,	Worcester, Mass.,	1
Smith, W. B.,	Machias, Maine,	1
Scammon, Hon. J. Young,	Chicago, Illinois,	5
Scammon, Franklin,	" "	1
Scammon, C. T.,	" "	1

STEVENS, E. B.,	Chicago, Illinois,	1
STEWART, R. L.,	New York City,	1
STEVENS, H. A.,	Boston, Mass.,	1
SIGOURNEY, Mrs. L. H.,	Hartford, Conn.,	2
SHANNON, RICHARD C.,	Biddeford, Maine,	1
SAWYER, GEO. B.,	Wiscasset, "	1
STEVENS, J. S.,	Chicago, Illinois,	1
SHORT, JOHN L.,	Portland, Maine,	1
THURSTON, B.,	Portland, Maine,	6
TEN BROECK, W. S.,	" "	1
TITCOMB, JOS.,	Kennebunk, Maine,	1
TALBOT, Hon. GEO. F.,	Machias, Maine,	1
TROWBRIDGE, C. A.,	Detriot, Mich.,	1
THOMPSON, DANIEL,	Chicago, Illinois,	1
UPHOLD, Rt. Rev. GEO., Bishop of Ind.,	Indianapolis, Ind.,	1
VEAZIE, JOHN W.,	Bangor, Maine,	1
WASHBURN, Hon. I., Jr.,	Orono, Maine,	1
WOODS, Rev. LEONARD, Pres. Bow. Col.,	Brunswick, Maine,	2
WILLIS, WILLIAM,	Portland, "	1
WHITTINGHAM, Rt. Rev. W. R.,	Baltimore, Md.,	1
WILLIAMS, PELHAM, Rec. Trinity Ch.,	Hartford, Conn.,	1
WALLBRIDGE, Hon. HIRAM,	New York City,	1
WINSLOW, J. N.,	Portland, Maine,	1
WHEELER, Rev. A. D.,	Topsham, "	2
WINSHIP, J. O.,	Gorham, "	1
WEEKS, J. L.,	Portland, "	1
WILLIAMSON, JOS.,	Belfast, "	1
WELLS, DANIEL, Jr.,	Milwaukee, Wis.,	1
WATERVILLE COLLEGE LIBRARY,	Waterville, Maine,	1

ERRATA.

Page 21, sixth line from bottom, for York read Knox; page 181, fifth line from bottom, for Hall read Hull; page 187, seventeenth line from bottom, for hath read had; page 224, note 2, read *nuces;* page 225, note 3, fourth line, after because, dele of; note 5, change to *Amberg*[*r*]*etie*[*m.*]

ENGLISH COLONIZATION IN AMERICA.

A

VINDICATION OF THE CLAIMS

OF

SIR FERDINANDO GORGES,

AS THE

FATHER OF ENGLISH COLONIZATION IN AMERICA.

BY JOHN A. POOR.

(Delivered before the Historical Societies of Maine, and New York.)

NEW YORK:
D. APPLETON AND COMPANY,
443 and 445 Broadway.
LONDON, 16 LITTLE BRITAIN.
MDCCCLXII.

N. A. Foster & Co., Print., Portland, Me.

MAINE HISTORICAL SOCIETY.

At a meeting of the Society, held in the new City Hall Building, Portland, on Wednesday, June 29th, 1859, JOHN A. POOR, Esq., read a paper on "*English Colonization in America*," in which he claimed for Sir Ferdinando Gorges, and his associates, the honor of English colonization on this continent, and disputed the claims set up by the Massachusetts historians, in behalf of the Pilgrims and the Puritans.

R. K. SEWALL, Esq., read a paper on the historical remains at Sheepscot and Sagadahoc, concurring in the views expressed by Mr. Poor as to the claims of the Pilgrims.

Votes of thanks were passed to Messrs. Poor and Sewall.

Extracts from the records.

EDWARD BALLARD,
Recording Secretary.

NEW YORK HISTORICAL SOCIETY.

At a stated meeting of the Society, held at the Library on Tuesday evening, October 4th, 1859:

The paper of the evening was read by Mr. John A. Poor, of Portland, Maine, entitled "English Colonization in America."

On its conclusion, Dr. John W. Francis submitted the following resolution, which, after some remarks by Messrs. Henry O'Reilly and Erastus C. Benedict, was adopted.

Resolved, That the thanks of the Society be presented to Mr. John A. Poor, for his able and interesting paper read this evening, and that a copy be requested for the Archives, and that the same be referred to the Executive Committee for publication, or such further disposition as they may deem expedient.

Extract from the minutes.

ANDREW WARNER,
Recording Secretary.

NOTE.

The following paper, as now printed, contains several paragraphs omitted for want of time, in the address before the New York Historical Society.

The authorities cited are few, compared with the works examined, having a direct bearing on the question, and confined mainly to such as have not, till recently been easily accessible to the public. The Documents found in the Appendix are such as seemed needful to the correction of the popular history of New England. The persistent efforts of modern writers to prejudice the name of Gorges, from the fact of his strong political and religious attachments to an unpopular sovereign and to an *established church*, ought by this time to cease, as the occasion that originally prompted them, has passed away. The fact that he was a royalist and a churchman would naturally excite the jealous hate of cotemporary rivals of dissenting opinions; but he did not seek to plant the established church of his nation, but *the people of his race*, with organized institutions of government, in the new world. If, as we have attempted to show, it is to him, that the English race owe the colonization of America, it is enough for our purpose; for all admit that he left to each community its choice, in all matters of civil polity, religion, and church government.

ADDRESS.

Two events, of ever increasing importance, have marked the progress of this continent, destined hereafter to be regarded, as the great epochs of its history — the grant of authority from the British Crown, under which Colonies were planted in America,[1] and the final surrender of the continent to the English race, by the conquest of Canada from France — the former obtained through the efforts of the sagacious and enterprising Sir Ferdinando Gorges, the latter achieved by the heroic valor of Wolfe. France, at one time, dividing with Spain the whole of North America,[2] saw its power broken,

1. See Appendix A.

2. On the evening in which this paper was read in New York, there was presented to the Historical Society, a Spanish Globe, dated 1542, engraved on copper, which shows the boundaries of Florida, and of "*Verrazzan or New France*"—Florida extending as high as the 33° north,—New France reaching north to Terra Corterealis. This Globe is one of the most valuable contributions yet made, to the history of North America. It was presented to the Society, by Buckingham Smith, Esq., late Secretary of Legation at Madrid.

Map of the world by Hondius. 1580.

and its dominion in the new world extinguished, when at the charge of the British bayonet, the hitherto invincible columns of Montcalm, broke and fled from the Plains of Abraham, and the morning sunlight of September 18, 1759, revealed to the disappointed soldiers of De Levis, the proud Cross of St. George, floating in triumph over the ancient Citadel of Quebec.[1]

The dominion of a continent was changed by a single encounter, and English institutions are now planted, as the fruits of that victory, over a region of territory greater than all Europe, extending from the northern ocean to the gulf of Mexico, and from the Atlantic to the Pacific seas.

The future of this conquering race, no statesman or philosopher of this day is able to foretell. My purpose is, to trace the earliest practical efforts to plant it in America, and to vindicate the claims of Sir Ferdinando Gorges, the Proprietor of my native State, to the proud title of FATHER OF ENGLISH COLONIZATION IN AMERICA.

The greatness of England is due to her colonization in America. She was but a second rate power at the commencement of the 17th century, till raised to greatness by the iron will of Cromwell. After the destruction of the Dutch fleet, the conquest of Acadia from France in 1654; of Jamaica from Spain in 1655; the establishment of her navigation

1. *Histoire Du Canada*, F. X. Garneau. Vol. i. p. 329.

laws, and her protective policy, she was admitted as an equal, into the community of nations. The Venetians and the Swiss sought the friendship of the Protector. All the northern nations respected his power, and the great Mazarin acknowledged his authority as the lawful sovereign of Great Britain.[1]

The necessity of encouraging the Colonies previously planted in North America, led to the navigation act of Cromwell, in 1651, which was the foundation of the maritime superiority of England. That statute remained for nearly two centuries,[2] and secured to England the entire trade of all her colonies. It stimulated the commercial enterprise of her people. It allowed strangers no importations, unless of their own products in their own vessels. This act fell with crushing weight on the trade of Holland, and left England mistress of the commerce of Europe. The protective policy of Cromwell, also, gradually drew to her own shores the manufactures of Holland and Flanders, and finally those of France after the revocation of the edict of Nantes, by Louis XIV., on the 24th of Oct., 1685. This celebrated edict of Henry IV., in 1598, secured liberty of conscience and perfect toleration to the Protestants of France, with a right to share the public offices; and

1. Heeren's Political History. Vol. i. p. 145 and seq.

2. The navigation Act of 1651 was repealed with the corn laws, June 26, 1846. Ch. 22, 9 and 10 Victoriæ.

its repeal inflicted a blow on France from which it has never recovered. Over 800,000 of her best people fled from the persecution that followed, most of them to Great Britain and her Colonies. The most skilful artizans of France sought refuge in England, over 50,000 taking up their residence in London. They established the manufacture of silks, jewelry, crystal glasses, and other fine works hitherto unknown in England, but since that time successfully prosecuted throughout the British realms.[1] Such has since, been the increase of the productive power of England, that according to the statement recently made by Lord Brougham in the British Parliament, the machinery of England, at this time employed, in the various branches of industry, equals in effective power, the labor of 800,000,000 of men, an aggregate three-fold greater than the entire laboring population of the globe. Yet England was the latest of all the European powers to encourage its subjects who came to America, by the direct aid of its government, or to take measures to plant its race in the new world. It was not so much the efforts of the government, as the genius of the people, and the enterprise of individuals, that gave to its sons the inheritance of this fair land, where free institutions have developed an expansive energy, that demands for its race, supremacy of the sea and dominion over the land.

1. Anderson's History of Commerce.

1497. The discovery of North America by Sebastian Cabot,[1] in the service of Henry VII., in 1497, seventeen months prior to the time when Columbus saw the mainland of the continent, and the exploration of its coast from latitude 67 deg., 30 m. north, to Florida, has often been urged in modern times, as giving to England claim of title. But it was followed by no act of jurisdiction, or of occupation for nearly a century,[2] while all the other maritime powers of Europe were engaged in schemes of colonization.

1500. Emmanuel, King of the Portuguese, whose subjects, at that time, were the great navigators of Europe, and whose vessels had visited the East, by the way of the Cape of Good Hope, mortified at his neglect of the offer of Columbus, determined to make up for it, by new conquests in the

1. Memoir of Sebastian Cabot, with review of the History of Maritime Discovery. *London*, 1831.

2. The Government of England was the first to lay down the true doctrine as to the right to newly discovered countries. They distinctly affirmed in 1580, in the reign of Elizabeth, that discovery and prescription are of no avail unless followed by actual occupation. "*Prescriptio sine possessione haud valeat.*" Camden, Eliz. Annales, 1580. Hearne's Ed., 1717, p. 360.

"Occupation confers a good title by nature, and the laws of nations." Parl. Debates, 1620–1, p. 250.

Denonvilles' Memoir, on French Limits in America. N. Y. Doc. His. Vol. ix. p 378.

"The first discoverers of an unknown country, not inhabited by Europeans, who plant the arms of their Prince, acquire the property of that country."

new world. He dispatched Gaspar Cortereal[1] to North America in 1500; who described its shores and forests, its stately pines, suitable for masts, &c.

But traffic in slaves, then an established
1501. business of the Portuguese, being esteemed the more profitable, he sailed northward, took in, by kidnapping, a cargo of over fifty natives, whom he carried to Europe and sold for slaves.[2] But the Portuguese did not maintain their claim to the country.

Juan Ponce de Leon, in the service of Spain,
1512. took possession of Florida in the name of his Sovereign, in 1512; published a map of the country as far north as Newfoundland, and claiming it as a possession of the Spanish Crown. But the Spaniards chiefly sought, at that time, mines of gold and silver, and never extended their occupancy of the country north of Florida, at about 33° north latitude.

France, on the contrary, sent out fishing
1504. vessels manned by the Bretons and Normans, to Newfoundland, as early as 1504.[3] Those who

1. The country of Labrador is laid down as "Corterealis," on the Spanish Globe, spoken of in a previous note, and in cotemporary maps of North America.

2. Bancroft, Vol. i., p. 16.

3. Relations Des Jesuites. Contenant ce qui s'est passé de plus remarquable dans Les Missions des pères de la compagnie de Jésus dans la nouvelle France. Ouvrage publiè sous les auspices de Gouvernement Canadien, 3 vols., 8 vo., 1858. Quebec. Augustine Cotè, Editeur imprimeur. Vol. i. p. 1. Relation 1611.

Documentary History of New York. Vol. ix. pp. 1, 304, 378, 701, 781.

came earliest, named the country first visited, Cape Breton, from their own home. They discovered the Grand Banks of Newfoundland, visited all the creeks and harbors of the Gulf of St. Lawrence, gave names to the localities which they still retain, and published maps of the country.

1506. Jean Denys of Honfleur, made a map on his return in 1506, and Thomas Aubert, of Dieppe, brought back natives and a plot of the country in 1508. The ocean they crossed was named the sea of the West, 800 leagues broad in its narrowest strait from France. The Western ocean they called the sea of China.[1]

1524. In 1524, Giovanni Verrazzani, a Florentine navigator in the service of Francis I., returned from his last voyage of discovery to America. According to Champlain,[2] he made two voyages to the new world, but we have no narrative from his own pen of more than one. He sailed to the coast of Carolina, in a direct passage, where he found a native population more refined in its manners, than that of any other country of the new world. It had never before been visited by Europeans. Verrazzani, sailing northward, explored the coast, penetrated its various harbors, entered the bay of New York, and spent fourteen days in the harbor of Newport, Rhode Island.

1. Relations Des Jesuites. Vol. i. p. 2. 1611.
2. N. Y. Doc. Hist. Vol. ix. p. 2.

At each place visited, he made acquaintance with the native population, which proved more and more warlike and unamiable as he advanced northward. Following the general line of the shore, he sailed 150 leagues along the coast of Maine, clearly defining that great Bay or Gulf extending from Cape Cod to Cape Sable, known afterward, as the *Bay* or *Gulf of Maine.*[1] To the entire tract of country never before discovered or frequented by Europeans, he gave the name of *New France.* On reaching the 50th parallel of latitude, he sailed to France, and published a most interesting narrative of his voyage.[2] France in this way established her claims to the country. It was not Cartier, as is commonly asserted, but Verrazzani, that gave the name of New France[3] to the country he discovered, which extended from the 30th to the 50th degree of north latitude. This claim France maintained, and named Carolina for Charles IX. During his reign in 1562, Ribaut built a fort there, which was called *Carlesfort* in honor of the King.[4]

1. Edingburgh Encyclopedia. Vol. xviii. p. 263.

2. New York Historical Collections, vol. i. p. 39, et seq., *new series*, contains the full narration of Verrazzani's voyage, addressed to the French Monarch, translated by J. G. Coggswell, Esq., of the Astor Library.

3. Relations Des Jesuites. Vol. i. p. 14. Champlain, N. York Documents. Vol. ix. p. 1–4. Do. vol. ix. p. 266. Harris' Voyages, Vol. i.

4. Garneau's History of Canada. Vol. i. p. 118.

Curiosity has been awakened the past, year in regard to the location of Charles-fort from the naval and military expedition to the same

It is a singular fact that neither Spain, France or England had furnished up to this time, any great navigator in the discovery of America. They were all Italians; Columbus a Genoese, Cabot a Venetian,[1] and Verrazzani a Florentine.

1534. The French Monarch, following out his plans for the colonization of America, sent out Jacques Cartier in 1534, who, sailing from St. Malo on April 20, with two ships and 122 men, on May 10th, 1534, came in sight of Bonavista, Newfoundland, a spot discovered by Cabot in 1497.

In the "Relations of the Jesuits," recently published under the patronage of the Government of Canada, it is stated, that Cartier had been on this coast ten years before,[2] and it is fair to conjecture that he was in the expedition of Verrazzani. But we find no other account of any such voyage. Cartier was most fortunate in his expedition. He

region, under command of Commodore Dupont and Gen. Sherman. No traces of the old fort have yet been found, by those in the army of the Beaufort expedition. Gen. Peter Force of Washington, whose authority is most valuable, places the site of Charles-fort on the north side of St. Helen's Island.

1. John Cabot, the father of Sebastian, undoubtedly was a Venetian. There is much evidence lately brought to light, tending to prove that Sebastian Cabot was born in Bristol. In Grafton's Chronicles of England, page 1323, we find the following notice of Cabot of Bristol: "A native of that city, but who with his father removed to Venice at the age of four years."

Sebastian Cabot, son of a merchant of Cathay, in London. Eden, 249.

Eden says, "Sebastian Cabot told me he was born at Bristol, and at four years of age went to Venice." Page 255.

2. Vol. i. p. 2.

found the localities of the Gulf of St. Lawrence already known to the fishermen, having the names they now bear. He sailed around Newfoundland, took possession in various places, both on the main land and the island of Newfoundland. Taking with him two young natives of Gaspé, by their full consent, he sailed for France and reached St. Malo on the 5th day of September, 1534.[1]

1535. The report of Cartier's voyage and discoveries, excited great curiosity and interest; and with a more ample equipment in three ships, provided at the Royal expense, he sailed on another expedition for the new world on the 19th of May, 1553, carrying back to America his two young savages, who became useful as interpreters to the natives.

Cartier on this voyage sailed up the Gulf and into the river St. Lawrence, where he spent the following winter at the fortified town of Hochelaga, to which he gave the name it still bears, *Montreal*.[2]

1536. The next spring, erecting the cross in the name of his Sovereign at various points, and taking with him the Chief of the savages at Quebec, Donacana, and his two young interpreters, he returned to France on the 6th of July, 1536.

1. Cartier's Voyages.
Garneau's History of Canada.

2. Cartier's Voyages. Garneau's History. Vol. i. p. 21.

He made his third voyage in 1540, but no new discoveries were made; and for nearly fifty years, the more northern portions of North America were apparently forgotten by the Governments of both France and Fngland.

Spain, at that time the great Europeon power, subjugated to her dominion, and planted colonies in the rich countries of tropical and southern America, held the Gulf of Mexico, and Florida to the 30th parallel of latitude.

The spirit of adventure had only led the French and English to take fish in the northern seas, and fur and timber from the coast of Maine—though the coast of America, from Labrador to the Equator, was accurately delineated on maps published in Europe within fifty years of its first discovery by Columbus. The French sent Ribaut, in 1562, to Florida, and joined with him Laudonniere, in 1564 but no results of importance came of these expeditions, as the French were driven out by the Spaniards.

The French asserted their right to the country north of Florida, for nearly one hundred years after its discovery, previous to any substantial claim to it being set up on the part of England.

1548. The first act of the British Parliament, concerning America, was passed in the second year of the reign of Edward VI., in 1548, entitled "an act against the exaction of money, or other dues, for licence to traffic into Iceland, Newfoundland," &c.[1]

England seemed more intent on religious
1577. disputes than on the extension of her dominions in America, during the reigns of Henry VIII., Edward VI., and Mary. No returns of the English fishery are found prior to 1577. Those of the French date back to 1527—three years after the expedition of Verrazzani. In 1577 there were found one hundred and fifty French fishing vessels on the coast of Newfoundland, engaged in the cod-fishery, and only fifty English ones.

The heroic exploits of Drake, the first Eng-
1578. lishman that circumnavigated the globe—who, sailing on this voyage from Plymouth, Nov. 15, 1577, returned to the same port, Sept. 26, 1580—and the *Discourse* of Sir Humphrey Gilbert, " to prove a passage by the north west *to Cathaia*," printed in 1576, had filled the youthful mind of England with enthusiasm for noble undertakings, and stimulated the ambition of all classes; and Sir Humphrey Gilbert led the way in the plans of colonizing the new world. He obtained from Queen Elizabeth a charter "for planting our people in America," June 11, 1578, in the 20th year of her reign. Under this grant, he took possession of Newfoundland, and planted the city of St. John, in the presence of thirty Europeans, of various nations—fishermen, who

1. Statutes at large.

accidentally, but not unfrequently, assembled in that secure seaport, at that early day. This port, long after this, retained the name of "the English port," and is so mentioned by the historian L'Escarbot, in his history of the voyage of De Monts to Acadia, in 1604.

But the loss of Sir Humphrey Gilbert, at sea, proved fatal to his plans, and it was some years before Newfoundland became a permanent settlement, or colony.[1]

In 1584, the Queen granted letters patent for the planting of a colony in Virginia to the gallant and accomplished Sir Walter Raleigh, whose heroic efforts for the honor of his country, and whose melancholy fate, excite at this day, the sympathy of all generous minds. But the first colony he transported to Virginia, returned—the second, perished by some unknown means; and thus was reserved for another, the glory of *first* planting the Saxo-Norman race in the new world.[2]

1. John Guy was sent out as Governor of Newfoundland in 1610, and began the Colony at Conception Bay. (*Purchase.*)

The Newfoundland Colony is the oldest of the present Colonies of Great Britain.

2. Since the writing of this paper, a work of great interest to the student of English history has been undertaken, "A CALENDAR OF STATE PAPERS." Edited by W. Noel Sainsbury. London, 1860. Longman, Green, Longman & Roberts." It is sub-divided into three great branches, or divisions—"Domestic," "Colonial," and "Foreign." The first volume of each, is already published. That containing an

Such is, in brief, the history of European
1600. attempts at colonization in North America, to the close of the sixteenth century. There was not an European settlement from Florida to the Northern Ocean. Two hundred and fifty years ago, England, a second rate power in Europe, had not a colonial possession on the globe. France and Holland were then the great maritime nations; and well did Sir Ferdinando Gorges say in the House of Com-

abstract of colonial documents, embraces the period from 1574 to 1660, from which we condense the following, viz:

1. 1574. Points stated in reference to proposed efforts to plant settlements in the northern parts of America. Petition to the Queen, dated March 22, 1574, to allow of an enterprise for the discovery of sundry rich and unknown lands "*fatally reserved for England, and for the honor of your Majesty.*" Endorsed, Sir Humphrey Gilbert, Sir Geo. Peckham, Mr. Carlile, and Sir Richard Grenville. p. 1.

Sir Humphrey Gilbert's commission and charter are dated June 11, 1578.

2. 1580. Fragment of a report of persons who had travelled in America, with John Barros, Andrew Thevett, and John Walker. Sir Humphrey Gilbert did confer in person. In 1580, John Walker and his company discovered "a silver mine within the river Norumbega." p. 2.

1600. Consideration on "a proposition for planting an English colony in the northwest of America.. If the Prince would assist it, in part, his Majesty's merchants go liberally into it—the country be stirred to furnish men; some gentlemen moved to be adventurers, and a worthy general chosen, qualified to judge by sight, of the strength of the places; it might be a glorious action for our Prince and country, honorable for the general welfare, and adventurers, and in time profitable." p. 4.

(This paper bears internal evidence, that Sir Ferdinando Gorges was its author.)

1603, Nov. 8. Copy of patent by the French King to De Monts, of Acadia, from the 40th° to the 46th° of north latitude. p. 4.

(The early filing of this copy in the British State Paper office, shows how complete was the information of the government as to the movements of the French towards colonizing the New World.)

1606, April 10. Grant of charter to Geo. Popham and als. by King Charles, from 34° to 45°. p. 5. (See Appendix A.)

1607, March 9. Ordinance enlarging the number, and augmenting the authority of the council for the two several colonies and plantations mons, when called on to show why he should not surrender the charter of New England, "*That so valuable a country could not long remain unpossessed, either by the French, Spaniard, or Dutch, but for his efforts here to settle a flourishing plantation.*[1]

The throne of England was filled by Elizabeth, from 1558 to 1603. That of France from 1589 to 1610, by the liberal-minded and chivalric Henry IV., who of all the Sovereigns of his time, seems most fully to appreciate the importance of American colonization.

1602. In the autumn of 1602, an expedition was fitted out by the merchants of Rouen, under charge of Seigneur du Pont Gravé, of St. Malo, and in the early part of 1603, Henry sent Champlain,[2] the great French navigator, to the St. Law-

in Virginia and America. Thirty members for the first colony, from 34° to 41° north latitude; and ten members for the second colony, between 38° and 45° north latitude.

1607, March 13. Letter of Gorges to Challong. (See later note.)

1607, Dec. 13. Geo. Popham to King James. Maine Hist. Coll. Vol. v. p. 341.

1613, Oct. 18–28. Montmorency Admiral of France to King James. Complains of Argall at Mt. Desert. Requests compensation, &c.

The following are found in the Calendar of "Domestic State Papers:"

1603, July 26. Warrant, &c., to N. Parker, (Warrant Book, p. 102,) take possession of the office and papers of Sir Ferdinando Gorges on his suspension from office.

1603, Sept. 15. Warrant to pay 56s. per annum to Sir F. Gorges, who is restored to his former post of Captain of the new fort at Plymouth. (Warrant Book, fol. 18.)

1608. *Letter*. Sir F. G. to Thomas Gamel of Salisbury. Escape of Challoner (Challong) out of Spain. Bad feelings of the Spaniards towards the English.

1609, July 31. Warrant to deliver Ordnance Stores to Sir F. G., Captain of the forts at Plymouth Island.

1. Gorges' Brief Narration. Maine His. Coll. Vol. ii. p. 36.

2. Champlain's Voyages, p. 40, edit., 1632.

rence, who visited on his return from Quebec, Gaspè, the Bay of Chaleur, and the other places occupied by the fishermen in the Gulf. He encountered icebergs of prodigious length, between the 44th and 45th degrees north latitude, and obtained from the savages a description of the St. Lawrence, above Hochelaga.

On the return of Champlain in 1603, Hen-
1603. ry had granted to Pierre du Gas, Seigneur De Monts, a French Protestant, and a member of his household, all that part of North America lying between the 40th and 46th parallels of north latitude, and confirmed it by letters patent, Nov. 8th, 1603.[1]

In this grant the King says, "fully confiding in your great prudence, and in the knowledge you possess of the quality, condition, and situation of the said country of Acadia, from the divers voyages, travels, and visits you have made into these parts, and others neighboring and circumjacent, &c., &c., we do appoint you our Lieut. General, to represent our person in the country, coasts and confines of Acadia, from the 40th to the 46th degree of latitude." The design was, *the occupancy of the country.*

De Monts sailed from Havre De Grace,
1604. March 17, 1604, with two vessels, in one of

1. L'Escarbot Historie de la nouvelle France, 1609.
Champlain's Voyages (Ed. 1632,) p. 44.
Hazard's Coll. Vol. i. p. 45.
Williamson's History of Maine. Vol. i. app.
Sainsbury's Calender of Colonial State Papers. Vol. i. p. 4.

which, Capt. Timothy, of New Haven, Master, were De Monts, Champlain, Poutrincourt, and the accomplished scholar and historian L'Escarbot.[1] In the other, commanded by Capt. Morell, of Honfleur, was Du Pont Gravé the companion and associate of De Monts. They called at Isle Sablon, and reached the coast May 16, 1604, where they found a ship trading with the natives contrary to the di-

1. L'Escarbot's History of New France, is by far the most valuable of all the works on America of that date. His first edition, published in 1608–'9, 12 mo., contained a map of the country explored, a copy of which we give. This work was translated into English, and published by P. Erondelle, London, in 1609, as an original work without any allusion to the author. A 2d edition was published in Paris in 1612, under the following title, which we translate from the copy recently placed in the Astor Library.

"HISTORY OF NEW FRANCE,

Containing the Voyages, Discoveries and Settlements made by the French, in the West Indies and New France, with the consent and authority of our Most Christian King, and the diverse fortunes of those engaged in the execution of these things, from a hundred years ago, till to-day.

In which is comprised the History, Moral, Natural and Geographical, of the said Province: with the Tables and Pictures of the same.

By MARC L'ESCARBOT, Lawyer in Parliament; Eye Witness of a part of the things here recited.

Multa renascentur qua iam occidere cadent que.

PARIS:

JOHN MILLOT, in front of St. Bartholomew with the three crowns, and in his shop, on the steps of the great hall of the Palace.

1612.

WITH PATENT FROM THE KING."

In the Library of Congress is a copy of the 3d Edition, published at Paris, in 1627.

The Dutch and the French adopted the names of the rivers and places given them by De L'Escarbot.

I am aware that Warburton and others assert, that L'Escarbot came out in the 2d Expedition in the ship IONAS, in 1606; but I find nothing to justify this statement from his own writings.

rections of the King, which they seized and confiscated, giving the master's name, Rossignol, to the Port, his only return for the voyage. The port is now called Liverpool, but a Lake in the interior still bears the name of the unlucky master.

Exploring the coast westward, De Monts reached port Mouton, where they landed, waiting the arrival of Du Pont Gravé. The company of Planters, those who designed to remain in the country, was one hundred in number, and here they erected tents, and planted the ground with grain, which two years later, was found bearing a good crop.

Champlain, impatient at the delay, proceeds west in a shallop, explored the coast, and discovered the beautiful island, which he named St. Croix — from the fact, that just above it, the streams formed a natural cross, one on each side, entering at right angles with the main river — which river finally retained the name of St. Croix, or Holy Cross, and now divides New Brunswick from Maine. Champlain rejoined his companions at Port Mouton, after exploring as far west as the Penobscot.

On the arrival of Du Pont Gravé and Captain Morell, both ships sailed west, entered the Bay St. Marie, discovered the Bay of Fundy, then sailing north, reached Port Royal.

Poutrincourt, who came out to select for himself a place of settlement, was so delighted with Port Royal, that he solicited, and obtained from De Monts a promise of a grant of it, and with Du Pont Gravé, returned to France, in the autumn of 1604, to arrange for his removal to this country, and for a fresh supply of planters.

Under the advice of Champlain, De Monts' company proceeded west, discovered the river St. John, followed the coast westward, and planted themselves in the spot he had selected, known at this day as Neutral Island, in the St. Croix river, within the limits of the State of Maine. This was the first settlement of Europeans north of Florida. Here they laid out a town, and planted the ground. During the autumn of 1604, habitations were erected, a fort built, a magazine constructed, and a chapel finished.[1]

1. "Leaving the river St. John, they came, following the coast twenty leagues, to a great river—properly a sea—where they fortified themselves in a little Island, seated in the midst of this river, that the said Lord Champlain had been to reconnoitre; and seeing it strong by nature, and easily guarded; and in addition, seeing that the season was beginning to pass, and the necessity of seeking a lodging without going further, they resolved to stop there.

"The Island of St. Croix is difficult to find for one who has not been there—there are so many Islands and great bays to pass, before reaching it. * * * * * * * *

"There are three or four mountains high above the others on the sides, but on the side of the north, from which the river descends, is a pointed one, two leagues distant. The woods of the main land handsome, and the grass likewise. There are streams of fresh water, very agreeable, opposite the Island, where several of the people of De Monts made their home, and had built cabins there. The said Island is about half a league in circuit, and at the end of the side towards the sea, there is a mount, or small hill, and like a separate Island, where we placed the cannon of Lord De Monts; and there also the chapel, built after the savage fashion.

"At the foot of this, there are some muscles, so many that it is a wonder, which can be picked up at low tide, but they are small.

"Lord De Monts caused the people to work upon his fort, which he had fixed at the end of the Island, opposite that where he had planted

1605. The winter of 1604–'5 was long and severe, and thirty-five of their number died of the scurvy. In the spring, De Monts, disappointed at the rigor of the winter, seeking a milder climate, proceeded to explore the country west and south, designing to settle four degrees south of St. Croix. He visited Mount Desert, the Penobscot, the Kennebec,[1] Casco,[2] and Saco; and coasted as far south as Cape Malabar, twelve miles south of Cape Cod.

his cannon. This was prudently considered to command all the river, above and below.

"But there was one difficulty. The fort was on the northern side, where there was no shelter, except the trees on the bank of the Island. Without the fort was the lodgings for the Swiss, and other little houses, like a suburb of a city. Some had built cabins on the main land, near the brook. But in the fort was the house, or dwelling, of Lord De Monts, made of good carpenter work, with the flag of France floating above it. On the other side was the magazine, where reposed the safety and life of all—similarly made of good carpenter work, and covered with shingles; and opposite the magazine were the houses of Lord Orville, Champlain, Champdore, and other noble personages, and on the opposite of the dwelling of De Monts, was a covered gallery, for the exercise of play, and for workmen in rainy weather; and between the said fort and the platform where the cannon was, all filled with gardens. Each one amused himself, or worked with a gay heart. All the autumn passed with this, and it was doing well to have lodged ourself, and cleared up the Island before the coming on of the winter."

L'Escarbot, book iv. ch. 4, p. 469—2d edition, 1812.

1. "Sailing west, 1605, to find a place of settlement, they, De Monts, Champlain and Champdore, came to Norumbega, the river of Pentagouet, (Penobscot,) and thence to Kinnibeki, (Kennebec,) which shortens the way to the great river of Canada. There are a number of savages settled there, and the lands begin to be better peopled."

L'Escarbot, book iv. ch. 7, p. 497.

2. "From Kinnibeki, in going farther on, they found the Bay '*Marchin*,' (Portland,) from the captain who commands there."

L'Escarbot, book iv. ch. 15, p. 557.

"In 1606, Poutrincourt arrived at *Marchin*, which is the name of the savage captain, who, on the arrival of the said Poutrincourt, cried *he! he!* To which they replied in the same way. He replied, asking in his language, "*Who are you?*" To which they replied, "*We are friends.*" On the approach of Poutrincourt, he made with him a treaty of friendship, and gave him presents of knives, axes and hatchets, made of paternosters, or glass tubes, (tuyaux,) white and blue, of which he was

Portland harbor, which he named "Marchin," from the Chief, or Sagamore, who then resided here, and who was killed in 1607, took the name of Machigonne. De Monts sailed into all the bays, harbors, and arms of the sea, from St. Croix to Cape Malabar, a distance of over four hundred leagues, "searching to the bottom of the bays." Saco still retains the name "*Chouaquet*," given to it by De Monts, in 1605. South of "*Pescadouet*," Piscataway, (Portsmouth,) the harbors were less and less satisfactory, and the country less and less inviting; and after reaching Cape Malabar, De Monts despaired of finding a suitable place of settlement, as he had designed. While at Cape Cod, in 1605, they carried on shore a large kettle for cooking, which the Indians seized in the absence of the cook. On discovering the theft, he attempted to rescue it from their hands; but he was slain by them, and the kettle carried off.[1] This was undoubtedly the same kettle that Bradford speaks of, which the Plymouth people found, in their first explorations in 1620.[2]

delighted; also, of the treaty, knowing well that that would make him a great deal of support. He distributed to some of the great number around him, the presents of Lord Poutrincourt, to whom he brought much flesh of deer, to support the company with. Thence they proceeded to Chouaquèt, the river of the Captain Olmuchin, where took place the next war between the Souriquois and the Etchemins.

"This Marchin was killed the year we departed from New France. 1607. Idem."

1. L'Escarbot. p. 498.

2. Bradford's History of Plymouth. Mass. Hist. Soc. Coll. 1856. p. 82.

In the Spring of 1605, Du Pont Gravé arrived at St. Croix with supplies and a reinforcement of forty men, for the colony, which gave great joy. At his suggestion, the establishment was broken up at St. Croix, and they removed to Port Royal. Here, under the advice of L'Escarbot, they cleared and cultivated the lands, and built a mill for the grinding of their corn. Though Port Royal was destroyed by Argall, in 1613, it was rebuilt, and has ever since been peopled. A settlement was made on the St. John, above the Falls, by Du Pont Gravé, and St. Croix was also soon re-occupied.

In 1611, when the Jesuits, Biard, and Masse, visited the Kennebec, for the purchase of grain, but without success, Plastrier, who lived at the Island of St. Croix, gave them, on their return, two hogsheads of beans, which rendered important aid, in supplying Port Royal with food, in the winter of 1611–'12. Four French ships were at that time taking fish, at the White Rock, twenty-two leagues west of St. Croix.

The whole country was familiar to the French fishermen. Champlain, and Champdore the pilot of De Monts, remained four years in the country.

On the return of L'Escarbot to France, he published his invaluable history, with a very accurate map of Acadia, or New France, as far south as Cape Malabar. Acadia became well known throughout

Europe. In 1609, the work of L'Ecsarbot was translated and published in England.[1]

De Monts sailed up the Kennebec river, as is reported, in 1605, in the expectation of reaching Hochelaga, or Montreal, by water, led into this attempt by the reports given him by the Indians. Though claiming the country as far south as the 40th parallel of latitude, there is no evidence that De Monts ever sailed south of, or attempted to extend his jurisdiction south of Cape Malabar. All east of this, was claimed as within the control of France. The country east of French Bay, or the Bay of Fundy, was called ACADIA; between that and Canada, NORUMBEGA.[2]

1600. At the commencement of the 17th century, the Dutch were the most commercial and the most powerful nation of Europe, if superiority in wealth and enterprise, is to be regarded as the true measure of greatness. Small in territory and inferior in point of numbers to France or England, Holland had grown superior to either in all the arts of civilized life. Tolerant of religious opinion, and enjoying unrestricted commercial freedom, the people of the low countries had accumulated wealth, reclaimed their marshes from the invasions of the sea, and cultivated the arts of peace. Their prosperity excited the jealousy of England, and they

1. See note ante, page 21.
2. Relations of the Jesuits.

were finally compelled to yield to the iron will of the Protector, who infused new life into all pursuits, not only of commerce, but of war.

The people of Holland had learned to practice religious toleration long before those of any other nation, and were the first to recognize the commercial code, or what is commonly called the "Law of nations." They were equally in advance of other powers, in all commercial ideas and undertakings. As early as 1581, the Dutch merchants had established a profitable trade with the West Indies, and in 1597, had a still more lucrative one with the East Indies. In 1600, the realized wealth of Holland surpassed that of France, England or Spain. Her Batavian provinces had yielded abundant returns to her merchants, though following long and tedious voyages around the Cape of Good Hope, and other nations sought to reach the same coveted treasure by a shorter route across the Atlantic, by the long-hoped for *northwest passage* to Cathay. With this view the famous British East India Company was chartered December 31st, 1600, with a capital of £70,000. In 1602, the Dutch East India Company was chartered with vastly greater capital.

An expedition for the colonization of North America was one of the early objects of the Dutch government and people, and they claimed the country from the 41st° to the 45th° of north latitude. Their ship, in command of Henry Hudson, was off the mouth of the Penobscot river, July 18, 1609, and from that year they had actual and permanent possession of *Manatte,* or New York Island. So that France, Holland and England, started almost simultaneously in a career of colonization in the new world.

1603. At this time appeared on the public stage, Sir Ferdinando Gorges. Born 1573, at Ashton Philips, in Somersetshire, he became a distinguished naval officer in the Spanish war prior to 1603, when, on the accession of James I., he was made Governor of Plymouth. How early he became interested in the colonization of America, does not quite clearly appear, but being an intimate friend of Sir Walter Raleigh, though 21 years younger, it is fair to suppose that he possessed the same adventurous spirit, and in his "Briefe Narration," speaking in later times of the grant to himself of the *Province of Mayne,* which was dated April 3d, 1639, he says, "Being now 'seized, of what I had travailed, for *above forty* (40) *years,* together with the expenses of many thousand pounds, and the best time of my age; laden with troubles and vexations from all parts, as you have heard, I will now give you an account in what order I have settled my affairs, in that, my Province of Mayne, with the true form and manner of the Government, according to the authority granted me by his Majesty's Royal Charter."

"First. I divided the whole into eight Bailiwicks or Counties, and these again into sixteen, several hundreds, consequently, into Parishes and Tithings as people did increase and the provinces were inhabited," &c.[1]

Gorges speaks in familiar terms, at the commencement of his narrative, of the efforts of Sir Humphrey Gilbert and of Sir Richard Grenville to plant colonies in America, the last of which terminated 1585, so that his mind was evidently familiar, at an early day, with their plans for American Colonization.

It has been recently made to appear that he was directly concerned in the great voyage of George Weymouth, in 1605, regarded as the initial point in the history of New England; and probably, in the previous ones of Gosnold, in 1602,[2] and of Pring, in 1603.

1. Briefe Narration. Maine Hist. Coll. Vol. ii. p. 54.

2. Interest has of late been awakened as to the route, and the purposes of Gosnold's voyage, which at this time deserves notice.

On the 26th of March, 1602, Capt. Bartholomew Gosnold, in the 42d year of the reign of Elizabeth, sailed from Falmouth, in the County of Cornwall, for a voyage into the north part of Virginia, in the bark CONCORD, with thirty-two persons on board—twelve of them sailors, and twenty "to remain in the country for population." So that the priority of the English, in efforts to colonize the country, is clearly established.

The country that invited rival efforts at colonization by the Dutch,

The information, recently brought to light by a publication of the Hon. Geo. Folsom, "A Catalogue of Original Documents in the English Archives, relating to the early History of Maine," proves, what

French and English, extended from Cape Breton to the head of Delaware bay.

Of those who came out with Gosnold, who was chief in command, and who died in Virginia in 1607, the only names preserved to us are Bartholomew Gilbert, second officer; John Angel; William Street, ship master; Robert Solterne, who came out with Pring the following year—afterwards a licensed clergyman; John Tucker; John Brereton, gentleman, and journalist of the voyage; James Rosier, the journalist of Weymouth's voyage in 1605, and Gabriel Archer, gentleman, and also journalist of the voyage, who subsequently went to Virginia.

The land-fall of Gosnold is thus described by Archer:

"On Friday, the fourteenth of May, early in the morning, we made the land, being full of fair trees—the land somewhat low—certain hammocks, or hills, lying into the land; the shore full of white sand, but very stony, or rocky. And standing fair along by the shore, about twelve of the clock the same day, we came to an anchor, where eight Indians, in a Biscay shallop, with mast and sail, and iron grapple, and a kettle of copper, came boldly aboard us; one of them apparelled with a waistcoat and breeches of black serge, made after our sea-fashion; hose and shoes on his feet; all the rest (saving one that had a pair of breeches of blue cloth) were naked. These people are of tall stature, broad and grim visage; of a black swart complexion; the eyebrows painted white; their weapons are bows and arrows. It seemed, by some words and signs they made, that some basques of St. John de Luz, have fished or traded in this place, being in the latitude of 43 degrees.

"But riding here, in no very good harbor, and withal doubting the weather, about three of the clock the same day in the afternoon, we weighed, and standing southerly off into the sea the rest of that day, and the night following, with a fresh gale of wind; in the morning, we found ourselves embayed within a mighty headland," &c.

This headland was Cape Cod, a name given to it by Gosnold, from the abundance of cod taken there, and which it still retains, despite the efforts of subsequent voyagers and writers, to affix to it the name of Cape James, in honor of the King.

John Brereton, the fellow passenger and historian of the voyage, thus describes Gosnold's land-fall:

"The 13th day, we landed in seventy fathoms, and observed great beds of weeds, much woods, and divers things close floating by us, when was before only a matter of conjecture, that Gorges was the chief promoter of Weymouth's voyage. In Gorges' letter, on file in the State Paper Office, published in full by Mr. Folsom, dated March 13,

as we find smelling of the shore as from some southern cape and Andalusia in Spain.

"The 14th, about six o'clock in the morning, we discovered land, that lay north, and the northerly part we called the Northland, in which to another rock, upon the same, lying twelve leagues west, that we called Savage rock; for six leagues toward the said rock is an outpoint of rising ground, the trees thereof were high and straight from the rock, east northeast.

"But finding ourselves short of our purposed place, we set sail westward, leaving them and their coast about sixteen leagues S. W.; from thence we perceived in that course two small Islands, the one lying eastward from Savage rock, the other to the southward of it. The coast we left was full of goodly lands, fair plains, with little green round hills above the cliffs, appearing unto us.

"The 15th day we had again sight of the land, which made ahead; being, as thought, an Island," &c.

This proved to be Cape Cod.

From these accounts, Dr. Belknap supposed Savage rock to be on the northerly shore of Massachusetts Bay, about Nahant. Drake, in his elaborate history of Boston, expresses the belief that "Savage rock" was in the vicinity of Great Boar's Head, in Hampton, and that Gosnold's land-fall was at Boon Island, on the Isle of Shoals, from the fact that they are nearer to the 43° of latitude than any Island on the coast.

The late John McKeen, Esq., of Brunswick, a thorough and accurate observer and explorer, in a paper read before the Maine Historical Society, exposes the errors of modern writers, and shows that the statement of Strachey, that Gosnold's land-fall was at the mouth of the Sagadahoc, is the true one. Strachey was a cotemporary, and undoubtedly wrote with the narrations of Archer and Brereton before him; and in constant intercourse with those who shared this adventurous voyage.

R. K. Sewall, Esq., in his able work, "Ancient Dominions in Maine," concurs in fixing the land-fall of Gosnold at Sagadahoc.

Mr. McKeen sums up the case in the following brief statement:

"The bark Concord, Capt. Gosnold, sailed from Falmouth, England, on the 26th of March, O. S., 1602, and on the 14th of April, had sight of the Island of St. Mary, one of the Azores. On the 23d of April, they were in north latitude 37°. On the 7th of May, they first saw birds of various kinds, which was an indication that they were approaching the land. On the 9th of May, they were near north latitude 43°. On

1607, addressed to Mr. Chalinge (Challong) he speaks of the return of the former voyage, of *but*

the 12th of May, they had the "smell of land," by which it was likened they were not far from it. But on the 14th, being in north latitude 43°, pursuing their course westerly, *at six o'clock in the morning*, they discovered land, which lay directly north from the ship, and which Strachey says was "land about Sagadahock." Pursuing their course westerly, they observed the land full of fair trees, and somewhat low; certain hammocks, or hills, lying into the land; the shores full of white sand, but very stony, or rocky. They had not proceeded far, when they discovered land ahead, over the starboard bow. This point of land called by the natives *Semiamis*, and by the English, Cape Elizabeth, after the name of the reigning queen. Finding this land not what was expected, "being short of their proposed place," they named it *Northland*, and pursued their course. From Cape Elizabeth, they veered a little south, and now commenced estimating their distances. They continued their course a fair distance from the land, till they came opposite an out-point of wooded land; the trees tall and straight. The distance from Cape Elizabeth they estimated at five leagues. This point is now called on our maps, "*Fletcher's Point*." It is situated near Saco, and the estimated distance from the Cape is very nearly correct.

"From this point, they shaped their course W. S. W., and sailed seven leagues to a great rock in the land, where they came to an anchor. This rock they called Savage Rock, and it is now named on our maps, *York Nubble*.

"This, likewise, corresponds to the course and distance as now estimated on the maps. I am indebted for the two last suggestions to a communication in the Temperance Journal (a newspaper printed in Portland) of January, 1859, which was over the signature of '*Rockport*.'

"To this place, 'the great rock in the land,' the Concord arrived at twelve o'clock at noon, having sailed from six o'clock in the morning, from the first point discovered, bearing north to this place about forty-eight miles. This rock was called Savage Rock."

The opinion that the land-fall of Gosnold was upon the coast of Maine, between Monhegan and Cape Elizabeth, is strongly confirmed by the fact that Pring in his voyage the next year with Robert Salterne as a companion, followed the same general direction. He followed the track of Gosnold, having on board some of Gosnold's party. Pring came in sight of land further east, between 43° and 44° of latitude, at the mouth of the Penobscot Bay, and gave the name of Fox Islands to the group still bearing the name, from the fact of taking a silver-grey fox upon it. The only objection to this theory is the supposition that this rock was found in the precise latitude 43°, which would bring them into the neighborhood of the Isle of Shoals, or Boon Island. But the intelligent reader will perceive from the language as quoted from Archer, that the place "where the Basques fished" was in 43°—a loose form of expression as applied to a fishing region, extending indefinitely for a con-

the five savages," whom Weymouth took as "*the chief return* TO US, WHO FIRST, sent to the coast."[1]

siderable space along the coast. There is reason to suppose they were not particular in determining the exact latitude of the places named, from the fact, that their place fixed on for settlement, Elizabeth Isle, is

1. 1607, Mar. 13. Plymouth. Letter of Sir Ferdinando Gorges to Mr. Chalinge.

Mr. Chalinge — I received your lrê sent me by the Mr. Nicholas Hines by whom I rest satisfied for your pte of the proceedinge of the voyadge and I doubte not but you willbe able to answer the expectacon of all your freindes. I hoope you shall receive verie shortlie, if alreadie you have not, an attestation out of the highe Courte of Admiraltie to give satisfacon of the truthe of our intent, yt sett you out, let me advise you to take heede that you be not ov'shott in acceptinge recompence for wrongs received, for you know that the jorney hath bene noe smale chardge to us, *yt first sent to the Coast and had for our returne but the five salvages whereof two of the principal you had with you and since within* in two months after your depture we sent out an other shippe to come to your supplie, and now again we have made a nue preparacon of divers others, all of wch throughe your misfortune is likely to be frustrate and our time and chardge lost, therefore your demands must be answerable hereunto, and accordinglie seeke for satisfacon which cannot be lesse than five thousande poundes and therefore before you conclude for lesse attende to receive for resolucon from hence, if they answere you not thereafter, for if their condicon be not such as shallbe reasonable, we do know howe to right ourselves, for rather then we will be loasers a penny by them we will attend a fitter time to gott us our content, and in the mean time leave all in their hands, therefore be you careful herein, and remember yt it is not the buisness of merchants or rovers but as you knowe of men of another ranke and such as will not preferre manie complayntes nor exhibite divers petitions for that they understande a shorter way to the woode, soe comendinge you to God and continuing my selfe

your most assured and lovinge friende
Ferdinando Gorges

Plymoth 13 of
Marche 1607

Postcript

I pray you use the meanes that the salvages and the companie be sent over with as muche speede as is possible and yt you hasten yourself away if you see not likelihoode of a present ende to be had for we will not be tired with their delaies and endlesse sutes such as commonlie they use but leave all to time and God the just revenger of wrongs

Ferdinando Gorges

(Endorsed) The Coopie of Sr. Ferdinando Gorges his lrê to Mr. Chalens.

Received ye 6 day."

An abstract of this letter is given in the "Calender of State Papers." See note, page 19.

This voyage of Weymouth was nominally undertaken to find the long sought for north-west passage to India, and " as set forth" by the Earl of Southampton, and Arundell, Lord Wardour. But this was undoubtedly a pretence to mislead the French who claimed the country, and were at this time, occupying the territory, and coasting along the shores of Maine. De Monts and Weymouth were in the same waters in 1605.[1]

1605. Weymouth sailed from the Thames, March 31, 1605, explored the coast of Maine, and west as far as Nantucket.

As Weymouth had been familiar with the coast in a previous naval service of twelve years, and knew that any idea of finding, by this route, a north-west passage to India, was absurd, the con-

put down by the same authority — Brereton — as in latitude 41° 10′, when it is found to be many minutes north of that point. We think the evidence fully establishes the fact we assume, that Gosnold's land-fall was at Sagadahoc; that on the 13th day of May, 1602, he sighted the Islands from Seguin to Cape Elizabeth, and gave to the latter, the name it still bears, in honor of his Queen,—that the name of Falmouth, subsequently adopted for the site of the present city of Portland, was so affixed in compliment to the port from which the first voyage of exploration sailed. It was a favorite idea with the English, from the first, to give the name of their former home, or their place of embarkation, to the places visited in the new world, as in case of Bristol, Plymouth, Falmouth, Yarmouth, Portsmouth, Dartmouth, York, Wells, &c. The French, on the contrary, generally adopted the local names of the country, attempting to express in language, the sounds gathered from the lips of the natives.

1. Weymouth's voyage. Mass. Hist. Coll. Vol. viii. 3d Series, p. 125.

clusion is inevitable, that Weymouth's voyage was designed to lay the foundation of the Royal Grant, which secured the Continent to Great Britain. In fact, Weymouth proposed to plant a Colony, and Owen Griffin and another man had agreed to remain.

A most interesting discussion is now going on by many able writers in Maine, as to the river visited by Weymouth, and which of the noble harbors of that wonderful coast, was the Pentecost harbor, in which he anchored his ship Archangel, in 1605.[1]

Weymouth carried back to England, in 1605, five natives of Pemaquid, from whom Gorges obtained full "particulars of its stately islands, and safe harbors, what great rivers ran up into the land, what men of note were seated on them, what power they were of, how allied, what enemies they had, and the like."[2]

By his glowing descriptions of the beauties of the country, he satisfied the Royal inquiry, and laid

1. Gorges calls the river Pemaquid; but the river, at this time, bearing that name, does not answer to the descriptions of Weymouth's narrative. It is a historical and geographical question, of interest, and we are gratified in being able to say, that an accurate exploration of these localities is to be made by the officers of the United States' Coast Survey, when on duty in that region; and that Professor Bache, its accomplished Superintendent, with the consent of the Government, has agreed to place a steamer of his command at the service of the Maine Historical Society for this purpose.

2. Gorges' Narration, p. 17.

the foundation for the subsequent grant from the King.[1]

1606. It was through the efforts of Gorges that King James made the Royal Grant or Charter, dated April 10, 1606, granting to "the Council of Virginia" the Continent of North America, from the 34th to the 45th degrees of north latitude, and all the Islands within one hundred miles of the shore.

Sir Ferdinando Gorges and the Earl of Southampton petitioned the King for this Charter, but no copy of this interesting Document has as yet been brought to light.

The attacks on Sir Ferdinando Gorges, for "grasping cupidity," in obtaining charters from King James, and the Stuarts, are among the striking evidences of the intolerance of the times. He, or any one, who would sacrifice his private fortune, to establish plantations in America, deserved the gratitude of the nation, and the warmest commendations of modern times. Instead of this, the historians of New England—those even, of our times, or such as follow Puritan authorities, unjustly represent Gorges as a man of a selfish and grasping spirit, whose only ambition was private advantage.

The grants to Sir Humphrey Gilbert, and to Sir Walter Raleigh, by Elizabeth, were as obnoxious to the charge of monopoly, as those subsequently

1. See Appendix A.

given to Sir Ferdinando Gorges and his associates, which the Puritans attacked; but no complaint was made against Elizabeth, for these grants; although others lavishly bestowed by her, in various departments of trade and manufactures, were boldly attacked by the Commons. The Queen, with instinctive sagacity, yielding to their demands—revoked the grants, and thanked the Commons for their zeal in the public welfare.

This charter of April 10, 1606, is the foundation of the title of England to North America. It was followed up by immediate acts of jurisdiction and possession.

In May, 1606, the Lord Chief Justice of England, Sir John Popham, having become associated in the enterprise, sent out Captain Haines, "in a tall ship belonging to Bristol and the river Severne, to settle a plantation in the river of Sagadahoc," but from the failure of the master to follow the course ordered, the ship fell into the hands of the Spaniards, by capture, and the expedition failed of success.[1]

In August, of the same year, a ship, sent out by Sir Ferdinando Gorges, under command of Henry Challong, with two savages as pilots, for the same purpose—the two designed to form one expedition—shared a similar fate.[2]

Another vessel, sent by the Chief Justice, in

1. Strachey, p. 290, vol. iii. Me. His. Coll.

2. Gorges' Briefe Narration, p. 19.

command of Hanam, under charge of Martin Pring as master, sailed two months later, reached the coast of Maine; but not finding Challong, made a perfect discovery of all the rivers and harbors, and brought back a most exact description of the coast; which so encouraged the company that they determined to send out a greater number of planters, with better provisions for the planting of a colony at Sagadahoc, the next year.

In consequence of these mishaps, Virginia was occupied prior to Maine. The expedition of Capt. Newport, to the Chesapeake, which sailed December 19, 1606, landed at Jamestown, May 13, 1607.

1607. On the 31st of May, 1607, the first Colony to New England, sailed from Plymouth for the Sagadahoc, in two ships — one, called the "*Gift of God*," whereof George Popham, brother of the Chief Justice, was commander; the other, the "*Mary and John*," whom Raleigh Gilbert commanded — on board which ships were one hundred and twenty persons for planters. They came to anchor under an Island, supposed to be Monhegan, the 31st of July, and in two hours after, eight savages in European apparel, came to them from the shore in a Spanish shallop, and after rowing about the vessels awhile, boldly came on shipboard, where three of them stayed all night. The next day the others returned with three women, in another Biscay shallop, bringing beaver skins, for the purpose of trade, so familiar had those people become with the habits and designs of their European visitors.

The fish of Monhegan were already more esteemed than those of Newfoundland, and this spot was the common resort of all the trading vessels on the coast. By this means, undoubtedly, the Indians became possessed of French and Spanish shallops prior to 1607.

After exploring the coast and Islands, on Sunday, the 9th of August, 1607, they landed on an Island they called St. George, where they had a sermon delivered unto them by Mr. Seymour, their preacher, and returned aboard again. On the 15th of August, they anchored under Seguin, and on that day the "Gift of God" got into the river of Sagadahoc. On the 16th, both ships got safely in, and came to anchor. On the 17th, in two boats, they sailed up the river—Captain Popham in his pinnace, with thirty persons, and Captain Gilbert in his long boat, with eighteen persons, and "found it a very gallant river; many good Islands therein, and many branches of other small rivers falling into it," and returned. On the 18th, they all went ashore, and there made choice of a place for their plantation, at the mouth, or entry, of the river, on the west side, (for the river bendeth towards the nor-east and by east,) being almost an Island, of good bigness, in a province called by the Indians "Sabino"—so called of a Sagamo, or chief commander, under the grand bashaba. On the 19th, they all went ashore, where they had made choice of their plantation, and where they had a sermon delivered unto them by their preacher, and after the sermon, the President's commission was read, with the laws to be observed and kept.

George Popham, gent., was nominated President.
Captain Raleigh Gilbert,
James Davies,
Richard Seymour, Preacher,
Captain Richard Davies,
Captain Harlowe,

were all sworn assistants; and so they returned back again.

Thus commenced the first occupation and settlement of New England, and from which date, the title of England to the new world was maintained.[1]

1. The charter of De Monts was revoked by the King, in 1607, on account of the intense jealousy of his rivals. This loss of title by the French, allowed the English charter of April 10, 1606, to take precedence of all French grants.

In all subsequent contests with rival nations, the Dutch and the French, the occupation by the Popham colony, in 1607, was put forward as the ground of title. In 1632, the Dutch West India Company, in their address to the States' General, under date of May 5th, say:

"In the year 1606, his Majesty of Great Britain granted to his subjects under the names of New England and Virgina, north and south of the river, (Manhattoes,) on express condition that the companies should remain one hundred miles apart. Whereupon the English began about the year 1607 to settle by the river of Sagadahoc. The English place New England between 41° and 45° of north latitude."

Holland Doc., N. Y., p. 51.

This act of formal possession of the country under their charter, August 29, 1607, was the consummation of England's title to New England, and the foundation of her future greatness, and the day

The Dutch contended that they had the right to occupy the one hundred miles, reserved by the charter as open territory.

Count De Tillieres, French Ambassador, writing to Secretary Conway, under date of April, 1624, admits the claim of England to Virginia and to the Gulf of Mexico, south five hundred leagues; but denies all right north. In answer to Tillieres, the charter of King James, in 1606, to the two companies is quoted to show that the claim of both is equally valid.

Calender of Colonial State Papers, i. p. 60.

In 1631, Champlain, in his great Memoir to the King, giving a statement of he rival claims of the French and English, says:

"King James issued his charter twenty-four years ago, for the country from the 33d° to the 45th°. England seized the coast of New France, where lies Acadia, on which they imposed the name of New England."

French Doc. N. Y., vol. ix, pp. 1 and 2.

In 1630, September 9th, the Scotch adventurers addressed a letter to the King, from the Council of Scotland—those claiming title under the grant to Sir William Alexander, afterwards Lord Stirling—in which they assert that "the planting of New England in the north," was by Chief Justice Popham.

Cal. of Colonial State Papers, i., p. 119.

In a work entitled "An Encouragement to Colonies," by William Alexander Knight, printed by William Stanly, London, 1625, it is said:

"One of them, Sir John Popham, sent the first company that went, of purpose to inhabit there, near to Sagadahoc." p. 30.

Capt. John Mason, writing to Sir Edward Coke, Secretary of State, under date of April 2, 1632, says:

"Plantations in New England have been settled about twenty-five years." London Doc., N. Y., vol. iii, p. 16.

In the work of Sir Ferdinando Gorges, grandson of the original proprietor of Mayne, entitled "A Description of New England,—America Painted to the Life," published in London, in 1659, he says:

"New England is between 41° and 45° of north latitude. In 1606, the country began to be possessed by the English by public authority.

should be observed as an epoch wherever there exists a community, who enjoy the common law of England, or speak our mother tongue.

This charter, of April 10, 1606, was *"for the planting of colonies or plantations in North America."* It placed the power in a council of thirteen.[1] To encourage competition, and excite rivalry, it provided for the planting of two distinct and separate colonies, each having a local government, of north and south Virginia, the former subsequently known as the Plymouth, the latter as the London Company; each company not to colonize or establish a plantation within one hundred miles of each other. Neither Gorges or the Chief Justice had their names inserted, for fear of exciting, as it would seem, the jealousy of rivals. Eight persons only

* * * * A peninsula at the mouth of the river Sagadahoc, where they built a fortress, which they named St. George." p. 18.

Sir John Popham was ridiculed in his time for his efforts to plant colonies in America.

"Chief Justice Popham not only punished malefactors, but provided for them, and first set up the discovery of *New* England, to maintain and employ those, that could not live honestly in the *Old.*"

Lloyd's State Worthies, p. 46.

1. The King ordained a Council, called the Council of Virginia, November 20, 1606, consisting of the following persons:

Sir William Wade,	Sir Thomas Smith,
Sir Walter Cope,	Sir George More,
Sir Francis Popham,	Sir Ferdinando Gorges,
Sir John Trevor,	Sir Henry Montague,
Sir William Romney,	John Doddridge,
Thomas Warr,	John Eldred,
Thomas James,	James Bagg.

The records of this company have never been published. It is hoped that the effort now making to recover them, will yet prove successful.

were named in the charter; four for each colony, who might be expected to join the expeditions.

The history of this Popham Colony is very imperfectly known. They called their settlement "*Fort St. George*;" the remains of which are still in existence; from which place, George Popham writes to King James, under date of Dec. 13, 1607, in the Latin language, in which he says: "My well considered opinion is, that in these regions the glory of God may be easily evidenced, the empire of your Majesty enlarged, and the welfare of Great Britain speedily augmented."

1608. They finished their vessel, of fifty tons, in the winter and spring, called the Virginia, of Sagadahoc, in which they returned to England that year. They lost their governor, George Popham, during the winter, who died February 5, 1608. Captain Gilbert, who succeeded to the command, was compelled to return, to settle the estate of his brother, Sir John Gilbert, who had deceased, and to whose estate he was heir. Added to these, the death in England of the venerable Chief Justice Popham, who died June 10, 1607, and the terrible severity of the winter through which they had passed, threw discouragements in their way, which they had not the courage to surmount.

This was the critical period in the history of the English race, in the new world. Both France and

England were claiming title. The occupation of the territory could alone determine the rights of the parties. Poutrincourt, inflamed with all the zeal of the Catholic faith, kept his hold on Acadia, and returning to France, with De Monts, in 1607, obtained from him a grant of Port Royal. He
1610. came out at the instance of the King, with a new grant, in 1610, with Fathers Biard and Masse, and being free from the annoyance of the Huguenots, he despatched his son Biancourt to France, to bring further recruits to his Colony. The flower of their youth were cheerfully engaged for this service, from all the Jesuit Colleges of France.

As they were about to embark for Acadia, the merchants of Dieppe, who had furnished the supplies for the ship, refused the Jesuits admission on board, on account of their religion, so strong was the Protestant faith at that time in France.

1611. The zealous and elevated Madame de Guerchville, moved to anger by this refusal of the merchants, raised the entire sum required for the voyage by contributions among the Catholic nobility, and despatched Biancourt, and his Jesuit missionaries, who arrived at Port Royal just in time to save Poutrincourt and his party from starvation. Meanwhile Champlain had in 1608 laid the foundation of Quebec, and held actual possession of the St. Lawrence under a new charter.

Emboldened by the breaking up of Popham's Colony, at Sagadahoc, the French pushed forward their possessions, claiming the territory as far south as Cape Cod. Gorges knew the importance of maintaining possession of the country, and while "*all his associates gave up to these discouragements,*" his heroic spirit, so far from yielding, rose with the occasion that demanded still greater sacrifices; and, as he says, "Finding I could no longer be seconded by others, I became an owner of a ship myself, fit for that employment, and under color of fishing and trade, I got a master and company for her, to which I sent Vines and others, my own servants, appointing them to leave the ship and ship's company for to follow their business in the usual places. By these and the help of those natives, formerly sent over, I came to be truly informed, of so much as gave me assurance, that in time, I should want no undertakers, though as yet, I was forced to hire men, to stay there; the winter quarters, at extreme rates," &c.[1]

We may therefore fairly claim that the occupancy of Vines and others under Gorges, saved the country from falling into the hands of the French. We find the English at Pemaquid in 1608 and 1609.[2] Thither the Virginia Colony sent annually for fish,

1. Gorges' Briefe Narration.

2. Relations Des Jesuites.

from 1608 and onward. Sir Francis Popham, the son of the Chief Justice, continued to send his ships to Pemaquid, and the same ship was found there by Capt. John Smith, on his first visit to the coast, in 1614.

Belknap says, that Vines came over a long time before the settlement at Plymouth, and the authorities concur in fixing it in 1609. Sir Ferdinando Gorges, though he does not name the year, speaking of events in the order of their occurrence, places the settlement of Vines before the voyage of Hobson, and tradition has assigned to Vines the honor of holding Pemaquid, Monhegan and Sagadahoc, from 1609, till he removed to Saco, where he spent the winter of 1616–17.

Capt. Hobson came over as early as 1611. Gorges says in connection with this voyage, "for some years together, nothing to my private profit was realized, for what I get one way, I spent another."

1613. In 1613, Argall, from the Virginia Colony, on visiting the coast for fish, learned that the French had a trading house at Penobscot, and a settlement at Mount Desert, or St. Saviour, another at St. Croix, and one at Port Royal. After procuring a sufficient force, he broke up these posts, and destroyed St. Saviour and Port Royal, carrying the Jesuits and some of their adherents to Virginia as prisoners, many of the French settlers fled to the woods, but returned and re-occupied the places thus laid waste by Argall.[1] French fishing and trading ships were constantly visiting these places.

1614. In June, 1614, Capt. Henry Harley, one of Popham's Colony at Sagadahoc, sailed in Gorges' employ with Assacumet, one of those natives first taken by Weymouth, and the famous Indian Epenow, of Martha's Vineyard, who proposed to show them valuable mines of gold. He was as Gorges says, "a person of goodly stature, strong and well proportioned," but he escaped from them as soon as they came to the coast, and the expedition was productive of no useful results.

It is not necessary to narrate all the events connected with the expeditions to the country, prior to 1614, when the eccentric but intrepid Captain John Smith appeared on the coast, in command of four ships.

This venture of Smith paid a profit of £1,500, "by traffic in otter and beaver skins, salt fish, train oil and such other like gross commodities." Smith at this time, made a plot or map of the country, since known as Smith's map of New England, published in 1616, and he was made Admiral of New England by the Company.

1615. In 1615, Smith sailed again for New England, in two ships, which voyage proved disastrous. He lost his masts in a gale, returned to

1. Seé note on page 19. Also Appendix B.

Plymouth, and again sailing, was taken prisoner by the French. One of the vessels, however, in command of Capt. Dermer, made its way to New England, and returned well laden.[1]

1616. In the same year, Sir Richard Hawkins, President of the Plymouth Company, departed for these parts, and took in a cargo for Spain, principally fish, which proved a profitable business. In 1616, eight ships from London and Plymouth made profitable voyages to New England, and the value of the fisheries of Monhegan was fully established. There can be no doubt, that Monhegan was occupied with a trading, though changing, population, many years before Plymouth was settled, and when Edward Winslow, of the Plymouth flock, visited it, in May, 1622, as he says, "*to obtain victuals for our famishing plantation*," he found there thirty ships. He also says, "I found there, kind entertainment, and good respect; with a willingness to supply our wants; through provident and discreet care, we were recovered, and preserved, till our own crop in the ground was ready."

1616. Such was the condition of New England affairs in 1616, before war had broken out among the Indian tribes, pestilence destroyed the native population, or the Pilgrim settlement been initiated. The country was well known along the

1. See Appendix C.

coast, from the Bay of Fundy to Cape Cod, and the fisheries yielded abundant profit.

It was comparatively full of people, a native population, subsisting not only on game and the products of the soil, but on oysters, salmon, and the choicest fish, in which the harbors, rivers and coves abounded.

The territory, now known as the State of Maine, with its numerous and well sheltered harbors; its noble rivers, swarming with the most valuable fish; its forests, of unrivaled beauty, surpassing, in the estimation of the navigators, those of the north of Europe; its soil, bearing readily the choicest grains of Europe, in addition to Indian corn, and the potato, indigenous to this continent; the charming variety of scenery; its undulating surface; its climate, that for healthfulness and salubrity, left nothing to desire; attracted the most skilful of the European voyageurs to its shores.

The region lying between Cape Porpoise (Kennebunk) and the Penobscot, was the most frequented of all, for it is by far the most beautiful portion of New England, and the possession of it excited the ambition of the French and English alike.

It was the seat of Indian Empire, more populous than any portion of the Continent, the home of the Bashaba, whose authority extended to Narragansett Bay.

The Indians always occupied the best portions of the Continent until driven from them by superior force, as seen in our day in the case of the Cherokees and Choctaws, of the South, and the Penobscots of our own State. The French were the first to perceive this great fact, and their possessions followed closely the grounds held by the Indians. We have not time to pursue this inquiry, but we hazard nothing in predicting, that the seats of Empire on this Continent, of the European races, will eventually coincide, with those of the aboriginal inhabtants.

The coast was at that time well delineated on maps in common use; the Dutch had a flourishing Colony on the Hudson river, and on the same day that John Smith was exhibiting to Prince Charles, for his approval of the names upon it, his map of New England, the Dutch Figurative map of New Netherlands, extending east to the Penobscot, was laid before the States General for their inspection and adoption. The early navigators saw nothing inviting between Cape Cod and Manhattan, while all the harbors east of Cape Porpoise, were filled with voyageurs from the Old World.

In 1602, when Gosnold came to New England, the Indians, clothed in Indian apparel, visited his ships without any signs of surprise, as at Pemaquid in 1607, the aborigines came fearlessly on board the vessels of Popham and Gilbert; and the famous Indian Sagamore Samoset, went from Pemaquid to greet the Pilgrims at Plymouth, in March, 1621, with hearty welcome in their own language, "*Welcome, Welcome, Englishmen,*" said Samoset, and proved his friendship to the end of his life. The welcome of Samoset was sincere, because the Indian tribes, who valued goodly rivers, fertile fields, and abundant forests, as the best hunting grounds, felt no jealousy of men who sought a resting place on the barren and deserted sands of Cape Cod;—where the native population had been swept off by the plague. And the French looked with equal indifference on that feeble band of fishermen whose location at Plymouth in no way interfered with their plans of dominion in the new world.

About this time, 1616, a bloody war broke
1616. out between the Tarratines, who lived east of the Penobscot, supposed to be incited to it by the French, and the Bashaba of Pemaquid. He was slain, and his people destroyed. At the same time, a devastating pestilence swept off the Indian race without injuring the whites. Gorges says, "Vines and the rest with him, that live in the cabins with these people that died, not one of them ever felt their heads to ache."

The year 1616 brings us to what may be called the Pilgrim Period; for at this time were initiated those measures that resulted in what Mr. Webster called the first settlement of New England.

The history of the times would disprove the popular theory, that "religious impulse accomplished the early settlement of New England;" by which is meant the settlement therein of the Pilgrims. But the plan of colonizing America did not originate with them, nor were they in any sense the leaders of the movement. They resorted thither from necessity, and while they profited by the labors and enterprise of others, achieved nothing beyond those in a subordinate position.

The settlement of New England was the work of many years, and was achieved by the same influences as those still at work, to extend the Saxo-Norman race. It was the legitimate result of the commercial ideas and adventurous spirit of the times.

The Protestant faith was struggling to maintain its foothold in the British Isles in the reigns of Henry VIII., of Edward VI., and of Mary, and not till the reign of Elizabeth was it fully established. This consummation gave internal repose to the nation, and allowed the spirit of enterprise to expand and ripen. This spirit sought employment in the new world, and drew from Elizabeth the earliest charters.

The English Puritans exhibited the restless spirit of change that had grown up in the English character, under the influence of the last fifty years; and not in the reign of the despotic Queen, but in the reign of the weak James, those who had not property, or Court favor, naturally preferred a life of adventure with the hopes of profit, or preferment in a new country.

It was the age of private enterprise, and of intellectual freedom. The East India Company was laying the foundation of English empire in the East, while the Council of Virginia was planting the seeds of a more glorious dominion over the wilds of nature in the West. The same spirit that has filled the valley of the Mississippi and the Pacific shore, with natives of New England and of Europe, within the last fifty years, led to the first emigration to America.

That "religious impulse" led the followers of Robinson to Leyden, in 1608, is, undoubtedly, true, but religious persecution in England soon ceased, and no one there suffered death, for that cause, after 1611. The forms of the church service were as harmless then as now, and were originally adopted, after long debate, by a majority of *one* only, in a full convention of the English Clergy, in the reign of Elizabeth.[1] The articles of the church were Calvinistic, and in no wise differed in doctrines from those of the Puritans.

Elizabeth was a far greater stickler for observance of church ceremonies than any one of her suc-

1. Sanford's History of the Great Rebellion, p. 67.

cessors. But the Leyden flock did not leave England in her reign.

It is time to vindicate the truth of history; to do justice to the claims of Gorges, and to repel the calumnious charges of the men who founded the Theocracy of New England; who persecuted alike Quakers, Baptists, and Churchmen. Fifty years after the putting of men to death for errors of doctrine had ceased, in Old England, from which the Massachusetts Puritans pretended to have fled "for conscience sake," they executed men of the most blameless lives for the slightest differences of opinion, or doctrine, in religion. On finding that Baptists and Quakers and Churchmen were only mulplied the more, by this means, as persecution grew more severe, they finally passed a statute, that Quakers should be treated as vagabonds, whipped from town to town by the Magistrates, till driven beyond the boundaries of the Colony. In point of fact, within the boundaries of the Colony of Massachuchusetts Bay, from the time they first landed, till the arrival of Sir Edmund Andros as Governor in 1686, the Government of Massachusetts Bay, was more arbitrary and intolerant than any despotism from which they fled from England. Stripes, imprisonment and even death itself were inflicted, on those who regarded baptism as a sacrament, fit only to be administered to those capable of understanding its import. The banishment of Wheelwright and others for antinomian heresy and his escape into Maine, show the character of the times.

The Plymouth flock, a portion of those whom Robinson had gathered at Leyden, were an amiable and pious people. They gladly sought the protection of Sir Ferdinando Gorges, the founder of the New England Company, prior to their removal from Holland, came out in view of his promise of a charter, from whom they obtained it in 1621. 1620. But they never, in fact, exerted any considerable political influence on the history of the Continent.

The Colony of Massachusetts Bay, on the other hand, was guided by the boldest set of adventurers that ever set foot on American soil. The fathers of this Colony, who first met in Nottinghamshire, 1627, and those who led the way afterwards, were men whom Charles had imprisoned for their too great freedom of speech in the House of Commons, and who gladly escaped to America to avoid a worse fate at home.

1629. Sir Ferdinando Gorges readily gave them a charter, March 19, 1629. They came over the same year. One condition, as Gorges says, of the grant was, that it should not be prejudicial to the previous grant to his son, Robert Gorges, made in 1622, then in the actual occupation of his grantees. But writing secretly to Endicott, their first Governor, under date of April 17, 1629, "the

Governor and Deputy of the New England Company for a plantation in Massachusetts Bay," residing in England, advise him, that Mr. Oldham had become the grantee of Robert Gorges, and that the Rev. Mr. Blackstone and Mr. Wm. Jeffreys had been duly authorized to put Oldham in possession of the premises, yet they held it void in law, and advised that "they should take possession of the chiefe part thereof," and thus destroy the value of the grant previously given to Gorges. This was done, and Gorges' grantees were driven out — a fair specimen of the sense of justice of that Company. To mislead the people of England, as to their true designs, after leaving England, while on ship-board, they publicly requested the prayers of the *English Church*, for their success in planting "the Protestant faith in America." But on landing, they forcibly expelled the two brothers Brown, who came over highly recommended by the Company in London, and against all protestations and reason they were sent back to England by the first vessel that returned, because they absented themselves from their meeting on the Sabbath. These men, in the privacy of their own chamber, were guilty of following in their devotions, the form of the English Liturgy. For this they were driven out of the country.

The Massachusetts Bay Company sent their charter with the great seal of the King to America, to render its recall the more difficult; and when it was subsequently vacated by writ of *quo warranto*, refused to comply with the order of Court for its return. The disputes at home which resulted in the beheading of Charles and the Revolution of 1688, in England, alone saved the leaders and their followers from punishment. The Royal Charter, uniting the Colonies of Plymouth, Massachusetts Bay, the Province of Maine, and all the territory east of it, under the Governorship of Sir William Phipps, a native of Pemaquid, put an end to the Theocracy of New England in 1691.

The modern popular history of New England, has sought to conceal the exact truth, and to throw apology over the grossest offences.

Those who trust to such early writers as the Cottons, the Mathers and Hubbards of former days, on whom the modern historians of Massachusetts seem mainly to rely, may find abundant means of correcting their opinions.

We may, at this time, venture to speak of these men as they deserve. The accurate and accomplished historian of Rhode Island, in his recent history, speaking of the Massachusetts historians, justly says:—

"The opinions of men who maligned the purity of Williams, of Clarke, and of Gorton, who bore 'false witness' to the character and the acts of some of the wisest and best men who ever lived in New

England ; who strove to blast the reputation of people whose liberal views they could not comprehend; who collected evidence to crush the good name of their more virtuous opponents by casting upon them the odium of acts wherein they were themselves the guilty parties; who committed outrages in the name of God, far more barbarous than the worst with which they ever charged 'the usurper;' the opinions of such men, we say, are not to be received without a challenge." — [*Arnold's History of Rhode Island. Vol. I. p.* 514.

The impartial and graphic Macauley, thus describes the Puritans of that day :—

" The persecution which the separatists had undergone, had been severe enough to irritate, but not severe enough to destroy. They had not been tamed into submission, but bated into savageness, and stubborness. After the fashion of oppressed sects, they mistook their own vindictive feelings for emotions of piety; encouraged in themselves in reading and meditation, a disposition to brood over their wrongs, and when they had worked themselves up into hating their enemies, imagined that they were only hating the enemies of Heaven. In the New Testament there was little indeed which, even when perverted by the most disingenuous exposition, could seem to countenance the indulgence of malevolent passions. But the Old Testament contained the history of a race selected by God, to be witnesses of his wrath and ministers of his vengeance, and especially commanded by him to do many things which, if done without his special command, would have been atrocious crimes. In such a history, it was not difficult for fierce and gloomy spirits to find much that might be distorted to suit their wishes. The extreme Puritans, therefore, began to feel for the Old Testament a preference, which, perhaps, they did not distinctly avow, even to themselves; but which showed itself in all their sentiments and habits. They paid to the Hebrew language a respect which they refused to that tongue in which the discourses of Jesus, and the Epistles of Paul, have come down to us. They baptized their children by the names, not of christian saints, but of Hebrew patriarchs and warriors. In defiance of the express and reiterated declarations of Luther and Calvin, they turned the weekly festival by which the church had from the primitive times, commemorated the resurrection of her Lord, into a Jewish Sabbath. They sought for principles of jurisprudence in the Mosaic law, and for precedents to guide their ordinary conduct, in the books of Judges and Kings. Their thoughts and discourses ran much on acts which were assuredly not recorded as examples for our imitation. The prophet who hewed in pieces a captive King, the rebel general who gave the blood of a Queen to the dogs, the matron, who, in defiance of plighted faith, and of the laws of Eastern hospitality, drove the nail into the brain of the fugitive ally who had just fed at her board, and who was sleeping under the shadow of her tent, were proposed, as models, to Christians, suffering under the tyranny of princes and prelates."—[*Macauley's History of England. Vol. I. p.* 62.

The most odious features of Puritan intolerance were developed in Massachusetts, with the rise of that party to power in England, and when the Commonwealth passed away at home, the weak counsels of the Stuarts were unable to control the people of New England. We find the Massachusetts Puritans persecutors from the outset of their career, denying the rights of citizenship to all but actual church members, and refusing to others protection even against the Indians. When the first New England league was formed in 1643, for better protection against savage warfare the Delegates of Maine were excluded because they were Churchmen, and those of Rhode Island, because they were Baptists.[1]

The settlement of Plymouth is clearly due to an act of Sir Ferdinando Gorges. His aim from the first was the settlement of the country, not advantage to himself. He sought, by putting other men prominently forward, and in every

1. Bradford's History of Plymouth Plantation, p. 416.
Brodhead's History of New York, pp. 361, 362.

other way to disarm the jealousy that always follows upright public action. As Gorges says, "the planting of Colonies in America, was undertaken for the advancement of religion, the enlargement of the bounds of our nation, the increase of trade, and the employment of many thousands of all sorts of people." The grant obtained on his request, says, "*was never intended to be converted to private uses,*" and in answer to the Commons, who sought to abrogate his charter, he publicly offered to surrender it; "not only in behalf of himself, but of the rest of those interested in the Patent, so they would prosecute the settling of the plantation as was first intended." "Wherein," he said, "we would be their humble servants in all that lay in our power, without looking to the great charge that had been expended in the discovery and seizure of the coast, and bringing it to the pass it was come unto."

This was "after they had found by our constant perseverance therein, some profit by a course of fishing upon that coast."

All writers agree, that after 1616, the New England Fisheries were successful and profitable to the English.

At this time, or prior to March 1617, Gorges, in pursuance of his policy of settling the country, invited the Leyden church to emigrate to America. He says, "before the unhappy controversy happened between those of Virginia and myself, they were forced, through the great charge they had been at, to hearken to any propositions, that might give ease and furtherance to so hopeful a business. For that purpose it was referred to their consideration, how necessary it was that means might be used *to draw into those enterprises* some of those families that had retired themselves into Holland for scruple of conscience, giving them such freedom and liberty as might stand with their likings. This advice being hearkened unto, there were, that undertook the putting it in practice and accordingly brought it forth," &c. "Such as their weak fortunes were able to provide," and they "with great difficulty recovered the coast of New England," &c., &c.

The Council of Virginia still held the country under the original charter of 1606, and it was the work of Gorges to draw the Leyden flock to America. Bradford says, "they liked not the idea of going South." They had confidence in the success of Gorges' plan of a separate charter for New England.

The Leyden flock early saw that they must soon become extinct if they remained in Holland. They could not remain longer in that country, or return to England to reside. They had little or no means of support, and trusted to the chances of obtaining it, in the new employment of fishing and trading to New England, then so popular at home. Robert Cushman and John Carver were sent to the King, asking permission to "enjoy liberty of conscience in America, where they would endeavor the advancement of His Majesty's dominions, and the enlargement of the gospel." "This," his Majesty King James said, "was a good and honest motive," and asking "what profit might arise in the part we intended, (the most northern parts of Virginia,") 'twas answered "Fishing." "So God have my soul," said James, "'tis an honest trade, 'twas the Apostles own calling." Winslow says, "some one of the Plymouth Colony lent them £300 gratis, for three years, which was repaid." Winslow further says, "some of the chief of the Plymouth Company doubted not to obtain our suit of the King, for liberty in religion." Bradford says, "some others wrought with the Archbishop, and they prevailed in sounding his Majesty's mind, that he would connive at them, and not molest them, provided they carried themselves peaceably."[1]

A still greater difficulty remained, the raising of money for the expedition. This was finally done through Mr. Thomas Weston, a merchant of London, who with others, 70 in all, "some gentlemen, some merchants, some handicraftsmen; some ad-

1. The date of their application was in 1618, as appears by the following:

1618. Seven articles which the Church of Leyden sent to the Council of England to be considered of, in respect of their judgments, occasioned about their going to Virginia. *Endorsed* "Copy of Seven articles sent unto the Council of England by the Brownists of Leyden."
[*Calendar of Colonial Papers. Vol. I. p.* 21.

venturing great sums, some small, as their estates and affections served." By the hard conditions agreed to, the whole Leyden Company, adventured their persons, as well as their estates. Hutchinson says, "they had no notion of cultivating any more ground than would afford their own necessary provisions, but proposed that their chief secular employment should be, commerce with the natives." It was a trading Company, not designing a community of goods, but a fair adventure in business. Any idea of founding a Colony or of remaining in the country beyond the seven years of their partnership, no where appears in their earlier movements or writings.

Having made up their minds to emigrate from Holland, they formed a partnership for seven years, to pursue fishing and traffic in the new world. They then applied to the Council of Virginia for a charter. Bradford says, "by the advice of some friends, the Patent was not taken in the name of any of their own Company, but in the name of Mr. John Wincob, a religious gentleman, belonging to the Countess of Lincoln, who intended to go with them."[1]

The statement explains fully the relations of the parties. This Countess of Lincoln had the most intimate relations with the New England settlements. Some of her children afterwards emigrated

1. Bradford's History of Plimouth Plantation, p. 41.

to America, and her daughter Frances was at that time the wife of John Gorges, the eldest son and heir of Sir Ferdinando.

Their departure from. Deft Haven, their arrival in England, and their trials in getting to sea, have been narrated with a minuteness and particularity that leaves nothing unsaid, and the voyage of the Mayflower is as famous as that celebrated one of ancient times, in quest of the Golden Fleece.

Capt. Smith says the Brownists found his chart or map "cheaper than his employment as a pilot," and with that in their hands they sailed to New England and sought Milford Haven, conspicuously laid down in it, now Cape Cod Harbor. Here they came to anchor, and sought New Plymouth, the precise spot designated on Smith's map, four years before.

When the Pilgrims sailed, Gorges had not obtained the charter for New England. On the return of the Mayflower, they sent to Gorges for their charter. In speaking of it, he says:—

"They found that the authority they had from the Company of Virginia could not warrant their abode in that place; * * They hastened away their ship with orders to their Solicitor to deal with me, to be a means, they might have a grant from the Council of New England's affairs, to settle in the place,—which was performed to their particular satisfaction, and good content of them all."

Their Charter was dated, June 1, 1621, granting to John Pierce, a clothworker of London, and his associates: One hundred acres of land to each settler, with a nominal rent, commencing at the end of seven years, the termination of their partnership; with liberal grants of land for public uses; and also certain rights of hunting, fishing, &c. It did not profess to grant any civil rights, or confer on them the power of making laws.[1] In that respect it differs from the charter granted to Robert Gorges in 1622, which vested ample powers for governing the country by means of a Parliament, one branch, like the Commons of England chosen by the freeholders of New England, the other appointed by authority of the Crown, with an Executive under the name of Governor.[2]

In this Charter to Robert Gorges, we find the model, or pattern, of the British Colonial Governments of later times. The division of the powers of Government into three branches was unknown to the Pilgrims, or to the Puritans for a long period, and this accounts for the despotic character of their governments. It was a quarrel in the General Court of Massachusetts about Mrs. Sherman's Pig, that led to the breaking up of the General Court and its division into two branches, in 1645.[3]

1. This long lost Charter has been recovered, and is printed in full in vol. ii., 4th Series of Mass. Historical Coll.

2. This Charter to Robert Gorges is found in full, in Gorges' Briefe Narration, p. 44, vol. ii., Maine Hist. Coll.

3. This amusing story is found in Winthrop's Journal, vol. ii. p. 260.

The Pilgrim government at Plymouth, which continued till the charter of William and Mary in 1692, never attained to the knowledge of a division of the Legislative power into two independent branches. Their government was through the church.

The first charter granted to the Plymouth flock, came, therefore, from the original Council of Virginia, who held at that time the entire country. Through Thomas Weston they had heard of the plan of Gorges for a separate grant of New England, and they sailed for North Virginia, trusting to Gorges for a grant.

The petition of Gorges for the New England charter, was dated March 3, 1620. An order in Council was made July 23, 1620, directing the preparation of the new charter, and it passed, the seals, Nov. 3, 1620. In this charter it says:—

"We have been humbly petitioned unto, by our trusty and well beloved servant, SIR FERDINANDO GORGES, Knight, Captain of our Fort and Island by Plymouth, and by certain the principal Knights and Gentlemen Adventurers of the said Second Colonye, and by divers other Persons of Quality, who now intend to be their Associates divers of which have been at great and extraordinary charge, and sustained many losses in seeking and discovering a Place fitt and convenient to lay the Foundation of a hopeful plantation, and have years past, by God's assistance and their own Endeavors, *taken actual Possession of the Continent hereafter mentioned in our name and to our use as Sovereign Lord thereof, and have settled already some of our people in places agreeable to their Desires in those places;* and in Confidence of prosperous Success therein, by the Continuance of God's Devine Blessing, and our Royall permission, have resolved in a more plentiful and effectual manner to prosecute the same."[1]

That Gorges had complete possession of the country before the Plymouth people came over, is also shown by the complaints against him for a monopoly in fishing. He had brought the country sufficiently into notice to attract thither the Pilgrim flock.

To deny to Gorges, therefore, the glory of being the founder of New England because his own Colony was overshadowed by that of Massachusetts Bay, is as unjust as it would be to deny to Columbus credit as the discoverer of America, and to assign the glory of it to Sebastian Cabot, simply because Cabot first discovered the main land of the Continent seventeen months before it was seen by Columbus. All fair minds agree, that it was the far-sighted and gifted Genoese, who by inspiration, looked through the darkness of ages, forecast the future, and pointed the way for Cabot and Vespucci to the new world across the ocean, though his modesty permitted the name of another to be given

2. See Appendix D.

to it, that of Cabotia, which for a time gained favor, yielding to that of America. Still more clearly than Columbus did the instinctive sagacity of Gorges foresee and predict the fruits of his own great endeavor, and beheld a rising State in America free from European control. And yet for the last thirty-nine years, or since Mr. Webster's great speech at Plymouth on the 22d of Dec., 1820, the truth of severe history has been overlooked, in admiration of the creations of his genius.

As an Epic Poem, Mr. Webster's speech stands in the same relation to history as the Iliad of Homer or the Æneid of Virgil. The war of the gods on Olympus, and the flight of Anchises, regarded at one time as historic truths, were just as real and true to history as Mr. Webster's description of the landing of the Pilgrims.

Among all the achievements of Mr. Webster, there is nothing that shows his real greatness, so much as those efforts, by which, in the style and manner of the ancient historians, he embodies in an impressive form, the great facts and ideas that are supposed to govern human affairs. It is fair to apply to this composition the definition of "Classical History," so clearly and beautifully expressed in his address before the New York Historical Society of Feb. 23, 1852. This Pilgrim speech is a true specimen of Classical History; "not," as he says, "a memoir, or a crude collection of acts, occurrences, and dates; it is a composition, a production, which has unity of design, like a work of statuary or of painting." As such, his Plymouth speech bears the impress of his creative mind. He transferred to the Plymouth Panorama a representation of the heroic achievements of Gorges, of Popham, and of Vines.

Mr. Webster's poetry has been regarded as history. But it is such history as are the writings of Livy, or the historic plays of Shakspeare.

The mission of the Poet precedes that of the historian, and the imaginary characters of a poetic mind continue for a while to walk the earth under the shadow of a great name. The Pilgrims have richly enjoyed this distinguished honor.

The Hon. Edward Everett, evidently on the authority of Mr. Webster, says in his Plymouth speech, four years later, "This, the source of our being, the Birth Day of all New England,—this grand undertaking was accomplished on the spot where we now dwell." "A continent for the *first time* explored, a vast ocean traversed by men, women and children, voluntarily exiling themselves from the fairest portions of the Old World," &c.

Modern historians of the Massachusetts school, have since then, taken these flights of poetic fancy for historic verities, and sought to elevate them into the dignity of history. They might as well insist, that a modern fourth of July oration was the cause of our Revolutionary war, though uttered some years after that event had taken place.

Regarded as a political event, the Plymouth settlement was not of the slightest consequence or importance. It neither aided or retarded the settlement of the country, and is of no moment except as the actors in that work were concerned, or those who claim thence their inheritance. As a tale of individual and personal heroism, in which patient resignation was mingled with superstitious confidence, it deserves sympathy and respect. But those who seek to give it political importance, confound the Plymouth settlement with that of the Puritan Commonwealth of Massachusetts Bay, two events as independent of each other in every respect as was the settlement of New Netherlands from that of Lord Baltimore, on the Chesapeake.

The Pilgrims had at the outset no idea of founding a Colony. The idea may have been suggested to them by the language of the charter of June, 1621. It is true, they dignified their head officer with the title of "Governor," a term formerly applied to the head of any family or company. He had no civil authority whatever, and the fact that for the first seven years no records of any sort were kept, and not a scrap of written history made prior to 1627, shows how primitive were all their ideas of government and of property.

Bradford began his history in 1630, and at a later

date, rejoicing over the downfall of the Bishops, in the days of the Commonwealth, he appends thereto the following comments: "when I began these scribbled writings, which was about the year 1630, and so peeced up at times of leasure, afterwards; little did I think their downfall was so near," &c.[1]

The compact signed on board the Mayflower, under date of November 11, 1620, which has been eulogized as "the germ of republican freedom," was, as Bradford says, "a combination, occasioned partly by the discontented and mutinous speeches that when they come ashore, they would use their own libertie," &c.[2]

In 1632, the first records of Plymouth Colony were commenced, but they had before them the example of the Colony of Massachusetts Bay, whose Records are of the same date as their settlement.

The famous Capt. John Smith, a cotemporary, says, "about one hundred Brownists went to Plymouth, whose humorous ignorance caused them to

1. Bradford's History of Plimouth, p. 6.

2. Bradford thus explains the matter:—

"I shall a little returne backe and begine with a combination made by them before they came ashore, being ye first foundation of their governmente in this place; occasioned partly by ye discontented and mutinous speeches that some of the strangers amongst them had let fall from them in ye ship. That when they came ashore they would use their own libertie; for none had power to command them; the patente they had being for Virginia, and not for New-england, which belonged to another Government, with which ye Virginia Company had nothing to doe. And partly that such an acte by them done (this their condition considered) might be as firme as any patent, and in some respects more sure." The form was as followeth. p. 89.

endure a wonderful deal of misery, with infinite patience."

It was under the charter given to John Wincob, and in the protection of the original Virginia Company, with the map of Smith for their guide, they came to America, too poor to own their vessel, or to pay for the land they should here occupy, and yet these obligations were never repaid, or acknowledged. The representations of Mr. Everett and others would lead us to suppose, that the Pilgrims embarked for America across an unknown sea, to seek a resting place in thickest darkness of ignorance, like that deep mystery that shrouded the Atlantic, when the vessel of Columbus first turned its prow Westward from the Canaries, one hundred and twenty-eight years before.

Oratory, painting and poetry, have brought their richest gifts to the Pilgrim altar, and raised this feeble band of unlettered men to the rank of statesmen and heroes. The genius of Webster, the oratory of Everett, the industry of Bancroft, and the zeal of Palfrey, have not failed to offer incense to the pride of Massachusetts as the leading community of the Western world;—and in their devotion to her, overlooked the great influences that for a whole generation, had been preparing the way, for the secure occupation of her soil. And they have too readily followed the authority of those partizan writers, whose zeal for their own cause, has outrun their sense of justice. And historic truth demands that the view of the character of Gorges as drawn by the two latter, should be corrected by the light of more recently discovered information. Gorges' defence against the charge of having unjustly betrayed the Earl of Essex, refutes it altogether, and should dispel the prejudice that Mr. Palfrey's recent work is calculated to perpetuate. The long lost history of Bradford, recovered in 1855, and published in 1856, since the first issue of Mr. Bancroft's earliest volumes, will, undoubtedly, lead to a modification of the views expressed by him as to the claims of Gorges.

It seems strange that the Pilgrims should have been advanced to the condition of heroes, while the services of Gorges, in a long and illustrious life of duty should have been overlooked and forgotten. But this is not difficult of explanation. By force of accident, not now needful to relate, the Colony of Massachusetts Bay, became the leading one of New England, and its population have always, beyond any other people, indulged their pride of ancestry. Mr. Webster easily sympathized with that spirit of Massachusetts that demanded for her the proud title of Parent Commonwealth. He enstamped on his time, beyond any man of this country, the impress of his own proud and heroic spirit. He inspired a love of country, a pride of home, a feeling of contentment and satisfaction favorable to industry, to religious sentiment, and the accumulation of property. The industrial superiority of that State, the growth of the last thirty years, is largely due to the elevated sentiments by him inspired.

With the progress of refinement, and the increase of wealth in every civilized community, in every age, there is a tendency to exaggerate the past, to undervalue the present, and to question all anticipations for the future. As weary age looks at existing facts as the limit of human experience, the poetic mind encourages future hopes, reproducing from the past, all the varied forms of beauty or grandeur that the page of romance has foreshadowed—and every cultivated community must have its classic and romantic age, demanding a corresponding history. It glories in after years in the fabled greatness of a remote, but heroic ancestry, till severe history dispels the poetic charm.

The Egyptian tradition pointed in after years to the days of its earlier grandeur a thousand years before those of Manetho, the founder of the temple of Karnac, whose dynasty commenced thirty-four centuries before the Christian Era. The Grecian poets, of its more modern times, constantly dwelt on the fabled glories of the past, the age that preceded the days of Homer and Hesiod, and the Roman orators in the proudest days of its luxurious civilization, pointed back to the foundation of Rome, whose fabled city was but the rudest structure of savage life. England glories still in the crude institutions of Alfred, while France with greater glory recounts the heroic deeds of Charlemagne.

New England has had her days of hero worship, and brought her devout offerings in the same spirit to the shrine of the Pilgrims, and raised them from the humble condition of artizans and laborers to the rank of founders of Empires, and the sentimental Mrs. Hemans, under the spell of Mr. Webster's genius, has thrown the charms of her poetic fancy around the rude homes of its early settlers.

All this is a pure myth. The war of the Gods on Olympus, and the mythic tales of the love of Sapho, are just as real. Had the Pilgrims landed on the rocky cliffs of Sagadahoc, of Donaquet, or of Pemaquid, the poetic fancy of Mrs. Hemans might have had the color of the truth. But to talk of "the rock bound coast" of Plymouth, amid the sands of Cape Cod, and of "the giant branches" of the scrubby pines on the south shore of Massachusetts Bay, is simply a flight of fancy. "The bleak and death-like desolation of nature" which, as Mr. Everett truly says, "met the eyes of the Pilgrims on their approach to land, are changed by the exuberant fancy of Mrs. Hemans into charming spots like those which the voyageurs had found in the rich forests, of that Norumbega, whose praises had been sung by John Milton.

The beautiful retreats at Diamond Cove and

Pentecost Harbor,—the rich forests on the banks of the Penobscot, the Sheepscot and the Kennebec, had attracted thither numerous voyagers from the old world, before the Leyden Church had been gathered, under the charge of the pious Robinson.

New England had all the attractions described by the early navigators answering the poetic descriptions of Mrs. Hemans. It had "good harbors, very good fishing, much fowl, noble forests, gallant rivers, and the land as good ground as any can desire." But this does not apply to the region where the Pilgrims made their home.

Let every one read the poetic description of the landing of the Pilgrims by Mr. Webster, and study the picture of it by Sargent, with the simple history of Bradford in his hands, and he is lost in admiration, like that which the student of classic history feels, in the perusal of the works of the great master of Epic poetry. According to Bradford, they embarked at Deft Haven, July 21, 1620, sailed from Southampton, Aug. 5, put back twice,—persevered in their plans, and espied Cape Cod, Nov. 9, 1620, old style, and came to anchor in Cape Cod harbor, Nov. 11, 1620, and on the same day, signed their compact of Government, and chose or rather confirmed, John Carver, Governor.

Their ship remained at Cape Cod, till Dec. 25, 1620, new style. Prior to this, Bradford, Standish and others, had explored the country, setting out on the 16th of Dec. On the 21st of Dec., they passed through Plymouth, and returned to the ship on the 24th. After much doubt and difficulty, and days of wandering, on Wednesday the 30th of Dec., they determined on their place of settlement. On the 4th of January, 1621, they went first on shore, and began to cut timber for a house. The *May-flower* remained in the harbor till April 15, when she departed for England. Till then, a large portion of them lived on shipboard, and there is no account of any distinct or specific act of landing. The winter was mild beyond example, and when Samoset "the Sagamore of Moratiggon arrived, March 26, he was stark naked, only a leather about his waist, with a fringe about a span long, or a little or more." Had the winter been as usual, or severe as that of 1607, when Popham wintered at Sagadahoc, not a soul of them could have survived.

Modern historians have accidentally fixed on the 22d of December as the landing day of the Pilgrims, and they attempt to justify it by the statement of Bradford, that on that day, the explorers passed through Plymouth and pitched upon it as one spot, to be recommended for the settlement. But unfortunately for their accuracy, this day was the 21st, and the adoption of the 22d, is not justified by any fact whatever.[1]

1. "And this being the last day of ye week, (Saturday, Dec. 19, n. s.) they prepared 'ther to keep y^e^ *Sabbath*. On Munday they sounded y^e^

The great misfortune of Gorges was, that, as a man of true honor, he was compelled to support the fortunes of the weak and decaying Stuart dynasty, to which he remained true to the last. He also suffered in his fortunes in not emigrating to America.

In a paper on file in the English State Paper Office, quoted in the recent volume of Mr. Folsom, it is stated that Gorges came to New England with Mason in 1619,[1] but we find no confirmation of

harbor, and founde it fitt for shipping; and marched into ye land, and found diverse cornfeilds, and litle runing brooks, a place (as they supposed) fitt for situation; at least it was ye best they could find, and ye season, and their presente necessitie, made them glad to accepte of it. So they returned to their shipp again with this news to ye rest of their people, which did much comforte their harts.

On ye 15, (25 n. s.) of Desem^r^, they wayed anchor to go to ye place they had discovered, and came within 2 leagues of it, but were faine to bear up againe; but ye 16 (26) day ye winde came faire, and they arrived safe in this harbor. And after wards tooke better view of ye place, and resolved wher to pitch their dwellings; and ye 25 day (Jan. 4, 1621, n. s.) begane to erecte ye first house for common use to receive them and their goods."—[*Bradford's History, pp.* 88, 89.

The above contains all that relates to the famous *Landing of the Pilgrims on Plymouth Rock.* The intelligent reader instinctively smiles at this recital, when he contrasts this simple statement, with the gorgeous decoration of the event by Mr. Webster. When the anniversary of the Landing of the Pilgrims was instituted, in 1769, the authors added *eleven* days for differencc of style, instead of *ten* the true difference. They fixed on Monday, the day "*they sounded the harbor and marched into the land,*" as the one most deserving of commemoration. From this has grown the magnificent conception of the Landing of the Pilgrims!

1. 1674–5 March

The title and case of Robert Mason touching the province of New Hampshire in New England.

A^o^ 1616 King James I. sends John Mason Esq. as Governor to Newfoundland, who after remaining there two years was ordered to New England and with *Sir Ferdinando Gorges made a voyage along the coast in* 1619, *account of which they furnished to his Majesty. A^o^* 1620 the King grants by Charter to some of the nobility under the title of the Council of New England the teritory called New England with divers privileges &c.

Folsom's Catalogue, p. 12.

this statement, elsewhere. He was commissioned it is true, by the King as Governor of New England in 1637,[1] but from the accidental loss of the ship in which he was to embark, he did not set sail for America.

But he persevered in his great work, and lived to see in New England prosperous communities, and his Province of Mayne, the best governed of all. He not only established the Pilgrims at Plyouth, but subsequently caused to be granted to them, a large and valuable tract of land on the Kennebec, with an enlargement of their Charter, January 13, 1629.[2] Nova Scotia was also granted to Sir William Alexander afterwards Lord Stirling, in 1621. He established his son, Robert Gorges, by grant at Nahant and Boston, in 1622. After this he planted Agamenticus, and when Christopher Levett came over in 1623 for the purpose of fixing on a place of settlement, he found that Monhegan Pemaquid and Cape Newagan had been already taken up, and he selected the Peninsula of Machegonne, now the site of the City of Portland, for himself. There he built his house, and gave to what is now known as Fore River, his own name, calling it Levett's River. The Cape Anne settlement was made in 1625, under a charter from Lord Sheffield, but not continued; and finally, the

1. See appendix F.

2. Hazard, Vol. i. p. 298.

Company of Massachusetts Bay came over in 1629, whose men of deed and daring finally overrun the whole of New England, and led Gorges to predict the final separation of their Government from that of the British Crown. He says, "some of the discreeter sort, to avoid what they found themselves subject unto, made use of their friends to procure from the Council for the Affairs of New England to settle a Colony within their limits; to which it pleased the thrice-honored Lord of Warwick to write to me, then at Plymouth, to condescend that a Patent might be granted to such as then sued for it. Whereupon I gave my approbation so far forth as it might not be prejudicial to my son Robert Gorges' interests, whereof he had a Patent under the seal of the Council. Hereupon there was a grant passed as was thought reasonable; but the same was after enlarged by his Majesty, and confirmed under the great seal of England, by the authority whereof the undertaking proceeded so effectually, that in a very short time numbers of the people of all sorts flocked thither in heaps, that at last it was specially ordered by the King's command, that none should be suffered to go without license first had and obtained, and they to take the oaths of supremacy and allegiance. So that what I long before prophesied, when I could hardly get any for money to reside there, was now brought to pass in a high measure. The reason of that restraint was grounded upon the several complaints, that came out of those parts, of the divers sects and schisms, that were amongst them, all contemning the public government of the ecclesiastical state. And it was doubted that they would, in short time, wholly shake off the royal jurisdiction of the sovereign magistrate."[1]

Gorges seems to have reached that conviction, common to our race, at this time, that it is capable of shaping its government to the wants of the people, and that Episcopalian or Puritan theology, cannot for any length of time, find cause of difference.

He never persecuted; on the contrary, he welcomed those whose escaped Puritan persecution in New England, or those who sought refuge from priestly domination at home. He granted lands in Maine to Rev. John Wheelwright and others, who fled from Massachusetts, first into New Hampshire, and then into Maine, banished on account of errors of doctrine; and was earlier than Rhode Island in the practical adoption of unlimited freedom of opinion. That he should have suffered in the estimation of the Puritans, and be denounced by them in opprobrious terms for being a loyalist and a churchman, ought not at this time to diminish from the respect fairly due for his great services.

But for Gorges, the western continent must have fallen under the dominion of Roman Catholic

1. Briefe Narration, p. 51.

France, and Celtic civilization would have changed its destiny; for all New England was in possession of the French prior to 1606. They had secured the favor of the savages, and held the country from Cape Malabarre to the St Lawrence. They do not seem to have been aware of the voyages of Gosnold, of Pring, or of Weymouth, though fully alive to the danger that threatened their possessions by the planting of the colony of Popham, at Sagadahoc.[1]

With all the efforts of Gorges, the labors of the Puritans, and the zeal of the British race, from 1606 to 1759, the French held twenty times the extent of the English territory on the continent, till the great struggle took place, one hundred years ago, on the Plains of Abraham, and the power of France passed from the continent forever.

Compare the services of Gorges with those of Wolfe, and all will agree that the claims of the former far surpass in real magnitude those of the latter. Yet the name of Wolfe is immortal, while

1. In a previous note, page 42, we have referred to the correspondence between the French Ambassador, Count De Tillieres, and the British government. In Gorges' Briefe Narration, he thus speaks of this matter:

"The French Ambassador made challenge of those territories granted us by the King, our sovereign, in the behalf of the King of France, his master, as belonging to his subjects, that by his authority were possessed thereof as a part of New France. To which I was commanded by the King to give answer to the Ambassador his claim, which was sent me from the Lord Treasurer, under the title of *Le Memorial de Monsieur Seigneur le Conte de Tillieres, Ambassadeur pour le Roy de France.* Whereupon I made so full a reply (as it seems) there was no more heard of that their claim." P. 40.

that of Gorges is comparatively unknown. As the heroic soul of Wolfe was just ready to take its flight to the world of spirits, from the field of battle, as the light had faded from his vision, his ear caught the words, "They fly!" "They fly!" "Who fly," said the dying hero. "The French," said the attendant. "What, so soon," said Wolfe; "then I die content;" and expired at the moment of victory. He knew that he had gained an undying fame.

The glory accorded to Wolfe for the conquest of Canada followed at once, as the fruits of that victory. But those like Columbus, or Gorges, who labor for their country, or for mankind in the less brilliant pursuits of peace, must wait the slow but ever faithful recorder of severe history, to do them justice.

When Columbus in old age, worn out in the service of his adopted country, died amid poverty and neglect, they placed over his grave these words, "Columbus has given a new world to the kingdom of Castile and Leon." But alas for human pride, the fame of Columbus has arisen higher and higher year by year in the admiration of men, while the Empire of Spain has passed from the Continent of America, and a weak and decaying dynasty fills the throne of Ferdinand and Isabella.

When Sir Ferdinando Gorges closed his life, in 1647, his countrymen should have placed over his grave these words, "Gorges saved North America to England." Instead of this, a cloud of obloquy rested on his name in both countries; at home because he supported the monarchy, and in New England because he had not done homage to the Puritan Theocracy. And to this hour the meed of praise has been selfishly withheld.

When George Popham, the able and accom-
1608. plished Governor of the Colony at Sagadahoc, knew that the hour of his departure had come, he was consoled in the thought that his name would be imperishably connected with the history of New England, for he was the *first* of his race whose bones should be laid on American soil. Like Wolfe he says, "I die content, for my name will always be associated with the first planting of the English race in the new world; my remains will not be neglected away from the home of my fathers and my kindred." And yet to this hour, two hundred and fifty-two years from the time that Popham died, the place of his burial is unknown.[1]

1. While these pages are going through the press, measures are in progress to commemorate the first settlement of New England, and to preserve the memory of the man who led hither the first English Colony.

Congress having made an appropriation for a Fort at the mouth of the Kennebec — the ancient Sagadahoc — the following correspondence, copied from the files of the War Office, shows the action of the Secretary of War in the matter, and the fitness of the name selected for the new Fort, which is called FORT POPHAM:

"TO THE HON. SIMON CAMERON, SECRETARY OF WAR:—

The undersigned, citizens of Maine, respectfully request that the new

Mr. Webster said, "the record of illustrious action is safely deposited, in the universal remembrance of mankind," and while we admit the truth of this maxim, we cannot forget that the record is rarely exhibited till the generations that knew their actors had passed away. Homer's words were not listened to in his life time, nor till history and even his birth-place were forgotten. He still lives, not in history, but in his own immortal writings. The greatest names of England, Milton and Cromwell, were a by-word and a reproach for years after their death. So it has been with the Father of English

Fort to be erected at the mouth of the Kennebec river, in Maine, may be named FORT POPHAM, in honor of Capt. George Popham, brother of the learned Chief Justice Popham, of England.

Capt. George Popham, as the Governor of the first English Colony in New England, built a fort at or near the site of the proposed fort, in the year 1607, where he died, February 5, 1608, and was buried, being the first person of his race whose bones were laid beneath the soil of New England, and whose grave will be appropriately marked by the fort that rises over his place of burial.

(Signed) JOHN A. POOR.
REUEL WILLIAMS.

Washington, Nov, 18, 1861."

This proposal for a name was favorably received at the Engineer Bureau, by Gen. Totten, who laid the matter before the Secretary of War.

On the 23d of November, General Cameron acted on the foregoing Petition, and entered thereon:—" Name approved.

SIMON CAMERON, *Secretary of War.*

WAR DEPARTMENT, *Washington, Nov.* 23, 1861."

A memorial stone, with an appropriate inscription, is to be inserted in the wall of this new Fort, and this event made the occasion of a public Celebration on the 29th of August, 1862, on the 255th anniversary of the Founding of Popham's Colony.

Colonization in America. Loaded with reproach by all the Pilgrim and Puritan writers of his time, his only crime was that he never countenanced persecution. The narrow and illiterate Bradford, the arrogant and bigoted Winthrop, the leading cotemporary writers of the times of Gorges, were incapable of doing justice to his motives or his conduct.

Within the last forty years, the growth and development of the English race in America, and the importance of the United States in the community of nations, have stimulated inquiry into its early history. The earliest settlement of the country, and the influences by which it was achieved, have become matters of the deepest interest. Events which were supposed to be of the least apparent moment, at the time, have influenced the direction of human affairs and permanently affected the history of the race.

Two hundred and fifty-six years ago, the first European settlement north of Florida, was made at St. Croix, in our State, by the French, with every assurance of permanently holding the Continent. In that same year, 1605, George Weymouth returned to England, after having explored the coast of Maine and of New England, not made known before, by the voyages of Gosnold and Pring. The leading minds of England, selected their place of settlement, looking simply at the natural advantages of the country. From Mount Desert to Cape Elizabeth, was the fairest land, and the most inviting sea coast, that had tempted an Atlantic voyage. There, they made their first effort to plant a Colony, as the means of enlarging the dominion of their nation. The seat of Empire accidentally passed farther west, for a time, to avoid the dangers of Indian and French hostility, and in the struggle for control of the Continent between England and her Colonies, a large portion of Maine was the subject of controversy. Her position became a subordinate one in the time of the Commonwealth, and not till our day has she been able to vindicate her just position.

But we already see the initiatory steps that shall realize the idea on which the thrice honored and renowned Warwick, and the sagacious Gorges, set on foot this Empire of the West;—and that chosen spot they selected became the seat of its power. Within the last sixteen years we have witnessed the great minds of England uniting with those of our own land, in cementing anew the ties of lineage which the the folly of an unwise ruler less than a century ago had severed. Already the iron arm of the railway has joined States and Provinces into one community of interests, and the iron locomotive departs from Casco Bay on an unbroken line of iron to the distant waters of Michigan and Huron, yet to be extended to the far distant shores of the Pacific. A giant work, greater than the Pyramids, now spans the waters of the St. Lawrence, while the ocean has been bridged by such lines of steamers that have practically annihilated space and time in the operations of business. It was the belief of those who first planted our State, that it would be the fairest portion of America, and that the deep waters of our bays should float the richest treasures of an expanding commerce. The realization of these visions is not far distant from our day; and if the sons of Maine are true to themselves and to their State, the dawn of that day may be speedily ushered in.

As it was the foresight of Gorges that planted the Saxo-Norman race in America, so it was the wisdom of Cromwell, that saw in them the great strength of the nation. Both these great men have in their own time suffered from the persecutions of their enemies, so that a future age only could do justice to their memories. Gorges, a devoted royalist, a persistent friend of the Stuart dynasty, has been as obnoxious to Puritan prejudice, as was Cromwell and the Independents, to that of the restored monarchy and its followers. But Gorges' fame shall yet eclipse that of any other name in our American annals. My native State has been remiss in the discharge of this duty, and supinely allowed the history of New England to cluster around the Rock of of Plymouth instead of standing clearly out in the earlier deeds of the great minds that saved New England and the Continent from the grasp of the French.

The high position and character of Gorges are vouched by his intimacy with the Chief Justice of England, and the chief noblemen of the realm, whose confidence he enjoyed to the close of his long and illustrious life, and his entire freedom from intolerance is shown in every act. His ambition was to people these realms with the best countrymen of England, though he foresaw their early independence of the Crown, and though a zealous Episcopalian, he gave equal encouragement to Puritan and Churchmen.

If the greatness of an individual is to be measured by his influence, on human affairs, the name of Gorges should be ranked with that of Cromwell and of Peter the Great of Russia, the men who have exerted most influence in shaping the history of modern times. The English, or Saxo-Norman race less than 5,000,000 in 1620, to-day is supreme on the ocean, and holds one-sixth of the habitable globe. It governs one-fourth part of the human race, four times in number the population of the Roman Empire when its eagles overshadowed the world.

The strength of a nation like that of an individual, is its history, and while we recount with pride the deeds of the great men who have preceded us, we should reflect on the value to us, of that larger theatre on which we are called to act, nor forget him whose genius and fidelity planted the English race in America. While this Saxo-Norman race learns more and more, and day by day sympathise with whatever is good and true in old England, we find in England's great men a corresponding sympathy with whatever is worthy of respect in the New England of our day so well expressed by Mr. D'Israeli, in a speech at Aylesbury, in the last Parliamentary election: "Whatever may be the fate of the England of the old world," said D'Israeli, "all that she has accomplished for good, in art, science, or political economy, and all that is glorious in her history, her literature or her institutions, is destined to still higher development in the hands of that race she has planted, springing from our loins, and enjoying a common ancestry with us, on the distant shores of New England and Australia.

APPENDIX A.

The FIRST CHARTER *of* VIRGINIA.

JAMES, by the Grace of God, King of *England*, *Scotland*, *France* and *Ireland*, Defender of the Faith, *&c.* WHEREAS our loving and well-disposed Subjects, Sir *Thomas Gates*, and Sir *George Somers*, Knights, *Richard Hackluit*, Clerk, Prebendary of *Westminster*, and *Edward-Maria Wingfield*, *Thomas Hanham*, and *Ralegh Gilbert*, Esqrs. *William Parker*, and *George Popham*, Gentlemen, and divers others of our loving Subjects, have been humble Suitors unto Us, that We would vouchsafe unto them our Licence, to make Habitation, Plantation, and to deduce a colony of sundry of our People into that part of *America* commonly called VIRGINIA, and other parts and Territories in *America*, either appertaining unto us, or which are not now actually possessed by any *Christian* Prince or People, situate, lying, and being all along the Sea Coasts, between four and thirty Degrees of *Northerly* Latitude from the Equinoctial Line, and five and forty Degrees of the same Latitude, and in the main Land between the same four and thirty and five and forty Degrees, and the Islands thereunto adjacent, or within one hundred Miles of the Coast thereof;

And to that End, and for the more speedy Accomplishment of their said intended Plantation and Habitation there, are desirous to divide themselves into two several Colonies and Companies; the one consisting of certain Knights, Gentlemen, Merchants, and other Adventurers, of our City of *London* and elsewhere, which are, and from time to time shall be, joined unto them, which do desire to begin their Plantation and Habitation in some fit and convenient Place, between four and thirty and one and forty Degrees of the said Latitude, alongst the Coasts of *Virginia*, and the Coasts of *America* aforesaid: And the other consisting of sundry Knights, Gentlemen, Merchants, and other Adventurers, of our Cities of *Bristol* and *Exeter*, and of our Town of *Plimouth*, and of other Places, which do join themselves unto that Colony, which do desire to begin their Plantation and Habitation in some fit and convenient Place, between eight and thirty Degrees and five and forty Degrees of the said Latitude, all alongst the said Coasts of *Virginia* and *America*, as that Coast lyeth:

We, greatly commending, and graciously accepting of, their Desires for the Furtherance of so noble a Work, which may, by the Providence of Almighty God, hereafter tend to the Glory of his Divine Majesty, in propagating of *Christian* Religion to such People, as yet live in Darkness and miserable Ignorance of the true Knowledge and Worship of God, and may in time bring the Infidels and Savages, living in those parts, to human Civility, and to a settled and quiet Government: DO, by these our Letters Patents, graciously accept of, and agree to, their humble and well-intended Desires;

And do therefore, for Us, our Heirs, and Successors GRANT and agree, that the said Sir *Thomas Gates*, Sir *George Somers*, *Richard Hackluit*, and *Edward-Maria Wingfield*, Adventurers of and for our City of *London*, and all such others, as are, or shall be, joined unto them of that Colony, shall be called the *first Colony*; And they shall and may begin their said first Plantation and Habitation, at any Place upon the said Coast of *Virginia* or *America*, where they shall think fit and convenient, between the said four and thirty and one and forty Degrees of the said Latitude; And that they shall have all the Lands, Woods, Soil, Grounds, Havens, Ports, Rivers, Mines, Minerals, Marshes, Waters, Fishings, Commodities, and Hereditaments, whatsoever, from the said first Seat of their Plantation and Habitation by the Space of fifty Miles of *English* Statute Measure, all along the said Coast of *Virginia* and *America*, towards the *West* and *Southwest*, as the Coast lyeth, with all the Islands within one hundred Miles directly over against the same Sea Coast; And also all the Lands, Soil, Grounds, Havens, Ports, Rivers, Mines, Minerals, Woods, Waters, Marshes, Fishings, Commodities, and Hereditaments, whatsoever, from the said Place of their first Plantation and Habitation for the Space of fifty like *English Miles*, all alongst the said Coasts of *Virginia*, and *America*, towards the *East* and *Northeast*, or towards the *North*, as the Coast lyeth, together with all the Islands within one hundred Miles, directly over against the said Sea Coast; And also all the Lands, Woods, Soil, Grounds, Havens, Ports, Rivers, Mines, Minerals, Marshes, Waters, Fishings, Commodities, and Hereditaments, whatsoever, from the same fifty Miles every way on the Sea Coast, directly into the main Land by the Space of one hundred like *English* Miles; And shall and may inhabit and remain there; and shall and may also build and fortify within any the same, for their better Safeguard and Defence, according to their best Discretion, and the Discretion of the Council of that Colony; And that no other of our Subjects shall be permitted, or suffered, to plant or inhabit behind, or on the Backside of them, towards the main Land, without the Express License or Consent of the Council, of that Colony, thereunto in Writing first had and obtained.

And we do likewise, for Us, our Heirs, and Successors, by these Presents, GRANT and agree, that the said *Thomas Hanham*, and *Ralegh Gilbert, William Parker*, and *George Popham*, and all others of the Town of *Plimouth* in the County of *Devon* or elsewhere, which are, or shall be, joined unto them of that Colony, shall be called the *second Colony*; And that they shall and may begin their said Plantation and Seat of their first Abode and Habitation, at any Place upon the said Coast of *Virginia* and *America*, where they shall think fit and convenient, between eight and thirty Degrees of the said Latitude, and five and forty Degrees of the same Latitude; And that they shall have all the Lands, Soils, Grounds, Havens, Ports, Rivers, Mines, Minerals, Woods, Marshes, Waters, Fishings, Commodities, and Hereditaments, whatsoever, from the first Seat of their Plantation and Habitation by the Space of fifty like *English* Miles, as is aforesaid, all alongst the said Coasts of *Virginia* and *America*, towards the *West* and *Southwest*, or towards the *South*, as the Coast lyeth, and all the Islands within one hundred Miles, directly over against the said Sea Coast; And also all the Lands, Soils, Grounds, Havens, Ports, Rivers, Mines, Minerals, Woods, Marshes, Waters, Fishings, Commodities, and Hereditaments, whatsoever, from the said Place of their first Plantation and Habitation for the Space of fifty like miles, all alongst the said Coast of *Virginia* and *America*, towards the *East* and *Northeast*, or towards the *North*, as the Coast lyeth, and all the Islands also within one hundred Miles directly over against the same Sea Coast; And also all the Lands, Soils, Grounds, Havens, Ports, Rivers, Woods, Mines, Minerals, Marshes, Waters, Fishings, Commodities, and Hereditaments, whatsoever, from the same fifty Miles every way on the Sea Coast, directly into the main Land, by the Space of one hundred like *English* Miles; And shall and may inhabit and remain there; and shall and may also build and fortify within any the same for their better Safeguard, according to their best Discretion, and the Discretion of the Council of that Colony; And that none of our Subjects shall be permitted, or suffered, to plant or inhabit behind, or on the back of them, towards the main Land, without express Licence of the Council of that Colony, in Writing thereunto first had and obtained.

Provided always, and our Will and Pleasure herein is, that the Plantation and Habitation of such of the said Colonies, as shall last plant themselves, as aforesaid, shall not be made within one hundred like *English* Miles of the other of them, that first began to make their Plantation, as aforesaid.

And we do also ordain, establish, and agree, for Us, our Heirs, and Successors, that each of the said Colonies shall have a Council, which shall govern and order all Matters and Causes, which shall arise, grow, or happen, to or within the same several Colonies, according to such Laws, Ordinances, and Instructions as shall be, in that behalf, given and signed with Our Hand or Sign Manual, and pass under the Privy Seal of our Realm of *England*; Each of which Councils shall consist of thirteen Persons, to be ordained, made, and removed, from time to time, according as shall be directed and comprised in the same Instructions; And shall have a several Seal, for all Matters that shall pass or concern the same several Councils; Each of which Seals, shall have the King's Arms engraven on the one side thereof, and his Portraiture on the other; And that the Seal for the Council of the said first Colony shall have engraven round about, on the one side, these Words: *Sigillum Regis Magnæ Britanniæ, Franciæ, & Hiberniæ;* on the other side this Inscription round about: *Pro Concilio primæ Coloniæ Virginiæ*. And the Seal for the Council of the said second Colony shall also have engraven, round about the one side thereof, the aforesaid Words: *Sigillum Regis Magnæ Britanniæ, Franciæ, & Hiberniæ;* and on the other side: *Pro Concilio fecundæ Coloniæ Virginiæ:*

And that also there shall be a Council established here in *England*, which shall, in like Manner, consist of thirteen Persons, to be, for that Purpose, appointed by Us, our Heirs and Successors, which shall be called our *Council of Virginia*; And shall, from time to time, have the superior Management and Direction, only of and for all Matters that shall or may concern the Government, as well of the said several Colonies, as of and for any other Part or Place, within the aforesaid Precincts of four and thirty and five and forty Degrees, abovementioned; Which Council shall, in like manner, have a Seal, for Matters concerning the Council or Colonies, with the like Arms and Portraiture, as aforesaid, with this Inscription, engraven round about on the one side: *Sigillum Regis Magnæ Britanniæ, Franciæ, & Hiberniæ;* and round about on the other side, *Pro Concilio ſuo Virginiæ.*

And moreover, we do GRANT and agree, for Us, our Heirs and Successors; that the said several Councils of and for the said several Colonies, shall and lawfully may, by Virtue hereof, from time to time, without any Interruption of Us, our Heirs or Successors, give and take Order, to dig, mine, and search for all Manner of Mines of Gold, Silver, and Copper, as well within any Part of their said several Colonies, as of the said main Lands on the Backside of the same Colonies; And to HAVE and enjoy the Gold, Silver, and Copper, to be gotten thereof, to the Use and Behoof of the same Colonies, and the Plantations thereof; YIELDING therefore to Us, our Heirs and Successors, the fifth Part only of all the same Gold and Silver, and the fifteenth Part of all the same Copper, so to be gotten or had, as is aforesaid, without any other Manner of Profit or Account, to be given or yielded to Us, our Heirs, or Successors, for or in Respect of the same:

And that they shall, or lawfully may, establish and cause to be made a Coin, to pass current there between the people of those several Colonies, for the more Ease of Traffick and Bargaining between and amongst them and the Natives there, of such Metal, and in such Manner and Form, as the said several Councils there shall limit and appoint.

And we do likewise, for Us, our Heirs, and Successors, by these Presents, give full Power and Authority to the said Sir *Thomas Gates*, Sir *George Somers*, *Richard Hackluit*, *Edward-Maria Wingfield*, *Thomas Hanham*, *Ralegh Gilbert*, *William Parker* and *George Popham* and to every of them, and to the said several Companies, Plantations, and Colonies, that they, and every of them, shall and may, at all and every time and times hereafter, have, take, and lead in the said Voyage, and for and towards the said several Plantations, and Colonies, and to travel thitherward, and to abide and inhabit there, in every the said Colonies and Plantations, such and so many of our Subjects, as shall willingly accompany them or any of them, in the said Voyages and Plantations; With sufficient Shipping, and Furniture of Armour, Weapons, Ordinance, Powder, Victual, and all other things, necessary for the said Plantations, and for their Use and Defence there: PROVIDED always, that none of the said Persons be such, as shall hereafter be specially restrained by Us, our Heirs, or Successors.

Moreover, we do, by these Presents, for Us, our Heirs, and Successors, GIVE AND GRANT Licence unto the said Sir *Thomas Gates*, Sir *George Somers*, *Richard Hackluit*, *Edward-Maria Wingfield*, *Thomas Hanham*, *Ralegh Gilbert*, *William Parker*, and *George Popham*, and to every of the said Colonies, that they, and every of them, shall and may, from time to time, and at all times forever hereafter, for their several Defences, encounter, expulse, repel, and resist, as well by Sea as by Land, by all Ways and Means whatsoever, all and every such Person and Persons, as without the especial Licence of the said several Colonies and Plantations, shall attempt to inhabit within the said several Precincts and Limits of the said several Colonies and Plantations, or any of them, or that shall enterprise or attempt, at any time hereafter, the Hurt, Detriment, or Annoyance, of the said several Colonies or Plantations:

Giving and granting, by these Presents, unto the said Sir *Thomas Gates*, Sir *George Somers*, *Richard Hackluit*, *Edward-Maria Wingfield*, and their Associates of the said first Colony, and unto the said *Thomas Hanham*, *Ralegh Gilbert*, *William Parker*, and *George Popham*, and their Associates of the said second Colony, and to every of them, from time to time, and at all times for ever hereafter, Power and Authority to take and surprise, by all Ways and Means whatsoever, all and every Person and Persons, with their Ships, Vessels, Goods, and other Furniture, shall be found trafficking, into any Harbour or Harbours, Creek or Creeks, or Place, within the Limits or Precincts of the said several Colonies and Plantations, not being of the same Colony, until such time, as they, being of any Realms or Dominions under our Obedience, shall pay, or agree to pay, to the Hands of the Treasurer of that Colony, within whose Limits and Precincts they shall so traffick, two and a half upon every Hundred, of any thing, so by them trafficked, bought, or sold; And being Strangers, and not Subjects under our Obeyance, until they shall pay five upon every Hundred, of such Wares and Merchandises, as they shall traffick, buy, or sell, within the Precincts of the said several Colonies, wherein they shall so traffick, buy, or sell, as aforesaid; WHICH Sums of Money, or Benefit, as aforesaid, for and during the Space of one and twenty Years, next ensuing the Date hereof, shall be wholly emploied to the Use, Benefit, and Behoof of the said several Plantations, where such Traffick shall be made; And after the said one and twenty Years ended, the same shall be taken to the Use of Us, our Heirs, and Successors, by such Officers and Ministers, as by Us, our Heirs, and Successors, shall be thereunto assigned or appointed.

And we do further, by these Presents, for Us, our Heirs and Successors, GIVE AND GRANT unto the said Sir *Thomas Gates*, Sir *George Somers*, *Richard Hackluit*, and *Edward-Maria Wingfield*, and to their Associates of the said first Colony and Plantation, and to the said *Thomas Hanham*, *Ralegh Gilbert*, *William Parker*, and *George Popham*, and their Associates of the said second Colony and Plantation, that they, and every of them, by their Deputies, Ministers, and Factors, may transport the Goods, Chattels, Armour, Munition, and Furniture, needful to be used by them, for their said Apparel, Food, Defence, or otherwise in Respect of the said Plantations, out of our Realms of *England* and *Ireland*, and all other our Dominions, from time to time, for and during the Time of seven Years, next ensuing the Date hereof, for the better Relief of the said several Colonies and Plantations, without any Customs, Subsidy, or other Duty, unto Us, our Heirs, or Successors, to be yielded or payed for the same.

Also we do, for Us, our Heirs, and Successors, DECLARE, by these Presents, that all and every the Persons being our Subjects, which shall dwell and inhabit within every or any of the said several Colonies and Plantations, and every of their Children, which shall happen to be born within any of the Limits and Precincts of the said several Colonies and Plantations, shall HAVE and enjoy all Liberties, Franchises and Immunities, within any of our other Dominions, to all Intents and Purposes, as if they had been abiding and born, within this our Realm of *England*, or any other of our said Dominions.

Moreover, our gracious Will and Pleasure is, and we do, by these Presents, for Us, our Heirs, and Successors, declare and set forth, that if any Person or Persons, which shall be of any of the said Colonies and Plantations, or any other, which shall traffick to the said Colonies and Plantations, or any of them, shall, at any time, or times hereafter, transport any Wares, Merchandises, or Commodities, out of any of our Dominions, with a Pretence to land, sell, or otherwise dispose of the same, within any the Limits and precincts of any of the said Colonies and Plantations, and yet nevertheless, being at Sea, or after he hath landed the same within any of the said Colonies and Plantations, shall carry the same into any other foreign Country, with a purpose there to sell or dispose of the same, without the Licence of Us, our Heirs, and Successors, in that Behalf first had and obtained; That then, all the Goods and Chattles of such Person or Persons, so offending and transporting, together with the said Ship or Vessel wherein such Transportation was made, shall be forfeited to Us, our Heirs, and Successors.

Provided always, and our Will and Pleasure is, and we do hereby declare to all Christian Kings, Princes, and States, that if any Person or Persons which shall hereafter be of any of the said several Colonies and Plantations, or any other, by his, their, or any of their Licence and Appointment, shall, at any Time or Times hereafter, rob or spoil, by Sea or Land, or do any Act of unjust or unlawful Hostility to any the Subjects of Us, our Heirs, or Successors, or any the Subjects of any King, Prince, Ruler, Governor, or State, being then in League or Amitie with Us, our Heirs, or Successors, and that upon such injury, or upon just Complaint of such Prince, Ruler, Governor, or State, or their Subjects, We, our Heirs, or Successors, shall make open Proclamation, within any of the Ports of our Realm of *England*, commodious for that purpose, That the said Person or Persons, having committed any such Robbery, or Spoil, shall within the term to be limited by such Proclamations, make full Restitution or Satisfaction of all such Injuries done, so as the said Princes, or others so complaining, may hold themselves fully satisfied and contented; And, that if the said Person or Persons, having committed such Robery or Spoil, shall not make, or cause to be made Satisfaction accordingly, within such Time, so to be limited, That then it shall be lawful to Us, our Heirs, and Successors, to put the said Person or Persons, having committed such Robery or Spoil, and their Procurers, Abettors, and Comforters, out of our Allegiance and Protection; And that it shall be lawful and free, for all Princes, and others to pursue with hostility the said offenders, and every of them, and their and every of their Procurers, Aiders, abettors, and comforters, in that behalf.

And finally, we do for Us, our Heirs, and Successors, GRANT and agree, to and with the said Sir *Thomas Gates*, Sir *George Somers*, *Richard Hackluit Edward-Maria Wingfield*, and all others of the said first colony, that We, our Heirs and Successors, upon Petition in that Behalf to be made, shall, by Letters Patent under the Great Seal of *England*, GIVE and GRANT unto such Persons, their Heirs and Assigns, as the Council of that Colony, or the most part of them, shall, for that Purpose, nominate and assign all the Lands, Tenements, and Hereditaments, which shall be within the Precincts limited for that Colony, as is aforesaid, To BE HOLDEN of Us, our heirs and Successors, as of our Manor of *East-Greenwich*, in the County of *Kent*, in free and common Soccage only, and not in Capite:

And do in like Manner, Grant and Agree, for Us, our Heirs and Successors, to and with the said *Thomas Hanham*, *Ralegh Gilbert*, *William Parker*, and *George Popham*, and all others of the said second Colony, That We, our Heirs, and Successors, upon Petition in that Behalf to be made, shall, by Letters-Patent, under the Great Seal of *England*, GIVE and GRANT, unto such Persons, their Heirs and

Assigns, as the Council of that Colony, or the most Part of them, shall for that Purpose nominate and assign, all the Lands, Tenements, and Hereditaments, which shall be within the Precincts limited for that Colony, as is aforesaid, To BE HOLDEN of Us, our Heirs, and Successors, as of our Manor of *East-Greenwich*, in the County of *Kent*, in free and common Soccage only, and not in Capite.

All which Lands, Tenements, and Hereditaments, so to be passed by the said several Letters-patent, shall be sufficient Assurance from the said Patentees, so distributed and divided amongst the Undertakers for the Plantation of the said several Colonies, and such as shall make their Plantations in either of the said several Colonies, in such Manner and Form, and for such Estates, as shall be ordered and set down by the Council of the said Colony, or the most part of them, respectively, within which the same Lands, Tenements, and Hereditaments shall lye or be ; Although express Mention of the true yearly Value or Certainty of the Premises, or any of them, or of any other Gifts or Grants, by Us or any of our Progenitors or Predecessors, to the aforesaid Sir *Thomas Gates*, Knt. Sir *George Somers*, Knt. *Richard Hackluit*, *Edward-Maria Wingfield*, *Thomas Hanham*, *Ralegh Gilbert*, *William Parker*, and *George Popham*, or any of them, heretofore made, in these Presents, is not made; Or any Statute, Act, Ordinance, or Provision, Proclamation, or Restraint, to the contrary hereof had, made, ordained, or any other Thing, Cause, or Matter whatsoever, in any wise notwithstanding. IN WITNESS whereof, we have caused these our Letters to be made Patent; Witness Ourself at *Westminster*, the tenth Day of *April*, in the fourth Year of our Reign of *England, France*, and *Ireland*, and of *Scotland*, the nine and thirtieth.

Lukin
Per breve de privato Sigillo.

APPENDIX B.

RELATIONS OF THE JESUITS,

Containing the most remarkable events in the Mission of the Company of Jesus in NEW FRANCE.

AN ACCOUNT OF NEW FRANCE ; the land, nature of the country, and its inhabitants, from a copy preserved in the Imperial Library of Paris.

Printed by LOUIS MUGUET, Lyons, June 23, 1616.

EXTRACTS:

CHAPTER XI.

On what account the Jesuits went to New France in 1611, *and what the French had done there from* 1608 *until their coming.*

" It has been narrated, how at the end of the said year 1607, all the train of Sr. de Monts, returned to France, and this New France was then entirely abandoned by the French. Nevertheless, the following year, 1608, Sr. de Monts appointed Sr. Champlain his Lieutenant, and sent him to explore along the great river St. Lawrence. Champlain did bravely there, and founded the city of Quebec. But as to the acts, voyages and discoveries of the said Champlain, there is no need to paint them to you, since he himself has so well and so long described them in his books.

Now Sr. Jean de Biencourt, called de Potrincourt, before Sr. de Monts had left New France, had asked him for the gift of Port Royal. Sr. de Monts gave it to him on condition that within the two following years, the said de Potrincourt should transport himself there with several families to cultivate, and inhabit it which he promised to do.

Then in 1607, all the French having returned, as above stated, Sr. de Potrincourt informed the late Henry the Great, of immortal memory, of the deed of gift made to him by Sr. de Monts, humbly petitioning his Majesty to ratify it. The King was pleased with the said petition, and promising himself to send a powerful French Colony. He said to Father Coton that he wished to make use of this Company for the conversion of the savages; that he should write about it to the Father General, and that some should be designated for these voyages; that he would call on them, on the first opportunity, promising from this time 2000 livres for their support.

Father Coton obeyed his Majesty, and soon through all the Colleges of France, it was heard that some should be chosen for this mission. Many presented themselves to join the band, as usual in such expeditions of much hardships and little glory; and among others, Father Pierre Biard, then teaching Theology at Lyons. It was God's will that the said Father should be chosen and sent to Bordeaux at the end of 1608, because at Lyons they thought that as the project of so powerful a Prince had been known for so many months, its execution could not [illegible] be near. But Father Biard was as much deceived in the place as the time. [illegible], at Bordeaux they were astonished when they heard why he had come. No news of the embarking for Canada, or of the past check, upon which every one philosophized in his own fashion.

At the end of the following year, 1609, Sr. de Potrincourt came to Paris, when his Majesty learned that, contrary to his opinion, the said Nobleman had not stirred from France, (for the King believed that he had crossed the sea as soon as he had obtained confirmation of Port Royal.) He was angry with him. Deeply touched at that, the Nobleman replied, that since his Majesty had the affair so much at heart, from that moment he would take leave of him, and go to equip the expedition. Then Father Coton, who was anxious about Father Biard, and the great summons he had made in the name of the King, knowing that Potrincourt had taken leave of the King, went to find Potrincourt and offered him the company of several members of his order. He received the reply, that it would be better to wait till the following year; that as soon as he had arrived at Port Royal, he would send back his son to France; and that, with him, everything being better arranged, those might go whom the King should please to send. At this, he left Paris and spent the winter in preparation.

The following year, 1610, he embarked, towards the last of February, and arrived late at Port Royal, viz: at the beginning of June, when having assembled as many savages as he could, he caused to be baptized about 24 or 25 of them on St. John's day, by a priest named Josse Flesche, entitled the Patriarch. Shortly after he sent back to France Sr. de Biencourt, his son, about 19 years old, to carry the news of the baptism of the savages, and to bring back succor speedily, for they were unprovided against hunger for the coming winter."

Then follows a minute account of the difficulties in fitting out their ships and supplying the Jesuits, and obtaining leave for them to go on board, but at last they sailed on the 26th January, 1611, and reached Port Royal the 22d of June, 1611, Pentecost day. Then he describes the life of the Jesuits on shipboard, and then comes

CHAPTER XIV.

The condition of Sr. de Potrincourt at their arrival, and his journey to the Etchemins.

"The joy at our arrival was great on both sides; great to the new comers, from the fatigue of so long a sea-voyage, but redoubled to Sr. de Potrincourt, who had been in great trouble and anxiety all the winter. Having with him 23 persons without sufficient provisions to support them, he had been obliged to send away some of them to live with the savages. The rest had been wanting bread for six or seven weeks, and without the help of the savages he did not know but they would all have perished miserably.

How the aid he brought them was almost, one may say, like a drop of water to a thirsting one: first because there were 36 in one ship, which, added to the 23 persons there, 59 mouths found themselves every day at table, and also Membertou, the savage, with his daughter and her companions; Second, we had been four months at sea, and thus our provisions were much diminished. Seeing also that our vessel was very small, about 50 or 60 tons, and provisioned more for fishing than for anything else. In this situation then, it was rather necessary for Sr. de Potrincourt to think how he should promptly send back so large a family, lest they should consume everything, than to obtain fishing and barter, in which, nevertheless lay every resource for a second voyage. But they did not wholly neglect bartering, for it was necessary to make some money to pay the wages of his men, and their coming and going to France.

For these purposes then, he sailed in his own ship, some days after, with almost all his people, for a port of the Etchemins, called the White Rock, 22 leagues due west from Port Royal. He hoped to find there some help of provisions from the French ships which he knew traded there. Father Biard wished to accompany him to explore the country and discover the character of the natives, which was granted him. He found there four French vessels; one belonging to Sr. de Monts, one from Rochelle, one from St. Malo belonging to du Pont Grave, and commanded by a relative of his called Captain La Salle, of whom we shall soon speak, and another bark from St. Malo. Sr. de Potrincourt, calling each one of these four after the other, caused them to acknowledge his son for Vice Admiral; and then asked them for assistance, showing the need to which he had been reduced the last winter, promising to repay them in France. Each one contributed. But God pardon the men from Rochelle; for he deceived the Excise, and gave us barrels of spoiled bread for good." Then comes an account of the pardon of Sir Pont Du Grave, and then

CHAPTER XV.

The return of Sr. de Potrincourt to France, and the difficulty of teaching the language to the Savages.

"He explained above the necessity which pressed upon Sr. de Potrincourt to send his people immediately back to France. He wished to conduct them in person in order to make better arrangements for everything, and principally for a new revictualling: for without this, those left behind at Port Royal, would have no means of passing the winter in manifest danger of being pierced by famine. For this cause then, he sailed about the middle of July of the same year, 1611, and arrived in France at the end of the August following. He left his son in his place, Sr. de Potrincourt, with two persons including the two Jesuits."

Then is a long account of the difficulty of teaching the language to the natives. Then we resume.

"One expedient presented itself to the Jesuits to rid them happily of all these perplexities; it was to find young du Pont Grave, whom they had heard had resolved to winter at the river St. Johns, some 18 or 20 leagues from Port Royal. Inasmuch as the said du Pont Grave had lived a long time in the country, and among the natives, it was thought that he must understand the language very well. Father Biard resolved to seek the said du Pont Grave, determining rather to pass French Bay in a canoe than to lose such an opportunity of doing good. But Sr. de Biencourt opposed strongly this determination, taking great offence, to which it was necessary to yield for peace."

CHAPTER XVI.

A voyage made to the river St. Croix, and the death of the Sagamore Membertou.

"At the end of August of the same year, 1611, Sr. de Biencourt having heard that the ship of Captain Plastrier of Honfleur, was fishing at Port aux Coquilles, (Shell Harbor,) 21 leagues west from Port Royal, decided to go and find him in order to introduce to him one of his men whom he was sending to France to hasten the expected aid, and to represent how pitiable their condition was. Father Biard accompanied him, and they met the ship so apropos, that if they had been a quarter of an hour later, the favorable opportunity would have been lost, for already he had set sail for France. He learned that Captain Plastrier had decided to pass the winter at St. Croix. This news decided Sr. de Biencourt to go to St. Croix on this very passage, before Captain Plastrier should fortify himself there, for he wished to obtain from him the fifth of all his trade and merchandise, because he wintered in the country. St. Croix is 6 leagues from Port aux Coquilles in the middle of a river. Sr. de Biencourt went there accompanied by 8 persons, and entered armed, having left Father Biard on one end of the Island. * * * * Thanks to God, everything passed off happily. Plastrier treated us as well as he could; by his aid Sr. de Biencourt recovered a bark which was at Port aux Coquilles, with which he returned to Port Royal." * * * *

Then the account of the death of Membertou. Then

CHAPTER XVII.

The journey to the river St. John, and the quarrels that came of it.

"I said above, that Sr. de Biencourt brought a bark from Port aux Coquilles, with which he might make a voyage to the Armouchiquois. So are called the people who are at the 43° lower down towards the south west. They begin at

Chouaquet, and from what is said, they are very numerous. Famine pressed Sr. de Biencourt to this voyage; because as these people worked and stored grain, he hoped by means of barter or otherwise, to draw some help from them against the famine, who was waiting for us in the winter. His bark was prepared too late for so long a voyage, for we were not ready till the 3d October, and he still wished to go to the river St. John before taking the former route. The river St. John is at northeast of Port Royal having between the two, French Bay, 14 leagues wide. The entrance of this river is very narrow and exceedingly dangerous, for it is necessary to pass between two rocks, one of which throws upon the other the current of the tide, which is swift as an arrow. To the rocks succeeds a frightful precipice, which, if you do not pass at the precise time, out of a hundred thousand barques, not a hair will escape, but dies and property will perish. Young du Pont Grave and Captain Merbeville had settled some 6 leagues within the St. John, being in all seven or eight persons, all from St. Malo. Sr. de Biencourt wished to obtain from them the fifth of all their merchandise, because they lived in the country as we have said. On this account he had mistaken the journey. We were in all 16 Frenchmen and 2 natives as guides."

Then an account of the skirmish and the submission of du Pont Grave and Merbeville.

CHAPTER XVIII.

The voyage to Quinnibequi and the return to Port Royal.

"We remarked above that this voyage to the St. John was only a detour from the greater expedition to the Armouchiquois to get corn. When we had thus acted with the Malhouins we set sail taking the route towards the Armouchiquois. We arrived at Kinibequi at the end of October. Kinibequi is a river near the Armouchiquois, 43⅔ degrees of elevation, and Southeast of Port Royal 70 leagues or thereabouts. It has two mouths, tolerably large, at least two leagues distant the one from the other; also many inlets and islands which divide it. For the rest, though the river is large and beautiful, we saw no good land, nor neither at the St. John. It is said, however, that above, far from the sea, the land is very fine, and the situation pleasant, and people work there. We did not ascend more than 3 leagues. We made so many quick turns, and leaped so many precipices, that it is a great miracle that we had not perished, several times. Some of our men cried two different times that they were lost; but they cried too soon, the Lord be praised. The savages flattered us with the hope of grain, then they changed their promise of grain into barter of beavers."

Then follows an account of the entrance of the natives to the ship.

"This tribe does not appear to be mischievous or malicious, although they defeated and overthrew the English who wished to settle among them in 1608 and 1609. They excused themselves to us for this, and related the outrages that they had suffered from the aforesaid English, and flattered us, saying they loved us well, because they knew that we would not shut our doors on the savages as the English, nor chase them from our table with clubs, nor let our dogs bite them. They are not thieves like the Armouchiquois, and they are the greatest speech-makers in the world; they do nothing without that. Father Biard went twice to see them, and (as he did everywhere) prayed to God in their presence, and showed them images, and the signes of our faith, which they kissed willingly, making the sign of the Holy Cross on their children, whom they offered to him that he might baptise them, and heard with attention and respect what was told them.

We were at Kinibequi till the 4th or 5th of November, a season too advanced for us to go farther according to our first plan. That is why Sr. de Biencourt returned, the more because he thought it better to endure the winter and the famine at Port Royal, being well lodged and warmed there, and trusting the mercy of God, than risking ourselves on the ocean, in a stormy season, among savages and enemies, having beside, hunger to fear, for our provisions commenced to fail greatly; thus then, we turned towards Pentagoet to return from there to Port Royal.

At Pentagoet we found a fleet of 80 Indian canoes, and one shallop, in all about 300 souls. From there we passed on to the Island of St.Croix, where Plastrier gave us 2 barrels of peas or beans; both were a very great present for us. * *

While we were on the voyage no one remained at the settlement at Port Royal except Father Enemond Masse and a young Parisian called Valentine Pageau. * * * *

Snow began the 26th of November and with it, (which annoyed us most,) the retrenchment of provisions. They gave to each person for the whole week only about 10 ounces of bread, ½ pound of lard, 3 porringers full of peas or beans and one of dried prunes. The Jesuits had never more, nor other than each one of the company, and it is an impudent falsehood which some disturber alleges to the contrary. All this time, the savages did not come to see us, except occasionally some one of the family of Membertou, to bring us some present of the chase. Then was joy and feasting, our people took heart a little."

CHAPTER XIX.

How the Marchioness Guerchville obtained from the King the land of New France, and the aid she procured for it.

* * * * * * A long account. Then

"The ship thus fitted out and freighted, sailed from Dieppe the 31st of December, in the depth of winter, and happily appeared at Port Royal the 23d of January in the following year, 1612."

CHAPTER XX.

The beginning of the disputes between Sr. de Biencourt and the Jesuits, and the causes of them; the accusation of Gilbert du Thet, and his defense.

CHAPTER XXIII.

Arrival of La Saussaye at Port Royal and then at St. Saviour.

"An expedition had been prepared in France, to remove the Jesuits from Port Royal and found a new settlement of French in some more convenient place. The chief of the expedition was Captain La Saussaye with 30 persons who were to winter in the country. The ship was 100 tons and commanded by Charles Flory de Hableville, a man brave, wise and peaceable.

This prepared expedition sailed from Honfleur the 12th of March, 1613, and touched land first at Cape of the Have in Acadia, May 16th. There they celebrated Mass and raised the Cross, fastening to it the arms of Mme. de Guercheville, to show they had taken possession in her name. Then putting out to sea, they came to Port Royal. There they found only five persons. Contrary winds detained them five days at Port Royal, then a favoring northeast wind arising, we set sail, with the design of going to the river Pentagoet, to a place called Kadesquit, which we had decided upon for our new settlement, as having great advantages for this purpose. But God willed otherwise; for as we were at the Southeast of the Island of Menamo, the weather changed, and there arose on the sea so thick a fog then we could see neither day nor night. We dreaded this danger greatly, because in this place there are many breakers and rocks, against which we were afraid we would strike, in the darkness. As the wind did not permit to put to sea again, we remained in this manner, two days and two nights, tacking first to one side, then to the other, as God inspired us. This affliction disposed us to pray to God that he would be pleased to deliver us from danger, and direct us to some safe place, for his glory. Of his goodness, he heard our vows, for that evening even we began to see the stars, in the morning the fog cleared, we discovered that we were over against Mount Desert, an Island that the savages called Pemetiq. The pilot turned to the eastern side of the island where we anchored in a large and beautiful harbor, and we gave thanks, raising the Cross and singing praises to God with the sacrifice of holy Mass. We called this place and harbor, St. Saviour."

CHAPTER XXIV.

On what account we stopped at St. Saviour, and the beauty of the place.

"Soon the natives made a smoke, which signified that we should seek them if we needed them. The Pilot took occasion to tell them that the Fathers from Port Royal were on board. The Savages replied that they would willingly see those whom they had known two years before, at Pentagoet; one was Father Biard, who went immediately to them and inquired about the route to Kadesquit, signifying that he wished to settle there. But said they, if you wish to settle in this part of the world, why do you not rather remain with us, who have quite as good a place as Kadesquit? And they began to sound the praises of their settlement, assuring us that it was so healthy and so agreeable, that when Savages are ill in other places, they bring them there to cure them. These commendations had no effect on Father Biard, because he knew well enough that the Savages are not wanting in what everybody else abounds, valuing one's own possessions.

But they knew how to arouse him, "for," said they, "you must come, because Asticou our Sagamore, is sick unto death, and if you do not come, he will die without baptism, and will not go to Heaven; you will be the cause. On his part, he wishes to be baptised." This reason so simply given, astonished Father Biard and persuaded him entirely to go there, especially as there were only three leagues to go, and it would cause but little loss of time, only an afternoon. Thus he entered one of their canoes, with Sr. de La Motte and Simon the interpreter, and went.

Arrived at the cabin of Asticou, we found him ill, but not dangerously, for it was only a cold which tormented him ; and we had abundant leisure to visit this place so praised, as better than Kadesquit for a French settlement, and indeed we found that the Savages had some reason for praising it so highly, for we ourselves were astonished at it. Having given an account of it to the leaders of our expedition, and they having come and examined it, all unanimously agreed that we had better stop there, and seek no further.

This place is a pretty colline rising gently from the sea and bathed on its sides by two springs. The land is grubbed for 20 or 25 acres, grassy in some places, as high as a man. Its aspect is towards the south and east, almost to the mouth of Pentagoet, where several large rivers, full of fish, discharge. The soil is black, fat and fertile. The port and haven are as fine as can be seen, and in a situation to command the entire coast ; the haven especially is as safe as a pond, for beside being separated from the large island of Mount Desert, it is also separated from certain small islets which break the winds and the waves, and fortify the entrance. There is no fleet for which it would not be sufficient, nor vessel so high which it might not approach land to unload within a cable's length. Its situation is $44\frac{1}{3}°$ of elevation, less northern than that of Bordeaux.

Having landed on this spot, and planted the Cross, we began to work, and with our work began our disputes. The cause of these, was that our Captain La Saussaye amused himself too much in cultivating the earth, and all the principal men begged him not to take off our workmen for that, but to apply ourselves without delay to dwellings and fortifications, which he did not wish to do. From these quarrels sprang others, till the English came to reconcile us, as you will see."

CHAPTER XXV.

Our capture by the English.

"Virginia is that continent of the earth which the ancients called Morosa, between Florida and New France, at the 36°, 37°, 38° of elevation. The country was first discovered by Giovanni Verrazzani, in the name of Francis I., as we said above, but the English having claimed it since 1593 or 1594, at last came to settle there, 7 or 8 years before this time. Their principal settlement, which they call Jamestown, is distant from St. Saviour, where we were, settled about 250 leagues in a straight line. See then, if they had any reason to pick a quarrel with us.

These English, from Virginia, have the habit of coming every year to the islands of PEMCUIT,* which are 25 leagues from St. Saviour, to get shell fish (moulues) for the winter."

The account is condensed by Garneau in his History of Canada, which we give in full.

GARNEAU'S HISTORY OF CANADA.

EXTRACT FROM CHAPTER I.

The destruction of St. Saviour and Port Royal.

"England claimed the country to the 45° of North latitude, as far as the heart of Acadia. France, on the contrary, pretended to claim as far South as the 40°. From this strife it happened that, while La Saussaye believed himself to be within the boundaries of New France, at St. Saviour, the English said they had advanced far into their territory. To support their claim, Captain Argall of Virginia, resolved to dislodge them, spurred on by the hope of rich booty, and by his prejudices against the Catholics.

He suddenly appeared before St. Saviour, with a vessel of 14 cannon, and struck terror into the defenceless inhabitants, who took him for a pirate at first. Father Gilbert du Thet in vain opposed some resistance. He was killed and the establish-

---

* Pemaquid.

ment given up to plunder. Everything was taken or sacked, Argall himself setting the example. The French clung to Acadia on account of the fisheries. The English, because it was on their route. Argall did not hesitate to attack in time of profound peace. Apart from his personal motives, he well knew the opinion of his countrymen, who wished to settle the question by taking actual possession.

To legitimatise this act of piracy, for it was so, he stole La Saussaye's commission, and affected to regard him and his people, as vagabonds. Gradually he appeared to relent, and proposed to those who had trades to follow him to Jamestown, where, after having labored a year, they should be sent back to their country. One dozen accepted the offer. The others with La Saussaye and Father Masse, prepared to risk themselves upon a frail vessel, to reach the Have, where they found a ship from St. Malo, which carried them back to France.

Those who had Argall's promises, were greatly surprised on arriving at Jamestown, to find themselves thrown into prison, and treated like pirates. They vainly claimed the fulfilment of the treaty they had made with him, they were condemned to death. Argall, who had not dreamed that his theft of La Saussaye's commission would end so seriously, would carry his dissimulation no farther; sent the commission to the Governor, Sir Thomas Dale, and confessed everything.

This document and information drawn out in the course of the affair, determined the Government of Virginia to drive the French from all the points they occupied south of the line 45. A squadron of 3 ships was put under the command of the same Argall, to carry out this design, and the prisoners of St. Saviour were embarked there with Father Biard. Later, Father Biard was accused, without doubt, too hastily, of having served as pilot of the enemies to Port Royal, from hatred to Biencourt, who was Governor, and with whom he had had difficulties while in Acadia.

The fleet commenced by destroying all that was left of the old settlement of St. Croix ; useless vengeance, since that had been deserted for several years; then sailed with a fair wind toward Port Royal where he found nobody; everybody being in the fields two leagues away: and in less than two hours all the houses were reduced to ashes as well as the fort. In vain Father Biard wished to persuade the inhabitants, drawn to the shore by the flames which devoured their shelter, to go away with the English, telling them that their ruined chief could no longer support them; they rejected his advice with anger, and one of them even raised an axe to kill him, accusing him of causing all their misfortunes. It was the third time, in its short existence, that Port Royal had been destroyed by different accidents, but this time the destruction was complete. One part of the inhabitants scattered in the woods, or mingled with the natives; another reached the settlement that Champlain had founded on the St. Lawrence. Potrincourt himself, who had remained in Acadia, overwhelmed by this last disaster, had to abandon America forever.

Potrincourt may be regarded as the real founder of Port Royal, and of Acadia itself; for the destruction of Port Royal did not cause the whole province to be abandoned; it was always occupied in one place or another by a part of its former colonists, to whom numerous adventurers came and united themselves."

APPENDIX C.

LETTER OF JOHN SMITH TO LORD BACON, 1618.

(S. P. O., Am. & W. I., N. Eng.)

To the Right Honble Sr. Francis Bacon, Knt. Baron of Verolam, & Lord High Chancellor of England.

Right Honorable :

Having noe better meanes to acquaint yor Lp. wth my meaning than this paper the zeale love and dutie to God my Country and yor honor I humbly crave may be my apoligie. This 19 yeares I have encountered noe fewe dangers to learne what here I write in these fewe leaves, and though the lines they containe are more rudely phrased then is meete for the viewe of so great a judgment, their frutes I am certayne may bring both wealth & honor for a Crowne & a kingdom to his Ma[ties] posterity. The profitts already returned wth so small charge & facilitie according to proportion emboldens me to say it.

With a stock of £5000 I durst venture to effect it, though more than £100,000 hath been spent in Virginia & the Barmudas to small purpose, about the procuring whereof many good men knowes I have spent noe small tyme labor nor mony : but all in vaine. No[twth] standing within these fower yeares I have occasioned twice £5000 to be employed that way: But great desyres to ingross it hath bred so many particular humors, as they have their willes, I the losse and the generall good the wrong.

Should I present it to the Biskayners, French or Hollanders, they have made me large offers. But nature doth binde me thus to begg at home, whome strangers have pleased to make a Comander abroad. The busines being of such consequence I hold it but my duty to acquaint it to yo[r] honor, knowing you are not only a chiefe Patron of yo[r] Countrie & state, but also the greatest favorer of all good designes and their authors.

Noe more, but humbly beseeching yo[r] goodness to pardon my rudeness & ponder my plaine meaning in the ballance of goodwille I leave the substance to the discretion of your most admired judgment, ever resting Yo[r] honors

ever most truly devoted,

Jo Smith.

Newe England is a part of America betwixt the degrees of 41 & 45 the very meane betweene the North Pole and the line, from 43 to 45. The Coast is mountaynous, rockye, barren & broken Isles that make many good harbours, the water being deepe, close to the shore. There is many Rivers & fresh springs, a fewe Savages, but an incredible aboundance of fish, fowles, wilde fruits & good store of Timber.

From 43 to 41½ an excellent mixed coast of stone sand & clay, much corne, many people, some Isles, many good harbors, a temperate aire yron & steele, oare & many other such good blessings, that having but men skillful to make them simples there growing, I dare ingage myself to finde all things belonging to the building & rigging of shippes of any proportion & good Merchandize for their fraught within a square of 10 or 14 leagues. 25 harbors I sounded: 30 severall Lordshipps I sawe, and as nere as I could imagine 3000 men, I was up one River fortie myles, crossed the mouthes of many whose heads the Inhabitants report, are great Lakes, where they kill their beavers inhabited wth many people that trade with them of Newe England and those of Canada.

The Benefit of Fishing.

The Hollanders raise yearly by fishing (if recordes be true) more than	£2,000,000
From Newfoundland at the least	£ 400,000
From Island & North Seea	£ 150,000
From Hamborough	£ 20,000
From Cape Blanke	£ 10,000

These five places doe serve all Europe as well the Land Townes as Ports & all the Christian shipping with these sorts of staple fish which is transported from whence it is taken many a thousand myle—Herring, Poor John, Saltfish, Sturgeon, Mullett, Pargos, Caviare, Buttargo.

Now seeing all these sortes of fish may be had in a land more fertile, temperate & plentifull of natural things for the building of Shipps, boates, howses & the nourishment for man only for a little labour or the most part of the chiefe materially, the seasons are so proper and the fishing so neare the habitations we may there make.

That New England hath much advantage of the most of those parts to serve all Europe farr cheaper, than they can who have neither wood, salt nor food but at a great rate, nothing to helpe them but what they carry in their shipps 2 or 300 leagues from their habitacons noe Port or Harbour but the mayne sea: Wee the fishing at our dores & the help of the land for woods, water, fruites, fowle, Corne or what we want to refresh us when we list. And the Terceras Maderas, Canaries, Spaine, Portugall, Province, Savoy, Cecilia, and all Italye as convenient Markets, for our drye fish, green fish, sturgeon, mullett and Buttargo as Norway, Swethland, Luttvania, Polonia, Denmarke or Germany for their Herring which is here also in aboundance for taking; they retourning but Wood, Pitch, Tarre, Soape Ashes, Cordage & such grosse comodities: we wynes, oyles, sugars, silkes & such merchandize as the Straits afford, whereby our profitt may equalize theirs. Besides the infinite good by increase of shipping & Marriners this fishinge would breede And imployment for the surplusage of many of his Ma[ties] unruly subjects. And that this may be, these are my proofes, (viz[t]):

1 Proofe. 1614. } In the year 1614 with two shipps I went from the Dounes the third of March arrived in New England the last of Aprill. I had but 45 men & boyes, we built seven boates, 37 did fish, myself with 8 others raunging the

Coast. I made this Mappe, gott the acquainntance of the Inhabitants, 1000 Beaver skins 100 martins and as many Otters. 40,000 of drye fish we sent for Spaine with Saltfish, Traine oyle & furrs. I retourned for England the 18th of July & arrived safe with my Company in health in the latter end of August. Thus in Six months I made my voyage out and home & by the labour of 45 men got nere the value of 1500£ in lesse than three moneths in those grosse Comodityes.

2 PROOFE. 1615. } In the year 1615 the Londoners uppon this sent 4 good shipps & intertayned the men who retourned wth me. They set sail in Januarye & arrived there in March & found fish enough till half June, fraughted a shipp of 300 Tonnes which they sent for Spaine, one went to Virginia to relieve that Collony & two came home with saltfish, Trayne oyle, furres & the salt—remayned within six moneths.

3 PROOFE. 1615. } The same year I sett forth from Plymouth wth a shippe of 200 & one of 50 to inhabit the Countrie according to the Tenor of his Maties Commission granted to the West parts of England. But ill weather breaking all my Mastes forced me to retourne againe to Plymouth where reimbarking myself in a small barke but of 60 Tonnes I passed the English Pyrats and the French; but at last I was betrayed by four frenchmen of warr who kept me prisoner that sommer & so overthrew my voyage & Plantation During wch tyme my Vice Admirall that sett forth in March arrived there in May, came home fraught with fish, Trayne oyle, Beavers skinnes, and all her men safe in August within 6 monethes and odd dayes.

4 PROOFE. 1616. } The Londoners ere I returned sent two shippes more in July to trye the Winter: but such courses they took by the Canaries, and the Indies, it was 10 moneths ere they arrived wasting in that time their seasons, victuall & healthes yet within 3 months after the one retourned were fraughted with fish Trayne oyle & Beavers.

5 PROOFE. 1616. } From Plymouth went 4 shipps only to fish and trade some in February some in March one of 200 Tonnes got thither in a moneth and went full fraught for Spaine wth drye fish, the rest retourned all well & safe and all full fraught with fish, furres and oyle in 5 moneths and odd dayes.

6 PROOFE. 1616. } From London went two more one of 220 tonnes got thither in 6 weekes & within 6 weekes after wth 44 men was fraughted with fish, furres and oyle & was again in England within 5 monethes & a few dayes.

7 PROOFE. 1617. } Being at Plymouth provided wth 3 good shippes I was winde bounde nere 3 monethes as was many a 100 sayle more so that the season being past I sent my shippes to Newfoundland whereby the adventures had noe losse. 1618. There is 4 or 5 saile gone thither this year to fish and trade from London also there is one gone only to fish and trade, each shippe for her particular designe and their private endes, but none for any generall good, where neither to Virginia, nor to the Bermudas they make such hast.

By this yor Lop may perceive the ordinary performance of this voyage in 6 monethes, the plenty of fish that is most certainly approved & if I be not misinformed from Cannada & New England within these 4 yeares hath been gotten by the French and English nere 36,000 Beavers skinnes: That all sorts of Timber for shipping is most plentifully there; All those wch retourned can testifye and if ought of this be untrue is easily proved.

The worst is of these 16 shippes 2 or 3 of them have been taken by Pyrates, wch hath putt such feare in poore fishermen, whose powers are but weake. And the desyre of gaine in Merchants so violent; every one so regarding his private, that it is worse than slaverye to follow any publique good, & impossible to bring them into a bodye, rule or order, unless it be by some extraordinary power. But if his Matie would be please to be perswaded to spare us but a Pinnace to lodge my men in and defend us & the Coast from such invasions the space of eight or ten monethes only till we were seated, I would not doubt but ere long to drawe the most part of Newfound Land men to assist us if I could be so provided but in due season: for now ere the Savages grow subtle and the Coast be too much frequented with strangers more may be done wth £20 than hereafter with a £100.

THE CHARGE.—The Charge of this is only Salt, Netts, Hooks, Lynes, Knives, Course Cloth, Beades, Glasse, Hatchetts and such trashe, only for fishing & trade wth the savages, that have desyred me to inhabitt where I wille and all these shippes have been fished within a square of two leagues the Coast being of the same Condition the length of two or three hundred leagues, where questionles within one hundred 500 sayle may have their fraught better than in Iseland Newfoundlande or elsewhere, and be at their marketts ere the other can have their fish in their shippes. From the west part of England the shippes goe for the third part that is when the voyage is done the goods are divided into three parts (viz.) one third for the Shippe: one for the Company the other for the Victualler, whereby with a stock of £5000 I goe forth wth a charge of £15000 for the transporting this Collonye will cost little or nothing but at the first, because the fishing will goe forward whether we plant it or noe, for the fishers report it to be best they knowe in the Sea and the land in a short time may be more profitable.

The facilitye of the Plantation.

Now if a Shippe can gain 50 or £60 in the 100 only by fishing, spending as much tyme in going & coming as in staying there were I there planted seing the fish in their seasons serveth the most part of the yeare and wth a litle labour I could make all the salt I need use I can conceive noe reason to distrust, but double & triple their gaines that are at all the former charge & can fish but two monethes. And if those do give 20, 30 or 40s for an acre of ground or Shipp Carpenters, Forgers of yron or steele, that buy all thinges at a dear rate grow rich when they may have as good of all needful necessaryes for taking in my opinion should not growe poore and no comoditye in Europe doth decay more than wood.

Thus Right honble & most worthy Peere I have thrown my Mite into the Treasure of my Countries good beseeching your Lop well to consider of it & examine whether Columbus could give the Spaniards any such certaintyes for his grounds, when he got 15 saile from Queene Isabell of Spaine when all the great judgments of Europe refused him! And though I can promise noe mynes of gold the Hollanders are an example of my project whose endeavoures by fishing cannot be suppressed by all the Kinge of Spaines golden powers. Truth is more than wealth & industrious subjects are more available to a king than gold. And this is so certaine a course to get both as I thinke was never propounded to any State for so small a charge, seeing I can prove it, both by example, reason, and experience. How I have lived spent my tyme & bene employed, I am not ashamed who will examine. Therefore I humbly beseech Yor Honr seriously to consider of it and lett not the povertie of the author cause the action to be less respected, who desyres no better fortune than he could find there.

In the interim I humbly desyre yor Honr would be pleased to grace me wth the title of yor Ldps servant. Not that I desyre to shut upp the rest of my dayes in the chamber of ease and idleness, but that thereby I may be better countenanced for the prosecution of this my most desyred voyage, for had I the patronage of so mature a judgment as yor honors it would not only induce those to believe what I know to be true in this matter who will now hardly vouchsafe the perusall of my relations, but also be a meanes to further it to the uttermost of their powers wth their purses. And I shal be ever ready to spend both and goods for the honor of my Country & yor Lops service, with wch resolution I doe in all humility rest

At Yor Honors service.

To show the difference betwixt Virginia and New England I have annexed mappes of them both and this schedule wch will show the difference of the old names from the new on the Map of New England:

The Ould Names.	*The New.*
Cape Cod,	Cape James, Milford Haven.
Chawum,	Barwick,
Accomack,	Plimouth.
Sagoquas,	Oxford.
Massachusetts mount,	Chevit Hill.
Massachusetts river,	Charles River.
Totant,	Fawmoth.
A country not discovd,	Bristow.
Naemkeeke,	Bastable.
Cape Trabigranda,	Cape Anne.
Aggawom,	Southampton.
Smithes Isles,	Smiths Isles.
Passataquack,	Hull.
Accominticus,	Boston.
Sassanowco Mount,	Snoddon Hill.
Sowacatuck,	Ipswtch.
Bahana.	Dartmouth.
Aucociscoes Mount,	Sandwich. Shooters Hill.
Aucocisco,	The Base.
Aumonghcawgen,	Cambridge.
Kinebeck,	Edenborough.
Sagadahock,	Leeth.
Pemmaquid,	St. Johns Towne.
Monahigan,	Barties Isles.
Sagocket,	Norwich.
Mattinnock,	Willoughbyes Isles.
Mettinicus,	Houghtons Isles.
Mecadacut,	Dunbarton.
Penobscot,	Aborden.
Nasket,	Lowmonds.

ARTICLES OF THE LEYDEN CHURCH, 1618.

PUBLIC RECORD OFFICE, LONDON.

COLONIAL, VOL. I. NO. 43.

[The following Paper is referred to in note 1, page 64, ante.]

Seven artikles wch ye Church of Leyden sent to ye Counsell of England to bee considered of in respect of theer judgments occationed about theer going to Virginia, ann^o^ 1618.

1. To ye confession of fayth published in ye name of ye Church of England & to every artikell theerof wee do wth ye reformed-churches wheer wee live, and also ellswhere assent wholy.

2. As wee do acknolidg ye docktryne of fayth theer tawght so do wee ye fruits & effeckts of ye same doctryne to ye begetting of saving fayth in thowsands in ye land (conformists and reformists) as ye ar called wth whom also as wth our bretheren wee do desyer to keepe speritual communion in peace and will pracktiz in our parts all lawfull things.

3. The Kings Maiesty wee acknolidg for Supreme Governer in his dominions in all causes over all parsons, & y^t^ none maye deklyne or apeale from his authority or judgment in any cause whatsoever, but y^t^ in all things obedience is dewe ounto hime, ether active if ye thing commanded bee not agaynst gods word, or passive yf itt bee except pardon can be obtayned.

4. Wee judg itt lawfull for his Maiesty to apoynt bishops civill overseers or officers in awthoryty onder hime, in ye severall provinces, dioses, congregations, or parishes to oversee ye churches and governe them civilly according to ye lawes of ye land untto whom ye ar in all things to geve an account & by them to be ordered according to godlynes.

5. The authority of ye present bishops in ye land wee do acknowlidg so far forth as ye same is indeed derived from his Maiesty untto them and as ye proseed in his name, whom wee will also therein honor in all things and hime in them.

6. Wee beleeve y^t^ no sinod, classes, convocation or assembly of eclesiasticall officers hath any power or authority att all but as ye same by ye maiestraet geven unto them.

7. Lastly wee desyer to geve unto all superiors dewe honnor to preserve ye unity of ye Speritt wth all y^t^ feare god, to have peace wth all men what in us lyeth and wheerin wee err to bee instruckcd by any.

Subscribed by John Robinson and Willyam Bruster.

indorsed. Copy of Seven Artikles sent untto ye Counsell of England by ye Brownists of Leyden.

APPENDIX D.

TRADE PAPERS, STATE PAPER OFFICE, V. 55.

To the Kinges most excellent Majestie.

The most humble peticon of y^r^ Maties councell for the second colonie, and other the adventurers in the Western partes of England for the plantation in the North partes of Virginia in America.

May it please yor Most excellent Majestie,

Whereas it pleased yor Matie by y^r^ most gratious L^res^ patentes bearing date the 10th of Aprill in the fowerth yeare of yor Matie most blessed raigne to give lycence for the establishinge of two colonies in Virginie in America, the one called the First Colonie undertaken by certaine noble men knightes and merchants about London; the other called the Second Colonie likewise undertaken by certaine knightes gentlemen and merchants of the Western partes; by vertue whereof some of the Western parts hath at their greate charg and extreme hazard continued to endeavour to discov^r a place fitt to entertaine such a designe, as also to find the meanes to bring to passe soe noble a worke; in the constant pursuit whereof it hath pleased God to ayde them with his blessing so far as in the confidence of the continewance of His Grace, they are resolved to pursue the same with all the power and meanes they are able to make, to His glorie, yor Maties honour and the publique good of the countrye.

And as it pleased y^r Matie to be gracious to those of the first colonie in enlarginge of the first patent two seav^rall times with many privileges & immunities according to y^r princely bountye, wherebye they have bin incouraged in their proceedings: yor Peticoners do in all humilitie desire that yor Matie will voutchafe unto them the like, that they may wth more boldness go on as they have begun, to the satisfaction of y^r Maties most religious expectacon, with the alteracon only of some few things and the additions here insueing.

First, that territories where yor peticoners make their plantacon may be caled (as by the Prince His Highness it hath bin named) NEW ENGLAND, that the boundes thereof may be setled from 40 to 45 degress of Northerly latitude and soe from sea to sea through the maine as the coast lyeth, and that yor Ma^ts counsell residing here in England for that plantacon may consist of a President, Vice President, Treasurer, Secretary, and other their associates, to be chosen out of the noble men and knights adventurers home about London, & others the adventurers both knightes gentlemen and merchants in the Western countryes; so as the said councell does not exceede the number of 40 who as one incorporate bodye may as often as neede requires be assembled when and where the P'sident or Vicp'sident, wth the Treasurer and Secretary or any two of them, to be assisted wth five or three others of the counsell shall think most convenient for that Service; whereby yor Ma^ts most humble peticoners doth verily hope, by Gods holy assistance to settle their plantacon to the imployeing of many of yor Ma^ts Subjects and the content of all that are well disposed to the prosperitie of yor Ma^ts most happy raigne.

And soe yor Ma^ts most humble peticoners shalbe bound as in duty they are to pray for all increase of glory & perpetuall happiness to yor Matie blessed posteritie for ever.

March, 1619. Upon readinge of this peticon, their Llps. did order that the Lo. Duke of Lenox, Lo. Steward of his Ma^ts Household, and the Earl of Arundell shall take notice of the peticon, consider of the demands for privileges, and thereupon certifie their opinions to their Llps. that such further order may be taken as shalbe meete.

(Signed) C. EDMONDES.

WARRANT TO PREPARE A PATENT FOR THE NORTHERN COMPANY OF VIRGINIA.

Present.—Lo. Chancellor
Lo. Privy Seale
E. of Arundell
E of Southampton
Lo B^p of Winton
Lo. Digby
Mr Comptroler
Mr Secy Calvert
Mr Secy Nauton
M^r of the Roles
M^r of the Wardes.

A LET^R TO S^R THOMAS COVENTRIE, KNIGHT, HIS MAJES SOLICITOR GENERAL.

WHEREAS it is thought fitt that a Patent of Incorporation be granted to the Adventurers of the Northern colonye in Virginia to containe the like liberties, priviledges, powers, authorities, Lands, and all other things within their lymits vizt between the degrees of 40 and 48 as were heretofore granted to the companie of virginia. Excepting only that whereas the said companie have a freedom of custome and subsidie for xxi yeares, and of impositions for ever, this new companie is to be free of custome and Subsidie for the like term of yeares, and of Impositions for so long tyme as his Matie shall be pleased to grant unto them. These shall be therefore to will and require you to prepare a Patent readie for his ma^ies royall signature, to the purpose aforesaid, leaving a blank for the tyme of freedom of impositions to be supplied and put in by his Matie and for which this shall be your Warrant. Dated, &c.

THE NEW ENGLAND CHARTER.

JAMES, by the Grace of God, King of *England, Scotland, France*, and *Ireland*, Defender of the Faith, *&c.* to all whom these Presents shall come, *Greeting*, Whereas, upon the humble Petition of divers of our well disposed Subjects, that intended to make several Plantations in the Parts of *America*, between the Degrees of thirty-ffoure and fforty-five; We according to our princely Inclination, favouring much their worthy Disposition, in Hope thereby to advance the in Largement of Christian Religion, to the Glory of God Almighty, as also by that Meanes to streatch out the Bounds of our Dominions, and to replenish those Deserts with People governed by the Lawes and Majestrates, for the peaceable Commerce of all, that in time to come shall have occasion to traffique into those Territoryes, granted unto Sir *Thomas Gates*, Sir *George Somers*, Knights, *Thomas Hanam*, and *Raleigh Gilbert*, Esquires, and of their Associates, for the more speedy Accomplishment thereof, by our Letters-Patent, bearing Date the Tenth Day of Aprill, in the Fourth Year of our Reign of *England, France*, and *Ireland*, and of *Scotland* the ffourtieth, free Liberty to divide themselves into two several Colloneys; the one called the first Collonye, to be undertaken and advanced by certaine Knights, Gentlemen, and Merchants, in and about our Cyty of London; the other called the Second Colonye, to be undertaken and advanced by certaine Knights, Gentlemen, and Merchants, and their Associates, in and about our Citties of Bristoll, Exon, and our Towne of Plymouth, and other Places, as in and by our said Letters-Pattents, amongst other Things more att large it doth and may appeare. And whereas, since that Time, upon the humble Petition of the said Adventurers and Planters of the said first Collonye, We have been graciously pleased to make them one distinct and entire Body by themselves, giving unto them their distinct Lymitts and Bounds, and have upon their like humble Request, granted unto them divers Liberties, Privileges, Enlargements, and Immunityes, as in and by our severall Letters-Patents it doth and may appeare. Now forasmuch as We have been in like Manner humbly petitioned unto by our trusty and well beloved Servant, Sir *ffердinando Gorges*, Knight, Captain of our ffort and Island by Plymouth, and by certain the principal Knights and Gentlemen Adventurers of the said Second Collonye, and by divers other Persons of Quality, who now intend to be their Associates, divers of which have been at great and extraordinary Charge, and sustained many Losses in seeking and discovering a Place fitt and convenient to lay the Foundation of a hopeful Plantation, and have divers Years past by God's Assistance, and their own Endeavours, taken actual Possession of the Continent hereafter mentioned, in our Name and to our Use, as Sovereign Lord thereof, and have settled already some of our People in Places agreeable to their Desires in those Parts, and in Confidence of prosperous Success therein, by the Continuance of God's Devine Blessing, and our Royall Permission, have resolved in a more plentifull and effectual Manner to prosecute the same, and to that Purpose and Intent have desired of Us, for their better Encouragement and Satisfaction herein, and that they may avoide all Confusion, Questions, or Differences between themselves, and those of the said first Collonye, We would likewise be graciously pleased to make certaine Adventurers, intending to erect and establish ffishery, Trade, and Plantacion; within the Territoryes, Precincts and Lymitts of the said second Colony, and their Successors, one several distinct and entire Body, and to grant unto them, such Estate, Liberties, Priveleges, Enlargements, and Immunityes there, as in these our Letters-Patents hereafter particularly expressed and declared. And forasmuch as We have been certainly given to understand by divers of our good Subjects, that have for these many Yeares past frequented those Coasts and Territoryes, between the Degrees of Fourty and Fourty-Eight, that there is noe other the Subjects of any Christian King or State, by any Authority from their Soveraignes, Lords, or Princes, actually in Possession of any of the said Lands, or Precincts, whereby any Right, Claim, Interest, or Title, may, might, or ought by that Meanes accrue, belong, or appertaine unto them, or any of them. And also for that We have been further given certanly to knowe, that within these late Yeares there hath by God's Visitation raigned a wonderfull Plague, together with many horrible Slaughters, and Murthers, committed amoungst the Sauages and bruitish People there, heertofore inhabiting, in a Manner to the utter Destruction, Deuastacion, and Depopulacion of that whole Territorye, so that there is not left for many Leagues together in a manner, any that doe claime or challenge any Kind of Interests therein, nor any other Superior Lord or Souveraigne to make Claime thereunto, whereby We in our Judgment are persuaded and satisfied that the appointed Time is come in which Almighty God in his great Goodness and Bountie towards Us and our People, hath thought fitt and determined, that those large and goodly Territoryes, deserted as it were by their naturall Inhabitants, should be possessed and enjoyed by such of our Subjects and People as heertofore have and hereafter shall by his Mercie and Favour, and by his Powerfull Arme, be directed and conducted thither. In Contemplacion and serious Consideracion whereof, Wee have thought it fitt according to our Kingly Duty, soe much as in Us lyeth, to second and followe God's sacred Will, rendering reverend Thanks to his Divine Majestie for his gracious favour in laying open and revealing the same unto us, before any other Christian Prince or State, by which Meanes without Offence, and as We trust to his Glory, Wee may with boldness goe on to the settling of so hopefull a Work, which tendeth to the reducing and Conversion of such Sauages as remaine wandering in Desolacion and Distress, to Civil Societie and Christian Religion, to the Inlargement of our own Dominions, and the Aduancement of the Fortunes of such of our good Subjects as shall willingly intresse themselves in the said Imployment, to whom We cannot but give singular Commendations for their soe worthy Intention and Enterprize; We therefore, of our especiall Grace, mere Motion, and certaine Knowledge, by the Aduice of the Lords and others of our Priuy Councell have for Us, our Heyrs and Successors, graunted, ordained, and established, and in and by these Presents, Do for Us, our Heirs and Successors, grant, ordaine and establish, that all that Circuit, Continent, Precincts, and Limitts in America, lying and being in Breadth from Fourty Degrees of Northerly Latitude, from the Equnoctiall Line, to Fourty-eight Degrees of the said Northerly Latitude, and in Length by all the Breadth aforesaid throughout the Maine Land, from Sea to Sea, with all the Seas, Rivers, Islands, Creekes, Inletts, Ports, and Havens, within the Degrees, Precincts, and Limitts of the said Latitude and Longitude, shall be the Limitts, and Bounds, and Precincts of the second Collony: And to the End that the said Territoryes may forever hereafter be more particularly and certainly known and distinguished, our Will and Pleasure is, that the same shall from henceforth be nominated, termed, and called by the Name of New England, in America; and by that Name of New-England in America, the said Circuit, Precinct, Limitt, Continent, Islands, and Places in America, aforesaid, We do by these Presents, for Us, our Heyrs and Successors, name, call, erect, found and establish, and by that Name to have Continuance for ever. And for the better Plantacion, ruling, and governing of the aforesaid New-England, in America, We will, ordaine, constitute, assigne, limitt and appoint, and for Us, our Heyrs and Successors, Wee, by the Advice of the Lords and others of the said priuie Councill, do by these Presents ordaine, constitute, limett, and appoint, that from henceforth, there shall be for ever hereafter, in our Towne of Plymouth, in the County of Devon, one Body politicque and corporate, which shall have perpetuall Succession, which shall consist of the Number of fourtie Persons, and no more, which shall be, and shall be called and knowne by the Name the Councill established at Plymouth, in the County of Devon for the planting, ruling, ordering, and governing of New-England, in America; and for that Purpose Wee have, at and by the Nomination and Request of the said Petitioners, granted, ordained, established, and confirmed; and by these Presents, for Us, our Heyres and Successors, doe grant, ordaine, establish, and confirme, our right trusty and right well beloved Cosins and Councillors Lodowick, Duke of Lenox, Lord Steward of our Household, George Lord Marquess Buckingham, our High Admiral of England, James Marquess Hamilton, William Earle of Pembroke, Lord Chamberlaine of our Household, Thomas Earl of Arundel, and our right trusty and right well beloved Cosin, William Earl of Bathe, and right trusty and right well beloved Cosin and Councillor, Henry Earle of Southampton, and our right trusty and right well beloved Cousins, William Earle of Salisbury, and Robert Earle of Warwick, and our right trusty and well beloved John Viscount Haddington, and our right trusty and well beloved Councillor Edward Lord Zouch, Lord Warden of our Cinque Ports, and our trusty and well beloved Edmond Lord Sheffield, Edward Lord Gorges, and our well beloved Sir Edward Seymour, Knight and Barronett, Sir Robert Manselle, Sir Edward Zouch, our Knight Marshall, Sir Dudley Diggs, Sir Thomas Roe, Sir fferdinando Gorges, Sir Francis Popham, Sir John Brook, Sir Thomas Gates, Sir Richard Hawkins, Sir Richard Edgcombe, Sir Allen Apsley, Sir Warwick Hale, Sir Richard Catchmay, Sir John Bouchier, Sir Nathaniel Rich, Sir Edward Giles, Sir Giles Mompesson, and Sir Thomas Worth, Knights; and our well beloved Matthew Sutcliffe, Deane of Exeter, Robert Heath, Esq; Recorder of our Cittie of London, Henry Bourchier, John Drake, Rawleigh Gilbert, George Chudley, Thomas Hamon, and John Argall, Esquires, to be in and by these Presents; We do appoint them to be the first moderne and present Councill established at Plymouth, in the County of Devon, for the planting, ruling, ordering, and governing of New-England, in America; and that they, and the Suruiuours of them, and such as the Suruiuours and Suruiuor of them shall, from tyme to tyme elect, and chuse, to make up the aforesaid Number of fourtie Persons, when, and as often as any of them, or any of their Successors shall happen to decease, or to be removed from being of the said Councill, shall be in, and by these Presents, incorporated to have a perpetual Succession for ever, in Deed, Fact, and Name, and shall be one Bodye corporate and politicque; and that those, and such said Persons, and their Successors, and such as shall be elected and chosen to succeed them as aforesaid, shall be, and by these Presents are, and be incorporated, named, and called by the Name of the Councill established at Plymouth, in the County of Devon, for the planting, ruling, and governing of New-England, in America; and them the said Duke of Lenox, Marquess Buckingham. Marquess Hamilton, Earle of Pembroke, Earle of Arundell, Earle of Bathe, Earle of Southampton, Earle of Salisbury, Earle of Warwick, Viscount Haddington, Lord Zouch, Lord Sheffield, Lord Gorges, Sir Edward Seymour, Sir Robert Mansell, Sir Edward Zouch, Sir Dudley Diggs, Sir Thomas Roe, Sir fferdinando Gorges, Sir ffrancis Popham, Sir John Brooks, Sir Thomas Gates, Sir Richard Hawkins, Sir Richard Edgcombe, Sir Allen Apsley, Sir Warwick Heale, Sir Richard Catchmay, Sir John Bouchier, Sir Nathaniell Rich, Sir Edward Giles. Sir Giles Mompesson, Sir Thomas Wroth, Knights; Matthew Suttcliffe, Robert Heath, Henry Bourchier, John Drake, Rawleigh Gilbert, George Chudley, Thomas Haymon, and John Argall, Esqrs. and their Successors, one Bodye corporate and politick. in deed and Name, by the Name of the Councell established att Plymouth, in the County of Devon, for the planting, ruling, and governing of New-England, in America. Wee do by these Presents, for Us, our Heyres and Successors, really and fully incorporate, erect, ordaine, name, consitute, and establish, and that by the same Name of the said Councill, they and their Successors for ever hereafter be incorporated, named, and called, and shall by the same Name have perpetual Succession. And further, We do hereby for Us, our Heires and Successors, grant unto the said Councill established att Plymouth, that they and their Successors, by the same Name, be and shall be, and shall continue Persons able and capable in the Law, from time to time, and shall by that Name, of Councill aforesaid, have full Power and Authority, and lawful Capacity and Hability; as well to purchase, take, hold, receive, enjoy, aud to have, and their Successors for ever, any Manors, Lands, Tenements, Rents, Royalties, Privileges, Immunities, Reversions, Annuities, Hereditaments, Goods and Chattles whatsoever, of or from Us, our Heirs and Successors, and of or from any other Person or Persons whatsoever, as well in and within this our Realme, of England, as in and within any other Place or Places whatsoever or wheresoever; and the same Manors, Lands, Tenements, and Hereditaments, Goods, or Chattles, or any of them, by the same Name to alien and sell, or to do, execute, ordaine and performe all other Matters and Things whatsoever to the said Incorporation and Plantation concerning and belonging. And further, our Will and Pleasure is, that the said Councill, for the time being, and their Successors, shall have full Power and lawful Authority, by the Name aforesaid, to sue, and be sued; implead, and to be impleaded; answer, and to be answered, unto all Manner of Courts and Places that now are, or hereafter shall be, within this our Realme and elsewhere, as well temporal as spiritual, in all Manner of Suits and Matters whatsoever, and of what Nature or Kinde soever such Suite or Action be or shall be. And our Will and Pleasure is, that the said ffourty Persons, or the greater Number of them, shall and may, from time to time, and at any time hereafter, at their owne Will and Pleasure, according to the Laws, Ordinances, and Orders of or by them, or by the greater Part of them, hereafter in Manner and forme in these Presents mentioned, to be agreed upon, to elect and choose amongst themselves one of the said ffourty Persons for the Time being, to be President of the said Councill, which President soe elected and chosen, Wee will, shall continue and be President of the said Councill, for so long a Time as by the Orders of the said Councill, from time to time to be made, as hereafter is mentioned, shall be thought fitt, and no longer; unto which President, or in his Absence, to any such Person as by the Order of the said Councill shall be thereunto appointed, Wee do give Authority to give Order for the warning of the said Council, and summoning the Company to their Meetings. And our Will and Pleasure is, that from time to time, when and so often as any of the Councill shall happen to decease, or to be removed from being of the said Councell, that then, and so often, the Survivors of them the said Councill, and no other, or the greater Number of them, who then shall be from time to time left remaininge, and who shall, or the greater Number of which that shall be assembled at a public Court or Meeting to be held for the said Company, shall elect and choose one or more other Person or Persons to be of the said Councill, and which from time to time shall be of the said Councill, so that the Number of ffourty Persons of the said Councill may from time to time be supplied: Provided always that as well the Persons herein named to be of the said Councill, as every other Councillor hereafter to be elected, shall be presented to the Lord Chancellor of England, or to the Lord High Treasurer of England, or to the Lord Chamberlaine of the Household of Us, our Heirs and Successors for the Time being, to take his and their Oath and Oathes of a Councellor and Councellors to Us, our Heirs and Successors, for the said Company and Collonye in New-England. And further, Wee will grant by these Presents, for Us, our Heires and Successors, unto the said Councill and their Successors, that they and their Successors shall have and enjoy for ever a Common Seale, to be engraven according to their Discretions; and that it shall be lawfull for them to appoint whatever Seale or Seales, they shall think most meete and necessary, either for their Uses, as they are one United Body incorporate here, or for the publick of their Gouvernour and Ministers of New-England aforesaid, whereby the Incorporation may or shall seale any Manner of Instrument touching the same Corporation, and the Manors, Lands, Tenements, Rents, Reversions Annuities, Hereditaments, Goods, Chattles, Affaires, and any other Things belonging unto, or in any wise appertaininge, touching, or concerning the said Councill and their Successors, or concerning the said Corporation and Plantation in and by these our Letters-Paents as aforesaid founded, erected, and established. And Wee do further by these Presents, for Us, our Heires and Successors, grant unto the said Councill and their Sccuessors, that it shall and may be lawfull to and for the said Councill, and their Successors for the Time being, in their discretions, from time to time to admitt such and so many Person or Persons to be made free and enabled to trade traffick unto, within, and in New-England aforesaid, and unto every Part and Parcel thereof, or to have, possess, or enjoy, any Lands or Hereditaments in New-England aforesaid, as they shall think fitt, according to the Lawes, Orders, Constitutions, and Ordinances, by the said Councill and their Successors from time to time to be made and established by Virtue of, and according to the true Intent of these Presents, and under such Conditions, Reservations, and agreements as the said Councill shall set downe, order and direct, and not otherwise. And further, of our especiall Grace, certaine Knowledge, and mere Motion, for Us, our Heires and Successors, Wee do by these Presents give and grant full Power and Authority to the said Councill and their Successors, that the said Councill for the Time being, or the greater Part of them, shall and may, from time to time, nominate, make, constitute, ordaine, and confirme by such Name or Names, Sale or Sales, as to them shall seeme Good; and likewise to revoke, discharge, change, and alter, as well all and singular, Governors, Officers, and Ministers, which hereafter shall be by them thought fitt and needful to be made or used, as well to attend the Business of the said Company here, as for the Government of the said Collony and Plantation, and also to make, ordaine, and establish all Manner of Orders, Laws, Directions, Instructions, Forms, and Ceremonies of Government and Magistracy fitt and necessary for and concerning the Government of the said Collony and Plantation, so always as the same be not contrary to the Laws and Statutes of this our Realme of England, and the same att all Times hereafter to abrogate, revoke, or change, not only within the Precincts of the said Collony, but also upon the Seas in going and coming to and from the said Collony, as they in their good Discretions shall thinke to be fittest for the good of the Adventurers and Inhabitants there. And Wee do further of our especiall Grace, certaine Knowledge, and mere Motion, grant, declare, and ordain, that such principall Governor, as from time to time shall be authorized and appointed in Manner and Forme in these Presents heretofore expressed, shall have full Power and Authority to use and exercise martiall Laws in Case of Rebellion, Insurrection, and Mutiny, in as large and ample Manner as our Lieutenants in our Counties within our Realme of England have or ought to have by Force of their Commission of Lieutenancy. And for as much as it shall be necessary for all our lovinge Subjects as shall inhabit within the said Precincts of New-England aforesaid, to determine to live together in the Feare and true Worship of Almighty God, Christian Peace, and Civil Quietness, each with other, whereby every one may with more Safety, Pleasure, and Profitt, enjoye that whereunto they shall attaine with great Pain and Perill, Wee, for Us, our Heires and Successors, are likewise pleased and contented, and by these Presents do give and grant unto the said Council and their Successors, and to such Governors, Officers, and Ministers, as shall be by the said Councill constituted and appointed according to the Natures and Limitts of their Offices and Places respectively, that they shall and may, from time to time for ever heerafter, within the said Precincts of New-England, or in the Way by the Seas thither, and from thence have full and absolute Power and Authority to correct, punish, pardon, governe, and rule all such the Subjects of Us, our Heires and Successors, as shall from time to time adventure themselves in any Voyage thither, or that shall att any Time heerafter inhabit in the Precincts or Territories of the said Collony as aforesaid, according to such Laws, Orders, Ordinances, Directions, and Instructions as by the said Councill aforesaid shall be established; and in Defect thereof, in Cases of Necessity, according to the good Discretions of the said Governors and Officers respectively, as well in Cases capitall and criminall, as civill, both marine and others, so always as the said Statutes, Ordinances, and Proceedings, as near as conveniently may be, agreeable to the Laws, Statutes, Government and Policie of this our Realme of England. And furthermore, if any Person or Persons, Adventurers or Planters of the said Collony, or any other, att any Time or Times heereafter, shall transport any Moneys, Goods, or Merchandizes, out of any of our Kingdoms, with a Pretence or Purpose to land, sell, or otherwise dispose of the same within the Limitts and Bounds of the said Colony, and yet nevertheless being att Sea, or after he hath landed within any Part of the said Collony shall carry the same into any other fforaigne Country with a Purpose there to sell and dispose thereof, that then all the Goods and Chattles of the said Person or Persons so offending and transported, together with the Ship or Vessell wherein such Transportation was made, shall be forfeited to Us, our Heires and Successors. And

Wee do further of our especiall Grace, certaine Knowledge, and meere Motion for Us, our Heirs and Successors for and in Respect of the Considerations aforesaid, and for divers other good Considerations and Causes, us thereunto especially moving, and by the Advice of the Lords and Others of our said Privy Councill have absolutely giuen, granted, and confirmed, and do by these Presents absolutely give, grant, and confirm unto the said Councill, called the Councill established att Plymouth in the County of Devon for the planting, ruling, and governing of New-England in America, and unto their Successors for ever, all the aforesaid Lands and Grounds, Continent, Precinct, Place, Places and Territoryes, viz. that aforesaid Part of America, lying, and being in Breadth from ffourty Degrees of Northerly Latitude from the Equinoctiall Line, to ffourty-eight Degrees of the said Northerly Latitude inclusively; and in Length of, and within all the Breadth, aforesaid, throughout all Maine Lands from Sea to Sea, together also, with the Firme Lands, Soyles, Grounds, Havens, Ports, Rivers, Waters, Fishings, Mines, and Mineralls, as well Royall Mines of Gold and Silver, as other Mine and Mineralls, precious Stones, Quarries, and all, and singular other Comodities, Jurisdictions, Royalties, Priveliges, Franchises, and Preheminences, both within the same Tract of Land upon the Maine. and also within the said Islands and Seas adjoining: Provided always, that the said Islands, or any of the Premises herein before mentioned, and by these Presents intended and meant to be granted, be not actually possessed or inhabited by any other Christian Prince or Estate, nor be within the Bounds, Limitts, or Territoryes, of that Southern Collony heretofore by us granted to be planted by diverse of our loving Subjects in the South Part, to have and to hold, possess and enjoy, all, and singular, the aforesaid Continent, Lands, Territoryes, Islands, Hereditaments and Precincts, Sea Waters; Fishings, with all, and all Manner their Commodities, Royalties, Liberties, Preheminences, and Profitts, that shall arise from thence, with all and singular, their Appertenances, and every Part and Parcell thereof, and of them, to and unto the said Councell and their Successors and Assignes for ever, the sole only and proper Use, Benefit, and Behooffe of them the said Council and their Successors and Assignes for ever, to be holden of Us, our Heires, and Successors, as of our Manor of East Greenwich, in our County of Kent, in free and comon Soccage and not in Capita, nor by Knight's Service; yielding and paying therefore to Us, our Heires, our Successors, the fifth Part, of the Ore of Gold and Silver, which from time to time, and att all times heereafter, shall happen to be found, gotten, had, and obtained, in or within any the said Lands, Limitts, Territoryes, and Precincts, or in or within any Part or Parcell thereof, for, or in Respect of all, and all Manner of Dutys, Demands, and Services whatsoever, to be done, made, or paid to Us, our Heires, and Successors. And Wee do further of our especiall Grace, certaine Knowledge, and meere Motion, for Us, and our Heires, and Successors, give and grant to the said Councell, and their Successors for ever by these Presents, that it shall be lawfull and free for them and their Assignes, att all and every time and times hereafter, out of our Realmes or Dominions whatsoever, to take, load, carry, and transport in, and into their Voyages, and for, and towards the said Plantation in New-England, all such, and so many of our loving Subjects, or any other Strangers that will become our loving subjects, and live under our Allegiance, as shall willingly accompany them in the said Voyages and Plantation, with Shipping, Armour, Weapons, Ordinance, Munition, Powder, Shott, Victuals, and all Manner of Cloathing, Implements, Furniture, Beasts, Cattle, Horses, Mares, and all other Things necessary for the said Plantation, and for their Use and Defence, and for Trade with the People there, and in passing and returning to and fro, without paying or yeilding, any Custom or Subsidie inward or outward, to either Us, our Heires, or Successors, for the same, for the Space of seven Years, from the Day of the Date of these Presents, provided, that none of the said Persons be such as shall be hereafter by special Name restrained by Us, our Heires; or Successors. And for their further Encouragement, of our especiall Grace and Favor, Wee do by these Presents for Us, our Heires, and Successors, yield and grant, to and with the said Councill and their Successors and every of them, their Factors and Assignes, that they and every of them, shall be free and quitt from all Subsidies and Customs in New-England for the Space of seven Years, and from all Taxes and Impositions for the Space of twenty and one Yeares, upon all Goods and Merchandizes att any time or times hereafter, either upon Importation thither, or Exportation from thence into our Realme of England, or into any our Dominions by the said Councill and their Successors, their Deputies, ffactors, and Assignees, or any of them, except only the five Pounds *per Cent.* due for Custome upon all such Goods and Merchandizes, as shall be brot and imported into our Realme of England, or any other of our Dominions, according to the ancient Trade of Marchants; which five Pounds *per Cent.* only being paid, it shall be thenceforth lawful and free for the said Adventurers, the same Goods and Merchandize to export and carry out of our said Dominions into fforaigne Parts, without any Custom, Tax, or other Duty to be paid to Us, our Heires, or Successors, or to any other Officers or Ministers of Us, our Heires, or Successors; provided, that the said Goods and Merchandizes be shipped out within thirteene Months after their first Landing within any Part of these Dominions. And further our Will and Pleasure is, and Wee do by these Presents charge, command, warrant, and authorize the said Councill, and their Successors, or the major Part of them, which shall be present and assembled for that Purpose, shall from time to time under their comon Seale, distribute, convey, assigne, and sett over, such particular Portions of Lands, Tenements, and Hereditaments, as are by these Presents, formerly granted unto each our loveing Subjects, naturally borne or Denizens, or others, as well Adventurers as Planters, as by the said Company upon a Commission of Survey and Distribution, executed and returned for that Purpose, shall be named, appointed, and allowed, wherein our Will and Pleasure is, that Respect be had as well to the Proportion of the Adventurers, as to the speciall Service, Hazard, Exploit, or Meritt of any Person so to be recompensed, advanced, or rewarded, and wee do also, for Us, our Heires, and Successors, grant to the said Councell and their Successors and to all and every such Governours, or Officers, or Ministers, as by the said Councill shall be appointed to have Power and Authority of Government and Command in and over the said Collony and Plantation, that they and every of them, shall, and lawfully may, from time to time, and att all Times hereafter for ever, for their severall Defence and Safety, encounter, expulse, repel, and resist by Force of Arms, as well by Sea as by Land, and all Ways and Meanes whatsoever, all such Person and Persons, as without the speciall Licence of the said Councell and their Successors, or the greater Part of them shall attempt to inhabitt within the said severall Precincts and Limitts of the said Collony and Plantation. And also all, and every such person or Persons whatsoever, as shall enterprize or attempt att any time hereafter Destruction, Invasion, Detriment, or Annoyance to the said Collony and Plantation; and that it shall be lawfull for the said Councill, and their Successors, and every of them, from Time to Time, and att all Times heereafter, and they shall have full Power and Authority, to take and surprize by all Ways and Meanes whatsoever, all and every such Person and Persons whatsoever, with their Ships, Goods, and other Furniture, Trafficking in any Harbour, Creeke, or Place, within the Limitts and Precinctes of the said Collony and Plantation, and not being allowed by the said Councill to be Adventurers or Planters of the said Colony. And of our further Royall Favor, Wee have granted, and for Us, our Heires, Successors, Wee do grant unto the said Councill and their Successors, that the said Territoryes, Lands, Rivers, and Places aforesaid, or any of them, shall not be visited, frequented, or traded unto, by any other of our Subjects, or the Subjects of Us, our Heires, or Successors, either from any the Ports and Havens belonging or appertayning, or which shall belong or appertayne unto Us, our Heires, or Successors, or to any foraigne State, Prince, or Potentate whatsoever: And therefore, Wee do hereby for Us, our Heires, and Successors, charge, command, prohibit and forbid all the Subjects of Us, our Heirs, and successors, of what Degree and Quality soever, they be, that none of them, directly, or indirectly, presume to visitt, frequent, trade, or adventure to traffick into, or from the said Territoryes, Lands, Rivers, and Places aforesaid, or any of them other than the said Councill and their Successors, ffactors, Deputys, and Assignees, unless it be with the License and Consent of the said Councill and Company first had and obtained in Writing, and the comon Seal, upon Pain of our Indignation and Imprisonment of their Bodys during the Pleasure of Us, our Heires or Successors, and the Forfeiture and Loss both of theire Ships and Goods, wheresoever they shall be found either within any of our Kingdomes or Dominions, or any other Place or Places out of our Dominions. And for the better effecting of our said Pleasure heerin, Wee do heereby for Us, our Heires and Successors, give and grant full Power and Authority unto the said Councill, and their Successors for the time being, that they by themselves, their Factors, Deputyes, or Assignees, shall and may from time to time, and at all times heereafter, attach, arrest, take, and seize all and all Manner of Ship and Ships, Goods, Wares, and Merchandizes whatsoever, which shall be bro't from or carried to the Places before mentioned, or any of them, contrary to our Will and Pleasure, before in these Presents expressed. The Moyety or one halfe of all which Forfeitures Wee do hereby for Us, our Heires and Successors, give and grant, unto the said Councill, and their Successors to their own proper Use without Accompt, and the other Moyety, or halfe Parte thereof, Wee will shall be and remaine to the Use of Us, our Heires and Successors. And we likewise have condiscended and granted, and by these Presents, for Us, our Heires and Successors, do condiscend, and grant to and with the said Councill and their Successors, that Wee, our Heires or Successors, shall not or will not give and grant any Lybertye, License, or Authority to any Person or Persons whatsoever, to saile, trade, or trafficke unto the aforesaid parts of New-England, without the good Will and Likinge of the said Councill, or the greater Part of them for the Time beinge, att any their Courts to be assembled. And Wee do for Us, our Heires and Successors, give and grant unto the said Councill, and their Successors, that whensoever, or so often as any Custome or Subsidie shall growe due or payable unto Us, our Heires or Successors, according to the

Limitation and Appointment aforesaid, by Reason of any Goods, Wares, Merchandizes, to be shipped out, or any Returne to be made of any Goods, Wares, or Merchandizes, unto or from New-England, or any the Lands Territoryes aforesaid, that then so often, and in such Case the ffarmers, Customers, and Officers of our Customes of England and Ireland, and every of them, for the Time being, upon Request made unto them by the said Councill, their Successors, ffactors, or Assignees, and upon convenient Security to be given in that Behalfe, shall give and allowe unto the said Councill and their Successors, and to all Person and Persons free of the said Company as aforesaid, six Months Time for the Payment of the one halfe of all such Custome and Subsidie, as shall be due, and payable unto Us, our Heires and Successors for the same, for which these our Letters Patent, or the Duplicate, or the Enrolment thereof, shall be unto our said Officers a sufficient Warrant and Discharge. Nevertheless, our Will and Pleasure is, that if any of the said Goods, Wares, and Merchandizes, which be, or shall be, att any Time heereafter, landed and exported out of any of our Realmes aforesaid, and shall be shipped with a Purpose not to be carried to New England aforesaid, that then such Payment, Duty, Custome, Imposition, or Forfeiture, shall be paid, and belong to Us, our Heires, and Successors, for the said Goods, Wares, and Merchandizes, so fraudulently sought to be transported, as if this our Grant had not been made nor granted: And Wee do for Us, our Heires and Successors, give and grant unto the said Councill and theire Successors for ever, by these Presents, that the said President of the said Company, or his Deputy for the Time being, or any two others of the said Councill, for the said Collony in New-England, for the Time beinge, shall and may, and att all Times heereafter, and from time to time, have full Power and Authority, to minister and give the Oath and Oathes of Allegiance and Supremacy, or either of them, to all and every Person and Persons, which shall at any Time and Times heereafter, goe or pass to the said Collony in New-England. And further, that it shall be likewise lawful for the said President, or his Deputy for the Time being, or any two others of the said Councill for the said Collony of New-England for the Time being, from time to time, and att all Times heerafter, to minister such a formal Oath, as by their Discretion shall be reasonably devised, as well unto any Person and Persons imployed or to be imployed in, for, or touching the said Plantation, for their honest faithfull, and just Discharge of their Service, in all such Matters as shall be committed unto them for the Good and Benefit of the said Company, Collony, and Plantation, as also unto such other Person or Persons, as the said President or his Deputy, with two others of the said Councill, shall thinke meete for the Examination or clearing of the Truth in any Cause whatsoever, concerning the said Plantation, or any Business from thence proceeding, or thereunto belonging. And to the End that no lewd or ill-disposed Persons, Saylors, Soldiers, Artificers, Laborours, Husbandmen, or others, which shall receive Wages, Apparel, or other Entertainment from the said Councill, or contract and agree with the said Councill to goe, and to serve, and to be employed, in the said Plantation, in the Collony in New-England, to afterwards withdraw, hide, and conceale themselves, or refuse to go thither, after they have been so entertained and agreed withall; and that no Persons which shall be sent and imployed in the said Plantation, of the said Collony in New-England, upon the Charge of the said Councill, doe misbehave themselves by mutinous Seditions, or other notorious Misdemeanors, or which shall be employed, or sent abroad by the Governour of New-England or his Deputy, with any Shipp or Pinnace, for Provision for the said Colony, or for some Discovery, or other Business or Affaires concerninge the same, doe from thence either treacherously come back againe, or returne into the Realme of Englande by Stealthe, or without Licence of the Governour of the said Collony in New-England for the Time being, or be sent hither as Misdoers or Offendors; and that none of those Persons after theire Returne from thence, being questioned by the said Councill heere, for such their Misdemeanors and Offences, do, by insolent and contemptuous Carriage in the Presence of the said Councill shew little Respect and Reverence, either to the Place or Authority in which we have placed and appointed them and others, for the clearing of their Lewdness and Misdemeanors committed in New-England, divulge vile and scandalous Reports of the Country of New-England, or of the Government or Estate of the said Plantation and Collony, to bring the said Voyages and Plantation into Disgrace and Contempt, by Meanes whereof, not only the Adventurers and Planters already engaged in the said Plantation may be exceedingly abused and hindered, and a great Number of our loveing and well-disposed Subjects, otherways well affected and inclined to joine and adventure in so noble a Christian and worthy Action may be discouraged from the same, but also the Enterprize itself may be overthrowne, which cannot miscarry without some Dishonour to Us and our Kingdome: Wee, therefore, for preventing so great and enormous Abuses and Misdemeanors, Do, by these Presents for Us, our Heires, and Successors, give and grant unto the said President or his Deputy, or such other Person or Persons, as by the Orders of the said Councill shall be appointed by Warrant under his or their Hand or Hands, to send for, or cause to be apprehended, all and every such Person and Persons, who shall be noted, or accused, or found at any time or times heereafter to offend or misbehave themselves in any the Affaires before mentioned and expressed; and upon the Examination of any such Offender or Offenders, and just Proofe made by Oathe taken before said Councill, of any such notorious Misdemeanours by them committed as aforesaid, and also upon any insolent, contemptuous, or irreverent Carriage or Misbehaviour, to or against the said Councill, to be shewed or used by any such Person or Persons so called, convened, and appearing before them as aforesaid, that in all such Cases, our said Councill, or any two or more of them for the time being, shall and may have full Power and Authority, either heere to bind them over with good Sureties for their good Behaviour, and further therein to proceed, to all Intents and Purposes as it is used in other like Cases within our Realme of England, or else at their Discretions to remand and send back the said Offenders, or any of them, to the said Collony of New-England, there to be proceeded against and punished as the Governour's Deputy or Councill there for the Time being, shall think meete, or otherwise according to such Laws and Ordinances as are, and shall be, in Use there, for the well ordering and good Government of the said Collony. And our Will and Pleasure is, and Wee do hereby declare to all Christian Kings, Princes and States, that if any Person or Persons which shall hereafter be of the said Collony or Plantation, or any other by Licence or Appointment of the said Councill, or their Successors, or otherwise, shall at any time or times heereafter, rob or spoil, by Sea or by Land, or do any Hurt, Violence, or unlawfull Hostility to any of the Subjects of Us, our Heires, or Successors, or any of the Subjects of the King, Prince, Ruler, or Governour, or State, being then in League or Amity with Us, our Heires and Successors, and that upon such Injury, or upon just Complaint of such Prince, Ruler, Governour, or State, or their Subjects, Wee, our Heires, or Successors shall make open Proclamation within any of the Ports of our Realme of England commodious for that Purpose, that the Person or Persons having committed any such Robbery or Spoile, shall within the Term limited by such a Proclamation, make full Restitution or Satisfaction of all such Injuries done, so as the said Princes or other, so complaining, may hold themselves fully satisfied and contented. And if that the said Person or Persons, having committed such Robery or Spoile, shall not make or cause to be made Satisfaction accordingly within such Terme so to be limited, that then it shall be lawful for Us, our Heires and Successors, to put the said Person or Persons out of our Allegiance and Protection; and that it shall be lawful and free for all Princes to prosecute with Hostility the said Offenders and every of them, their, and every of their Procurers, Aidors, Abettors, and Comforters in that Behalfe. And also, Wee do for Us, our Heires, and Successors, declare by these Presents, that all and every the Persons beinge our Subjects, which shall goe and inhabitt within the said Collony and Plantation, and every of their Children and Posterity, which shall happen to be born within the Limitts thereof, shall have and enjoy all Liberties, and ffranchizes, and Immunities of free Denizens and naturall Subjects within any of our other Dominions, to all Intents and Purposes, as if they had been abidinge and born within this our Kingdome of England, or any other our Dominions. And lastly, because the principall Effect which we can desire or expect of this Action, is the Conversion and Reduction of the People in those Parts unto the true Worship of God and Christian Religion, in which Respect, Wee would be loath that any Person be permitted to pass that We suspected to affect the Superstition of the Chh of Rome, Wee do hereby declare that it is our Will and Pleasure that none be permitted to pass, in any Voyage from time to time to be made into the said Country, but such as shall first have taken the Oathe of Supremacy; for which Purpose, Wee do by these Presents give full Power and Authority to the President of the said Councill, to tender and exhibit the said Oath to all such Persons as shall at any time be sent and imployed in the said Voyage. And Wee also for Us, our Heires and Successors, do covenant and grant to and with the Councill, and their Successors, by these Presents, that if the Councill for the time being, and their Successors, or any of them, shall at any time or times heereafter, upon any Doubt which they shall conceive concerning the Strength or Validity in Law of this our present Grant, or be desirous to have the same renewed and confirmed by Us, our Heires and Successors, with Amendment of such Imperfections and Defects as shall appeare fitt and necessary to the said Councill, or their Successors, to be reformed and amended on the Behalfe of Us, our Heires and Successors, and for the furthering of the Plantation and Government, or the Increase, continuing, and flourishing thereof, that then, upon the humble Petition of the said Councill for the time being, and their Successors, to Us, our Heires and Successors, Wee, our Heires and Successors, shall and will forthwith make and pass under the Great Seale of England, to the said Councill and theire Successors, such further and better Assurance, of all and singular the Lands, Grounds, Royalties, Privileges, and Premises aforesaid granted, or intended to be granted, according to our true Intent and Meaning in these our Letters-patents, signified, declared, or mentioned, as by the learned Councill of Us, our Heires, and Successors, and of the said Company and theire Successors shall, in that Behalfe, be reasonably devised or advised. And further our Will and Pleasure is, that in all Questions and Doubts, that shall arise upon any Difficulty of Instruction or Interpretation of any Thing contained in these our Letters-pattents, the same shall be taken and interpreted in most ample and beneficial Manner, for the said Council and their Successors, and every Member thereof. And Wee do further for Us, our Heires and Successors, charge and command all and singular Admirals, Vice-Admirals, Generals, Commanders, Captains, Justices of Peace, Majors, Sheriffs, Bailiffs, Constables, Customers, Comptrollers, Waiters, Searchers, and all the Officers of Us, our Heires and Successors, whatsoever to be from time to time, and att all times heereafter, in all Things aiding, helping, and assisting unto the said Councill, and their Successors, and unto every of them, upon Request and Requests by them to be made, in all Matters and Things, for the Furtherance and Accomplishment of all or any the Matters and Things by Us, in and these our Letters-pattents, given, granted, and provided, or by Us, meant or intended to be given, granted, and provided, as they our said Officers, and the Officers of Us, our Heires and Successors, do tender our Pleasure, and will avoid the contrary att their Perills. And Wee also do by these Presents, ratifye and confirm unto the said Councill and their Successors, all Privileges, ffranchises, Liberties, Immunities granted in our said former Letters-patents, and not in these our Letters-patents revoaked, altered, changed or abridged, altho' express Mention, &c.

In Witnes *&c.*

Witnes our selfe at *Westminister*, the Third Day of November, in the Eighteenth Yeare of our Reign over England, &c.

Par Breve de Privato Sigillio, &c.

This is a true Copy from the Original Record remaining in the Chapel of the Rolls having been examined.

HEN. ROOKE, *Clerk of the Rolls.*

THE FIRST PLYMOUTH PATENT.

THIS INDENTURE MADE THE FIRST DAY OF JUNE 1621 AND IN THE yeeres of the raigne of our Sovraigne Lord JAMES by the grace of god King of England Scotland Fraunce and Ireland defendor of the faith &c That is to say of England Fraunce and Ireland the Nynetenth and of Scotland the fowre and fiftith, Betwene the President and Counsell of New England of the one ptie And John Peirce Citizen and Clothworker of London and his Associate of the other ptie WITNESSETH that whereas the said John Peirce and his Associates haue already transported and vndertaken to transporte at their coste and chardges themselves and dyvers psons into New England and there to erect and build a Towne and settle dyvers Inhabitants for the advancem^t of the genall plantacon of that Country of New England NOW THE SAYDE President and Counsell in consideracon thereof and for the furtherance of the said plantacon and incoragem^t of the said Vndertakers haue agreed to graunt assigne allott and appoynt to the said John Peirce and his associates and euy of them his and their heires and assignes one hundred acres of grownd for euy pson so to be transported besides dyverse other pryvileges Liberties and comodyties hereafter menconed, *And* to that intent they haue graunted allotted assigned and confirmed, And by theis pnts do graunt allott assigne and confirme vnto the said John Peirce and his Associates his and their heires & Assignes and the heires & assignes of euy of them seually & respectyvelie one hundred seuall acres of grownd in New England for euy pson so transported or to be transported (Yf the said John Peirce or his Associate contynue there three whole yeeres either at one or seuall tymes or dye in the meane season after he or they are shipped with intent there to inhabit The same Land to be taken and chosen by them their deputies or assignes in any place or places wheresoeu not already inhabited by any English and where no English pson or psons are already placed or settled or haue by order of the said President and Councell made choyce of, nor within Tenne myles of the same (vnles it be on the opposite syde of some great or Navigable Ryver to the former pticuler plantacon, together with the one half of the Ryver or Ryvers, that is to say to the middest thereof as shall adioyne to such lands as they shall make choyce of together with all such Liberties pryviledges pffits & comodyties as the said Land and Ryvers which they shall make choyce of shall yield together with free libtie to fishe in and vpon the Coast of New England and in all havens ports and creekes Therevnto belonging and that no pson or psons whatsoeu shall take any benefitt or libtie of or to any of the grownds or the one half of the Ryvers aforesaid (excepting the free vse of highways by land and Navigable Ryvers, but that the said vndertakers & planters their heires & assignes shall haue the sole right and vse of the said grownds and the one half of the said Ryvers with all their pffitts & app'tennces. AND forasmuch as the said John Peirce and his associates intend and haue vndertaken to build Churches, Schooles, Hospitalls, Towne houses, Bridges and such like workes of Charytie As also for the maynteyning of Majestrates and other inferior Officers. In regard whereof and to the end that the said John Peirce and his Associates his and their heires and assignes may haue wherewithall to beare & support such like charge. THEREFORE the said President & Councell aforesaid do graunt vnto the said Vndertakers their heires & assignes Fifteene hundred acres of Land more-over and aboue the aforesaid proporcon of one hundred the pson for euy vndertaker & Planter to be ymployed vpon such publiq vses as the said Vndertakers & Planters shall think fitt. AND they do further graunt vnto the said John Peirce and his Associates their heires and assignes, that for euy pson that they or any of them shall transport at their owne prop coste & charge into New England either vnto the Lands hereby graunted or adioyninge to them within Seven Yeeres after the feast of St John Baptist next coming Yf the said pson transported contynue there three whole yeeres either at one or seuall tymes or dye in the meane season after he is shipped with intent there to inhabit that the said pson or psons that shall so at his or their owne charge transport any other shall haue graunted and allowed to him & them and his & their heires respectyvelie for eny pson so transported or dyeing after he is shipped one hundred acres of Land, and also that euy pson or psons who by contract & agreemt to be had & made with the said Vndertakes shall at his & their owne charge transport him & themselves or any other and setle and plant themselves in New England within the said Seaven Yeeres for three yeeres space as aforesaid or dye in the meane tyme shall haue graunted & allowed vnto euy pson so transporting or transported and their heires & assignes respectyvely the like nomber of one hundred acres of Land as aforesaid the same to be by him & them or their heires & assignes chosen in any entyre place together and adioyning to the aforesaid Lands and not straglingly not before the tyme of such choyce made possessed or inhabited by any English Company or within tenne myles of the same (except it be on the opposite side of some great Navigable Ryver as aforesaid YIELDING and paying vnto the said President and Counsell for euy hundred acres so obteyned and possessed by the said John Peirce and his said Associates and by those said other psons and their heires & assignes who by Contract as aforesaid shall at their owne charge transport themselves or others the Yerely rent of Two shillings at the feast of St. Michaell Tharchaungell to the hand of the Rentgatherer of the said President & Counsell and their successors foreu, the first paymt to begyn after the'xpiracon of the first seven Yeeres next after the date hereof AND further it shalbe lawfull to and for the said John Peirce and his Associates and such as contract with them as aforesaid their Tennts & srvants vpon dislike of or in the Country to returne for England or elsewhere with all their goods and chattells at their will and pleasure without lett or disturbance of any paying all debts that iustly shalbe demaunded AND likewise it shalbe lawfull and is graunted to and for the said John Peirce and his Associates & Planters their heires & assignes their Tennts & srvants and such as they or any of them shall contract with as aforesaid and send and ymploy for the said plantacon to goe & returne trade traffiq in port or transport their goods & mchaundize at their will & pleasure into England or elsewhere paying onely such duties to the Kings matie his heires & successors as the President and Counsell of New England doe pay without any other taxes Imposicons burthens or restraints whatsoeu vpon them to be ymposed (the rent hereby resved being onely excepted) AND it shalbe lawfull for the said Vndertakes & Planters, their heires & successors freely to truck trade & traffiq with the Salvages in New England or neighboring thereabouts at their wills and pleasures without lett or disturbance. As also to haue libtie to hunt hauke fish or fowle in any place or places not now or hereafter by the English inhabited. AND THE SAID President & Counsell do covennt & promyse to and with the said John Peirce and his Associates and others contracted wth as aforesaid his and their heires & assignes, That vpon lawfull srvey to be had & made at the charge of the said Vndertakers & Planters and lawful informacon geven of the bowndes, metes, and quantitie of Lands so as aforesaid to be by them chosen & possessed they the said President & Counsell vpon srrender of this pnte graunt & Indenture and vpon reasonable request to be made by the said Vndertakers & Planters their heires & assignes within seaven Yeeres now next coming, shall and will by their Deede Indented and vnder their Comon seale graunt infeoffe & confirme all and euy the said lands so sett out and bownded as aforesaid to the said John Peirce and his Associates and such as contract with them their heires and assignes in as large and beneficiall manner as the same are in theis ptnts graunted or intended to be graunted to all intents and purposes with all and euy pticuler pryviledge & freedome resvacon and condicon with all dependences herein specyfied & graunted ; *And* shall also at any tyme within the said terme of Seaven Yeeres vpon request vnto the said President & Counsell made, graunt vnto them the said John Peirce and his Associates Vndertakers & Planters their heires & assignes, Letters & graunts of Incorporacon by some vsuall & fitt name & tytle with Liberty to them and their successors from tyme to tyme to make orders Lawes Ordynaunces & Constitucons for the rule government ordering and directing of all psons to be transported & settled vpon the lands hereby graunted, intended to be graunted or hereafter to be graunted and of the said Lands & proffitts thereby arrysing ; *And* in the meane tyme vntill such graunt made, Yt shalbe lawfull for the said John Peirce his Associate Vndertakes & Planters their heires & assignes by consent of the greater pt of them, To establish such Lawes & ordynances as are for their better governem^t^, and the same by such Officer or Officers as they shall by most voyces elect & choose to put in execution. AND lastly the said President and Counsell do graunt and agree to and with the said John Peirce and his Associates and others contracted with and ymployed as aforesaid their heires & assignes. That when they haue planted the Lands hereby to them assigned & appoynted, That then it shalbe lawfull for them with the pryvitie & allowaunce of the President & Counsell as aforesaid to make choyce of to enter into and to haue an addition of fiftie acres more for euy pson transported into New England with like resvacons condicons & priviledges as are aboue graunted to be had and chosen in such place or places where no English shalbe then settled or inhabiting or haue made choyce of and the same entered into a booke of Acts at the tyme of such choyce so to be made or within tenne Myles of the same (excepting on the opposite side of some great Navigable Ryver as aforesaid ; *And* that it shall and may be lawfull for the said John Peirce and his Associates their heires and assignes from tyme to tyme and at all times hereafter for their seuall defence & savetie to encounter expulse repell & resist by force of Armes aswell by Sea as by Land and by all wayes and meanes whatsoeu all such pson & psons as without the especiall lycense of the said President or Counsell and their successo[rs] or the greater pt of them shall attempt to inhabit within the seuall psincts & lymytts of their said Plantacon, Or shall enterpryse or attempt at any tyme hereafter distrucon, Invation, detryment or annoyaunce to the said Plantacon. AND THE SAID John Peirce and his associates and their heires & assignes do covennt & promyse to & with the said President & Counsell and their successo[rs], That they the said John Peirce and his Associates from tyme to tyme during the said Seaven Yeeres shall make a true Certificat to the said President & Counsell & their successors from the chief Officers of the places respectyvely of euy pson transported & landed in New England or shipped as aforesaid to be entered by the Secretary of the said President & Counsell into a Register book for that purpose to be kept AND the said John Peirce and his Associates Jointly and seually for them their heirs & assignes do covennt promyse & graunt to and with the said President & Counsell and their successors That the psons transported to this their pticuler Plantacon shall apply themselves & their Labors in a large and competent mann to the planting setting making and procuring of good & staple comodyties in & vpon the said Land hereby graunted vnto them as Corne & silk grasse hemp flaxe pitch and tarre sopeashes and potashes Yron Clapboard and other the like materialls. IN WITNESS whereof the said President & Counsell haue to the one pt of this pnte Indenture sett their seales And to th'other pt hereof the said John Peirce in the name of himself and his said Associates haue sett to his seale geven the day and yeeres first aboue written.

LENOX (Seale.)
BK. (Seale.)
HAMILTON (Seale.)
WARWICK (Seale.)
SHEFFIELD (Seale.)
FERD. GORGES (Seale.)

On the *Verso* of the instrument is the following indorsment:—

Sealed and Delivered by my Lord Duke in the Psence of

EDWARD COLLINGWOOD, CLERK.

NOTE. The signatures, are those of the Duke of Lenox, the Marquis of Buckingham, the Marquis of Hamilton, the Earl of Warwick, Lord Sheffield, and Sir Ferdinando Gorges.

PUBLIC RECORD OFFICE, LONDON.

Colonial, Entry Book, No. 59. pp. 101—108.

A Grant of the Province of Maine to Sr Ferdinando Gorges, and John Mason, Esqr. 10th of August, 1622.

This Indenture made the 10th day of August Anno Dom: 1622, & in the 20th yeare of the Reigne of our Sovereigne Lord James by the grace of God King of England, Scotland, France and Ireland, Defender of the Faith, &c^a. Betweene the President & Councell of New England on ye one part, and Sr Ferdinando Gorges of London, Knight and Captaine John Mason of London Esquire on ye other part Wittnesseth that whereas our said Sovereigne Lord King James for the makeing a Plantacon & establishing a Colony or Colonyes in ye country called or knowne by ye name of New England in America hath by his Highness Letters Patents under the Great Seale of England bearing date at Westm^r: the 3^d day of Novembe^r. in the 18th yeare of his Reigne given granted and confirmed vnto the Right Honorable Lodowick Duke of Lenox George Marquiss of Buckingham, James Marquiss Hamilton, Thomas Earle of Arundell, Robert Earle of Warwick, Sr Ferdinando Gorges Kn^t. and diverse others whose names are expressed in ye said Letters Patents, their successors and assignes that they shalbe one Body Politique and Corporate perpetuall and that they should have perpetuall Succession & one Comon Seale or Seales to serve for the said Body and that they and their Successors shalbe knowne called and incorporated by the name of the President & Councill established at Plymouth in the County of Devon for the planting ruling and governing of New England in America. And also hath of his especiall grace certaine knowledge and meer motion for him his heyres and successo^rs : & given granted and confirmed vnto the said President and Councill and their successo^rs: under the reservacons, limitacons and declaracons in the said Letters Patents expressed. All that part or porcon of that country now comonly called New England wch is situate lying and being between the Latitude of 40 and 48 Degrees northerly Latitude together wth the Seas and Islands lying wth in one hundred miles of any part of the said Coasts of the Country aforesaid and also all ye Lands, Soyle, grounds, havens, ports, rivers, mines as well Royal mines of Gold and Silver as other mines minerals pearls and pretious stones woods, quaryes, marshes, waters fishings hunting, hawking fowling comodities and hereditaments whatsoever together wth all prerogatives jurisdictions royaltys privileges franchises and preheminences within any of the said Territoryes and precincts thereof whatsover, To have hold possess and enjoy all and singular the said lands and premises in the said Letters Patent granted or menconed to bee granted unto ye said President and Councill their Successo^rs and assignes for ever to be holden of his Ma^ty his heyeres and successo^rs as of his highness Mano^r of East Greenwich in the County of Kent in free and common Soccage and not in capite or by Kn^ts service — Yeelding & paying to the King's Matie his heyers and successo^rs the one fifth part of all Gold and Silver oare that from time to time and att all times from the date of the said Letters Patents shall be there gotten had or obtayned for all services dutyes or demands as in & by his highnes said Letters Pattents amongst other divers things therein contayned more fully and at large it doth appeare, And whereas the said President & Councill have upon mature deliberacon thought fitt for the better furnishing and furtherance of the Plantacon in those parts to appropriate and allott to severall and particuler persons diverse parcells of Lands within the precincts of the aforesaid granted p^rmisses by his Ma^ts said Letters Patents. Now this Indenture witnesseth that ye s^d President and Councill of their full free and mutuall consent as well to the end that all the Lands, woods, lakes, rivers, waters, Islands and fishings wth all other the Traffiques proffits & comodityes whatsover to them or any of them belonging and hereafter in these presents menconed may be wholly and intirely invested appropriated severed and settled in and upon ye said Sr Ferdinando Gorges & Capt John Mason their heyres and assignes for ever as for diverse speciall services for the advancem^t of the s^d Plantacons and other good and sufficient causes and consideracons them especially thereunto moveing have given granted bargained sould assigned aliened sett over enfeoffed & confirmed — And by these presents doe give grant bargaine sell assigne alien sett over and confirme unto ye s^d Sr Ferdinando Gorges & Capt John Mason their heirs and assignes all that part of ye maine land in New England lying vpon ye Sea Coast betwixt ye rivers of Merimack & Sagadahock and to ye furthest heads of ye said Rivers and soe forwards up into the land westward untill threescore miles be finished from ye first entrance of the aforesaid rivers and half way over that is to say to the midst of the said two rivers wch bounds and limitts the lands aforesaid togeather wth all Islands & Isletts wth in five leagues distance of ye premisses and abutting vpon ye same or any part or parcell thereoff. As also all the lands, soyle, grounds, havens, ports, rivers, mines, mineralls, pearls, pretious stones woods quarryes marshes waters fishings hunting hawking fowling and other comodityes and hereditam[ts] whatsoever wth all and singular their apurtenances together wth all prerogatives rights royaltyes jurisdictions privileges franchises libertyes preheminences marine power in and vpon y[e] said seas and rivers as alsoe all escheats and casualtyes thereof as flotson petson lagon wth anchorage and other such dutyes immunityes sects isletts and apurtenances whatsover wth all ye estate right title interest claime and demands whatsoever w[ch] y[e] said President and Councell and their successo[rs] of right ought to have or claime in or to y[e] said porcons of lands rivers and other y[e] premisses as is aforesaid by reason or force of his highnes said Letters Patents in as free large ample and beneficiall maner to all intents constructions and purposes whatsoever as in and by the said Letters Patents y[e] same are among other things granted to y[e] said President and Councell afores[d] Except two fifths of y[e] Oare of Gold and Silver in these pnts hereafter expressed w[ch] said porcons of lands wth y[e] appurtenances the said S[r] Ferdinando Gorges and Capt. John Mason wth the consent of y[e] President & Councell intend to name y[e] PROVINCE OF MAINE To haveand to hould all the said porcons of land, Islands rivers and premises as aforesaid and all and singler other y[e] comodytyes and hereditam[ts] hereby given granted aliened enfeoffed and confirmed or menconed or intended by these presents to be given granted aliened enfeoffed and confirmed wth all and singuler y[e] appurtences and every part and parcell thereof unto y[e] said S[r] Ferdinando Gorges and Capt. John Mason their heyres and assignes for ever, To be holden of his said Ma[tie] his heyres and successo[rs] as of his Highnes Mano[r] of East Greenwich in y[e] County of Kent in free and common Soccage and not in capite or by Kn[ts] service. Neverthelesse wth such exceptions reservacons limitacons and declaracons as in y[e] said Letters Patents are at large expressed yeelding & paying unto our Soveraigne Lord the King his heyres & successo[rs] the fifth part of all y[e] oare of gold and silver that from time to time and att all times hereafter shall be there gotten had and obtayned for all services dutyes and demands. And alsoe yeelding and paying unto the said President and Councell and their Successors yerely the sum of Tenn shillings English money if it be demanded. And the said President and Councill for them and their Successo[rs] doe covenant and grant to and wth the said S[r] Ferdinando Gorges and Capt. John Mason ther heires and assignes from and after the ensealing and delivery of these presents according to y[e] purport true intent and meaning of these presents that they shall from henceforth from time to time for ever peaceably and quietly have hold possess and enjoye all y[e] aforesaid Lands Islands rivers and premises wth y[e] appurtenences hereby before given and granted or menconed or intended to be hereby given and granted and every part & parcell thereof wth out any lett disturbance denyall trouble interrupcon or evicon of or by y[e] said President and Councill or any person or persons whatsoever claiming by from or under them or their successo[rs] or by or under their estate right title or Interest, And y[e] said President and Councill for them and their Successo[rs] doe further Covenant and grant to & wth y[e] said S[r] Ferdinando Gorges & Capt. John Mason their heyres and assignes by these presents that they y[e] said President and Councill shall at all times hereafter vpon reasonable request at y[e] only proper cost and charges in the Law of y[e] said S[r] Ferdinando Gorges & Capt. John Mason their heyres and assignes doe make performe suffer execute and willingly consent unto any further act or acts conveyance or conveyances assurance or assurances whatsoever for y[e] good and perfect investing assuring and conveying and sure making of all the aforesaid porcons of Lands Islands rivers and all and singuler their appurtences to y[e] said S[r] Ferdinando Gorges and Capt. John Mason their heyres and assignes as by them their heyres and assignes or by his their or any of their Councill learned in y[e] Law shall bee devised advised or required. And further it is agreed by and between the said partyes to these presents and y[e] said S[r] Ferdinando Gorges and Captaine John Mason for them their heyres executors administrators and assignes doe covenant to and wth y[e] said President and Councill and their successo[rs] by these presents that if at any time hereafter there shall be found any oare of gold and silver within y[e] ground in any part of y[e] said premises that then they y[e] said S[r] Ferdinando Gorges and Capt. John Mason their heyres and assignes shall yield & pay vnto y[e] said President and Councill their successo[rs] and assignes one fifth part of all such gold and silver oare as shall be found within and vpon y[e] premises and digged and brought above ground to be delivered above ground & that always within reasonable and convenient time if it be demanded after y[e] finding getting and digging vp of such oare as aforesaid wth out fraud or covin and according to y[e] true intent and meaning of these Presents. And ye s[d] S[r] Ferdinando Gorges and Capt. John Mason doe further covenant for them their heyres and assignes that they will establish such government in y[e] s[d] porcons of lands and Islands granted unto them and y[e] same will from time to time continue as shall be agreeable as nere as may be to y[e] Laws and Customs of y[e] realme of England, and if they shall be charged at any time to have neglected their duty therein that then they will reforme the same according to y[e] directions of the President and Councill or in defaulte thereof it shall be lawfull for any of y[e] agrieved inhabitants or planters being tenn[ts] vpon y[e] said Lands to appeale to y[e] Chief Courts of Justices of y[e] President and Councill. And y[e] s[d] S[r] Ferdinando Gorges and Capt. John Mason doe covenant and grant to and wth y[e] said President and Councill their successors & assignes by these presents, that they ye said Sr Ferdinando Gorges and Capt. John Mason shall and will before ye expiracon of three years to be accompted from ye day of ye date hereof have in or vpon the said porcons of lands or some pt thereof one parte wth a competent guard and ten famillyes at ye least of his Mats subjects resident and being in and vpon ye same premises or in default thereof shall and will forfeite and loose to the said President & Councill the sum of one hundred pounds sterling money and further that if ye said Sr Ferdinando Gorges and Capt. John Mason their heires and assignes shall at any time hereafter alien these premises or any part thereof to any forraigne nations or to any person or persons of any forraigne nation without ye speciall licence consent and agreement of ye said President and Councill their successors and assignes that then ye part or parts of the said lands so alienated shall immediately returne back againe to ye use of ye said President and Councill. And further know yee that ye said President and Councill have made constituted deputed authorized and appointed and in their place & stead doe put Capt. Robt Gorges or in his absence to any other person that shall be their Governor or other officer to be their true and lawfull attorney and in their name and stead to enter the said porcons of Lands and other the premises wth their appurtences or into some part thereof in ye name of ye whole, for them and in their name to have and take possession and seizin thereof, or some part thereof in ye name of ye whole soe had and taken there for them and in their names to deliver the full and peaceable possession and seizin of all and singuler the said granted premises unto ye said Sr Ferdinando Gorges and Capt. John Mason or to their certaine attorney or attorneys in that behalf according to ye true intent and meaning of these presents, ratifying confirming all and allowing and whatsoever their said attorney shall doe in or about ye premises by these presents. In Witnesse whereof to one parte of these present Indentures remaining in the hands of Sr Ferdinando Gorges and Captaine John Mason the said President and Councill have caused their comon seale to be affixed and to the other of these present Indentures remaining in the custody of the said President and Councill the said Sr Ferdinando Gorges & Capt. John Mason have put to their hands and seales. Given ye day and yeare first above written.

PUBLIC RECORD OFFICE, LONDON.

Colonial Vol. II. No. 6. pp. 5—7.

MINUTES OF THE COUNCIL OF NEW ENGLAND.

Wednesday ye 24th of July 1622.

The Earle of Arundell. Sr. Ferd: Gorges.
Mr. Secretary Calvert. Sr. Saml. Argall.

Lord Dukes devition. It is ordered and agreed that the Lord Duke of Lenox have for his devident and part of the mayne Land of New England in America, from ye middle of Sawahquatock towards Sagadahoc, and his bounds that way to reach mid way betweene Sawahquatock and Sagadahoc upon ye Coast. And to reach 30 miles backward into ye Mayne. And 3 Leagues into ye sea.

Mr. Secretary Calverts devident. Mr. Secretary Calvert to begin his devident ye middle of Sagadahoc and to goe close to ye Lord Duke his bounds. And to have further into his devident the Island called by ye name of Setquin.

The Earle of Arundles devidt. The Earle of Arundele to have for his devident from ye middle of Sagadahoc, and to goe Northeast soe much on his side, as Mr. Secretary goes on ye other side upon ye Coast. And to reach miles backward into ye Mayne, and 3 leagues into ye Sea. And to have further into his Devident ye Iland called Menchigan.

Tenure of the grand pattent. It is propounded that ye Tenure in ye grand pattent is thought meet to bee held of ye Crowne of England by ye sword.

Tenure of private planters. And that private Planters shall hold of the Chamber of State to bee established there, and shall have power to create their owner Tenures to such as shall hold under them.

Nova Albion. The Country to bee called Nova Albion. That there may bee power given in the grand pattent to create Titles of Honour and precedency, soe as ye differ in nominacon from the titles used heere in England.

Touching the staying of the Timber. Mr. Ratcliffe is sent for by a Messinger of the Chamber to attend Earle of Arundell, to morrow by two of ye clock, touching Timber stayd by his appointment in ye woods at Whiteby.

Two Islands reserved for publike plantacon. It is thought meet that the two great Islands lying in ye river of Sagadahoc bee reserved for the publike plantacon.

A place for the publike Citty. Further that a place bee reserved betweene the branches of the two rivers for a publike Citty.

Touching ye renewing of the pattent. Mr. Thompson is appointed to attend the Lords for a Warrant to Mr. Attorney generall for drawing ye new Pattents, and Sr. Henry Spilman is desired to attend Mr. Attorney thereabouts.

The Lord Dukes and ye Earle of Arundells devidents, sett downe by Sr. Ferd: Gorges upon view of ye mapps.

The Lord Dukes Devident. The Lord Duke of Lenox is to have for a part of his Devident of ye lands in New England, from the midst of the river called Sawahquatock 15 English Miles in a straight line upon the sea coast, to ye Eastward of ye River. And 30 English miles backward of all the breadth afore-sd upp into the Mayne Land, North or North and by west, as ye Coast and River of Sawahquatock lyeth, accounting 1760 yards to every mile, with all ye fishings, Bayes, Havens, Harbours and Islands lyeing or being within 9 miles directly into ye sea (Excepting such Island, as are allready granted etc. All lyeing betweene the degrees of 43 and 44 etc.)

The Earle of Arundles Devidt. The Earle of Arundell to have for a part of his divident from ye Southermost poynt of Pethippscott East 12 Miles in a straight lyne as the coast lyeth on ye sea shoare. And 30 miles by all that breadth upp into the Mane Land due North. accounting 1760 yards to every mile, with all ye Fishings, Havens, Islands, etc. Lying and being within 9 miles directly into the sea, etc. Together with ye Islands of Menehiggan etc. All lyeing betweene the Degrees of 43 & 44.

PUBLIC RECORD OFFICE, LONDON.

Colonial, Vol. II. No. 16.

A Cattalogue of such Pattentes as I know granted for making Plantacons In New England.

The Councell of New England. Imps the Originall Patent granted to divers Lords some times in the Custody of Tho. Eyres, The Lords granted others.

1622. 1. A Pattent to David Thompson M Jobe, M Sherwood of Plimouth for a pt of Piscattowa Riuer in New England

2. A Pattent for a Plantation att New Plimouth to make a Corporation wch is pformed (See ante p 118)

1628. 3. A Pattent of the bay of the Massechusets Bay 3 my. South of Charles Riuer and 3 myles North of Merrimake 50 myles by sea shore but now haue subiugated most of the Cuntery wthin thes 10 yeares

4. A Pattent granted to Capt. Jo. Mason of Agawam now pos'sed by the peple of the Massechusets.

5. A Pattent granted to Capt. Jo. Mason and Sir Fir: Gorges for discouery of the Great Lakes. nothing ther in done

6. A Pattent to Sir Fir: Gorges Capt Norton and others for the Riuer of Accamenties wch was renewed by Edward Godfrey 1638: & p'palated wth inhabitance most att his charge and regulated 25 years, but now ould by the vnlimated power of the Mathesusets and by them caled Yorke as by pet'os may appeer.

7. A Pattent to Sir Fir: Gorges and divers others of a plantation and the sea coast of Pascatowae now . . . . it and sundery others, vnder the Massechusets.

8. A Pattent granted to Ed. Hilton, by him sould to mchants of Bristoll they sould it to my Lo. Say and Brokes, they to sume of Shrusbery: in Passatowa many towns now gouerned by ye Mathesusets

9. A Pattent granted to Jo. Stratton for Cape Porpase.

11, 12. Two Pattents to Ric. Vines & Tho: Lias for pt of Saco Riuer.

13. A Pattent to Capt. Tho: Camoke (Cammock) for Blake (Black) poynt.

14. A Pattent to Mr. Trelany of Plimouth for Cape Elizabeth.

15. A Pattent to Capt Leint for a Plantation att Casco.

16. A Pattent for a plantation att Pechipscot.

17. A Pattent for the Corporation of New Plimouth for Kenebecke (Jan. 13, 1629.)
21. A Pattent to Oliuer Godf . . . & others for Cap. Nosick, (Neddick.)
18. A Pattent for Mr Crispe and others for Sagadahock.
19. A Pattent for Mr Aldsworth and other of Bristoll for a plantation att Pemaquard
20. A Pattent of Richmonds Iland and 1500 ackers one the Mayne.

Quere what other Pattents haue binne granted by the Earle of Warwick, Lord Gorges, Sir: Gorges and others presidents of New England Company.

Noat in all thes Pattents ther is conditions to bee pformed and bounded wth reservations of Rentes

And sundery places yet to grant, as I humbly conceue by this Ho. Stat and not by the State of the Mathesusets wch yf not louked into may bee the inuinsible State of Amerrica

The Pattents aboue out of the bounds of The Mathesusets or the vnited Collones and of whome the sd vnited Collones as Conecticut, Ilands, of Erras Newhaven and The rest had ther Pattents noe appeales suffered from the Mathesusets in New England to ould England.

neather the Pattents to the Estwards euer had 1d. of their vast beneualence they haue had out of England and yearly haue what hath binne collected and heere disposed of is knowne to them and ther Agents heere, wheather Godfreys letter to the Ho. State heere ware soe Capitall a crime as to lose his Estate

yf the Mathesusets bee suffered to bee a free State the danger great

may as yet onely by letter bee pruented yf by Comittion or a generall Gouernor at prsent the consequence I leave.

indorsed. A List of sundery Pattents that haue binne granted for New England.

APPENDIX E.

[The popular belief has been that the Plymouth Colony designed to settle within the limits of the Dutch territory in the neighborhood of Manhattan, and such is the statement of Bradford. They negotiated with the Dutch for this purpose prior to their departure from Holland, and the application in their behalf was rejected. This is shown by the following papers, copied from the Holland Documents, published by the State of New York. Doc. Hist. Vol. 1.]

PETITION OF THE DIRECTORS OF THE NETHERLAND COMPANY.

To the Prince of Orange, &c.

Referred to the Deputies of the Board of Admiralty who are invited here for the 15th instant. Done 12th Feb. 1620. (signed) C. Aerssens 1620.

The Directors of the Company trading to New Netherlands, situate in latitude from 40 to 45 degrees, between New France and Virginia, reverently represent that they, the petitioners, have, as discoverers and first finders of said countries, traded hither now several years, in virtue of a certain general Charter from the High and Mighty Lords States General, dated the 10th March 1614; that they, also, have delivered to their High Mightinesses their written report, with a map of the situation and usefulness of said countries.

And whereas the petitioners' Charter has expired so that every one is now at liberty to trade there, they have again sent thither two ships, in order to preserve the reputation of said trade; some vessels have been likewise sent by others traders, exclusive of the Company.

Now it happens, that there is residing at Leyden a certain English Preacher, versed in Dutch language who is well inclined to proceed thither to live, assuring the petitioners that he has the means of inducing over four hundred families to accompany him thither, both out of the country and England, provided they would be guarded and preserved from all violence on the part of other potentates, by the authority and under the protection of your Princely Excellency and the High and Mighty Lords States General, in the propagation of the true, pure Christian religion, in the instruction of the Indians in that country in true learning, and in converting them to the Christian Faith, and thus through the mercy of the Lord, to the greater glory of this country's government, to plant there a new Commonwealth, all under and command of your Princely Excellency and the High and Mighty Lords States General. And whereas they, the Petitioners, have experienced that his Majesty of Great Britain would be disposed to people the aforesaid with the English nation, and by force to render fruitless their possession and discovery, and thus deprive this State of its right and apparently with ease surprise the ships of this country which are there, and are ordered to remain there the whole year; wherefore they, the petitioners, pray and request that your Princely Excellency may beningly please to take all the aforesaid into favorable consideration, so that, for the preservation of this country's rights, the aforesaid Minister and the four hundred families may be taken under the protection of this country, and that two ships of war may be provisionally despatched to secure to the State the aforesaid Countries, inasmuch as they would be of much importance, whenever the West India Company is established, in respect to the large abundance of timber fit for ship building &c., as may be seen by the accompanying report. On all which

(Endorsed) Petition of the Directors of the Company trading to New Netherlands.
12 February, 1620.

Further Resolution of the States General on the preceding Petition.

Tuesday, the 10th March 1620.

Folio 75. New Netherland Company. Resolved that the opinion of his Excellency shall be first obtained on the Petition presented by the Directors of the Company trading to New Netherland, before acting on it and on the advice of the Deputies from the Board of Admiralty.

Further Resolutions of the States General.

Friday the 10th of April, 1620.

Folio 113. New Netherland Company. Read the Petition of the Directors of the New Netherland Company, that their request should be favorably disposed, and resolved to obtain his Excellency's opinion thereon.

Resolution of the States General on the Petition of the New Netherland Company.

Saturday, the 11th April, 1620.

Folio 115. New Netherland Company. The petition of the Directors of the New Netherland Company, that they, for the people of said Island, may be assisted with two ships of war, is again rejected.

APPENDIX F.

COMMISSION TO SIR FERDINANDO GORGES AS GOVERNOR OF NEW ENGLAND. BY THE KING.

Many festing Our Royall pleasure for the establishing a generall Govern'mt in Our Territorye of New England for prevention of those evils that otherwise might ensue for default thereof.

Forasmuch as we have understood and been credibly informed of the many inconsistencies and mischiefs that have growne and are like more and more to arise amongst Our Subjects already planted in the parts of New England by reason of the severall opinions differing humors, and many other differences springing up between them and daily like to encreass and for that it rested not in the power of the Councill of New England (By our Gracious ffather's royall Charter established for those affaires) to redress the same, without we take the whole managing thereof into Our owne hands, and apply vnto Our immediate power and authority, which being perceived by the principall undertakers of those businesses, They have humbly resigned the said Charter unto us, that thereby there may bee a speedy order ta ken for reformation of the aforesaid Errors and mischiefs. And knowing it to be a Duty proper to our Royall justice not to suffer such numbers of Our people runne to ruine and so religious and good intents to languish for want of timely remedie and Soueraigne assistance Wee have therefore graciously accepted of the said Resignation and doe approve of their good affections to a service soe acceptable to God and to Us, And we have seriously advised with Our Councill both of the way of Reformation and of a person meet and able for that employment by whose grauity, moderation and experience wee have hopes to repair what is amiss and settlemt of those affaires to the good of Our people and honour of our Government. And for that purpose we have resolved with Our selfe to imploy Our Servant fferdinando Gorges Knight, as well for that Our Gracious ffather of blessed memory as Wee have had for a long time good experience of his fidelity, circumspection and knowledge of his Governmt in Martiall and Civill affaires, besides his understanding of the state of those Countryes wherein he hath been an immediate mover, and a principall Actor, to the great prejudice of his estate, long troubles and the loss of many of his good ffriends and servants in making *the first discovery of these Coasts*, and taking *the first seizure thereof* as of right belongs to Us Our Crowne and dignity, and is still resolved according to his Gracious pleasure to prosecute the same in his own person, which resolution and most comendable affection of his to serve Us therein, as We highly approve. So We hold it a property of Our princely care to second him with Our Royall and ample authority Such as shall bee meet for an employment soe eminent and the performance of Our Service therein, whereof Wee have thought it fitt to make publick declaration of Our said pleasure That thereby it may appear to our good Subjects the resolution We have graciously to provide for the peace and future good of those whose affection leads them to any such vndertaking, and withall to signifye that Our further will and pleasure is, That none bee permitted to goe into any those parts to plant or inhabit. But that they first acquaint our said Gouernor therewith, or such other as shall bee deputed for that purpose during his aboad heer in England. And who are to receive from him or them allowance to pass with his or their further directions where to sitt downe most for their perticuler commodityes and publick good of our Service (saving and reserving to all those that have joyned in the Surrender of the Great Charter of New England and have grants immediately to bee holden of Us, for their severall plantations in the said Countrye, ffree liberty at all times hereafter to go to themselves and also to send such numbers of people to their Plantations as by themselves shall be thought convenient,) Hereby strictly charging and commanding all our Officers and others to whom it shall or may appertaine, to take notice of this our pleasure and to be careful the same bee firmly observed as they or any of them shall answer the same at their uttermost perill. Given at the Court of Whitehall the 23d day of July 1637, and in the Sixteenth Yeare of Our Raigne.

APPENDIX G.

The following paper filed in the British State Paper Office, in the year 1600, was brought to notice by *Sainsbury*, in his Calender of Colonial State Papers, Vol. 1, page 4, a copy of which has been obtained since the foregoing pages were in type. It is referred to in note 2 on page 18, as bearing internal evidence that Sir Ferdinando Gorges was its author.

PUBLIC RECORD OFFICE, LONDON, A. D. 1600.

Colonial Correspondence, Vol. I. No. 9.

Yt beinge a verrye noble action to inlarge a dominion, wheath[r] yt be by ope conquest, wheare resistance is made, or by plantinge vpon plases neclected thorroughe the barbarousnes of the inhabitaints or neyghbors, the most vertuous minds are easly taken w[th] falseste hopes, ambision makinge a quicke sence of the good and easeines, and conferminge the minds againste all difficulties, and th[r]fore in this proposition of planting an Englishe Collonee in the no[r]the weste of America: conceivinge that the vttermoste argumentts w[th] the greateste hopes are expreste for the actio[n], I thincke yt is intended that the difficulties should be examined, thatt by the comparison; the possibility or glory of the worke mighte be for scene: yt is graunted the strengthe o[r] navy giues vs, the necessity of th maintenance butt how owre State stands more dangerous than eu[r] is not proved, and as itt is to bee wishte, that wee had plases of o[r] owne to furnishe soe necessary a comoditye as apertinentts to o[r] shippinge, soe muste yt be examined, wheath[r] o[r] cuntry should not bee as muche wrested or more to record them thence then by the wayes they haue them; and to the argument that god foresawe o[r] necessities to come of these provisions and therfore discouered to henry the 7th thes cuntries, yt weare to be ansured largely, butt heare this only god foresaw from the beginninge, his purpose to haue loue amongeste all men. and therefore gaue abondaunce and necessitie to countries to mak traffike, and expresse an vse one of anoth[r]., by which way of traffike wee are furnishte plentiouslye of all those commodities, neth[r] is yt to bee feared, that any tyme canne bringe forth a matter sav of trade to us except all the world att once should torne againste vs, and then wee muste keepe the new gotten by miracle and defend the ould hardly, and many examples make plaine and nowe wth vs wee see, thatt soe longe as a State resists the sword and cane furnishe mony or oth[r] matter for exchange, trafficke, will bringe the enemies moste forbidden comoditye in sufficiently, soe as yf the only benefitt weare the havinge a land from whence to fetche things necessary for our shippinge, yt weare like to bee boughte to deere, since wth the bringinge in of those trades from the easte, wee carry out our aboundinge commodities to the inrichinge of o[r] state w[ch] is sayde should likewyse bee downe this way, in two kindes, one by trafficke wth those nations that come theth[r] for fishe, and then over land, both w[ch] wayes require much tyme to bringe them to a ripenes, and in the trade ouer land theare riseth many difficulties, first accordinge to the expression made yt seemed to bee an infinite greate mayne of land, & wheare yt is said the inhabitants speake of a bitter water wth affection would vnderstand for salte yt may rightlier be conceaved to bee some lake w[ch] are common in waste countries and of suche nature, the watters of them, thorrowe the seprament of the earth, and the saileinge in of the levcs havinge noe currantes to clense, that they euer yeld a bitter taste. & all thoughe at the firste and vpon the vttermoste skirte of a land wee find butt a naked people, & suche as while wee stay not to giue them law[e] butt flatter them wth toyes, and exchange to theyre advantange, & so depte, apear well inclined & apte to reseue vs, yett by the comparison of this plasses wth others that haue bine discouered yt may be conseaved that they haue more with in land townes peopled, & will when they shall see that wee attempte vpon them, as a people that, will p'swade accordinge to owre knowledges theyre good or forse yt, then will they putt them selves into resistance, nothinge beinge able to change the forme of religion in the moste barbarous; but the spirite of revelation or an absolute conqueste; neythr is example only in many ages able to alter the habite of a lyfe confirmed in libertye and idleness to order & industrye, espessially in could regions wch brings forth a dull inflexible people, obstinately affectinge barbarous liberty, & jelious of all authority throughe much to theyre good, yf they had sence of civility to examine yt by; soe as I finde little foundation for hope of trafficke into eythr partts untell longe tyme had made vs masters of att least all the convenient passages & those secured by fortifications or inhabitants subjecte to or lause wch must firste haue a beginninge, & that is to bee examined how yt may rise from commodities of the fisheinge & exchange of trafficke & to invite vs the rathr lett vs admitt, the trafficke to Muscouia, is a hevey jorney to or marchants, in respecte of the lengthe of the voyage & couldness of the region wch suffers but one voyage in a yeare, & there owne marchants subiecte att pleasure of the prinse to arrests of thr psons & goods and to passe by a straighte sea of the denmarks stronge in shippinge and of whome wee cane haue noe security, and thatt the easterlings may increase in there mislike and injuries towards vs wheareof they have given aparent marks, and from hence lett vs conclude that anothr trade were more convenient for vs, and that this land of new found land, for the shortenes of the passage and openesse of the sea, & lesse intemperate could then Muscouia, havinge the commodities necessary for shippinge & trade settled there is more convenient, admittinge the necessities for ower navye to be there in abundance lett vs examine how a trade may be settled there & whatt may be the difficulties in their trade as well as in the settlinge; wherein wee mustee somethinge examnine the nature of the countrey, wth the state and inclinacon of or people, & the correspondansye of that contry wth othr new discoueries, peopled wch p'adventure at the firste aprehension make this worke seeme the easier: The contrye seems by the preposicon to be coulde, and to bringe forth commodities as coulde countries doth wth industery, or contry people, havinge euer bine bred wth plenty in a more temperate ayre, and naturally not very industrious, att home and lesse to seeke out plases, wheare thr labors are present and ther hopes a littell differed, wheareof we have too good experience by Ireland, wch beinge neere vs, a temperate and fertile contrye, subjecte to our owne lawes and halfe sivill, the portts and many plases friendly inhabited, notwthstandinge many of good reputacon, became undertakers there in the tyme of pease, could not invite our people, neyther in any compotent numbers, nor constantly in thr action, the reason beinge cheefely that in climatts that bringe forthe, butt yearely riches and that wth labor, a stocke and industrie must be adventured vpon expectacon; or able men are in the same trade at home allreddy, and loue ease and securitie and the poore men wantts welthe to disburse any thinge, wants wisdome to foresee the good, & wants vertu to haue patiens, and constantly to attend the reward of a good worke & industry: Those new discoueries inhabited by the portingalls & Spaniards, was in regions that althoughe they were intemperately hotte, yett bringe forthe by reason of there heate and fertillity, gould, silver, pretious stones, spises, riche dies & druggs, wch they have eyther for the gatheringe or by trafficke for small exchange wch was such a profitable increase, as att there returne both the prinses and people we are incurraged to inhabite not only there butt vpon all the passages and borders, that mighte eythr winne those cuntries to them or serue to keep out others or them in thr trade theathr, the countries for the most p'te all wheare they doe inhabite yieldinge abundance of all things both for vse and pleasure wth small industry; and for the intemperateness of the some for heate, by caues and forme of thr howses they wth as little labor and coste saue themselues fro that ayre, as wee in america are to doe by stoues from the could. The generall discouery beinge made, a particular discovery is to be made, of the plase wheare or nation should settle, yf there be hope eyther of mines or other good returne that may draw one a secondinge of the action, wch is moste to be doubted; for yf her Matie shall only countenance yt and recommende yt to her marchtts whoe may have for incorragmt the difficulties of the esterne fruits and a gratious fredo' of the trafficke of America to bee only rescued to the firste adventurers, yett when soe great a charge muste be firste issued as the sendinge of a compotent nomber to inhabite wth all necessaries requisitt for new inhabitants, and victualls for a hole yeare for them, & that thr retorne shall bringe home nothinge aboue the ordinarye frayte of fish and a narration of the sighte of Cuntrey and hope of better by the next adventure, yt is feared that the ordinary wayes of traed, beinge less chargeable, they will content themselves, and looke vpon the dangers and alterations a farr of, and eyther slowlye or not all giue second ; and wheare yt is propounded that or poore of England, may be easly sent thethr by the shippes that go to fishe yearely they beinge deliuered a . . . the portts, wth victualls for a yeere, or common people of England are not riche, & doe almoste repine att those most behoufull impositions wch are layed vpon them, for leveinge of souldiers & yett those willinge subsidies and payments they graunt to her Matie for juste reasons deputed in open p'liment, then we muste remember whatt pore they are thatt arre requisite to people a new Conqueste, not the impotente they muste remaine burden to the p'rishes, and then what charge would be requsite to eu'y man, wch is not onely compotent ap'rell for one yeare, money to bringe hime to the porte, &

armes of defence and offence, butt victualls for a year & to plante and build wth all, for wantinge eyther sufficiensy vntill the freute of there labors shalbe reapte to them, or wantinge indvstry to make sufficensy, & not havinge wheare-wth to exchange for victualls wth the savadge people they shalbe forste to doe outrages wch will shutt vp all way of trafficke or intelligens wth those people, and cause them to stand vpon force, before we . . . shalbe able to force them, or well to defend or selves: the number for the firste and seconde is likewyse to bee had in consideration, for the firste ytt cannott be lesse then may bee thoughte competent, to fortefye and secure the harboare, to plante and geather provision for the nexte yeare, & to defend what soeuer they shall take for theyrs wth out they bee lodgings, and att the firste to avoyde the losse of tyme in the trade, there would bee builded convenient lodgings and storehowses, for the safe-keepinge and exchanginge of suche commodities, and should a trafficke betweene vs the people or others toe fishe, & the second moste p'forme as much wth an increase furthr of a compotent troope or troopes, to discouer the riuers and the lande, wheather wth mines or other marchandise may bee presently putt in vse to giue incorragemt to th . . . adventurers, for certaine charge & vncertaine retornes will quickely quaile . . . an action thowghe well founded, and this may well bee lookte for, that the inhabitants, will giue vs noe better way then wee can forse, & will easly insulte vpon or weakenes yf they can find an advantage, besids wee are to conceaue, thatt the frenche whoe haue pretenses, & haue a secreat trafficke thethr; will repine & resiste yf they can or dare, all vnder the subiection of the Spaniards are declared opositts, & wee muste resolue that the kinge & thatt state will have his eyes open vpon ower actions, and will yf hee cane forse vs from any benifite, att leaste wee muste looke that from all his partts or wheare his seas thatt hee can com'and . . . lett vs in any trafficke from the sowthe he will barr thatt, neyther shall he need any of those traffiicks thatt plase will yeald vs, since bothe the easterlinges and dutches whoe haue greater trade into muscouia then . . . will furhishe hime of all needfull things thence thatt are to bee had in th . . . p'te of America we pretend toe. Now thorowe all these difficulties, yf the prinse would assiste yt in p'te & her marchants thatt are well affected goe liberallye into yt, & that the countries mighte bee stirred to an assistance by men in some meante measure, and some gentlemen moued to bee venturers, thatt should foresee not only the vndertakinge butt the secondinge; then I conceave that a worthye generall beinge chosen thatt mighte haue a Royall commission, and weare quallifide to judge of the sighte of plases for strengthe, & for comodities, would exercise justice in the to the presise the merchants adventurers & gentlemen or others that should thr p'sone . . . would keepe his troopes in obedience, industrye, & vse clemensy & justice to the inhabitinge, and yt mighte be a glorious action, for or prinse and countrie, honorable for the generall and adventurers and in tyme profitable, to the generall and p'ticular, & I doubte not an acceptab. service to god, the purpose and execution beinge to Magnifie his name in the extending of his worde, thoughe the example of or savior and his desiples is preachinge, butt not compellinge, vnlesse we may make vse of this thatt the firste tyme he sente forthe his desiples hee willed them to carry nothinge nor to care for any thinge, and the nexte tyme he commanded hime thatt had a Coate to sell itt and buy

APPENDIX H.

On page 42, note, reference is made to a paper addressed to the King, by the Scotch adventurers, REASONS ALLEDGED FOR HOLDING PORT ROYAL, which is of so much historic interest and value that we give the same in full, copied from the British State Paper Office, and not heretofore published.

PUBLIC RECORD OFFICE, LONDON.

COLONIAL, VOL. 5. NO. 102. T

Immediately about the time that Columbus discovered the Isle of Cuba, Sebastian Chabot set out from England by Henrie the seuenth did first discouer the continent of America, beginning at the Newfoundland, and thereafter going to the Gulph of Canada and from thence hauing seene Cap Bretton all along the Coast to Florida, By which discouery his Ma[tie] hath the title to Virginia, New England and New Scotland, as being then first discouered by Chabot at the charges of the K of England.

The French after this neglecting the knowledge they had thereafter by Jaques Cartier of the riuer of Canada as a cold climate, or as it may bee in regard it was challenged as first discouered by the English, having a great desire to possesse themselues in some part of America, they planted first a Colony vnder the charge of Mons[r] Villegas now in Brasill, and an other vnder the charge of Mons[r] Laudoniere in Florida, from both which they were expelled by the Spaniards.

Then giving ouer all hope of attempting anything that was belonging to the Spaniards and pressing by all meanes to have some interest in America, notwithstanding that the English (though they were not able to possesse the whole at first) had possessed themselves of that continent, discouered by them, by a Colonie in the South part thereof now called Virginia, and by an other in the North part thereof now called New England and New Scotland planted by Justice Popham.

The French in the time of Henry the Fourth vnder the charge of Mons[r] Poutrincourt hauing seene all the coasts of Newengland and Newscotland to both which parts they did then beginne to claime right. They seated themselues in Port Royal, out of which as soone as it was made knowne to the English they were displanted by S[r]. Samuel Argall, as having wrongfully intruded themselues within those bounds, which did belong to this Crowne, both by discouery and possession.

The remainder of this French Collony not hauing occasion to bee transported to France, stayed still in the Countrie, yet they were so neglected by the State, not owning them any more and hardly supplied in that which was necessary for them by voluntary adventurers, who came to trade in hope of their commodities in exchange of what they brought, and during the time of King James there was no complaint made vpon S[r.] Samuel Argall for hauing displanted them, and they were now lately glad to demand that protection from his Ma[te] which was not afforded them from any other. Whereby it may euidently appeare that his Ma[tes] title was thought good. Otherwise it is likely that the French King, if any wrong had beene done unto him, would haue sought to haue had the same repaired, either by Treatie or otherwise. But without making either any priuat complaint, or yet doing any publick Act against the same, They went next and seated themselues vpon the Northside of the river of Canada at Kebeck, a place whereunto the English by a preceding title might likewise haue claimed right. But small notice was taken thereof till during the time of the late warre, a Commission was giuen by his Ma[tie] to remoue them from thence, which was accordingly performed, the place being taken a little after the peace was concluded, which at that time had not come to the takers knowledge, and a Colonie of Scottish was planted at Port Royal, which had neuer beene repossesed nor claimed by the French since they were first remoued from the same.

This businesse of Port Royall cannot be made lyable to the articles of the peace, seeing there was no Act of hostilities comitted thereby, a Colonny onely beeing planted vpon his Ma[ts] owne ground, according to a patent granted by his Ma[ts] late deare father and his Ma[ts] self, hauing as good right thereunto as to any part of that Continent, and both the patent and possession taken thereupon was in the time of his Ma[ts] late deare father, as is set-downe at length in the voyages written by Purchas. But neither by that possession nor by the subsequent pla-ta'on hath any thing beene taken from the French whereof they had any right at all, or yet any possession for the time, and what might haue beene done either before the warre or since the warre without a breach of peace, cannot justly bee complained vpon for being done at that time.

After that the Scottish Colony was planted at Port Royal, they and the French who dwelled there hauing met with the Commanders of the Natives, called by them Sagamoes did make choice of one of the cheefe of them called Sagamo Sigipt to come in name of the rest to his Ma[tie] for acknowledging of his title, and to become his Ma[ts] subjects, crauing onely to bee protected by his Ma[tie] against their enemies, which demand of his was accepted by his Ma[tie] who did promise to protect them, as he reported to the rest at his returne.

Mons[r.] La Tour, who was cheefe comand[r] of the few French then in that countrie beeing neglected (as is said) by his owne Countriemen, and finding his Ma[ties] title not so much as questioned after theyr beeing expelled from Port Royall and the coming in of the Scottish necessary for his securitie did come along with the same Sagamo offring and demanding the like in name of the French who liue there, so that his Ma[te] hath a good right to New Scotland by discouere, by possession of his Ma[ts] subjects, by remouing of the French who had seated themselves at Port Royall and by Mons. La Tour the comander of them there his turning Tenant and by the volontarie turning tenants of the rest to his Ma[tie]. And that no obstacle might remaine the very Sauages by their Commissioner willingly offering their obedience vnto his Ma[te] so that his Ma[tie] now is bound to maintaine them both in regard of his subjects that have planted there vpon his warrant and of the promise that he made to the Commissioner of the Natiues that came to him from thence, as he promised to the Commissioner of the Natiues, and as all the subjects of his Ma[ts] ancient Kingdome of Scotland did humbly entreat at their last conuention, as may appeare by a letter to his Ma[te] from his Counsel to that effect.

indorsed. Reasons alleaged by the Scottish adventurers for the holding of Port Royal.

Discours
Concerning his Ma[ts] right and title to the port Royall and whole Canada, &c.
9 Sept[e] 1630.
Canada.

APPENDIX I.

CONSTITUENT CODE OF LAWS.

On page 94, Appendix A., Section 7 of the Virginia Charter of April 10, 1606, will be found a provision, that each of the Colonies is to have a Council which shall govern "*according to such Laws, Ordinances and Instructions as shall be in that behalf, given and signed by our Hand, or Sign Manual, and pass under the Privy Seal of our nation of England,*" &c.

This Constituent Code is contained in the following papers, under which the government at Sabino was ordained and established.

On the 19th of August, O. S., 1607, after taking possession, first came acts of religious worship — the Commission of Governor Popham was then read, authorizing the conducting hither of a Colony — then the Charter of April 10, 1606; after that, the "Laws to be observed and kept." Then followed the election of President and other officers, in conformity with the instructions of the following Constituent Code of Laws, signed by King James, under date of Nov. 20, 1606, and of March 9, 1607.

Articles, Instructions and Orders made, sett down and established by us, twentieth day of November, in the year of our raigne of England, France, and Ireland the fourth and of Scotland the fortieth, for the good Order and Government of the two several Colonies and Plantations to be made by our loving subjects, in the Country commonly called Virginia and America, between thirty four and forty five degrees from the Æquinoctial line —

Istructions, &c for the 2 Colonies of Virginia

Wheras, wee, by our letters pattents under our great seale of England, bearing date att Westminster, the tenth day of Aprill, in the year of our raigne of England, France, and Ireland the fourth, and of Scotland the 39th have given lycence to sundry our loving subjects named in the said letters pattents and to their associates, to deduce and conduct two several collonies or plantations of sundry our loving people willing to abide and inhabit in certaine parts of Virginia and America, with divers preheminences, privileges, authorities and other things, as in and by the same letters pattents more particularly it appeareth,

Recital of former charter

wee according to the effect and true meaning of the same letters pattents, doe by these presents, signed with our hand, signe manuel and sealed with our privy seale of our realme of England, establish and ordaine, that our trusty and well beloved Sir William Wade, Knight, our Lieutenant of our Tower of London, Sir Thomas Smith, Knight, Sir Walter Cope, Knight, Sir George More, Knight, Sir Francis Popham, Knight, Sir Ferdinando Gorges, Knight, Sir John Trevor, Knight, Sir Henry Montague, Knight, recorder of the City of London, Sir William Romney, Knight, John Dodderidge, Esq. Sollicitor General, Thomas Warr, Esqr. John Eldred of the citty of London, merchant, Thomas James of the citty of Bristol, merchant, and James Bagge of Plymouth, in the countyof Devonshire, merchant, shall be our councel for all matters which shall happen in Virginia of any the territories of America, between thirty-four and forty-five degrees from the æquinoctial line northward, and the Islands to the several collonies limited and assigned, and that they shal be called the King's Councel of Virginia, which councel or the most part of them shal have full power and authority, att our pleasure, in our name, and under us, our heires and successors, to give directions to the councels of the several collonies which shal be within any part of the said country of Virginia and America, within the degrees first above mentioned, with the Islands aforesaid, for the good government of the people to be planted in those parts, and for the good ordering and disposing of all causes happening within the same, and the same to be done for the substance thereof, as neer to the common lawes of England, and the equity thereof, as may be, and to passe under our seale, appointed for that councel,

Nov. 20th 4th James 1st.

Councillors, how nominated—

which councel, and every or any of them shall from time to time be increased, altered or changed, and others put in their places, att the nomination of us, our heires and successors, and att our and their will and pleasure, and the same councel of Virginia, or the more part of them, for the time being shall nominate and appoint the first severall concellours of those several councells, which are to be appointed for those two several colonies, which are to be made plantations in Virginia and Amerca, between the degrees before mentioned, according to our said letters pattents in that behalfe made;

Each Council to choose a president; his continuance in office.

and that each of the same councels of the same several colonies shal, by the major part of them, choose one of the same councel, not being the minister of God's word, to be president of the same councel, and to continue in that office, by the space of one whole year, unless he shall in the mean time dye or be removed from that office;

Vacancies how supplied.

and wee doe further hereby establish and ordaine, that it shal be lawful for the major part of either of the said councells, upon any just cause, either absence or otherwise to remove the president or any others of that Councel, from being either president or any of that councel, and upon the deathes or removal of any of the presidents or councel, it shal be lawfull for the major part of that councel, to elect another in the place of the party soe dying or removed, so alwaies, as they shal not be above thirteen of either of the said councellours, and we doe establish and ordaine, that the president shal not continue in his office of presidentship above the space of one year; and wee doe specially ordaine, charge, and require, the said presidents and councells, and the ministers of the said several colonies respectively, within their several limits and precincts, that they, with all diligence, care, and respect, doe provide, that the true word, and service of God and Christian faith be preached, planted, and used, not only within every of the said several colonies, and plantations but alsoe as much as they may amongst the salvage people which doe or shall adjoine unto them, or border upon them, according to the doctrine, rights, and religion now professed and established within our realme of England, and that they shall not suffer any person, or persons to withdrawe any of the subjects or people inhabiting, or which shall inhabit within any of the said several colonies and plantations from the same, or from their due allegiance, unto us, our heirs and successors, as their immediate soveraigne under God, and if they shall find within any of the said colonies and plantations, any person or persons soe seeking to withdrawe any of the subjects of us, our heirs or successors, or any of the people of those lands or territories, within the precincts aforesaid, they shall with all diligence, him or them soe offending, cause to be apprehended, arrested, and imprisoned, until he shall fully and throughly reforme himselfe, or otherwise, when the cause so requireth, that he shall, with all convenient speed be sent into our realme of England, here to receive condigne punishment for his or their said offence or offences, and moreover wee doe hereby ordaine and establish for us, our heirs and successors, that all the lands, tenements, and hereditaments to be had and enjoyed by any of our subjects within the precincts aforesaid, shal be had and inherited and injoyed, according as in the like estates they be had and enjoyed by the lawes within this realme of England; and that the offences of tumults, rebellion, conspiracies, mutiny and seditions in those parts which may be dangerous to the estates there, together with murder, manslaughter, incest, rapes, and adulteries committed in those parts within the precincts of any the degrees above mentioned (and noe other offences) shal be punished by death, and that without the benefit of the clergy, except in case of manslaughter, in which clergy is to be allowed, and that the several presidents and councells, and the greater number of them, within every of the several limits and precincts, shall have full power and authority, to hear and determine all and every the offences aforesaid, within the precinct of their several colonies, in manner and forme following, that is to say, by twelve honest and indifferent persons sworne upon the Evangelists, to be returned by such ministers and officers as every of the said presidents and councells, or the most part of them respectively shall assigne, and the twelve persons soe returned and sworne shall according to their evidence to be given unto them upon oath and according to the truth, in their consciences, either convict or acquit every of the said persons so to be accused and tried by them, and that all and every person or persons, which shall voluntarily confesse any of the said offences to be committed by him, shall, upon such his confession thereof, be convicted of the same, as if he had been found guilty of the same, by the verdict of any such twelve jurors, as is aforesaid; and that every person and persons which shall be accused of any of the said offences, and which shall stand mute, or refusing to make direct answer thereunto, shall be, and he held convicted of the said offence, as if he had been found guilty by the verdict of such twelve jurors, as aforesaid; and that every person and persons soe convicted either by verdict, his own confession, or by standing mute, or by refusing directly to answer as aforesaid of any the offences beformentioned, the said presidents, or councells, or the greatest number of them within their several precincts and limits, where such conviction shall be had and made as aforesaid, shall have full power and authority, by these presents, to give judgment of death upon every such offender without the benefit of the clergy, except only in case of manslaughter, and noe person soe adjudged, attainted, or condemned shall be reprieved from the execution of the said judgment, without the consent of the said president and councel or the most part of them by whom such judgment shall be given; and that noe person shall receive any pardon or be absolutely discharged of any the said offences, for which he shall be condemned to death as aforesaid, but by pardon of us, our heirs and successors, under our great seale of England; and wee doe in like manner establish and ordaine, if any either of

Christian religion to be preached among the colonists and the savages.

Penalty for withdrawing any of the people from their religion or allegiance.

How lands to descend and pass.

How certain offences to be punished.

Trial by jury.

Judgement on standing mute, or by confession.

President and Councel to pronounce judgment.

Reprieve by the president and council—pardoning by the King.

Offenders to be tried in their colony.

the said collonies shall offend in any of the offences before mentioned, within any part between the degrees aforesaid, out of the precincts or his or their collony, that then every such offender or offenders shall be tried and punished as aforesaid within his or their proper collony; and that every the said presidents and councells, within their several limits and precincts, and the more part of them shall have power and authority by these presents, to hear and determine all and every other wrongs, trespasses, offences, and misdemeanors whatsoever, other than those before mentioned, upon accusation of any person, and proofe thereof made, by sufficient witness upon oath; and that in all those cases the said president & councel, and the greater number of them, shall have power and authority, by these presents respectively, as is aforesaid, to punish the offender or offenders, either by reasonable corporal punishment and imprisonment, or else by convenient fine, awarding damages or other satisfaction, to the party grieved, as to the said president and councell, or to the more part of them, shall be thought fitt and convenient, having regard to the quality of the offence, or state of the cause; and that also the said president and councel, shall have power and authority, by virtue of these presents, to punish all manner of excesse, through drunkennesse or otherwaise, and all idle loytering and vagrant persons, which shall be found within their several limits and precincts, according to their best discretion and with such convenient punishment, as they or the most part of them shall think fitt; alsoe our will and pleasure, concerning the judicial proceedings aforesaid, that the same shall be made and done summarily, and verbally without writing, until it come to the judgment or sentence, and yet nevertheless our will and pleasure is, that every judgment and sentence hereafter to be given in any causes the aforesaid, or in any other of the said several presidents and councells or the greater number of them, within their several limits and precincts, shall be breifely and summarily registered into a book, to be kept for that purpose, together with the cause for which the said judgment or sentence was given; and that the said judgment and sentence, so registered and written, shall be subscribed with the hands or names of the said president, and councel, or such of them as gave the judgment or sentence; alsoe our will and pleasure is, and wee doe hereby establish and ordaine, that the said several collonies and plantations, and every person and persons of the same, severally and respectively, shall within every of their several precincts, for the space of five years, next after their first landing upon the said coast of Virginia and America, trade together all in one stocke or devideably, but in two or three stocks at the most, and bring not only all the fruits of their labours there, but alsoe all such other goods and commodities which shall be brought out of England, or any other place, into the same collonies, into severall magazines or store houses, for that purpose to be made, and erected there, and that in such order, manner and form, as the councel of that colony, or the more part of them shall sett downe and direct: and our will and pleasure is, and wee doe in like manner ordaine, that in every of the said collonies and plantations there shall be chosen there, elected yearely, by the president and councell of every of the said several colonies and plantations or the more part of them, one person, of the same colony and plantation, to be treasurer or cape-merchant of the same collony and plantation to take charge and manageinge of all such goods, wares and commodities which shall be brought into or taken out of the severall magazines or store houses; the same treasurer or cape-merchant to continue in his office by the space of one whole year, next after his said election, unless he shall happen to dye within the said year, or voluntarily give over the same or be removed for any just or reasonable cause; and that thereupon the same president & councell, or the most part of them, shall have power and authority to elect him again or any other or others in his room or stead, to continue in the same office as aforesaid; and that alsoe there shall be two or more persons of good discretion within every of the said colonies and plantations elected and chosen yearely during the said terme of five years, by the president and councell of the same collony, or the most part of them respectively, within their several limits and precincts, the one or more of them to keep a book in which shall be registered and entred all such goods, wares, and merchandizes, as shall be received into the several magazines or store houses within that collony, being appointed for that purpose, and the other to keep a like book, wherein shall be registered all goods, wares, and merchandizes which shall issue or be taken out of any the several magazines or store-houses of that collony, which clarks shall continue in their said places but att the will of the president and councell of that colony, whereof he is or of the major part of them; and that every person or

President & council to have power to hear and determine all civil causes.

To punish excesses and drunkenness.

How judicial proceedings to be entered.

How the colonists are to trade for the first 5 years.

Cape-merchant.

Clerks.

Books.

Magazines.

every the said several colonies, and plantations shall be furnished with all necessaries out of those several magazines or storehouses which shall belong to the said colony and plantation, in which that person is, for and during the terme and time of five years, by the appointment, direction and order of the president and councell there, or the said cape merchant and two clerks or of the most part of them, within the said several limits and precincts of the said colonies and plantations; alsoe our will and pleasure is, and wee doe hereby ordain, that the adventurers of the said first colony and plantation, shall and may during the said terme of five years, elect and choose out of themselves one or more companions, each company consisting of three persons att the least who shall be resident att or neer London, or such other place, and places, as the councell of the colony for the time being, or the most part of them during the said five years shall think fitt, who shall there from time to time take charge of the trade an accompt of all such goods, wares and merchandizes, and other things which shall be sent from thence to the company of the same colony, or plantation in Virginia, and likewise of all such wares, goods and merchandizes, as shall be brought from the said colony or plantation unto that place within our realme of England, and of all things concerning the mannaging of the affaires and profits concerning the adventurors of that company which shall soe passe out of or come into that place or port; and likewise our will and pleasure is, that the adventurors in the said second colony and plantation shall and may during the said terme of five years elect out of themselves, one or more companies, each company consisting of three persons att the least, who shall be resident att, or near Plymouth in our county of Devon, within our realme of England, and att such one, two, or three other places or ports, as the councell of that colony, or the most part of them shall think fitt, who shall there, from time to time, take care and charge of the trade and account of all such goods, wares; merchandizes and other things, which shall be sent from thence from the same colony and plantation in Virginia, and likewise of all such goods, wares and merchandizes as shall be brought from the said colony and plantation in Virginia, into our realme of England, and of all things concerning the mannaging of the affaires and profits of the adventurors of that company; alsoe our will and pleasure is, that no person or persons shall be admitted into any of the said colonies and plantations there to abide and remaine, but such as shall take not only the usual oath of obedience to us, our heirs, and successors, but alsoe the oath which is limited in the last session of Parliament holden at Westminster in the fourth year of our raigne, for their due obedience unto us our heirs and successors, that the trade to, and from any the colonies aforesaid may be managed to, and from such ports and places, within our realme of England, as is before in these articles intended, any thing set down heretofore to the contrary notwithstanding, and that the said President and Councell of each of the said colonies, and the more part of them respectively shall and may lawfully from time to time constitute, make and ordaine such constitutions, ordinances, and officers, for the better order, government and peace of the people of their several collonies, soe alwaies as the same ordinances, and constitutions doe not touch any party in life or member, which constitutions, and ordinances shall stand, and continue in full force, untill the same shall be otherwise altered, or made void, by us, our heirs, or successors, or our, or their councel of Virginia, soe alwaies as the same alterations, be such as may stand with, and be in substance consonant unto the lawes of England, or the equity thereof; furthermore, our will, and pleasure is, and wee doe hereby determine and ordaine, that every person and persons being our subjects of every the said collonies and plantations shall from time to time well entreate those salvages in those parts, and use all good means to draw the salvages and heathen people of the said several places, and of the territories and countries adjoining to the true service and knowledge of God, and that all just, kind and charitable courses, shall be holden with such of them as shall conforme themselves to any good and sociable traffique and dealing with the subjects of us, our heires and successors, which shall be planted there, whereby they may be the sooner drawne to the true knowledge of God, and the obedience of us, our heirs, and successors, under such severe paines and punishments, as shall be inflicted by the same several presidents, and councells of the said several colonies, or the most part of them within their several limits and precincts, on such as shall offend therein, or doe the contrary; and that as the said territories and countries of Virginia and America within the degrees aforesaid shall from time to time increase in plantation by our subjects, wee our heires and successors will ordaine and give such order, and further in-

Margin notes: Companies. — Adventurors in the 2d colony may within five years elect out of themselves one or more companies. — Their power and duty. — Colonists to take certain oaths. — President and Council. — May pass ordinances, &c. — Must promote civilization among the Indians. — Provision for further ordinances, &c.

structions, lawes, constitutions, and ordinances for the better order, rule and government of such, as soe shall make plantations there, as to us, our heires and successors, shall from time to time be thought fitt and convenient, which alwaies shall be such, as may stand with, or be in substance, consonant unto the lawes of England, or the equity thereof, and lastly wee doe ordaine, and establish for us, our heires and successors, that such oath shall be taken by each of our councellors here for Virginia concerning their place and office of councell, as by the privy councell of us, our heires and successors of this our realme of England, shall be in that behalf limited and appointed; and that each councellor of the said colonies shall take such oath, for the execution of their place and office of councel, as by the councel of us, our heires and successors here in England, for Virginia shall in that behalfe be limited and appointed, and as well those several articles and instructions herein mentioned and contained, as alsoe all such as by virtue hereof shall hereafter be made and ordained, shall as need shall require, by the advice of our councel here for Virginia shall be transcripted over unto the said several councells of the said several colonies, under the seale to be ordained for our said councell here for Virginia. In witnesse, &c.

Councillors to take an oath.

March 9. 4th James 1st.

An Ordinance and Constitution enlarging the number of our Councel for the two several Colonies and Plantations in Virgina and America, betweeen thirty-four and forty-five degrees of northerly latitude, and augmenting their authority, for the better directing and ordering of such things as shall concerne the said Colony.

Recital.

James, by the grace of God, &c. Whereas wee, by our letters pattents, under our great seale of England, bearing date the tenth day of April last past, have given lycence to sundry our loving subjects, named in the said letters patents, and to their associates, to deduce and conduct two several colonies or plantations of sundry our loving people, willing to abide and inhabit in certain parts of Virginia and America, and divers preheminences, priviledges, authorities and other things as in and by the said letters patents more particularly it appeareth; and whereas wee, according to the effect and true meaning of the said letters patents, have, by a former instrument signed with our hand and signe manuel, and sealed with our privy seal of our realme of England, established and ordained, that our trusty and well-beloved Sir William Wade, Knight, our Lieutenant of our Tower of London, Sir Thomas Smith, Knight, Sir Walter Cope, Knight, Sir George More, Knight, Sir Francis Popham, Knight, Sir Ferdinando Gorges, Knight, Sir John Trevor, Knight, Sir Henry Montague, Knight, recorder of our citty of London, Sir William Romney, Knight, John Dodderidge, Esq[r]. our solicitor general, Thomas Warr, Esqr. John Eldred of our city of London, merchant, Thomas James of our citty of Bristol, merchant, and James Bagge of Plymouth, in our county of Devon, merchant, should be our councel for all matters which should happen in Virginia or any territories of America aforesaid, or any actions, businesse or causes for and concerning the same, which councel is from time to time to be increased, altered, or changed att the nomination of us, our heirs and successors, and att our and their will and pleasure; and whereas our said councel have found by experience, their number being but fourteen in all, and most of them dispersed by reason of their seval habitations far and remote the one from the other, and many of them in like manner far remote from our citty of London, where, if need require, they may receive directions from us and our privy councel, and from whence instructions and directions may be by them left and more readily given, for the said colonies, that when very needful occasion requireth, there cannot be any competent number of them, by any meenes be drawne together for consultation; for remedy whereof our said loving subjects of the several colonies aforesaid, have been humble suitors unto us, and have to that purpose offered unto our royal consideration, the names of certaine sage and discreet persons, and having with the like humility entreated us, that the said persons or soe many of them, as to us should seem good, might be added unto them, and might (during our pleasure) be of our councel for the foresaid colonies of Virginia, wee therefore, for the better establishing, disposing, orderring and directing of the said several colonies, within the degrees aforesaid, and of all such affaires, matters, and things, as shall touch and concerne the same, doe by these presents, signed with our hand and signe manuel, and seal-

Ordinance &c. enlarging the councils.

Former councillors.

Their number.

ed with our privy scale of our realme of England, establish and ordaine, that our trusty and well beloved Sir Thomas Challonor, Knight, Sir Henry Nevil, Knight, Sir Fulks Grevil, Knight, Sir Jo'n Scot, Knight, Sir Robert Mansfield, Knight, Sir Oliver Cromwell, Knight, Sir Morrice Berkeley, Knight, Sir Edward Michelbourne, Knight, Sir Thomas Holcroft, Knight Sir Thomas Smith, Knight, clerk of our privy councel, Sir Robert Kelligrew, Knight, Sir Robert Croft, Knight, Sir George Kopping, Knight, Sir Edwyn Sandys, Knight, Sir Thomas Row, Knight, and Sir Anthony Palmer, Knight, nominated unto us by and on the behalfe of the said first colony ; Sir Edward Hungerford, Knight, Sir Jo'n Mallet, Knight, Sir John Gilbert, Knight, Sir Thomas Freake, Knight, Sir Richard Hawkings, Knight, Sir Bartholomew Mitchel, Knight, Edward Seamour, Esqr. Bernard Greenville, Esqr. Edward Rodgers, Esqr. and Matthew Sutcliffe, Doctor of Divinity, nominated to us by and on the behalfe of the said second colony shall, together with the persons formerly named, be our councel for all matters, which shall or may conduct to the aforesaid plantations, or which shall happen in Virginia or any the territories of America, between thirty-four and forty-five degrees of northerly latitude from the æquinoctial line, and the Islands to the several colonies limited and assigned. That is to say, the first colony, from thirty-four to forty-one degrees of the said latitude, and the second colony between thirty-eight and forty-five degrees of the said latitude; and our further will and pleasure, and by these presents for us, our heires and successors, wee doe grant unto our said councel of Virginia, that they or any twelve of them att the least for the time being whereof six att the least to be members of one of the said colonies, and six more att the least to be members of the other colony, shall have full power and authority, to ordaine, nominate, elect, and choose any other person, or persons at their discretion to be and to serve as officer or officers, to all offices and places, that shall by them be thought fitt and requisite for the businesse and affaires of our said councel, and concerning the plantation or plantations aforesaid, and for the summoning, calling, and assembling of the said councel, together when need shall require, or for summoning and calling before the said councel, any of the adventurors, or others which shall passe on unto the said several colonies to inhabit or to traffick there or any other such like officer, or officers, which in time shall or may be found of use, behoofe or importance unto the councel aforesaid [And the said councel or any twelve of them as is aforesaid shall have full power and authority from time to time to continue or to alter or change the said officers and to elect and appoint others in their roomes and places, to make and ordain acts and ordinances for the better ordering disposing and marshalling of the said several colonies and the several adventurers or persons going to inhabit in the same several colonies, or of any provision or provisions for the same, or for the direction of the officers aforesaid, or for the making of them to be subordinate or under jurisdiction one of another, and to do and execute all and every of their act and things which by any our grants or letters patents heretofore made they are warranted or authorised to do or execute so as always none of the said acts and ordinances or other things be contrary or repugnant to the true intent and meaning of our said letters patents granted for the plantation of the said several colonies in Virginia and territories of America as aforesaid, or contrary to the laws and statutes in this our realme of England, or in derogation of our prerogative royal. Witness ourself at Westminster, the ninth day of March, in the year of our reign of England, France and Ireland the fourth, and of Scotland the fortieth, &c.]

Additional councillors nominated by the 1st Colony.

By the 2d colony.

Any 12 may act.

Their power

May change their officers.

APPENDIX J.

On page 81, reference is made to the grant of January 13, 1629, to William Bradford, for the benefit of the Plymouth Colony, establishing their territorial boundaries, and adding largely to their means of support, by the donation of the large and valuable tract on the Kennebec, extending fifteen miles on each side of that river, from the Cobbessee-Contee (Gardiner) to the Nequamkike (Waterville.) To show under what circumstances this Charter was given, and as evidence of the estimation in which Sir Ferdinando Gorges was held by the Plymouth Company, we give below two letters from Governor Bradford to him, in 1627 and 1628, taken from Bradford's Letter Book, printed in the Massachusetts Historical Collections, 1st series, vol. III, pages 57 and 63. The letters, in connection with the subsequent grant, show how noble and generous was Gorges' conduct to this Plymouth Colony, and refutes the assertions subsequently made by Bradford, of his lack of friendship for them. The Plymouth Company at the outset, was made up of sincere and worthy people, but gradually assimilated toward the fierce characters that ruled the Colony of Massachusetts Bay.

LETTER TO SIR FERDINANDO GORGES.

Honorable Sir :

My humble duty remembered ; we have of late received letters from the Dutch Plantation, and have had speech with some of them. I hold it my duty to acquaint your worship, and the rest of the Honorable Council, therewith, unto whom we have likewise writ, and sent, the copies of their letters, that together with their, and your honorable directions, we may know how to order ourselves herein. They have used trading there this six or seven and twenty years, but have begun to plant of later time, and now have reduced their trade to some order, and confined it only to their company, which heretofore was spoiled by their seamen and interlopers, as ours is this year most notoriously ; of whom we have made some complaint in our letters to the Council, not doubting but we shall find worshipful furtherance therein. We are now upon concluding with our adventurers, and shall be put upon hard straits by great payments which we are enfored to make for sundry years, or else to leave all, which will be to us very difficult : and, to say the truth, if these disorders of fishermen and interlopers be not remedied, no plantations are able to stand, but will decay, whereas otherwise they may subsist and flourish : Thus in all humbleness, I take leave, and rest

At your service, William Bradford.

Plymouth, June 15, Anno 1627.

P. S. Beside the spoiling of the trade this last year, our boat and men, had like to have been cut off by the Indians, after the fishermen were gone, for the wrongs which they did them, in stealing their skins, and other abuses offered them, both the last year and this : and besides, they still continue to truck pieces, powder and shot with them, which will be the overthrow of all, if it be not looked unto.

TO SIR FERDINANDO GORGES.

Honorable Sir :

As you have ever been, not only a favorer, but also a most special beginner and furtherer of the good of this country, to your great cost and no less honor, we, whose names are underwritten, being some of every plantation in the land, deputed for the rest, do humbly crave your worship's help and best assistance, in the speedy, (if not too late,) redress of our almost desperate state and condition in this place, expecting daily to be overrun and spoiled by the savages, who are already abundantly furnished with pieces, powder and shot, swords, rapiers and javelins : all of which arms and munition is this year plentifully and publicly sold unto them by our own countrymen ; who under the pretence of fishing come a trading amongst them: yea, one of them (as your worship may further understand by our particular informations) hath for his part sold twenty or twenty-one pieces, and one hundred weight of powder, by which you may conceive of the rest. For we hear the savages have above sixty pieces amongst them : besides other arms : in a word, there is almost nothing vendible amongst them, but such munitions so they have spoiled the trade in all other things. And as vice is always fruitful, so from the greedy covetousness of the fishermen, and their evil example, the like hath began to grow amongst some, who pretend themselves to be planters, though indeed they intend nothing less but to take opportunity of the time and provide themselves and begone, and leave others to quench the fire which they have kindled, of which number, Mr. Thomas Morton is one, being of late a dweller in the Massachusetts Bay, and the head of a turbulent and seditious crew, which he had gathered unto him, who dwelling in the midst of us, hath set up the like practice in these parts and hath sold sundry pieces to the natives, who can use them with great dexterity, excelling our English therein, and have been vaunting with them at Sowams, Narragansett and many other places, so as they are spread both North and South all the land over to the great peril of all our lives. In the beginning of this mischief we sought friendly to dissuade him from it, but he scorned us therein, and prosecuted it the more; so as we were constrained for the safety of ourselves, our wives and innocent children, to apprehend him by force (though with some peril) and now have sent him to the Council of New England to receive according to his demerits, and be disposed of as their honors shall think fit, for the preventing of further mischief, the safety of our lives, and the terror of all other delinquents in the same kind. Now our hope and humble request is, that your Worship and those honorable of his Majesty's Council for New England will commiserate our case, tender our lives and pity our infants; and consider the great charges and expenses that we and our assistants and associates have been at, besides all the miseries and hardships that we have broken through in these beginnings which have hitherto happily succeeded for the planting of this country which is hopeful, if it be cherished and protected against the cankered covetousness of these licentious men; if not we must return and quit the country: Wherefore we beseech your Worship to afford us your favorable assistance and direction in bringing this man to his answer before those whom it may concern; and to credit our true informations sent by this bearer, lest by his audacious and colored pretences he deceive you which know not things as we do: As likewise that such fishermen may be called to account for their great abuses offered this year and the last, as many as have been known to offend in this case; and that your Worship for the time to come would be a means in what you may, that we may be strengthened with some authority or good order amongst ourselves for the redressing of the like abuses which may arise amongst us, till some general government be established in the land: Thus in hopeful assurance that your Worship will make a favorable construction of these our honest intendments and humble requests, we commend you to the protection of the Highest, and rest,

At your service, &c.

June 9, Anno 1628.

[This letter, Bradford says, was subscribed by some of the chief of every plantation, Plymouth, Naumkeag, (Salem,) Pascataquack and Natascot.]

APPENDIX K.

The 3d Edition of L'Escarbot's "*History of New France*," published in Paris, in 1618, contains an Address to the King, which we here re-produce in full, and which confirms the views maintained by the writer, as to the effect of the revocation of De Mont's Charter, on the destinies of the new world. That revocation according to L'Escarbot worked "*the ruin of a fine Enterprise, which promised the speedy establishment of a new kingdom.*"

To the very Christian King of France and of Navarre, LOUIS XIII, Duke of Milan, Count of Ast, Lord of Genoa.

Sire:—There are two principal things which ordinarily incite Kings to make conquests: zeal for the glory of God, and the augmentation of their own. In this double subject, our Kings, your predecessors, have been for a long time invited to extend their dominion beyond the ocean, and to form new empires there, at little expense, by just and lawful ways. They have expended some sums, and are now expending, in different places. But after having discovered the country they have been satisfied with that and the French name is fallen into contempt, not through want of virtuous men who might carry it upon the wings of the loftiest winds, but by the plots, arts and practices of the enemies of your Crown, who have been able to govern the minds of those whom they have felt, were able to do something to forward such an affair. Meanwhile, the Spaniard, formerly weak, by our indifference, has rendered himself powerful in the East, and in the West, without our having had the honorable ambition, not to precede him, but to second him, not to second him, but to avenge the insults done by them to our French, who under the consent of our Kings, wished to have a share in the inheritance of those new and immense lands that God presented to the men of these parts about twenty-six years ago. It was a thing worthy of the late King of glorious memory, your father, *Sire*, to reform these things; but having lofty designs for the welfare of the Christian republic he had left to your young years, these exercises and the establishment of a new kingdom in the new world: whilst on this side he would labor to reunite different religions, and bring to a good understanding the Christian Princes much prejudiced between themselves. Now the jealousy of his enemies having begrudged him this glory, and us, such a possession, it may be said, that the burden which you have taken of governing kingdoms which have fallen to you weighs upon you sufficiently without seeking occupations for pleasure, which are not necessary. But, *Sire*, I think on the contrary; that as the grand Alexander begun, almost at your age, the conquest of the first empire of the world, so extraordinary enterprises are very becoming to your Majesty, who for six months has given so many proofs of your prudence and of your courage, that the heavens have been charmed, and the earth so much astonished, that there is not any among men who does not admire, love and fear you to-day, nor deem you capable of governing not only what you possess, but all the universe.

This being so, *Sire*, and God so abundantly bestowed his favors upon you, they ought to be acknowledged by some action worthy of a very Christian King; which is to make Christians and to bring to the fold of Jesus Christ the people from beyond the sea, who are not yet subjected to any Prince; or, to efface from our books and from the memory of man, this name of *New France*, of which in vain we boast. *Sire*, you will not want good captains upon the spot, if you may please to help and sustain them and pay the expenses for those only who are willing to settle in the country. But, *Sire*, it is necessary to wish, and to command and not to allow that that which has once been granted, should be revoked, as has been done heretofore, to the ruin of a fine enterprise which promised the speedy establishment of a new kingdom in those lands beyond, and the work would be well advanced to-day if the envy and the avarice of certain people who would not give a stroke of their sword for your service, had not prevented it. The late Lord de Poutrincourt, gentleman of immortal memory, burned with immutable desire (as he had well begun) the lands fallen to his share; and in that he has alway been crossed; (as also his eldest son, who inhabited the country ten years ago,) having never found but very little support in a thing so lofty, so Christian, and which belongs only to Christian Herculi.

Lord de Monts and de Razille make the same complaint in regard to them. I leave out the enterprises farther back in our memory, of the voyages of Jacques Quartier, Villegagnon and Laudonniere, to Canada, to Brazil and to Florida. What, then, *Sire*, shall the Spaniard boast that wherever the sun shines, from his rising to his setting, he shall command? and you, first King of the earth, eldest son of the Church, will not be able to say the same? What, have the old Greeks and Romans in their paganism, had the praise of having civilized many nations and sent great colonies, to that effect: and shall not we, born in the knowledge of the true God, and under a law wholly of charity, have the zeal not only to civilize, but to bring to the way of safety so many wandering people, capable of every thing good, who are beyond the ocean, without God, without law, without religion, living in pitiable ignorance? What, *Sire*, have the Kings, your great ancestors, exhausted the men and treasures of France, and exposed their lives to death, to keep religion among the people of the East, and shall not we have the same zeal to make Christians of those of the West, who have voluntarily given us their land, and extended their arms to us for a hundred years past? Can we find any available excuse before the throne of God, when they accuse us of the want of pity which we have had towards them, and attribute to us their failure to be converted? If we did not know the condition in which they are, we should be beyond reproach. But we see it, we touch it, we feel it, and we have no anxiety about it. If some new people come to us from Italy or from Spain, with a new garment or a new song, we go to meet them, we embrace them, we admire them, in a moment we make them overflow with riches. I do not blame this, *Sire*, since the bounty of Kings has no other bounds than their good pleasure, and since in your kingdom every one is mastor of his own property. But to my mind, they should pay as much attention to the work of which I speak, a work without a parallel which exceeds everything pious which can be conceived in the actions of men. One single confiscation, one single good benefice, one single sum of one hundred thousand crowns, counted and numbered (among several) since the death of the late King, your father, *Sire*, to a company who should only have to act in the matter, could supply that, and cause you to rule within the torrid zone, and beyond in the West. But every one wishes to draw to himself and so far from their representing that to you, on the contrary, results make us believe, that all means are tried to enervate and cause to lose courage, those who busy themselves in such generous actions; without taking care that to-day, your kingdom is at stake in such matters. And if we wait a century more, France will no longer be France but the prey of the stranger who undermines us every day; corrupts your allies, and makes himself powerful to our ruin in a new world, which will all belong to him. And to dazzle us, treasures all made ready in those lands are demanded, as if the way to enter when you please was not open to your Majesty from one tropic to the other; as if the glory and strength of Kings consisted in anything except the multitude of men; and as if your ancient France had not noble treasures in its wheat, wine, cattle, cloth, wool, woad and other provisions which are native to it: which are also the treasures to hope for from your *New France*, more neighboring to us, which for so long a time, such as it is, supports with its fish all Europe, as much by sea as by land, and gives to Europe its skins from which our Newfoundlanders, and merchants draw good profit.

Sire, if there is a King in the world, who can, and ought to rule over the sea and the land, it is you who have innumerable men, part of whom are languishing for want of occupation. And were there only two or three kinds of people who abound in your kingdom, you would have much advantage, which would be no less powerful in making you feared at the extremities of the earth than the old Gauls who conquered Asia and Italy; and there occupied the provinces called by their name; and more recently still, our fathers, the first French who possessed the Rhine as much on the other side as on this. But you, (beside this,) have harbors for the East and the West under your command. In addition, wood for ships; provisions, sails and cordage to freight them in such abundance that you furnish all the nations near your kingdom,.

There are many other things to say on this subject, *Sire*, which I abstain, at this time, from representing to your Majesty, when you have considered the importance of the above, and will manifest that you wish seriously to hear what concerns the good of your service and the glory of God in those Western lands.

Thus may God deign to inspire you, *Sire*. Thus may God aid you, and strengthen your arm to re-enter your former inheritauce, and to subdue your enemies. Thus may God help us, soon to see your greatness served and obeyed through all the earth. I shall deem myself honored in contributing to this all which ought, such a man as I am,

Sire,

of your Majesty,
a very humble, very obedient
and very faithful subject,
Mark L'Escarbot,
of Vervin.

APPENDIX L.

Explanation of L'Escarbot's Map of New France.

On page 21, reference is made to the Map of New France which accompanied the 1st Edition of L'Escarbot's great work, the *History of New France*, a *fac simile* of which Map is herewith given. This Map was reproduced in England in 1609, by *P. Erondelle*, whose work was a compilation from L'Escarbot's History, without awarding any credit, or making any reference to the original. The work of L'Escarbot has never been translated into English.

The information contained in this Map and the accompanying Catalogue of Explanations, will be valued and appreciated by all students of American History.

TO THE READER.

My reader, not having been able to arrange well, in so little space, so many harbors, islands, capes, gulfs, or bays, straits and rivers, of which mention is made in the voyages which I have henceforward to represent to thee, in this third book, I have esteemed it better and more convenient, to indicate them by figures, having only burdened the map which I give thee, with the most famous names which may be in Newfoundland, and the great river of Canada.

PLACES IN NEWFOUNDLAND.

1. *Cap de Bonne-veue*—First landing of Captain Jacques Quartier.
2. *Port de Sainte Catherine.*
3. *Ile aux Oiseaux.*—In this island there is such a quantity of birds that all the ships of France could load themselves with them without its being perceived; Captain Jacques Quartier said this, and I believe it, indeed, for I have almost seen the same thing.
4. *Golfe des Chateaux.*
5. *Port de Carpunt.*
6. *Cap Raze*, where there is a harbor, called *Rougnenst.*
7. *Cap and Port de Degrad.*
8. *Ile Sainte Catherine*, and there even the *Port des Chateaux.*
9. *Port des Gouttes.*
10. *Port des Balances.*
11. *Port de Blanc-sablon.*
12. *Ile de Brest.*
13. *Port des Ilettes.*
14. *Port de Brest.*
15. *Port Saint Antoine.*
16. *Port Saint Servain.*
17. *Fleuve Saint Jacques*, and Port de Jaques Quartier.
18. *Cap Tiennot* .
19. *Port Saint Nicholas.*
20. *Cap de Rabast.*
21. *Baye de Saint Laurent.*
22. *Ile Saint Guillaume.*
23. *Ile Sainte Marthe.*
24. *Ile Saint Germain.*
25. *Les Sept Iles.*
26. *Riviere* called *Chischedec*, where there is a great quantity of aquatic horses called Hippopotami.
27. *Ile de L'Assumption*, otherwise called *Anticosti*, which is about 30 leagues long, and is at the entrance of the great river of *Canada.*
28. *Detroit Saint Pierre.*

Having pointed out the places in Newfoundland which look towards the East, and those which are along the main land on the North, let us return to the said Newfoundland and go entirely round it. But we must know that there are two principal passages to enter the great gulf of *Canada*. Jacques Quartier, in his two voyages, went by the Northern passage. To-day, to avoid the ice and for the shortest way, several people take the Southern passage, through the Strait which is between Cape Breton and Cape de Raye. And this route having been followed by Champlain, the first land discovered on his voyage was

29. *Cap Sainte Marie.*
30. *Iles Saint Pierre.*
31. *Port du Saint Esprit.*
32. *Cap de Lorraine.*
33. *Cap Saint Paul.*
34. *Cap de Raye*, which I consider to be the *Cap pointu* of Jacques Quartier.
35. *Les Mons des Cabanes.*
36. *Cap double.*

Now let us pass to the other land towards Cap Saint Laurent, which I should willingly call the island of *Bacaillos*, that is to say, of codfish, (as Postel has very nearly marked,) to give it a proper name, although I may name thus all around the Golfe de Canada: for, as far as Gachepe, all the harbors are suitable for the fishery of the said fish, and also, even the harbors which are outside and look towards the South; such as the harbor of the English, of *Campseau*, and of *Savalet*. Now, beginning at the Strait between *Cape de Raye* and *Cap Saint Laurent* (which is 18 leagues broad) are found:

37. *Les Isles St. Paul.*
38. *Cap Saint Laurent.*
39. *Cap Saint Pierre.*
40. *Cap Dauphin.*
41. *Cap Saint Jean.*
42. *Cap Royal.*
43. *Golfe Saint Julien.*
44. *Passage*, or *Detroit* of the bay of *Campseau*, which separates the island of *Bacaillos* from the main land.

Since so many years, this Strait is scarcely known, and nevertheless, it serves very much to shorten the way (or at least will serve when New France is inhabited) to the great river of *Canada*. We saw it last year, being ourselves in the harbor of Campseau going to look for some stream to supply us with fresh water before our return. We found one little one which I marked near the end of the said baye of *Campseau*, at which place I had great fishing of cod. Now, when I consider Jacques Quartier's route, in his first voyage, I find it so obscure, that nothing is more so, for want of having noticed this passage. For our sailors the oftenest use the names placed by the Savages, such as *Tadoussac, Anticosti, Gachepe, Tregate; Miramichis, Campseau, Kebec, Batiscan, Sayeunay, Chitshedec, Mantaune*, and others. In this obscurity I have thought that what he calls the Iles Colombaires, are the Islands called Ramees, which are several in number, as he had said in his speech that a tempest had carried them from Cap pointu to 37 leagues distance, for he had already passed from the Northern bend towards the South.

45. *Iles Colombaires* alias *Ramees*.

46. *Iles Margeaux*. There are three islands filled with these birds like a meadow with grass, as Jacques Quartier said.

47. *Ile de Brion*, where there are *Hippopotami*, or sea horses.

48. *Ile d' Alezay*.

From there it is said that they sailed 40 leagues and found

49. *Cap d'Orleans*.

50. *Fleuve des Barques*, which I take to be *Miramichis*.

51. *Cap des Sauvages*.

52. *Golfe Saint Laurent*, which I take to be Tregate.

53. *Cap d' Esperance*.

54. *Baye* or *Golfe de Chaleur*, at which it is hotter, Jacques Quartier says, than in Spain. In which I shall not voluntarily believe him, until another voyage has been made, as regards the climate. But it may be that accidentally it was very warm there when he was there, which was in the month of July.

55. *Cap du Pre*.

56. *Saint Martin*.

57. *Baye des Morues*.

58. *Cap Saint Louis*.

59. *Cap de Montmorency*.

60. *Gachepe*.

61. *Isle percee*.

62. *Ile de Bonaventure*.

Let us now enter the great river of *Canada* in which we shall find few harbors in the space of more than 350 leagues, for it is very full of rocks. At the bend of the South, Gachepe being passed, there is:

63. *Cap a L'Evegue*.

64. *Riviere de Mantaune*.

65. *Les Ileaux Saint Jean*, which I take to be *Le Pic*.

66. *Riviere des Iroquois*. At the bend of the North, after *Chischedec*, placed above at number 27.

67. *Riviere Sainte Marguerite*.

68. *Port de Lesquemin*, where the Basques go to fish for whales.

69. *Port de Tadoussac*, at the mouth of the river of *Saguenay*, where is the greatest traffic in skins of all the country.

70. *Riviere de Sageunay*, at 100 leagues from the mouth of the river of *Canada*. This river is so hollow that the bottom is almost not to be found. Here the great river of *Canada* is only 7 leagues broad.

71. *Ile de Lievre*.

72. *Ile aux Coudres*. These two islands were thus named by Jacques Quartier.

73. *Ile d' Orleans*, which Jacques Quartier named *Ile de Bacchus*, on account of the great quantity of vines which are there. Here the water of the great river is fresh, and the tide flows more than 40 leagues beyond.

74. *Kebec*. It is a Strait of the great river of *Canada*, which Jacques Quartier named Achelaci, where Sire De Monts made a fort, and a settlement of French. Near which place there is a stream which falls from a rock very high, and very straight.

75. *Port de Saincte Croix*, where Jacques Quartier wintered, and Champlain says that he did not pass beyond; but he is mistaken, and the remembrance of those who have done well ought to be kept.

76. *Riviere de Batiscan*.

77. *Ile Saint Eloy*.

78. *Riviere de Foix*, named by Champlain *Les Trois Rivieres*.

79. *Hochelaga*, a city of the Savages, from whose name Jacques Quartier called the great river that we name *Canada*.

80. *Mont Royal*. Mountain near *Hochelaga*, from which the great river of *Canada* is seen till lost from sight beyond the *Grand Saut*.

81. *Saut* of the great river of *Canada*, which lasts a league, this river falling among the rocks below with a strange noise.

82. *La grande Riviere de Canada*, whose source is not known. More than 800 leagues of which are known, either from actual sight, or from the report of the Savages. I find in Jacques Quartier's second voyage, that it is 30 leagues broad at its entrance, and more than 200 fathoms deep. This river has been called *Hochelaga*, by the same Jacques Quartier, from the name of the people who, in his time, inhabited about this *Saut*.

www.ingramcontent.com/pod-product-compliance
Lightning Source LLC
LaVergne TN
LVHW021312110826
845150LV00003B/553